इंग्लिश भाषा के Errors, Mistakes एवं Blunders से कैसे बचें

SC Gupta
BSc, MA, LLB, DLL, MCom, CAIIB

Arihant Publications (I) Pvt Ltd, Meerut

Delhi Office: 4577/15, Ramchhaya, Agarwal Road, Darya Ganj, New Delhi - 2
Phone : 011-23280316, 47630600 ; Fax : 011-43540876

Head Office : Kalindi, TP Nagar, Meerut
Phone : 0121-2401479, 2512970, 2402029 ; Fax : 0121-2401648, Email : arihant_meerutbranch@yahoo.co.in

卐 **Zonal & Regional Offices :**

North Zone **Agra**: 8/195, New Engineers' Colony, Kaushalpur, Agra, Ph. 0562 – 6451531, Email: arihant_agra02@yahoo.co.in **Delhi–1 (for Delhi & NCR) :** 4577/15, Ramchhaya, Agarwal Road, Darya Ganj, New Delhi – 110002, Ph. 011 – 23280316, Fax. 011 – 43540876, Email: arihant_delhi07@yahoo.co.in; **Delhi–2 (for Haryana, Himachal, J&K & Punjab) :** 4577/15, Ramchhaya, Agarwal Road, Darya Ganj, New Delhi – 110002, Ph. 011 – 23280316, Fax. 011 – 43540876, Email: arihant_delhi07@yahoo.co.in **Jaipur**: C–8, Link Road, Jalupura MD Road, Near Hotel Apoorva, Jaipur – 302 001 (Raj), Ph. 0141 – 4033077, Email : deepmahur85@gmail.com; **Kota**: 5-J-18, Talwardi, Behind T.T. Hospital, Kota–324009 (Rajasthan.), 0744–2406760, Email : arihant_kota@yahoo.co.in; **Lucknow**: C – 22,Vijay Laxmi Transport Building, Transport Nagar, Kanpur Road, Lucknow – 226 012 (UP), Ph. 0522 – 6459009, Fax : 0522-4028575, Email : arihant_lko@yahoo.com; **Haldwani**: Raja Enterprises, Varun Complex, Rampur Road, Haldwani (Uttarakhand), Ph. 05946 – 235456 ; Email : arihant_kashipur@yahoo.co.in; **Meerut**: Kalindi, TP Nagar, Meerut, Ph: 0121-6534323, Email: arihant_meerutbranch@yahoo.co.in.

East Zone **Bhubaneshwar**: 14, Shahid Nagar, Bhubaneshwar – 751007 (Orissa), Ph. 064 – 2503050, 09938211103, Email : bhubaneshwar@arihantbooks.com; **Kolkata**: 4, Tottee Lane, Kolkata – 700016 (WB), Ph. 033 – 22526713, Fax. 033 – 22523564, Email: arihant_kol@yahoo.co.in; **Guwahati**: Aastha Towers, Ist Floor, Module No. XIII, CK Road, Pan Bazar, Guwahati – 781 001, (Asom) Ph. 0361 – 2731599, E-mail : arihant_guwahati@yahoo.co.in; **Patna**: Gangotri Complex, U/465, Lohia Nagar, Kankarbagh, Patna – 20 (Bihar), Ph. 0612 – 2360623, Email: cafpatna@rediffmail.com.

Central Zone **Nagpur**: 27, Nathuji Pise Complex, Opp. Mokshadham, New Gate, Beside Hanuman Mandir, Great Nag Road, Nagpur – 14, (Maharashtra), Ph. 0712 – 2748211 ; Email : arihant_nagpur1@yahoo.co.in.

South Zone **Hyderabad**: Plot No.–115, SBI Colony, Kavadiguda, Near Sri Satya Sai Temple, Hyderabad–500020, Ph. 040 – 65347774, 66107772, Email: hyd.arihant@gmail.com; **Bengaluru**: 362, 10th Main, 2nd Cross, Ist Block, Basaveshwara Nagar, Bengaluru-560079, Mob : +919242693192

卐 **Price** : Rs 150.00

卐 **Laser Typesetting** : Arihant DTP Unit, Meerut

Printed & Bound in India
by Arihant Publications (India) Limited

For further information on
Arihant Group, log in : www.arihantbooks.com

Preface

यह Book मुख्य रूप से उन छात्रों के लिए बहुत उपयोगी है जो विभिन्न प्रतियोगी परीक्षाओं में बैठ रहे हैं एवं इन परीक्षाओं में अंग्रेजी प्रश्न पत्रों में Errors से सम्बन्धित पूछे जाने वाले प्रश्नों को हल करने में स्वयं को असफल पाते हैं। इस Book में हमने लगभग सभी प्रकार की Error/Mistakes/Blunders को समाहित करने का प्रयास किया है। यह Book चार Parts में विभाजित है।

Part I– Grammar Part with exercises relating to errors/mistakes/blunders.

Part II– Practice Exercises Spotting Errors, Sentences Correction & Miscellaneous exercises.

Part III– Know these words. Know the English fundamentals.

Part IV– This part contains following very important chapters:
Words Often Create Confusion (Homonyms)
Specific Use of Words (Similar Meaning)
Words Used In A Good Sense
Words Not Used In A Good Sense
Some Peculiar Expressions
One Word Substitutions
Related Pair Of Words
Synonyms, Antonyms
Foreign Words, Group Terms

इस Book का उद्देश्य छात्रों को अंग्रेजी से लगने वाले भय से छुटकारा दिलाना तथा अंग्रेजी प्रश्न पत्र में अच्छे अंक प्राप्त करने में आपको सहयोग प्रदान करना है।

"Heights by the great man reached and kept,
Were not attained by sudden flight,
But while their companions slept,
They were toiling upwards in the night."

इस Book को इस स्थिति में प्रस्तुत करने के लिए मैं श्री दीपेश जैन (अरिहन्त पब्लिकेशनस, मेरठ) का आभारी हूँ जिनके सक्रिय एवं रचनात्मक सहयोग के बिना यह पुस्तक इतनी शीघ्रता से आपके हाथों में उपलब्ध होना सम्भव नहीं था।

इस Book में further improvement हेतु आपके सुझाव हमेशा आमन्त्रित हैं।

SC Gupta
129-South West Block
Near Eidgah
Alwar (Rajasthan)
Ph.: 0144-2700438

Contents

1

Articles

Articles का प्रयोग छात्रों को बहुत सरल प्रतीत होता है लेकिन जितनी गलतियाँ Articles के प्रयोग में की जाती हैं, उतनी शायद अन्यत्र कहीं नहीं की जाती हैं । वे स्थितियाँ, जहाँ Articles का प्रयोग नहीं किया जाता है, 'Zero Articles' या 'No Articles' के नाम से जानी जाती हैं। परीक्षा में Errors से सम्बन्धित प्रश्न अधिकांशतया इन्हीं में से पूछे जाते हैं । अत : छात्रों को इन्हें अच्छी तरह याद कर लेना चाहिये ।

Use of A/An

(1) A / An का प्रयोग अनिश्चित (Indefinite) Singular Noun से पूर्व किया जाता है ; निश्चित होने पर Noun के पूर्व 'The' का प्रयोग किया जाता है। इसी कारण से A/An को Indefinite Articles कहा जाता है। जैसे:

(a) I have a purse. (b) He sang a song.

उपरोक्त उदाहरणों में, यह निश्चित नहीं है कि कौन सा विशेष निश्चित purse या song है; अत: purse और song अनिश्चित singular nouns हैं, इसलिये इन से पहले 'a' का प्रयोग किया गया है।

(2) जिस शब्द से पूर्व A/An का प्रयोग करना है, उस शब्द के उच्चारण की प्रथम ध्वनि (First sound of pronunciation) यदि स्वर है तो An का प्रयोग होगा, अन्यथा A का प्रयोग होगा।

Note

(a) अंग्रेजी भाषा में A, E, I, O, U, को स्वर (Vowels) माना गया है। कई शब्द इन Vowels से तो शुरू हो सकते हैं , लेकिन मुख्य बात है, उस शब्द के उच्चारण की। यदि प्रथम ध्वनि व्यंजन है, तो 'a' का प्रयोग होगा। यदि यह ध्वनि स्वर है, तो 'an' का प्रयोग करना होता है। जिस शब्द के पूर्व हमें 'a' या 'an' प्रयुक्त करना है, यदि उसके उच्चारण की प्रथम ध्वनि, हिन्दी वर्णमाला के स्वर से उच्चारित है तो 'an' का प्रयोग करें अन्यथा 'a' का प्रयोग करें।

हिन्दी वर्णमाला में ; अ, आ, इ, ई, उ, ऊ, ए, ऐ .... स्वर माने जाते हैं।

An umbrella -अम्ब्रेला, A university - यूनिवर्सिटी

A one rupee note-वन, An honest-ऑनेस्ट

शब्द का प्रथम letter क्या है, यह महत्त्वपूर्ण नहीं है; महत्त्वपूर्ण है, उसके उच्चारण की प्रथम ध्वनि (First sound of pronunciation) I

(b) अंग्रेजी भाषा में एक अक्षर, कई प्रकार की ध्वनि हेतु प्रयुक्त होता है। जिन अक्षरों को स्वर (A, E, I, O, U) माना गया है, उनका प्रयोग बहुत बार व्यंजनों (Consonants) की तरह होता है। बहुत से व्यंजन (Consonants) स्वर का कार्य करते हैं। ***हो सकता है, शब्द का प्रथम अक्षर M, F, N, X, S, L, H हो, लेकिन उच्चारण की प्रथम ध्वनि (First sound of pronunciation) स्वर हो, तो ऐसे शब्दों के पूर्व an का प्रयोग होगा। जैसे :***

(a) He is an MLA / MP. (एम.एल.ए. / एम. पी.)

(b) He lodged an FIR. (एफ.आई.आर.)

(c) Shashi is an NCC officer. (एन. सी. सी.)

Correct use of A/An

1. An hour.
2. An hourly meeting.
3. An hour's daybreak.
4. An honour.
5. An honorary post
6. An honourable person.
7. An honest man.
8. An heir
9. An honorarium.
10. A house
11. A historical fair.
12. A humble person.
13. A husband
14. A heinous crime.
15. A young man.
16. A ewe
17. A university
18. A unity
19. A union
20. A eulogy
21. A one rupee note.
22. A one eyed man.
23. A uniform.
24. A useful book .
25. A useful feature.
26. A unique decision.
27. A united front.
28. A unified plan.
29. A year.
30. A USA ally.
31. An FO.
32. A forest officer.
33. An MP/MLC
34. A member of parliament.
35. An IAS / IPS / ILO
36. An SP / SDO.
37. An M.A./M.Sc/M.Com..
38. An RTS / RTC / RO.
39. An RC worker.
40. A UK ship / European.

Articles; A/An के सन्दर्भ में निम्न महत्त्वपूर्ण बिन्दुओं पर गौर करें। अधिकांश प्रश्न इन्ही के सन्दर्भ में पूछे जाते हैं।

(3) Exclamatory वाक्यों में 'What' के बाद Singular, Countable nouns से पूर्व 'a' / 'an' का प्रयोग किया जाता है :

(a) What a grand building! (b) What a pretty girl !

(4) 'प्रति माह' या 'प्रति वस्तु कीमत' के सन्दर्भ में प्रयोग करने पर A/ An का प्रयोग किया जाता है :

(a) I earn Rs. twenty thousand a month.
(b) This train runs seventy kms an hour.

(5) कुछ गिनती बताने वाले शब्द, जैसे :

A hundred, A thousand, A million, A dozen, A couple से पूर्व '*a*' प्रयुक्त होता है। 'Half' से पूर्व 'a' का प्रयोग इस प्रकार किया जाता है; जैसे- 3½ kilo - Three and a half kilos, 2/½ meters - Two and a quarter meters.

(a) I have a hundred pens. (b) He has a thousand rupees.

(6) किसी विशिष्ट व्यक्ति की विशेषताओं के सम्बन्ध में किसी अन्य व्यक्ति को पहचान दी जाये तो a / an का प्रयोग किया जाता है :

(a) He is a Hitler. (A despot like Hitler)
(b) He is a second Dara Singh. (A wrestler as great as Dara Singh)

(7) जब वाक्य में Verb (क्रिया) का प्रयोग Noun की तरह किया जाता है, तब उससे पहले a / an लिखा जाता है।

(a) He goes for a walk daily. ['Walk' (verb) used as noun]
(b) Last Sunday, I had a long talk with him. ['Talk' is a verb used here as noun]
(c) I want to have a rest /a drink / a bath. ['rest/drink/bath' are verbs used as noun]

(8) 'Many / rather / quite / such' के बाद यदि singular noun आता है, तो उससे पूर्व 'a/an' का प्रयोग किया जाता है :

(a) Many a woman would welcome such a chance.
(b) It is rather a pity , I say.
(c) It was quite an impossible task.
(d) It was a foolish argument.

(9) यदि Adjective से पहले 'so, as, too, how, quite' का प्रयोग होता है तो उसके बाद 'a/an' (Indefinite Article) का प्रयोग निम्न प्रकार किया जाता है :

(a) It is too heavy a parcel for me to carry.
(b) She is as beautiful a girl as you are ever likely to meet.
(c) Ram is not so big a fool as you think.
(d) How serious a crime had been committed was not realised by him.

(10) कुछ विशेष Phrases में 'a / an' का प्रयोग होता है :

In a fix, in a hurry, in a nutshell, make a noise, make a foot, keep a secret, as a rule, at a discount, at a stone's throw, a short while ago, at a loss, take a fancy to, take an interest in, to have a drink, go for a walk, have a good education, tell a lie, take a bath, half a kilo, a matter of chance etc. :

(a) He has a good knowledge of Sanskrit.
(b) Do not make a noise.
(c) Twelve inches make a foot.

Note ***'A / An' का प्रयोग निम्न स्थिति में नहीं करना चाहिये :***

(a) किसी भी Plural noun से पूर्व 'A / An' का प्रयोग नहीं किया जाता है।

(b) Proper noun से पूर्व 'A/An' का प्रयोग नहीं किया जाता है। किसी देश, राज्य, शहर, दिन, माह, व्यक्ति या वस्तु के नाम को Proper noun कहा जाता है।

(c) Uncountable nouns से पूर्व 'A/An' का प्रयोग सामान्यतया नहीं किया जाता है। जैसे : Advice, Accommodation, Baggage, Luck, Luggage, News, Permission, Progress, Scenery, Weather, Traffic, Knowledge, Music, Milk, Homework, Stone, Brick, Wine, Beauty, etc. :

(a) The wall is made of stone and brick.
(b) Enjoy your vacations! I hope you have good weather.
(c) No news is good news.
(d) India has made good progress in the field of I.T.

Uncountable nouns के पूर्व जब 'a/an' का प्रयोग किया जाता है, तो इन्हें कुछ शब्दों का (जैसे: a piece of, a bar) प्रयोग करके, Countable बनाया जाता है; इनके प्रयोग से ही Noun के Countable होने का पता चलता है :

(a) I have a good news for you.
(b) I have a piece of bread.
(c) I have a milk bar.
(d) He gave me a piece of information.

(d) Inchoate Verb, 'turn' का प्रयोग जब noun के साथ किया जाता है, तो noun से पूर्व Indefinite Article A/An का प्रयोग नहीं किया जायेगा :

(a) I hope you will never turn traitor.
(b) Is it wise for a great general to turn politician?
(c) When her husband left she had to turn cook.

यहाँ nouns; traitor, politician, cook के पूर्व 'a/an' का प्रयोग नहीं किया गया है।

ARTICLES : 'A/AN' AND 'ONE' - DIFFERENCE

(1) A/An Articles हैं, जबकि One एक Adjective है।

(2) Hundred, Thousand, Million, Billion etc. के पूर्व 'a' का प्रयोग 'one' से ज्यादा उचित माना गया है; 100 = a hundred, 1000 = a thousand ,100000 = A hundred thousand. हम A hundred one से a hundred and ninety nine तथा A thousand one से a thousand and ninety nine तक में 'a' का प्रयोग कर सकते हैं। लेकिन 1160 = One thousand one hundred sixty में 'one' का प्रयोग ही किया जायेगा।

(3) 'प्रतिदिन', 'प्रति सप्ताह', 'प्रति किलो' कीमत या दर के लिए 'a' का प्रयोग ही किया जायेगा 'one' का नहीं: Sixty rupees a kilo, Rs. five thousand a week, four times a day, sixty kilometres an hour, ten rupees a dozen **उक्त में 'a/an' की जगह 'one' का प्रयोग नहीं किया जा सकता है।**

(4) 'A' एवं 'one' का noun के साथ प्रयोग करने पर भिन्न-भिन्न अर्थ निकलता है। 'A/an' का अर्थ 'any' या 'every' से भी होता है :

One screw driver is not enough. (We need two or more screw drivers.)
A screw driver is a useful tool. (Screw drivers are useful tools.)

(5) 'One' का प्रयोग उस another/other के साथ किया जा सकता है, 'a' का प्रयोग नहीं :

(a) One student wants to read, another wants to play.
(b) One day he came early, another day he was very late.

(6) 'One' का प्रयोग day/week/month/year/summer/winter etc. या महिनों / दिनों के नाम के पूर्व किया जा सकता है, जो उस दिन / समय होने वाली किसी घटना के सन्दर्भ में प्रयुक्त होता है :

(a) One night there was a terrible storm.

(7) One day का प्रयोग 'किसी दिन' के अर्थ में भी किया जाता है :

(a) One day you'll realise your mistake.

(8) 'One' का प्रयोग a/an के pronoun के समरूप भी किया जाता है :

(a) Did you get a ticket? Yes I managed to get one.
'One' का बहुवचन (plural) उक्त स्थिति में some है। जैसे :
Did you get tickets? Yes I managed to get some.

DEFINITE ARTICLE 'THE'

Use of 'The'

इसका प्रयोग उस noun से पूर्व किया जाता है, जो निश्चित है, विशेष है या जिसकी चर्चा पूर्व में की जा चुकी है। 'The' को इसीलिए Definite article कहा जाता है।

Some Important Rules

(1) **जब किसी पूर्व निर्धारित वस्तु के बारें में कहा जाता है। जैसे:-**

(a) I found a bag. The bag contained a coin. The coin was made of gold.
वाक्य संख्या (a) में 'bag' से पूर्व सर्वप्रथम 'a' का प्रयोग किया गया है, बाद में 'the' का प्रयोग किया गया है; क्योंकि यह bag पूर्व निर्धारित, निश्चित हो गया है। इसी तरह आरम्भ में coin से पहले 'a' का प्रयोग किया है, बाद में 'the' का, क्योंकि अब coin पूर्व निर्धारित, निश्चित हो चुका है। अन्य उदाहरण देखें-

(a) This is the hotel where she lives. (b) The man in blue dress is my brother.

(2) **Comparative degree से पूर्व, जब इसका प्रयोग adverb की तरह किया जाये :**

(a) The more she gets, the more she demands.
(b) The sooner he completes, the better it is.

(3) जब Comparative degree से पूर्व कोई Selection व्यक्त करना हो या Comparison व्यक्त करना हो तो 'The' का प्रयोग होता है :

(a) He is the stronger of the two. (b) This is the better of the two novels.

(4) शरीर के अंगों (Parts of the body) के नामों के पूर्व 'The' का प्रयोग निम्न प्रकार से होता है :

(a) He was wounded in the arm. (b) Ram hit him in the head.

(5) Superlative degree से पूर्व 'The' का प्रयोग किया जाता है :

(a) He is the best student of our class.
(b) She is the most beautiful girl in this school.

लेकिन यदि Superlative degree 'most' का प्रयोग 'very' के अर्थ में हो तो उससे पहले 'The' नहीं प्रयुक्त होता है :

(a) She is a most beautiful girl. (b) This is a most useful reference book.

(6) धार्मिक समुदाय के नाम, साम्राज्य के नाम, इतिहास की घटनाओं, वंशजों के नाम, राजनैतिक दलों के नाम, ट्रेन, जहाज, अखबार के नाम, महत्त्वपूर्ण भवनों के नाम, नदियों के नाम, नहरों के नाम तथा समुद्र के नाम, आदि के पूर्व 'The' का प्रयोग किया जाता है :

(a) The Ganga / the Godawari / The Satluj.
(b) The Pacific, The Red Sea, The Indian Ocean.
(c) The Hindus, the Muslims, the Sikhs.
(d) The Intercity, The Rajdhani Express.
(e) The B J P, the Congress, the Communist party.
(f) The Boeing, the Vikrant.
(g) The Bay of Bengal, the gulf of Mexico.
(h) The Taj Mahal, The Char Minar.
(i) The French Revolution, the Quit India Movement.
(j) The Hindustan Times, The Indian Express.

(7) जो वस्तुएँ Unique हैं, उनसे पूर्व 'The' का प्रयोग होता है :

The sun, The earth, The world, The universe, etc. लेकिन Heaven, Hell, Paradise, God, Parliament आदि के पूर्व 'The' का प्रयोग नहीं होता है :

(a) The sun sets in the west. (b) The earth revolves round the sun.
(c) Go to hell. (No 'the') (d) Gods reside in heaven. (No 'the')

(8) धार्मिक ग्रन्थों के नाम के पूर्व 'The' का प्रयोग किया जाता है ; The Ramayan, The Quran, The Bible etc. :

(a) The Ramayan is a sacred book. (b) The Quran is also a sacred book.

लेकिन Valmiki's Ramayan, Banbhatt's Kadambari, जैसी स्थिति में, इनके पूर्व 'The' नहीं प्रयुक्त होता है।

(9) व्यक्ति के पद के पूर्व 'The' का प्रयोग निम्न प्रकार किया जाता है :

(a) The Chairman will decide the matter.
(b) The meeting was presided over by the Executive Director.

(10) Nationality (राष्ट्रीयता) व्यक्त करने वाले शब्दों से पूर्व 'The' का प्रयोग किया जाता है :

(a) The English defeated the French.

(11) जब Adjective का प्रयोग Noun की तरह किया जाता है, तो उससे पहले 'The' प्रयुक्त होने पर वह पूरे समुदाय को दर्शाता है :

(a) The young and the old, the poor and the rich, the male and the female all loved Gandhi ji.
(b) Three percent posts are reserved for the disabled.

(12) जब कोई वस्तु Understood होती है, तो उससे पूर्व 'The' का प्रयोग किया जाता है :
(a) Kindly return the book. (That I gave you.)
(b) Can you turn off the light? (The light in the room.)

(13) Ordinals से पूर्व 'the' का प्रयोग किया जाता है ; first, second, third .....ordinals तथा one, two, three... cardinals कहलाते हैं :
(a) The second lesson of this book is very difficult.
(b) He is the first to arrive in the meeting.

(14) Musical Instrument, किसी आविष्कार (Invention) के नाम के पूर्व 'the' का प्रयोग किया जाता है:
(a) She can play the tabla / violin / trumpet.
(b) Who invented the telephone/telescope?

(15) 'Go to the cinema', 'Go to the theatre' में 'cinema' एवं 'theatre' से पूर्व 'The' आता है :
(a) He went to the cinema yesterday. (b) She is going to the theatre.

(16) Plural Nouns से पहले 'The' का प्रयोग किया जाता है, यदि वाक्य के reference के अनुसार Plural Noun, particular/ definite हो गया हो :
(a) The boys of this college are very intelligent.
(b) The girls of this hostel are very beautiful.

(17) जब कोई Noun, किसी गुण या भाव को व्यक्त करे तो उससे पूर्व भी 'the' का प्रयोग होता है :
(a) The judge (moral of judge) in him, prevailed upon the husband (love of husband) and he sentenced his wife to death.
(b) The moralist (spirit of moralist) in Gandhi revolted against the tyranny of the British.

(18) 'Same' से पूर्व 'The' का प्रयोग comparison हेतु निम्न प्रकार से होता है :
(a) These books are the same as we saw in that shop.

(19) यदि दो या अधिक Nouns एक ही व्यक्ति या वस्तु के लिए प्रयुक्त हुए हों तो, 'The' का प्रयोग प्रथम noun के पूर्व किया जाता है :
(a) The secretary and treasurer was present there.
यहाँ Secretary and treasurer एक ही व्यक्ति है।

(20) 'The' का प्रयोग Country के नाम के पूर्व नहीं होता है, लेकिन यदि Country के नाम के साथ Republic, Kingdom, या States जुड़े हुए हों तो 'The' का प्रयोग इनसे पूर्व किया जाता है। जैसे:- The Republic of Ireland, the Dominican Republic, the United States, the United Kingdom etc.
(a) He visited India and the United States.

(21) 'The' का प्रयोग Plural names of : countries/ islands / mountains/ persons के साथ होता है :
The Netherlands, The Laccadiv islands, The Philippines, The Andes, The Alps, The Himalayas, The Johnsons, the Raymonds, the Ambanis etc.

Note *Sicily island, Bermuda island, Java island; Everest, Etna, Abu (Name of Mountain) इत्यादि के साथ 'The' का प्रयोग नहीं होगा।*

(22) East, West, North, South के साथ 'The' का प्रयोग होता है लेकिन यदि इनके साथ कोई Place का नाम जोड़ा गया हो तो 'The' का प्रयोग नहीं होगा। इसी तरह Northern, Southern , Eastern, Western से पूर्व 'The' नहीं आता है :

(a) The sun rises in the east. (b) He is going to North America.
(c) Rajasthan is in western India. (d) Sweden is in northern Europe.

(23) **बहुत-सी महत्त्वपूर्ण Buildings एवं Institutions के नाम, दो शब्दों से मिलकर बने होते हैं, जिनमें से एक शब्द किसी व्यक्ति या स्थान का नाम होता है, ऐसे नाम के साथ 'The' कर प्रयोग नहीं किया जाता है।** जैसे: Delhi Airport, Victoria Station, London Zoo, Jaisingh Palace, Indira Gandhi Airport, Edinburgh Castle, Jaipur Place इत्यादि। इनके साथ 'The' का प्रयोग नहीं किया जाता है। **लेकिन अन्य नाम; जैसे : The Royal Palace, The Char Minar, The White House, The Red Square, The Taj Mahal, इनके साथ 'The का प्रयोग होता है। (Note:- This is a generally accepted rule; there are several exceptions.)**

(24) **Sky, Moon, World, Sea, Country, Environment से पूर्व 'The' का प्रयोग किया जाता है :**
(a) The sky is dark and the moon in shinning.
(b) The sea seems calm today.
लेकिन Space से पूर्व 'The' नहीं आता है, जब Space का अर्थ 'अंतरिक्ष' से होता है, **लेकिन यदि Space 'जगह' के अर्थ में प्रयुक्त हुआ है तो 'The' प्रयोग होता है :**
(a) There are laces of stars in space.
(b) He tried to park his car there but the space was too small.
लेकिन 'sea' के साथ निम्न स्थिति में 'the' का प्रयोग नहीं होगा :
(a) We go to sea as sailors. (b) He is at sea now-a-days (on a voyage).

(25) **Sentence Structure:- The+Name+of+....**
में 'The' का प्रयोग किया जाता है :
(a) The tower of London is a great tower.
(b) The great wall of China is a historical monument.

NO ARTICLE ZERO ARTICLE

Articles का प्रयोग, छात्रों को बहुत सावधानी से करना चाहिए। नीचे दी गई स्थितियों में Article का प्रयोग नहीं किया जाता है :

(1) **'School, College, University, Bed, Church, Court, Hospital, Prison, Market', आदि से पूर्व article 'the' का प्रयोग उस स्थिति में नहीं किया जाता, जब उक्त स्थानों पर जाने का उद्देश्य वही हो, जिस हेतु इनका निर्माण किया गया है :**
(a) I go to college at 10 AM. (for the purpose of study)
(b) He went to Church on Sunday. (for offering prayer)
लेकिन यदि इन स्थानों पर जाने का उद्देश्य अन्यथा हो, तो इनसे पहले 'The' प्रयुक्त होता है :
(a) The school is near Ram's house.
(b) I will meet you near the court.

(2) **'Appoint, made, nominate, elect, declare' के बाद यदि कोई Noun आता है, तो उससे पूर्व article का प्रयोग नहीं होता है :**
(a) He was elected MLA. (b) He was appointed supervisor.

(3) **खाने के नाम (lunch, dinner, supper, breakfast) के पूर्व article का प्रयोग, सामान्य स्थिति में नहीं किया जाता है :**
(a) I couldn't have breakfast this morning. (b) He was invited to dinner.

लेकिन यदि खाने के नाम के साथ कोई adjective प्रयुक्त हो या खाना particular हो गया हो तो article का प्रयोग किया जाता है :

(a) He arranged a nice dinner. (b) The dinner hosted by the queen was superb.

(4) बिमारियों (Diseases) के नाम से पूर्व सामान्यतया कोई article नहीं प्रयुक्त होता है :

(a) She is suffering from fever. (b) He died of cholera.

लेकिन यदि diseases का नाम Plural में हो जैसे– Mumps, Measles आदि, तो इनके पूर्व 'The' का प्रयोग किया जाता है :

The measles is a contagious disease.

(5) भाषा के नाम व रंग के नाम के पहले article का प्रयोग नहीं होता है :

(a) I can speak Hindi, but I can't speak English.

(b) He likes blue and white colour.

लेकिन यदि colour का नाम एक adjective की तरह किसी countable noun के साथ प्रयुक्त हुआ है, तो article का प्रयोग किया जाता है :

(a) She has a blue saree.

(6) कुछ Titles जैसे : Emperor Ashoka, President Abdul Kalam, Queen Victoria, Captain Cook आदि के साथ भी article 'the' का प्रयोग नहीं होता है। ('The Emperor Ashoka' लिखना गलत है, लेकिन 'The ' का प्रयोग Title 'The Duke of York' के साथ तो होता है ।

(7) यदि दो अलग-अलग adjectives एक ही Countable Noun के लिए प्रयुक्त हों, तो article का प्रयोग पहले वाले adjective के साथ ही होगा :

(a) This is a Hindi and English learning book.

(b) This is a English and Hindi dictionary.

(8) 'The' का प्रयोग noun + number के साथ नहीं होता है :

(a) Our train arrives at platform 6. (b) I need shoes in size 18.

(9) सामान्यतया 'watch television' में 'television' से पूर्व 'The' का प्रयोग नहीं होता है। लेकिन 'listen to the radio' में 'radio' से पूर्व 'The' प्रयुक्त होता है।

(a) I heard the news on the radio. (b) I watched the news on television.

(10) कई Shops, Restaurants, Hotels, Banks के साथ उन व्यक्तियों के नाम जुड़े रहते हैं, जिन्होंने इन्हें शुरू किया है। इनके साथ 'The' का प्रयोग नहीं किया जाता है :

Lloyds Bank, Mcdonalds, Jack's Guest House, Harrods (Shop), Raymonds (shop). etc.

(11) Church के नाम के साथ Saints के नाम जुड़े रहते हैं , इनके साथ भी 'The' का प्रयोग नहीं किया जाता है :

St. John's Church, St. Paul's Cathedral.

(12) कम्पनियों के नाम व Airlines के नाम के साथ भी 'The' का प्रयोग नहीं होता है :

Fiat (not the Fiat), Sony, Kodak, British Airways, IBM, Reliance etc.

(13) विषयों (Subjects) के नाम के पूर्व सामान्यतया articles का प्रयोग नहीं करते हैं :

(a) I am student of Political Science. (b) He is learning French.

(14) 'Kind of' के बाद 'The' का प्रयोग नहीं किया जाता है :

(a) What kind of bird it was! (b) What kind of girl she is!

(15) कुछ ऐसे Phrases हैं, जिनमें Preposition के बाद object आता है, इनमें article का प्रयोग नहीं होता है :

at hand, by name, by bus, by train, by plane, in jail, at dinner, underground, in jest, by water, on horseback, at sunset, in debt, in hand, all day, all night, at noon, at night, by post etc.

(16) कुछ ऐसे Phrases हैं, जिनमें Transitive verb के बाद object आता है, इनमें article का प्रयोग नहीं होता है :

to catch fire, to leave school / college, to give ear, to bring word, to lay size, to lose heart, to set sail, to send word, to cast anchor etc.

(17) जब किसी abstract noun द्वारा feelings या emotions को कथन की तरह व्यक्त किया जाये, तो article का प्रयोग नहीं किया जाता है :

(a) Honesty is the best policy. (b) Virtue has its own reward.

लेकिन यदि Abstract noun द्वारा किसी व्यक्ति / जीव या वस्तु की qualities से सम्बन्ध स्थापित किया जाये तो उसके पूर्व article 'the' प्रयुक्त होता है :

(a) He possesses the swiftness of a tiger.
(b) He has the cunningness of crow.

(18) जब Common Noun का प्रयोग विस्तृत अर्थ में किया जाता है तो उससे पूर्व article नहीं प्रयुक्त होता है :

(a) Man is an intelligent animal. (b) Birds fly.

(19) सामान्यतया Proper noun से पूर्व articles का प्रयोग नहीं किया जाता है लेकिन यदि Proper noun का प्रयोग एक Common noun की तरह होता है तो उससे पहले article का प्रयोग किया जाता है :

(a) Akbar was a great king. (b) Agra is a beautiful city.

यहाँ 'Akbar', और 'Agra', proper nouns हैं।

(a) Jaipur is the Paris of India. (b) Kashmir is the Switzerland of Asia.

यहाँ 'Paris' और 'Switzerland' का प्रयोग common noun की तरह हुआ है।

(20) 'Nature' का प्रयोग जब प्रकृति के अर्थ में हो तो इसके पूर्व 'the' का प्रयोग नहीं होगा :

(a) If you interfere with nature you will suffer for it.

(21) 'Games'के नाम के पूर्व 'The' का प्रयोग नहीं होता :

(a) I play golf. (b) He plays cricket.

(22) 'Seasons ' के नाम के पूर्व 'The' का प्रयोग नहीं होता :

(a) In spring we like to clean the house.

(23) 'Time of day ' के नाम के पूर्व 'The' का प्रयोग निम्न स्थिति में नहीं होता :

(a) We travelled mostly by night. (b) We'll be there around midnight.

ERRORS, MISTAKES AND BLUNDERS IN USE OF ARTICLES

Exercise : ***Find the errors and justify your answer.***

1. Of the two (A)/solutions the second was (B)/definitely better (C)./No Error (D).
2. I have been (A)/informed that (B)/ Mr. Clinton visits Rajasthan (C)/following month (D)./No Error (E).
3. In the field of invention (A)/the credit goes to a man (B)/ who convinces the world (C)/with his arguments (D)/ not to the man who simply thinks (E)./No Error (F).
4. He claims to be a scientist (A)/but in reality he (B)/does not know even (C)/ABC of science (D)./ No Error (E).

5. Her father (A)/forbade her to go (B)/to cinema (C)/with Mohan (D)./ No Error (E).
6. It is an impossile task (A)/to calculate number (B) /of creatures living (C)/ on earth. (D)./No Error (E).
7. The man (A)/ is the only living creature (B)/that can speak (C)/and smile (D)./No Error (E).
8. He is an atheist (A)/but today he is going (B)/to the church (C)/for offering prayer (D)./No Error (E).
9. You should not spend (A)/ good part of the day (B)/ in marketing only (C)./No Error (D).
10. Whatever little (A)/milk left in the bottle (B)/was drunk by your cat (C)./No Error (D).
11. She leads (A)/a luxurious life (B)/so she visits everywhere (C)/by a car (D)./No Error (E).
12. The principal instructed (A)/the girls to return (B)/to the college (C)/before the sunset (D)./ No Error (E).
13. You must (A)/be true to your words (B)/in order to enjoy (C)/the real reputation in the life (D)./No Error (E).
14. She is the (A)/most beautiful girl (B)./No Error (C).
15. It was an insight (A)/and perseverance of the lady doctor (B)/that many women were (C)/ able to lead normal life (D)./No Error (E).
16. It is a pity (A)/that the daughter of millionaire (B)/is involved in (C)/the bank robbery (D)./No Error (E).
17. He was in a trouble (A)/when he saw (B)/a truck running (C)/towards his car (D)./No Error (E).
18. The fruits of (A)/all the modern luxuries (B)/lie in the science (C)./No Error (D).
19. I advised him (A)/to take the heart (B)/in all odd circumstances (C)./No Error (D).
20. Little knowledge (A)/of computers that she possessed (B)/proved a boon for her (C)/in getting job (D)./No Error (E).
21. We (A)/saw (B)/a elephant (C)/in the zoo (D)./No error (E).
22. It is (A)/a most (B)/beautiful (C)/painting of the gallery (D)./No Error (E).
23. Mr. Gaurav Sharma (A)/is (B)/coming to (C)/dinner (D)./No Error (E).
24. I (A)/go (B)/to cinema (C)/every Sunday (D)./No error (E).
25. He (A)/ went there(B)/ a hour(C)/ ago(D)./ No error(E).
26. He (A)/always speaks (B)/ truth(C)./No Error (D).
27. Kashmiri (A)/shawls (B)/are made of (C)/the hair of sheep (D)./No Error (E).
28. The Tajmahal (A)/is (B)/situated (C)/at the Agra (D)./No error.
29. Bible (A)/said that (B)/the sun (C)/goes round the earth (D)./No Error (E).
30. An horse (A)/is (B)/running (C)/on the ground (D)./No error (E).
31. An European (A)/dish (B)/is (C)/very famous (D)./No error (E).
32. Rome (A)/was (B)/not built (C)/in a day (D)./No error (E).
33. Ritika (A)/helps (B)/poor and (C)/the sick people (D)/No error (E).
34. The Sapna (A)/ is a very (B)/beautiful (C)/girl (D)./No error (E).
35. I (A)/saw (B)/an one rupee note (C)/on the road (D)./No error (E).
36. The boy (A)/is (B)/swimming (C)/in the pool (D)./No error (E).
37. Here is a red (A)/ shirt (B)/ which Sapna gave me (C)/yesterday (D)./No error (E).
38. Shatabdi Express (A)/runs (B)/very (C)/fast (D)./No error (E).
39. Parul (A)/was also invited (B)/to the lunch hosted by the queen (C)/ at her cottage yesterday (D)./No error (E).
40. My uncle (A)/is (B)/ a (C)/ S.P. (D)./ No error (E).
41. Gold (A)/ is (B)/an useful (C)/metal (D)./No error (E).
42. This is (A)/a good dress (B)/but (C)/that's a better one (D)./No error (E).

43. Rupam (A)/presented me (B)/a ring (C)/the ring is lost (D)./No error (E).
44. The Punjabi (A)/is (B)/a sweet language (C)/of Punjab (D)./No error (E).
45. Adnan Sami (A)/is the (B)/most popular (C)/singer in Indian film industry (D)./No error (E).
46. The sun (A)/rises (B)/in (C)/east(D)./No error (E).
47. The teaching (A)/profession (B)/ is (C)/good for women (D)./No error(E).
48. The milk (A)/is (B)/good (C)/for health (D)./No error (E).
49. I (A)/think (B)/a baby (C)/is crying (D)./No error (E).
50. Kunal (A)/was (B)/sent to (C)/a prison (D)./No error (E).
51. I(A)/ will go (B)/there (C)/ by train or bus (D)./ No error (E).
52. My parents (A)/sometimes (B)/come to school (C)/to see the principal (D)./No error (E).
53. Riya (A)/went home (B)/very late (C)/last Monday (D)./No error (E).
54. The winters (A)/are (B)/generally very (C)/cold here (D)./No error (E).
55. The monkeys (A)/jump (B)/on (C)/the trees (D)./No error (E).
56. The dog (A)/is (B)/a (C)/faithful animal (D)./No error (E).
57. Chief Minister (A)/will (B)/decide (C)/the matter (D)./No error (E).
58. Kshitiz (A)/is (B)/ a (C)/honest boy (D)./No error (E).
59. The sun (A)/ rises in (B)/the east (C)/ is an universal truth (D)./No error (E).
60. Times of India (A)/is a most popular (B)/newspaper (C)/of these days (D)./No error (E).
61. Three children (A)/died (B)/in a (C)/bus accident yesterday (D) ./No error (E).
62. The Mahatma Gandhi (A)/was (B)/also called (C)/ 'Bapu'(D)./ No error (E).
63. Chinese (A)/are (B)/fond of (C)/ chowmin (D)./No error(E).
64. Taj Mahal (A)/ is a(B)/ beautiful (C)/ building in Agra (D)./ No error (E).
65. The capital (A)/ of(B)/ U.K. is (C)/ London (D)./ No error(E).
66. My mother (A)/ is cooking (B)/ in a (C)/ kitchen (D)./ No error (E).
67. The teacher (A)/ called a (B)/ last boy (C)/ standing in the queue (D)./ No error (E).
68. The apple (A)/ a day (B)/ keeps (C)/ the doctor away (D)/ No error (E).
69. The more (A)/ I learn history(B)/ the more (C)/ I get bored (D)./ No error (E).
70. The intelligent(A)/ should (B)/ help (C)/ the duffer (D)./ No error (E).
71. Shreya (A)/gave (B)/me (C)/the watch (D)/.No error (E).
72. In the conclusion it (A)/ may be said (B)/ that the writer has surpassed (C)/ the ethical norms (D)./No Error (E).
73. It is the most (A)/ important point that (B)/ you have to (C)/ understand well. (D)./No Error (E).
74. He said to me, (A)/ "I think you (B)/ will never (C)/ turn a traitor."(D)./No Error (E).
75. Ramesh told me (A)/ that he first went (B)/ to the Mexico and(C)/ then to the Netherlands.(D)./ No Error (E).
76. My mother forbade (A)/ my sister to (B)/ go to theatre (C)/ at night.(D)./No Error (E).
77. One should be true (A)/ to one's words in (B)/ order to earn good name (C)/ and fame in the life (D)./No Error (E).
78. I have been waiting (A)/ for her (B)/ for more than (C)/ half an hour. (D)./No Error (E).
79. You should not spend (A)/good part of the day (B)/ in gossiping and wandering (C)/ here and there (D)./No Error (E).
80. Will you please (A)/ give me (B)/ little milk (C)/ for my cat ? (D)./No Error (E).
81. She informed me (A)/ that he had gone (B)/ to the church(C)/ to offer prayers(D)./No Error (E).

Explanations

1. (C) 'better' से पहले 'the' का प्रयोग करें। Comparative degree के adjective द्वारा जब कोई choice का निर्धारण होता है तो उससे पहले 'the'का प्रयोग करना होता है; जैसे : He is the stronger of the two wrestlers.
2. (D) 'following' से पूर्व 'the' लिखें। यहाँ following month - particular हो गया है।
3. (B) 'a man', की जगह 'the man' का प्रयोग करें । यहाँ 'man', particular हो गया है।
4. (D) 'ABC' के पूर्व 'the' लिखें। To emphasise use of 'the' is necessary.
5. (C) 'Cinema' से पूर्व 'the' प्रयुक्त होता है। 'go to the cinema', 'go to the theatre' जैसे phrases में 'the' का प्रयोग होता है।
6. (B) 'number' से पहले 'the' लिखें। 'the number' का अर्थ निश्चित संख्या होता है। 'the number of' वैसे भी phrase की तरह प्रयुक्त होता है।
7. (A) 'man' से पहले 'the' को Delete करें। 'man' का प्रयोग जब मानव जाति (in broader sense)के लिए होता है, तो उससे पहले 'the' प्रयुक्त नहीं होता है :

   Man is a social animal.

   Man is mortal.
8. (C) 'Church' के पहले 'the' का प्रयोग उस स्थिति में गलत है जब कि वहाँ जाने का उद्देश्य प्रार्थना करना हो। यदि church जाने का अन्य कोई उद्देश्य हो तो 'the' प्रयुक्त होगा।
9. (B) 'good part' से पहले 'a' लिखें। 'a good part of the day', phrase की तरह प्रयुक्त होता है।
10. (A) 'Little' से पहले 'the' प्रयुक्त होगा। यहाँ 'the little' से अर्थ - 'जो भी थोड़ा' से है।
11. (D) 'by a car', नहीं होगा, 'by car' होगा। 'by car, by bus, by train' के बीच में article उपयुक्त नहीं लगता है।
12. (D) 'Before sunset' होगा ('the' को delete करें)। 'before sunset, before noon, after day break' में 'the' का प्रयोग नहीं होता है। निम्न वाक्यों में अंतर समझने का प्रयास करें :

    He returned home after sunset.

    He returned home after the sun had set.
13. (D) 'life' से पहले 'the' नहीं लिखा जायेगा। जब 'life' का प्रयोग व्यापक अर्थ में हो तो 'the' का प्रयोग नहीं होता है। लेकिन life का प्रयोग यदि particular अर्थ में हो तो article का प्रयोग करना होता है:

    He is leading a happy life.

    The life of this patient is spoiled by the doctor.
14. (A) 'the' की जगह 'a' का प्रयोग करें। यहाँ 'a most' का अर्थ 'a very beautiful' से है। जब 'most' का अर्थ comparison के लिये न किया जाकर, 'very' के अर्थ में होता है तो 'a' का प्रयोग किया जाता है।
15. (A) 'an' की जगह 'the' का प्रयोग होगा। किसी भी चीज को महत्त्व देने हेतु 'the' का प्रयोग किया जाता है।
16. (B) 'Millionaire' से पहले 'a' प्रयुक्त होगा। यह एक countable noun है अत: article प्रयुक्त करना होगा।
17. (A) 'trouble' से पहले 'a' नहीं प्रयुक्त होगा। 'in danger, in trouble, in detail, in debt, in comparison, in fact' जैसे phrases के बीच में article का प्रयोग नहीं होता है।
18. (C) 'Science' से पहले 'the' का प्रयोग नहीं होगा। 'science, life', का प्रयोग जब व्यापक अर्थ में होता है, तो इनसे पहले 'the' का प्रयोग नहीं होता है।

19. (B) 'take heart' होगा। 'take heart, take care' जैसे phrases के बीच में article का प्रयोग नहीं होता है।
20. (A) 'Little' से पहले 'the' का प्रयोग होगा। 'the little का अर्थ – जो भी थोड़ा से है।
21. (C) Here 'a' is used with elephant instead of 'an'. 'An elephant' is correct.
22. (B) 'It is a most beautiful painting' – Use 'the' before 'most', being superlative.
23. (E) No error.
24. (C) 'I go to the cinema every Sunday'. When 'club', 'cinema', 'pictures', 'theatres', are used for their primary purpose of entertainment, 'The' is used before them.
25. (C) Replace 'a' by 'an'. Here 'an' will be used instead of 'a' because 'h' (in 'hour') is silent.
26. (C) He always speaks the truth.
27. (A) 'The Kashmiri shawls'; 'The' is used before nouns which name the inhabitants of a country or city collectively.
28. (D) Delete 'The' before Agra, being proper noun.
29. (A) The Bible said. 'The' is used before the names of renowned books on religion or litera ture.
30. (A) 'A horse is running on the ground'. 'A' is used with the singular countable nouns which are pronounced with the consonant sound.
31. (A) 'A' European dish is very famous; Here 'European' begins with vowel 'E' even then it sounds 'yoo' or 'u'.
32. (E) No Error. 'A' is used with certain numerical terms to give the sense of 'one'.
33. (C) Ritika helps the poor and the sick people.
34. (A) "Sapna is a very beautiful girl." 'The' is not used before proper noun.
35. (C) "I saw a one rupee note on the road." 'A' is used with nouns pronounced with consonant sound.
36. (A) A boy is swimming in the pool. 'A' is used with the singular countable nouns.
37. (A) Here is the red shirt which Sapna gave me yesterday. 'Red shirt' has become particularised.
38. (A) The Shatabdi Express. 'The' is used before the names of well-known trains.
39. (E) No error. 'The' is used before names of particular meals.
40. (C) 'My uncle is an S.P.' Here, 'An' is used before a consonant–'s' (of. S.P.), which sounds like a vowel ('ess').
41. (C) Gold is a useful metal. Before useful we should put 'a' instead of 'an'.
42. (E) No error. 'A' is used with positive and comparatives but not with superlatives.
43. (E) No error. 'The' is used before a noun which is repeated after it has been introduced once.
44. (A) 'The' is not used before name of the language (*i.e.,* Punjabi).
45. (E) No error. 'The' is used with the superlative degree of adjective.
46. (D) In the east. 'The' is used with the name of 'directions' like east, west, north, south.
47. (E) No error. 'The' is used with the professions like the nursing, the medical profession.
48. (A) Milk is good for health; 'The' article are omitted before proper nouns, material nouns, uncountables etc. in general.
49. (C) 'the baby'.
50. (D) 'Kunal was sent to prison'. 'The' article is omitted before 'church, prison, hospital, college, school and bed', when the visit to these places is for the purpose they are primarily built.
51. (E) No error. Article 'the' is omitted before modes of transportation or travel. Always use 'by bus, by car, by train', etc.
52. (C) Insert 'the' before school. When the visit to places : school, church, hospital, prison are for the purpose other than what they are primarily built for, always use 'the' before these nouns.

53. (E) No error. 'The' is not used before names.
54. (A) Remove 'the' before 'Winters'. Do not use articles before names of the seasons.
55. (A) Monkeys jump on the trees. Article 'the' is omitted before plural countable nouns when they tell about class or cast etc.
56. (E) No error. 'The' is used before a singular countable noun meant to represent a whole class or kind.
57. (A) Insert 'The' before Chief Minister. Use 'the' before designation.
58. (C) Kshitiz is an honest boy. Here 'an' is used before a word (honest) beginning with silent 'H'.
59. (D) 'The sun rises in the east' is a universal truth. 'A' is used before a word beginning with the sound 'u' (pronounced as 'yoo'or 'u').
60. (A) The "Times of India" .... 'The' is used before the names of the newspapers and magazines.
61. (E) No Error.
62. (A) Delete 'the' before Mahatma Gandhi. Article is not used before any name (proper noun).
63. (A) The chinese........... 'The' is used before nationality.
64. (A) The Taj Mahal .... 'The' is used before such names of Monuments.
65. (C) "The" is used before names of countries like U.K., U.S.A. etc.
66. (C) My mother is cooking in the kitchen; Here 'The' is used before the noun (kitchen) which can be undersdtood easily.
67. (B) The teacher called the last boy.......... 'The' is used before the ordinals.
68. (A) An apple...... 'An' is used here before a word beginning with a vowel (a,e,i,o,u,) sound.
69. (E) No error 'The' is here used twice, with comparatives to show that two things increase or decrease in the same proportion.
70. (E) No error. (Here 'the intelligent' means intelligent person and the 'duffers' means duffer persons.
71. (D) Shreya gave me a watch. 'A' is used with indefinite nouns, pronounced with consonant sound.
72. (A) Conclusion के पहले 'the' नहीं प्रयुक्त होगा। कुछ Phrases; जैसे – In detail, in fear, in hope, in problem, in conclusion का प्रयोग करते समय ध्यान दें, इनमें बीच में 'the' का प्रयोग नहीं होगा।
73. (A) most से पहले 'the' की जगह 'a' लिखना होगा। जब Superlative degree 'most' का प्रयोग Comparison हेतु किया जाता है तो 'the' लिखना होगा। यहाँ 'most' का प्रयोग 'very' के अर्थ में हुआ है अत: 'a' प्रयुक्त होगा। जैसे:
    Sarla is the most beautiful girl in the college.
    Sarla is a most beautiful girl.
74. (D) Inchoative Verb, 'Turn' के साथ noun (traitor) के पूर्व 'a' का प्रयोग नहीं किया जायेगा।
75. (C) 'Mexico' से पूर्व 'the' का प्रयोग नहीं होगा। Plural name of countries या जिन countries के नाम के साथ States or Republic जुड़ा हो, उनके नामों के पूर्व ही 'the' का प्रयोग किया जाता है।
76. (C) 'theatre' से पूर्व 'the' लिखें। 'go to the cinema/go to the theatre' आदि phrases, का इसी तरह प्रयोग किया जाता है।
77. (D) Life से पहले 'the' नहीं लिखें। Life का प्रयोग जब विस्तृत अर्थ में हो, तो life से पूर्व 'the' नहीं प्रयुक्त होता है। विशेष अर्थ में life से पूर्व article प्रयुक्त होता है। जैसे:
    She leads a happy life.
    The life of villagers is paralysed due to earthquake.

78. (D) 'hour' से पूर्व 'a' की जगह 'an' प्रयुक्त होगा।

79. (B) 'a good part of the day'. 'Good part' से पहले 'a' प्रयुक्त होगा।

80. (C) 'little' से पूर्व 'a' प्रयुक्त होगा। 'a little' का अर्थ होता है 'थोड़ा-सा'।

81. (C) 'Church' से पूर्व 'the' का प्रयोग गलत है; जब वाक्य में Church, Hospital, School, Prison, इत्यादि जाने का उद्देश्य भी वही हो कि जिसके लिए इन संस्थाओं का निर्माण हुआ है, तो इनसे पूर्व 'the' नहीं प्रयुक्त होता है।

BLUNDERS IN USE OF ARTICLES

Exercise : ***Rewrite the sentences after correction.***

1. I have a umbrella of blue colour.
2. He is an union leader.
3. Sarla is a best student of our class.
4. The honesty is the best policy.
5. Jaipur is a Paris of India.
6. We went to the Agra.
7. He is a President of our society.
8. The Sunita is a also a beautiful girl in our class.
9. This is a better of the two novels.
10. The Akbar was a great king.

Explanations

1. 'वाक्य' में 'a' की जगह 'an' आना चाहिए।
2. 'an' की जगह 'a' का ही प्रयोग होगा।
3. 'best' से पूर्व 'a' की जगह 'The' आयेगा।
4. 'honesty' से पूर्व 'The' का प्रयोग गलत है।
5. यहाँ Paris से पूर्व 'a' की जगह 'The' आयेगा।
6. Proper noun 'Agra' से पहले 'the' का प्रयोग गलत है।
7. 'a' की जगह 'the' का प्रयोग होगा। पद के नाम के पूर्व 'the' का प्रयोग होता है।
8. 'Sunita' के पूर्व (नाम के पूर्व) 'the' का प्रयोग गलत है।
9. 'better' के पूर्व a की जगह 'the' आयेगा।
10. 'Akbar' (नाम) के पूर्व 'the' का प्रयोग गलत है।

❑❑❑

2

Noun

English Grammar में Noun का बहुत महत्त्व है। बहुत से nouns, दिखने में Singular प्रतीत होते हैं लेकिन प्रयुक्त Plural की तरह होते हैं, बहुत से nouns दिखने में Plural लगते हैं, लेकिन इनका प्रयोग Singular की तरह होता है। बहुत से nouns, का रूप Singular एवं Plural form में एक समान रहता है। ध्यान रखें, किस Noun के साथ Verb Singular या Plural प्रयुक्त होगी, यह Grammar के दृष्टिकोण से बहुत महत्त्वपूर्ण है। Noun के प्रयोग के नियमों को जानने के साथ ही यह जानना भी आवश्यक है कि किसी Noun का Feminine एवं Pluralised रूप क्या है। इसके अतिरिक्त Apostrophe के सही प्रयोग हेतु विभिन्न नियमों का अध्ययन बहुत आवश्यक है। परीक्षा में Errors से सम्बन्धित पूछे जाने वाले प्रश्न अधिकांशतया इन नियमों पर ही आधारित होते हैं।

Rules

1. **कुछ nouns हमेशा Plural form में ही रहती हैं। इन Nouns के अन्त में लगे s को हटाकर, इन्हें Singular नहीं बनाया जा सकता है। ये दिखने में भी Plural लगते हैं, एवं इनका प्रयोग भी Plural की तरह होता है। ऐसे nouns निम्न है :**

   Alms, amends, annals, archives, ashes, arrears, auspices, caves, species, scissors, trousers, pants, clippers, bellows, gallows, fangs, eyeglasses, goggles, belongings, breeches, bowels, braces, binoculars, customs, congratulations, dregs, earnings, entrails, embers, fetters, fireworks, lodgings, odds, outskirts, particulars, proceeds, proceedings, regards, riches, remains, savings, shambles, shears, spectacles, surroundings, tidings, troops, tactics, thanks, tongs, vegetables, valuables, wages etc.

   (a) Where are my pants.
   (b) Where are the tongs.
   (c) The proceeds were deposited in the court.
   (d) All his assets were seized.

Note

Means' - (Singular) यदि इसके साथ 'a' या 'every' का प्रयोग हो, या इसका प्रयोग 'way to an end' 'तरीका/रास्ता' के अर्थ में किया जाये।

'Means' - (Plural) यदि इसका प्रयोग Income के अर्थ में किया जाये।

(a) My means were reduced substantially.

(b) Every means is good if the end is good.

2. **कुछ noun दिखने में Plural लगते हैं लेकिन अर्थ में Singular होते हैं। इनका प्रयोग हमेशा Singular में ही होता है। जैसे : News, Innings, Politics, Summons, Physics, Economics, Ethics, Mechanics, Mathematics, Mumps, Rickets, Billiards, Measles, Draughts, athletics etc.**

   (a) No news is good news.
   (b) Draughts is a good game.
   (c) Economics is a good subject.
   (d) Ethics demands honesty in working.

3. **कुछ nouns दिखनें में Singular लगते हैं लेकिन इनका प्रयोग हमेशा Plural में होता है; जैसे : cattle, clergy, cavalry, infantry, poultry, peasantry, children, gentry, police etc. इनके साथ कभी भी 's' नहीं लगाया जाता, जैसे cattles, childrens लिखना गलत है क्योंकि ये noun स्वंय में ही plural हैं:**

   (a) Cattle are grazing in the field.
   (b) Our infantry have marched forward.

4. **कुछ nouns का प्रयोग, केवल Singular form में ही किया जाता है। ये uncountable nouns हैं। इनके साथ Article 'A / An' का प्रयोग भी नहीं किया जाता है। जैसे :**
Scenery, Poetry, Furniture, Advice, Information, Hair, Language, Business, Mischief, Bread, Stationery, Crockery, Luggage, Baggage, Postage, Knowledge, Wastage, Money, Jewellery, Breakage.
(a) The scenery of Darzeeling is very charming.
(b) I have no information about her residence.

ध्यान रखें
(i) उक्त Nouns को कभी भी 's' लिखकर pluralise नहीं किया जाता है। जैसे : Sceneries, informations, furnitures, hairs इत्यादि लिखना गलत है।
(ii) यदि उक्त Nouns को Singular या Plural forms में बताना आवश्यक हो तो, इनके साथ कुछ शब्द जोड़कर ऐसा किया जा सकता है। जैसे :-
(a) He gave me a piece of information.
(b) Many kinds of furniture are available in that shop.
(iii) यदि 'Hair' का प्रयोग 'Countable' की तरह हो तो 'hairs' हो सकता है। जैसे : one hair, two hairs :
(a) I need your two grey hairs.

5. **कुछ nouns, plural एवं singular दोनों वचनों में एक ही रूप में रहते हैं। जैसे : deer, fish, crew, family, team, jury, pike, trout, aircraft, counsel etc. :**
(a) Our team is the best.
(b) Our team are wearing their new uniform.
(c) The jury is considering its judgement.
(d) The jury are considering their verdict.

6. **कुछ Nouns अर्थ में तो Plural होते हैं, लेकिन यदि इनके पूर्व कोई निश्चित संख्यात्मक विशेषण (Definite numeral adjective) का प्रयोग किया जाता है, तो इन nouns को Pluralise नहीं किया जाता है। जैसे : Pair, score, gross, stone, hundred, dozen, thousand, million, billion, etc.**
(a) I have two pair of shoes.
(b) I have two hundred rupees only.
(c) She purchased three dozen pencils.
लेकिन यदि इनके साथ Indefinite countable का प्रयोग हो, तो इन्हें Pluralise किया जाता है। जैसे :- Dozens of women, Hundreds of people, Millions of dollars, scores of shops, many pairs of shoes, thousands, millions etc.

7. **यदि किसी Noun के बाद Preposition आता है एवं फिर वही Noun आता है, तो वह noun singular रहता है।**
(a) Town after town was devastated.
(b) Row upon row of pink marble looks beautiful.

NOUN NUMBER (SINGULAR-PLURAL)

सामान्यतया Noun की वर्तनी (spelling) के अन्त में 's' जोड़ने से उसका Plural बन जाता है। जैसे : Boy- Boys, Table- Tables,
इस सम्बन्ध में निम्न नियमों एवं इनके अपवादों को ध्यान में रखें :

(1) जिन nouns के अन्त में s, ss, ch, sh, z या x आता है, उनका plural बनाने के लिये अन्त में 'es' जोड़ दिया जाता है :

Singular	**Plural**	**Singular**	**Plural**
Bus	Buses	Class	Classes
Fox	Foxes	Church	Churches

इस नियम के कुछ अपवाद भी हैं। जैसे :

Singular	Plural	Singular	Plural
Stomach	Stomachs	Locus	loci
Radius	Radii	Ox	Oxen

(2) कुछ Nouns के अन्त में 'o' आता है, यदि उससे पूर्व कोई व्यंजन (consonant) हो, तो उसका plural बनाने के लिये noun के अन्त में 'es' जोड़ते हैं :

Singular	Plural	Singular	Plural
Hero	Heroes	Mango	Mangoes
Potato	Potatoes	Cargo	Cargoes

इस नियम के कुछ अपवाद हैं :

Singular	Plural	Singular	Plural
Canto	Cantos	Piano	Pianos
Dynamo	Dynamos	Solo	Solos

(3) यदि किसी noun के अन्त में double vowel लगे हुये हों, तो उसका plural बनाने के लिये उसके अन्त में 's' जोड़ दिया जाता है :

Singular	Plural	Singular	Plural
Bee	Bees	Radio	Radios
Zoo	Zoos	Portfolio	Portfolios

(4) यदि Noun के अन्त में 'y' आये एवं 'y' से पूर्व कोई व्यंजन आता हो तो 'y' की जगह 'ies' लिखने से उसका plural बनता है :

Singular	Plural	Singular	Plural
Country	Countries	Dictionary	Dictionaries
Family	Families	Lorry	Lorries

(5) यदि Noun के अन्त में 'y' आये एवं 'y' से पूर्व कोई Vowel आता हो तो उसके अन्त में 's' जोड़ने से उसका plural बनता है :

Singular	Plural	Singular	Plural
Key	Keys	Way	Ways
Donkey	Donkeys	Valley	Valleys

(6) यदि noun के अन्त में 'f' या 'fe' आये, तो plural बनाने के लिये 'f' या 'fe' को हटाकर 'ves' लिखते हैं :

Singular	Plural	Singular	Plural
Calf	Calves	Life	Lives
Half	Halves	Leaf	Leaves

इस नियम के कुछ अपवाद निम्नलिखित हैं :

Singular	Plural	Singular	Plural
Belief	Beliefs	Proof	Proofs
Chief	Chiefs	Roof	Roofs
Cliff	Cliffs	Safe	Safes

(7) Compound noun में मुख्य शब्द के साथ 's' लगाने पर उसका plural बनता है :

Singular	Plural	Singular	Plural
Brother-in-law	Brothers-in-law,	Bed-room	Bed-rooms
Commander-in-chief	Commanders-in-chief	Step-daughter	Step-daughters
Maid-servant	Maid- servants,	Pea-hen	Pea-hens

**Man servant	Men servantss	**Woman conductor	Women conductors
*Woman lover	Woman lovers	*Man lover	Man lovers

Note the difference among the plurals of nouns with single star(*) and with double star(**)

(8) निम्न आठ Nouns ऐसी हैं, जिनका Plural बनाने के लिए Inside Vowels में परिवर्तन करते हैं, ये हैं :

Singular	Plural	Singular	Plural
Man	Men	Mouse	Mice
Woman	Women	Louse	Lice
Foot	Feet	Goose	Geese
Tooth	Teeth	Dormouse	Dormice

(9) निम्नलिखित चार Nouns ऐसी हैं, जिनका Plural बनाने के लिए इनके अन्त में 'en' या 'ne' जोड़ते है :

Singular	Plural	Singular	Plural
Child	Children	Cow	Kine (Cows)
Ox	Oxen	Brother	Brethren

(10) कुछ nouns के दो तरह के plural बनते हैं जिनका अर्थ भी भिन्न होता है :

(1) Brother - Brothers - Sons of the same parents.
brethren - Members of a society or community.

(2) Cloth - Cloths - Unstitched cloth.
Clothes- Stitched clothes (Garments).

(3) Die - Dies - Stamps used for printing and coining.
Dice - Small cubes used in games.

(4) Index - Indexes - Tables of contents in a book.
Indices - Signs used in Algebra.

SOME TYPICAL NOUNS

(A) Latin words :- Latin के कुछ शब्द, जिनके अन्त में 'um' आता है, एकवचन होते हैं; इनको Plural बनाने के लिये 'um' हटाकर 'a' लगाया जाता है। जैसे :

Singular	Plural	Singular	Plural
Addendum	Addenda	Agendum	Agenda
Datum	Data	Dictum	Dicta

Note

*आजकल **Agenda** एवं **Data** का प्रयोग Singular एवं Plural दोनों वचनों में किया जाने लगा है; यथा:*

(a) The agenda has been finalised. *(b) The agenda of the meeting are drawn today.*

(c) The data is incomplete. *(d) More data are required.*

***'Medium'** का प्रयोग जब means या agency के रूप में किया जाता है तो इसका Plural - media होता है।*

लेकिन जब medium का प्रयोग spiritual sense में किया गया हो तो इसका Plural, mediums होगा।

IMPORTANT

Latin के निम्न शब्दों पर ध्यान दें : इन शब्दों के अन्त में भी 'um' आता है, लेकिन इनका Plural बनाने हेतु इनके अन्त में 's' जोड़ा जाता है :

Singular	Plural	Singular	Plural
asylum	asylums	forum	forums
museum	museums	pendulum	pendulums
premium	premiums	quorum	quorums
petroleum	petroleums	formula	formulae / formulas

(B) कुछ Latin words केअन्त में 'us' आता है। इनका plural 'us' को 'i' में बदलकर बनाया जाता है :

Singular	Plural	Singular	Plural
Radius	Radii	Locus	Loci
Syllabus	Syllabi	Genius	Genii

(C) कुछ Greek शब्दों केअन्त में 'is' आता है, इनका Plural, 'is' को 'es' में बदलकर बनाया जाता है :

Singular	Plural	Singular	Plural
Analysis	Analyses	Basis	Bases
Crisis	Crises	Thesis	Theses
Hypothesis	Hypotheses	Parenthesis	Parentheses.

(D) कुछ Greek शब्दों के अन्त में 'on' आता है इनका Plural 'on' को 'a' में बदलने से बनता है :

Phenomenon	Phenomena	Criterion	Criteria

(E) अन्य कई प्रकार के nouns के Plural निम्न प्रकार बनते हैं :

Singular	Plural	Singular	Plural
If	Ifs	But	Buts
I	I's	T	T's
5	5s	10	10s
P	P's	MP	MPs
BA	BAs	MA	MAs
ATM	ATMs	UPC	UPCs

(F) कुछ nouns का Singular में अर्थ, इनके Plural form के अर्थ से पूर्णतया अलग होता है, अत: इनका प्रयोग सावधानीपूर्वक करना चाहिए :

Singular	Plural	Singular	Plural
Air (हवा)	Airs (दिखावटी)	Alphabet (वर्णमाला)	Alphabets (भाषायें)
Compass (सीमा)	Compasses (एक यंत्र)	Manner (तरीका)	Manners (व्यवहार)
Number (संख्या)	Numbers (मात्रायें)	Pain (तकलीफ)	Pains (प्रयत्न)
Physic (दवा)	Physics (भौतिकी)	Premise (प्रस्तावना)	Premises (भवन)
Quarter (चौथाई भाग)	Quarters (छोटे मकान)	Iron (लोहा)	Irons (जंजीरें)
Return (वापसी)	Returns (हिसाब,आय)	Effect (प्रभाव)	Effects (सामान)
Force (शक्ति)	Forces(सेना)	Good (अच्छा)	Goods (सामान)
Sand (बालू)	Sands (रेगिस्तान)	Water (पानी)	Waters (समुद्र)
Wood (लकड़ी)	Woods (जंगल)	Ground (जमीन)	Grounds (कारण)
Abuse (दुरुपयोग)	Abuses(कुरीतियाँ)	Advice (सलाह)	Advices (सूचनायें)

USE OF APOSTROPHE WITH 'S

सामान्य रूप से Possessive Case के लिए Apostrophe का प्रयोग Noun के साथ 's' लगाकर किया जाता है।

इस सम्बन्ध में निम्न बिन्दुओं पर गौर करें :

(A) यदि plural शब्द का अन्तिम अक्षर 's' है तो apostrophe का प्रयोग करते समय 's' नहीं लगाते हैं, केवल apostrophe comma (') का ही प्रयोग करते है :

1. Horses' tail,
2. Boys' college,
3. Girls' school,
4. Working girls'hostel.

Words with hissing sound of 's' में भी 's नहीं लगता है:

for peace' sake, for conscience' sake, for goodness' sake, for Jesus' sake.

(B) कुछ शब्द ; **his, hers, yours, mine, ours, its, theirs** के साथ **apostrophe** नहीं लगाते हैं :

Yours faithfully, Yours truly, Ours garden , his pen, hers purse, theirs room.

(C) निम्न **titles** को **Plural** बनाते समय **apostrophe** इनके अन्तिम शब्द के साथ ही लगाते हैं :

1. Governor-General's instructions.
2. Commander-in-Chief's orders.
3. My son in law's sister.
4. Ram and Sons's shop.

(D) Do not use 'double apostrophe'. We should avoid use of double apostrophe in a sentence:

1. My wife's secretary's mother has expired. — Incorrect

   इसकी जगह हमें लिखना चाहिये :

   The mother of my wife's secretary has expired. — Correct
2. Mrs Kuwrani's now chairperson of society's proposal was rejected. — Incorrect

   The proposal of Mrs Kuwrani, now chairperson of society was rejected.— Correct

(E) Anybody/Nobody/Everybody/Somebody/Anyone/Someone/No one/Everyone के साथ **Apostrophe 's** का प्रयोग किया जाता है। जैसे:

1. Everyone's concern is no one's concern.
2. Everybody's business is nobody's business.

Note *यदि इनके बाद 'else' का प्रयोग हो, तो apostrophe को 'else' के साथ लगाते हैं। जैसे:*

(a) I can rely on your words, not somebody else's.

(b) I obey your orders and nobody else's.

(यहाँ Somebody's else या Nobody's else लिखना गलत होगा- ध्यान रखें।)

ERRORS, MISTAKES AND BLUNDERS IN USE OF NOUN

Exercise : ***Following sentences have some errors/ mistakes. Rewrite these sentences after correction :***

1. Her hairs are curly.
2. Our elders gave us many advices.
3. I have many work to do.
4. Sita has sold all her furnitures.
5. She gave me informations about this bank.
6. The sceneries of Himachal Pradesh are very charming.
7. The peoples are hard working.
8. The cattles are grazing in the field.
9. I want a paper.
10. I bring fruits and vegetables from the market.
11. You must continue your study.
12. These news are false.
13. They go to Agra during the summer vacations.
14. Her spectacle is very nice.
15. She has a twenty rupees note.
16. He got only passing marks.
17. Ram was true to his words.
18. Ten miles are a long distance.
19. They want two dozens apple.
20. I want two pairs of white shoes.
21. Rahul has finished two third of his work.
22. The chair's legs are broken.
23. Good night , I am so glad to meet you.
24. There is no space in the car.
25. We should help the poors.
26. She left for Delhi by 8.30 O'clock bus.
27. One of his son is a teacher.
28. 'Amazing stories' are an interesting book.
29. This is my son's in law house.
30. I brought my furnitures by goods train.
31. I saw two beautiful fishes in the pond.
32. Thomson's poetries are very charming.
33. Is your scissors dull?
34. Light travel faster than sound.

35. All the furnitures of my house have been stolen.
36. A poet and writer are dead.
37. The committee was divided on this issue.
38. Mathematics are not a dificult subject.
39. My sympathies are always with the poor.
40. The mother both carried her son and daughter from the burning house .
41. My sister serves in boy's school.
42. Rohan's and Mohan's house is very far from here.
43. There are many news published in local paper.
44. The teacher has taught the alphabets.
45. Please reply, your's faithfully.
46. I go for a two miles walk daily.
47. She loves either you or I.
48. There are four breads in the kitchen.
49. One should not hate the poors.
50. The magistrate passed order of his release.
51. She has committed not one but many mischiefs.
52. The first inning is going to over now.
53. There is no place in this compartment.
54. He bought some stationeries.
55. My mother's brother's son has come.
56. There are a few peoples who are really honest.
57. Give me ten pices.
58. There were no gentries in that function.
59. He is a sixty years old man.
60. A five men committee had a three hours meeting yesterday.
61. An all parties meeting was called to consider the drought situation in the country.
62. There is two ways traffic here, so no problem of traffic blockage.
63. How can our country accept the two nations theory?
64. He has gone to market to purchase vegetable.
65. He said, "Riches has wings".
66. I asked him where was his spectacles
67. She said that she was suffering from measle.
68. She said, "Please give him an alm".
69. Shelly's poetries are great.
70. I saw beautiful sceneries in Kashmir last year.
71. He has purchased new machineries.
72. He said, "He has purchased very costly crockeries".
73. There were very heavy traffics on the road.
74. She has bought very beautiful furnitures.
75. He gave me many informations.
76. I am going to purchase some stationeries.
77. Ram said, "The hair of Sita are black".
78. This house is made of bricks and stones.
79. Cities after cities were destroyed by the army.
80. Hours after hours were passed,but she didn't turn up.
81. Raju said, "I beg from doors to doors daily".
82. Ships after ships were sailing by those days.
83. Rows upon rows of pink marble are soothing to the eyes.
84. I gave her three and a half apples.
85. The meeting was held for three and a quarter hours.
86. The length of this hall is three times and a half to that hall.
87. His salary is two times and a half to that of mine.
88. I have two and a half rupees only.
89. What the peoples think , I can't say .
90. Who owns these poultries?
91. He is my cousin brother.
92. How many 3s are there in 31313 ?
93. How many cattles you have?
94. I have only ten five rupees's notes.
95. He has written a nice poetry.
96. Today I have received two month's wages.
97. What is this book's price.
98. There are only two females in the garden.

Explanations

1. Her hair is curly
2. Our elders gave us many pieces of advice.
3. I have much work to do.
4. Sita has sold all her furniture.
5. She gave me information about this bank.
6. The scenery of Himachal Pradesh is very charming.
7. The people are hard working .
8. The cattle are grazing in the field.
9. I want a piece of paper.
10. I bring fruit and vegetables from the market.
11. You must continue your studies.
12. This news is false.
13. They go to Agra during the summer vacation.
14. Her spectacles are very nice.
15. She has a twenty rupee note.
16. He got only pass marks.
17. Ram was true to his word.
18. Ten miles is long distance.
19. They want two dozen apples.
20. I want two pair of white shoes.
21. Rahul has finished two thirds of his work.
22. The legs of the chair are broken.
23. Good evening ,I am so glad to meet you.
24. There is no room in the car.
25. We should help the poor.
26. She left for Delhi by 8.30 bus.
27. One of his sons is a teacher.
28. 'Amazing stories' is an interesting book.
29. This is my son -in-law's house.
30. I brought my furniture by goods train.
31. I saw two beautiful fish in the pond.
32. Thomoson's poetry is very charming.
33. Are your scissors dull?
34. Light travels faster that sound.
35. All the furniture of my house have been stolen.
36. A poet and writer is dead.
37. The committee were divided on this issue.
38. Mathematics is not a dificult subject.
39. My sympathy is always with the poor.
40. The mother carried both her son and daughter from the burning house.
41. My sister serves in boys' school.
42. Rohan and Mohan's house is very far from here.
43. There are many items of news published in the local paper.
44. The teacher has taught the letters of alphabet.
45. Please reply, yours faithfully.
46. I go for a two mile walk daily.
47. She loves either you or me.
48. There are four pieces of bread in the kitchen.
49. One should not hate the poor.
50. The magistrate passed orders of his release.
51. She has committed not one but many acts of mischief.
52. The first innings is going to be over now.
53. There is no room in this compartment.
54. He bought some stationery.
55. The son of my mother's brother has come.
56. There are few people who are really honest.
57. Give me ten pice.
58. There were no gentry in that function.
59. He is a sixty year old man.
60. A five man committee had a three hour meeting yesterday.
61. An all party meeting was called to consider the drought situation in the country.
62. There is two way traffic here so no problem of traffic blockage.
63. How can our country accept the two nation theory ?
64. He has gone to market to purchase vegetables.
65. He said, "Riches have wings".
66. I asked him where were his spectacles.
67. She said that she was suffering from measles.
68. She said, "Please give him alms".

69. Shelly's poetry is great.
70. I saw beautiful scenery in Kashmir last year.
71. He has purchased new machinery.
72. He said, "He has purchased very costly crockery".
73. There was very heavy traffic on the road.
74. She has bought very beautiful furniture.
75. He gave me a lot of information.
76. I am going to purchase some stationery.
77. Ram said, "The hair of Sita is black".
78. This house is made of brick and stone.
79. City after city was destroyed by the army.
80. Hour after hour was passed but she didn't turn up.
81. Raju said, "I beg from door to door daily."
82. Ship after ship was sailing by those days.
83 Row upon row of pink marble is soothing to the eyes.
84. I gave her three apples and a half.
85. The meeting was held for three hours and a quarter.
86. The length of this hall is three and a half times to that hall.
87. His salary is two and a half times to that of mine.
88. I have two rupees and a half only.
89. What the people think I can't say.
90. Who owns these poultry?
91. He is my cousin.
92. How many 3's are there in 31313.
93. How many cattle you have?
94. I have only ten five rupee notes.
95. He has written a nice poem. or
He has written nice poetry.
96. Today I have received two months wages.
97. What is the price of this book?
98. There are only two women in the garden.

SPOTTING ERRORS (NOUN)

Exercise : *Find the errors and justify your answer.*

1. He acted not(A)/ as per my advice(B)/ but somebody else(C).
2. Pakistan's problems(A)/ are also as(B)/ serious as(C)/ that of India(D).
3. When I reached(A)/ at the gate of his(B)/ house I found his(C)/ locking up the gate(D).
4. Many of the question(A)/ appeared in this question paper(B)/ are too difficult(C)/ to solve(D).
5. I visited(A)/ Ram's and Sita's house(B)/ and found the couple missing(C).
6. All the girls students (A)/ are advised to (B)/ attend the meeting positively (C).
7. She gave me (A)/ two important informations(B)/ I had been waiting for(C)/ the last two months(D).
8. The English teacher(A)/ gave him a home work (B)/ to complete that (C)/ by night positively(D).
9. She could not complete(A)/ even the two third(B)/ of the book(C)/ owing to her busy schedule(D).
10. All the woman teachers(A)/ are agitating(B)/ against the haughty attitude(C)/ of the Principal(D).
11. He informed that(A)/ he had lost a packet(B)/ of the hundred(C)/ rupees notes(D).
12. He has ordered(A)/ bricks for the proposed(B)/ shopping complex(C).
13. She has ordered(A)/ two dozens of copies(B)/ of English Book by Mr. Gupta(C).
14. She uses a good(A)/ quality of shampoo(B)/so her hairs are(C)/ black (D).
15. I known nothing(A)/ about her (B)/ whereabout (C).

Explanations

1. (C) 'else' की जगह 'else's' लिखना होगा। यहाँ 'somebody else's' का अर्थ किसी अन्य की 'advice' से है, न कि किसी अन्य व्यक्ति से। अत: apostrophe का use करना होगा।
2. (D) 'India' की जगह 'India's' होगा, क्योंकि यहाँ Pakistan की problems की तुलना India की problems से की जा रही है, न कि India से।

3. (C) 'his' की जगह 'him' का प्रयोग होगा। यहाँ 'locking' एक participle की जगह प्रयुक्त हुआ है अत: इससे पहले objective case (him) का प्रयोग होगा न कि possessive case (his) का; जैसे :
Swimming is a good exercise.
I found him swimming in the pool.
'Swimming/walking' का प्रयोग जब gerund के रूप में होता है, तो इनका अर्थ होता है- 'तैरना, टहलना।' लेकिन जब इनका प्रयोग participle के रूप में होता है, तो इनका अर्थ होता है - तैरते हुऐ, टहलते हुऐ।

4. (A) 'question' के स्थान पर 'questions' आयेगा। After phrases : 'of the like', 'one of the', 'many of the', plural noun is used.

5. (B) 'Ram's and Sita's' के स्थान पर 'Ram and Sita's' होना चाहिये। जब दो nouns एक ही वस्तु के possession को बता रहे हों, तो एक ही apostrophe का प्रयोग होगा।

6. (A) girls students के स्थान पर 'girl students' होना चाहिये। एक compound noun में मुख्य शब्द को ही plural किया जाता है। जैसे :
   1. boy friend - boy friends.   2. maid servent - maid servants.

7. (B) 'two important informations' के स्थान पर 'two important pieces of information' होगा। 'information' एक uncountable noun है अत: इसके साथ a, two, three etc. नहीं लगता है।

8. (B) 'gave him a home work' के स्थान पर 'gave him home work' होगा। 'home work', uncountable noun है, अत: इससे पहले article (a / an) का प्रयोग गलत है। ध्यान रखें home work, class work, 'urgent work' के पहले 'a' या 'an' का प्रयोग नहीं होता है। यदि 'work' का प्रयोग किसी author की किसी रचना के सन्दर्भ में हुआ है, तो article का प्रयोग कर सकते है। जैसे -
   (a) Hamlet is a popular work by Shakespeare.
   (b) All the works of Bernard Shaw are worth reading.
   (c) 'An easy approach to English' is a good work by Mr S.C. Gupta .

9. (B) 'two third' की जगह 'two thirds' होगा। यहां 'Book' के एक part के बारे में बात हो रही है, अत: 'two thirds' लिखा जायेगा।

10. (A) 'Woman teachers' की जगह 'women teachers' होगा। man, woman के साथ यदि कोई अन्य plural noun (teacher) आता है तो men, women हो जाता है। जैसे :
   Man supervisor – Men supervisors
   Woman cleaner – Women cleaners.

11. (D) 'rupees' की जगह 'rupee' लिखें। साधारणतया हम one hundred rupees कहते हैं। यहाँ 'one hundred' adjective की तरह कार्य कर रहा है, अत: 'rupee' singular ही रहेगा।

12. (B) 'Bricks' की जगह 'pieces of brick' होगा। क्योंकि 'brick, stone, iron, chalk' etc. uncountable, material noun हैं।

13. (B) 'two dozen copies' होगा। Question No. 11 का Explanation देखें।

14. (C) 'hairs are' की जगह 'hair is 'होगा। 'hair' is used in singular.

15. (C) 'whereabout' की जगह 'whereabouts' (पता) होगा।

BLUNDERS IN USE OF NOUN

Exercise : *Correct the following sentences, justifying your answers.*

1. There are three childrens in the park.
2. He gave me many informations .

3. Ram brought his furnitures by goods train.
4. Every candidate should write their names neatly .
5. Your's faithfully.
   P. K. Sharma.
6. I want to purchase ten knifes.
7. Three young mans and two young womans were present in the hall .
8. How many MP's were present in the meeting ?
9. This is a girl's hostel.
10. My son's in law sister is coming tomorrow.

Explanations

1. 'Children' होगा। 'Children, Cattle, Infantry' etc. आदि nouns हैं, जो हमेशा Plural में ही प्रयुक्त होते हैं। इनमें 's' नहीं जोड़ा जा सकता है।
2. 'Information' होगा। 'Information, Language, Furniture, Money' इत्यादि ऐसे nouns हैं, जिनको 's' जोड़कर Pluralize नहीं किया जा सकता है।
3. 'Furnitures' की जगह 'Furniture' होगा। वाक्य (2) का explanation देखें।
4. 'their' की जगह 'his' होगा। 'Every, Each' के साथ Singular Pronoun Third person का प्रयोग होता है।
5. 'Yours faithfully' होगा। 'Yours' में apostrophe का प्रयोग गलत है।
6. 'Knifes' की जगह 'knives' होगा। 'knife' का plural- 'knives' होता है।
7. 'Men' एवं 'women' होगा। 'man' का plural - men तथा 'women' का plural - women होता है।
8. 'MPs' होगा। 'MP' का Plural 'MPs' होता है। इसी तरह 'BA' का plural 'BAs' होता है।
9. 'Girls' hostel' होगा।
10. 'My son in law's sister' होगा। Apostrophe गलत जगह प्रयोग की गई है।

3

Tense

English Grammar में प्रवीणता प्राप्त करने हेतु Tense के नियमों की जानकारी, उनके उचित प्रयोग का ज्ञान होना परम आवश्यक है। Tense के सन्दर्भ में निम्नलिखित महत्त्वपूर्ण बिन्दुओं पर गौर करें। परीक्षाओं में Tense के Errors से सम्बन्धित प्रश्न, अधिकांशतया इन्हीं के सम्बन्ध में पूछे जाते हैं।

Tenses are the base for writing and speaking English correctly.

PRESENT TENSE

(A) Present Indefinite Tense

(a) Present Indefinite का सबसे महत्त्वपूर्ण बिन्दु यह है, कि जब वाक्य में subject,- singular number, third person है तो verb के साथ 's' या 'es' जोड़ दिया जाता है।

Verb के साथ 'es' का प्रयोग कब किया जायेगा ?

यदि Verb का अंतिम अक्षर ss, o, z, x, ch, sh है, तो subject- singular number, third person के साथ 'es' जोड़ा जाता है। सामान्यतया अन्य स्थिति में verb के साथ 's' जोड़ा जाता है:

1. I go - He goes.
2. I kiss - She kisses.
3. They fetch - She fetches.
4. We clash - He clashes.

सामान्यतया अन्य सभी verbs के साथ केवल 's' लगता है। जैसे:–

1. We play - He plays.
2. I pray - He prays.
3. You say - He says.
4. I pay - He pays.

(b) जब Verb का अंतिम अक्षर 'y' है एवं इससे पूर्व का अक्षर व्यंजन (Consonant) है, तो subject- singular number third person के साथ Present Indefinite में 'y' को 'ies' में बदला जाता है। जैसे:–

1. They fly kites.- He flies kites.
2. I try. - Sita tries.
3. Girls cry. - Suman cries.
4. I verify. - She verifies.

Important Points About the Use of Present Indefinite Tense :

(1) 'Here' एवं 'There' से शुरू होने वाले exclamatory वाक्यों में Present Tense का प्रयोग किया जाता है:

(a) There she lives!
(b) There goes the bell!
(c) Here comes the train!
(d) Here she comes!

(2) Simple Present Tense का प्रयोग always, never, occasionally, sometimes, often, usually, every week, on Sunday, twice a year, every year etc. के साथ निम्न प्रकार से किया जाता है:

(a) She always speaks the truth.
(b) He sometimes goes for a walk.
(c) He never tells a lie.
(d) Rahim often comes late.

(3) 'Whenever' एवं 'When' के साथ Simple Present Tense का प्रयोग निम्न प्रकार से होता है:

(a) Whenever it rains, the roof leaks.
(b) When you open the window, a light goes on.

(4) जब main verb, future tense में हो, तो Conditional sentences में if, till, as soon as, when, unless, before, until, even if, in case, as के बाद Present Indefinite का प्रयोग किया जाता है :

(a) We shall wait till she arrives.
(b) I shall not go there even if it rains.
(c) When he comes, I shall give him a gift.
(d) I shall go to Jaipur in case she asks me.

(B) Present Continuous Tense

Important points about the use of Present Continuous Tense :

(1) ऐसे कार्य हेतु भी Present Continuous का प्रयोग किया जाता है जो at the time of speaking नहीं हो रहा होता है, लेकिन regular process में लगातार हो रहा है। जैसे :

(a) He is writing a novel now a days. (b) Sita is learning English grammar now a days.

(2) Near future में सम्पन्न होने वाले planned or arranged action हेतु भी Present Continuous का प्रयोग किया जाता है :

(a) They are going to Delhi tomorrow. (b) She is coming by 7 A.M. train on Monday.

(3) 'Always, continually, constantly, forever' के साथ Present Continuous का प्रयोग ऐसे कार्य हेतु किया जाता है, जो कि व्यक्ति आदतन, दूसरों की इच्छा के विपरीत frequently करता है :

(a) She is always complaining. (c) You are forever finding faults with others.

(4) Stative and Dynamic Verbs

कुछ Verbs का प्रयोग सामान्य स्थिति में Continuous form में नहीं किया जाता है। इस तरह की Verbs को Stative Verbs कहा जाता है।

Stative Verbs को पाँच भागों में वर्गीकृत किया जा सकता है :

1. **Verbs of Perception:-** See, hear, smell, taste, feel etc. : जब इन verbs का प्रयोग, बिना किसी विशेष प्रयास के, सामान्य स्थिति में होता है, तो इन्हें Present Simple में ही प्रयोग किया जाना उचित है। खुली आँख से स्वत: ही देखने (see) का कार्य होता है, उसी तरह नाक, कान, जीभ (smell, hear, taste हेतु) का उपयोग व्यक्ति स्वत: ही करता है। स्पर्श (feel) भी एक स्वत: अनुभव होने वाला कार्य है। लेकिन अगर इन verbs का प्रयोग किसी विशेष उद्‌देश्य हेतु किया जाता है, तो इनको continuous tense में प्रयोग किया जा सकता है। इन verbs की सूचि में 'notice, recognise' भी शामिल कर लिये गये हैं।
2. **Verbs of appearance:-** look, resemble, seem, appear etc.
3. **Verbs of emotions:-** want, desire, wish, hate, hope, like, refuse, hope, believe, doubt, loathe, mind, care, detest, adore, appreciate, admire, fear, expect etc.
4. **Verbs of thinking:-** think, suppose, agree, consider, trust, remember, forget, know, understand, perceive, realise, recollect etc.
5. **Verbs of possession:-** belong, owe, own, possess, contain, have etc.

ये verbs, stative verbs या **Non-conclusive verbs** भी कहलाती हैं। इनका प्रयोग सामान्य अर्थ में Present Continuous में करना गलत है। इनका प्रयोग सामान्यतया Simple Present में किया जाता है।

निम्न वाक्यों को देखें :

Incorrect	**Correct**
1. We are seeing with our eyes.	1. We see with our eyes.
2. Are you hearing a strange noise?	2. Do you hear a strange noise?
3. We are smelling with our nose.	3. We smell with our nose.
4. I am feeling you are worng.	4. I feel you are wrong.
5. The water is feeling cold.	5. The water feels cold.
6. The coffee is tasting bitter.	6. The coffee tastes bitter.

7. How much am I owing you? — 7. How much do I owe you?
8. I am hating it. — 8. I hate it.
9. I am having a car. — 9. I have a car.
10. I am thinking. — 10. I think.

लेकिन निम्न स्थितियों में इन Verbs का प्रयोग Continuous form में करना उचित है :-

1. The Session Judge is hearing our case.
2. We are thinking of going to USA next year.
3. He is minding (looking after) the children, while his wife is away.
4. I am seeing my lawyer today.
5. I am having some difficulties with this puzzle.

Dynamic Verbs:- Dynamic का अर्थ होता है-क्रियाशील गतिशील। यह Stative का विपरीतार्थक शब्द है। जब कोई Verb; Temporary, Momentary या Dynamic कार्य हेतु प्रयुक्त होती है, तो वह Dynamic Verb कहलाती है। जैसे: He is swimming., She is going., Ram is coming.

IMPORTANT Stative Verbs का प्रयोग, किन्हीं अवस्थाओं में जब Continuous form में होता है, तो ये Dynamic Verbs बन जाती हैं (जब इनका प्रयोग Temporary/Dynamic कार्य हेतु होता है।), जैसे:

1. We see with our eyes (Permanent-Stative Verb 'see'.)
2. I am seeing the teacher tomorrow (Temporary- Dynamic Verb)
3. I have a Maruti car. (Permanent- Stative verb- 'have')
4. I am having a nice time (Temporary- Dynamic verb)
5. This apple tastes sweet. (Permanent- Stative verb 'taste')

(C) Present Perfect Tense

Important points about the use of Present Perfect Tense :

(1) जब कोई कार्य भूतकाल में शुरू हुआ हो, एवं अब भी जारी हो तो Present Perfect का प्रयोग किया जा सकता है। ऐसी स्थिति में Present Perfect के साथ 'since/for' का प्रयोग किया जाता है।

(a) He has lived in this house for five years.(He is still living.)
(b) He has taught in this college for three years. (He is still teaching.)

IMPORTANT **जो कार्य Past में शुरू हुआ हो एवं अभी भी चल रहा हो, उसके लिये दो Tenses प्रयोग किए जा सकते हैं :**

Present Perfect Continuous एवं Present Perfect : कुछ Verbs जिनका प्रयोग Continuous form में नहीं किया जा सकता है, उनके लिये Present Perfect का प्रयोग करना उचित रहता है। ऐसी Verbs के बारे में पूर्व में Present Continuous के अन्तर्गत बताया गया है :

I have been knowing her for three years. *—Incorrect*
I have known her for three years. *—Correct*

(2) 'Yet, always, never, already, upto now, to day, often, several times, lately, recently, so far, ever' का प्रयोग Present Perfect में निम्न प्रकार किया जाता है :

(a) Have the children gone to school yet? (b) Has Ramesh left yet?
(c) I have already visited Agra. (d) Have you ever been to Russia?
(e) Hari hasn't come to college this morning. (f) She hasn't been well lately.

(3) निम्न प्रकार के Sentence Structures में भी Present Perfect का प्रयोग किया जाता है :

'This / It / That' is the 'first /second/ third / only / best /worst' + ...

(a) This is the best whisky, I have ever drunk.
(b) This is the easiest job, I have ever had.
(c) This is the third time you have asked me the same question.

(4) 'It is' के साथ Present Perfect का प्रयोग निम्न Sentence Structures में किया जा सकता है :
(a) It is three years since I have seen her.
(b) It is two months since I have smoked a cigarette.

(5) वाक्य में Conditional Clause के साथ Present Perfect Tense का प्रयोग Future Time को व्यक्त करता है। जैसे :
(a) I can't decide until I've discussed the matter with my wife.
(b) I will come as soon as I've finished writing this letter.

The Present and Present Perfect Tenses may indicate future time in temporal and conditional clauses : *Guide to patterns and usage in English* page 98 — *A.S. Hornby*

IMPORTANT यद्यपि Present Perfect Tense, Past एवं Present का मिश्रण है, तथापि यह ध्यान रखें कि Present Perfect Tense में Past time के adverbs; जैसे- last night/ last year/month/week, ago, short while ago, yesterday, day before yesterday इत्यादि का प्रयोग नहीं किया जाता है :

(a) He has gone to Jaipur last night. — *Incorrect*
He went to Jaipur last night. — *Correct*
(b) Ram has arrived shortwhile ago. — *Incorrect*
Ram arrived shortwhile ago. — *Correct*

Past time के adverbs के साथ Simple Past का प्रयोग किया जाता है।

(D) Present Perfect Continous Tense

ऐसे कार्यों हेतु, जो कुछ समय पूर्व से लगातार जारी हैं एवं अभी तक पूर्ण नहीं हुए हैं, के लिये Present Perfect Continuous का प्रयोग किया जाता है।

Sentence Structure in Present Perfect Continuous:

Subject + has/have been + V-IV +.... + since/for +...

(a) 'For/Since':- Present Perfect Continuous में समय व्यक्त करने हेतु 'for, since' का प्रयोग किया जाता है। 'for' का प्रयोग Period of time, जैसे: for two hours, for 15 days, for 10 years, for a long time, for a long period, for some time, आदि व्यक्त करने हेतु किया जाता है; 'for' अवधि को बताता है। जबकि 'Since' का प्रयोग Point of time; जैसे – since 2 O'clock, since morning, since Monday, since January, since 1997, तथा since last night etc. व्यक्त करने हेतु किया जाता है।

(b) Has been का प्रयोग singular number third person, (He, She, It, Name, My borther, My friend etc.) के साथ, तथा have been का प्रयोग I एवं II person तथा Plural Subject के साथ किया जाता है।

PAST TENSE

(A) Past Indifinite Tense

Important points about the use of Past Indifinite Tense :

(1) भूतकाल की आदत को व्यक्त करने हेतु भी Simple Past का प्रयोग किया जाता है :
(a) He always carried this bag. (b) She never went to church.

(2) Conditional Sentences में भी 'if' के साथ Past Indefinite का प्रयोग किया जाता है :
(a) If I had a map I would give it to her.
(But I haven't a map. The meaning is 'Present')

(b) If he tried to blackmail me, I would inform you.
(But I don't expect that he will try to blackmail me. The meaning here is future.)

(3) जब दो कार्य sequence में घटित हों तथा एक के बाद दूसरा कार्य तुरंत समाप्त हो जाता हो, तो Past Indefinite का प्रयोग किया जाता है। ऐसे वाक्यों में सामान्यतया 'before', conjunction का प्रयोग होता है :

(a) He switched on the light before he opened the door.
(b) The train started just before I reached the station.

(4) जब दो घटनाएँ साथ-साथ घटित होती हैं, तो भी Past Indefinite का प्रयोग किया जाता है :

(a) When the queen entered the hall, the orchestra played the National Anthem.
(b) When the P.M. entered the meeting room, all congratulated him.

(5) 'Wish' एवं 'If only' के साथ Simple Past का प्रयोग एक Unreal past एवं Present की स्थिति को स्पष्ट करता है :

(a) I wish I were a millionaire. (I am not a millionaire)
(b) I wish I knew her. (I don't know her)

(B) Past Continous Tense

Important points about the use of Past Continuous Tense :

(1) Past Continous Tense का प्रयोग ऐसे कार्यों को दर्शाने के लिये करते हैं, जो कि व्यक्ति past में आदतन एवं frequently करता रहा था। ऐसे वाक्यों में always, continually, constantly जैसे adverbs का प्रयोग किया जाता है :

(a) He was always abusing others.
(b) She was constantly crying those days.
(c) They were continually threatening us.
(d) She was always grumbling.

(2) ऐसी स्थिति में भी Past Continuous का प्रयोग किया जाता है, जब कोई दूसरी घटना घटित हुई हो, एवं अन्य कोई कार्य भी जारी रहा हो। जैसे :

(a) When he arrived, his wife was washing her clothes.
(b) The boy was knocked down by a car, while he was crossing the road.

(3) एक साथ दो कार्य होते रहने की स्थिति में भी Past Continuous का प्रयोग दोनों कार्यों हेतु किया जाता है :

(a) While she was cooking, I was washing the clothes.
(b) While I was singing, Ramesh was reading.

'While' is used - When both the actions were going on simultaneously.
'When' is used- When one action was completed and the other action was going on.

(C) Past Perfect Tense

(1) जैसा कि पूर्व में बताया गया है का Past Perfect Tense प्रयोग, दो ऐसी घटनाओं या कार्यों को दर्शाने हेतु किया जाता है, जहाँ एक निश्चित समय या घटना के बाद, दूसरी घटना या कार्य पूर्ण हुआ हो :

(a) I had reached college, before the principal came.
(b) When I reached the station, the train had already left.
(c) They ran out to play after they had completed their class work.

(2) Past Perfect का प्रयोग Verbs; 'hope, expect, think, intend, want, suppose' के साथ ऐसी Past आशाओं, इच्छाओं, कल्पनाओं के सन्दर्भ में किया जाता है जो पूर्ण नहीं हुई हों :

(a) We had hoped that you would cooperate us. (but you didn't cooperate.)
(b) I had intended to go to USA last year. (but I couldn't go.)
(c) She had thought of paying us a visit. (but due to some reasons she couldn't visit.)

(3) **निम्न प्रकार के Conditional Sentences में भी Past Perfect का प्रयोग किया जाता है :**

(a) यदि वह मुझसे मिलता तो मैं उसकी मदद करता।

If he had met me, I would have helped him.

(b) यदि वह मुझे सूचित करता तो मैं वहाँ अवश्य जाता।

If he had informed me, I would have gone there positively.

इस तरह के वाक्य यह स्पष्ट करते हैं कि कार्य नहीं हुआ। यह एक महत्त्वपूर्ण Structure है; छात्रों को इसे ध्यान से समझना चाहिये :

If +Subject + had + V-III +....+ would have +V-III +...

इस तरह के वाक्यों के पहले भाग में had + V-III तथा दूसरे भाग में would have के साथ Verb की III form का प्रयोग किया जाता है।

ध्यान रखें

If he had come to me, I would have helped him.

or

Had he come to me, I would have helped him.

इन दोनों वाक्यों का अर्थ समान है, कोई अन्तर नहीं है।

(D) Past Perfect Continuous Tense

(1) **Past Perfect Continuous का प्रयोग, ऐसे actions हेतु किया जाता है जो Past में किसी समय बिन्दु (Point of time) या अवधि (Period of time) से लगातार जारी थे :**

(a) He had been working since dawn. (b) She had been waiting for him for two hours.

(2) **Past perfect के repeated action को भी Past Perfect Continuous में व्यक्त किया जा सकता है:**

(a) He had tried five times to contact her. — Past perfect

He had been trying to contact her. — Past perfect continuous

(b) He had tried many times to get the job there. — Past perfect

He had been trying to get the job there. — Past perfect continuous

An action in the past perfect can some times be expressed as a continuous action in the past perfect continuous.

—A Practical English grammar: A.J.Thomson, A.V.Martin

FUTURE TENSE

(A) Future Indefinite Tense

Use of Future Indefinite Tense in various situations:

(1) **Clause of condition एवं clause of time वाले वाक्यों में Future Indefinite का प्रयोग किया जाता है। इस सम्बन्ध में विस्तार से Present Indefinite के अध्याय में बताया गया है।**

(a) I shall go to market, if it rains. (b) I shall go to Jaipur in case she asks me.

(2) **Will be / Shall be का प्रयोग निम्न प्रकार किया जाता है :**

(a) Tomorrow will be Monday. (b) He will be twenty five in January.

(B) Future Continuous Tense

Future Continuous Tense का प्रयोग सामान्यतया ऐसे कार्यों हेतु किया जाता है, जो भविष्य में जारी रहेगें :

I shall be writing the thesis in the evening.

Ram will be playing at this time tomorrow.

इस तरह के वाक्य में future continuous tense का प्रयोग भविष्य में जारी रहने वाले कार्य को व्यक्त करता है। इस तरह के वाक्यों हेतु निम्न Sentence Structure प्रयुक्त होता है :

Subject + will/ shall be + V-4 + object.

इस तरह के वाक्यों में will / shall be के बाद Verb की IV form (Verb की first from + ing) प्रयुक्त की जाती है।

Difference between Present Continuous and Future Continuous:

(a) I am seeing the principal tomorrow. — Present continuous
(b) I'll be seeing the principal tomorrow. — Future continuous

वाक्य (a) एक Planned action या arrangement (पहले से तय)को बताता है। जबकी दूसरा वाक्य normal course में कार्य होने को बताता है, हो सकता है वह उसी office में कार्य करता हो।

(C) Future Perfect

(1) जब कोई एक कार्य दूसरे कार्य के पूर्ण होने के बाद पूर्ण होगा तब इस तरह के वाक्यों में पहले पूर्ण होने वाले कार्य के लिये Future perfect एवं जो कार्य बाद में पूर्ण होगा उसके लिए Present Indefinite का प्रयोग होता है :

(a) The student will have left the class before the teacher comes.
(b) The Principal will have started before I reach there.

(2) ऐसे कार्यों हेतु जिनके बारे में हम यह समझते हैं कि उनका ज्ञान अन्य के पहले से ही होगा :

(a) You will have heard about Mother Teressa.
(b) You will have heard about our plans of investment.

(D) Future Perfect Continuous Tense

Future Perfect Continuous का प्रयोग ऐसे कार्यों का विवरण करने हेतु होता है, जो भविष्य में किसी समय तक जारी रहेंगे। ऐसे वाक्यों में समय का सन्दर्भ आवश्यक है :

(a) सात बजे वे दो घंटे से खेल रहे होंगे।
They will have been playing for two hours by 7 O' clock.

(b) वह अगले माह में इस कार्यालय में चार वर्ष से कार्य कर रही होगी।
She will have been working in this office for four years by the next month.

(c) 15 अगस्त 2009 को वह इस मकान में सात वर्ष से रह रहा होगा।
He will have been living in this house for seven years on 15th August 2009.

(1) इस तरह के वाक्यो में 'will / shall' के साथ 'have been' (has been का नहीं) का प्रयोग होता है।

(2) 'Since' का प्रयोग Point of time व्यक्त करने के लिये (जैसे – Since January, since 2 O'clock, since morning, since 2005 etc.) तथा 'For' का प्रयोग Period of time (जैसे – for two hours, for 15 years, for sometime etc.) के लिये होता है।

(3) समय-सीमा व्यक्त करने हेतु सामान्यतया 'by' का प्रयोग किया जाता है। लेकिन 'on' का भी प्रयोग वाक्य के सन्दर्भ को ध्यान रखकर किया जा सकता है, जैसा कि वाक्य (c) में दर्शाया गया है।

ERRORS, MISTAKES AND BLUNDERS IN USE OF TENSE

Exercise-1

Following sentences have some errors/ mistakes. Rewrite these sentences after correction.

1. I writes a letter.
2. He go to temple daily.
3. Rita crys.
4. He flys kites.
5. He do not play.
6. Does I write a letter?

7. Do she swims?
8. Does she goes to school?
9. Ram does not tells a lie.
10. He never verifys the bills.

Explanations

1. I write a letter.
2. He goes to temple daily.
3. Rita cries.
4. He flies kites.
5. He does not play.
6. Do I write a letter?
7. Does she swim?
8. Does she go to school?
9. Ram does not tell a lie.
10. He never verifies the bills.

REMEMBER

1. जब Subject, Singular number third person है तो verb के साथ 's' या 'es' जोड़ते हैं।
2. जब verb का अन्तिम अक्षर o, z, ss, x., ch, sh है तो 'es' जोड़ते हैं।
3. यदि verb का अन्तिम अक्षर 'y' एवं उससे पूर्व कोई व्यंजन (Consonant) आया है तो Subject, Singular number, Third Person की स्थिति में 'y' -'ies' में बदल जाता है।

Exercise-2 (Present Tense)

Following sentences have some errors/ mistakes. Rewrite these sentences after correction.

1. You is playing.
2. I is reading.
3. They are read.
4. She does not swimming.
5. Is it rains?
6. Are she cooking?
7. Am he playing?
8. Is you coming?
9. I is going to play.
10. She are speaking.
11. I am seeing.
12. I am having a car.
13. I am understanding.
14. He is knowing me.
15. He is resembling his brother.

Explanations

1. You are playing.
2. I am reading.
3. They are reading.
4. She is not swimming.
5. Is it raining?
6. Is she cooking?
7. Is he playing?
8. Are you coming?
9. I am going to play.
10. She is speaking.
11. I see.
12. I have a car.
13. I understand.
14. He knows me.
15. He resembles his brother.

REMEMBER

1. Present Continuous Tense में helping verb का प्रयोग निम्न प्रकार से किया जाता है : 'I' के साथ 'am': 'You, we, they, any plural' subject के साथ 'are' तथा 'He, she, it, name, any singular' के साथ 'is' लगता है तथा verb की IV form (1st form + ing) लगती है।
2. कुछ verbs, जैसे: see, hear, have, own, understand ; इत्यादि का प्रयोग सामान्य स्थिति में continuous form में नहीं किया जाता है।

Exercise-3 (Present Tense)

Following sentences have some errors/ mistakes. Rewrite these sentences after correction.

1. He have gone to Jaipur.
2. I has played.
3. They have arrived yesterday.
4. Have he played a match?

5. Ram has gone two minutes ago.
6. He not has taken food.
7. He was ill since Monday.
8. I have been playing since two hours.
9. He has been swimming for 2'O clock.
10. Has she cooking for two hours?
11. Have I been not playing for one hour?
12. She have just arrive.
13. Raju is playing for three hours.
14. I known him.
15. They have been not reading since an hour.

Explanations

1. He has gone to Jaipur.
2. I have played.
3. They arrived yesterday.
4. Has he played a match?
5. Ram has just gone.
6. He has not taken food.
7. He has been ill since Monday.
8. I have been playing for two hours.
9. He has been swimming since 2 O'clock.
10. Has she been cooking for two hours?
11. Have I not been playing for an hour?
12. She has just arrived.
13. Raju has been playing for three hours.
14. I have known him.
15. They have not been reading for an hour.

REMEMBER

1. Present Perfect में 'I, You, We, They' एवं Any plural subject के साथ 'have' तथा He, She, It, Name, Any singular subject के साथ 'has' का प्रयोग किया होता है।
2. Verb की III form प्रयुक्त होती है।
3. Present Perfect में, Past time के adverbs जैसे – yesterday, ago इत्यादि का प्रयोग कभी नहीं होता है।
4. Present Perfect Continuous में 'since' का प्रयोग, Point of time; जैसे : morning, evening, 2 O'clock, January, February etc. के साथ होता है। 'For' का प्रयोग अवधि; जैसे – 2 hours, 15 days etc. के साथ होता है। Verb की IV form प्रयुक्त होती है।

Exercise-4 (Past Tense)

Following sentences have some errors/ mistakes. Rewrite these sentences after correction.

1. He gone to Jaipur.
2. He just went to Jaipur.
3. He did not went to Jaipur.
4. Did he came yesterday?
5. He did not opened the door.
6. He were not going.
7. I were not doing that.
8. You was making a noise.
9. She did not asked me.
10. Did he not reminded you?
11. Was you not playing?
12. Were not you writing?
13. Was not I watching movie?
14. Were she not cooking?
15. Were they playing not football?

Explanations

1. He went to Jaipur.
2. He went to Jaipur a short while ago.
3. He did not go to Jaipur.
4. Did he come yesterday?
5. He did not open the door.
6. He was not going.
7. I was not doing that.
8. You were making a noise.
9. She did not ask me.
10. Did he not remind you?
11. Were you not playing?
12. Weren't you writing?
13. Wasn't I watching movie?
14. Was she not cooking?
15. Were they not playing football?

Exercise-5 (Past Tense)

Following sentences have some errors/ mistakes. Rewrite these sentences after correction.

1. I had knew her for five years.
2. If he had come to me, I would help him.
3. If I had a pen, I will give you.
4. She had not play.
5. Ram told Sita that I have seen your photos
6. The train had departed before I reach the station.
7. Had she warn you before ?
8. Ram had been waiting for me since two hours.
9. Had Sita been not cooking since morning?
10. Suresh had been writing a book since three months.
11. It had been raining for last evening.
12. He told that he has been writing a letter for the last one hour.
13. Had not he been waiting for you for two hours?
14. Maya had already inform me.
15. Gita not had been waiting for you since January.

Explanations

1. I had known her for five years.
2. If he had come to me, I would have helped him.
3. If I had a pen, I would give you.
4. She had not played.
5. Ram told Sita that he had seen her photos.
6. The train had departed before I reached the station.
7. Had she warned you before ?
8. Ram had been waiting for me for two hours.
9. Had Sita not been cooking since morning?
10. Suresh had been writing a book for three months.
11. It had been raining since last evening.
12. He told that he had been writing a letter for the last one hour.
13. Hadn't he been waiting for you for two hours?
14. Maya had already informed me.
15. Gita had not been waiting for you since January.

REMEMBER

1. Past Perfect में 'had' के साथ verb की III form प्रयुक्त होती है।
2. Conditional Sentences में had + V-3 के साथ would have + V-3 का प्रयोग होता है।
3. Conditional Sentences में had + noun के साथ will का प्रयोग नहीं होगा, would का प्रयोग होगा।
4. Past Perfect Continuous में had been के साथ Verb की IV form का प्रयोग होता है।
5. Since का प्रयोग, Point of time के दर्शाने हेतु होता है तथा For का प्रयोग अवधि अर्थात् 'Period of time' दर्शाने हेतु होता है।
6. Indirect narration में यदि reporting verb past में है तो, reporting speech में 'have been' की जगह 'had been' का प्रयोग होगा।

Exercise-6 (Past Tense)

Following sentences have some errors/ mistakes. Rewrite these sentences after correction.

1. The students will have left the school before the principal came.
2. The train will have arrived before I reaches the station.
3. He would have reached here before the sun set.

4. Will he has completed his work by tomorrow?
5. Will he have not repaired the car by 7 P.M.?
6. He will has been waiting for you for three days.
7. Will not he have been waiting for you since morning?
8. Ram will have not been playing at this time tomorrow.
9. Will the girls have played the game at 7 P.M.?
10. He will have finish the work by 8 P.M.

Explanations

1. The students will have left the school before the principal comes.
2. The train will have arrived before I reach the station.
3. He will have reached here before the sun sets.
4. Will he have completed his work by tomorrow?
5. Will he not have repaired the car by 7 P.M.?
6. He will have been waiting for you for three days.
7. Won't he have been waiting for you since morning?
8. Ram will not have been playing at this time tomorrow.
9. Will the girls have played the game by 7 P.M.?
10. He will have finished the work by 8 P.M.

REMEMBER

1. जब दो कार्यों के सन्दर्भ में Future Perfect का प्रयोग किया जाता है तब एक भाग में will / shall have + Verb III form का प्रयोग होता है तथा दूसरे भाग में Present indefinite tense प्रयुक्त होता है (sentences 4, 6 above)।
2. Future tense के वाक्यों में 'will/ shall' के साथ 'has' का प्रयोग नहीं किया जाना है। हमेशा 'have' का ही प्रयोग किया जाता है।
3. Will not/ Shall not से यदि प्रश्न शुरू किया जाता है तो Won't / Shan't से शुरू किया जायेगा (देखें उपरोक्त वाक्य संख्या 5, 7)।
4. Negative वाक्यों में 'not' का प्रयोग 'will' के बाद होगा। 'Will have' के बाद 'not' लिखना गलत है (as in sentences 5, 9, 10 above)।
5. Future में समय के सन्दर्भ हेतु सामान्यतया by का प्रयोग किया जाता है।

Exercise-7 (Present Tense)

Correct the following sentences.

1. Sarita go to office at 10 A.M.daily
2. She has been cooking meal from 7 A.M.
3. Nisha is playing tabla for 2 hours.
4. Rani have just come from college.
5. They have been residing here since four years.
6. They goes to field at 5 A.M.
7. Ram do his work in time.
8. He drink coffee in the morning.
9. Mr Sharma teachs us English grammar.
10. Sakshi catchs the train at 8 O'clock.
11. He flys kite on Sunday.
12. We takes bath together in the river .
13. We have been playing for 12 O'clock.
14. Raheja has been singing since one hour.
15. He pass all the tests without fail.

Explanations

1. Change 'go' to 'goes'.
2. Change 'from' to 'since'.
3. Change 'is' to 'has been'.
4. Change 'have' to 'has'.

5. Change 'since' to 'for'.
6. Change ' goes' to 'go'.
7. Change 'do' to 'does'.
8. Change 'drink' to 'drinks'.
9. Change 'teachs' to 'teaches'.
10. Change 'catchs' to 'catches'.
11. Change ' flys' to 'flies'.
12. Change 'takes' to 'take'.
13. Change ' for' to 'since'.
14. Change 'since' to 'for'.
15. Change 'pass' to 'passes'.

Exercise-8 (Past Tense)

Correct the following sentences.

1. Tejpal and his friends were playing chess for two hours.
2. Sita had been cooking for 2 0'clock.
3. Rahim gone to market.
4. The teacher was taught us Hindi at that time.
5. Ramesh had took your purse.
6. The girl had been crying since an hour.
7. We had been playing chess since two hours.
8. The train arrived before we reached there.
9. The patient had fainted than the doctor came.
10. My friends was coming by bus.

Explanations

1. Change 'were' to 'have been'.
2. Change 'for' to 'since'.
3. Change 'gone' to 'went'.
4. Change 'taught' to 'teaching'.
5. Change 'took' to 'taken'.
6. Change 'since' to 'for'.
7. Change 'since' to 'for'.
8. Insert 'had' after 'train'.
9. Change 'than' to ' before'.
10. Change 'was' to 'were'.

SPOTTING ERRORS (TENSE)

Exercise : *Find the errors and justify your answers; write 'No Error' if you find none.*

1. I came to(A)/ know that(B)/ his father has died(C)/ three days ago.(D)
2. When you will find(A)/out a solution (B)/ to this problem,(C)/ you will be awarded a prize.(D)
3. Before the alarm had stopped(A)/ ringing (B)/ Nisha had telephoned(C)/the police. (D)
4. This is (A)/ the first time (B)/ that I see such (C)/ an interesting movie. (D)
5. Whenever he is coming (A)/ here, he brings (B)/ many (C)/ gifts for me. (D)
6. Now a days (A)/ he teaches English (B)/ because the teacher of English (C)/ has gone for a month's leave (D)
7. "It is high time (A)/ you are starting (B)/this business" (C)/ said Ram to Mahesh.(D)
8. I will let you know(A)/ as soon as I (B)/will get (C)/ any news in this regard. (D)
9. When I will cross (A)/ fifty, my (B)/wife will cross (C)/forty five. (D)
10. The secret of his good health (A)/ lies in the fact (B)/ that he is getting up early (C) and goes to bed early.(D)
11. The students sitting on the dais, (A)/ studied here (B)/for three years, but (C)/ they have never created any problem. (D)
12. A philogynist is a person(A)/ who loves woman (B)/ but a mysogynist is a person (C)/ who is hating woman (D)
13. It is appearing to me (A)/ that you are (B)/ trying to destabilise (C)/the present committee. (D).

14. I have been knowing her (A)/ for many years (B)/ but I don't know (C)/where she works.(D)
15. If he would have done this, (A)/he would have done wrong (B)/and would have deceived (C)/many of his relatives. (D)
16. The victim tried to tell us (A)/ what has happened (B)/ but his words (C)/ were not audible. (D)
17. I want you to (A)/ pick up the box of eggs gently (B)/ and kept it in (C)/ the corner carefully.(D)
18. She came to (A)/ the party much (B)/ later than (C)/I expect. (D)
19. I lived here(A)/for five years, (B)/ so I know about the (C)/ problems of this colony. (D)
20. The chairman had not taken (A)/ any decision until (B)/he had studied (C)/the case thoroughly. (D)
21. They got everything(A)/ready for the visitors(B)/long before(C)/they reached there. (D)
22. He switched on (A)/the light before (B)/he entered(C)/the room. (D)
23. I have been admiring (A)/her for the (B)/voice with which(C)/she is gifted.(D)
24. He was with me (A)/ uptil now, (B)/so don't (C)/punish him for the delay. (D)
25. Several survey reports (A)/indicate that (B)/the number of (C)/drug addicts is grown gradually. (D)
26. "Here is coming up Bachchan!", (A)/said he (B)/when he was (C)/waiting for him.(D)
27. I could not recall(A)/ when she has told me(B)/about her(C)/affair with Gopal.(D)
28. Four and four(A)/always made eight(B)/cannot(C)/be questioned by anyone.(D)
29. She hopes to(A)/become an engineer(B)/after she will complete.(C)/her education.(D)
30. I have been working (A)/ in this firm (B)/ for the last twenty years (C).
31. When you will find (A)/ a solution to this problem (B)/ you will be able (C)/ to get this project (D).
32. The teacher told us (A)/ that we should remain (B)/ in the hostel (C)/ if it rains (D).
33. I could not recall (A)/ what she has advised me (B)/ in this matter (C).
34. By this time tomorrow (A)/ she has had reached (B)/ there positively (C).
35. I will inform (A)/ you as soon as (B)/ I will get any news (C)/ about his health (D).
36. A recent survey (A)/ indicates (B)/ that the number of drug addicts (C)/ grew day by day (D).
37. Before the alarm (A)/ had stopped ringing (B)/ Reena had pulled up the shade (C).
38. If I was you (A)/ I would have told (B)/ the principal (C)/ to keep his mouth shut (D).
39. If we had Ramesh (A)/ in our team, we (B)/ would have won the match (C).
40. My friend said to me, (A)/"When have (B)/ you come here?(C).
41. I have been knowing (A)/ him for the last five years (B)/ but now I don't know (C)/ where he lives (D).
42. He lived here (A) since 1998, (B)/ so he knows everything (C)/ about this town (D).

Explanations

1. (C) 'has died' की जगह केवल 'died' लिखा जायेगा। Present perfect के साथ past time के adverb (यहाँ three days ago) का प्रयोग नहीं किया जाता है।
2. (A) 'When' के बाद 'will' का प्रयोग नहीं किया जायेगा, जबकि main clause में भी 'will' का प्रयोग किया गया है। 'When you find out a solution ....' लिखें ।
3. (A) 'Had stopped' की अपेक्षा 'stopped' ही लिखा जायेगा। Past perfect tense में जो कार्य पहले होता है, उसके लिये Past perfect (had telephoned) एवं बाद में पूर्ण होने वाले कार्य के लिये Past indefinite (stopped) का प्रयोग किया जाता है।

4. (C) 'I see' की जगह 'I have seen' लिखा जायेगा। ध्यान रखें निम्नलिखित expresions के साथ present perfect tense प्रयोग किया जाता है :
(a) This/that/ it is the first/second/third .... time/chance.
(b) That/this/ it is the only ....
(c) This/that/it is the best/worst/finest/most interesting.... जैसे :
This is the first time that I have heard her sing in public.
5. (A) 'Whenever he comes here' लिखा जायेगा। यह आदतन किया जाने वाला act है जिसके लिए present indefinite का प्रयोग होगा।
6. (B) 'he teaches' की जगह 'he is teaching' लिखा जायेगा। Temporary कार्य हेतु present continuous का प्रयोग होता है।
7. (B) 'you started' लिखाा जायेगा। ध्यान रखें 'It is high time / It is time / I wish / If /As if' आदि के साथ सामान्यतया past indefinite का प्रयोग किया जाता है।
8. (C) 'Will get' की जगह 'get' ही आयेगा। जब main clause में will का प्रयोग किया गया है, तो if / as soon as / when / before /as / in case etc. के साथ present indefinite का प्रयोग होता है।
9. (A) 'I will cross' की जगह 'I cross' ही आयेगा। प्रश्न (8)का explanation देखें।
10. (A) 'he is getting up' की जगह 'he gets up' होगा। आदतन किए जाने वाले कार्यों हेतु Present Indefinite का प्रयोग होता है।
11. (B) 'studied' की जगह 'have studied' होगा। 'sitting on the dais' एवं 'have never created' का प्रयोग यह व्यक्त करता है कि वाक्य को Present tense में माना गया गया है।
12. (D) 'who is hating' की जगह 'who hates' लिखा जायेगा। Universal truth/ eternal truth के लिए Present indefinite का प्रयोग होता है।
13. (A) 'it is appearing' की जगह 'it appears' लिखा जायेगा। यहाँ 'appear' का प्रयोग 'seem' के अर्थ में हुआ है, अत: present continuous का प्रयोग नहीं किया जायेगा; Present indefinite का प्रयोग किया जायेगा। 'appear' का प्रयोग यदि 'जनता' के सामने आने या प्रकाशित होने के सन्दर्भ में हो तो continuous में इसका प्रयोग किया जा सकता है। जैसे :
(a) His next novel is appearing this month.
(b) Now an eminent author is appearing on the stage.
14. (A) 'I have been knowing' की जगह 'I have known' लिखा जायेगा। 'know', verb का प्रयोग continuous नहीं में किया जाता है।
15. (A) 'If he had done this' लिखा जायेगा। इस तरह के conditional वाक्यों का Structure निम्न होगा।
It + subject + had + V-3 ....would have + V-3
16. (B) 'has happened' की जगह 'had happened' लिखा जायेगा। जब वाक्य में सब जगह past tense है तो present perfect का प्रयोग गलत है।
17. (C) 'kept it' की जगह 'keep it' होगा। वाक्य में past tense का प्रयोग अनावश्यक किया गया है।
18. (D) 'I expect' की जगह 'I had expected' आयेगा। कार्य past में हुआ है, अत: expect के साथ had expected (past to past) का प्रयोग होगा ।
19. (A) 'I lived' की जगह 'I have lived' होगा। सारा वाक्य present tense (kept) में है; एवं वाक्य का सन्दर्भ बताता है कि वाक्य का वक्ता आज भी वहाँ रहता है।
20. (A) 'The chairman did not take' लिखा जाना चाहिए। जब वाक्य में एक clause में 'had + V-3' का प्रयोग होता है तो दूसरे clause में past Indefinite का प्रयोग होता है।

21. (A) 'They got' की जगह 'They had got' लिखा जाएगा, क्योंकि जब वाक्य में दो कार्य होते हैं, व एक के बाद दूसरा कार्य पूर्ण होता है, तो पहले पूर्ण होने वाले कार्य के लिए past perfect प्रयोग किया जाता है।
22. No Error. वाक्य सही है ।
23. (A) 'I have been admiring' की जगह 'I admire' लिखा जाना चाहिए; क्योंकि know, admire, adore, trust, believe, rely, hope etc. का प्रयोग सामान्यतया continuous form में नहीं किया जाता है।
24. (A) 'He was' की जगह 'He has been with me' लिखा जायेगा। क्योंकि 'uptil now', के साथ past tense का प्रयोग नहीं होता है।
25. (D) 'Is grown' की जगह 'is growing' आयेगा ।
26. (A) 'Here is coming' की जगह 'Here comes' लिखा जायेगा। Exclamatory वाक्यों में present indefinite का निम्न प्रकार से प्रयोग होता है :
Here comes the tram! There works Sita!
27. (B) 'she has told' की जगह 'she had told' लिखा जाना चाहिए। जब वाक्य में past tense का प्रयोग है तो present perfect का प्रयोग नहीं होगा।
28. (B) 'Made' की जगह 'makes' लिखें; universal truth / mathematical calculations / historical facts हेतु present indefinite का प्रयोग किया जाता है।
29. (C) 'She will complete' की जगह 'she has completed' लिखा जाना चाहिए। she hopes का प्रयोग future अर्थ के लिए किया गया है, चूँकि engineer बनने से पूर्व education पूर्ण करनी है अत: present perfect का प्रयोग होगा। निम्न वाक्यों को देखें :
I'll come as soon as I have finished writing this letter.
I can't decide until I have discussed the matter with my wife.
I'll buy it for you when I have the money.
The present and present perfect tense may indicate future time in temporal and conditional clause : *A.S. Hornby (Guide to Pattern and Usage in English* page 98.)
30. No Error. वाक्य सही है ।
31. (A) 'Will' को delete करें । 'When' के बाद वाक्य में will का प्रयोग नहीं करते हैं । When, if, before, after, until के बाद will का प्रयोग नहीं किया जाता है ।
32. (D) 'if it rains' की जगह 'if it rained' होना चाहिये । जब reporting verb, past tense में है तो reported speech भी past tense में होगी।
33. (B) 'she has' की जगह 'she had' होना चाहिये। Principal clause में यदि past की घटना है तो subordinate clause में भी past tense ही आवेगा।
34. (B) 'has had reached' की जगह 'will have reached' होगा। यह Future perfect का वाक्य है ।
35. (C) 'Will' को delete करें । Conditional clauses में as soon as, when, after, before if, के बाद future tense का प्रयोग नहीं होता है ।
36. (D) 'grew' की जगह 'is growing' होगा। The sentence is in present tense.
37. (B) 'had stopped' की जगह केवल 'stopped' होगा। जैसे:
He had died before the doctor came.
Conditional sentences में जो कार्य बाद में होता है उसमें past indefinite tense का प्रयोग होता है ।
38. (A) 'If I was' की जगह 'If I were' होगा; इस तरह के conditional वाक्यों में 'were' का प्रयोग किया जाता है।
39. (A) 'We had' की जगह 'we had had' होना चाहिये। जैसे:

If he had come to me, I would have helped him.
If he had had in our group, we would have won the shield.

40. (B) 'When have' की जगह 'when did' लिखा जायेगा । Past में कोई question पूँछने हेतु 'when did' का प्रयोग होता है ।
41. (A) 'I have been knowing' की जगह 'I have known' होगा । verbs: know, see, appear, believe आदि का प्रयोग continuous tense में करना अनुचित है ।
42. (A) 'lived' की जगह 'has been living' होगा। वाक्य की संरचना से अभी भी वाक्य-वक्ता का उस town में निवास जाहिर होता है।

BLUNDERS IN APPLICATION OF TENSES

Exercise ***: Find the errors/mistakes in following sentences.***

1. I plays football daily.
2. He do not go to school by bus.
3. He go to office at 10 A.M. .
4. They does not play hockey.
5. I are watching TV. .
6. He has gone to Delhi yesterday .
7. Sita has arrived two days ago.
8. We are reading for two hours.
9. He has been playing now.
10. Ram is waiting for you since 2 O' clock.
11. He didn't played yesterday.
12. I didn't asked him any question.
13. I were not abusing him.
14. She was watching TV for two hours.
15. Ramesh had been watching TV serials since a long time.
16. If he had invited me I had attended the function.
17. The train is about to be started.
18. The train will have departed before I reached the station.
19. Ram will has passed his graduation by the next year.
20. He will be playing for two hours.
21. Sita will have been washing clothes since an hour.

Explanations

1. 'plays' की जगह 'play' लिखना चाहिए।
2. 'He' के साथ 'does not' लिखना चाहिए।
3. 'He' के साथ 'goes' लिखना चाहिए।
4. 'They do not' लिखना चाहिए।
5. 'I' के साथ 'am' लिखना चाहिए।
6. Present perfect के साथ Past tense adverbs; जैसे – 'yersterday, ago' etc., का प्रयोग नहीं होगा। सही वाक्य होगा : He went to Delhi yesterday .
7. वाक्य (6) का Explanation देखें। सही वाक्य होगा - Sita arrived two days ago.
8. यहाँ Present Perfect Continuous का प्रयोग किया जाना चाहिए । सही वाक्य होगा – We have been reading for two hours.
9. यहाँ Present Continuous का ही प्रयोग होगा । सही वाक्य होगा – He is playing now.
10. वाक्य (8) का explanation देखें। सही वाक्य होगा – Ram has been waiting for you since 2 O'Clock.
11. 'didn't play' लिखना चाहिए। Past Indefinite में negative interrogative sentence में verb की Ist form प्रयुक्त होती है।
12. 'didn't ask' लिखना चाहिए।

13. 'I' के साथ 'were' के स्थान पर 'was' का प्रयोग होगा।
14. यह Past Perfect Continuous का वाक्य है अत: सही वाक्य होगा- She had been watching TV for two hours.
15. 'for a long time' होगा। 'for' का प्रयोग period के लिये तथा 'since' का प्रयोग point of time के लिये किया जाता है ।
16. सही वाक्य होगा - If he had invited me I would have attented the function.
17. सही वाक्य होगा – The train is about to start.
18. सही वाक्य होगा – The train will have departed before I reach the station..
इस प्रकार के वाक्यों में, जो कार्य बाद में पूर्ण होता है उसमें Present Indefinite का प्रयोग किया जाता है।
19. Future Perfect में 'will have' का प्रयोग होता है। 'has' का प्रयोग गलत है।
20. यहाँ Future Perfect Continuous का प्रयोग किया जाना चाहिए। सही वाक्य होगा-He will have been playing for two hours.
21. 'for an hour' होगा। 'for' का प्रयोग period हेतु तथा 'since' का प्रयोग point of time हेतु किया जाता है।

4

Verb

'Verb' वाक्य का सबसे महत्त्वपूर्ण Part है। कोई भी वाक्य, बिना Verb के अपूर्ण है। न केवल Main Verbs अपितु Auxiliary verbs के भी सही प्रयोग का ज्ञान, English Grammar में प्रवीणता प्राप्त करने हेतु परम आवश्यक है। जितनी गलतियाँ Verbs के प्रयोग में की जाती हैं, उतनी शायद अन्यत्र कहीं नहीं की जाती हैं। Verbs का अध्ययन आपको पूरी गंभीरता से करना है।

Verb से कार्य का करना या होना स्पष्ट होता है। Verb को निम्न प्रकार से वर्गीकृत किया जा सकता है :

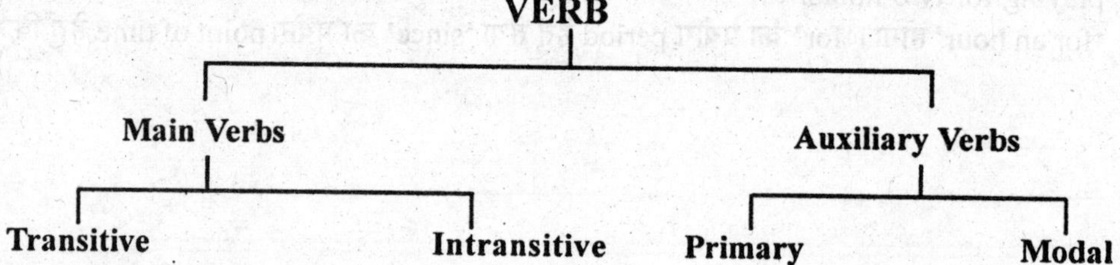

नीचे लिखे वाक्यों को देखें :

(a) I am playing - am (auxiliary verb), play (main verb).

(b) He is writing -is (auxiliary verb), write (main verb).

TRANSITIVE AND INTRANSITIVE VERB

Transitive verbs (सकर्मक क्रियाएँ) : ऐसी verbs जिनके साथ object प्रयुक्त हो, Transitive verbs कहलाती है। Transitive का अर्थ है- passing over अर्थात इन verbs में action, कर्ता तक ही सीमित नहीं रहकर, Object (किसी अन्य वस्तु) पर pass over होता है। जैसे :

(a) Ramesh hits a ball.

(b) He rings the bell.

यहाँ 'hits' एवं 'rings', transitive verb की तरह प्रयुक्त है, जिनमें action, कर्ता तक ही सीमित नहीं रहा है अपितु Object ; 'ball' एवं 'bell' पर pass over हुआ है।

Intransitive verbs (अकर्मक क्रियाएँ) : Intransitive verbs में action कर्ता तक ही सीमित रहता है, object पर pass over नहीं होता है। जैसे :

(a) He sleeps in the bed.

(b) Shyam speaks loudly.

इन वाक्यों में verbs; sleeps एवं speaks, intransitive verbs हैं, इनमें action कर्ता तक ही सीमित रह गया है।

IMPORTANT

अधिकांश verbs का प्रयोग, Transitively एवं Intransitively, दोनों प्रकार हो सकता है :

	Verbs used transitively.		*Verbs used intransitively*
(a)	*He **speaks** the truth.*	*(a)*	*Sita **speaks** slowly.*
(b)	*The students **rang** the bell.*	*(b)*	*The bell **rang** loudly.*
(c)	*He **flies** kites.*	*(c)*	*A bird **flies**.*

ध्यान रखें (a) जब Verb का प्रयोग Transitively होता है तो इसके साथ object अवश्य आता है लेकिन जब verb का प्रयोग Intransitively होता है तो इसके साथ कोई object नहीं आता है।

(b) किसी भी verb के लिए यह कहना कि यह transitive verb है, या intransitive verb है, गलत है, इसकी बजाय हमें यह कहना चाहिए कि verb का प्रयोग Transitively या Intransitively हुआ है।

AUXILIARY VERB

Auxiliary Verbs को हम Primary Auxiliary Verbs एवं Modal Auxiliary Verbs में वर्गीकृत कर सकते हैं :

1. Primary Auxiliary Verbs, 2. Modal Auxiliary Verbs.

Primary Auxiliary Verbs को तीन भागो में वर्गीकृत किया गया है :

1. **Verbs 'to be ':- is, am , are ,was , were**
2. **Verbs 'to have' :- have, has ,had**
3. **Verbs 'to do':- do, does, did**

Auxiliary Verb 'To be' (Is/ Am/ Are/ Was/ Were)

'Is /Am/ Are', तीनों verbs का प्रयोग present tense में तथा 'was /were' का प्रयोग past tense में होता है। 'Is' का प्रयोग present में singular number third person 'subject' के साथ होता है। 'Am' का प्रयोग केवल 'I' के साथ होता है। 'Are/were' का प्रयोग Plural Subject के साथ होता है। 'Was' का प्रयोग past में Singular subject के साथ होता है।

इन Auxiliaries का प्रयोग present / past continuous के Affirmative/ Negative /Interrogative वाक्यों में होता है; इसके लिये Tense का अध्याय देखें। इनका प्रयोग Active Passive, Direct/Indirect Structures में भी होता है। यह आगे सम्बन्धित अध्याय में बताया जायेगा।

Some Important Uses of 'to be' form of Verbs

(1) Auxiliary 'to be ' के बाद to infinitive का प्रयोग निम्न प्रकार किया जाता है। ऐसे वाक्यों का structure निम्न होता है :

Subject + to be form of verb + to infinitive....

(a) He is to come on Sunday. उसे रविवार को आना है।
(b) I am to complete this work. मुझे यह कार्य पूरा करना है।
(c) They are to assemble in the hall. उन्हें हॉल में एकत्र होना है।
(d) They were to attend the party. उन्हें पार्टी में उपस्थित होना था।
(e) He was to go to Jaipur. उसे जयपुर जाना था।

(2) There के साथ Auxiliary 'to be ' का प्रयोग एक महत्त्वपूर्ण वाक्य संरचना है :

There + is /am/are/was/were + subject (or),
There + is/am/are/was/were + subject + adverbial adjective.

इन दोनों sentence structures का English writing एवं speaking में काफी प्रयोग होता है :

(a) There is a cow. वहाँ एक गाय है।
(b) There was a large crowd. वहाँ बहुत भीड़ थी।
(c) There are three tables in the room. कमरे में तीन मेज हैं।

(3) जब वाक्य का Subject एक Infinitive (+to) के रूप में होता है , तो इस प्रकार Sentence structure का प्रयोग उचित लगता है -To meet you is nice. की जगह It is nice to meet you. लिखना एवं बोलना अपेक्षाकृत अधिक उचित है :

It + be + adjective/noun + to infinitive....

(a) It is so nice to walk here with you.

(b) It was a pleasant surprise to talk with her.

(4) जब उक्त वाक्यों को 'How / what' का प्रयोग करके exclamatory वाक्यों में परिवर्तित किया जाता है तो ऐसे वाक्यों का structure निम्न होता है :

How /What + adjective /noun + (it +be) + to infinitive....

(a) How nice to walk here with you!

(b) What a pleasant surprise to talk with her!

(5) Auxiliary verb 'to be 'का प्रयोग निम्न प्रकार के वाक्य बनाने में भी किया जाता है :

Subject + is/am/are/was/were + adverbial adjunct....

(a) He is here in the room.

(b) The magazine you are looking for is here on the table.

Note *'Here / there' को सामान्यतया वाक्य के अन्त में लिखते हैं लेकिन exclamatory वाक्यों में इन्हें वाक्य के प्रारम्भ में लिखा जाता है :*

(a) Here is your friend! *(b) Here comes the bus!*

(6) जब वाक्य का subject ; for + noun /pronoun + to infinitive होता है तो ऐसे वाक्य में auxiliary 'to be' का प्रयोग It के साथ निम्न structure में होता है :

It + to be .... + for + noun/pronoun + to infinitive....

(a) It was very difficult for him to live in this cold region.

(b) It is very easy for anyone to talk to her.

(7) Auxiliary verb 'were' के प्रयोग का एक महत्त्वपूर्ण sentence structure निम्न है :

If + subject + were + complement.

(a) If I were a king ! यदि मैं राजा होता। (काश! मैं राजा होता।)

(b) If she were a bird! यदि वह पक्षी होती। (काश! वह पक्षी होती।)

इस तरह के वाक्यों को निम्न structure द्वारा भी समान अर्थ में लिखा जा सकता है :

Were + subject + complement.

(a) Were I a king! (b) Were I young again!

Auxiliary Verb 'to have' (Have/ Has/ Had)

Have / Has/ Had का प्रयोग Present, Past एवं Perfect Continuous Tenses में विभिन्न स्थितियों में किया जाता है। इस विषय में आपको Tense के अध्याय में विस्तृत रूप से हर प्रकार के sentence structure (Affirmative, Negative, Interrogative एवं Interrogative Negative) में स्पष्ट किया गया है। **Have/Has/Had के Tense में प्रयोग के अतिरिक्त अन्य use निम्न हैं :**

(1) Have/Has/Had का प्रयोग, किसी वस्तु पर मालिकाना हक, स्वामित्व (Possession, ownership) व्यक्त करने हेतु किया जाता है। वाक्य का structure निम्न होता है :

Subject + have/has/had + noun

Or

Subject + have/has/had + got + noun :

'Have' के साथ 'got' का प्रयोग करने से वाक्य में उस प्राप्त वस्तु का महत्त्व बढ़ जाता है :

(a) I have a car. (b) I have got a car.

Note

(A) उपरोक्त sentence structure का प्रयोग Relationship (संबंध) को व्यक्त करने हेतु भी किया जाता है :

(a) I have two sisters. (b) She has two sons.

(B) इस sentence structure द्वारा किसी व्यक्ति या वस्तु के पास उसके अनेक भागों (अंगों) के होने को भी व्यक्त किया जा सकता है :

(a) A man has two legs. (b) A cow has four legs.

(C) 'Have/had' का प्रयोग take/receive/experience हेतु भी निम्न प्रकार किया जाता है :

(a) I have my dinner at 9 PM. (take)

(b) I had no problem in searching his house. (experience)

(2) 'Have/Has/Had' का प्रयोग, कार्य की अनिवार्यता (Urgency), करने की बाध्यता (force or compulsion of doing) को भी व्यक्त करता है। ऐसे वाक्यों का structure निम्न होता है :

Subject + have/has/had+ infinitive

(a) He has to complete this work today. उसे यह कार्य आज पूरा करना है। (अनिवार्यता)

(b) I had to sell my house. मुझे अपना मकान बेचना पड़ा था। (बाध्यता)

(c) He will have to come here. उसे यहाँ आना पड़ेगा। (बाध्यता)

इस तरह के वाक्य , अनिवार्यता,बाध्यता को स्पष्ट करते हैं। इस तरह के वाक्य दैनिक जीवन में बहुत प्रयोग में आते हैं। छात्रों को इस structure को अच्छी तरह समझ लेना चाहिये।

(3) 'Have/has/had' का causative verb की तरह प्रयोग भी होता है। Causative verb की तरह प्रयोग का अर्थ है - कर्ता स्वंय कार्य नहीं करता है, अपितु वह कार्य होने का कारण (cause) है, अर्थात् वह दूसरों से कार्य करवाता है :

(a) I had him punished for his negligence.

(b) Suresh has his thesis written by somebody else.

इस तरह के वाक्यों में 'get/made' का भी प्रयोग किया जाता है। आगे 'causative verb' शीर्षक के अन्तर्गत यह बताया गया है।

(4) 'Have been/has been' का निम्न प्रकार के structure में प्रयोग देखें :

Subject + have/has been + noun (noun with preposition).

(a) I have been a professor.

उपरोक्त वाक्य यह स्पष्ट करता है कि भूतकाल में वक्ता एक Professor रह चुका है, लेकिन अब नहीं है।

I have been to U.S.A. में यह अर्थ निहित है कि - मैं अमेरिका रह चुका हूँ लेकिन अब वहाँ उपस्थित नहीं हूँ।

(5) 'have/had' के साथ had का प्रयोग देखने को मिलता है :

(a) I have had my lunch.

(b) He has had her breakfast.

(c) She had had her breakfast early in the morning.

(d) He will have had his lunch by now.

उपरोक्त वाक्यों में पहले 'have' या 'had' का प्रयोग present perfect या past perfect के अनुसार होता है तथा दूसरे 'had' का प्रयोग verb की III form (जो present /past perfect में लगानी आवश्यक है) की तरह (have = take के लिये) हुआ है।

Auxiliary Verb 'to do' (Do/ Does/ Did)

(1) Do/does/did का प्रयोग negative एवं interrogative वाक्यों में present एवं past tense में सामान्यतया किया जाता है। इस तरह का प्रयोग tense के अध्याय में विस्तृत रूप से वर्णित किया गया है।

(2) Do, Does, Did, का प्रयोग affirmative वाक्यों में निम्न स्थितियों को व्यक्त करता है :

(a) I do go to her. मै उसके पास जाता तो हूँ।

(b) She does come here. वह यहाँ आती तो है।

(c) He did come yesterday. वह यहाँ कल आया तो था।

(3) निम्न वाक्यों में 'do, does, did' का प्रयोग emphasis देने हेतु किया गया है। देखें :

(a) Have a cup of tea. (b) Do have a cup of tea.

(c) Have a seat please. (d) Do have a seat please.

(e) Write to me. (f) Do write to me.

उपरोक्त वाक्यों में 'Do' का प्रयोग ,वाक्यों को Interrogative नहीं बनाता है, बल्कि यह वक्ता की अधिक आग्रहयुक्त विनम्रता प्रदर्शित करता है।

Note ***The so-called emphatic 'do' has many uses in English :***

(1) To add emphasis to an entire sentence:

(a) He does like eggs. He really does!

(2) To add emphasis to an imperative:

(a) Do come in. (actually softens the command)

(3) To add emphasis to a frequency adverb:

(a) He never did understand his mother.

(b) She always does manage to hurt her mother's feelings.

(4) To contradict a negative statement:

(a) You didn't do your homework, did you? Oh, but I did finish it."

(5) To ask a clarifying question about a previous negative statement:

(a) Raju didn't take the purse. Then who did take the purse ?

(6) To indicate a strong concession:

(a) Although Jack denied any wrong-doing, they did return some of the presents.

(4) 'Do' का प्रयोग adequacy, suitability बताने हेतु भी निम्न प्रकार किया जाता है :

(a) I haven't got a torch.

Will a match box do? क्या माचिस उपयुक्त रहेगी?

No a matchbox won't do. I am trying to find out the gas leak.

(A match box will be unsuitable.)

(b) Would Rs. 100/- do? (= be adequate)

No it wouldn't. I need Rs. 1000.

(5) Forms of 'do' are useful in expressing similarities in conjunction with 'so' and 'neither'.

(a) My wife hates eggs and so does my son. (b) My wife doesn't like eggs ; neither do I.

(6) 'Do' is also used to avoid the repetition of the verb:

(a) Shalini excelled in language studies; **so did** his brother.

(b) Rahul studies as hard as his sister **does**.

One Principal Verb + Two Auxiliaries

कई वाक्यों में एक Principal Verbs के साथ दो Auxiliaries का प्रयोग किया जाता है। जैसे-

(a) She neither can nor will help him. (b) He did not and should not talk to him.

उपरोक्त वाक्यों में Principal verb (help, talk) एक ही है लेकिन auxiliaries दो हैं। यहाँ दोनों auxiliary verbs के साथ principal verb की एक अवस्था का ही प्रयोग किया गया है। कुछ परिस्थितियों में यदि दोनों auxiliaries के साथ main verb को अलग-अलग रूप से भी प्रयोग करें तो भी सही प्रयोग होगा। लेकिन निम्न वाक्यों को देखे।

(a) He neither has talked nor will talk to me. (b) They have not helped and will not help you.

उपरोक्त वाक्यों में Principal verb का रूप दोनों auxiliaries के साथ बदला हुआ दिखाई दे रहा है। प्रथम वाक्य में 'has' के साथ talked तथा will के साथ talk का ही प्रयोग होगा। इसी तरह दूसरे वाक्य में 'have' के साथ 'helped' था 'will' के साथ 'help' का ही प्रयोग सही है। **यदि इन वाक्यों को निम्न प्रकार लिखा जावे तो गलत होगा :**

(a) He neither has nor will talk to me. *—incorrect*

(b) They have not and will not help you. *—incorrect*

छात्रों को इस प्रकार की त्रुटि से बचना चाहिये। यह एक महत्त्वपूर्ण बिन्दु है।

CAUSATIVE VERBS

Causative verbs show that somebody/something is indirectly responsible for an action; The subject doesn't perform the action itself, but causes someone/something else to do it instead.

For example:

Yesterday I *had* my hair cut. (I didn't cut my own hair, but I made someone else do it for me instead.)

(a) I *made* her sing a song. (b) I *got* my clothes washed by him.

इन वाक्यों में कर्ता स्वयं कार्य नहीं करता है, बल्कि वह अन्य से कार्य करवाता है। कार्य अन्य से करवाने हेतु जो verbs प्रयुक्त होती हैं, वे causative verbs कहलाती हैं। इस तरह की verbs हैं- get,make, have,keep etc.

(a) I *made* him laugh. (b) I *kept* her waiting.

Active voice में सामान्य रूप से 'make, keep' का प्रयोग किया जाता है। तथा Passive voice में 'have, get' का प्रयोग किया जाता है। जैसे :

(a) I *got* my shoes polished by him. (b) I *had* the thesis written by him.

सामान्यतया 'get' का प्रयोग विनम्रता, अनुरोध को व्यक्त करता है एवं 'make, have' का प्रयोग बाध्यता, दबाव, विवशता आदि के सन्दर्भ में होता है।

Let (as causative verb)

'Let' can be used as a causative verb :

(a) I can let this car cool. (b) Would you let me join your party?

Help (as causative verb)

'Help' can also be used as a causative verb :

(a) I helped her to pack the luggage. (b) Would you help me deliver this box?

The most common error with causatives is using 'to' unnecessarily. For example :

(a) We made Jack to finish his supper. *—Incorrect*

We made Jack finish his supper. *—Correct*

LINKING VERBS OR NOTIONAL VERBS

जब Auxiliary (helping) verbs किसी वाक्य में मुख्य verb को support नहीं करते हैं बल्कि मुख्य verb की तरह प्रयुक्त होते हैं तो उस स्थिति में इन्हें Linking verbs या Notional verbs कहा जाता है; जैसे:

1. I **have** a book and a pencil
2. She **is** a beautiful girl.
3. He **has** a table made of wood.
4. You **do** your work now .

उपरोक्त वाक्यों में Bold type में लिखे verbs, Linking verbs या Notional verbs हैं।

A handful of verbs that reflect a change in state of being are sometimes called **Resulting Copulas. They, too, link a subject to a predicate adjective:**

See the following sentences:

(a) His face turned purple. (b) She became older.
(c) The dogs ran wild. (d) The milk has gone sour.

INCHOATIVE VERBS

वे Verbs जो किसी कार्य के प्रारम्भ होने को व्यक्त करती हैं, Inchoative verbs कहलाती हैं।

The term Inchoative verb is used for a verb that denotes the beginning, development or final stage, of a change of condition.

— Guide to patterns and usage in English by A.S. Hornby

इस तरह की मुख्य verbs हैं : Get, Become, Grow etc.

(a) My father is getting weaker. (b) It is growing dark.

इस तरह की अन्य verbs हैं - come, go, turn etc.

(a) The paper of the book turned yellow. (b) Will his dream come true?
(c) Ram soon fell asleep. (d) The carpet is wearing thin.

(A) Get :

Inchoative verb - 'get' का प्रयोग सर्वाधिक किया जाता है। 'Get' का प्रयोग अधिकांशत: Continuous form में होता है। Get का प्रयोग Adjective की Positive एवं Comparative degree के साथ तथा Participles के साथ किया जाता है :

(a) Sugar is getting scarcer. (b) It is getting dark.
(c) He is getting weaker. (d) She is getting older.

(B) Become :

'Get' की भाँति 'become' का प्रयोग भी काफी प्रचलित है। 'Become' का प्रयोग Adjective की Positive एवं Comparative degree के साथ तथा Participle के साथ निम्न sentence structures में किया जाता है :

(a) How did you become acquainted with her? (b) He became suspicious.

'Become'का प्रयोग Noun के साथ भी होता है।

(a) On leaving school she became an actress. (b) He soon became the richest man in the town.

(C) Grow :

'Grow' का प्रयोग भी 'get' एवं 'become' की तरह Adjective की positive एवं comparative degree के साथ तथा participle के साथ निम्न sentence structure में किया जाता है। जैसे:-

(a) Time is growing short. (Time is getting short.)
(b) It is growing dark. (or It is getting dark or It is becoming dark.)

(D) Come :

'Come' का प्रयोग adjective की positive एवं comparative degree के साथ तथा past participle की 'un' form (undone, unstitched, untied etc.) के साथ किया जाता है। Past participle के साथ come का प्रयोग एक unsatisfactory or undesirable position को बताता है।

(a) My dreams have come true. (b) The hinge has come loose.

(c) The knot came united. (d) The seam came unstitched.

(E) Go :

'Go' का प्रयोग adjective के साथ एक निश्चित परिवर्तन को व्यक्त करता है। जैसे:

(a) His hair has gone white. (b) He went mad.

'Go'का प्रयोग कुछ prepositional phrases; जैसे – go to bed, go to pieces में सामान्यतया प्रचलन में है।

(a) They started to go off the idea.(Go off - not like)

(b) He went to sleep.(fell asleep)

(F) Turn :

'Turn' का प्रयोग adjective की positive एवं comparative degree के साथ निम्न structure में होता है :

(a) The weather has turned much colder. (b) The oranges are turning red.

'Turn' का प्रयोग nouns के साथ भी किया जाता है। ऐसी स्थिति में noun के साथ indefinite article का प्रयोग नहीं किया जाता है :

(c) I believe you'll never turn traitor.

ERRORS, MISTAKES AND BLUNDERS IN USE OF VERBS

Exercise : ***Rewrite the sentences after correction.***

1. I made my clothes washed by her.
2. I got him polish my shoes.
3. My wife hates eggs and so my son does.
4. Ramesh studies as hard as his younger brother.
5. He neither has nor will complete this work today.
6. My mother doesn't like meat; neither I do.
7. I got her laugh.
8. I let Raju to clean up the room.
9. I kept her to wait.
10. They made me to repair the car.
11. The milk has gone to sour.
12. The cloth of the curtains turned to yellow.
13. Both of them first got to words and then blows.
14. After leaving school she become an actress.
15. I believe you will never turn a traitor.
16. It is common for bureaucrats to turn a politician after retirement.

Explanations

1. I got my clothes washed by her.
2. I made him polish my shoes.
3. My wife hates eggs and so does my son.
4. Ramesh studies as hard as his younger brother does.
5. He neither has completed nor will complete this work today.
6. My mother doesn't like meat; neither do I.
7. I made her laugh.
8. I let Raju clean up the room.
9. I kept her waiting.
10. They made me repair the car.
11. The milk has gone sour.
12. The cloth of the curtains turned yellow.
13. Both of them first got to words and then to blows.
14. After leaving school she became an actress.
15. I believe you will never turn traitor.
16. It is common for a bureaucrat to turn politician after retirement.

❑❑❑

5

Modals

Modals के सही प्रयोग के सम्बन्ध में अधिकांश छात्रों को बहुत परेशानी होती है। Writing and Speaking में प्रवीणता हेतु, Modals की पूर्ण जानकारी व उनके उचित प्रयोग का ज्ञान होना परम आवश्यक है।

Modals, Auxiliary verbs होती हैं, ये verbs के mood (अवस्था भाव) को व्यक्त करती हैं। Mood या modes, एक ही बात है। चूँकि ये verbs के भाव, क्रियाविधि को व्यक्त करती हैं- अत: इन्हें modals कहा जाता है।

विशेषताएँ

(1) इनका प्रयोग एक helping verb की तरह, मुख्य क्रिया के साथ होता है।

(2) Modals पर कर्ता के Number; singular या plural होने, या कर्ता के person (I, II, III person) का कोई प्रभाव नहीं पड़ता है; जैसे :

1. I can do it. **2. They can do it.**
3. He can do it. **4. You can do it.**

(3) Modals के साथ हमेशा verb की first form प्रयुक्त होती है।

(4) 'Ought' एवं 'Used' के बाद 'to' का प्रयोग आवश्यक है।

(5) कुछ modals; जैसे - need, dare, used का प्रयोग main verbs की तरह भी हो सकता है, अत: इन्हें marginal modals या semi-modals कहा जाता है।

USE OF MODALS

May/might

May : इसका प्रयोग निम्न अवस्थाओं में किया जा सकता है।

(1) अनुमति (permission) माँगने एवं अनुमति देने के लिये :-

(a) May I go now? (Permission माँगना)
Yes you may. (Permission देना)

(2) 'May' का प्रयोग Informal request हेतु किया जाता है।

May I have the salt please?

(3) 'May' का प्रयोग किसी घटना के घटित होने की अनिश्चितता को सम्भावना के साथ व्यक्त करता है; जबकि 'Might' का प्रयोग एक Remote possibility को व्यक्त करता है :

(a) The sky is cloudy, it may rain today.
(b) The sky is not cloudy but a change in weather is always possible it might rain today (remote possibility)

इस तरह 'may' का प्रयोग संभावना तथा 'might' का प्रयोग दूरस्थ सम्भावना (Remote possibility) व्यक्त करता है।

(4) 'May' का प्रयोग good wishes, desires प्रदर्शन हेतु किया जाता है :

(a) May God bless you ! (b) May you live long !

(5) Purpose व्यक्त करने के लिये भी 'may/might' का प्रयोग किया जा सकता है :

(a) We eat so that we may live.

(b) He works hard so that he may earn good livelihood.

(6) आश्चर्य व्यक्त करने एवं जानकारी प्राप्ति हेतु भी 'may' का प्रयोग निम्न प्रकार होता है :

(a) Who may be my friend here? (आश्चर्य)

(b) How old she may be? (जानकारी)

Might

(1) 'Might' का request हेतु प्रयोग more politeness व्यक्त करता है। यह वक्ता की hesitation, आत्म-विश्वास की कमी, एवं request के स्वीकार न होने की आशंका वाली स्थिति को व्यक्त करता है :

(a) Might I borrow your golden necklace?

(2) 'Might', may का past tense भी है । 'Might' का प्रयोग, present tense में भी हो सकता है । Direct से Indirect narration में परिवर्तन करते समय 'may' को 'might' में बदला जाता है :

(a) He asked if he might come in.

(3) 'May' एवं 'might' का perfect tense में प्रयोग :

(a) He may have been wounded.

(We do not know so far, but he is perhaps injured, possibility exists.)

(b) He might have been wounded. [that was a possibility in the past. (but he was not wounded.)] इसका अर्थ है कि – वह घायल हो सकता था।

Perfect tense में 'may' का प्रयोग, वर्तमान में एक सम्भावना को व्यक्त करता है जबकि 'might' का प्रयोग, past में किसी घटना के घटित होने की सम्भावना (जो वास्तव में घटित नहीं हुई) को बताता है ।

Can

(1) 'Can' का प्रश्न में प्रयोग, वक्ता का आश्चर्य (Astonishment), अधीरता (Impatience) तथा क्रोध (Anger), आदि दर्शाता है :

(a) What can he do ? (b) What can she say, I wonder?

(c) Where can he go? (d) How can she resign?

(2) 'Can' का प्रयोग परिस्थितिजन्य सम्भावना (Circumstantial possibility) को व्यक्त करता है :

(a) You can ski on the hills now a days. (As there is enough snow)

(3) 'Can' का प्रयोग शारीरिक क्षमता (Physical capacity), मानसिक योग्यता (capability) एवं ज्ञान के कारण प्राप्त योग्यता (Mental ability) को व्यक्त करता है । :

(a) I can solve this puzzle. (b) Can you lift this suitcase?

(4) 'Can' का प्रयोग परिस्थितिजन्य योग्यता या दूसरे व्यक्ति की योग्यता (Capacity, capability) **के सन्दर्भ में किया जाता है :**

(a) Can you lend me ten lac rupees?

(Are you in a position to do so ? Are you having this much amount surplus?)

May and Can

(1) Second Person के साथ 'may' का प्रयोग तब किया जाता है, जब वक्ता (speaker) द्वारा अनुमति दी गई हो :

You may park your vehicle here.(इसका भावार्थ यह हुआ कि, 'I give you permission to park your vehicle here.It does not mean that you have authority to park your vehicle here'.)

'Can' का प्रयोग II Person के साथ उसकी authority को व्यक्त करता है :

You can park your vehicle here.(You have authority to park your vehicle here.)

'Can' का इस तरह प्रयोग, 'I allow you / the police allow you / you have an authority or a right to park your vehicle here.' के अर्थ में होता है।

(2) Third Person के साथ 'may' का प्रयोग Speaker द्वारा दी गई permission को व्यक्त करता है।
He may take my umbrella.
इस तरह के वाक्यों का भावार्थ यह हुआ कि 'I give him permission ....'
ऐसे वाक्यों में 'Can' का प्रयोग भी किया जा सकता है :
He can take my car.
यहाँ 'Can' का अर्थ subject की authority व्यक्त करता है, अर्थात उसे car ले जाने हेतु कोई Formal Permission की आवश्यकता नहीं है; Subject और वक्ता में परस्पर relation इतने informal एवं close हैं।

DIFFERENCE BETWEEN 'MAY NOT' AND 'CANNOT'

'May not' का प्रयोग Improbability (सम्भावना नहीं लेकिन सम्भावना है भी) को व्यक्त करता है। जबकि, cannot का प्रयोग असंभाव्यता (Impossibility) को व्यक्त करता है ।

(a) The news may not be true. (may or may not be true)
(b) You cannot go there by water. (As there is no water route)

Can / Could

(1) 'Can' एवं 'Could' दोनों का प्रयोग Request हेतु किया जा सकता है । 'Could' से more politeness व्यक्त होती है।

(a) Can you give me your umbrella?
(b) Could you please send me an application form?
('Could you' is a very good way of introducing a request. It is an alternative to would you ?' And a little more polite. ***A practical English Grammar-Thomson and Martin***)

(2) 'Could' का प्रयोग past ability को व्यक्त करता है :

(a) When I was young, I could climb any tree.

(3) 'Could' का प्रयोग present perfect में एक ऐसी past possibility को भी व्यक्त करता है, जो पूर्ण नहीं हुई :

(a) He could have caught the train, if he had hurried. (But he didn't catch the train)

(4) 'Can' के past tense के रूप में 'could' का प्रयोग होता है :

(a) Ramesh told me that he could lend me his umbrella.

(5) काल्पनिक (Unreal) conditions में 'could' का प्रयोग निम्न प्रकार होता है :

(a) If I had more money, I could build a temple.

Shall /Will

(1) Traditional Grammar के अनुसार 'I /we' (I person) के साथ 'Shall' तथा II, III person के साथ 'will' का प्रयोग मान्य है ।

(2) I person (I / we) के साथ जब 'will' का प्रयोग तथा II and III person के साथ जब 'shall' का प्रयोग किया जाता है तो यह determination, threat, warning, promise को व्यक्त करता है ।
आजकल will / shall के प्रयोग में उक्त अन्तर लगभग समाप्त हो गया है। लेकिन हमें Modals के सन्दर्भ में Traditional Grammar के अनुसार ही चलना है ।

Shall

(1) Shall का प्रयोग I person के साथ एक सामान्य future action को व्यक्त करता है। II एवं III person के साथ 'shall' का प्रयोग promise, determination, threat, warning के भावों को व्यक्त करता है :

(a) I shall go to market tomorrow. (Future action)
(b) He shall pay you on Monday. (Promise)

(c) He shall work hard to achieve success. (Determination)

(d) Anyone find involved shall be punished. (Warning, threat)

(2) II एवं III person के साथ 'shall' का प्रयोग 'determination, compulsion, bindings', एवं 'force' व्यक्त करता है :

(a) You shall go to meet him tomorrow. (you are instructed to go and meet him)

(b) She shall complete her work by tommorrow. (She has to complete her work by tomorrow)

(3) 'Shall not' का II एवं III person के साथ प्रयोग prohibition (निषेध) को व्यक्त करता है :

(a) You shall not meet him .

(b) Nobody shall write on the table.

(c) She shall not attend the night party.

(4) 'Shall' का I person के साथ एक प्रश्न के रूप में प्रयोग, दूसरे की इच्छा जानने हेतु या अपनी सेवाएँ देने हेतु किया जाता है :

(a) Shall I open the door?

(b) Shall I carry this box into the room for you?

(c) Shall I thread the needle for you?

(d) Shall I assist you?

(5) 'Shall' का III person के साथ प्रयोग या एक noun के साथ प्रयोग दूसरे की इच्छानुसार कार्य करने को व्यक्त करता है :

(a) Shall Rahim wait for you ? (Do you want him to wait for you?)

(b) Shall the messenger wait out side ? (Do you want the messenger to wait out side?)

Will

(1) 'Will' का प्रयोग II & III person के साथ सामान्य future action को बताता है , जबकि I person के साथ will का प्रयोग threat, warning, promise, determination के भाव को व्यक्त करता है :

(a) He will go tomorrow.

(b) You will work here.

(c) I will see you. (threat, warning)

(d) I will pay you on Monday. (promise)

(e) I will achieve my goal. (determination)

(f) I will never speak to him. (determination)

(2) 'Will' का प्रयोग प्रश्न के प्रारूप में formal request को व्यक्त करता है :

(a) Will you close the door?

(b) Will you bring me a glass of water?

(3) 'Will' का प्रयोग सभी persons के साथ सम्भावना (Probability) व्यक्त करता है। 'will not' (won't) का प्रयोग refusal (इन्कार) को व्यक्त करता है :

(a) I won't go there.

(b) He will not sanction your leave.

(c) He will be in the park.

(d) Today is 15th Aug; schools will be closed.

(4) 'Won't' (will not) का प्रयोग जब प्रश्न के रूप में किया जाता है, तो यह Invitation को व्यक्त करता है:

(a) Won't you have a cup of tea?

(b) Won't you meet her?

(c) Won't you stay for a day?

(5) 'Will' का प्रयोग Instruction, command को भी व्यक्त करता है :

(a) All the cadets will attend the parade. (Instruction, command)

(b) The girls will not wear the shorts. (Instruction, command)

(c) You will deliver the welcome speech. (Instruction, command)

(6) 'Will' का प्रयोग III person के साथ, सामान्य आदत को व्यक्त करता है :

(a) The women will not keep mum. (habit)

(b) The girls will talk. (habit)

(c) He will smoke. (habit)

(d) The minister will come late. (habit)

Should/ Would

Should

(1) 'Should' का प्रयोग Duty (कर्तव्य) Responsibility (दायित्व, जिम्मेदारी), Advice (सलाह) probability (संभावना), Expectation (आशा) Presumption(पूर्व अनुमान), Moral obligation (नैतिक दायित्व) तथा Mild Command (नम्र आदेश) व्यक्त करता है :

(a) One should obey one's elders. (Duty)
(b) You should obey your parents. (Moral obligation)
(c) The rich should help the poor. (Expectation)
(d) You should work hard. (Advice)

(2) Conditional sentences में 'lest' के साथ 'should' का प्रयोग किया जाता है । यह एक Important use है :

(a) Work hard lest you should fail.
मेहनत करो, कहीं ऐसा न हो कि, तुम असफल हो जाओ ।

'Lest' का अर्थ –'कहीं ऐसा न हो कि', होता है ।

(3) 'Should' का प्रयोग जब purpose व्यक्त करने हेतु किया जाता है, तब वह 'may' एवं 'might' के अर्थ से समानता रखता है :

(a) I taught her so that she should pass. (She might pass)

(4) 'Should' का perfect tense में प्रयोग, इस आशय को स्पष्ट करता है कि जो कार्य जिस रूप में किया जाना चाहिये था, वह नहीं किया गया :

(a) He should have gone by morning bus. (but he didn't go)

Would

(1) 'Would' का प्रयोग 'will' की अपेक्षा अधिक polite request को दर्शाता है। Request हेतु 'will' की अपेक्षा 'would' का प्रयोग अधिक मान्य है। 'Would' का प्रयोग दूसरे की इच्छा (Willingness) जानने हेतु भी किया जाता है :

(a) Would you accompany me to the railway station? (Polite request)

(2) 'Would' का प्रयोग likelihood, presumption एवं probability को भी व्यक्त करता है :

(a) He would be in the field. (likelihood)
(b) She would be in the club at this time (probability)

(3) 'Rather' के साथ 'would' का प्रयोग, preference (प्राथमिकता) को व्यक्त करता है :

(a) I would rather study than see a movie.

(4) 'Wish' के साथ 'will' का प्रयोग नहीं किया जाता है। 'wish' के साथ 'would' का प्रयोग strong desire / willingness को स्पष्ट करता है ।

(a) I wish, you would fight this election.

(5) Unreal (काल्पनिक) परिस्थितियों को व्यक्त करने हेतु भी 'would' का प्रयोग, conditional sentences में किया जाता है :

(a) If I had one crore rupees, I would donate fifty lacs to the trust.
(b) If I had wings I would fly to Europe.

(6) Conditional sentences में past perfect के sentences में 'would' का प्रयोग, किसी कार्य के past में न होने को व्यक्त करता है :

(a) If she had asked me, I would have helped her. (But she didn't ask me.)
यदि वह मुझे कहती तो मैं उसकी सहायता करता ।

(7) 'Would' - 'will' का past है, Direct से Indirect narration में परिवर्तन करते समय, reporting verb past में होने पर 'will' को 'would' में बदलते हैं :

(a) He told me that he would go to Jaipur the next day.

IMPORTANT **'Should, could, would, might' का प्रयोग, past tense एवं present tense दोनों में किया जाता है । लेकिन 'shall, will, may, can' का प्रयोग past tense में नहीं किया जाता है । कई बार परीक्षाओं में प्रश्न will /would, shall /should , may / might, can / could के reference में आते हैं ; इस बिन्दु का ध्यान रखकर answer लिखें।**

Must

'Must' का प्रयोग present time एवं future time, दोनों प्रकार के Actions व्यक्त करने हेतु किया जा सकता है। 'Must' का कोई past tense नहीं होता है। Reported speech में direct से indirect में परिवर्तन करते समय, कई स्थितियों में 'must' को 'had to' में भी परिवर्तित किया जाता है।

(1) 'Must' का प्रयोग command, compulsion, order (निर्देश, दबाव, आदेश) का भाव दर्शाता है :

(a) Soldiers must obey orders without any question.

(2) 'Must' से moral duty / obligation भी व्यक्त होता है :

(a) We must respect our elders.

(3) 'Must' से necessity, urgency, circumstancial compulsion (जरूरत, आवश्यकता, पारिस्थितिक, दबाव) भी व्यक्त होता है :

(a) I must leave now, otherwise I may miss the train.

(4) 'Must not' का प्रयोग prohibition, Emphatic advice (निषेध एवं दबाव युक्त सलाह) की अभिव्यक्ति हेतु भी प्रयोग किया जाता है :

(a) Students must not resort to copying. (prohibition)
(b) You must not miss the classes. (emphatic advice)

(5) 'Must' से strong probability / likelihood को भी व्यक्त किया जाता है :

(a) She must be eighty now.

(6) जब प्रश्न 'must' से शुरू किया जाता है, एवं उसका answer यदि affirmative में हो, तो answer में 'must' का प्रयोग किया जाता है । लेकिन यदि answer, negative में दिया जाये तो 'Needn't' का प्रयोग करना चाहिये :

(a) Must I attend the meeting ?
Yes, you must.
No, you needn't

(7) 'Must' का perfect tense में प्रयोग भूतकाल में किसी कार्य के होने की प्रबल सम्भावना को व्यक्त करता है:

(a) He must have passed the test in first attempt.

NEED

'Need' का प्रयोग Ordinary verb एवं Modal Auxilidry verb, दोनों की तरह किया जा सकता है। इसीलिए इसे ***Semi Modal*** या ***Marginal Modal*** कहा जाता है ।

(1) Modal के रूप में 'Need' का प्रयोग सामान्यतया Interrogative एवं Negative वाक्यों में किया जाता है :

(a) He need not talk to her. (b) Need he talk to her?

(2) Present tense में 'needn't' का प्रयोग ऐसे कार्य को व्यक्त करता है, जो वास्तव में नहीं किया जाना ही उचित था। 'Needn't' का अर्थ होता है – 'आवश्यक नहीं होना' या 'जरूरत नहीं होना' :

(a) He needn't have written such a detailed essay. (The essay was to be written is 300 words only.)
(b) You needn't have bought such a costly gift (waste of money).

(3) जब 'need' से कोई प्रश्न आरम्भ किया जाता है एवं उसका answer यदि affirmative में है, तो answer में must का प्रयोग किया जाना चाहिये । Negative में answer हेतु needn't का प्रयोग होता है :

Need I go there? Yes, you must.
No, you needn't.

(4) Principal verb की तरह 'need' का प्रयोग निम्न प्रकार से होता है :

(a) He needs my assistance. (b) He needed my help.
(c) He does not need my help. (d) I do not need your advice in the matter.

जब 'need' का प्रयोग principal verb की तरह होता है तो सामान्यतया Affirmative sentences में जरूरत या आवश्यकता (meaning) के सन्दर्भ में होता है। 'Need' का principal verb की तरह प्रयोग जब Negative, में या Interrogative में किया जाता है तो 'Do, Does, Did' का प्रयोग Ordinary verb की तरह करते हैं।

Used to

यह भी एक Marginal or Semi Modal है। 'Used to' का Negative form 'used not to' होता है। 'Used to' के negative हेतु 'didn't use to' का भी प्रयोग किया जाता है। इसी तरह 'used to' को Interrogative में प्रयोग करते समय **Did+subject + use to + verb** की तरह भी प्रयोग किया जा सकता है ।

(1) 'Used to' का प्रयोग यह व्यक्त करता है कि भूतकाल में कोई कार्य आदतन किया जाता था, लेकिन अब नहीं किया जाता है :

(a) He used to drink daily. (Now he does not drink.)

(2) 'Used to' का वर्तमान काल में अभ्यस्त (accustomed) होने के सन्दर्भ में प्रयोग निम्न प्रकार किया जाता है :

(a) I am used to take tea in the morning . मैं सुबह चाय पीने का अभ्यस्त हूँ।

(3) 'Used to' का Negative एवं Interrogative वाक्यों में प्रयोग निम्न प्रकार किया जा सकता है :

(a) He used to play chess at college. – Affirmative.
He didn't use to play chess at college – Negative
Used he to play chess at college ? – Interrogative.
Did he use to play chess at college? – Interrogative.

Dare

'Dare' का प्रयोग principal verb एवं modal verb दोनों प्रकार से होता है, इसीलिए 'dare' को भी **Marginal modal or Semi modal** कहा जाता है।

Use of 'Dare' as Modal :

(1) 'Dare' का modal की तरह प्रयोग सामान्यतया Negative एवं Interrogative sentences में होता है । जब इसका Modal की तरह प्रयोग होता है तो इसके साथ 'to' का प्रयोग नहीं होता है, तब 'dare' का अर्थ होता है, दुस्साहस करना, चुनौती देना :

(a) He dare not say like this. (b) Dare he not say like this ?

(2) 'How' के साथ 'dare' का प्रयोग, वक्ता का आश्यर्य, गुस्सा एवं सदमा (surprise, anger or shock) व्यक्त करता है :

(a) How dare you speak like this ?
(b) How dare my wife leave without my permission?

(3) 'Nobody, any body', एवं 'somebody' etc. के साथ जब 'dare' का प्रयोग modal की तरह किया जाता है, तो इसके साथ 'to' का प्रयोग किया भी जा सकता है एवं नहीं भी किया जा सकता है :

(a) Nobody dare to comment like that. (b) Some body dare complain in the matter.

(4) 'Daresay' का अर्थ होता है - शायद, संभवतया (perhaps, it is expected, I expect); 'Daresay' का प्रयोग 'I' के साथ /ही किया जाता है :

(a) I daresay he will come. (b) I daresay she may agree.

(Daresay को साथ-साथ एवं अलग-अलग (dare say) दोनों प्रकार से लिखा जा सकता है ।

(5) 'Dare' का प्रयोग जब principal verb की तरह किया जाता है, तो इसके साथ 'to' का प्रयोग किया जाता है। Singular number third person: subject के साथ 'dare' में 's' जोड़ा जाता है एवं Do, Does का प्रयोग Negative एवं Interrogative वाक्यों में किया जाता है :

(a) He dares to oppose you . (b) He does not dare to oppose you.

(c) Does he dare to oppose you? (d) Do you dare to speak against him?

Ought to

'Ought' के साथ हमेशा 'to' लगता है । **'Ought to' एवं 'should' का प्रयोग एवं अर्थ लगभग समान है।**

(1) 'Ought to' का प्रयोग, Advice (सलाह), moral obligation (नैतिक दायित्व), Duty (कर्तव्य) को व्यक्त करता है :

(a) You ought to consult a physician. (Advice)

(b) We ought to respect our parents. (Moral duty)

(2) 'Ought' के साथ 'not' का प्रयोग किसी दायित्व को पूर्ण न करने के सन्दर्भ में किया जाता है या Advice के रूप में किया जाता है :

(a) You ought not to treat your friends like this.

(b) Children ought not to watch T.V. so long.

(3) 'Ought to' का perfect tense में प्रयोग यह व्यंक्त करता है कि जो कार्य सम्पन्न होना चाहिये था वह कार्य सम्पन्न नहीं किया गया :

(a) She ought to have invited him in the function. (But she didn't invite him.)

(4) सामान्यतया ought to एवं should को समान अर्थ एवं समान प्रयोग के सन्दर्भ में एक जैसा माना जाता है लेकिन formal notices, या अन्य कोई सूचना देने के लिये 'should' का प्रयोग किया जाता है, 'Ought to' का नहीं :

(a) Students should be prepared to donate the blood.

(b) Travellers should be in possession of the following documents.

(c) On hearing the alarm bell, the students should leave their rooms immediately .

उपरोक्त वाक्यों में 'Ought to' का प्रयोग नहीं होगा ।

ERRORS, MISTAKES AND BLUNDERS IN USE OF MODALS

Exercise : ***Rewrite the sentences after correction.***

1. The sky is cloudy, it can rain today.
2. He said that she may have missed the train
3. He said, "Can I come in please?
4. You will be transferred if you don't complete your work in time.
5. Move fast lest you may miss the train.
6. I would rather played than rest.
7. You could obey your parents.
8. Passengers should cross the line by the footbridge.
9. Must I attend the court? No, you must not.
10. Dares she complain against you?
11. You ought to have help her in that matter.

Explanations

1. The sky is cloudy it may rain today.
2. He said that she might have missed the train.
3. He said, "May I come in please?
4. You shall be transferred if you don't complete your work in time.
5. Move fast lest you should miss the train.
6. I would rather play than rest.
7. You should obey your parents.
8. Passenger must cross the line by the footbridge.
9. Must I attend the court? No, you need not.
10. Dare she complain against you?
11. You ought to have helped her in that matter.

SPOTTING ERRORS (MODALS)

Exercise : ***Find the errors and justify your answers.***

1. If allowed an accused (A)/ can appeal (B)/ against the judgement of (C)/ the High Court in civil cases (D).
2. May you get (A)/to the top of (B)/ this mountain (C)/ in eight hours (D).
3. If you have (A)/ got the ticket (B)/ you may(C)/ park your car here(D).
4. There is no water route (A)/ between India and Mexico, (B)/ you may not (C)/go to Mexico by water (D).
5. He can have (A)/ caught the train, (B)/ if he had hurried (C).
6. When I was young (A)/ I can climbe up (B)/ this mountain in (C)/ six hours (D).
7. She wouldn't have opened (A)/ the letter, (B)/ it wasn't addressed to her (C).
8. Doctor: If the pain has gone (A)/ you mustn't take (B)/ any more of these pills (C).
9. You needn't read (A)/ the whole book (B)/ but you should read (C) / the first two chapters (D).
10. I am use to (A)/ take wine (B)/ with my meals (C)/ so I find this lunch unrelishing (D).

Explanations

1. (B) 'can appeal' की जगह 'may appeal' का प्रयोग होगा। 'may' shows the authority, given by someone else, while 'can' shows authority lying with the subject.
2. (A) 'may' की जगह 'can' लिखें। 'can' shows capability.
3. (C) 'may' की जगह 'can' का प्रयोग होगा। 'can' shows 'right' of the subiect.
4. (C) 'may not' की जगह 'cannot' का प्रयोग होगा। 'cannot' shows impossibility.
5. (A) 'can' की जगह 'could' का प्रयोग होगा।
6. (B) 'can' की जगह 'could' का प्रयोग होगा। 'could' shows, past possibility.
7. (A) 'wouldn't' की जगह 'shouldn't' का प्रयोग होगा। इसका अर्थ है कि 'उसे पत्र नहीं खोलना चाहिए था'।
8. (B) 'mustn't' की जगह 'needn't' का प्रयोग होगा।
9. (C) 'should' की जगह 'must' का प्रयोग होगा।
10. (A) 'use to' की जगह 'used to' का प्रयोग होगा।

❑❑❑

6

Verbs Arrangements

प्रत्येक वाक्य में Verb एवं Subject के मध्य एक Agreement होता है; जब Subject singular है, तो verb भी singular होगी। Main Verbs के प्रयोग के नियम एवं विभिन्न Parts of Sentence, जैसे : Noun, Pronoun, Preposition, Conjunction etc. के साथ Verb का प्रयोग किस तरह किया जायेगा, यह English Grammar का बहुत ही महत्त्वपूर्ण बिन्दु है। यद्यपि 'Verbs' का सही प्रयोग करने हेतु विभिन्न नियमों को बताया गया है तथापि ध्यान रखें नियमों को रटने से अंग्रेजी में प्रवीणता हासिल नहीं की जा सकती है। नियमों को बार-बार पढ़ें, तथा Exercises को solve करें। **"Practice alone can make you Perfect."**

The verb must agree with its subject in number and person- Nesfield

(a) I am playing.
(b) They are playing.
(c) He is playing.
(d) We are playing.

वाक्य संख्या (a) एवं (c) में subject singular है अत: verb 'am', 'is' singular है तथा वाक्य संख्या (b) एवं (d) में subject plural है अत: verb 'are' plural है।

ध्यान रखें

(1) सभी Verbs को Plural एवं Present Tense में माना जाता है। Verbs के साथ Present Tense में s या es लगाने से वह Singular बनती है। Verbs - Singular या Plural , Present Tense में ही होती हैं।

(2) 'To be' form of Verbs (is, am, are, was, were); इन Verbs में से Singular में अलग-अलग Persons के साथ अलग-अलग Verb काम आती है। जैसे- I के साथ am, 'you' के साथ 'are', 'He' के साथ 'is'; जबकि Plural में इनका रूप एक ही रहता है। Present Tense में 'are' तथा Past Tense में were, जैसे - We are, You are, They are एवं We were, You were, They were.

(3) 'Shall, Will, Should' एवं 'Would' के साथ हमेशा 'Have' का प्रयोग किया जाता है, इनके साथ कभी भी 'Has' का प्रयोग करने की गलती न करें।

SUBJECT - VERB AGREEMENT V/S RULES OF CORRECT USE OF VERBS

Exceptions to the Rule

1. कुछ वाक्य ऐसे होते हैं जिनमें Singular subject होते हुए भी, Plural verb का प्रयोग किया जाता है :

(A) जब वाक्य में 'कल्पना' का भाव या असंभव प्राय: शर्त का भाव प्रदर्शित होता है। जैसे :-

(1) I wish I were the Prime Minister.
(2) I wish I were a bird.

(B) जब वाक्यों में verbs; bless, save, help, live, का प्रयोग, इच्छा, अभिलाषा (desire, wish) या आशीर्वाद का भाव प्रकट करता है तो singular subject के साथ भी 'bless, save, help, live' की plural form का प्रयोग होता है (अर्थात blesses, saves, helps या lives की तरह इनका प्रयोग नहीं किया जा सकता है।); जैसे :-

(1) God save the queen.
(2) Gop help you .

(C) जब वाक्य में 'Dare' एवं 'Need' का प्रयोग Modals की तरह किया जाता है, तो Subject, Singular होने पर भी 'Dare' एवं 'Need' ही रहते हैं ; 'Dares' या 'Needs' नहीं होते हैं :

(a) He need not to go there .
(b) She dare not oppose your proposal
(c) Dare she oppose you?
(d) He dare not speak like this.

2. यदि दो अलग-अलग Nouns, एक ही व्यक्ति या वस्तु के लिये प्रयुक्त हों, तो Verb- Singular प्रयुक्त होती है :

(a) The poet and painter has died.
(b) The Project Director and Additional Collector is on tour.

यहाँ poet, painter; Project Director तथा Additional Collector एक ही व्यक्ति के लिये प्रयुक्त हुऐ हैं। यह भी ध्यान रखें, कि ऐसे वाक्यों में Article का प्रयोग पहले Noun के साथ ही होता है।

3. जब दो Nouns, जो लगभग एक सा भाव या अर्थ रखते हैं, का प्रयोग एक दूसरे का महत्त्व बढ़ाने हेतु किया जाता है, तो भी Verb -Singular प्रयुक्त होती है। जैसे :

(a) The scheme and plan of my life differs from that of yours.
(b) The benefit and advantage from this business is enormous.

4. दो Noun जो यद्यपि समानार्थक नही हैं लेकिन एक Phrase की तरह प्रयुक्त होते हैं तो भी Verb -Singulr रहती है। Actually ये दो Nouns, एक ही idea को व्यक्त करते हैं :

(a) Bread and butter is a good breakfast.
(b) "Early to bed, early to rise" is a good habit.

5. जब दो या अधिक singular nouns; or ,either...or, neither ...nor से जोड़े गये हों, तो Verb- singular रहती है :

(a) No man or woman was present there.
(b) Either Sita or Ram was present in the party.
(c) Neither he nor she is responsible for this loss.

6. जब दो या अधिक noun अलग-अलग Number के हों (अर्थात् कोई Plural हो, कोई Singular हो), तो Plural number वाला Nouns ही Verb के साथ लिखना चाहिये एवं Verb भी Plural ही प्रयुक्त होती है :

(a) Neither the Principal nor the teachers were present in the function
(b) Either Ramesh or his friends have stolen the watch.

7. यदि दो या अधिक Subjects; Either ...or, Neither...nor, or से जुड़े हुए हों तथा different persons के हों, तो Verb अपने पास वाले Person के अनुसार ही प्रयुक्त होती है :

(a) Either you or I am to go there.
(b) Neither he nor you are to attend them.

8. जब एक Collective noun, जैसे -Committee, Army, Crowd, Mob, Society, Assembly, Parliament, Council, Crew, Staff, Jury, Fleet, Majority, आदि इस तरह से प्रयुक्त होती है जैसे एक Unit (इकाई) हो तो Verb-Singular प्रयुक्त होती है :

(a) The Parliament has passed the bill.
(b) The jury has taken a unanimous decision.

Note *लेकिन यदि collective Noun एक Unit की तरह action नहीं लेती हो, बल्कि वाक्य से divided प्रतीत होती हो या समूह के विभिन्न सदस्यों में एकमत नहीं हो तो plural verb प्रयुक्त की जाती है :*

(a) The committee are divided over the proposal.
(b) The jury are divided in their opinion.

9. यदि एक Plural noun, एक निशचित quantity या amount को एक Unit की तरह व्यक्त करता है तो Verb-singular प्रयुक्त होती है :

(a) Five kilograms is not a heavy weight.
(b) Hundered rupees is a big amount for him.

10. 'Each' एवं 'Every' के साथ जुड़े हुये singular noun (each एवं every के साथ हमेशा Singular noun ही आता है) के साथ Verb singular प्रयुक्त होती है :

(a) Each boy and girl has to attend the function.
(b) Every man, woman and child was happy to meet with the President.

11. जब दो Subjects, 'Not only ....but also' से जुड़े हों तो Verb, अपने पास वाले subject के अनुसार प्रयुक्त की जाती है :

(a) Not only the principal but also the teachers were playing the match.

12. जब एक Subject के साथ beside, as well as, and not, in addition to, like, with, together with जैसे जोड़ने वाले conjunctions से अन्य subject या कोई शब्द जुड़े हुए हों, तो Verb वाक्य में पहले आने वाले subject के अनुसार प्रयुक्त होती है :

(a) Ram and not his friends was present there.
(b) The house with all its belongings was sold.
(c) The president as well as the members has come.
(d) The pigeon like other birds has wings.

13. 'The poor, The rich, The disabled, The young, The old, The English, The French' इत्यादि पूरी Class को व्यक्त करते हैं (The poor का अर्थ है- सभी गरीब लोग ,The rich का अर्थ होता है - सभी धनी लोग) इनके साथ Plural verb का प्रयोग किया जाता है एवं 'The poors, The riches' लिखना गलत है :

(a) The poor are trustworthy. (b) The rich are generally unkind to the poor.

14. Hair (बाल) का प्रयोग singular में किया जाता है एवं singular verb प्रयुक्त होती है, लेकिन यदि बालों की Counting का सन्दर्भ हो, तो Verb plural प्रयुक्त होगी :

(a) His hair is black. (b) Five hairs of the horse are needed by him.

15. सामान्यत: 'All' एवं 'Some' के साथ यदि Countable noun आता है तो वह Noun भी Plural होगा एवं verb भी Plural प्रयोग की जायेगी। लेकिन यदि 'All' एवं 'Some' के साथ कोई Uncountable noun आता है तो Verb-Singular प्रयोग की जाती है :

(a) All the tigers are wild animals. (b) All the money was taken away by the thief.
(c) Some animals are faithful. (d) Some milk in needed.

लेकिन यदि 'all' का प्रयोग वाक्य में एक Unit की तरह हो रहा है, तो इसके साथ singular verb प्रयुक्त होगी :

(a) He informed the police all that happened last night.
(b) I would inform you all that was discussed in the meeting.
(उपरोक्त वाक्यों में 'all' का प्रयोग एक Unit की तरह हो रहा है।)

16. यदि एक वाक्य में 'Most of/Half of' of के बाद Countable noun आता है तो ध्यान रखें, वह Plural ही आयेगा तथा उसके बाद Verb भी Plural ही प्रयुक्त होगी, लेकिन Noun यदि Uncountable आता है तो Verb-Singular प्रयुक्त होती है :

(a) Most of the persons are dishonest. (b) Most of the milk was impure.
(c) He said that half of the hostlers were absent. (d) Half of the milk was spoiled.

17. 'There' के बाद आने वाली Verb Plural या Singular होगी, यह इस तथ्य पर निर्भर है कि वाक्य का Subject, Plural है या Singular जैसे:

(a) There is a girl in the room. (b) There are ten students in the class.

18. कई वाक्यों में Singular noun का repetition, preposition के बाद होता है, ऐसे वाक्यों में Singular Verb प्रयुक्त होती है :

(a) Man after man was coming there. (b) Ship after ship is arriving regularly.

19. यदि किसी वाक्य में infinitive, gerund, phrase, या कोई clause, subject का कार्य करता है, या subject की तरह प्रयोग में आया है, तो singular verb का प्रयोग किया जाता है :

(a) Swiming is a good exercise. — Gerund
(b) To swim is good for you. — Infinitive
(c) How to start it is a big question. — Phrase
(d) That she is poor is known to me. — Clause

20. 'More than one' के साथ किसी noun का प्रयोग किया जाये, तो Verb-singular प्रयुक्त होगी। जैसे :

(a) More than one worker was absent.
(b) More than one student was killed .

More than one यद्यपि एक Plural संख्या को व्यक्त करता है लेकिन उसके साथ singular verb का ही प्रयोग किया जाता है; इस संबंध में Mr. Fowler ने Modern English usage में लिखा है :

'More than one', though its sense is necessarily plural, is treated as a sort of compound of 'one', following its construction, and agrees with a singular noun and takes a singular verb- More than one workman was killed, not 'workmen' or 'were'. —Fowler.

21. कई वाक्यों में 'more' का प्रयोग निम्न प्रकार होता है :

(a) More books than one have been purchased by her.
(b) More girls than one were present in the party.

इस तरह के वाक्यों में Plural verb का प्रयोग किया जाता है :

22. कुछ वाक्यों में noun के बाद Preposition एवं फिर noun आता है, जैसे :

(a) The quality of these goods is well known.
(b) Financial help from all the countries was received.
(c) The colour of these shirts is liked by all.
(d) Your views on this matter are supported by all.
(e) The details of the accident are not received by us so far.
(f) The cost of production of steel goods is increasing.
(g) Economic co-operation between India and Pakistan is increasing.
(h) The smell of these flowers is liked by all.

उपरोक्त वाक्यों का Structure: noun + preposition + noun की तरह का है। ऐसे वाक्यों में verb, preposition से पहले आने वाले noun के अनुसार प्रयुक्त होती है। वाक्य संख्या (d) एवं (e) के अतिरिक्त सभी वाक्यों में preposition के पहले आने वाला noun singular है अत: verb singular प्रयुक्त की गई है।

Note *यदि वाक्य में एक से अधिक nouns, preposition के साथ आये तो भी verb, सबसे पहले आने वाले preposition के पहले आने वाले noun के अनुसार लगाई जाती है । जैसे :*

(a) The manager's remarks in a newspaper about the conduct of the player were not appreciated by any one.
(b) The cost of production of steel items is increasing everywhere.

23. जब वाक्य में इन phrases का प्रयोग होता है— a number of, lots of, a lot of, plenty of, a quarter of, part of, percent of, proportion of, none of, remainder of, two third of, most of, some of, majority of, much of, many of, a good deal of, a great deal of, heaps of तो 'of' के बाद आने वाले noun के अनुसार verb प्रयुक्त की जाती है। यदि 'of' के बाद आने वाला noun plural है तो verb भी plural प्रयुक्त की जाएगी :

(a) Plenty of sugar is required. (b) Plenty of chairs have been purchased.
(c) A lot of books were destroyed in fire. (d) A lot of milk was sent there .

यदि 'of' के बाद कोई Countable noun है तो वह Plural होगा एवं यदि uncountable noun है तो वह singular होगा :

(a) A number of boys, plently of books. (Boys and books are countables.)
(b) Plenty of milk, a lot of sugar. (Milk and sugar are uncountables.)

24. यदि वाक्य में 'A number' या 'The number' का प्रयोग हुआ है तो ध्यान रखें 'the number' के साथ हमेशा singuler verb प्रयुक्त होती है तथा 'A number' के साथ हमेशा Plural verb प्रयुक्त होती है। 'The number' का अर्थ होता है एक निश्चित संख्या। यह collective noun की तरह प्रयुक्त होता है एवं Singular verb का प्रयोग किया जाता है ।

A number का अर्थ होता है 'बहुत' (many) तो इसके साथ Plural verb ही प्रयोग में लाई जायेगी :

(a) The number of students opted English in Administrative services is generally small.
(b) A number of English books are available in library.

25. 'None' के साथ सामान्य रूप से Singular verb का प्रयोग सही माना जाता है। लेकिन Modern English में 'none' के साथ Plural verb का भी प्रयोग किया जाने लगा है; इस संबंध में grammarians में काफी मतभेद हैं। देखें :

(a) It is mistake to suppose that the pronoun 'none' is singular only and must at all costs be followed by singular verb.
— Fowler

(b) 'None' was originally used only as singular but it has also acquired a plural meaning.
—Nesfield

(3) 'None' is an abbreviated form of not one or no one and would therefore seem to be singular, but in its context it usually has a plural sense.
— Vallins

इस तरह 'none' का प्रयोग singular एवं plural दोनों ही स्थितियों में किया जा सकता है।

नीचे लिखे वाक्यों पर गौर करें :

(1) None of the minor characters were present on the day of rehersal. (Plural)
(2) None of his works shows his capabilities and his calibre. (Singular)

26. यदि किसी वाक्य का Subject, कोई Relative pronoun, जैसे : 'who, which, that' है, तो verb, इस Relative Pronoun के Antecedent के अनुसार प्रयोग की जाती है (Antecedent का अर्थ होता है पहले आने वाला), अत: Relative pronoun के पहले आने वाला noun या pronoun यदि Singular है तो Verbभी Singular, यदि Plural है तो Verb Plural प्रयुक्त होगी या यह कहें कि Relative Pronoun से पूर्व आने वाला noun या pronoun ही verb को अनुशासित करता है :

(a) It is I who have telephoned you. (b) It is he who is responsible for this loss.
(c) The book that is here is mine. (d) The books that are here are mine .

27. जब वाक्यों में 'Nothing but' आता है तो Verb हमेशा Singular ही प्रयुक्त होगी चाहे 'Nothing but' के बाद आने वाला noun; singular हो या plural.

(a) Nothing but hill is seen. (b) Nothing but birds is seen.

28. यदि दो Singular nouns के पहले 'no' का प्रयोग हो तो verb- singular प्रयुक्त होगी :

(a) No boy and no girl was present in the party.
(b) No man and no woman was swimming at that time.

29. जब दो अंकगणितीय figures, 'and' से जोड़े जाते हैं तो verb-singular भी हो सकती है और plural भी :

(a) Four and four is eight. (b) Four and four are eight.

जब Singular verb का प्रयोग होता है तो इसका अर्थ है कि 'and' से संयुक्त इन अंकों को एक Unitary Concept माना गया है; जब Plural Verb का प्रयोग किया जाता है तो इन्हें अलग अलग माना गया है। इस संबंध में Norman Lewis के निम्न कथन पर ध्यान दें :

Five and Five is ten :- Right --- But don't jump to the conclusion that 'five and five are ten' is wrong both verbs are equally acceptable. ***(Norman Lewis)***

साधारणतया Singular verb का प्रयोग उचित रहता है।

30. 'Everyone, Every body, Nobody, Somebody, No one, Each one, Someone' के साथ Singular Verb प्रयुक्त होती है :

(a) Everyone was happy to get this news. (b) Somebody is coming here.
(b) Each one was given a gift. (c) Someone is there in the hall.

31. 'Either of, Each of, Neither of' के साथ भी singular verb का प्रयोग होता है। ध्यान रखें, Either of, 'Each of' एवं 'Neither of' के बाद Subject (noun) plural आता है :

(a) Each of the students was given a gift. (b) Either of the magazines is useful.
(c) Neither of the books is cheap. (d) Neither of the girls was beautiful.

32. कुछ Verbs के बाद 'as' अवश्य आता है। ये verbs हैं- regard, describe, represent, portray, depict, mention, define, treat आदि; जैसे :

(a) You ought to have regarded him as your brother.
(b) He was described by his wife as the most harmless man.

33. कुछ Verbs के बाद 'as' नहीं आता है। ये verbs हैं - name, call, term, think, consider, nominate, appoint; आदि :

(a) The Chairman nominated Hari secretory of the society.
(b) Ram called him a fool, a rogue and a crook.
(c) Ram calls his wife 'Situ.'

INVERSION

What is 'Inversion' ?

Affirmative वाक्यों का Structure सामान्यतया निम्न प्रकार का होता है :

Subject + Verb + ...

सामान्यतया वाक्यों में Verb का प्रयोग Subject के बाद किया जाता है।

Interrogative वाक्यों में सामान्यतया Verb का प्रयोग Subject से पूर्व निम्न प्रकार होता है :

Verb + Subject + ...

Interrogative वाक्यों के अतिरिक्त अन्य बहुत से वाक्यों में Adverbs एवं Adverbial expressions का प्रयोग जब clause के प्रारम्भ में होता है, तो भी Verb, Subject के पहले आती है। **वाक्यों में Verb का Subject के पहले आना Inversion कहलाता है।**

Inversion of the Verb

"Certain adverbs and adverb phrases, most with a restrictive or negative sense, can for emphasis be placed first in a sentence or clause and are then followed by the inverted (i.e. interrogative) form of the verb." ***Thomson and Martinet.***

Inversion दो प्रकार का होता है।

Examples of Inversion

1. **'Hardly, rarely, scarcely, seldom, never' का प्रयोग जब वाक्य को शुरू करने के लिए होता है, तो Verb का Inversion होता है। जैसे :**
   (a) Hardly does she go to church.
   (b) Seldom had I seen such a healthy baby.
   (c) Never does she go to temple.
   (d) Scarcely ever did they manage to meet the deadline.
2. **'Not only .... but also' का प्रयोग जब Verbs के पूर्व किया जाता है :**
   (a) Not only did she watch TV but she also cooked meal.
   (b) Not only does he rob her but he also smashes everything.
3. **'No sooner' का प्रयोग जब वाक्य को शुरू करने हेतु किया जाता है तब भी Verb का Inversion होता है :**
   (a) No sooner had she seen her husband than she hugged him
4. **'No........' से बने expressions, जैसे :**
   Under no circumstances, In no way, On no account, On no condition, At no time के साथ Inversion का प्रयोग किया जाता है :
   (a) Under no circumstances shall I accept this proposal.
   (b) On no condition will she sell the house.
5. **'Only' के साथ प्रयुक्त Adverbial expressions, जैसे: Only yesterday, Only the day before yesterday, Only last month, Only last fortnight, Only after a month/ year, Only then, Only in this way, Only when, Only by doing this thing, Only in a few schools/colleges/ countries/continents etc. के साथ Inversion का प्रयोग किया जाता है :**
   (a) Only yesterday did he buy that car.
   (b) Only by taking risk did he save the life of the minister.
   (c) Only by accepting the condition, did he join this job.
   (d) Only by shouting was she able to make herself heard.
6. **Adverbial expressions showing place(स्थान) के साथ verb का Inversion apply होता है। ऐसे expressions : 'Outside the gate, under the table, In the valley, Along the border, Round the Corner, On a hill' etc. है :**
   (a) In the valley did I see a strange man.
   (b) Out side the gate did he notice something moving.
   (c) On a hill did he find a new revolver.
7. **'Here/There/Away/Out/Up/Indoor/Out doors/In/down' इत्यादि से शुरू होने वाले वाक्यों में Inversion प्रयुक्त होता है। जैसे :**
   (a) Down fell a dozen apples. (b) In came the child weeping.
   (c) Here comes the train. (d) There goes Sita.
   जब इस तरह के वाक्यों में Subject के रूप में pronoun आये तो Verb, उस Subject के बाद आता है :
   (a) There she goes. (b) Here she comes.
8. **'So' के साथ Adverb of manner का प्रयोग वाक्य के शुरू में होने पर भी Inversion होता है :**
   (a) *So well did* he organise the function, that everyone started praising him.
   (b) *So absurdly did* he speak that everyone was offended.

9. **'To such a degree/To such an extent/ To such a point/To such a length' से जब वाक्य शुरू होता है तो Inversion प्रयुक्त होता है :**

(a) To such an extent he made the investment that people started trusting him.

(b) To such a degree they made a noise that Principal had to call the police.

10. **निम्न प्रकार के वाक्यों में भी Inversion प्रयुक्त होता है :**

(a) Were I a bird!

(If I were a bird एवं were I a bird का एक ही अर्थ है।)

(b) Had he come to me, I would have helped him.

(If he had come to me, I would have helped him; वाक्य(b)को इस तरह भी लिखा जा सकता है।)

ERRORS , MISTAKES AND BLUNDERS IN USE OF VERBS

Exercise : ***Rewrite the following sentences after correction.***

1. Either he or I is to represent the school.
2. Neither you nor he are to go now.
3. The mob move towards the collectorate.
4. The second innings were spoiled due to fire.
5. Each hour and each minute are to be utilised by you.
6. Every young and every old were happy to receive a gift.
7. Not only the Tajmahal but also other monuments is worth seeing.
8. The house with all its furniture were auctioned at a very low bid.
9. The peacock like other birds have wings to fly.
10. There is another schools better than this.
11. More than one girl were killed in the accident.
12. God blesses you with success!
13. Financial help from all the quarters were received.
14. The quality of these items are appreciated by everyone.
15. The fragrance of these beautiful flowers are liked by all.
16. More workman than one are not traceable.
17. He said, "Plenty of milk are required for the party."
18. A lot of books and magazines was destroyed by the fire.
19. The number of students opted Hindi in RAS are generally large.
20. A number of English magazines is available in the college library.
21. It is I who is responsible for the loss in the business.
22. The women who is standing there are my sisters.
23. He is one of those who does not know anything about the incident.
24. It is one of the problems that was taken care of by the civil administration.
25. Nothing but monkeys are seen.
26. No man and no woman were allowed to enter without payment.
27. Much of the time were wasted by the students.
28. More than one man were killed there.
29. Economic cooperation between India and China are decreasing day by day.
30. More students than one has participated in the annual function.
31. About half of the girls was present in the hall.
32. Half of the sugar were spoiled due to heavy rains.

33. The apparatus purchased by the Nagar Parishad were very old.
34. The advice of his friend are indeed valuable.
35. Men after men were coming to visit the art gallery.
36. One month after another have passed.
37. His shoes is shining.
38. Approximately ten sheeps were grazing in the college ground.
39. A pair of shoes are purchased by her for her husband.
40. There are many fishes in the aquarium.
41. Each of the sports women were given a certificate.
42. I wish I will be the minister.
43. She ordered as if she is my elder sister.
44. God saves our queen!
45. He needs not go to market.
46. The poors are never reliable.
47. All the milk were used in the preparation of sweets.
48. All the animal were given the proper diet.
49. She apprises the inspector all that have happened tonight.
50. Most of the person are reliable.

Explanations

1. Either he or I am to represent the school.
2. Neither you nor he is to go now.
3. The mob moves towards the collectorate.
4. The second innings was spoiled due to fire.
5. Each hour and each minute is to be utilised by you.
6. Every young and every old was happy to receive a gift.
7. Not only the Tajmahal but also other monuments are worth seei
8. The house with all its furniture was auctioned at a very low bid.
9. The peacock like other birds has wings to fly.
10. There is another school better than this.
11. More than one girl was killed in the accident.
12. God bless you with success!
13. Financial help from all the quarters was received.
14. The quality of these items is appreciated by everyone.
15. The fragrance of these beautiful flowers is liked by all.
16. More workman than one is not traceable.
17. He said, "Plenty of milk is required for the party."
18. A lot of books and magazines were destroyed by the fire.
19. The number of students opted Hindi in RAS is generally large.
20. A number of English magazines are available in the college library.
21. It is I who am responsible for the loss in the business.
22. The women who are standing there are my sisters.
23. He is one of those who do not know anything about the incident.
24. It is one of the problems that were taken care of by the civil administration.
25. Nothing but monkeys is seen.
26. No man and no woman was allowed to enter without payment.

27. Much of the time was wasted by the students.
28. More than one man was killed there.
29. Economic cooperation between India and China is decreasing day by day.
30. More students than one have participated in the annual function.
31. About half of the girls were present in the hall.
32. Half of the sugar was spoiled due to heavy rains.
33. The apparatus purchased by the Nagar Parishad was very old.
34. The advice of his friend was indeed valuable.
35. Man after man was coming to visit the art gallery.
36. One month after another has passed.
37. His shoes are shining.
38. Approximately ten sheep were grazing in the college ground.
39. A pair of shoes is purchased by her for her husband.
40. There are many fish in the aquarium.
41. Each of the sports women was given a certificate.
42. I wish I were the minister.
43. She ordered as if she were my elder sister.
44. God save our queen!
45. He need not go to market.
46. The poor are never reliable.
47. All the milk was used in the preparation of sweets.
48. All the animals were given the proper diet.
49. She apprises the inspector all that has happened tonight.
50. Most of the persons are reliable.

SPOTTING ERRORS(VERBS)

Exercise : ***Find the errors and justify your answers.***

1. He ordered(A)/ as if he(B)/ was my master(C).
2. God saves(A)/ the queen Victoria(B).
3. If it was so(A)/ poetry(B)/would cease to matter(C).
4. The merit(A)/ of these books(B)/ are known to everyone(C).
5. The condition of (A)/ people living in(B)/ rural area(C)/ are very bad (D).
6. The smell(A)/of these rose(B)/ flowers are(C)/ very sweet.
7. The condolence messages(A)/ received on the (B)/ death of Mrs. Gandhi(C)/ speaks highly of her greatness (D).
8. Economic cooperation (A)/ between the two countries (B)/have increased substantially(C).
9. A band of musicians (A)/ have been engaged(B)/ for the inaugurational function(C).
10. The number(A)/of persons interested(B)/in psychology are (C)/generally small(D).
11. The manager's comments(A)/ on the preparation of the test matches(B)/ for this tour(C)/ has been generally praised(D).
12. The details(A)/of the incident(B)/was not known(C)/to me (D).
13. The majority of (A)/ writers never(B)/ passes this stage(C).
14. A large part of(A)/ the distinctive features(B)/ of the mind is due to its being (C)/ an instrument of communication(D).
15. A part of (A)/ the mango (B) / are rotten(C).
16. A part of (A)/ the mangoes(B)/ are rotten(C).
17. The governing body at (A)/ its first meeting(B)/ have decided (C)/ to conduct the test again (D).

18. The banker's association (A)/ has submitted a memorandum(B)/ for the fulfilment of(C)/ their demands(D).
19. Five quintals of wooden coal (A)/ are (B)/ his annual requirement(C) for the unit(D).
20. Dickens have criticised(A)/the philosophy (B)/in'Hard Times'.
21. All his money(A)/ is spent(B)/ and all his(C)/ hopes ruined(D).
22. This rule may(A)/ and ought to be(B)/disregarded for the time being(C).
23. He is one of the(A)/ richest man(B)/ if not the richest man(C)/ in the world(D).
24. We can almost get(A)/ everything in(B)/ this market(C).
25. Every(A)/ Tom, Dick and Harry(B)/ drink wine these days(C).
26. He and I(A)/ is partners in(B)/ this firm(C).
27. He is one of the(A)/ great man(B)/ that have ever lived(C).
28. The magistrate and collector(A)/ were (B)/ present there(C)/on the spot (D).
29. Horse and Carriage(A)/are(B)/waiting there(C)/for the couple(D).
30. Rice and fish(A)/are(B)/ my favourite dish(C).
31. "Under no circumstances (A)/I can help you in(B)/ this venture"(C)/, said Sita(D).
32. "I don't like(A)/ such a bright colour(B)/nor she does"(C)/, he said to Ram(D).
33. Every member of(A)/his family is (B)/ addicted to gambling (C)/and so John is(D).
34. Never before (A)/ I had been asked(B)/ to go there (C)/by bus (D).
35. On no account (A)/ this switch must (B)/ be touched (C).
36. "Seldom I had seen (A)/ such a (B)/beautiful girl",(C)/said Mohanti (D).
37. Under a tree(A)/was sleeping an (B)/ old lady (C)/with her young child (D).
38. To such a degree (A)/ he created (B)/ the problems that (C)/people thrashed him(D).
39. Not only she watched (A)/the news(B)/ but she also (C)/cooked food(D).
40. No sooner the plane landed at the (A) /airport than(B)/a group of armed (C)/commandos surrounded it (D).

Explanations

1. (C) 'was' की जगह 'were' आयेगा। जब वाक्य में कल्पना (imagination) का भाव हो तो, singular subject के साथ 'were' कर प्रयोग होता है :
   I wish I were a king.
   I wish it were possible.
2. (A) 'saves' की जगह 'save' आयेगा। ऐसे वाक्य जिनमे कोई इच्छा (desire), अभिलाषा (wish) या आशीर्वाद (blessing) का भाव हो तो verbs; bless, live, save, एवं help हमेशा, plural में आती हैं अर्थात् इनके साथ 's' नहीं जोड़ा जाता है। जैसे – May Lord help you! Long live our friendship!
3. (A) was की जगह 'were' आयेगा। Question (1) का explanation देखें। 'If it was so' reflects imaginations.
4. (C) 'are' की जगह 'is' आयेगा। यहाँ subject 'merit' है जो singular है अत: verb singular होगी।
5. (D) 'are' की जगह 'is' आयेगा। यहाँ subject of the verb, 'condition' है, जो singular है, अत: verb भी singular ही प्रयुक्त होगी।
6. (C) 'are' की जगह 'is' लिखे। यहाँ subject of the verb is 'smell' 'which is singular अत: verb (is) भी singular ही लगेगी।
7. (D) 'speaks' की जगह 'speak' आयेगा verb (speak) का subject, condolence messages है ,जो plural है, अत: verb, plural होगी।
8. (C) 'have' की जगह 'has' आयेगा; subject– 'economic cooperation'-singular है, अत: verb भी singular ही प्रयुक्त होगी।

9. (B) 'have been' की जगह 'has been' आयेगा। 'A band' collective noun है, जिसके साथ singular verb का प्रयोग होगा।

10. (C) 'are' की जगह 'is' आयेगा। 'The number' एक निश्चित संख्या को बताता है, collective noun की जगह प्रयुक्त होता है, अत: इसके लिये हमेशा singular verb का प्रयोग किया जाता है।

11. (D) 'has been' की जगह 'have been' आयेगा। verb का subject, 'manager's comments' है, जो कि plural है, अत: verb भी plural होगी।

12. (C) 'was' की जगह 'were' आयेगा। subject of the verb - 'details', plural है अत: verb भी plural (were) ही प्रयुक्त होगी।

13. (C) passes की जगह pass आयेगा। The majority of, यहाँ 'of' के बाद में जो noun (writers) आया है, वह plural है, अत: verb भी plural ही रहेगी।

14. (C) 'mind is due' की जगह 'mind are due' आयेगा। 'of' के बाद (A large part of the distinctive features) आने वाला noun यहाँ plural (features) है अत: verb भी plural होगी।

15. (C) 'are' की जगह 'is' लिखें। 'of' के बाद (A part of the mango) आने वाला noun (mango) singular है, अत: verb भी singular लगेगी।

16. (E) No error. 'of' के बाद आने वाला noun (mangoes) plural है, अत: verb भी plural होगी।

17. (C) 'have' की जगह has लिखें; governing body, collective noun है, अत: verb-singular होगी।

18. (D) 'their' की जगह 'its' होगा। 'The banker's association' एक collective noun है, अत: यहाँ pronoun, 'its' आयेगा।

19. (B) 'are' की जगह 'is' लिखें; 'five quintals एक निश्चित weight को व्यक्त करता है, जो collective noun की तरह, singular noun का बोध कराता है, अत: verb singular (is) ही प्रयुक्त होगी।

20. (A) 'have' की जगह 'has' लिखें, Dickens एक व्यक्ति का नाम है।

21. (D) 'hopes' के बाद 'are' insert करें। जब वाक्य में पहले आने वाली verb (यहाँ 'is') दूसरे noun के number एवं person से मेल नहीं खाती है, तो दूसरे noun के अनुसार अलग से verb का प्रयोग करना होता है। Hopes, plural है अत: यहाँ plural verb प्रयुक्त होगी।

22. (A) 'may' के बाद 'be' का प्रयोग करें। प्रश्न (1) का Explanation देखें।

23. (B) 'richest *man*' की जगह 'richest *men*' आयेगा। 'one of' के बाद आने वाले adjective के साथ plural noun आता है।

24. (A) 'We can *almost get*' की जगह, 'we can *get almost*' लिखना चाहिये। Adverb के गलत जगह लिखने से वाक्य का अर्थ ही बदल जाता है।

25. (C) 'drink' की जगह 'drinks' आयेगा। 'Every, Each' के साथ इस तरह के वाक्यों में singular verb आती है।

26. (B) 'is' की जगह 'are' आयेगा। जब दो nouns को and से जोड़ा जाता है तो verb, plural आती है।

27. (B) 'one of the' के बाद adjective के बाद plural noun आता है; 'man' की जगह 'men' लिखें।

28. (B) 'were' की जगह 'was' लिखें। यहाँ magistrate एवं collector एक ही व्यक्ति को refer करते हैं।

29. (B) 'are' की जगह 'is' लिखें। Horse and carriage जोड़े की तरह एक ही वस्तु का ज्ञान कराते हैं अत: verb singular लिखें।

30. (B) 'are' की जगह 'is' लिखें। Rice and fish एक pair की तरह, एक चीज का ही संकेत करते हैं अत: verb, singular लिखें।

31. (B) 'I can help you' की जगह 'can I help you' होगा। 'under no circumstances' के साथ Inversion आता है।

32. (C) 'nor she does' की जगह 'nor does she' आयेगा। इस तरहे के वाक्यों में 'nor' के साथ Inversion आता है।
33. (D) 'so John is' की जगह 'so is John' लिखा जायेगा। इस तरहे के वाक्यों में 'so' के साथ Inversion आता है।
34. (A) 'Never' के साथ Inversion लगता है, अत: 'never had I been' लिखा जायेगा।
35. (B) 'On no account' के साथ Inversion लगता है अत: 'must this switch' लिखा जायेगा।
36. (A) 'Seldom had I seen' लिखा जायेगा। 'Seldom/Hardly/Rarely/Scaraly/Never' से वाक्य शुरू होने पर Inversion का प्रयोग होता है।
37. वाक्य सही है।
38. (B) 'To such a degree' के बाद Inversion लगता है। अत: 'he created ज्की जगह 'did he create' आयेगा।
39. (A) 'Not only' से वाक्य शुरू होने पर Inversion का प्रयोग होता है। अत: 'Not only did she watch' लिखा जाना चाहिए।
40. (A) 'No sooner' से वाक्य शुरू होने पर Inversion का प्रयोग होता है। अत: 'No sooner did the plane land' होना चाहिए।

BLUNDERS

Exercise : ***Rewrite the following sentences after correction.***

1. Slow and steady win the race .
2. Either you or I are to go there.
3. Five kilograms are a heavy weight.
4. Their advice in that matter were very useful.
5. Her hairs are black.
6. Plenty of sugar are needed.
7. Everyone were happy to get the news.
8. Hardly she reached the school when the bell rang.
9. No sooner did he saw his wife, he cried loudly.
10. Scarcely he managed to meet the dead line.

Explanations

1. जब दो nouns , (यहाँ 'slow' and 'steady') एक ही Phrase का part हैं तब: verb singular होगी। 'win' की जगह 'wins' लिखें ।
2. सही वाक्य होगा–Either you or I *am* to go there; इस तरह के वाक्यों में verbs अपने पास वाले subject के अनुसार आती है।
3. 'are' की जगह 'is' होगा। जब Plural noun, quantity को एक unit की तरह व्यक्त करे, तो verb-singuler आती है।
4. 'advice' के साथ singular verb-'was' प्रयुक्त होगी।
5. सही वाक्य होगा– Her hair *is* black. 'Hair' को इस तरह के वाक्यों में Pluralize नहीं किया जाता है, एवं 'Hair' के साथ singular verb आती है।
6. 'Plenty of', 'Most of', के बाद यदि Unconnlable noun आता है, तो verb- singular आती है; Change 'are' to 'is'.
7. 'Everyone' के साथ singular verb आती है; Change 'were' to 'was'.
8. 'Hardly' के बाद 'had' लिखकर वाक्य इस तरह से लिखा जाना चाहिए– Hardly had he reached the school when the bell rang. यह inversion का case है।
9. 'saw' की जगह 'see' होगा। जब वाक्य में 'did'का प्रयोग हो गया है, तो verb की First form आयेगी ।
10. 'scarcely' के बाद auxiliary verb 'did' आयेगी । सही वाक्य होगा– Scarcely did he mangage to meet the dead line. यह inversion का case है।

❑❑❑

7

Non-Finites

सामान्यतया Infinitive को to+ verb के रूप में जाना पहचाना जाता है। कुछ स्थितियों में Infinitive के साथ 'to' का प्रयोग नहीं होता है। कुछ verbs के साथ केवल Infinitive का प्रयोग ही होता है। Infinitive से सम्बन्धित नियमों का अध्ययन गमभीरतापूर्वक करें। छात्रों द्वारा infinitive के प्रयोग में बहुधा गलतियाँ की जाती हैं।

Verbs को Finite verbs एवं Non finite-verbs में भी वर्गीकृत किया जाता है :

VERB

FINITES | **NON-FINITES**

Finite verb

जिन verbs में subject के Number, Person एवं Tense के अनुसार परिवर्तन होता है, finite verbs कहलाती हैं।

Look at the following sentences :

(a) I like to play.
(b) He likes to play.
(c) They like to play.
(d) He liked to play.
(e) She liked to play.
(f) They liked to play.

उक्त वाक्यों में 'like', finite verb है, जो first person singular ('I') एवं third person plural ('they') के साथ तो 'like' ही है, लेकिन third person singular (he) के साथ 'likes' के रूप में है। इसी प्रकार past tense में इसका रूप 'liked' हो गया है। अत: like एक finite verb है।

NON-FINITES

उपरोक्त वाक्यों में 'to play' ; non-finite verb है, जिसका रूप subject के Number, person एवं वाक्य के tense से अप्रभावित है। अत: non finite verbs ऐसी verbs होती हैं, जिन पर वाक्य के tense एवं subject के person एवं number का कोई प्रभाव नहीं पड़ता है। एक और महत्त्वपूर्ण बिन्दु है - कि finite verb का एक subject अवश्य होता है। लेकिन Non-finite verb का स्वयं का कोई subject(कर्ता) नहीं होता, बल्कि यह एक object की तरह वाक्य में दिखाई पड़ती है जैसे कि उक्त वाक्यों में 'like' (Finite verb) का subject, I, He, They इत्यादि हैं, लेकिन Non-finite verb ; 'to play' एक object की तरह प्रयुक्त हुई है।

NON-FINITES

INFINITIVE	**GERUND**	**PARTICIPLE**
(With or with out 'to')	**(Verb+ing ; Verbal noun)**	**(Verb+ing ; verbal adjective)**

INFINITIVE

Infinitive को सामान्यतया 'to + verb' के रूप में जाना एवं पहचाना जाता है। जैसे: 'to play, to go, to walk', etc. लेकिन कभी-कभी 'to' नहीं भी आता है। इस प्रकार की Infinitive को **Bare Infinitive** (Infinitive without 'to') कहा जाता है, जैसे : 'I saw him *go*', 'I bade him *go*' etc. यहाँ 'go', bare infinitive है।

KINDS OF INFINITIVE

Infinitive को इनके प्रयोग के आधार पर दो भागों में वर्गीकृत किया जाता है :

(1) **Simple Infinitive or Noun Infinitive:** इनका प्रयोग वाक्य में noun की तरह होता है । जब हिन्दी वाक्य के अन्त में 'ना' या 'ने' लगा हो, तो सामान्यतया ये simple infinitive को व्यक्त करते हैं। जैसे :

(a) I am *to go.* — मुझे *जाना* है।

(b) He is about *to go.* — वह *जाने* को है।

(2) **Gerundial Infinitive :-** जब Infinitive का प्रयोग वाक्य में Adjective या Adverb की तरह होता है, तो उसे gerundial infinitive कहा जाता है, जैसे :

(a) The sweet is good *to eat.*

(b) This is the house *to let.*

BARE INFINITIVE OR INFINITIVE WITHOUT 'TO'

जैसा कि पूर्व में बताया गया है, बहुत सी स्थितियों में Infinitive केसाथ 'to' का प्रयोग नहीं किया जाता है।

Use of Bare Infinitive

(1) **अग्रलिखित Auxiliary verbs के साथ आने वाले Infinitives के साथ 'to' नहीं प्रयुक्त किया जाता है– shall, will, should, do, did, may, might, must, can, could, need.**

(a) I shall play .

(b) He will come.

(c) I should write.

(d) He would write.

ध्यान रखें ***'ought' एवं 'used' (ये भी Modal auxiliaries हैं) के साथ 'to' लगता है :***

(a) He ought to come here. ***(b) He used to smoke.***

'Dare, Need' का प्रयोग जब modals की तरह किया जाता है। (सामान्यतया Negative एवं interrogative वाक्यों में), तो इनके साथ 'to' नहीं आता है । लेकिन जब इनका प्रयोग principal verbs की तरह किया जाता है तो इनके साथ 'to' का प्रयोग होता है :

(a) He dare not speak so. (As modal)

(b) Dare she complain against you ? (As modal)

(2) **अग्रलिखित verbs के बाद आने वाले Infinitive के साथ 'to'का प्रयोग Active voice में नहीं होता है– 'Bid, let, make, feel, watch, behold, hear, overhear, notice, observe, see', etc. :**

(a) She bade me go.

(b) Let her sing.

लेकिन यदि उक्त verbs का प्रयोग passive voice में किया जाएगा तो Infinitive के साथ 'to' का प्रयोग होगा :

(a) He was made to sing .

(b) I was bidden to go.

लेकिन 'let' के साथ passive में भी 'to' नहीं प्रयुक्त होगा : She was let sing.

(3) **अग्रलिखित शब्दों के साथ Bare Infinitive का ही प्रयोग किया जाता है– 'had better, would rather, would sooner, sooner than, rather than, had sooner' etc.**

(a) He had better withdraw.

(b) He would sooner resign than fight with the boss.

उक्त वाक्यों के structure का ध्यान रखें। इस तरह के वाक्यों में verb की Ist form (Infinitive without 'to') का प्रयोग होता है। इस तरह के वाक्य परीक्षाओं में कई रूप में पूछे जाते हैं।

(4) **वाक्य में यदि conjunction, 'than' का प्रयोग हुआ है तो, उसके बाद Bare infinitive का प्रयोग ही होगा :**

(a) She is better able to speak than write.

(5) **Have / has /had के बाद यदि noun या pronoun आता है, एवं उसके बाद कोई Infinitive का प्रयोग होता है, तो वह Bare infinitive (Infinitive without 'to') होगा :**

(a) I will have him *realise* his mistake.

(b) I had him *know* his mistakes.

(6) निम्न प्रकार के वाक्यों में except / but के साथ 'to' नहीं प्रयुक्त होता है :

(a) They did nothing but weep.

(b) The dog does nothing except bark.

Specific use of Infinitives-Rules

(1) निम्न Verbs के बाद सीधे ही Infinitive (With 'to') का प्रयोग किया जा सकता है :

agree,appear,aim,arrange,target,attempt,ask,guarantee,bother,claim,happen,care,decide earn,choose,demand,pretend,condescend,determine, promise, consent, resolve, prove, decline, to be determined, seem, fail, swear, hesitate, threaten, hope, undertake, long, manage, neglect, offer, plan, prepare, be prepared, proceed, refuse, tend , trouble (negative), volunteer, vow, etc.

(a) He agreed *to pay* Rs. 250 only.

(b) They are preparing *to evacuate* the colony.

(c) He refused *to surrender*.

(d) I volunteered *to help* with bread and money.

(2) इन Verbs का प्रयोग Verb+Object+Infinitive या Verb+Infinitive किसी भी प्रकार किया जा सकता है- 'ask, beg, expect, would hate, help, intend, like, would like, would love, mean, prefer, want, wish'; जैसे :

(a) He likes to drink well.

(b) He likes his friends to drink well.

(c) I want to go.

(d) I want you to go.

Care, hate, like, love एवं prefer के बाद Gerund का भी प्रयोग किया जा सकता है।

(3) कुछ verbs का प्रयोग निम्न structure में किया जाता है :

Verb + Object + Infinitive

advise	forbid	entitle	allow
oblige	teach	bribe	order
tell	command	implore	permit
tempt	compel	induce	persuade
instruct	remind	urge	encourage
invite	request	train	enable
warn	force	make*	hear*
let*	see*	watch*	feel*
help*	notice*	observe*	look at*

ध्यान रखें : advise, allow, permit के साथ Gerund का प्रयोग भी किया जा सकता है।

(*) लगी हुई Verbs के साथ infinitive without 'to' (Bare infinitive) का प्रयोग होता है :

(a) He *pursuaded me to go* with her.

(b) I have *trained these dogs to sniff* out drugs.

(c) He *encouraged me to try* again.

(d) They *forbade us to pluck* the flowers.

(e) These goggles *will enable you to see* in dim light.

(f) We *watched* him clear* the table.

(g) They *heard* the thief crash* through the door.

(h) She *made* me* do it.

(i) We *helped* her finish* the homework.

In above sentences, italicised words show the structure '.... verb + object + infinite ....'

Note

Verbs; 'show, teach, tell' के साथ उक्त Structure में Infinitive का प्रयोग करते समय 'how' का प्रयोग करना आवश्यक है :

(a) He showed me how to operate the machine.

(b) He told me how to replace a fuse.

(c) He taught me how to light a cigarette without a match box.

जब कभी 'Skill' बहुत common हो तो 'how' का प्रयोग नहीं भी किया जाता है :

(a) He taught me to ride.

(b) He taught me to write my name.

(4) Verb + How/what/when/where/which/why + infinitive ......

उक्त structure में सामान्यतया verbs; 'ask, decide, discover, find out, forget, know, learn, remember, see (= understand, perceive), think,understand, want to know, wonder' etc. का प्रयोग किया जाता है। इसके अतिरिक्त उक्त structure में show+ object + 'wh' word + infinitive का भी प्रयोग होता है :

(a) He *knows how to swim.*

(b) He *discovered how to operate* the machine.

(c) I *asked him, where to buy* fruits at reasonable rate.

(d) I *remember when to switch* off the machine.

(e) I *showed him which button to press.*

(5) Verbs ; assume, believe, feel, suppose, consider, understand का प्रयोग निम्न structure में किया जाता है। Verb +object + to be

(a) I *assume him to be* the best athlete .

(b) I *consider him to be* an honest person.

(c) I *thought her to be* a dedicated teacher.

(d) He is supposed to be washing the car.

(6) निम्न nouns के बाद infinitive का प्रयोग सीधे ही किया जा सकता है :

ability	decision	effort	promise	willingness
ambition	demand	failure	refusal	wish
anxiety	determination	offer	request	desire
attempt	eagerness	plan	scheme	

(a) He made an attempt to walk without support.

(b) His ability to get the work done is his main assets.

(c) Failure to find the fault may result in termination.

(d) Their offer/plan/promise to rebuild the house was not taken seriously.

(7) Infinitive after 'too',

(I) too + adjective + infinitive .....

(a) He is *too weak to walk.* (He is so weak that he cannot walk.)

(b) He was *too young to get* married . (He is so young that he cannot get married.)

उपरोक्त वाक्यों में too के बाद adjective प्रयोग होनें के बाद infinitive का प्रयोग हुआ है।

(II) कई वाक्यों में 'too' के साथ infinitive का प्रयोग निम्न structure में होता है :

too + adjective +a + noun + infinitive

(a) He is *too shrewd a man to rely* on anybody.

(b) He is *too experienced a driver to mind* what anybody says.

(III) too + adverb + infinitive ....

(a) It is *too soon to say* whether the plan will run or not.

(b) He cried *too loudly to understand* by any one.

'too' के साथ infinitive का प्रयोग negativity show करता है। इस तरह के वाक्य दैनिक जीवन में बहुत प्रयोग में आते है।

(8) Infinitive after 'enough':-

(I) Adjective + enough+ infinitive........

(a) He is *matured enough to take* decisions. (b) She is *bold enough to travel* by herself

उपरोक्त वाक्यों में adjective के बाद enough का प्रयोग हुआ है एवं फिर infinitive का प्रयोग हुआ है।

(II) Adverb + enough +infinitive ....

(a) He jumped *high enough to win* the first prize

(b) He spoke *loudly enough to understand* by all.

उपरोक्त वाक्यों में high, loudly, quickly, fast ; adverbs हैं।

THE SPLIT INFINITIVES

(1) Infinitive के बीच में (to एवं infinitive के बीच में) कोई भी adverb या शब्द लिखना traditional grammar में गलत माना गया है। But as per modern grammarians, one adverb may be inserted between the infinitive :

I ask you *to kindly grant me* one day leave only.

Here insertion of adverb 'kindly' is well accepted now a days.

CONTINUOUS INFINITIVE

Continuous Infinitive की form- **to be+ Present Participle** होती है :

Ram *may be watching* TV at this time.

Use of Continuous Infinitive

(A) Auxiliary Verbs के बाद 'will/shall/may/might/can/could/must/would/should' के साथ Continuous Infinitive का प्रयोग निम्न प्रकार होता है :

(a) They'll be playing now.

(b) He might/may be watching TV.

(B) Verbs; 'appear, happen, pretend, seem' के साथ सामान्यतया continuous infinitive का प्रयोग होता है।

(a) I *happened to be looking* towards the road when their car stopped.

(b) She *seems to be following* us.

PERFECT INFINITIVE

Perfect Infinitive की form - **to have+ Past Participle** जैसे : **to have gone, to have completed** होती है।

Use of Perfect Infinitive

(1) Auxiliary Verbs के साथ Perfect Infinitive का प्रयोग :

was/were के साथ Perfect Infinitive का प्रयोग एक unfulfilled plan या arrangement को व्यक्त करता है; जैसे :

(a) The house was to have been ready so far. (But it is not ready.)

(b) She was to have gone. (But she has not gone.)

(2) 'Should/would/might/could' के साथ Perfect Infinitive का प्रयोग Conditional sentence में किया जाता है :

(a) If I had seen him, I would have invited him.

(b) If he had come to me, I might have helped him.

ये सभी वाक्य कार्य के पूर्ण न होने को व्यक्त करते हैं।

(3) 'May/ might' के साथ Perfect Infinitive का प्रयोग निम्न प्रकार किया जाता है :

He may/might have heard the news so far. (It is possible that he has heard the news by now.)

यह कार्य के पूर्ण होने की Probability को व्यक्त करता है।

(4) 'Must' के साथ Perfect Infinitive का प्रयोग एक निश्चितता (Certainity) को व्यक्त करता है :

The thief must have entered through this gate. (Here are his footprints.)

(5) 'Needn't' के साथ Perfect Infinitive का प्रयोग एक ऐसे Past action को व्यक्त करता है, जिसकी आवश्यकता नहीं थी :

(a) He needn't have watered the plants. (as it rained a day before.)

(b) You needn't have written him. (As I had telephonic discussions with him yesterday.)

Note Verbs; 'appear, hope, pretend, seem' का प्रयोग perfect infinitives के साथ निम्न प्रकार होता है :

(a) He pretended to have learned the lesson.

(b) He seemed to have been a great sportsman.

निम्न Verbs के साथ perfect Infinitive का प्रयोग Passive Voice में किया जाता है :

'acknowledge, believe, consider, find, how, know, report, say, suppose, think, understand' :

(a) They are understood to have left the village.

(b) He was believed to have been a great artist.

(c) She is thought to have information which will be useful to the police.

(d) She is known to have been a great leader.

PERFECT CONTINUOUS INFINITIVE

Perfect Continuous Infinitive की form- **to have been + Present Participle** होती है।

Use of Perfect Continuous Infinitive

Perfect continuous infinitive का प्रयोग verbs; 'appear, seem, happen, pretend' के बाद किया जाता है :

(a) He seems *to have been standing* there since morning.

(b) She appears *to have been waiting* a long time.

ERRORS, MISTAKES AND BLUNDERS IN USE OF INFINITIVE

Exercise : *Rewrite the sentences after correction.*

1. English is difficult to be learnt.
2. Do you dare refuse me?
3. I watched her to cross the road.
4. The act is easy to be performed.
5. He is better able to act than to sing.
6. She can do nothing but to abuse him.
7. Stop to write.
8. I had sooner run than to walk.
9. I have decided helping her.
10. Better to reign in hell than to serve in heaven.
11. I made him to polish my shoes.
12. She avoids to do her duties seriously.
13. I am looking forward to meet you soon.
14. I got a mechanic repairing my car.
15. A brave man does not fear dying.
16. The river is very deep to be crossed by the army.
17. Please tell me to close it.
18. I know swim.
19. I can't decide to get out of this trouble.
20. I chanced meeting her in the art gallery.
21. She appears recognising me.
22. Could you tell me to explain the situation?
23. There was no board to write.
24. She hopes of passing with distinction.
25. She is eager to meeting me.
26. He went to Jaipur seeing the Jantar Mantar.
27. She failed winning the prize.
28. I shall be glad meeting you.
29. I have no pen to write.
30. She has a house for furnishing.
31. I have no house to live.
32. He requested me going to Jaipur.
33. He did nothing but to talk and to laugh.
34. I will have you to remember me.
35. She was known having hidden the jewellery box.
36. I would study rather than to waste my time.
37. They bade me to go.
38. Let I sing a song.
39. I observed him to play.
40. We had him to know his mistakes.

41. He learned to operate the machine.
42. I asked him from where to buy shirts at reasonable rates.
43. I wonder whether go or not.
44. She pretended to look for some eatables.
45. Ramesh seems to follow us in his car.
46. He seemed to be a great musician.
47. His plan of rebuild the building was not approved by the municipality.
48. He made an effort to getting pass without copying.
49. She is too weak that she cannot walk.
50. She is enough matured to go alone.
51. She ran enough fast to catch the train.
52. He was so foolish as left his car unlocked.
53. Will you be so kind as sanction my leave?
54. She is the only one secure 95% marks.
55. She likes to completely change the colour.

Explanations

1. English is difficult to learn.
2. Do you dare to refuse me?
3. I watched her cross the road.
4. The act is easy to perform.
5. He is better able to act than sing.
6. She can do nothing but abuse him.
7. Stop writing.
8. I had sooner run than walk.
9. I have decided to help her.
10. Better reign in hell than serve in heaven.
11. I made him polish my shoes.
12. She avoids doing her duties seriously.
13. I am looking forward meeting you soon.
14. I got a mechanic to repair my car.
15. A brave man does not fear to die.
16. The river is very deep to cross by the army.
17. Please tell me how to close it.
18. I know how to swim.
19. I can't decide how to get out of this trouble.
20. I chanced to meet her in the art gallery.
21. She appears to recognise me.
22. Could you tell me how to explain the situation?
23. There was no board to write on.
24. She hopes to pass with distinction.
25. She is eager to meet me.
26. He went to Jaipur to see the Jantar Mantar.
27. She failed to win the prize.
28. I shall be glad to meet you.
29. I have no pen to write with.
30. She has a house to furnish.
31. I have no house to live in.
32. He requested me to go to Jaipur.
33. He did nothing but talk and laugh.
34. I will have you to remember me.
35. She was known to have hidden the jewellery box.
36. I would study rather than waste my time.
37. They bade me go.
38. Let me sing a song.
39. I observed him playing.
40. We had him know his mistakes.
41. He learned how to operate the machine.
42. I asked him where to buy shirts at reasonable rates.
43. I wonder whether to go or not.
44. She pretended to be looking for some eatables.
45. Ramesh seems to be following us in his car.
46. He seemed to have been a great musician.
47. His plan to rebuild the building was not approved by the municipality.
48. He made an effort to get pass without copying.
49. She is too weak to walk.
50. She is matured enough to go alone.
51. She ran fast enough to catch the train.
52. He was so foolish as to leave his car unlocked.
53. Will you be so kind as to sanction my leave?
54. She is the only one to secure 95% marks.
55. She likes to change the colour completely.

❑❑❑

8

Gerund

छात्रों द्वारा Gerund, Infinitive एवं Participle के प्रयोग में बहुधा त्रुटियाँ की जाती हैं। छात्र Gerund सम्बन्धित विभिन्न नियमों का अध्ययन ध्यान पूर्वक करें एवं दी गई Exercises solve करें।

Gerund, verb की एक ऐसी form है, जो verb में 'ing' (Verb + ing) जोड़ने से बनती है, एवं noun का कार्य करती है । Gerund को *Verbal Noun* भी कहते हैं। जैसे : Walking, Running, Reading, Writing etc.

Present Participle V/s Gerund

Present participle एवं Gerund का रूप एक जैसा होता है ; लेकिन जहाँ Gerund वाक्य में एक **Verb + noun** का कार्य करता है, वहाँ Participle ; **verb + adjective** का कार्य करता है। Gerund को Verbal Noun तथा Participle को Verbal Adjective कहते हैं।

Gerund V/ s Simple Infinitive

Gerund वाक्यों में Verb + Noun (Verbal Noun) की तरह function करता है, इसी प्रकार Simple Infinitive जिसे Noun Infinitive भी कहते हैं, वह भी वाक्य में verb + noun का कार्य करता है । इसी कारण से बहुत से वाक्यों में (with certain verbs) Gerund या Simple Infinitive किसी का भी प्रयोग किया जा सकता है; ऐसा करने से वाक्य के अर्थ में कोई अन्तर नहीं आता है ।

निम्नलिखित verbs के साथ Gerund या Infinitive किसी का भी प्रयोग किया जा सकता है :

advise	hate	propose	used to
agree	intend	recommend	want
allow	like	regret	be ashamed of
being	love	remember	afraid of
can / could bear	mean	require	sorry for
cease	need	start	go on
continue	permit	stop	prefer
forget	try		

GERUND	**INFINITIVE**
(a) They began *playing.*	(a) They began *to play.*
(b) We prefer *taking* tea.	(b) We prefer *to take* tea.
(c) He never ceased *complaining* about the quality.	(c) He never ceased *to complain* about quality.
(d) I can't bear *waiting* so long.	(d) I can't bear *to wait* so long.

Italicised words in above examples, are Gerunds and Infinitives.

SPECIFIC USE OF GERUND - RULES

(1) जब वाक्यों में - verb, preposition के तुरन्त बाद आती है , तो Gerund का प्रयोग किया जाता है :

(a) He is fond of *fishing.* (b) She is good at *swimming.*

(c) He is too afraid of *losing.* (d) I am tired of *arguing.*

उपरोक्त वाक्यों में - 'fish, lose, swim, argue', ये सभी verb Gerund from में प्रयुक्त हैं।

(2) कुछ verbs के साथ, verbs + preposition / adverb combination के बाद Gerund का ही प्रयोग किया जाता है । ऐसी verbs हैं –'care for, give up, keep on, look forward to, put off, see about, take to' etc.

(a) We do not *care for standing* in queues.
(b) We are *looking forward to meeting* you in the party.
(c) He has *given up smoking* since long.
Italicised words show the sentence structure mentioned above.

(3) 'To'का प्रयोग जब preposition की तरह होता है तो उसके बाद gerund का प्रयोग किया जायेगा । 'To'का प्रयोग preposition की तरह हुआ है , या नहीं इसको जानने के लिऐ , उसके बाद noun या pronoun लिखकर देखें, यदि उसके बाद noun या pronoun लिखा जा सकता है, तो 'to'का प्रयोग preposition की तरह हुआ है अन्यथा as part of Infinitive.

(a) I am looking forward to meeting you. ('To' used as preposition)
(b) I am accustomed to smoking. ('To' used as preposition)
(c) I want to go there. ('To' used as part of Infinitive)
(d) Will you like to come in? ('To' used as part of Infinitive)

(4) निम्न verbs के बाद Gerund का ही सामान्यतया प्रयोग किया जाता है :

admit	keep (= continues)	anticipate	loathe
appreciate	mean (= involve)	consider	miss
avoid	mind (= object)	defer	pardon
dislike	propose (= suggest)	delay	postpone
enjoy	remember (= recollect)	deny	practise
detest	prevent	dread	recollect
escape	resent	excuse	resist
risk	fancy (= imagine)	imagine	suggest
finish	save	involve	understand
forgive	stop (= cease)		

(a) He admitted taking the bribe.
(b) You should avoid overeating.
(c) He detests waiting.
(d) I dislike standing here.
(e) We dread getting old.
(f) I do not enjoy teaching.
(g) She is determined to get a seat even if it ***means standing*** in crowd all the night.

(5) यदि verb के साथ कोई possessive adjective (my) या possesive pronoun (him) आता है, तो उसके बाद Gerund का ही प्रयोग किया जाता है :

(a) He insisted on *my reading* the letter.
(b) He resented on *my refusing* the entry.
(c) I can't stop *him writing* to the editor.

(6) 'Forgive, excuse, pardon' एवं 'prevent' के तुरन्त बाद Gerund का प्रयोग नहीं किया जाता है, बल्कि Gerund से पहले possessive adjective / pronoun भी आता है :

(a) Please forgive my / me calling you so early.
(b) We can't prevent him wasting his own money.
(c) I indeed appreciate your giving me so much of your time.

Possessive case का प्रयोग Gerund के case में निम्न प्रकार किया जाता है :

(a) We do not remember our mother's protesting against this proposal.

Apostrophe's को omit करके भी Gerund का निम्न प्रकार प्रयोग किया जाता है। यह अधिक उचित प्रयोग है :

(b) We do not remember our mother protesting against this proposal.

(7) Perfect Gerund; जैसे- 'having worked, having spoken' etc. का प्रयोग एक past action हेतु निम्न प्रकार किया जाता है :

(a) He was accused of having deserted his ship.

(b) He denied having been involved in the murder.

(8) Verb : 'mind' - special case

(i) Verb mind के साथ कभी भी Infinitive का प्रयोग नहीं होता है।

(ii) 'Mind' का प्रयोग मुख्यतया Interrogative एवं Negative वाक्यों में किया जाता है :

(a) I don't mind waiting here. (b) Would you mind waiting for some time.

(iii) 'Mind' के बाद सामान्यतया या तो तुरन्त Gerund का या noun / pronoun / possessive adjective के बाद Gerund का प्रयोग किया जाता है :

(a) I don't *mind working* here. (b) I don't *mind his sitting* there.

(c) I didn't *mind her living* there.

(9) Gerundial form के साथ कई nouns संयुक्त होकर compound noun की तरह प्रयुक्त होते हैं, इन्हें Gerund ही माना जाता है :

ऐसे Compound nouns हैं :

'Sleeping child, freezing point, blotting paper, walking stick, a dancing master, dining room, retiring age' etc.

ERRORS, MISTAKES AND BLUNDERS IN USE OF GERUNDS

Exercise : ***Rewrite the sentences after correction.***

1. She is good at write.
2. He is afraid to lose the game.
3. I cannot forget you for you helping me.
4. It is totally useless to cry over the past misdeeds.
5. He said, "Don't give up to try again."
6. Would you mind to work with me?
7. She is fond of being admire.
8. I am sorry for me getting late.
9. I am happy at your arrival at schedule time.
10. To drink being his habit, we didn't go with him.
11. I enjoy to travel.
12. Check the air before to start the generator.
13. It is no good to work with him.
14. Some people prefer to spend money to earn it.
15. I am thinking to leave my job and going back to my native place.
16. She said to me, "Don't forget to lock the door before go to bed."
17. I heard someone crying but I failed seeing anyone.
18. She has finished to wash the clothes.
19. I prefer to play football to reading my course books.
20. A novice can't learnt to spelling without being help.
21. You cannot prevent me to go to the market.
22. She refrains to do this work.
23. I insisted him to attend the class.
24. He has a passion to learn English grammar.
25. She is negligent to attend the meetings.
26. She persisted to write again.
27. He is bent to fight again.
28. I am confident to win the match.
29. He succeeded to pass the examination this time.
30. I am proud to have a friend like Ram.
31. I cannot hinder her to enter the temple.
32. She is desirous to leave the place.
33. Ram was disqualified to compete in this tournament.
34. I cannot think to oppose him.

35. He was prohibited to enter the temple.
36. You should abstain to drink now.
37. He intends to go to Jaipur.
38. It is very difficult to dissuade him to go there.
39. He is fortunate to get a ticket.
40. I am hopeful to achieve success.

Explanations

1. She is good at writing.
2. He is afraid of losing the game.
3. I cannot forget you for your helping me.
4. It is totally useless crying over the past misdeeds.
5. He said, "Don't give up trying again."
6. Would you mind working with me?
7. She is fond of being admired.
8. I am sorry for my getting late.
9. I am happy at your arriving at schedule time.
10. Drinking being his habit, we didn't go with him.
11. I enjoy travelling.
12. Check the air before starting the generator.
13. It is no good working with him.
14. Some people prefer spending money to earning it.
15. I am thinking of leaving my job and going back to my native place
16. She said to me, "Don't forget to lock the door before going to bed."
17. I heard someone cry but I failed to see anyone.
18. She has finished washing the clothes.
19. I prefer playing football to reading my course books.
20. A novice can't learn to spell without being helped.
21. You cannot prevent me from going to the market
22. She refrains from doing this work.
23. I insisted him on attending the class.
24. He has a passion for learning English grammar.
25. She is negligent in attending the meeting.
26. She persisted in writing again.
27. He is bent on fighting again.
28. I am confident of winning the match.
29. He succeeded in passing the examination this time.
30. I am proud of having a friend like Ram.
31. I cannot hinder her from entering the temple.
32. She is desirous of leaving the place.
33. Ram was disqualified from competing in this tournament.
34. I cannot think of opposing him.
35. He was prohibited from entering the temple.
36. You should abstain from drinking now.
37. He intends on going to Jaipur.
38. It is very difficult to dissuade him from going there.
39. He is fortunate in getting a ticket.
40. I am hopeful of achieving success.

❑❑❑

9

Participle

Present Participle एवं Gerund की शक्ल-सूरत एक जैसी होती है। छात्रों को Participels से सम्बन्धित विभिन्न नियमों का अध्ययन ध्यान पूर्वक करना चाहिए; Dangling Participle/ Mis-related participle के कारण होने वाली गलतियों को अच्छी तरह समझ लें । परीक्षा में पूछे जाने वाले Errors से सम्बन्धित प्रश्न, अधिकांशतया इन्हीं के सम्बन्ध में पूछे जाते हैं।

Participle, verb का ऐसा रूप है, जिसमें verb के साथ-साथ Adjective के गुण पाये जाते हैं। Participles को इसीलिए **Verbal adjectives** भी कहा जाता है। Participle तीन प्रकार के होते हैं :

Participle

Present Participle	**Past Participle**	**Perfect Participle**
(Verb+ing)	**(Verb +d/ed/t)**	**(having+ Past Perfect)**
(Running, singing, walking)	**(Talked, burnt, hurt)**	**(Having done, having seen, having spent)**

(1) Present Participle: Verb की I form के साथ 'ing' जोड़ने से Present Participle बनता है, इससे कार्य का जारी रहना (पूर्ण नहीं होना) व्यक्त होता है :

(a) He is *reading.* (b) I am *playing.*

(c) Ram is *running.*

Present Participles are italicised in above examples.

(2) Past Participle: Past Participle द्वारा कार्य का Past में पूरा होना व्यक्त किया जाता है । जैसे : burnt, selected, striken etc.

(a) The owner gave a *written* notice to the tenant.

(b) A *burnt* child dreads the fire.

(c) *Driven* by hunger, he begged for food.

(3) Perfect Participle के द्वारा एक कार्य के समाप्त होने के बाद दूसरे कार्य के शुरू होने या पूर्ण होने को व्यक्त किया जाता है। सामान्यतया एक वाक्य में दो घटनाओं के मध्य सम्बन्ध (relation) Perfect Participle द्वारा स्पष्ट किया जाता है :

जैसे : Having finished, Having written, Having done, Having seen (Having + Past Participle = Perfect Participle)

Passive Voice में Perfect Participle – 'having been + Past Participle' द्वारा बनता है।

जैसे : having been failed, having been completed.

(a) *Having finished* my project, I went to play.

(b) *Having been failed* in BA, he joined the parental business.

(c) *Having passed* his MA, Ramesh enrolled for Ph.D.

ERRORS IN THE USE OF PARTICIPLES

छात्रों द्वारा Participles के प्रयोग में बहुत गलतियाँ की जाती हैं। परीक्षा में Participles से सम्बन्धित प्रश्न अधिकांशतया निम्न से सम्बन्धित होते हैं :

(1) Unattached or Dangling Participle

Participle वाक्यों में Adjective का कार्य करते हैं, अत: Participle के साथ एक noun या pronoun का सम्बन्धित (related) होना आवश्यक है। यदि Participle के साथ कोई noun या pronoun सम्बन्धित नहीं है तो वह Participle, Unattached or Dangling Participle है। जैसे :

(1) *Being* a cold morning I didn't go to office

(2) *Being* a rainy day, the school remained closed.

उपरोक्त दोनों वाक्यों में प्रयुक्त Participle- 'Being' Unattached Participle है, यहाँ Being के साथ कोई noun या Pronoun लिखना आवश्यक है। अत: इन वाक्यों को निम्न प्रकार लिखा जाना चाहिए :

(1) *It being* a cold morning I didn't go to office.

Or

The *morning being* cold, I didn't go to office.

(2) *It being* a rainy day, the school remained closed.

Or

The *day being* rainy, the school remained closed.

(2) Misrelated Participle

कई Participle वाले वाक्यों के दो भाग होते हैं। एक भाग में Participle होता है। जब Participle वाले भाग में कोई Subject नहीं है,तो दूसरे भाग के Subject को ही Participle का Subject माना जाता है। यहाँ यह ध्यान रखना आवश्यक है कि यदि वाक्य के दोनों भागों का Subject एक ही है तो वाक्य सही होगा। यदि वाक्य के दोनों भागों में अलग-अलग Subjects की आवश्यकता है, एवं Participle वाले भाग में Subject नहीं दिया गया है, तो यह वाक्य एक गलत (Incorrect) वाक्य होगा। यह Misrelated Participle का उदाहरण होगा। जैसे:-

Standing near the gate, a dog caught her. — *Incorrect*

इस वाक्य के दो भाग है, पहला:- Standing near the gate - इसका कोई Subject नहीं है।

दूसरा भाग : 'a dog caught her', इसका Subject-'dog' है। यदि 'dog' को ही पहले भाग का Subject माना जावे तो इसका अर्थ होगा कि Dog was standing near the gate .- जो कि गलत होगा। अत: यहाँ 'Standing' एक Misrelated Participle है। सही वाक्य होगा –

While she was standing near the gate, a dog caught her. — *Correct*

See more such sentences :

(a) *Waiting* for the train, a brick fell on my feet. — *Incorrect*

While I was waiting for the train, a brick fell on my feet. — *Correct*

(b) *When using* this machine it must be remembered to unlock it first. — *Incorrect*

When using this machine, you must remember to unlock it first. — *Correct*

(c) *Deciding* to join the navy, the recruiter happily pumped Jack's hand. — *Incorrect*

(The recruiter is not deciding to join the navy; Jack is.)

The recruiter happily pumped Jack's hand after learning that Joe had decided to join the navy. — *Correct*

(d) When *watching* films, commercials are especially irritating. — *Incorrect*

(i) To correct the above sentence, one option would be to change the subject so that it names the actor that the modifier implies:

When watching films, I find commercials especially irritating. — *Correct*

(ii) Another option would be, to turn the modifier into a word group that includes the actor:

When I am watching films, commercials are especially irritating. — *Correct*

IMPORTANT **लेकिन कुछ participles जैसे : 'considering, regarding, concerning, taking, speaking, touching' इत्यादि का प्रयोग बिना Noun / pronoun से सम्बन्धित (related) हुए भी किया जा सकता है :**

(a) Considering the price, the quality of the cloth is good.
(b) Speaking roughly, the distance between Delhi and Alwar is 150 Kms.
(c) Taking every point into consideration, the proposal is very attractive.

इस तरह Participles का से प्रयोग एक preposition की भाँति होता है ।

HOW TO DETECT ERRORS ?

(A) ध्यान रखें, Participle के साथ एक Subject का attached / related (सम्बन्धित) होना आवश्यक है। जब किसी वाक्य में एक Clause में Participle का प्रयोग किया हुआ हो तो इस Participle से पूर्व, दूसरे Clause में उपलब्ध Subject को लिखकर देखें। यदि उस Subject के साथ यह Participle सही, तर्क-संगत अर्थ देता है, तो Participle का सही प्रयोग किया गया है, अन्यथा वाक्य में गलती है। निम्न उदाहरण देखें:-

(i) Walking through the jungle, he saw a white tiger. *—Correct*

इस वाक्य में 'Walking' एक Participle है इसके साथ कोई Subject नहीं है। वाक्य के दूसरे Clause में 'he' Subject है। इसे Participle से पूर्व लिखने पर 'he walking (while he was walking) बनता है। जिसका अर्थ; सही, तर्क-संगत निकलता है। अत: Participle का सही प्रयोग किया गया है।

(ii) Walking towards the gate, a plate slipped from his hand. *—Incorrect*

इस वाक्य में 'Walking' Participle है। इसके साथ कोई Subject नहीं है, अत: दूसरे Clause के Subject 'plate' को इसके पूर्व लगाने पर a plate walking towards the gate (While a plate was walking towards the gate) बनता है, जिसका कोई तर्क-संगत अर्थ नहीं निकलता है, **अत: Participle के प्रयोग में गलती है।** यहाँ Participle का Subject, plate नहीं हो सकता है। वाक्य के दूसरे Clause को भी देखने से पता चलता है कि वाक्य को निम्न अर्थ देने का प्रयास किया गया है :

"जब वह दरवाजे की तरफ चल रहा था, तो एक प्लेट उसके हाथ से छूट गई।"

इस अर्थ को पूर्णता देने हेतु / अर्थ स्पष्ट करने हेतु ,वाक्य को निम्न प्रकार लिखा जाना चाहिए।

While he was walking towards the gate, a plate slipped from his hand. *—Correct*

(iii) Being a rainy day, he didn't go to the office.

यहाँ यदि 'Being' (Participle) के साथ दूसरे clause के subject 'he' का प्रयोग करें, तो He being a rainy day, एक अर्थहीन वाक्य बनता है। चूँकि rain, day, weather, time इत्यादि हेतु 'it' (Introductory Subject) का प्रयोग किया जाता है अत: Being से पूर्व 'it' लिखने से वाक्य सही बन जाता है एवं उसका सही अर्थ निकलता है :

It being a rainy day, he didn't go to the office. *—Correct*

(B) कई बार परीक्षा में Active एवं Passive के साथ Participle के प्रयोग के सन्दर्भ में प्रश्न पूछे जाते हैं; जहाँ Active का प्रयोग किया जाना चाहिए वहाँ Passive का प्रयोग करके प्रश्न दिया जाता है। निम्न उदाहरण देखें:

(i) Having been taken lunch, he went to Office. *—Incorrect*

यहाँ been का प्रयोग अनावश्यक / गलत किया गया है। यह Passive Structure में है। इसका अर्थ हुआ ' लंच लिए जाने के बाद, वह ऑफिस गया' । जबकि वाक्य का आशय है " लंच लेने के बाद वह ऑफिस गया", अत: इसे निम्न प्रकार लिखा जाना चाहिए - Having taken lunch, he went to office. *—Correct*

(ii) Having deserted by his wife, he became a hermit. *—Incorrect*

इस वाक्य में Having के बाद been का प्रयोग करना आवश्यक है। इस वाक्य में 'Having' का प्रयोग Participle'

की तरह हुआ है जिसके साथ Subject 'he' का प्रयोग करने पर 'he having deserted by his wife' बनता है जिसका कोई तर्क-संगत अर्थ नहीं निकलता है। यहाँ Participle का प्रयोग Passive में होना आवश्यक है अत: यहाँ Having been का प्रयोग करने पर -

Having been deserted by his wife, he became a hermit. (अर्थात पत्नि द्वारा छोड़ दिये जाने पर वह सन्यासी बन गया) यह Participle का सही प्रयोग है। Likewise:-

The sun having been risen, the fog dispersed. *—Incorrect*

The sun having risen, the fog dispersed *—Correct*

ERRORS, MISTAKES AND BLUNDERS IN USE OF PARTICIPLES

Exercise : ***Rewrite the sentences after correction.***

1. Being Sunday, I am thinking to go to a movie.
2. Remember the lessons teach by the teacher.
3. Where is the book wrote by Mr. Gupta ?
4. Ploughing his fields some old statues were found.
5. I want a wrote complaint.
6. There is no drink water in the office.
7. Having satisfied with his reply, I didn't take any action.
8. Tired, I couldn't work any more.
9. Left from hand to mouth, he yet maintains his standard of living.
10. Having referred to your application, I beg to write.
11. In regard to my qualification I beg to submit.
12. Sleeping in the house, a thief entered their house.
13. Having injured he went to hospital.
14. Turn to the left you can see the palace.
15. Walking in the forest a lion was seen.
16. Don't get off a ran bus.
17. The ship has sunken.
18. Having been worked hard he got tired.
19. Having opened the drawer she took out a knife.
20. We must provide good education to grown chil dren.

Explanations

1. It being Sunday, I am thinking to go to a movie.
2. Remember the lessons taught by the teacher.
3. Where is the book written by Mr. Gupta?
4. While ploughing his fields he found some old statues .
5. I want a written complaint.
6. There is no drinking water in the office.
7. Having been satisfied with his reply, I didn't take any action.
8. Being tired, I couldn't work any more.
9. Living from hand to month, he yet maintains his standard of living.
10. Referring to your application, I beg to write.
11. Regarding my qualification I beg to submit.
12. While they were sleeping in the house, a thief entered their house.
13. Having been injured he went to hospital.
14. Turning to the left you can see the palace.
15. While I was walking in the forest I saw a lion.
16. Don't get off a running bus.
17. The ship has sunk.
18. Having worked hard he got tired.
19. Opening the drawer she took out a knife.
20. We must provide good education to growing children.

INFINITIVE -PARTICIPLES (SPOTTING ERRORS)

Exercise : ***Find the errors and justify your answers.***

1. Being often ill (A)/ and frequently absent (B)/ she had no opportunity to complete his work (C)/ or do much of it in toto. (D)
2. Taking breakfast (A)/ he went to the office (B)/ and ordered the staff (C)/ to complete the work without any further delay (D) .
3. Without taking proper care (A)/ the doctors would (B)/ not have been saved (C)/ the life of this patient (D).
4. Going towards the gate (A)/ with a cup of tea (B)/ somebody switched off (C)/ the light (D) .
5. He does nothing (A)/ but to find faults (B)/ with others (C)/ and laugh at them (D).
6. The Chief Minister (A) should not let (B)/ the terrorist activities (C)/ to grow in our state (D).
7. Many persons are coming (A)/ to his concert (B)/ to hear him to sing (C)/ the religious songs (D).
8. Having had reached (A)/ the station, you (B)/ may make a telephone call (C)/ to your boss (D).
9. It is better to stay (A)/ at home than to go to market (B)/ when it is raining (C).
10. When he entered the home (A)/ he found the child sleeping (B)/ and the fan moves slowly (C).
11. He asked me to (A)/ completely forget her (B)/ but only I know it is not possible(D).

Explanations

1. (D) 'do'से पहले ' to' प्रयुक्त होगा। 'or' से पहले 'to complete' है तो 'or' के बाद भी 'to do'आयेगा।
2. (A) 'After taking breakfast' या 'Having taken breakfast' लिखा जायेगा ।
3. (C) 'been' का प्रयोग गलत है।
4. (A) 'While *he* was going towards the gate' होगा।
5. (B) 'Nothing but' के बाद 'to' का प्रयोग गलत है। जैसे : He does nothing but watch T.V.
6. (D) 'to' हटाना होगा। 'let' के बाद infinitive 'to' का प्रयोग नहीं होता है ।
7. (C) 'to sing' की जगह केवल 'sing' आयेगा; hear, see, make, know, feel के बाद infinitive 'to' का प्रयोग नहीं होता है । जैसे :

   (a) I see her walk. (b) I feel her presence .
8. (A) 'Had' का अनावश्यक प्रयोग किया गया है।
9. (B) 'than' के बाद 'to'का प्रयोग नहीं होता है। जैसे :-

   It is better to study than wander here and there
10. (C) 'fan *moving* slowly' होना चाहिए।
11. (B) 'Completely forget her' की जगह 'forget her completely' होगा। यहाँ infinitive को गलत split किया गया है।

BLUNDERS (INFINITIVE/GERUND/PARTICIPLE)

Exercise : ***Rewrite the sentences after correction.***

1. He had better to withdraw.
2. He did nothing but to cry bitterly.
3. He knows to operate the machine well.
4. Let she sing a song.
5. I need a boiling egg.
6. Standing near the church, a car hit her,
7. He is fond of swim.
8. Being a cold morning I didn't go to office.
9. This is the book wrote by him.
10. You cannot prevent her to go to the market.

Explanations

1. सही वाक्य होगा–He had better withdraw. यहाँ 'to' का प्रयोग गलत है।
2. यहाँ 'but' के बाद 'to' का प्रयोग गलत है। यहाँ bare infinitive 'cry' का प्रयोग होगा।
3. यहाँ 'knows' के बाद 'how' का प्रयोग होगा।
4. 'Let' के बाद 'she' की बजाय 'her' का प्रयोग होगा। 'Let' के बाद Objective case Pronoun ही प्रयुक्त होता है।
5. 'a boiling egg' की अपेक्षा 'a boiled egg' लिखें।
6. सही वाक्य होगा –'While she was standing near the church,a car hit her'. यहं dangling participle का case है।
7. Preposition के बाद verb की gerund form आती है। अत: 'of' के बाद 'swimming' लिखें।
8. सही वाक्य होगा – It being a cold morning, I didn't go to office. यह dangling participle का case है।
9. यहाँ 'wrote' की जगह Past Participle 'written' लिखा जायेगा।
10. सही वाक्य होगा – 'You cannot prevent her from going to the market'.यहाँ 'go' से पहले 'to' का प्रयोग गलत है।

❑❑❑

10

Adverbs

Adverb के सम्बन्ध में सामान्यतया Errors / Mistakes सम्बन्धित प्रश्न, वाक्य में Adverb की Position के सम्बन्ध में या उसके गलत प्रयोग के सन्बन्ध में पूछे जाते हैं। छात्र इन बिन्दुओं का विशेष ध्यान रखें।

Adverb वाक्य में ऐसा शब्द है जो verb या Adjective या अन्य Adverb या Adverbial phrase को विशेषता प्रदान करता है / संशोधित करता है / उसके अर्थ में कुछ वृद्धि / परिवर्तन करता है।

An adverb is that word in a sentence which modifies the meaning of verb or adjective or another adverb or adverbial phrase.

Look at the following sentences :

(a) He ran fast. — Verb 'ran' को संशोधित करता है।

(b) These are very sweet magoes. — Adjective, 'sweet' को संशोधित करता है।

(c) He speaks very loudly. — Adverb, 'loudly' को संशोधित करता है।

(d) He was sitting close beside her. — Adverbial phrase, 'beside her' को संशोधित करता है।

सभी underlined शब्द- Adverbs हैं। जब Adverb का प्रयोग वाक्य के शुरू में होता है तो वह सारे वाक्य को संशोधित करता है। जैसे -

(a) Certainly she is right. (b) Fortunately we escaped unhurt.

KINDS OF ADVERBS

(1) Simple, (2) Relative and (3) Interrogative.

Simple Adverbs : ये वाक्य में प्रयुक्त कुछ शब्दों (Verb, Adverb, Adjective, Adverbial phrase) को संशोधित करते हैं।

Relative Adverbs : ये शब्दों को भी संशोधित करते हैं एवं सम्पन्न कार्यो के मध्य relation भी व्यक्त करते हैं।

Interrogative Adverbs : ये प्रश्न भी करते हैं एवं शब्दों को भी संशोधित करते हैं।

Adverbs के सम्बन्ध में निम्न बिन्दुओं पर गौर करें :

Position and Rules of Adverbs

Adverbs का प्रयोग वाक्य में किस जगह किया जावे, यह एक महत्त्वपूर्ण बिन्दु है। Adverb को गलत जगह पर प्रयुक्त करने से, वाक्य का अर्थ ही परिवर्तित हो सकता है। नीचे लिखे वाक्यों से यह स्पष्ट हो जाता है:

(a) *Only* she can speak.
(केवल वह बोल सकती है।)

(b) She can *only* speak.
वह केवल बोल सकती है (लिख नहीं सकती।)

(c) She can speak *only*.
(वह केवल बोल सकती है, अन्य कोई कार्य, जैसे: घर का कोई कार्य, बाजार का कोई कार्य नहीं कर सकती है।)

इस तरह Adverb, 'only' की वाक्य में स्थिति परिवर्तन होने से, वाक्य का अर्थ बदल जाता है। अत: Adverb को वाक्य में कहाँ पर लिखना है (Position of Adverb) यह एक महत्त्वपूर्ण बिन्दु है।

1. **Adverb of manner,** जैसे ; slowly, quickly, carefully, easily, calmly, fast etc. वाक्य में verb के बाद लिखे जाते हैं, लेकिन यदि वाक्य में verbका object भी है, तो इन्हें object के बाद लिखना चाहिए :

Correct use	**Incorrect use**
(a) He talks well.	He well talks.
(b) He speaks English fluently.	He speaks fluently English.

2. Adverb of Time एवं Adverb of place :

Adverb of Time, (जैसे ; Now, then, soon, today, next day, yet etc,) एवं **Adverb of place** (जैसे ; Here, there, on etc.)भी verb के बाद प्रयुक्त होते हैं, लेकिन यदि verb का कोई object भी है तो ये object के बाद प्रयुक्त होते हैं।

Correct use	**Incorrect use**
(a) She will come soon.	She soon will come.
(b) He will go to Jaipur the next day.	He will next day go to Jaipur.
(c) He has not arrived yet.	He has yet not arrived.

3. Adverb of Frequency, जैसे : Always, often, daily, generally, never, rarely एवं अन्य कुछ Adverbs, जैसे : almost, just, hardly, nearly, already का प्रयोग सामान्यतया, subject एवं verb के बीच किया जाता है। यदि verb में एक से अधिक शब्द हैं जैसे: has advised, have seen तो इन adverbs का प्रयोग 'have / has', Auxiliary verb के बाद किया जाता है :

Correct use	**Incorrect use**
(a) His mother never cooks food.	His mother cooks food never.
(b) He always speaks the truth.	He speaks the truth always.
(c) He often comes late.	He comes late often.
(d) He *has never seen* the Taj.	He has seen the Taj never.

Note **(A) यदि वाक्य में 'is / am / are/ was / were' जैसी Auxiliary verbs का प्रयोग हुआ हो तो ये Adverbs इनके बाद आते हैं। जैसे :**

(a) He is always ready. (b) She is often late.
(c) They are generally late. (d) We are always happy.

(B) Auxiliary ; 'have to / used to' के साथ उक्त Adverbs का प्रयोग उनसे पूर्व किया जाता है :

(a) I often have to go on foot. (b) He always used to take umbrella.

(C) Adverb, 'Not' का प्रयोग हमेशा Auxiliary के बाद एवं Principal verb के पहले किया जाता है:

(a) I have not done my work. (b) He did not go to Jaipur.

4. Adverb 'Enough' का प्रयोग उस शब्द के बाद किया जाता है, जिसे वह qualify करता है। 'Enough से' पहले हमेशा positive degree का adjective या adverb रहेगा। Comparative degree के बाद 'enough' का प्रयोग नहीं होता है :

(a) I have money enough to buy a shirt.
(b) The building is large enough for the guest house.

जब 'enough' का प्रयोग adjective की तरह होता है तो यह noun की विशेषता बताता है और तब यह noun के पहले या बाद में आ सकता है, लेकिन जब यह adverb की तरह प्रयुक्त होता है, तो हमेशा बाद में आता है।

5. Adverbs 'only' एवं 'even' को हमेशा उस word से पहले लिखना चाहिए, जिसके लिये इनका प्रयोग किया जाता है :

(a) I cannot write even correct Hindi. (b) He has only one car.
(c) Only he has a car. (d) He cannot do even this work.

6. Order of Adverbs : यदि एक वाक्य में कई तरह के Adverbs का प्रयोग हुआ हो, तो सबसे पहले Adverb of manner, फिर Adverb of place एवं फिर Adverb of time आता है :

(a) She spoke loudly at the meeting yesterday.
1 2 3

(b) He is crying <u>loudly</u> <u>at the field</u> <u>now.</u>

1 2 3

M	P	T
1	2	3

उक्त वाक्यों में - 1 - Adverb of manner-M

2- Adverb of place -P

3 - Adverb of time- लाइन में T को व्यक्त करते हैं।

यदि वाक्य में कई Adverbs of time का प्रयोग हो तो सबसे पहले, सबसे छोटा Time, फिर उससे बड़ा, फिर सबसे बड़े Time को रखा जाना चाहिये।

(a) He came here at <u>7O'clock</u> in the <u>morning</u> on <u>Monday.</u>

7. यदि कोई adverb किसी Adverb / Adjective या Adverbial phrase को modify करता है तो उस Adverb को पहले लिखते हैं। जैसे :

(a) He likes <u>very</u> <u>sweet</u> mangoes.

(b) They were standing <u>close</u> <u>beside the canteen</u>.

8. जब Adverb सारे वाक्य को ही संशोधित करता है, तो उसे वाक्य के आरम्भ में प्रयोग करते हैं :

(a) <u>Certainly</u> she will meet us there.

9. जब किसी वाक्य में 'not' का प्रयोग किया गया हो, तो negative adverb का प्रयोग नहीं करना चाहिए। वाक्य में Double negative होना गलत है :

(a) I will not find her nowhere. —*Incorrect.*

I will not find her anywhere. —*Correct*

(b) No one scarcely visits here. —*Incorrect.*

No one visits here. —*Correct*

10. 'Else' के साथ हमेशा 'but' Adverb का प्रयोग किया जाता है, 'than'का प्रयोग करना गलत है :

(a) Go anywhere else than Pakistan —*Incorrect.*

Go anywhere else but Pakistan —*Correct*

11. वाक्य में Intransitive verbs होने की स्थिति में Adverb का प्रयोग verb के तुरन्त बाद ही किया जाता है :

(a) He died calmly. (b) She spoke softly.

(कई बार adverbs पर पूछे जाने वाले प्रश्न, specific Adverbs से सम्बन्धित होते हैं।

SOME IMPORTANT ADVERBS

Too

'Too' का अर्थ होता है – 'More than enough' अर्थात् excess (अतिशय)। 'Too' का प्रयोग 'very'के अर्थ में करना गलत है; 'very' का अर्थ होता है – 'बहुत', जबकि 'Too'का अर्थ होता है - excess (अतिशय)। **यदि हम किसी मित्र को देखकर यह कहें कि, "I am too glad to meet you". तो इसका अर्थ होगा कि, "मै आपसे मिलकर इतना खुश हूँ जितना नहीं होना चाहिए"।**

(A) Too + infinitive:

'Too' के बाद 'to'infinitive का प्रयोग एक negativity व्यक्त करता है :

(a) He is too weak to walk.

वह इतना अधिक कमजोर है कि चल नहीं सकता।

(B) 'Too'का प्रयोग 'भी' के लिए भी किया जा सकता है, जैसे :

(a) He too went to America. वह <u>भी</u> अमरीका गया।

(C) 'Too'का निम्न प्रयोग भी उचित है; यहाँ too का अर्थ 'अत्याधिक' से है :

(a) You are too weak in English. (b) He is too poor.

Much / Very

(A) 'Much' का प्रयोग comparative degree के Adverb या Adjective के पहले किया जाता है; जबकि 'very' का प्रयोग positive degree के Adverb / Adjective पूर्व होता है। **अर्थात् positive degree के Adverb / Adjective के पूर्व 'much' का प्रयोग नहीं होता तथा comparative degree के साथ 'very' का प्रयोग नहीं होता है :**

(a) Ram is much stronger than Rahim. (b) Ram is a very strong man.

(B) 'Very much' का प्रयोग comparative degree से पूर्व किया जा सकता है :

(a) He is very much stronger than Sonu. (b) Suresh is very much cleverer than Shalu.

(C) जब superlative degree के साथ 'much' का प्रयोग किया जाता है तो यह 'the'के पहले आता है; जबकि 'very' का प्रयोग 'the'के बाद तथा superlative के पहले होगा :

(a) Nisha is <u>much</u> the best girl in the college. (b) Nisha is <u>the very</u> best girl in the college.

(D) 'Much' एवं 'very' में एक महत्त्वपूर्ण अन्तर यह है कि 'much' का प्रयोग part participle या verb के साथ होता है जबकि 'very' का प्रयोग present participle के साथ किया जाता है। जैसे :

(a) He was much shocked. (past participle)
(b) The news is very interesiting (present participle)
(c) She talks much. (He talks very - यह गलत है।)

(E) कुछ phrases में past participle के साथ 'very' का स्वत: ही प्रयोग होता है। जैसे :

Very pleased, very tired etc.

Too much / much too / only too

'Too much' या 'much too' दोनों का अर्थ समान है। 'Too much' के प्रयोग के बाद noun का प्रयोग होता है एवं 'much too' के प्रयोग के बाद Adjective या participle का प्रयोग किया जाता है। **दोनों का अर्थ है – excess, more than limits, इतना ज्यादा, जितना नहीं होना चाहिए :**

(a) His behaviour gave me too much pain. (noun)
(b) His behaviour was much too <u>painful.</u> (adjective)

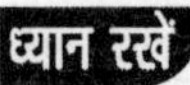

Only too : ''Only too' का अर्थ होता है – 'बहुत' (very) इसका प्रयोग 'very' के अर्थ में किया जा सकता है :

He will be <u>only</u> too happy to meet you.
Means = He will be <u>very</u> happy to meet you.
'only too' का अर्थ 'too' से पूर्णतया अलग है।

Since / Ever since

'Since' का प्रयोग perfect tense में किया जाता है; इसका अर्थ होता है – 'जब से, तब से'

(a) I have been playing football since 7 O'clock.

कभी-कभी वाक्य में 'since' का प्रयोग अंत में किया जाता है, एवं इससे पूर्व 'ever' का प्रयोग किया जाता है; 'ever', ''since' का अर्थ होता है – **'तब से'**, जैसे :

(b) I first met her three years ago and have remembered her face ever since.

Late / Lately

'Late' का अर्थ है – 'देरी से', जबकि 'Lately' का अर्थ होता है, 'अभी '(recently).

(a) He came late today. (b) He has come lately. (recently)

'Lately' का प्रयोग present perfect में होता है क्योंकि यह वर्तमान में पूर्ण होने वाले कार्य को व्यक्त करता है।

Hard / Hardly

'Hard' का अर्थ होता है 'कठिन', जबकि 'Hardly' का अर्थ Negative में – 'नहीं', से लिया जाता है :

(a) He works hard. — वह कड़ी मेहनत करता है।

(b) He hardly works. — वह कार्य लगभग नहीं करता है।

Most / Mostly

'Most' का अर्थ है सबसे अधिक; जबकि 'Mostly' का अर्थ है, अधिकांश भाग :

(a) He is the most intelligent student of all.

(b) The candidates were mostly from rural area.

Before / Ago

दोनों का अर्थ है – 'पहले' ; 'Before' का प्रयोग past या present perfect के साथ हो सकता है, जबकि 'Ago' का प्रयोग present perfect के साथ नहीं हो सकता है :

(a) I have never before seen such a beautiful lady. —*Correct*

(b) I arrived here two days ago. —*Correct*

(c) He *has arrived* here ten minutes *ago.* —*Incorrect*

(Present perfect के साथ 'Ago' का प्रयोग नहीं किया जा सकता है।)

Still / Yet / Already

(A) 'Still' का प्रयोग वर्तमान में हो रहे कार्य के लिये किया जाता है; भूतकाल (past) के लिये इसका सामान्यतया प्रयोग नहीं होता है :

(a) He is still asleep. (b) It is still raining.

(B) 'Not yet' का प्रयोग भविष्य में पूर्ण होने की आशा वाले कार्यों के लिए किया जाता है :

(a) Has she come? Not yet. (b) The jeep hasn't arrived yet.

(C) प्रश्न के साथ 'yet' का प्रयोग ऐसे कार्यों हेतु किया जाता है जिनके पूर्ण होने की आशा थी, वे पूर्ण हुए या नहीं यह अभी ज्ञात नहीं है।

(a) Is lunch ready yet? (b) Has the jeep arrived yet?

(D) सामान्यतया 'yet' वाक्य के अन्त में आता है। 'Yet' का प्रयोग अधिकांशतया Negative एवं Interrogative वाक्यों में किया जाता है। Affirmative वाक्यों में 'yet' का प्रयोग 'still' के समान ही किया जाता है :

We have yet to hear from the government. (;We are still waiting to hear from the government.)

(E) 'Already' का अर्थ है – 'पहले से'। जब कोई कार्य आशा से पहले पूर्ण हो चुका होता है तो सामान्यतया 'Already' का प्रयोग किया जाता है :

(a) When is she coming? She is already here.

(b) You must visit Agra? I have already visited.

Note

तीनों words(still, yet, already) का प्रयोग past moment बताने के लिये भी हो सकता है :

I went to see if she had woken up yet.But she was still asleep. This was irritating as her friends had already arrived.

Position in a sentence : 'Still' एवं 'already' का प्रयोग सामान्यतया वाक्य के मध्य में किया जाता है। कुछ स्थितियों में 'already' का प्रयोग वाक्य के अन्त में भी हो सकता है। जैसे:-

Are you here already? You must have come by some fast mode.

'Yet' सामान्यतया वाक्य के अन्त में आता है। 'Not' के साथ 'yet' उसके तुरन्त बाद आता है। जैसे :

(a) Don't eat the apples, they aren't ripe *yet*.

(b) The apples are *not yet* ripe.

Fairly/ Rather

'Fairly' का प्रयोग good sense में तथा 'Rather' का प्रयोग bad sense में होता है। दोनों का अर्थ 'मात्रा' को व्यक्त करता है:

(a) The weather is rather hot. *—Correct*
The weather is fairly hot. *—Incorrect*
(b) Coffee is fairly hot. *—Correct*
Coffee is rather hot. *—Incorrect*
(c) I like her as she is rather beautiful. *—Incorrect*
I like her as she is fairly beautiful. *—Correct*

Just

इसका अर्थ है 'अभी'। 'Just' का प्रयोग सामान्यतया Present Perfect में किया जाता है :

(a) He has just arrived.

'Just' का अर्थ- 'एकदम सही समय' हेतु भी किया जाता है। तब इसका प्रयोग Simple Past में भी किया जा सकता है :

(a) They just caught the train.

'Just' का प्रयोग समय इंगित करने हेतु निम्न प्रकार किया जाता है :

(a) It has just struck seven. अभी-अभी 7 बजे हैं।
(b) It has just struck three. अभी-अभी 3 बजे हैं।

Early/Soon/Quickly

'Early' का प्रयोग Adjective एवं Adverb दोनों तरह से किया जाता है:

(a) He came in early morning. (b) Roses blossomed early this spring.

'early' का यहाँ अर्थ है- **'सुबह शुरू होने के तुरंत बाद या बसंत शुरू होने के तुरंत बाद'।**

'Early' का प्रयोग 'निर्धारित समय से पूर्व' के लिए भी होता है :

(a) She came early in the meeting. (b) The Chief guest came early.

जबकि 'soon' का प्रयोग 'after a point of time' के अर्थ में किया जाता है :

(a) She came to meet me soon after Ram arrived.
(b) Get well soon.

'Soon' means a short time after a point of time.

Quickly : 'quickly' का अर्थ, कार्य करने की गति से लिया जाता है :-

Come and see us quickly. (Means-Make the arrangement fast.)
Come and see us soon. (Means-Come and see us before long.)

Seldom or never/ Seldom if ever

'Seldom' के साथ या तो 'or never' या 'if ever' आता है ('Seldom or ever' लिखना गलत है।) :

(a) She seldom or never tells lies.
(b) She seldom if ever asks the boys the reason of their absence.

ERRORS, MISTAKES AND BLUNDERS IN USE OF ADVERBS

Exercise : ***Rewrite the sentences after correction :***

1. She takes generally her breakfast at 8 AM.
2. Ram only came here last Saturday.
3. Ramesh was too tired when he came here.
4. Sita came quicker than I expected.
5. We wanted a better and efficient Office Assistant.
6. It was much cold last night.

7. I visited her frequently while in Newyork.
8. He will be quite sorry to know that.
9. The water of this tank is too cold.
10. He ran very fastly.
11. Hari was fortunately not available in the hostel.
12. It was nothing else than her arrogance.
13. He feels comparatively better today.
14. Come at 7 o'clock to my office.
15. I seldom or ever refused the leave.
16. He quickly ran away from the site.
17. Firstly you think over the words and then speak.
18. I go often to the Shani Temple.
19. No one hardly goes to church daily.
20. I care a straw for it.
21. We were very delighted to get the news.
22. Call me anything else than a fraud.
23. They could not find her nowhere.
24. I only solved two sums.
25. She peacefully died yesterday.
26. Do you know to drive ?
27. I went directly to Meerut.
28. It is very cold to go for a walk today.
29. Parul runs fastly than Nalini.
30. If you run fast, you would have won the race.
31. Hari speaks clear.
32. Sita writes neat.
33. Sarla hit the thief hardly on the head.
34. He is perfectly quite right.
35. The speaker spoke enough loud to be heard easily.
36. He is much old.
37. The story is much interesting.
38. Ram comes here seldom.
39. I am very satisfied with her conduct.
40. The train will arrive just now.
41. The film was mostly over when you entered.
42. He fared bad in the second innings.
43. Repeat again what you have said.
44. Breathe deeply when you walk.
45. He cautiously drives.
46. She heartily loves Ram.
47. There were every where flowers in the garden.
48. Ram comes at the field regularly every day.
49. She has been absenting herself frequently from the office.
50. Ram already has finished his work.
51. I see her frequently in the market.
52. She has often to go by tram.
53. He is intelligent wonderfully.
54. Sita regularly visits her friend Sarla.
55. I drive seldom after sunset.
56. He explained clearly the method of transplantation the heart.
57. The parents heartily love their children.
58. Three passengers were unfortunately injured.
59. You are forbidden not to write on the table.
60. The day is hot too.
61. I was too tired after the swimming.
62. Sita loves her only daughter too much.
63. The new medicines have given her too much relief.
64. I met none else than your real brother.
65. She quickly writes.
66. Unless you do not work hard, you can't succeed.
67. The news is much interesting.
68. He seldom or ever refuses a genuine request.
69. You seldom or ever find a grammatical error in this book.
70. Ram ran very fastly.
71. They last evening, went to Jaipur.
72. I only solved two sums in an hour.
73. The matter has been very discussed.
74. I do not know to swim.
75. They have gone to Jaipur yesterday.
76. He has left this place five minutes ago.

77. Do you know him? Yes, I do not.
78. Do you know him? No, I do.
79. The teacher asked him to not sleep in the class.
80. Could you lend me your umbrella? Oh, no, I can.
81. She will today go to Mumbai.
82. With most humbly and respectfully, I beg to apprise.....
83. I have not pen with me.
84. There was no an intelligent student to solve that question.

Explanations

1. Generally she takes her breakfast at 8 A.M..
2. Ram came here only last Saturday.
3. Ramesh was much tired when he came here.
4. Sita came quickly than I expected.
5. We wanted a better and more efficient Office Assistant.
6. It was very cold last night.
7. I frequently visited her while in Newyork.
8. He will be very sorry to know that.
9. The water of this tank is very cold.
10. He ran very fast.
11. Fortunately Hari was not available in the hostel.
12. It was nothing else but her arrogance.
13. He feels better today.
14. Come to my office at 7 o'clock.
15. I seldom or never refused the leave.
16. He ran away quickly from the site.
17. First you think over the words and then speak.
18. I often go to the Shani Temple.
19. Hardly any one goes to church daily.
20. I do not care a straw for it.
21. We were much delighted to get the news.
22. Call me anything else but a fraud.
23. They could not find her anywhere.
24. I solved only two sums.
25. She died peacefully yesterday.
26. Do you know how to drive ?
27. I went direct to Meerut.
28. It is too cold to go for a walk today.
29. Parul runs faster than Narlini.
30. Had you run fast you would have won the race.
31. Hari speaks clearly.
32. Sita writes neatly.
33. Sarla hit the thief hard on the head.
34. He is perfectly right.
35. The speaker spoke loud enough to be heard easily.
36. He is very old.
37. The story is very interesting.
38. Ram seldom comes here.
39. I am much satisfied with her conduct.
40. The train will arrive shortly.
41. The film was almost over when you entered.
42. He fared badly in the second innings.
43. Repeat what you have said.
44. Breathe deep when you walk.
45. He drives cautiously .
46. She loves Ram heartily.
47. There were flowers every where in the garden.
48. Ram comes regularly at the field every day.
49. She has been frequently absenting herself from the office.
50. Ram has already finished his work.
51. I frequently see her in the market.
52. She often has to go by tram.
53. He is wonderfully intelligent.
54. Sita visits her friend Sarla regularly.
55. I seldom drive after sunset.
56. He clearly explained the method of transplantation the heart.
57. The parents love their children heartily.
58. Unfortunately three passengers were injured.

59. You are forbidden to write on the table.
60. The day is too hot.
61. I was very tired after the swimming.
62. Sita loves her only daughter very much.
63. The new medicines have given her much relief.
64. I met none else but your real brother.
65. She writes quickly.
66. Unless you work hard, you can't succeed.
67. The news is very interesting.
68. He seldom or never refuses a genuine request.
69. You seldom or never find a grammatical error in this book.
70. Ram ran very fast.
71. They went to Jaipur last evening.
72. I solved only two sums in an hour.
73. The matter has been much discussed.
74. I do not know how to swim.
75. They went to Jaipur yesterday.
76. He left this place five minutes ago.
77. Do you know him? Yes, I do.
78. Do you know him? No, I don't.
79. The teacher asked him not to sleep in the class.
80. Could you lend me your umbrella? Oh, no, I can't.
81. She will go to Mumbai today.
82. Most humbly and respectfully, I beg to ap–prise.....
83. I have no pen with me.
84. There was not an intelligent student to solve that question.

SPOTTING THE ERRORS (ADVERBS)

Exercise : ***Find the errors and justify your answers.***

1. "Under no circumstances (A)/ we can help you (B)/ in this immoral project", (C)/ said the Chairman. (D)
2. Somebody informed (A)/ the contractor that his (B)/ brother had only died (C)/ five days before. (D)
3. She is very senior(A)/ to me, so I (B)/cannot defy her orders.(C)
4. Who can believe (A)/ that she was not (B)/ hardly hit (C)/ by the death of her son. (D)
5. Hardly she likes (A)/ to hear my name (B)/ after the dispute which occurred (C) / between us last year. (D)
6. Only by discussing with (A)/ the officer concerned (B)/ they found out (C)/ the person behind the fraud.(D)
7. The house is very good (A)/ but too much small (B)/ to accommodate (C)/ the full family. (D)
8. He does not (A)/ know to make (B)/ friends so he is leading (C)/ a lonely life. (D)
9. Every member of the family (A)/ is addicted to drinking (B) and so Asha is. (C)
10. He was very tired (A)/ of work so he said (B)/ that he would (C)/ not accompany us. (D)
11. Sakshi was exorbitantly paid (A)/ for how skilful she (B)/ welcomed the visitors. (C)
12. She is almost quite competent(A)/for the post of Marketing Executive(B)/so if given a chance(C)/ she can show the results (D).
13. The student requested (A)/ the principal to be enough kind (B)/ to grant him seven days' leave. (C)
14. He has been trying (A)/ to persuade her for several months (B)/ but he has (C)/ not still succeeded. (D)
15. Before the game he felt surely (A)/ of wining, but within five minutes (B)/ he realised that he was wrong. (C)
16. The amount which the company (A)/ paid to the dependents of (B)/ the deceased was (B)/ fairly unjustified. (D)
17. Although he only earns (A)/ sixteen hundred rupees per month (B)/ yet he manages his (C)/ family well. (D)

18. I liked that opportune moment (A)/ where the workers proved themselves (B)/ and came out victorious. (C)
19. Where else (A)/ did you go besides (B)/ the bank ? (C)
20. I hardly ever (A)/ see him (B)/ because in my opinion(C)/he is not a reliable man. (D)
21. He is a linguist (A)/ and always tries to(B)/ make his students (C)/ pronounce the words correctly. (D)

Explanations

1. (B) 'We can' की जगह 'can we' आयेगा। जब वाक्य 'Under no circumstances' से शुरू होता है, तो Verb, Subject से पहले (Inversion is applied)आती है ।
2. (C) 'only' का प्रयोग 'died' के बाद होगा; brother had died only five days before; 'He only died' का अर्थ है 'केवल वह मरा' He died only three days ago. का अर्थ है 'वह केवल तीन दिन पहले मरा'।
3. (A) 'Very senior' की जगह 'much senior' लिखें। 'very' का प्रयोग positive degree के adjective के पूर्व किया जाता है। much का प्रयोग comparative degree के adjective के पूर्व किया जाता है । जैसे :-
   He is a very strong boy.
   He is much stronger than you.
4. (C) 'Hardly hit' की जगह 'Hit hard' लिखें। 'hardly' का अर्थ 'न के बराबर' (negative) होता है; जबकि 'hard' का अर्थ 'कठिन'/ 'कड़ा' होता है।
5. (A) 'Hardly does she' लिखें । जब वाक्य Hardly, Seldom से शुरू होते हैं, तो Auxiliary verb, Subject से पहले (Inversion is applied) आती है ।
6. (A) 'Only' को 'with' से पहले लिखें; By discussing only with. 'Only' का प्रयोग सामान्यतया उस word से पहले किया जाता है जिसे महत्त्व दिया जा रहा है ।
7. (B) 'Too much' की जगह 'much too small होना चाहिए।
   सामान्यतया 'too much' का प्रयोग noun से पूर्व होता है, 'much too' का प्रयोग adjective से पूर्व होता है। जैसे :
   It gives me too much pleasure .
   It is much too pleasuresome.
8. (B) 'Know to make' की जगह 'know how to make' होगा। जैसे :
   I know how to swim.
   He knows how to cook.
9. (C) 'So Asha is' की जगह 'so is Asha' होगा। इस तरह के वाक्यों में सहायक क्रिया Subject से पहले आती है (Inversion is applied), जैसे :-
   I don't like such cheap things nor does she.
10. No Error वाक्य सही है।
11. (B) 'how skilfully' होगा। 'skilful' एक adjective है जबकि यहाँ 'skilfully' (Adverb), verb – 'received' को qualify कर रहा है ।
12. (A) 'almost' का प्रयोग गलत है। 'quite' से पहले किसी adverb का प्रयोग नहीं किया जाता है।
13. (B) 'to be kind enough' होगा। 'enough' (as adverb) का प्रयोग उस शब्द के बाद होता है, जिसे वह qualify कर रहा है । जैसे :
    He is intelligent enough to solve this problem .
    लेकिन enough का प्रयोग adjective के रूप में noun से पूर्व एवं बाद में दोनों तरह हो सकता है जैसे :-
    I have enough money.
    I have money enough to ......

14. (D) 'Still' की जगह 'yet' आयेगा; 'not succeeded yet'. 'Still' का प्रयोग affirmative वाक्यों में होता है जबकि 'yet' का प्रयोग सामान्यतया negative वाक्यों में किया जाता है।
15. (A) 'surely' की जगह 'sure' लिखें verbs of perception जैसे feel, small, appear, look, seem आदि अपने बाद Adjective लेते हैं, न कि Adverb.
16. (D) 'Fairly' की जगह 'rather' या 'quite' का प्रयोग करें। 'Fairly' का प्रयोग सामान्यतया good sense में होता है।
17. (A) 'He earns only' होगा 'only, almost, even' etc. का प्रयोग हमेशा उस Phrase या शब्द से पहले किया जाता है जिसे वह qualify करता है, जैसे :
    (a) Only she visited the temple .
    (b) She gave him only three rupees.
18. (B) 'Where' की जगह 'when' का प्रयोग होगा 'Where' - adverb of place है तथा time के लिए Adverb of time, 'when' का प्रयोग किया जाता है।
19. (A) 'else' delete करें यहाँ 'else' लिखने की आवश्यकता नहीं है, क्योंकि 'besides' का प्रयोग किया गया है; 'Besides' एवं 'else' का यहाँ एक ही अर्थ है।
20. No Error वाक्य सही है। 'Hardly ever' का अर्थ 'बहुत कम ' होता है।
21. (B) 'and so he always tries to' होना चाहिए, जैसे: She is intelligent, so she can solve it.

BLUNDERS

Exercise : ***Find the errors and justify your answers.***

1. He speaks the truth always.
2. I never have seen an aeroplane.
3. He came here in the morning at 8 A.M. on Monday.
4. She came more early than Sita.
5. He works hardly to earn more money.
6. He is to weak too walk.
7. I like her as she is rather beautiful .
8. I seldom or if ever asked the boys the reason of their failure.
9. Ram is very the best sportman in the town.
10. I am too glad to meet you.

Explanations

1. सही वाक्य होगा– He always speaks the truth, ध्यान रहे: Adverbs of frequency; जैसे: almost,often, never etc. का प्रयोग सामान्तया subject एवं verb के बीच किया जाता है । लेकिन यदि वाक्य में is/am/are जैसी auxiliary verbs का प्रयोग हो, तो ये Adverbs इनके बाद आते हैं; He is always ready; She is never late.
2. सही वाक्य होगा– I have never seen an aeroplane. ध्यान रखें : यदि वाक्य में verb में एक से अधिक शब्द हो; जैसे – have seen, have done etc., तो Adverb of frequency, जैसे : always, never etc. का प्रयोग have, has के बाद होता है। He has always cooperated me.
3. सही वाक्य होगा– He came here at 8 A.M. in the morning on Monday. यदि वाक्य में कई Adverbs of time का प्रयोग हो, तो सबसे पहले सबसे छोटा समय, फिर उससे बड़ा, फिर उससे बड़ा time आता है ।
4. सही वाक्य होगा–She came earlier than Sita; *early – earlier – earliest* होता है। 'more early' गलत है।

5. सही वाक्य होगा-He works hard to earn more money; 'hardly' का अर्थ 'नहीं' (negative) होता है ।
6. सही वाक्य होगा-He is too weak to walk.
7. सही वाक्य होगा-I like her as she is fairly beautiful.
   'Fairly' का प्रयोग good sense में तथा 'rather' का प्रयोग सामान्यतया bad sense में किया जाता है।
8. 'Seldom or if ever' कोई Phrase नहीं है, सही Phrase है - 'seldom or never' या 'seldom if ever'.
9. सही वाक्य होगा-Ram is much the best sportsman in the town .यहाँ 'very' का प्रयोग करना उचित नहीं है।
10. इस वाक्य का अर्थ हुआ कि 'मैं तुमसे मिलकर, इतना प्रसन्न हुआ जितना नहीं होना चाहिए'।
    अत: सही वाक्य होगा- I am very glad to meet You.

❑❑❑

11

Adjectives/Determiners

Adjectives/Determiners के सही प्रयोग से सम्बन्धित विभिन्न नियमों का गम्भीरता पूर्वक अध्ययन करें एवं विभिन्न, किन्तु समान से दिखाई देने वाले Adjectives के सही अर्थ एवं प्रयोग को ध्यान पूर्वक समझ लें। विभिन्न परीक्षाओ में Adjectives के सम्बन्ध में पुछे जाने वाले प्रश्न इसी प्रकार की Errors/Mistakes से सम्बन्धित होते हैं।

Traditional Grammar में Determiners को Adjective से अलग नहीं किया गया है। Determiners, Adjectives का ही भाग हैं, जिनमें निम्न विशेषताएँ पाई जाती है। जैसे :

1. **Determiners के रूप में परिवर्तन नहीं होता है ; जैसे :** A, An, the, some, All, much, both, few, whole, etc. में Suffix या prefix जोड़कर, कोई परिवर्तन नहीं किया जा सकता है; जबकि Adjectives के रूप में परिवर्तन सम्भव है, जैसे : 'black' से 'blackish', 'blackness'; 'good' से 'goodness', 'fast' को 'faster', 'fastest' बनाया जा सकता है।
2. **Determiners का प्रयोग हमेशा Noun से पहले होता है जबकि Adjectives का प्रयोग Noun के पहले भी हो सकता है एवं बाद में भी।** Determiner का प्रयोग होने पर यह निश्चित हो जाता है कि इसके बाद Noun अवश्य आयेगा।
3. **वाक्य में Determiner एवं Adjective दोनों का प्रयोग हो तो पहले Determiner फिर Adjective एवं फिर noun आता है। Adjective का प्रयोग Determiner के पहले नहीं किया जा सकता है :**

   (a) He is a boy.
   (b) He is a good boy.
   (c) I have some pencils.
   (d) I have some coloured pencils.

   उपरोक्त वाक्यों में 'a, some'; Determiners हैं तथा 'good' एवं 'coloured', adjectives हैं। वाक्य (a) एवं (c) में Determiners का प्रयोग Noun से पहले हुआ है। (b) एवं (d) वाक्यों में Determiner + adjective + noun का प्रयोग हुआ है।

ADJECTIVES

Adjective वह शब्द है, जो कि वाक्य में प्रयुक्त noun या pronoun को विशेषता प्रदान करता है।

An *Adjective* is a word, when used with a noun or pronoun adds something to the meaning of noun or pronoun.

Look at the following sentences :

(a) She is a good girl.
(b) Alwar is a small city.

उपरोक्त वाक्यों में Underlined words, Adjectives हैं।

Correct use of some 'Adjectives'

1. **Each / Every / Either / Neither :**

   Each / Every / Either / Neither के साथ हमेशा Singular Noun का प्रयोग होता है, एवं Verb भी Singular ही प्रयुक्त होती है। जैसे:

   (a) Each student gets a prize.
   (b) Every seat was occupied.

यदि वाक्य में Every के बाद कोई plural adjective of number (two, three, four etc) का प्रयोग हो तो उसके बाद आने वाला Noun, plural होगा।

(a) She takes medicine every three hours. (b) He visits here every two months.

2. **Each / Every :**

(A) 'Each' एवं 'Every' दोनों का अर्थ समान है; Each का प्रयोग दो एवं दो से अधिक के लिये भी होता है, जबकि 'Every' का प्रयोग दो से अधिक (प्रत्येक) के लिये ही होता है :

(a) Each of the two girls gets a prize.

(b) Each of the ten students gets a prize.

(c) Every candidate was given a certificate.

Each- Two and more than two.

Every- More than two.

(B) 'Each' का प्रयोग निश्चित संख्या हेतु, तथा 'Every' का प्रयोग अनिश्चित संख्या के सन्दर्भ में किया जाता है।

(C) 'Each' का प्रयोग उस समय किया जाता है जब, वस्तु या व्यक्ति की Individuality, या separate action व्यक्त करना हो। 'Every' का प्रयोग Group- Action को व्यक्त करता है :

(a) Each student was given a certificate by the Chief Guest one by one.

(d) Every student was happy.

(D) 'Each' एक pronoun भी है एवं एक adjective भी है अत: 'Each' के बाद 'of' का प्रयोग किया जा सकता है। लेकिन **'Every' केवल Adjective है अत: 'Every' के बाद 'of' का प्रयोग करना गलत होगा।**

Each of the teachers is doing his work. *—Correct.*

Every of the teachers is doing his work. *—Incorrect.*

(E) Each and every दोनों का इस तरह से प्रयोग दो से अधिक (व्यक्ति या वस्तु) हेतु ही किया जा सकता है, दो के लिये केवल each का ही प्रयोग करना होता है :

Each and every student received a prize.

3. **Either / Both :**

'Either' का अर्थ है : 'दोनों में से एक या दोनों' Both का अर्थ है : 'दोनों'

'Either' का अर्थ 'दोनों ' उस स्थिति में होता है, जब एक भाग, दूसरे भाग का ही complement होता है। जैसे: Either side of the road, Either hand etc.

'Both' का प्रयोग तब किया जाता है, जब वस्तु के इस प्रकार दो भाग नहीं होते हैं :

(a) There was water on either side of the highway.

(b) His either son went to America. *—Incorrect*

His both sons went to America. *—Correct*

4. **Little / A little / The little :**

'Little' का प्रयोग uncountable के साथ किया जाता है। 'Little' का अर्थ नकारात्मक ('नगण्य या कुछ नहीं') होता है। 'A little' का अर्थ 'कुछ ', 'थोड़ा सा ' होता है। जबकि 'The little' का अर्थ 'जो सब कुछ थोड़ा सा' (not much but all that is) होता है।

Use of little (नगण्य या कुछ नहीं) :

(a) We have little hope of his recovery. (उसके ठीक होने की आशा नगण्य, न के बराबर है।)

(b) He has little knowledge of computers. (उसकी कम्प्यूटर विषयक जानकारी न के बराबर, नगण्य है।)

'A little' (Not much but some - 'कुछ ही ', 'थोड़ा सा') :

(a) We have a little hope of his recovery. (उसके ठीक होने की कुछ ही आशा है।)

(b) A little knowledge is always dangerous. (थोड़ी जानकारी सदा खतरनाक होती है।)

'The little' : (Not much but all there is -'जो सब कुछ थोड़ा सा') :

(a) The little money she had, was also spent on medicines.
(जो कुछ थोड़ा सा धन था, सब, अब कुछ नहीं बचा है......)

(b) Use the little time you have in a proper way now.
(जो कुछ थोड़ा सा समय बचा है.....)

5. Few / A Few / The Few :

'Few' का प्रयोग countables के लिए किया जाता है। 'few' का अर्थ नकारात्मक (नगण्य, न के बराबर) होता है। 'A few' का अर्थ , 'कुछ' होता है, जबकि 'The few' का अर्थ 'जो भी थोड़ा सा सब' होता है :

(A) Use of 'Few': Means'—Hardly any' - नगण्य, न के बराबर :

(a) Few people are fully happy. (नगण्य व्यक्ति)

(b) Few men are free from any disease. (न के बराबर या कोई नहीं)

(B) Use of 'A few' means— 'थोड़े से ' (not many) :

(a) A few person can write correct English. (कुछ व्यक्ति)

(b)He asked me a few questions. (कुछ प्रश्न)

(C) Use of 'The few' means— 'not many but all there are' -'जो भी थोड़ा सा सब ' :

(a)The few utensils she had, were taken by the thief.
(थोड़े से सारे बर्तन - अब और बर्तन नहीं बचे हैं।)

(b)The few clothes he had, were burnt in fire. (थोड़े से कपड़े, सारे - अब और कपड़े नहीं है।)

ध्यान रखें

Few का अर्थ Negative(नगण्य) में होता है एवं 'A few' तथा 'The few' का अर्थ positive में होता है। इनका सही प्रयोग करना आना महत्त्वपूर्ण है।

6. Fewer / Less / Lesser :

(A) 'Fewer' का प्रयोग countables में ' कम संख्या ' हेतु किया जाता है :

(B) 'Less' का प्रयोग Uncountables हेतु ' थोड़ी मात्रा ' हेतु किया जाता है। Price एवं Number के साथ less का प्रयोग नहीं करना चाहिये।

(C) 'Lesser' का अर्थ होता है 'कम महत्त्वपूर्ण' :

(a) Fewer persons were present in the meeting.

(b) I have less time for my preparations.

(c) Many lesser speakers also came to speak.

Generally, when we're talking about countable things, we use the word 'fewer'; when we're talking about measurable quantities that we cannot count, we use the word 'less'.

7. Later / Latest / Latter / Last :

'Later' एवं 'Latest' का प्रयोग सामान्य रूप से समय के सन्दर्भ में किया जाता है। 'Latter' एवं 'Last' का प्रयोग स्थिति (क्रम) इंगित करने के सन्दर्भ में किया जाता है। जब दो के लिए स्थिति / क्रम के सन्दर्भ में प्रयोग किया जाना हो तो 'Latter' का, एवं दो से अधिक के सन्दर्भ में 'Last' का प्रयोग (बाद वाले को बताने के लिये) किया जाता है।

'Latest' का अर्थ होता है। - 'Last up to now only', अर्थात-'अब तक जो अन्तिम है', जबकि 'Last' का अर्थ होता है-'अन्तिम', उसके बाद कोई नहीं (finally last)।

Look at the following sentences :

(a) He came later than I (मेरे बाद, समय के क्रम अनुसार).

(b) Between Ram and 'Shyam, the latter is more intelligent'.
(क्रम से बाद में अर्थात् 'Shyam is more intelligent')

(c) This is the latest technology. (अब तक की सबसे अन्तिम – सबसे नई।)

(d) Lord Mountbatten was the last Governor General of India.(अन्तिम – उसके बाद कोई नहीं)

8. Elder / Eldest / Older / Oldest :

'Elder' एवं 'Eldest' का प्रयोग एक ही परिवार के सदस्यों हेतु किया जाता है। 'Older / Oldest' का प्रयोग व्यक्तियों एवं वस्तुओं दोनों के लिये किया जा सकता है। 'Elder' के साथ हमेशा 'to' preposition प्रयुक्त होता है, जबकि 'older' के साथ 'than' preposition प्रयुक्त होता है :

(a) Ram is my elder brother.

(b) My mother is the eldest member of our family.

(c) Ram is older than Shyam.

(d) Sunder and Purinder are real brothers. Sunder is elder to purinder.

(e) This is the oldest college in our city.

(f) The older people should be respected.

9. Farther / Further / Farthest :

'Farther' का अर्थ होता है-तुलनात्मक रूप से अधिक दूर। 'Farther' यह 'far' की Comparative degree है तथा 'Farthest', 'Far' की Superlative degree है, जिसका अर्थ है सबसे अधिक दूर। 'Further' का अर्थ होता है Additional (अतिरिक्त)। 'Farther' एवं **'Farthest' का प्रयोग दूरी के सन्दर्भ में तथा 'Further' का प्रयोग Action या सूचना आदि के सन्दर्भ में सामान्यतया किया जाता है :**

(a) Mumbai is farther from Alwar than that of Jaipur.

(b) No further action is required.

(c) Please don't make further delay.

(d) It is the farthest place from the railway station.

10. Some / Any :

'Some' का प्रयोग सामान्यतया Affirmative वाक्यों में Countables एवं Uncountables दोनों के साथ किया जा सकता है। Interrogative Sentence में 'Some' का प्रयोग Request या Commands के रूप में किया जाता है। 'Some' के साथ Request का अर्थ सामान्य रूप से मान ली जाने वाली Request के लिये होता है :

(a) I shall buy some books. (Countables)

(b) They have purchased some fruit. (Uncountables)

(c) Will you give me some milk? (Request)

(d) Can you lend me some rupees? (Request)

Any : 'Any' का प्रयोग सामान्यतया Negative एवं Interrogative वाक्यों में Countables एवं Uncountables दोनों के लिये किया जा सकता है :

(a) I don't have any pen.

(b) Have you any novel?

(c) He hasn't purchased any fruits.

(d) Did anyone come here?

11. No any :

'No any' कोई phrase नहीं है। अत: इसका प्रयोग गलत है। जैसे निम्न वाक्य अशुद्ध है :

(a) I have no any book. —*Incorrect*

(b) I have no pencil. —*Correct*

चूँकी 'No' एवं 'any' दोनों adjective हैं, अत: दोनों एक noun का गुण नहीं बता सकते अत: दोनों का एक साथ प्रयोग गलत है।

12. Near / Next :

'Near' का प्रयोग दूरी के सन्दर्भ में किया जाता है, जबकि 'Next' का प्रयोग क्रम (order) के सन्दर्भ में किया जाता है :

(a) Ram lives near to my school.

(b) She is sitting next to her father.

3. Much / Many :

Much - परिमाण (quantity) के लिए प्रयुक्त होता है।

Many - संख्या (Number) को व्यक्त करता है।

Much एवं many का प्रयोग सामान्यतया Negative एवं Interrogative वाक्यों में किया जाता है। जैसे:

(a) I haven't much patience. (b) She hasn't much money.

(c) Have you much money? (d) I haven't many chairs.

(e) He hasn't many cars. (f) Have you many friends?

Note (1) *Affirmative वाक्यों में much / many का प्रयोग subject के साथ हो सकता है लेकिन object के साथ नहीं होता है :*

(a) Many people came to see the temple. (b) Much milk was required.

यहाँ people एवं milk, subjects हैं, अत: इनके साथ many / much का प्रयोग उचित है। लेकिन यदि इनका प्रयोग object की तरह निम्न प्रकार किया जावे तो गलत होगा :

(a) I know many persons. (b) I learned many poems. — Incorrect

(c) He bought much sugar. (d) She put much water. — Incorrect

यहाँ many / much का प्रयोग एक object की तरह affirmative sentences में किया गया है जो गलत है।

(2) *Affirmative sentences में Object की तरह 'much / many' की अपेक्षा निम्न phrases का प्रयोग करना चाहिए– 'a lot of, lots of, a plenty of, a large quantity of, a large number of' etc.*

(3) *Much / many के साथ 'as, how, too' का प्रयोग करने पर, इनका (much / many का) प्रयोग subject एवं object के साथ भी किया जा सकता है। जैसे :*

(a) She has too many friends.

(b) I don't have too much milk.

(c) I don't remember how many persons came here.

(d) You can purchase as many books as you like.

(e) You can take as much water as you need.

(f) I don't know how much sugar is needed.

14. Whole / All :

(A) 'Whole' का प्रयोग जब एक adjective की तरह किया जाता है, तो इससे पहले 'the' का प्रयोग करना चाहिए, जैसे :

(a) He wasted the whole day. (b) I worked the whole day.

(B) 'Whole' का प्रयोग जब Proper noun के पहले किया जाता है, तो इससे पहले 'the' तथा बाद में 'of' का प्रयोग किया जाता है। जैसे :

(a) <u>The whole</u> of India mourned the death of Rajeev Gandhi.

(C) 'All' का प्रयोग जब plural noun के साथ किया जाता है तो 'All' के बाद 'the' का प्रयोग करना होता है। Possessive noun या pronoun के साथ 'All' हमेशा उससे पहले आता है :

(a) <u>All the</u> students were happy. (b) <u>All my</u> friends went to party.

15. Both :

(A) 'Both' का प्रयोग जब वाक्य में एक adjective की तरह किया जाता है तो इसके बाद 'the' का प्रयोग किया जाता है। **'The' कभी भी 'Both' के पहले नहीं लगता है। जैसे :**

(a) I know *both the* women. (b) She knows *both the* boys.

(B) Personal pronouns के साथ 'Both of' का प्रयोग किया जाता है :

(a) Both of them can come tomorrow. (b) She invited both of us.

(C) 'Both' का प्रयोग pronouns के बाद object की तरह भी किया जाता है :

(a) She invited us both. (b) She sends you both her love.

(D) 'Both .....not' के प्रयोग की जगह 'Neither of them' का प्रयोग करना चाहिए :

(a) Both of them are not here. *—Incorrect*

(b) Neither of them is here. *—Correct*

16. As ....as / So ....as :

'As.........as' का प्रयोग तुलनात्मक वाक्यों में Similarity / Likeliness व्यक्त करने हेतु किया जाता है।

'So ....as' का प्रयोग ऐसे वाक्यों में Unlikeliness, dissimilarity (negative वाक्यों में) व्यक्त करने हेतु किया जाता है। जैसे:

(a) He is as intelligent as his sister. (b) He is not so intelligent as his sister.

17. Another / Other / Any other :

'Another' का प्रयोग Singular noun के साथ, तथा 'other' का प्रयोग plural noun के साथ किया जाता है। 'Any other' का प्रयोग सामान्यतया negative वाक्यों में singular एवं plural दोनों तरह के nouns के साथ हो सकता है :

(a) He has purchased another book. (b) She has visited other places.

(c) I haven't seen any other place. (d) They haven't visited any other places.

18. First / Foremost :

'First' का प्रयोग क्रम में, 'प्रथम' को इंगित करने के लिये होता है, जबकि 'foremost' का अर्थ 'महत्त्वपूर्ण' होता है, जैसे:

(a) Ram was the first to arrive here.

(b) Indira Gandhi was the foremost politician of her time.

19. Verbal / Oral :

'Verbal' एवं 'oral' को आजकाल समान अर्थ में प्रयुक्त किया जाने लगा है। 'Oral' का अर्थ होता है 'जुबानी', 'मौखिक'; जबकि 'verbal' का अर्थ होता है 'शब्दिक'। a verbal picture, an oral message.

(a) There is verbal similarity in these two essays.

(b) He informed me orally, about his absence.

20. Due to / owing to :

(A) 'Due to' का अर्थ है 'result of'(कारण से) जबकि 'owing to' का अर्थ है 'Because of'(इस कारण)। 'Due to' में 'to' का प्रयोग एक preposition की तरह हुआ है।

(B) 'Due to' का प्रयोग subject + verb के बाद किया जाता है। 'owing to' का सामान्यतया प्रयोग वाक्य के शुरू में होता है।

Look at the following sentences :

(a) He failed due to his negligence. (b) Owing to his negligence, he failed.

(c) The accident was due to carelessness. (d) Owing to carelessness, there was an accident.

Important Rules

Determiners/Adjective के सम्बन्ध में निम्न नियमों का अध्ययन करें। परीक्षा में आने वाले अधिकांश प्रश्न इन्हीं में से पूछे जाते हैं।

1. जब किसी वस्तु का comparison किया जाता है तो compare करते समय उस वस्तु को exclude करना चाहिए, जैसे :

(a) This building is larger than any building in the town. — *Incorrect*
This building is larger than *any other* building in the town. — *Correct*
(b) Ram is stronger than all students. — *Incorrect*
Ram is stronger than *any other* student. — *Correct*

2. एक वाक्य में दो comparative adjectives का एक साथ प्रयोग करना गलत है। जैसे:

(a) He is *more wiser* than you. — *Incorrect*
He is *wiser than* you. — *Correct*

यदि एक adjective comparative degree में है तो उसके साथ positive degree का प्रयोग किया जाता है। **'Comparatively' शब्द के साथ भी comparative degree के Adjective का प्रयोग नहीं करना चाहिये। Comparative से पहले 'rather' का प्रयोग किया जा सकता है ;** She is rather better today. लेकिन ऐसे वाक्यों में 'fairly' का प्रयोग नहीं करना चाहिए ; She is fairly better today. यह गलत है।

3. कुछ Adjectives; जैसे : senior, junior, posterior, superior, inferior, anterior, prior इत्यादि के साथ preposition 'to' का प्रयोग किया जाता है। Elder, prefer एवं preferable के साथ भी 'to' का ही प्रयोग होता है :

(a) Ram is senior to Shyam. (b) He came prior to me.

Note *Major, minor, exterior, interior, outer, lower, ulterior, upper, former, inner इत्यादि शब्द दीखने में comparative degree adjectives लगते हैं। ये comparative degree नहीं हैं। इनका प्रयोग comparison हेतु नहीं किया जा सकता।*

4. जब एक ही व्यक्ति या वस्तु की दो qualities की तुलना की जाती है तो 'er' से बने comparative adjective का प्रयोग नहीं करना चाहिए, बल्कि 'more' का प्रयोग करना चाहिए। जैसे:

(a) Ram is more strong than intelligent. (यहाँ stronger का प्रयोग गलत होगा।)

5. जब दो वस्तुओं का comparison किया जाता है, तो वाक्य से उन वस्तुओं का ही comparison स्पष्ट होना चाहिऐ। कई बार comparison करते समय निम्न प्रकार की गलती की जाती है।

(a) The climate of Alwar is hotter than Jaipur. — *Incorrect*
The climate of Alwar is hotter than that of Jaipur. — *Correct*
अर्थात, अलवर की climate, जयपुर की **climate** की तुलना में अपेक्षाकृत Hotter है (न कि जयपुर शहर से)।

6. Comparative degree का प्रयोग, दो वस्तुओं या व्यक्तियों हेतु किया जाता है। दो से अधिक के लिये comparative degree का प्रयोग नहीं करना चाहिए। जैसे :

(a) Which is better ; Tea, coffee or milk? — *Incorrect*
(b) Which is easier, Physics, Chemistry or Math? — *Incorrect*
ये दोनों वाक्य गलत हैं।

7. दो वस्तुओं की तुलना हेतु superlative degree का प्रयोग नहीं किया जाता है :

(a) He is the best of the two students. — *Incorrect*
(b) Which is the cheapest ; silver or gold? — *Incorrect*
ये दोनों वाक्य गलत हैं।

8. वाक्य में दो superlatives का प्रयोग एक साथ किया जाना त्रुटिपूर्ण है :

(a) He is the most strongest of all. — *Incorrect*
He is the strongest of all. — *Correct*

9. Superlative के साथ 'other or else' का प्रयोग करना भी त्रुटिपूर्ण है :

(a) She is the most beautiful of all girls. (not all other girls)

10. कुछ वाक्य ऐसे होते हैं , जिनमें adjective की comparative degree का प्रयोग दोनों भागों में निम्न प्रकार से होता है :

(a) *The more* she gets, *the more* she demands.

(b) *The richer* a man is, *the larger* house he owns

इस प्रकार के वाक्यों में दोनों comparative degrees से पहले 'the' का प्रयोग होता है।

11. कई वाक्यों में 'a most' का प्रयोग 'very' के अर्थ में किया जाता है। जैसे :

(a) This is a most interesting book. (in the library)

(b) She is a most beautiful girl. (in the school)

ऐसे वाक्यों में superlative की तरह 'in the library', या 'in the school' का प्रयोग नहीं होगा।

12. जब एक से अधिक Adjectives को 'and' से जोड़ा जाता है तो सभी Adjectives एक ही degree में होने चाहिएँ; या तो सब comparative में हों या सब superlative में होने चाहिएँ। जैसे :

(a) Ram is *wiser and stronger* than Shyam —*Correct*

Ram is *wise and stronger* than Shyam —*Incorrect*

13. कई adjectives अपने meaning के कारण न तो comparative की तरह प्रयोग किये जा सकते हैं, न ही superlative की अन्य degree के साथ। इनके साथ very या अन्य कोई adverb, इनको emphasise करने के लिये प्रयुक्त नहीं किया जा सकता है; ऐसे Adjectives हैं :

Absolute, Perfect, Full, Complete, Entire, Whole, Chief, Extreme,. Unique, Universal, Circular, Square, Round ,Ideal, Flat, Impossible etc.

यद्यपि आजकल कुछ लेखक 'full, fuller, fullest', एवं 'perfect, more perfect एवं most perfect', तथा 'most impossible' एवं 'most universal' का प्रयोग करने लगे हैं; शेष adjective का इस तरह प्रयोग नहीं किया गया है।

14. 'Kind' एवं 'sort', singular number होते हैं। इनके साथ 'This' या 'That' का प्रयोग होता है। इनके साथ 'These' या 'Those' का प्रयोग करना गलत है :

(a) I don't like *this* kind of dresses. —*Correct*

(b) He doesn't like *that* kind of shirts. —*Correct*

(c) I don't like *these* kinds of shirts. —*Incorrect*

(d) I don't like *those* kind of shirts. —*Incorrect*

15. 'One of ....if not the........ Superlative –कुछ वाक्यों का Structure इस तरह का होता है। जैसे :

(a) He is one of the greatest writers, if not the greatest writer.

(b) This is one of the largest buildings, if not the largest in the world.

इस तरह के वाक्यों में 'one of the superlative' के बाद plural noun (writers, buildings) प्रयुक्त होती है तथा 'if not the superlative' के बाद singular noun प्रयुक्त होती है। साधारणतया ऐसे वाक्यो में 'if not the superlative' के बाद noun को नहीं लिखा जाता है।

16. कुछ वाक्यों का structure इस प्रकार का होता है, '........Comparative + and + comparative':

(a) He is getting richer and richer. (b) The weather is getting cooler and cooler.

ऐसे वाक्यों में comparative से पूर्व 'the' का प्रयोग नहीं होता है।

17. कुछ वाक्यों का structure निम्न प्रकार का होता है :

(a) She runs as fast as, if not faster than Shyam.

(b) He is as good as if not better than you.

ऐसे वाक्यों में 'as ....:as' (दोनों बार 'as') का प्रयोग होता है, तथा दूसरे भाग में Comparative degree का प्रयोग होता है।

ERRORS, MISTAKES AND BLUNDERS IN USE OF ADJECTIVES/DETERMINERS

Exercise : ***Rewrite the following sentences after correction.***

1. Whole girls were present in the function.
2. All the third books are in our course.
3. This is mine bed, which is your ?
4. None of these two books are useful.
5. A good deal of persons were present at the railway station.
6. All the sides of the coin are shining.
7. He alone lives in such a large house.
8. The both girls have arrived.
9. She is among the four first merit holders.
10. Lord Ram was an incarnate God.
11. Our all members are very cooperative.
12. His all books have been burnt in fire.
13. I bought tickets three for Delhi.
14. The Great Ashoka was a brave king.
15. This custom has been observed since immemorial time.
16. Have you new anything to tell me about the incident.?
17. Ram is as taller as his brother.
18. Sita is not more beautiful as Rita.
19. Gold is more precious than any metal.
20. She is not that all reliable.
21. To drive is as difficult as fishing.
22. It is as difficult to swim as driving.
23. It is not as easy to write as reading.
24. They had better died than surrender before the enemy.
25. I had rather read than wasting my time here.
26. He is junior than me.
27. According to Ram, milk is preferable than tea.
28. She is more wiser than her brother.
29. My house is better than Ram.
30. The climate of Udaipur is better than Jaipur.
31. There are lesser rooms in this hotel than that.
32. Take this tablet with a few milk.
33. Your problem is comparatively easier than that of mine.
34. The quality of this detergent powder is comparatively better.
35. He runs as faster, if not fast than you.
36. Sita is as beautiful as if not beautiful than her sister.
37. The more you hide something, the most you expose yourself.
38. This is all the more better.
39. The valley goes deep and deep after this point.
40. Ram said, "I am very better now."
41. The cloth of this suit is very inferior.
42. This is longest river in the world.
43. He is the richest of all man in the city.
44. He is the strongest of all other students in the college.
45. Ramesh is one of the best student in the college.
46. He is my the best friend.
47. Ramesh is one of the strongest person, if not the strongest in the town.
48. I shall purchase the bigger of all these houses.
49. Mr. Sharma is the most ideal teacher.
50. This is more the best college in the city.
51. I have the best and a cheaper magazine.
52. This is out and in the best. hospital.
53. Which of these books do you like the most ?
54. I don't like these kind of apples.
55. I don't like these sort of men.
56. The poors should be helped.
57. That was a most excellent opportunity to earn good money.
58. She reached here the earliest of both girls.
59. This is the much best school.
60. She is getting weak and weaker.
61. He is braver than stronger.
62. The quality of this shirt is superior than yours.
63. Ram came prior than me .
64. The Ghee of Haryana is better than Rajasthan.
65. He is more intelligent than any student of his class.

Explanations

1. All the girls were present in the function.
3. This is my bed, which is yours ?
5. A number of persons were present at the railway station.
7. He lives alone in such a large house.
9. She is among the first four merit holders.
11. All our members are very cooperative.
13. I bought three tickets for Delhi.
15. This custom has been observed since time immemorial.
17. Ram is as tall as his brother.
19. Gold is more precious than any other metal.
21. Driving is as difficult as fishing.
23. It is not as easy to write as read.
25. I had rather read than waste my time here.
27. According to Ram, milk is preferable to tea.
29. My house is better than Ram's.
31. There are fewer rooms in this hotel than that.
33. Your problem is comparatively easy than that of mine.
35. He runs as fast, if not faster than you.
37. The more you hide something, the more you expose yourself.
39. The valley goes deeper and deeper after this point.
41. The cloth of this suit is much inferior.
43. He is the richest of all men in the city.
45. Ramesh is one of the best students in the college.
47. Ramesh is one of the strongest persons, if not the strongest in the town.
49. Mr. Sharma is an ideal teacher.
51. I have the best and the cheapest magazine.
53. Which of these books do you like most ?
55. I don't like this sort of men.
57. That was an excellent opportunity to earn good money.
59. This is the very best school. or This is much the best school.
61. He is more brave than strong.

2. All the three books are in our course.
4. Neither of these two books is useful.
6. Both the sides of the coin are shining.
8. Both the girls have arrived.
10. Lord Ram was God inarnate.
12. All his books have been burnt in fire.
14. Ashoka the Great was a brave king.
16. Have you anything new to tell me about the incident.?
18. Sita is not as beautiful as Rita. or Sita is not more beautiful than Rita
20. She is not all that reliable.
22. It is as difficult to swim as drive
24. They had better die than surrender before the enemy.
26. He is junior to me.
28. She is wiser than her brother.
30. The climate of Udaipur is better than that of Jaipur.
32. Take this tablet with a little milk.
34. The quality of this detergent powder is comparatively good.
36. Sita is as beautiful as if not more beautiful than her sister.
38. This is all the better.
40. Ram said, "I am much better now."
42. This is the longest river in the world.
44. He is the strongest of all students in the college.
46. He is my best friend.
48. I shall purchase the biggest of all these houses.
50. This is much the best college in the city.
52. This is out and out the best hospital.
54. I don't like this kind of apples.
56. The poor should be helped.
58. She reached here the earliest, of all girls.
60. She is getting weaker and weaker.
62. The quality of this shirt is superior to yours.

63. Ram came prior to me.

64. The Ghee of Haryana is better than that of Rajasthan.

65. He is more intelligent than any other student of his class.

SPOTTING THE ERRORS

Exercise : *Find the errors and justify your answers.*

1. Kolkata is further (A) /from Alwar (B) /than Jaipur (C) /the capital of Rajasthan (D).
2. Ramesh is smarter (A) /enough to get (B) /selected for this (C) /post, without any recommendations (D).
3. He said, "Priyanka (A) /is the most unique (B) /singer of (C) /our college" (D).
4. This shirt is (A) /comparatively better (B) /than that (C) /we saw in corner shop yesterday (D).
5. Everyone was surprised to note (A) /that Rahim married a girl (B) /who was more beautiful and more tall (C) /than he (D).
6. A lots of books (A) /on English grammar are (B) /available with me but (C) /this one is the best (D).
7. I told her (A) /that it would be all (B) /the more better (C) /if she herself talked to the groom (D).
8. She does not have (A) /some money to buy (B) /a new refrigerator (C) /so she is worried (D).
9. Now a days (A) /the weather (B) /is getting more cold (C) /and colder (D).
10. All the books (A) /were indeed interesting (B) /but that one was (C) /the more interesting (D).
11. There were only two (A)/warriors but each and every (B)/warrior was equal (C)/to six persons (D).
12. Whole the chapter (A) /of this grammar book is full of errors (B) /that shows the (C) /carelessness of the proof reader (D).
13. Can we rely (A) /on this agency (B) /for the last news (C) /of the day (D)?
14. Ram is junior than (A) /Shyam and (B) Ram is older (C) /than Ganesh (D).
15. The militants (A) /entered the palace (B) /from the utmost gate (C) /with guns hidden in their clothes (D).
16. "She can't sing (A) /much than (B) /four songs at (C) /a stretch", he informed (D).
17. It is well know (A) /that Mrs Indira Gandhi (B) /was the first statesman (C) /of her time (D).

Explanations

1. (A) Change 'further' to 'farther'. Farther का अर्थ-'अधिक दूर', तथा 'further' का अर्थ 'आगे' होता है। 'Farther', 'far'की comparative degree है।
2. (A) 'smarter' की जगह 'smart' लिखा जायेगा। ध्यान रखें, enough के पूर्व, positive degree का प्रयोग होता है।
3. (B) unique के पूर्व, 'the most' को delete करें। ध्यान रखें: कुछ adjectives; unique, full, whole, square universal, etc. अपने अर्थ के कारण superlative degree की तरह प्रयुक्त होते हैं। इनको compare नहीं किया जा सकता है। 'more unique, more complete' या 'more square' लिखना एवं 'most unique, most complete' या 'most square' लिखना गलत है।
4. (B) 'Comparatively' के साथ positive degree के Adjective का प्रयोग होता है। अत: या तो 'comparatively good' लिखा जायेगा या केवल 'better' लिखा जायेगा।
5. (C) 'more tall' की जगह 'taller' होगा। सामान्यतया one syllable के adjective का comparative उसमें 'er'या 'r'जोड़कर बनाया जाता है।

6. (A) 'A lots of' की जगह या तो 'lots of' लिखें या 'A lot of' लिखें।
7. (C) 'more better' लिखना गलत है। Avoid double comparatives; 'more'को delete करें।
8. (B) 'some money' की जगह 'any money' लिखा जावेगा। इस तरह के negative वाक्यों में 'some' की जगह 'Any' का प्रयोग होता है।
9. (C) 'more cold' की जगह 'colder' लिखा जावेगा। इस तरह के वाक्यों में comparative degree of adjective का प्रयोग निम्न प्रकार से होता है :
   (a) He is becoming stronger and stronger.   (b) The weather is getting hotter and hotter.
10. (D) 'more' की जगह 'most' का प्रयोग किया जायेगा। जब दो से अधिक वस्तुओं की परस्पर तुलना हो, तो superlative degree of adjective का प्रयोग किया जाता है। दो वस्तुओं में तुलना हेतु comparative degree का प्रयोग होता है।
11. (B) Change 'each and every' to 'each'. ध्यान रखें 'each' का प्रयोग दो हेतु किन्तु 'each and every' या 'every' का प्रयोग हमेंशा दो से अधिक के लिए होता है।
12. (A) 'Whole the' की जगह 'The whole' लिखा जायेगा; 'whole' के पूर्व 'The' प्रयुक्त होता है।
13. (C) 'last' की जगह 'latest' लिखा जायेगा। समय के सन्दर्भ में 'late' की comparative एवं superlative degree 'later, latest' हैं।
14. (A) 'than' की जगह 'to'का प्रयोग होगा; junior, senior, prior, etc के साथ 'to' का प्रयोग किया जाता है।
15. (C) 'Utmost' की जगह 'outer most' लिखा जायेगा। 'out' का comparative, 'outer' एवं superlative; 'outer-most' होता है। 'Utmost' का अर्थ-'complete' (पूर्णतया) होता है। यहाँ 'Utmost' का गलत प्रयोग हुआ है।
16. (B) 'much' की जगह 'more' का प्रयोग होगा। 'Much'- positive degree का Adjective है, जिसका comparative 'more' है।
17. (C) यहाँ 'first' की जगह 'foremost' का प्रयोग किया जायेगा। 'first' का अर्थ-'प्रथम' होता है, जबकि 'foremost' का अर्थ 'most notable' (सर्वाधिक चर्चित) होता है। वाक्य के सन्दर्भ के अनुसार 'foremost' का प्रयोग ही उचित है।

BLUNDERS IN USE OF ADJECTIVES

Exercise : ***Correct the following sentences and justfy your corrections.***

1. Between Sita and Sarla, the later is more intelligent
2. Ram and Shyam are real brothers. Shyam is elder than Ram.
3. Rahul is stronger than any student of his class.
4. The scenery of Kashmir is more beautiful than Jaipur.
5. Ramesh is the most strongest of all students in the college.
6. Which is better ; tea, milk or coffee?
7. I didn't find more costlier gift than this one.
8. Rahim is junior than Shyam .
9. He is minor than you.
10. This glass in more square in shape among all the glasses .

Explanations

1. 'later' की जगह 'latter' का प्रयोग होगा। क्रम में बाद में आने हेतु 'latter' का प्रयोग होता है।
2. 'elder' के साथ हमेशा 'to' का प्रयोग होता है।

3. 'than any *other* student' होगा।
4. सही वाक्य होगा – The scenery of Kashmir is more beautiful than that of Jaipur.
5. एक वाक्य में दो Superlative degrees का प्रयोग न करें । 'Most' को delete करें ।
6. Comparative degree of adjective का प्रयोग दो वस्तुओं के comparison हेतु ही किया जा सकता है।
7. 'Costlier' का अर्थ ही 'अधिक Costly' है अत: इस वाक्य को इस तरह लिखा जाना चाहिये -I didn't find more costly gift than this one.
8. Junior के साथ हमेशा 'to' आता है। इसी प्रकार 'superior, elder, prefer' के साथ भी 'to' आता है।
9. 'minor', Comparative degree of adjective नहीं है। 'minor' का अर्थ है –'अवयस्क'। अत: सही वाक्य होगा –He is younger than you.
10. 'Square, Complete, Absolute' जैसे Adjectives को अपने अर्थ के कारण Compare नहीं किया जा सकता है। Square का More Square करके Comparative बनाना गलत है।
    अत: सही वाक्य होगा – 'This glass is square in shape among all the glasses.'

❑❑❑

12

Pronoun

Pronoun, English Grammar का बहुत महत्त्वपूर्ण concept है। विभिन्न प्रकार के Pronouns के सही प्रयोग के सम्बन्ध में नियमों का अध्ययन ध्यानपूर्वक करें। 'That/which' तथा 'who/whom' के उचित प्रयोग के सम्बन्ध में विभिन्न बिन्दुओं का भी ध्यानपूर्वक अध्ययन करें। Errors के सम्बन्ध में प्रश्न अधिकांशतया इन्हीं पर आधारित होते हैं।

Pronoun : जो शब्द Noun की जगह प्रयुक्त होता है, उसे Pronoun कहते हैं।
Generally (but not always) pronouns stand for (pro + noun) or refer to a noun, an individual or individuals or thing or things (the pronoun's antecedent) whose identity is made clear earlier in the text. For example:
Ramesh found a purse. He picked it up and gave it to Sarla. She threw it into a river.
इस वाक्य में 'He', Ramesh (Noun) के लिये, 'it', purse (Noun) के लिये तथा 'She', Sarla (Noun) के लिये प्रयुक्त हुऐ हैं। अत: He, it एवं she, pronouns हैं।

KINDS OF PRONOUN

Personal Pronoun

वे pronouns जो व्यक्ति का बोध कराते हैं, **Personal pronouns** कहलाते हैं। **'I, we,'** - first person, **'You'** second person pronoun तथा **'He, she, it, they'**, आदि third person pronoun हैं।

Personal Pronoun : Use and Rules

1. **यदि एक वाक्य में भिन्न - भिन्न Persons के pronouns एक ही verb के साथ प्रयुक्त होते हैं, तो उनको लिखने का क्रम (order) निम्न प्रकार होगा :-**

   (A) Singular : सबसे पहले 'you' (second person), उसके बाद 'he' (third person) एवं उसके बाद 'I' (First person), Good manners की दृष्टि से, लिखा जाता है। इसको याद रखने का तरीका है 2+3+1 (second + third + first person pronoun). जैसे :

   (a) You, he and I are partners. (b) He and I are good friends.

   (B) Plural में यह क्रम 1+2+3 होता है। जैसे :

   (a) We and you cannot live together. (b) We, you and they can purchase that complex.

   (C) यदि वाक्य में कोई गलती का सन्दर्भ आये या कोई भूल या अपराध का जिक्र हो या वाक्य का भाव सकारात्मक नहीं हो तो Pronouns का क्रम 1+2+3 की तरह होना चाहिये :

   (a) I and you are responsible for the loss.(b) You and he spoiled the party.

2. **यदि वाक्य में एक से अधिक भिन्न - भिन्न persons के pronouns का प्रयोग होता है एवं उनके लिये एक ही plural pronoun का प्रयोग किया जाये तो Third एवं First person के साथ First person plural ; Second एवं Third person के साथ Second person plural - एवं second एवं first के लिये, First person plural pronoun का प्रयोग होगा। यदि तीनों Persons का प्रयोग हुआ है, तो Pronoun- First Person Plural होगा।**

III + I ---------------- I Person plural
II + III --------------- II Person plural
II + I ----------------- I Person plural

(a) You and I have done our job. (b) You and he have completed your job.
(c) He and I have done our duty. (d) You he and I have completed our duty.

3. Collective Noun के साथ, Pronoun का प्रयोग उस स्थिति में Singular (and Neuter Gender) में होता है, जब Collective Noun का प्रयोग एक Unit के रूप में हो; यदि Collective Noun का प्रयोग Unit की तरह न होकर, dividedly हुआ होता है तो plural pronoun प्रयोग किया जाता है :

(a) The crew revolted and murdered its captain.
(b) After three days, the jury gave its verdict.

उपरोक्त वाक्यों में Collective Noun, एक unit की तरह प्रयुक्त है, अत: Pronoun, 'its', Singular एवं Neuter Gender में प्रयुक्त है।

Look at the following sentences :

(a) The jury were divided in *their* opinions.
(b) The society took the decision without leaving *their* seats.

4. जब दो Singular Nouns, 'and' से संयुक्त हों एवं दोनों के पूर्व 'each' या 'every' का प्रयोग हुआ हो, तो Pronoun भी singular होगा :

(a) Every soldier and every sailor was in his place.

5. जब एक Plural एवं एक Singular Noun, 'or' या 'nor' से संयुक्त किये जाते हैं, तो pronoun - plural प्रयुक्त होता है :

(a) Either the principal or the teachers failed in **their** duty.

6. 'to be' form of verb के बाद आने वाला Pronoun उसी case में होना चाहिए, जिस case में verb 'to be' के पहले आने वाला Noun या Pronoun प्रयुक्त हुआ है। जैसे :

(A) (a) It is I. (b) It is he.
(c) This is she.

उक्त वाक्यों में 'It' एवं 'This' का प्रयोग nominative case में हुआ है अत: Pronoun, 'I, he,' एवं 'she', nominative case में प्रयुक्त हैं। लेकिन कई विद्वान आजकल :

(B) (a) It is me. (b) This is me.
(c) This is her. (d) This is him.

को भी सही मानते हैं। अत: (A) एवं (B) दोनों ही वाक्य समूह सही हैं। दोनों ही प्रकार के वाक्य प्रचलन में हैं।

ध्यान रखें

यदि इस तरह के वाक्यों में 'Who/Which' के साथ clause का प्रयोग होता है तो, verb 'to be' के बाद आने वाला Pronoun हमेशा nominative case में आता है। जैसे:

(a) It is he who is responsible.
(b) It is she who refused the offer.

Verb 'to be' के पहले आने वाला noun/pronoun यदि objective case में है, तो इसके बाद आने वाला noun या pronoun भी objective case में ही आता है :

(a) I know the girl to be her.
(b) I recognised the student to be him.

यहाँ 'to be' से पहले आने वाले nouns 'girl' एवं 'student', verb; 'know' एवं 'recognised' के object हैं, अत: यहाँ Pronouns 'her' एवं 'him', objective case में हैं।

REFLEXIVE PRONOUN

Some Rules

1. **कुछ Transitive verbs के साथ Reflexive pronoun का प्रयोग किया जाता है। Transitive verb के साथ object का आना आवश्यक है, जब इन verbs के साथ कोई object नहीं होता है, तो Reflexive pronoun लगाकर object की पूर्ति करनी होती है। ऐसी verbs हैं : avail, absent, enjoy, resign, apply, revenge, exert, etc. :**
   (a) I absented myself from the office. (b) I revenged myself upon her.
2. **कुछ Verbs का जब intransitively प्रयोग किया जाता है, तो इनके साथ Reflexive pronoun का प्रयोग नहीं किया जाता है। ऐसी Verbs हैं : Keep, break, set, bathe, make, stop, steal, qualify, move, open, draw, rest, roll, burst, hide, feed, gather etc. सामान्यतया इन verbs का प्रयोग intransitively ही होता है। जैसे :**
   (a) He kept away from the function. —*Correct*
   He kept *himself* away from the function. —*Incorrect*
   (b) She hid in the room. —*Correct*
   She hid *herself* in the room. —*Incorrect*
3. **Reflexive pronoun का निम्न प्रकार से प्रयोग किया जाना गलत है :**
   (a) Myself is R.C. Gupta. (b) Himself will do it. —*Incorrect*

EMPHATIC PRONOUN

Reflexive pronoun एवं Emphatic pronoun बनावट व देखने में एक समान होते हैं। Emphatic pronoun का प्रयोग किसी noun / pronoun को emphasise (महत्त्व बढ़ाने) करने हेतु किया जाता है। जैसे :-
(a) I *myself* solved this question. (b) She *herself* found the solution.
इनका प्रयोग subject के तुरन्त बाद किया जाता है।

DISTRIBUTIVE PRONOUNS

'Each, Everyone, Either' एवं 'Neither'; Distributive Pronouns हैं। ये Pronouns एक व्यक्ति या वस्तु (one at a time) को व्यक्त करते हैं। ये singular होते हैं एवं इनके साथ singular verbs का प्रयोग किया जाता है।

1. 'Everyone' का प्रयोग हमेशा दो से अधिक के सन्दर्भ में होता है। जबकि 'Each' का प्रयोग दो या दो से अधिक के लिये हो सकता है। **दो के लिये Everyone का प्रयोग कभी नहीं किया जाता है।**
   (a) Each of the students gets a prize one by one.
   (b) Everyone of the students was happy to receive a prize.
   (c) Each of the two students received a medal.
2. 'Either' एवं 'Neither' का प्रयोग सामान्यतया दो (व्यक्ति या वस्तु) के सन्दर्भ में किया जाता है। दो से अधिक के लिये 'Any, No one, None' का प्रयोग करना चाहिये।
3. Distributive pronouns के साथ Third person, Singular pronoun, Masculine Gender (he, his, him) का प्रयोग किया जाता है :
   (a) *Everyone* should obey his parents.
   (b) *Neither* of there two students has received his prize.
4. यदि वाक्य में Distributive pronouns के बाद Feminine Gender के Noun का प्रयोग हुआ है, तो 'her' pronoun का प्रयोग करना आवश्यक है। ध्यान रखें, इस case में he, him, his का प्रयोग गलत होगा :
   (a) *Neither* of these two *girls* has deposited *her* fees.

(b) *Either* of the two *girls* has received *her* gift.

यदि feminine noun की जगह plural pronoun (us / them / you) का प्रयोग हुआ हो तो Singular, Masculine gender Pronoun का प्रयोग किया जायेगा। जैसे :

(a) Neither of them has done his duty. (b) Each of them has forgot his purse.

INTERROGATIVE PRONOUN

Who, Whom, Whose, Which, What ; Interrogative Pronouns हैं। इनका प्रयोग प्रश्न पूछने हेतु किया जाता है। The Interrogative pronouns are used for making querries or asking questions :

(a) What is that? (b) Who is he?

(c) Which is your pen? (d) Whose bag is this?

1. उपरोक्त वाक्यों में आये सभी underlined words, Interrogative Pronouns हैं।
2. 'What' का प्रयोग सामान्यतया वस्तुओं या कार्यों के लिये होता है जैसे :

   (a) What is your father? (Father का व्यवसाय क्या है ?)
3. 'Who, Whose, whom' का प्रयोग व्यक्तियों के लिये किया जाता है ; 'Who' का प्रयोग Nominative case में, 'whose' का प्रयोग Possessive case में एवं 'whom' का प्रयोग objective case में किया जाता है। जैसे:

   (a) Who is he? (b) Whom did you see today?

   आजकल कई विद्वान 'whom' की जगह 'who' का ही प्रयोग करने लगे हैं। जैसे :-

   (a) Who have you called? (b) Who do you want to meet?
4. 'Which' का प्रयोग व्यक्तियों एवं वस्तु के लिये selection / choice के लिये सामान्यतया किया जाता है। जैसे :

   (a) Which is your umbrella? (b) Which book is yours?
5. कभी-कभी 'what' एवं 'which' के साथ preposition का प्रयोग निम्न प्रकार होता है :

   (a) What is this table made of ? (b) Which year were you born in?

RELATIVE PRONOUN

Rules

1. **Relative Pronouns, 'who' एवं 'whom' का प्रयोग निर्जीव वस्तुओं के लिये नहीं किया जाता है। इनका प्रयोग व्यक्ति एवं अन्य living nouns हेतु किया जाता है। 'Who' का प्रयोग Nominative case में तथा 'whom' का प्रयोग objective case में किया जाता है। 'People' एवं 'those' के साथ 'who' का ही प्रयोग किया जाता है।**

   (a) I like the boy who helps the poor. (Nominative)

   (b) This is the girl whom all admire. (Objective case)
2. **'Whose' का possessive case में प्रयोग, सामान्यतया व्यक्ति एवं जानवर को इंगित करने के लिये किया जाता है। कई स्थितियों में 'whose' का प्रयोग Non- living nouns हेतु भी किया जाता है :**

   (a) This is the boy whose parents have died.

   (b) The sun, whose rays give us light, is adored like a God.
3. **'Which' का प्रयोग non living nouns एवं animals हेतु किया जाता है :**

   (a) The book which I purchased yesterday is useless.

   (b) The dog which was caught by the municipality has died.
4. **'What' का प्रयोग वस्तुओं के लिये किया जाता है। इससे पूर्व कोई antecedent नहीं आता है। वाक्य में Antecedent का प्रयोग होने पर 'what' की जगह 'that' का प्रयोग होगा :**

   (a) What can't be cured must be endured. (b) What he told you is not correct.

5. Use of 'That'.

(A) 'That' का प्रयोग living एवं non-living , nouns के लिये, singular वें plural दोनों nouns के साथ होता है :

(a) I have lost the book that you gave me.
(b) I haven't read the magazine that the teacher suggested to me.

(B) 'That' से पूर्व कोई preposition नहीं प्रयुक्त होता है यदि preposition प्रयोग करने की आवश्यकता हो तो वह वाक्य के अन्त में प्रयुक्त होता है :

(a) We know the hotel that she lives *in*.
(b) I understand the point that you are hinting *at*.

Superlative degree के बाद 'that' का प्रयोग 'who' या 'which' की अपेक्षा अधिक उचित माना जाता है :

(a) He is the most eloquent speaker that I have ever heard.
(b) Patel was the greatest man that India produced.

(C) निम्नलिखित शब्दों के साथ 'that' का प्रयोग किया जाता है।

All, any, anybody, anything, much, nothing, little, somebody, no one, none : Sentence structures :

the same + noun , the only + noun etc. में भी 'that' प्रयुक्त होता है :

(a) All that glitters is not gold.
(b) There was none that didn't support the cause.
(c) It is for nothing that I have been trying to find.
(d) There is much that he needs.
(e) This is *the same girl* <u>that</u> we met yesterday.
(f) This is *the* only girl <u>that</u> won a gold medal.

(D) Interrogative pronoun - 'who' एवं 'what' के बाद 'that' का ही प्रयोग किया जाता है :

(a) What is it that you can't solve. (b) Who am I that you should care for.

(E) जब दो Antecedents जिनमें एक व्यक्ति को एवं दूसरा जानवर या वस्तु को व्यक्त करे तो Relative pronoun 'that' का प्रयोग किया जाता है :

(a) The boy and his dog that entered the temple were caught by the people.

(F) 'Same' एवं 'such' के बाद 'as' या 'that' का ही प्रयोग होता है, 'who' या 'which' का प्रयोग नहीं करना चाहिये :

(a) This is the same fellow that came yesterday also.

6. वाक्य में Relative Pronoun का antecedent, possessive case में नहीं होना चाहिए। यह एक गलत structure है। जैसे :

(a) These are chairman's instructions that must be followed. —*Incorrect*
(b) I went to Sarla's house, who is my class fellow. —*Incorrect*

इन दोनों वाक्यों में Relative pronoun 'that' एवं 'who' के antecedents, 'chairman' एवं 'Sarla' है जो possessive case में हैं, **यह गलत structure है।** अत: इन वाक्यों को निम्न प्रकार से लिखा जाना चाहिए।

(a) These are the instructions of the chairman that must be followed. —*Correct*
(b) I went to the house of Sarla who is my class fellow. —*Correct*

Who/Whom

Relative Pronoun के विषय में अधिकांश प्रश्न 'who/whom' के प्रयोग के सम्बन्ध में पूछे जाते हैं, जैसे:

(a) The girl **whom** I met yesterday is Sarla's sister. —*Correct*

ऐसे वाक्यों में 'who' का प्रयोग करना गलत है।

(b) The girl **who** came yesterday is Sarla's sister. —*Correct*

इस तरह के वाक्यों में 'whom' का प्रयोग गलत है।

ध्यान रखें ***'Who', Nominative case Pronoun है तथा 'whom', objective case pronoun है। 'Who' के साथ verbs आना आवश्यक है, जबकि 'whom' के साथ verb नहीं आता है।***

जब अपको किसी वाक्य में 'who' एवं 'whom' के प्रयोग के मध्य कोई confusion हो तो आप, वाक्य में subjects एवं verbs की संख्या गिन लें। यदि verbs की संख्या, subjects से अधिक है, तो 'who' का प्रयोग करें। यहाँ यह भी ध्यान रखना होगा कि 'and' से संयुक्त verbs एक ही subject के लिये प्रयुक्त होते हैं, जैसे :

She came and spoke to me. यहाँ verb 'came' एवं 'spoke', 'and' से संयुक्त हैं अत: एक ही subject के लिये प्रयुक्त हैं।

Look at the following example:

The guests (s-1) whom we (s-2) were (v-2) talking about have arrived, (v-3) are (v-1) my relatives.

यहाँ दो subject हैं, 'Guests' एवं 'we' जो क्रमश: 'are' एवं 'were', verbs को लेते हैं। तीसरी verb है 'have arrived' इसके लिये कोई subject नहीं है। अत: इस वाक्य में 'whom' की जगह 'who' आयेगा, जो subject का कार्य करता है।

So, the correct sentence will be :

The guests, who we were talking about have arrived, are my relatives.

Other example:-

The candidates (s-1) whom we (s-2) have chosen (v-2) are (v-1) sincere and energetic.

यहाँ 'whom' का प्रयोग सही है। Here are two verbs and two subjects, so the use of 'Whom' is justified.

ERRORS, MISTAKES AND BLUNDERS IN USE OF PRONOUNS

Exercise : ***Rewrite the following sentences after correction.***

1. Let you and I go to play.
2. There is close relation between he and I.
3. You, he and I have done their job.
4. You and he could not complete his work.
5. He and I have fastened his belts.
6. I, you and he were present in the function.
7. I and you are strangers.
8. You and I are responsible for this loss.
9. He and I were the main accused.
10. You, he and I must beg sorry for the misconduct.
11. Neither of these four vehicles will do.
12. Anyone of the two girls can solve this puzzle.
13. Either of the three students is responsible for the loss.
14. None of the two girls could complete the job.
15. One should obey his elders.
16. One should respect not only his own parents but also other's.
17. One should take care not to make himself obnoxious to others.

18. Each girl and every madam tried their best to finish the work before 7P.M.
19. Every man and every woman have their own fascinations.
20. Every leader and every citizen have a duty towards their country.
21. Each of the employees have to arrange their own vehicle.
22. Every one of them were given their table and chair.
23. Either Ramesh or Sita have left their tiffin box.
24. Either the teacher or the students have left his classroom unlocked .
25. Please take the buffaloe to her shed.
26. The cow has hurt her legs.
27. This is easy to get her agreed.
28. This was he who arrived first in the meeting.
29. It is to certify that Mr. A. is our employee.
30. This is 8 O'clock by my watch.
31. All which she said was incorrect.
32. Who was the girl which came to meet you?
33. What is his opinion about the work which you have completed?
34. I always purchase the item which is best in the market.
35. This is the same shirt which I saw in the shop.
36. Who is she who can abuse me like this?
37. Only those employees should be promoted whom are sincere.
38. The leaders which do not love their country are not respected.
39. Those whose live in glass houses should not throw stones at others.
40. What was the reply, which she submitted?
41. It was me who telephoned you yesterday.
42. The girl whom you spoke to in the office is my friend.
43. My brother and myself are glad to get your greetings.
44. I am not one of those who cannot keep his promise.
45. It is not us who are responsible for the delay.
46. They admired his wife and he.
47. What place are you going?
48. Which house do you live?
49. She has absented from duty today again.
50. I could not avail of the opportunity I got last year.
51. The treatment received by me was such, which I never expected.
52. His expectation is the same which is hers.
53. One cannot bear his insult like this.
54. My house is bigger than their.
55. This is a secret between you and I.

Explanations

1. Let you and me go to play.
2. There is close relation between him and me.
3. You ,he and I have done our job.
4. You and he could not complete your work.
5. He and I have fastened our belts.
6. You, he and I were present in the function.
7. You and I are strangers.
8. I and you are responsible for this loss.
9. I and he are the main accused.
10. I, you and he must beg sorry for the misconduct.

11. None of these four vehicles will do.
12. Either of the two girls can solve this puzzle.
13. Anyone of the three students is responsible for the loss.
14. Neither of the two girls could complete the job.
15. One should obey one's elders.
16. One should respect not only one's own parents but also other's.
17. One should take care not to make oneself obnoxious to others.
18. Each girl and every madam tried her best to finish the work before 7 P.M.
19. Every man and every woman has his/her own fascinations.
20. Every leader and every citizen has a duty towards his country.
21. Each of the employees has to agrrange his own vehicle.
22. Every one of them was given his table and chair.
23. Either Ramesh or Sita has left his/her/this tiffin box.
24. Either the teacher or the students have left their class room unlocked.
25. Please take the buffaloe to its shed.
26. The cow has hurt its legs.
27. It is easy to get her agreed.
28. It was he who arrived first in the meeting.
29. This is to certify that Mr.A. is our employee.
30. It is 8 O'clock by my watch.
31. All that she said was incorrect.
32. Who was the girl that came to meet you?
33. What is his opinion about the work that you have completed?
34. I always purchase the item that is the best in the market.
35. This is the same shirt that I saw in the shop.
36. Who is she that can abuse me like this?
37. Only those employees should be promoted who are sincere.
38. The leaders who do not love their country are not respected.
39. Those who live in glass houses should not throw stones at others.
40. What was the reply that she submitted?
41. It was I who telephoned you yesterday.
42. The girl who you spoke to in the office, is my friend.
43. My brother and I are glad to get your greetings.
44. I am not one of those who cannot keep their promise.
45. It is not we who are responsible for the delay.
46. They admired his wife and him.
47. What place are you going to?
48. Which house do you live in?
49. She has absented herself from duty today again.
50. I could not avail myself of the opportunity I got last year.
51. The treatment received by me was such as I never expected.
52. His expectation is the same as is hers.
53. One cannot bear one's insult like this.
54. My house is bigger than theirs.
55. This is a secret between you and me.

SPOTTING THE ERRORS (PRONOUN)

Exercise : ***Find the errors and justify your answers.***

1. The board of directors (A)/ want the facilities (B)/ of car and accommodation (C)/for itself (D).
2. Every teacher (A)/ and every student (B)/ of this school is determined to do their best (C)/ for the benefit of all (D).
3. The officer(A)/ as well as the (B)/clerks absented themselves(C)/ from the office (D).
4. There were (A)/ five active workers (B)/ and three lazy one (C)/ in the factory (D).
5. There is none (A)/ who can support you (B)/ in this crucial period (C).
6. Any of the (A)/ two photos which reflect (B)/ the natural beauty of Kashmir (C)/ is worth seeing (D).
7. The guests (A)/ whom we were talking (B)/ about have arrived (C)/ are my relatives (D).
8. He introduced (A)/ to the chairman as (B)/ the president of the (C)/ workers association (D).
9. As a student(A)/of arts(B)/you are much better(C)/ than him(D).
10. He hates everybody (A)/ and everything who(B)/ reminds him(C)/of his blunder (D).
11. Whomever(A)/does not come in time(B)/will not be allowed (C) / to mark his presence (D).
12. The six partners(A)/are at daggers drawn(B)/so they do not talk(C)to each other (D).
13. If some one has(A)/completed the work (B)/ he may leave(C).
14. She lent me (A)/ some money with the condition (B)/ that I should return (C)/ the same within a month (D).
15. The teacher instructed (A)/ the peon to let (B)/ the students and I (C)/ go into the office of Principal (D).
16. The candidate (A)/ being a commerce graduate (B)/ she is eligible (C)/ for the post of accountant (D).
17. In all circumstances(A)/I have helped him(B)/and he knows(C).
18. I don't appreciate(A)/him who laugh (B)/at others without (C)/ any reason (D).
19. You and myself (A)/ will enjoy the function(B)/being arranged in honour of (C)/ the new Principal (D).
20. He asked for (A)/ permission to go to the cinema (B)/ but his mother (C)/ did not give (D).

Explanations

1. (D) 'itself' की जगह 'themselves' आयेगा। यहाँ Board of Directors का प्रयोग as collective noun नहीं हुआ है ।
2. (C) 'their' की जगह 'his' आयेगा। जब दो singular nouns, Each एवं Every से जुड़े होते हैं, तो singular verb एवं possessive pronoun भी singular (यहाँ 'his') आता है।
3. (C) 'themselves' की जगह 'his' आयेगा। यहाँ subject 'officer' है। जब दो nouns; as well as, besides, in addition etc. से संयुक्त होते हैं, तो verb एवं pronoun पहले वाले noun के अनुसार प्रयुक्त होते हैं।
4. (C) 'lazy one' की जगह 'lazy ones' होना चाहिये। 'one' का प्रयोग singular के लिये एवं 'ones' का प्रयोग plural हेतु किया जाता है ।
5. (B) 'Who' की जगह 'that'का प्रयोग करें । याद रखें, All/none/same/only/ के साथ सामान्यतया relative pronoun 'that' का प्रयोग होता है। जैसे:

   (a) All that glliters is not gold. (b) He is the same man that supported me.

   'Same' के साथ Relative pronoun 'as' का प्रयोग किया जायेगा, यदि इसके बाद verb का प्रयोग नहीं हुआ है; This is the same house as mine.
6. (A) 'Any' की जगह 'Either' का प्रयोग होगा। 'Either' का प्रयोग दो के लिये होता है।

7. (B) 'Whom' की जगह 'who' का प्रयोग किया जायेगा। 'Whom'-objective case है। 'Who', subjective case.

Note *जब आपको किसी वाक्य में 'Who' एवं 'whom' के प्रयोग के मध्य कोई confusion हो तो आप, वाक्य में subject एवं verbs की संख्या गिन लें। यदि verb की संख्या, subjects से अधिक है तो 'who' का प्रयोग करें। यहाँ यह भी ध्यान रखना होगा कि 'and' से संयुक्त verbs एक ही subject के लिये प्रयुक्त होते हैं। जैसे :*

She came and spoke to me यहाँ verb 'came' एवं 'spoke', 'and' से संयुक्त हैं अत: एक ही subject के लिये प्रयुक्त हैं। वाक्य सं (7) को देखें:

The guests whom we were talking about have arrived, are my relatives.
s-1 s-2 v-2 v-3 v-1

यहाँ दो subject हैं, 'Guests' एवं 'we' जो क्रमश: 'are' एवं 'were', verbs को लेते हैं। तीसरी verb है have arrived इसके लिये कोई subject नहीं है। अत: इस वाक्य में 'whom' की जगह 'who' आयेगा, जो subject का कार्य करता है। इस प्रकार सही वाक्य होगा :

The guests who we were talking about have arrived are my relatives.

Other example:-

The candidates whom we have chosen are sincere and energetic.
s-1 s-2 v-2 v-1

यहाँ whom का प्रयोग सही है। Here are two verbs and two subjects, so the use of 'Whom' is justified.

8. (A) 'introduced' के बाद Reflexive pronoun 'himself' भी प्रयुक्त करना होगा। ध्यान दें : कुछ verbs, जैसे absent, present, enjoy, introduce, confine, devote, sacrifice, prostrate etc, transitive verbs हैं, जिनके बाद या तो कोई object आता है या Reflexive pronoun का प्रयोग किया जाता है। जैसे:
She enjoyed the picnic. —*Incorrect*
She enjoyed herself in the picnic. —*Correct*
अन्य उदाहरण:
He prostrated before the king, who had returned after two years. —*Incorrect*
यहाँ prostrated एक transitive verb है, अत: इसके बाद 'himself' प्रयुक्त करना होगा। सही वाक्य होगा :
He prostrated himself before the king, who has returned after two years. —*Correct*

9. (D) 'him' की जगह 'he' आयेगा। 'than' के बाद यदि दो subjects के मध्य तुलना की जाये, तो nominative case का प्रयोग होगा न कि object case का। 'he' nominative case एवं 'him' object case है। देखें:
She was more surprised than me, to see the circus girl coming towards us.
यहाँ भी 'me' की जगह 'I' का प्रयोग होगा, क्योंकि तुलना दो subjects, 'she' एवं 'I' में है।

10. (B) 'Who' की जगह 'which' या 'that' का प्रयोग करना होगा। जब किसी pronoun के पहले आये दो Nouns, 'and' से संयुक्त होते हैं तो pronoun अपने पास आये noun से govern होता है। यहाँ पास वाला noun, 'everything' है अत: यहाँ 'which' या 'that' का प्रयोग होगा।

11. (A) 'Whomever' की जगह 'whoever' होगा। whomever, objective case है जबकि 'whoever'-nominative case है जो अपने साथ verb, does not come ले रहा है। Also see the explanation to question no. 7.

12. (D) 'Each other' की जगह 'one another' होगा। 'each other' का सामान्यतया प्रयोग दो के लिये किया जाता है।

13. (E) No Error. वाक्य सही है।

14. (D) 'the same' की जगह 'it' आयेगा। 'the same' का प्रयोग हमेशा एक adjective की तरह होता है। 'the same' का प्रयोग pronoun की तरह करना गलत है। निम्न दोनों वाक्य गलत हैं:
   (a) This is the same pen as mine. —*Incorrect*
   (b) It is the same chair as yours. —*Incorrect*
15. (C) 'I' की जगह 'me' होगा। 'Let' के साथ pronoun हमेशा objective case में आता है ; जैसे :
   (a) Let you and me go there. (b) Let you and him prepare a proposal.
16. (C) 'She' को delete करें । यहाँ 'She' लिखने की आवश्यकता ही नहीं है :
   This is the pen, which I lost it yesterday.; यहाँ भी 'it' का प्रयोग superfluous है, अनावश्यक है।
17. (C) 'Knows' के बाद 'it' लिखना आवश्यक है ।
18. (B) 'Laugh' की जगह 'laughs' होगा। 'Laugh', 'him' के लिये प्रयुक्त है जो singular pronoun है ।
19. (A) 'myself' के बदले 'I' होगा। ध्यान दें, Reflexive pronoun, कभी भी वाक्य में subject की तरह प्रयुक्त नहीं हो सकता है। साधारण बोलचाल में हम 'myself' को subject की तरह प्रयोग करते हैं; जैसे :
   (a) Myself is Suresh. —*Incorrect*
   (b) I am Suresh. —Correct
   (c) Yourself is responsible. —*Incorrect*
   (d) You are responsible. — Correct
20. (D) 'give' के बाद 'it' प्रयुक्त होगा। 'give' एक transitive verb है, इसके साथ object लिखना आवश्यक है।

BLUNDERS

Exercise : ***Rewrite the following sentences after correction.***

1. Every soldiers and every sailors were in their place.
2. Each of the students are ready to participate in the blood donation camp.
3. Either the principal or the teachers failed in his duties.
4. This is raining here.
5. Myself is Prakash Chand.
6. It is Ram, my younger brother.
7. Each of the girls has donated his pocket money.
8. This is the girl whom parents have died .
9. He asked "Who is him"?
10. Every one should obey their elders.

Explanations

1. सही वाक्य होगा-Every soldier and every sailor *was in his* place.
   इस तरह के वाक्यों में Singular verb (was) एवं Singular Pronoun (his) का प्रयोग होता है।
2. 'Each' के साथ भी Singular verb 'is' का प्रयोग होता है। सही वाक्य है –
   Each of the students *is* ready to participate in the blood donation camp.
3. Failed in *their* duties होगा। वाक्य में 'Either.... or' conjunction के द्वारा जब एक Singular एवं एक Plural Subject को संयुक्त किया जाता है, तो Pronoun अपने पास वाले Subject (यदि दो में से एक Plural Subject है, तो वह बाद में ही आता है) के अनुसार Plural होगा।
4. यहाँ 'This' की जगह 'It' का प्रयोग होगा ।
5. Reflexive Pronoun का इस तरह प्रयोग गलत है। सही वाक्य होगा – I am Prakash Chand.
6. It is Ram की जगह This is Ram होगा ।
7. 'girls' के लिये 'his' की जगह her, Pronoun प्रयुक्त होगा।
8. यहाँ 'whom' की जगह 'whose' (Possessive Pronoun) का प्रयोग होगा।
9. 'Who was *he*' होना चाहिए ।
10. 'Everyone' के साथ Singular Pronoun - 'his' प्रयुक्त होगा।

❑❑❑

13

Reported Speech

Reported speech के Errors सम्बन्धित अधिकांश प्रश्न, जब Reporting verb - past में हो तो Reported speech के Tense एवं Pronouns के change के सम्बन्ध में पूछे जाते हैं; या इनके अपवादों के सम्बन्ध में पूछे जाते हैं। छात्रों को इन बिन्दुओं पर विशेष तौर पर ध्यान देना चाहिए।

वक्ता के कथन को Narration या Speech कहा जाता है। किसी भी कथन को दो तरह से व्यक्त किया जा सकता है :

(i) Direct Speech, (ii) Indirect Speech.

(i) Direct Speech or Direct Narration :- जब वक्ता के कथन को 'ज्यों का त्यों '(हू - ब - हू), व्यक्त किया जाये तो उसे Direct Narration कहा जाता है। Direct Narration को Inverted Commas में बन्द किया जाता है।

(ii) Indirect Speech or Indirect Narration :- जब वक्ता के कथन को अपने शब्दों में व्यक्त किया जाये, तो उसे Indirect Narration कहा जाता है।

ध्यान रखें **Indirect Narration में वक्ता के कथन का आशय नहीं बदलता है, केवल कथन का तरीका बदल जाता है।**

REPORTER/REPORTING VERB/REPORTED SPEECH/VERB OF REPORTED SPEECH

Reporter : Direct Narration के वक्ता को Reporter कहा जाता है ।

Reporting Verb :- वक्ता द्वारा जिस verb का प्रयोग किया जाता है, उसे Reporting verb कहा जाता है।

Reported Speech :- Inverted Commas ("....") के भीतर जो वाक्य रहता है, उसे Reported speech कहा जाता है।

Verb of Reported Speech :- Reported Speech (Inverted commas के अन्दर के वाक्य) की verb को Verb of Reported Speech कहा जाता है :

She said to me, "I am going to Jaipur."

इस वाक्य में :- 'She' - Reporter है, 'said' - Reporting verb है।

"I am going to Jaipur"- Reported Speech है तथा 'am going' - Reported Speech की verb है।

ध्यान रखें

(a) Reported Speech हमेशा Capital letter से शुरू होता है, एवं Inverted commas में बन्द रहता है।

(b) Direct से Indirect में बदलने पर Inverted commas हटा दिये जाते हैं।

RULES OF CHANGING DIRECT SPEECH INTO INDIRECT SPEECH

Direct speech को Indirect Speech में परिवर्तित करने के नियमों को दो भागों में विभाजित किया जा सकता है :

1. **सामान्य नियम :- ये नियम सभी प्रकार के वाक्यों पर साधारणतया लागू होते हैं।**
2. **विशेष नियम :- ये नियम भिन्न-भिन्न प्रकार के वाक्यों के लिये भिन्न-भिन्न हैं।**

GENERAL RULES

1. Direct speech से Indirect Speech में परिवर्तन होने पर Inverted commas हट जाते हैं।
2. (a) यदि Direct narration में Reporting verb, Present या Future tense में है, तो Indirect में परिवर्तन करते समय Reported speech के tense में कोई परिवर्तन नहीं किया जाता है।

   (b) Reporting verb, के Past में होने की स्थिति में Rules आगे दिये गये हैं।
3. Indirect Speech में परिवर्तन होने पर, Reported Speech के Persons का परिवर्तन निम्न प्रकार होता है :

   (a) First person -Reporting verb के Subject के अनुसार बदलता है।

   (b) Second person -Reporting verb के Object के अनुसार बदलता है।

   (c) Third person -इसमें कोई परिवर्तन सामान्यतया नहीं होता है।

   Person का परिवर्तन करते समय यह ध्यान रखें कि यदि person बहुवचन है, तो परिवर्तन बहुवचन के अनुसार होगा। यदि person, possessive case में है, तो परिवर्तन उसी अनुसार होगा । Person का परिवर्तन, Direct से Indirect में परिवर्तन का एक महत्त्वपूर्ण भाग है। ध्यान रखें person का number एवं case नहीं बदला जाता है।
4. यदि Reporting verb 'say , says,will say' या 'said' रहे तो Indirect speech में भी 'say, says, will say' या 'said' ही रहेगी, लेकिन यदि Reporting verb के साथ 'to' लिखा हो तो परिवर्तन निम्न प्रकार होता है :

   say to - tell, says to - tells, said to - told
5. **Indirect Speech में बदलने पर reporting verb के बाद सामान्य वाक्यो में 'that' का प्रयोग किया जाता है।**

उक्त नियमों को ध्यान में रखते हुए निम्न वाक्यों के Direct से Indirect में परिवर्तन पर गौर करें :-

(a) He says, "I am going to Jaipur". — *Direct.*
He says that he is going to Jaipur. — *Indirect.*

(b) She says to me, " You are writing a letter to him." — *Direct.*
She tells me that I am writing a letter to him . — *Indirect*

(c) They say to Ram, " We will go to Jaipur." — *Direct*
They tell Ram that they will go to Jaipur. — *Indirect*

(d) Hari says to Shalu, "I am your brother and you are my sister." — *Direct*
Hari tells Shalu that he is her brother and she is his sister. — *Indirect*

यद्यपि Reported Speech का Tense नहीं बदलता है, तथापि Indirect Speech में pronoun या subject में परिवर्तन होने पर, Reported Speech की verb का रूप बदल जाता है। वाक्य (a) में 'am' का 'is', एवं वाक्य (d) में 'am' का 'is' में परिवर्तन हुआ है।

REPORTING VERB IN THE PAST

6. यदि Reporting verb, Past tense में है तो Reported Speech में जो भी Tense होता है, उसका past हो जाता है। Reported Speech में Tense में परिवर्तन निम्न प्रकार होगा :

Change in tense of Reported Speech

	Direct Narration	Indirect Narration
1.	Present Indefinite	Past Indefinite
2.	Present Continuous	Past Continuous
3.	Present Perfect	Past Perfect
4.	Persent Perfect Continuous	Past Perfect Continuous

5.	Past Indefinite	Past Perfect
6.	Past Continuous	Past Perfect Continuous
7.	Past Perfect	No change of tense
8.	Past Perfect Continuous	No change of tense

Change in Future Tense (Reported Speech)

1.	Will / shall	Would / should.
2.	Can	Could
3.	May	Might
4.	Could /should /would /might	No change

7. **जब Reporting verb, Past tense में है, तो Reported Speech में आये कुछ शब्दों में परिवर्तन निम्न प्रकार होता है :**

	Direct Narration	Indirect Narration
1.	This	That
2.	These	Those
3.	Here	There
4.	Hence	Thence
5.	Hither	Thither
6.	Now	Then
7.	Ago	Before
8.	Thus	So
9.	Today	That day
10.	Tomorrow	The next day / the following day
11.	Yesterday	The previous day
12.	Last week / month / year	The previous week / month / year
13.	The last fort night	The previous fort night
14.	The day before yesterday	The day before the previous day

SOLVED EXAMPLES : TENSE WISE

Present Indefinite

(1) He said to me, "I do not eat apples." *— Direct*
He told me that he did not eat apples. *— Indirect*

Present Continuous

(2) Ram said to Shyam, "I am watching T.V." *— Direct*
Ram told Shyam that he was watching T.V. *— Indirect*

Persent Perfect

(3) Sita said, "I have already cooked". *— Direct*
Sita said that she had already cooked. *— Indirect*

Present Perfect Continuous

(4) Sonu said to me, "I have been reading for an hour". *— Direct*
Sonu told me that he had been reading for an hour. *— Indirect*

Past Indefinite

(5) She said to Ram, "I went to Jaipur last week". *— Direct*
She told Ram that she had gone to Jaipur the previous week. *— Indirect*

Past Continuous

(6) She said to me, "I was waiting for you". — *Direct*
She told me that she had been waiting for me. — *Indirect*

Past Perfect

(7) He said to me, "I had completed my project". — *Direct*
He told me that he had completed his project. — *Indirect*

Past Perfect Continuous

(8) He said , "I had been playing chess for two hours". — *Direct*
He said that he had been playing chess for two hours. — *Indirect*

Future Indefinite

(9) Ram said to Meena, "I shall write a letter." — *Direct*
Ram told Meena that he would write a letter. — *Indirect*

Future Continuous

(10) Rahim said to Ram, "Sita will be waiting for you". — *Direct*
Rahim told Ram that Sita would be waiting for him (Ram). — *Indirect*

Future Perfect

(11) Sita said to Ram, "I will have completed my work". — *Direct*
Sita told Ram that she would have completed her work. — *Indirect*

Future Perfect Continuous

(12) Nisha said to me, "I shall have been reading the book." — *Direct*
Nisha told me that she would have been reading the book. — *Indirect*

ध्यान रखे ***यदि Reporting Verb, Past Tense में है तो Reported Speech के वाक्य का Tense भी नियमानुसार परिवर्तित किया जाता है । यह Important बिन्दु है ।***

8. यदि Reported Speech में कोई Universal Truth (सर्वकालिक सत्य), Proverb,(कहावत), Mathematical fact (गणितीय तथ्य), Historical Fact (ऐतिहासिक तथ्य), Habitual Act (आदतन क्रिया) या कोई Morality (नैतिकता) का सन्दर्भ हो तो , ऐसे वाक्यों को जब Indirect में परिवर्तित करते हैं, तो Reporting verb के Past Tense में होने पर भी इनका (Reported speech का) Tense नहीं बदलता है।

Look at the following Sentences :

1. He said, "The sun sets in the west". — *Direct*
He said that the sun sets in the west. — *Indirect*
2. He said, "Man is Mortal". — *Direct*
He said that the man is mortal. — *Indirect*
3. The teacher said, "India became Republic on 26th Jan 1950" — *Direct*
The teacher said that India became Republic on 26th Jan 1950. — *Indirect*
4. She said to me, "Honesty is the best policy. — *Direct*
She told me that honesty is the best policy. — *Indirect*
5. She said, "Two and two is four". — *Direct*
She said that two and two is four. — *Indirect*

INTERROGATIVE SENTENCES

Interrogative Sentences को दो भागों में विभाजित किया जा सकता है :

1. ऐसे प्रश्न जिनका Answer - 'Yes' या 'No' में दिया जा सकता है, जैसे : Are you happy?
2. ऐसे प्रश्न जिनका Answer - 'Yes' या 'No' में नहीं दिया जा सकता है। These are also called 'Wh' questions.
ये Interrogative Sentences, ऐसे प्रश्न होते हैं, जिनका Answer, Yes या No में नहीं दिया जा सकता है। ऐसे प्रश्नों में कुछ जानकारी चाही गई होती है, जैसे : (a) Where do you live? (b) What is your name?
इस तरह के प्रश्न, 'Wh' words, जैसे- What, Where, Which, Who, How, etc. से शुरू होते हैं।

Rules

1. प्रथम प्रकार के Interrogative Sentences जो Auxiliary verb से शुरू होते हैं, जिनका Answer, 'Yes' / 'No' में दिया जा सकता है, उनको Indirect में परिवर्तित करते समय 'that'की जगह **'if' या 'whether'** का प्रयोग किया जाता है।
2. Indirect Speech में बदलते समय Interrogative Sentences को Assertive Sentences में बदला जाता है; **अर्थात Indirect Speech में परिवर्तित होने के बाद, वाक्य, एक प्रश्न के रूप में नहीं रहता है** तथा वाक्य के अन्त में अंकित Question Mark (?) भी हट जाता है। वाक्य का Tense एवं Pronoun पूर्व में बताए नियमानुसार बदले जाते हैं।
3. **Reporting verb ; 'say, says, said' की जगह 'ask, asks, asked' प्रयोग किया जाता है।**
कई बार 'ask' की जगह 'inquire' या 'enquire of' का प्रयोग किया जाता है। 'enquire of' का प्रयोग तब किया जाता है जब इसके बाद object (जैसे - He enquired of me) आता है।

Look at the following solved examples :

1. She said to me, "Are you going to college?" — *Direct*
   She asked me whether I was going to college. — *Indirect*
2. She said to Shyam, "Have you an extra copy?" — *Direct*
   She asked Shyam if he had an extra copy. — *Indirect*

Interrogative वाक्य को Direct से Indirect में बदलते समय इसे Assertive बनाना आवश्यक है।

4. **यदि Interrogative Sentence के साथ वाक्य में उसका उत्तर भी जुड़ा हुआ हो, तो ध्यान रखें, 'Yes' में Answer देते समय assertive में answer देना होगा, एवं 'No' में answer देते समय Negative में answer देना होगा। जैसे :**
   (a) She said to me , "Can you solve this question?" "No", I said.
   She asked me if I could solve that question. I said , "I couldn't" or° I replied in negative.
   (b) He said to me , " Do you know me ? I said, "yes".
   He asked me if I knew him. I said, I did or I replied in affirmative.
5. **ऐसे Interrogative Sentences जो 'Wh' Words से शुरू होते हैं, उनको जब direct से Indirect में परिवर्तित करते हैं , तो Conjunction ; that / if / whether नहीं प्रयुक्त होता, बल्कि 'Wh' Word ही Conjunction का कार्य करते हैं । जैसा हमने पूर्व में बताया है , Indirect Speech में वाक्य Interrogative में नहीं रहता है, उसे Assertive बनाना आवश्यक है। वाक्य में आये Pronoun एवं Tense में परिवर्तन पूर्व में बताये गये नियमानुसार ही होता है।**

Look at the following solved examples :

(1) He said to her , "What do you want?" — *Direct*
He asked her what she wanted. — *Indirect*
(2) He said to me , "Why are you happy?" — *Direct*
He asked me why I was happy. — *Indirect*
(3) Ram said to Hari , "Where do you live?" — *Direct*
Ram asked Hari where he lived. — *Indirect*

(4) She said to Hari, "When will you come?" —Direct

She asked Hari when he would come. —Indirect

(5) He said to me , "What is your father ?" —Direct

He asked me what my father was. —Indirect

IMPERATIVE SENTENCES

Imperative Sentences ऐसे वाक्य हैं , जिनमें आदेश (order), निर्देश (direction , command), प्रार्थना (Request), सुझाव (Suggestion), सलाह (Advise) का भाव निहित रहता है। ऐसे वाक्यों को Indirect Narration में परिवर्तित करते समय निम्न नियमों का ध्यान रखें :

Rules

(1) Reporting verb को वाक्य के भाव के अनुसार, Order, Command, Advise, Suggest, Request, Warn etc. में से किसी एक verb में परिवर्तित करें ।

(2) Conjunction 'that' की जगह 'to'का प्रयोग करें । यदि वाक्य Negative है, तो 'not to' का प्रयोग करें।

(3) वाक्य में यदि 'Please', 'Kindly' जैसे शब्द हैं , तो इनको Indirect Speech में नहीं रखें । वाक्य के भावार्थ के अनुसार Reporting verb 'Request' का प्रयोग किये जाने से, 'Please', 'Kindly' का भाव स्वत: ही वाक्य के भाव में आ जाता है।

Look at the following solved examples :

(1) She said to Ramu, "Please bring my book." — Direct

She requested Ramu to bring her book . — Indirect

(2) She said to me, "Have a glass of milk". — Direct

She asked me to have a glass of milk. — Indirect

(3) Ram said to Sita, "Take medicines regularly." — Direct

Ram advised Sita to take medicines regularly. — Indirect

(4) I said to Hari, "Don't pluck the flowers". — Direct

I ordered Hari not to pluck the flowers. — Indirect

(5) The SP said to the SHO, "Shoot the robber". — Direct

The SP ordered the SHO to shoot the robber. — Indirect

(6) The Principal said to the students, "Get out from office". — Direct

The Principal ordered the students to get out from office. — Indirect

(7) He said , "Follow my instructions". — Direct

He ordered me to follow his instructions. — Indirect

(8) He said to Sarla, "Lend me your Physics book". — Direct

He requested Sarla to lend him her Physics book. — Indirect

Note **Negative Imperative वाक्यों में जो 'Do not' या 'Don't' जैसे शब्दों से शुरू होते हैं , उनमें जैसा हमने पहले बताया है, 'not to'का प्रयोग करते हैं । 'Not to'की जगह 'forbade' का प्रयोग भी किया जाता है। लेकिन 'forbade' के साथ वाक्य में 'not' का प्रयोग नहीं करना है , क्योंकि 'forbade' स्वयं ही Negative है, इसका अर्थ है - 'मना करना' । जैसे :**

(1) The teacher said to Hari, "Don't write on the table". —Direct

The teacher forbade Hari to write on the table —Indirect

or The teacher instructed Hari not to write on the table. —Indirect

(2) The Principal said , "Don't make a noise students". —Direct

The Principal forbade the students to make a noise. —Indirect

or The Principal instructed the students not to make a noise. —Indirect

(3) She said to me , "Don't park your car here". —Direct

She forbade me to park my car there. —Indirect

or She asked me not to park my car there. —Indirect

EMPHATIC IMPERATIVE (USE OF 'DO')

कई बार Imperative वाक्यों को आग्रहपूर्ण (Emphatic) बनाने के लिये 'Do' का प्रयोग किया जाता है। **यह 'Do' का प्रयोग, मात्र अधिक आग्रह या विनम्रता को प्रदर्शित करने हेतु होता है। ऐसे वाक्यों को Indirect में बदलते समय** 'Do'को हटा दिया जाता है एवं ऊपर बताए गये नियमानुसार वाक्य को Indirect में बदला जाता है। जैसे :

(1) He said to me, "Do have a cup of coffee please". — *Direct*
He requested me to have a cup of coffee. — *Indirect*

IMPERATIVE AND TAG QUESTION

कई बार Imperative Sentence के साथ एक Tag Question लगा रहता है। Tag Question का प्रयोग, अपनी बात का महत्त्व बढ़ाने के लिये, अथवा ध्यान आकृर्षित कर , उत्तर पाने की आकांक्षा से किया जाता है। इस प्रकार के वाक्यों को Indirect में बदलते समय, Tag Question को महत्त्व नहीं दिया जाता है। शेष वाक्य को पहले बताये नियमानुसार Indirect में बदलते हैं । जैसे :

(1) He said to me, "Open the door, will you ? — *Direct*
He asked me to open the door. — *Indirect*

(2) She Said to Ram , "Bring me a glass of water, won't you? — *Direct*
She asked Ram to bring her a glass of water. — *Indirect*

IMPERATIVE SENTENCES WITH 'LET'

(A) 'Let' से शुरू होने वाले वाक्य भी एक प्रकार के Impertive वाक्य ही होते हैं। 'Let' से कई भावार्थ व्यक्त होते हैं; सुझाव (Suggestion), प्रस्ताव (Proposal) हेतु 'Let' का प्रयोग मिम्न प्रकार होता है :

(1) She said to me, "Let us go to market".
She suggested to me to go to market. or
She suggested to me that we should go to market.

(2) He said to me, "Let us purchase this house".
He proposed to me to purchase that house. or
He proposed to me that we should purchase that house.

ध्यान रखें

(a) 'Let' से शुरू होने वाले वाक्यों में Imperative वाक्य की तरह 'to' का प्रयोग भी उपरोक्तानुसार कर सकते हैं। जब 'should' का प्रयोग किया जाता है, तो Conjunction 'that' का प्रयोग suggested / proposed के बाद करना होगा।

(b) यदि Reporting verb - 'said' है तो केवल 'Suggested' या 'Proposed' का प्रयोग होता है । एवं Reporting verb, 'said to' होने पर 'suggested to' या 'proposed to' का प्रयोग होगा।

(1) She said , "Let him complete his work first".
She suggested that he should complete his work first.

(B) 'Let' से व्यक्ति की इच्छा (Wish) भी व्यक्त की जाती है। ऐसे वाक्यों में Reporting verb, 'wish' का प्रयोग करना चाहिये :

(1) The student said, "Let me take food".
The student wished that he should take food.

(2) The lady said, "Let me have an ice cream pack".
The lady wished that she should have an ice cream pack.

(C) 'Let' से Order / Request का भाव भी व्यक्त किया जाता है। ऐसे वाक्यों में Reporting verb, 'order' या 'request' का प्रयोग करते हैं । ऐसे वाक्यों में जब अनुमति मांगी या दी जाती है तो 'to allow' का प्रयोग Conjunction की तरह किया जाता है :

(1) The boy said to the teacher, "Let me go home now."
The boy requested the teacher to allow him to go home then.

(2) The Principal said to the peon, " Let the students come in".
The Principal ordered the peon to allow the students come in.

Note 'Let' से शुरू होने वाले वाक्यों में कभी-कभी 'Let' का 'to let' में बदलकर Indirect Speech में परिवर्तित किया जाता है :

I said to her, "Let me go to market".
I requested her to let me go to market.

OPTATIVE SENTENCES

(A) ऐसे वाक्य, जिनसे Good wishes, प्रार्थना, अभिवादन या इच्छा व्यक्त की जाती है, Optative Sentences कहलाते हैं।

(a) यदि वाक्य में कोई Good wish व्यक्त की गई है, तो Reporting verb को 'wished' या 'prayed' में बदला जाता है , 'that', conjunction का प्रयोग किया जाता है तथा वाक्य को Assertive sentence में बदलते हैं। जैसे :

(1) My mother said to my friend, "May you live long !"
My mother wished my friend that he might live long.

(2) She said, "God grant you success !"
She prayed that God might grant me success.

(b) उपरोक्त वाक्य (2) में 'may' का प्रयोग नहीं हुआ है तब भी Indirect speech में 'might' का प्रयोग किया गया है। 'May' की existence ऐसे वाक्यों में स्वत: मानी जाती है।

(B) यदि वाक्य में Good morning, good evening, good day इत्यादि का प्रयोग अभिवादन स्वरूप किया गया है तो Reporting verb की जगह 'wished' का प्रयोग किया जाता है। यदि 'sir' या किसी अन्य शब्द द्वारा अभिवादन किया गया है और वह शब्द या 'sir' भी Inverted commas में है, तो उसे Inverted commas से बाहर निकाल लिया जाता है; जैसे :

(1) He said to the teacher, "Good morning !"
He wished the teacher good morning.

(2) She said, "Good morning, sir !"
She wished the sir good morning.

(C) यदि वाक्य में farewell (विदाई) सूचक शब्द, जैसे : Good bye, farewell इत्यादि का प्रयोग किया गया है तो Reporting verb - bade (bid) का प्रयोग किया जाता है, जैसे :

(1) She said to me, " Good bye".
She bade me good bye.

(2) The leader said, "Farewell my friends".
The leader bade his friends farewell.

EXCLAMATORY SENTENCES

ऐसे वाक्य जो अफसोस, घृणा, दुखः आश्चर्य, प्रसन्नता, शाबाशी देने के भाव व्यक्त करें, Exclamatory Sentences कहलाते हैं।

(A) इस तरह के वाक्यों को Indirect में बदलते समय, वाक्य के भावार्थ के अनुसार, exclaimed with joy, exclaimed with sorrow, exclaimed with surprise, exclaimed with applause, exclaimed with anger, exclaimed with contempt, जैसी Reporting verb का प्रयोग किया जाता है।

(B) Conjunction 'that'का प्रयोग किया जाता है।

(C) Alas, Bravo, Oh, Wow, Wah, Hurrah जैसे शब्दों को Indirect बनाते समय हटा दिया जाता है।

(D) Exclamatory वाक्यों को Assertive वाक्य में बदल दिया जाता है।

(E) यदि वाक्य में कोई इच्छा (जैसे- If I were the bird, If I were the P.M.) प्रगट की गई हो तो Reporting verb, 'wished' का प्रयोग किया जाता है।

Look at the following solved examples :

(1) She said, "If I were a bird !"
She wished that she would be a bird.

(2) He said, "If I were young again !"
He wished that he would be young again !"

(3) Raju said, "Alas ! I have been ruined".
Raju exclaimed with sorrow that he had been ruined.

(4) The lady said, "Oh ! My dog is dead".
The lady exclaimed with sorrow that her dog was dead.

(5) He said, "What a beautiful girl Sita is !"
He exclaimed with praise that Sita was a beautiful girl.

(6) The player said, "Hurrah ! We have won".
The player exclaimed with joy that they had won.

(F) Exclamatory वाक्यों को Assertive वाक्यों में कैसे बदलते हैं, निम्न वाक्यों पर गौर करने से यह समझ में आ जायेगा :

	Exclamatory	**Assertive**
(1)	What a beautiful girl she is !	She is a beautiful girl.
(2)	What a nice place it is !	It is a very nice place.
(3)	What a great fall !	It is a great fall.

MISCELLANEOUS SENTENCES

(A) जब वाक्यों में व्यक्ति का नाम Inverted commas के अन्दर, Reported Speech में सम्मिलित होता है :

(1) He said, "Rajeev, I am waiting for you."
He told Rajeev that he was waiting for him (Rajeev).

(2) She said, "Take your purse, Tony".
She asked Tony to take his purse.

ऐसे वाक्यों में व्यक्ति के नाम को Reporting verb के साथ लिख कर, शेष वाक्य को पूर्व में बताए गये नियमों के अनुसार Indirect Speech में बदला जाता है।

(B) जब वाक्यों में 'Sir', 'Madam' का प्रयोग Inverted commas के अन्दर Reported Speech के साथ किया गया हो :

(1) He said, "May I leave now Madam ?"
He asked the Madam if he might leave then.

(C) कुछ वाक्यों में Well, Okay, You, see, You know, आदि का प्रयोग किया गया होता है, जैसे :-

(1) The receptionist said, "Well, what can I do for you ? "
The receptionist asked politely what she could do for me.

(2) "Okay", She said, "I will consider your proposal."
She said that she would consider my proposal.

(D) वाक्यों में 'Must' का प्रयोग जब एक future action या present action में मजबूरी को प्रगट करता है तो ऐसे वाक्यों को Indirect Speech में बदलते समय, 'must' को 'had to' में बदलते हैं :

(1) She said, "I must leave at once."
She said that she had to leave at once.

(2) Ramesh said, "He must go to Jaipur tomorrow."
Ramesh said that he had to go to Jaipur the next day.

(E) 'Must not' एवं 'Need not' वाले वाक्यों को Direct से Indirect narration में बदलते समय उक्त शब्दों में कोई परिवर्तन नहीं होता है :

(1) He said, "You must not speak to anyone".
He said that I must not speak to anyone.

(2) She said, "You need not purchase this book".
She said that I need not purchase that book.

(F) 'Would, Should, Could, Might' वाले वाक्यों को Direct से Indirect narration में बदलते समय उक्त शब्दों में कोई परिवर्तन नहीं होता है :

He said, "She would / should / could / might attend the party".
He said that she would / should / could / might attend the party.

(G) वाक्य में यदि 'had to' का प्रयोग है तो वह 'had had to' में परिवर्तित हो जाता है। यहाँ 'had to' एक urgency को दर्शाता है :

The poet said, "After the function, I had to rush to my house"
The poet said that after the function he had had to rush to his house.
ध्यान दें, यहाँ had to का प्रयोग Past Perfect Tense की तरह नहीं किया गया है।

(H) Joint Sentences : जब कई वाक्य एक साथ होते हैं, तो speech इस प्रकार change करते हैं :

(1) She said, "I am a girl. I cannot stay here in night".
She said that she was a girl and added that she could not stay there in night.

(2) Ramesh said, "Sita is going to Jaipur tomorrow. I can also go with her."
Ramesh said that Sita was going to Jaipur next day and he could also go with her.

(3) Payal said, "I will not marry this year. I am preparnig for IAS examinations".
Payal said that she would not marry that year and further added that she was preparing for IAS examinations.

उपरोक्त प्रकार के वाक्यों में दूसरे वाक्य के लिये 'added, further added' या 'and' शब्द का प्रयोग कर, पूर्व में बताये गये नियमानुसार Indirect Speech में बदला जाता है :

See some more examples :

(1) He said, "Do you know who is he ?"
He asked me if I knew who he was.

(2) She said, "Can you find, where are the keys?
She asked me if I could find where the keys were.

ऐसे संयुक्त वाक्यों में, दोनों वाक्यों को ही Reporting verb के Tense के अनुसार बदला जाता है, पुनः देखें:

(3) He said, "Sarla is coming, wait here."
He said that Sarla was coming and asked me to wait there.

(4) He said, "Where is your purse, I have lost mine."
He asked me where my purse was and added that he had lost his.

(5) My father said, "I am going to office, where are you going."
My father said that he was going to his office and wanted to know where I was going.

उपरोक्त प्रकार के संयुक्त वाक्यों को पृथक-पृथक हमने पूर्व में Indirect Speech में आसानी से परिवर्तित किया है। जब इस तरह के वाक्य एक साथ आयें, तो पूर्व में बताए गये नियमानुसार ही परिवर्तित करें एवं बीच में 'added, wanted to know, etc.' का प्रयोग आवश्यकतानुसार करें।

(I) Indirect Commands :-कई वाक्य ऐसे होते हैं जो देखनें में Negative या Interrogative लगते हैं, लेकिन उनका अर्थ, आशय एक सलाह (advise), निमंत्रण (Invitation) या प्रार्थना (request) का होता है। इस तरह के वाक्य Indirect Commands कहलाते हैं ।

Look at the following sentences :

(1) She said, "If I were you, I'd stop smoking."
She advised me to stop smoking.

(2) He said, "Why don't you change your clothes ?"
He advised me to change my clothes.

(3) "Would / could you show me your ticket, please ?", the TC. said.
The TC. asked me to show him my ticket.

SOME SPECIFIC POINTS ABOUT REPORTED SPEECH

(A) यदि Past के वाक्य में कोई इस तरह का तथ्य है जो वर्नमान काल तक भी परिवर्तित नहीं हुआ है तो उसका Tense भी अपरिवर्तित रहता है।

(1) He said, "I decided not to purchage the house, because it was near the railway track."
He said that he had decided not to purchage the house because it was near the railway track.

(2) They said, "We decided not to buy the house as it is on the main road."
They said that they had decided not to buy the house as it is on the main road.

वाक्य (1) एवं (2) में जो 'fact' अपरिवर्तित है (it was near the railway track., it is on the main road.) उनके Tense में Indirect speech में भी कोई परिवर्तन नहीं हुआ है।

(B) 'Wish' एवं 'It is time' के बाद प्रयुक्त Unreal Past Tense के वाक्यों के Tense में, Indirect speech में Change करते समय परिवर्तन नहीं होता है :

(1) He said, "I wish I didn't have to take examination,"
He said he wished he didn't have to take examination.

(2) "It is time we began planning for our examinations,"he said.
He said that it was time they began planning for their examinations.

(C) ऐसे वाक्य जिनमें 'I/he/she/we/they/ had better' जैसा Structure मिलता है, Indirect Speech में परिवर्तित करते समय उनके Tense में कोई परिवर्तन नहीं होता है ; लेकिन 'You had better' वाले वाक्यों में Advised + Object का प्रयोग किया जा सकता है। (यदि 'Advised' का प्रयोग नहीं किया जाये, तो इसमें भी कोई परिवर्तन नहीं होगा ।) जैंसे:

(1) "The children had better go to bed early", said Ram.
Ram said that the children had better go to bed early.

(2) Sita said, "You had better give up smoking."
Sita said that I had better give up smoking.
Sita advised me to give up smoking.

(3) He said, "You had better not drink the tea."
He advised me not to drink the tea.
He said that I had better not drink the tea.

(D) अग्रलिखित प्रकार के Conditional Sentences की speech को Indirect में परिवर्तित करते समय उनके Tenses में कोई परिवर्तन नहीं होता है :

(1) He said, "If I had a permit I could get this job".
He said that if he had a permit he could get that job.

(2) She said, "If he had come to me, I would have helped him."
She said that if he had come to him, she would have helped him.

(3) He said, "When I was a boy, I could stay up as long as I liked".
He said that when he was a boy he could stay up as long as he liked.

ERRORS, MISTAKES AND BLUNDERS IN REPORTED SPEECH

Exercise : ***Find the errors and justify your answers.***

1. The Chief Minister assured the people (A)/ that the government (B)/ will do its (C)/ best for the welfare of the poor (D).
2. She exclaimed with sorrow (A)/that her younger (B)/ son died (C)/ six days before (D).
3. The father said to his daughter(A)/ that if she wants to secure(B)/ good marks, she (C)/had to work hard (D).
4. She asked me(A)/ how could she(B)/ help me (C)/ in that situation (D).
5. The teacher forbade (A)/ the students not (B)/ to pluck the flowers (C)/ in the school garden (D).
6. Sarla asked the teacher (A)/ how many girls (B)/ were there (C)/ in class X (D).
7. The boy requested (A)/ the teacher to (B) allow him to (C)/ go to his home now (D).
8. The captain exclaimed with (A)/ applause that (B)/ the players played (C)/ the match very well (D).
9. My father asked me (A)/ why you were (B)/taking that (C)/examination (D).
10. She asked Shyam (A)/ if I could (B)/ accompany him (C)/ to the market (D).
11. Ram told me (A)/ that he got up (B)/ early in the (C)/ morning daily (D).
12. The teacher told the students (A)/that (B)/India had attained freedom (C)/on 15th August 1947 (D).
13. He said that (A)/ he was tired and (B)/that he wants (C)/to go to bed (D).
14. The mother asked (A)/ her son where (B)/ he was all (C)/the afternoon (D).
15. The magistrate asked the accused (A)/ what was he doing (B)/ with his hand (C) /in gentleman's pocket (D).
16. The old man advised his sons (A)/ not to quarrel amongst themselves (B)/ when he is dead (C)/ but to remain united (D).
17. He asked them (A)/ whether he would (B)/ listen to (C)/ such a man (D).
18. He requested him (A)/ that to wait (B)/ there till he returned (C)/ from the office (D).
19. He urged them(A)/ to be quiet (B)/ and listen to (C)/ my words (D).
20. He asked his (A)/ father when the (B)/ next letter (C)/will come (D).
21. He told that (A)/ his father had gone(B)/ to Mumbai (C)/the previous week (D).
22. Sumit told his father that (A)/ he wanted to go abroad (B)/ after he finishes (C)/his studies there (D).
23. The station master told me (A)/ that I was very late (B)/ and it was an hour (C)/since the train left (D).
24. He respectfully (A)/ wished his teacher (B)/ good morning sir (C).
25. He asked his son (A)/ if he has seen (B)/ the Taj Mahal earlier (C).
26. The child asked his mother (A)/ whether (B)/ she was going (C)/ to office today (D).
27. The queen eagerly (A)/ wished that (B)/ she will be (C)/ young again (D).
28. The officer warned him that (B)/ he would be dismissed (B)/ if he does not attend (C)/ the office regularly (D).
29. Ram asked (A)/me as if (B)/ what (C)/I was doing (D).
30. Sarita said (A)/ that a (B)/ stitch in time (C)/saved nine (D).
31. He said that (A)/" Work hard (B)/ if I want to (C)/ secure good marks" (D).
32. He tells me (A)/ that he would go (B)/ to Mumbai the (C)/ next month (D).
33. Mohan told me (A)/ that I was (B)/ doing his work (C).
34. John asked James (A)/ if he had come there (B)/ just to see him or (C)/ there is some other reason (D).

35. He said that he had (A)/ decided not to buy (B)/ the house as (C)/ it was on the main road (D).
36. My wife being ill sent (A)/ a message to her boss (B)/ informing why could she (C)/ not attend the office on that day (D).
37. My mother prayed (A)/ that God may granted (B)/ me success (C).
38. She reminded me (A)/ that she has often (B)/ told me not to (C)/play tricks with water (D).
39. The teacher told, (A)/ "Never make mischief (B)/ again." (C).
40. I asked Sumit (A)/ why he wanted to (B)/ join Navy and (D)/ what he actually wants (D).

Explanations

1. (C) 'will' की जगह 'would' होना चाहिए। जब Reporting verb-past में है, तो Reported speech का Tense भी Past में परिवर्तित हो जाता है।
2. (C) 'son died' की जगह 'son had died' होना चाहिए। यहाँ Past indefinite, Past Perfect में परिवर्तित होता है।
3. (B) 'wants' की जगह 'wanted' होना चाहिए।
4. (B) 'how could she' की जगह 'how she could' होगा। Indirect narration में Reported Speech को Assertive बनाया जाता है।
5. (B) 'not' को हटायें। यदि Reporting Verb 'forbade' का प्रयोग किया जाता है तो 'not' का प्रयोग नहीं किया जायेगा। 'forbade' स्वयं में negative है।
6. (C) 'were there' की जगह 'there were' होना चाहिए। वाक्य (4)का उत्तर देखें।
7. (D) 'now' की जगह 'then' होना चाहिए। जब Reporting verb past में है तो 'now' का 'then', 'yesterday' का 'the previous day' हो जाता है। का
8. (C) 'played' की जगह 'had played' आयेगा। Question (1) का explanation देखें।
9. (B) 'why you were' की जगह 'why I was' आयेगा। Indirect narration में Pronoun II person, Object (me) के अनुसार परिवर्तित होगा।
10. (B) 'If I could' की जगह 'If she could' होना चाहिए। Indirect narration में Pronoun I person, subject (she) के अनुसार परिवर्तित होगा।
11. (B) 'that he gets up' होगा। Reported speech में जब कोई habitual fact आदि हो, तो Reported speech के tense में कोई परिवर्तन नहीं होता है।
12. (C) 'had attained' की जगह केवल 'attained' ही होगा। Indirect narration में बदलते समय historical fact के Tense में कोई परिवर्तन नहीं होता है।
13. (C) 'that he wants' की जगह 'that he wanted' होगा। जब Reporting verb, past में है, तो Reported speech का Tense भी Past में परिवर्तित हो जाता है।
14. (C) 'he was all' की जगह 'he had been all' होना चाहिए। वाक्य (13) का explanation देखें।
15. (B) 'what he was doing' होगा। Indirect narration में Assertive वाक्य बनता है।
16. (C) 'when he was dead' होगा। यहाँ Present Tense का प्रयोग (जब Reporting verb Past में है)गलत है।
17. (B) 'he' की जगह they आयेगा। Pronoun के परिवर्तन के नियमों का अध्ययन करें।
18. (B) 'that' को हटायें। imperative sentence में 'that' का प्रयोग नहीं होगा।
19. (D) 'my' की जगह 'his' आयेगा। Ist person pronoun subject (He) के अनुसार बदलता है।
20. (D) 'will' की जगह 'would' होगा। Reporting verb जब past में हो तो Indirect narration में 'will' का परिवर्तन 'would' में हो जाता है।

21. (A) 'told' के साथ Object आना आवश्यक है। यदि object नहीं आता है तो 'He *said'* ही होगा।
22. (C) 'finishes' की जगह 'finished' लिखा जाना चाहिए। जब Reporting verb past में हो तो Reported Speech का Tense भी past में बदला जाता है।
23. (D) 'the train had left' होगा। वाक्य (2) का explanation देखें।
24. (C) 'Sir' को हटायें।
25. (B) 'He has seen' की जगह 'he had seen' होगा। Reporting verb जब past में हो तो Reported Speech को Past में बदलते हैं।
26. (D) 'today' की जगह 'that day' होगा।
27. (C) 'will be' की जगह 'would be' या 'were' लिखा जाना चाहिए।
28. (C) 'does not' की जगह 'did not' आना चाहिए। जब Reporting verb past में हो, तो Reported Speech को Past में बदला जाता है।
29. (B) 'as if' को delete करना होगा।
30. (D) 'saved' की जगह 'saves' होगा। 'A stitch in time saves nine' एक कहावत है, जिसके Tense में कोई परिवर्तन नहीं होगा।
31. (A) 'that' को Delete करें। यह Direct narration का वाक्य है।
32. (B) 'he would go' की जगह 'he will go' होगा। जब Reporting verb, present में हो तो Reported Speech का Tense नहीं बदलता है।
33. (B) 'I was' की जगह 'he was' होगा।
34. (D) 'there is' की जगह 'there was' होगा।
35. (D) वाक्य सही है। इस वाक्य में Part 'D' में 'was' की जगह कुछ विद्वानों ने had been प्रयोग करने को बताया है। यदि house की location अब बदल गई है, जैसे कि-वह अब main road पर नहीं है या main road बदल गया है, तो ही had been आयेगा, अन्यथा 'was' ही रहेगा।
36. (D) 'why could she' की जगह 'why she could' होगा। Indirect narration में वाक्य Assertive होता है।
37. (B) 'God may granted' की जगह 'God might grant' होगा।
38. (B) 'she has often' की जगह 'she had often' होगा।
39. (A) 'told' की जगह 'said' होगा। 'told' के बाद object अवश्य होना चाहिए।
40. (D) 'wants' की जगह 'wanted' होगा।

BLUNDERS

Exercise : ***Correct the following sentences and justify the corrections.***

1. He told that he had won the match.
2. She said to me that Sita was playing chess the previous day.
3. Ram told Sita that I am alright.
4. The teacher said that India had attained freedom in 1947 .
5. The teacher forbade the students not to pluck the flowers.
6. She exclaimed with sorrow that it was a beautiful place.
7. She advised me that to stop smoking.
8. She wished the teacher very good morning sir.
9. She requested Ramu that to bring a glass of water.
10. She asked Shyam if you had an extra copy.

Explanations

1. सही वाक्य होगा – 'He told *me* that....' या 'He said that....' ध्यान रखें, 'told' के बाद Object आना आवश्यक है।
2. सही वाक्य होगा – 'She *told* me that .....' Indirect narration में 'said to' को 'told' में बदला जाता है।
3. सही वाक्य होगा – Ram told Sita that *he was alright.*
4. सही वाक्य होगा –The teacher said that India attained freedom in 1947; Historical Events व्यक्त करने वाली Reported speech का tense अपरिवर्तित रहता है।
5. वाक्य से 'not' हटायें। जब 'forbade' का प्रयोग किया जाता है तो 'not' का प्रयोग नहीं होगा। 'Forbade' स्वयं ही negative है।
6. 'She exclaimed with *pleasure*' होगा ।
7. 'that' को delete करें ।
8. वाक्य से 'sir' को delete करें ।
9. वाक्य से 'that' को delete करें ।
10. सही वाक्य होगा –She asked Shyam if *he* had an extra copy.

❑❑❑

14

Active Voice-Passive Voice

Active - Passive Voice के विषय में Error सम्बन्धित प्रश्नों में सामान्यतया verb की form की गलती या verb के साथ आने वाले Preposition से सम्बन्धित प्रश्नों का समावेश होता है। छात्र 'Active-Passive' विषयक इस अध्याय का अध्ययन करते समय इन बिन्दुओं पर विशेष ध्यान दें।

Voice: The voice of a verb tells whether the subject of the sentence performs or receives the action. In English language there are two voices; passive and active.

Active Voice :- Active Voice वाले वाक्यों में कर्ता (Subject) की प्रमुखता होती है। कर्ता Active होता है। Verb, Active voice में होती है।

Passive Voice :- Passive Voice वाले वाक्यों में कर्ता (Subject) की प्रमुखता नहीं होती बल्कि Object की प्रमुखता होती है, वाक्य Object से शुरू होता है, एवं Verb, Passive Voice में होती है।

GENERAL RULES TO CHANGE THE VOICE

1. **Active Voice से Passive में परिवर्तन करने पर Active Voice का Object, Passive Voice का Subject बन जाता है तथा Active Voice का Subject, Passive Voice में Objective form में बदलकर Object बनता है :**

   I write a letter. — *Active Voice*
   A letter is written by me. — *Passive Voice*

2. **Passive Voice में Verb III form में प्रयुक्त होती है, तथा उससे पहले is / am / are / was / were / been / being का प्रयोग वाक्य के Tense के अनुसार किया जाता है।**

3. **Passive के Subject (नये Subject) के अनुसार Verb, Singular या Plural लिखनी होती है ; यदि Subject - Singular है तो verb - singular एवं यदि नया subject - plural है तो verb भी plural लगती है। जैसे :**

   She is helping the students. — *Active Voice*
   The students are being helped by her. — *Passive Voice*

   यहाँ plural verb - 'are' नये subject - 'students' के अनुसार प्रयुक्त हुई है।

4. **Passive Voice में 'by' का प्रयोग उन वाक्यों में Agent हेतु किया जाता है जहाँ कार्य किसी के द्वारा कराया जाता है। 'by'का प्रयोग verb के बाद एवं agent (object) से पूर्व किया जाता है। कुछ स्थितियों में 'by' एवं agent का प्रयोग नहीं किया जाता है। इसको आगे समझाया गया है।**

5. **Passive Voice में Active Voice का कर्ता निम्न प्रकार से Objective form में बदलता है :**

Active Voice	Passive Voice	Active Voice	Passive Voice
I	Me	She	Her
He	Him	They	Them
You	You	It	It
We	Us	Who	Whom

6. **सामान्य रूप से Transitive verb (ऐसी verb जो अपने साथ object लेती है) का ही Passive बनता है,** जैसे : sleep, sit, stand, go, come, laugh, etc. का Passive नहीं बनता है; लेकिन Intransitive verbs के साथ कोई Preposition प्रयुक्त हो तो, उस स्थिति में इनको भी Passive बनाया जा सकता है।

	Active	**Passive**
(a)	They laughed .	No - Passive
(b)	They laughed at the teacher	The teacher was laughed at by them.
(c)	None had slept.	No- Passive.
(d)	None had slept in the bed.	The bed had not slept in.

7. **Present Perfect Continuous, Past Perfect Continuous, Future Perfect Continuous, एवं Future Continuous का Passive नहीं बनता है। इस प्रकार 12 में से 8 Tenses का Passive बनता है।**

Passive Voice बनाते समय Verb का Tense के अनुसार परिवर्तन निम्न प्रकार से होता है :

	Tense	**Verb (Active)**	**Verb (Passive)**
1.	Simple Present	write / writes	am / is / are written
2.	Simple Past	wrote	was / were written
3.	Simple Future	shall / will write	shall / will be written
4.	Present Continuous	is / am / are writing	is / am / are being written
5.	Past Continuous	was / were writing	was / were being written
6.	Present Perfect	has / have written	has / have been written
7.	Past Perfect	had written	had been written
8.	Future Perfect	will / shall have written	will / shall have been written

उक्त नियमों का ध्यान पूर्वक अध्ययन करें, एवं देखें कि किस तरह हर प्रकार के वाक्यों को Tense wise Passive में बदला जाता है :

VARIOUS TENSES AND CHANGE OF VOICE

Present Tense

1. **Present Indefinite :** Active Voice में Present Indefinite के वाक्य की structure निम्न प्रकार की होती है :

   Subject + V-I + Object.

   He writes a letter.

   इसको Passive Voice में बदलने पर निम्नलिखित वाक्य बनेगा :

   A letter is written by him.
   Subject + is + V – 3 + by + Object.

   इस तरह Passive Voice में वाक्य का Structure निम्न होगा :

   Subject + is / am / are+ V -3 + by + Agent (object).

2. **Present Continuous :-** Present Continuous में Active Voice वाक्य का Structure निम्न प्रकार का होता है :

   He is writing a letter.

   Subject + is / am / are + verb + ing + Object.

   इसको Passive Voice में बदलने पर :

   A letter is being written by him.
   Subject + is + being + V-3 + by Object (Subject of Active in objective form).

   इस तरह Passive Voice में वाक्य का structure होगा :

   Subject + is / am / are + being + V -3 + by + agent (object).

3. **Present Perfect :-**Active Voice में Present Perfect Tense में वाक्य का structure निम्न होता है :
I have written a letter; Subject + have / has +V-3 + Object.
इसको Passive में बदलने पर :-
A letter has been written by me.
Subject + has been + V -3 + by + Object.
इस तरह Passive में वाक्य का Structure होगा -
Subject + have / has been + V- 3 + by + Agent (Object).

Past Tense

1. **Past Indefinite :-** Active Voice में Past Indefinite Tense वाले वाक्य का Structure निम्न होता है :
I wrote a letter; Subject + V- 2 + Object.
Passive Voice में बदलने पर-
A letter was written by me.
Subject + was + V-3 + by + Object. (subject of Active).
इस तरह Passive वाक्य का Structure होगा,
Subject + was / were + V3 + by + agent (Object).
2. **Past Continuous :-** Active Voice में Past Continuous Tense वाले वाक्य का structure निम्न होता है :
Subject + was / were + (verb + ing) + object.
He was writing a letter.
इसे Passive में बदलने पर :-
A letter was being written by him.
Subject +was + being + V-3 + by + object.
इस तरह Passive का structure होगा,
Subject + was / were + being + V - 3 + by + Agent (Object).
3. **Past Perfect :-** Active Voice में Past Perfect Tense वाक्य का structure निम्न होता है :
He had written a letter. (Subject + had + V - 3 + object.)
इसे Passive Voice में बदलने पर :
A letter had been written by him.
इस तरह Passive Voice में वाक्य का structure होगा,
Subject + had been + V-3 + by + (Agent) Object.

Future Tense

1. **Future Indefinite :** Active Voice में Future Indefinite Tense में वाक्य का structure निम्न होता है:
I shall write a letter (Subject + shall / will + V - 1+ Object). इसे Passive में बदलने पर-
A letter will be written by me. [Subject +will be+ V- 3 + by + Object (Subject of Active).]
इस तरह Passive में वाक्य का structure होगा
Subject + will / shall be + V - 3 + by + (Agent)Object.
2. **Future Perfect :-**Active Voice में Future perfect Tense में वाक्य का structure निम्न होता है।
I shall have bought a pen. (Subject+ will / shall have+V-3+ Object.)
इसे Passive Voice में बदलने पर :-
A pen will have been bought by me. (Subject + will have been + V- 3 + by + agent)
इस तरह Passive Voice में वाक्य का structure होगा :
Subject + will / shall have been + V- 3 + by + Agent (Object).

PASSIVE OF INTERROGATIVE SENTENCES

Interrogative Sentences मुख्यतया दो प्रकार के होते हैं :

(1) 'Yes' / 'No' questions (2) 'Wh' words questions.

Yes / No questions

'Yes' / 'No questions' : को निम्न भागों में विभाजित किया जा सकता है।

(a) 'Is / am / are' से शुरू होने वाले questions- इस तरह के Active Voice वाले प्रश्नों के Passive Voice के वाक्यों का Structure होगा :

Is / am / are / + subject + being + V -3 + by + agent ?

Active	**Passive**
(1) Is he writing a letter?	Is a letter being written by him.
(2) Are they ploughing the field.	Is the field being ploughed by them.

(b) 'Do / Does' से शुरू होने वाले questions-इस तरह के Active Voice के प्रश्नों के Passive Voice वाक्यों का Structure होगा :

Is / am / are / + subject + V -3 + by + agent ?

Active	**Passive**
(1) Does he need a pen?	Is a pen needed by him?
(2) Do you like the rooms?	Are the rooms liked by you?

(c) 'Did' से शुरू होने वाले Active Voice questions-इस तरह के प्रश्नों के Passive Voice वाक्यों का Structure होगा :

Was / Were + subject + V -3 + by + agent ?

Active	**Passive**
(1) Did he write a letter?	Was a letter written by him?
(2) Did she help you?	Were you helped by her?

(d) 'Was / Were' से शुरू होने वाले Active Voice questions-इस तरह के प्रश्नों का Passive Voice में वाक्यों का Structure होगा :

Was/Were + subject + being + V -3 + by + agent ?

Active Voice	**Passive Voice**
(1) Was she cooking food?	Was food being cooked by her?
(2) Were they playing chess?	Was the chess being played by them?

(e) Have / Has / Had से शुरू होने वाले questions-इस तरह के प्रश्नों में Passive Voice वाक्यों का Structure होगा

Has/Have/Had + subject + been+ V -3 + by + agent ?

Active Voice	**Passive Voice**
(1) Has he written a book?	Has A book been written by him?
(2) Have they played a match?	Has a match been played by them?
(3) Had she written a letter?	Had a letter been written by her?

(f) **Modal Auxiliary verbs से शुरू होने वाले questions**-इस तरह के प्रश्नों में Passive Voice वाक्यों का Structure होगा।

Modal Auxiliary + Subject + be + V -3 + by + agent ?

Active Voice	**Passive Voice**
(1) Can she control the situation ?	Can the situation be controlled by her ?
(2) May he cross the river?	May the river be crossed by him?
(3) Should he cut the wood ?	Should the wood be cut by him?

An Easy Way

ऐसे Interrogative sentences जिनका Answer 'Yes / No' में दिया जा सकता है, helping verbs से शुरू होते हैं। ऐसे वाक्यों को Passive में बदलने हेतु हमने ऊपर structure भी बताया है एवं solved example भी दिये हैं। इसका बहुत सरल तरीका यह है, कि (i) Interrogative वाक्यों को Assertive में बदलें। (2) अब उस वाक्य का Passive बनावें (3) इस Passive वाक्य में प्रयुक्त helping verb को subject से पहले लिखें, एवं प्रश्न वाचक चिन्ह वाक्य के अन्त में अंकित करें। यह Interrogative वाक्य का Passive होगा।

जैसे :- Does he write a letter?

Assertive- He writes a letter. Passive- A letter is written by him.

इस Passive वाक्य की helping verb (is) को subject से पहले लिखें, एवं प्रश्न वाचक चिन्ह वाक्य के अन्त में अंकित करें :

Is a letter written by him? यह (A) वाक्य का Passive है। इसी तरह :

Has he written a letter?

Assertive- He has written a letter. Passive- A letter has been written by him.

अब; Has a letter been written by him? (Passive Voice)

'Wh' words

'Wh' Words : 'What, Why, When, Where' etc. से शुरू होने वाले। प्रश्नों का उत्तर 'Yes / No' में नहीं दिया जा सकता है, ऐसे प्रश्नों का Passive निम्न प्रकार से बनाया जा सकता है -

सामान्यतया Wh words, Active वाक्य के शुरू में आते हैं। उसके बाद helping verb आती है। यदि वाक्य से 'Wh' word हटाकर देखें तो जो वाक्य बचता है, उसका जवाब 'Yes / No' में दिया जा सकता है। इस वाक्य को पूर्व में बताये नियमानुसार Passive में बदलें। अब 'Wh'word को इस वाक्य के पहले लिखने से, Passive वाक्य बन जाता है। जैसे :

1. Why have you broken the mirror? इस वाक्य में से 'Wh' word हटाने पर शेष वाक्य रहता है: **Have you broken the mirror?** इस वाक्य का Passive बनाना हमनें सीख लिया है। यह एक 'Yes/No' question sentence है। इसका Passive बनेगा: **Has the mirror been broken by you?**

   अब इस वाक्य के शुरू में 'Wh' word लिखने से यह नया वाक्य, वाक्य (1) का Passive Voice रूप बन जायेगा, यथा :

   Why has the mirror been broken by you?

Active Voice	**Passive Voice**
(1) Why have you broken the mirror?	Why has the mirror been broken by you?
(2) Why do you write a letter?	Why is a letter written by you?
(3) When will you return my pen?	When will my pen be returned by you?
(4) Why are you laughing at her?	Why is she being laughed at by you?

'Who' से प्रारम्भ होने वाले Interrogative sentences : इस तरह के वाक्यों में 'By whom' का प्रयोग सामान्यतया वाक्य के शुरू में करके Passive बनाया जाता है। जैसे :

Active Voice	Passive Voice
(1) Who broke this beautiful glass?	By whom was this beautiful glass broken (2)
Who solved that problem?	By whom was that problem solved?

'Whom' से शुरू होने वाले Interrogative sentences :-इनमें 'Who' का प्रयोग करके इन्हें Passive Voice में बनाया जाता है जैसे :

Active Voice	Passive Voice
(1) Whom have you invited?	Who has been invited by you?
(2) Whom has he abused?	Who has been abused by him?

PASSIVE WITHOUT AGENT

Passive Voice बनाते समय वाक्य के अन्त में किन्हीं-किन्ही परिस्थितियों में 'by + Agent' का प्रयोग नहीं किया जाता है, जैसे : जब कर्ता नहीं है या कर्ता का बिना प्रयोग करे भी कार्य चल सकता है या कर्ता understood है, अर्थात यदि Active वाक्य में someone, somebody, nobody, people, आदि कोई कर्ता है :

Active Voice	Passive Voice
(1) People speak English all over the world.	English is spoken all over the world.
(2) Police arrested the thieves.	The thieves were arrested. (कर्ता understood है)
(3) Someone has stolen my watch.	My watch has been stolen.

"In all passive voice exercises the use of 'by' with an agent must be rigorously suppressed, except in those examples where our interest in the predicate has led us to use the passive voice - we should omit the agent where the agent is vague or unknown."

W.S. Allen (Living English Structure)

SENTENCES WITH MODALS

(1) यदि वाक्य में किसी Modal Auxiliary verb का प्रयोग किया गया है, तो इसकी Passive Voice में Helping verb हमेशा 'be' ही आता है।

(2) Modal की स्थिति में कोई परिवर्तन नहीं होता है। शेष वाक्य की Passive Voice पूर्व निर्धारित नियमानुसार बनायें :

Active Voice	Passive Voice
(1) Sita could help him.	He could be helped by Sita.
(2) I will write a letter.	A letter will be written by me.

IMPERATIVE SENTENCES

Imperative Sentences ऐसे वाक्य होते हैं, जिनमें आदेश (order), प्रार्थना (Request) या सलाह (advice, suggestion) आदि का भाव व्यक्त होता है। ऐसे वाक्य सामान्यतया मुख्य क्रिया (Principal verb) से शुरू होते हैं :

(A) Sentences with Order, Command :

Active Voice	Passive Voice
(1) Shut the window.	Let the window be shut.
(2) Bring a glass of water.	Let a glass of water be brought.
(3) Finish this work.	Let this work be finished.

Order / Command वाले Imperative वाक्यों में, साधारणतया passive sentences का structure निम्न प्रकार का होता है : **Let + Subject + be + III form of verb.**

कभी-कभी 'You are ordered' से भी Passive Voice में वाक्यों को शुरू किया जाता है। जैसे :-

(1) Get out of this office. — *Active*
You are ordered to get out of this office. — *Passive*
(2) Bring some glasses of water for them. — *Active*
You are ordered to bring some glasses of water for them. — *Passive*

इस प्रकार के Passive Voice वाले वाक्यों का structure निम्न होता है :

You are ordered to + verb I + object.

(B) Sentences containing Request :-

Active Voice	**Passive Voice**
(1) Please open the door.	You are requested to open the door.
(2) Please help that old lady.	You are requested to help that old lady.

इस प्रकार के Passive Voice वाक्यों का structure निम्न प्रकार का होता है:

You are requested to + I form of verb + object.

(C) Sentences with Suggestion:- Suggestion वाले Imperative sentences को Passive Voice में बदलते समय should be का प्रयोग निम्न प्रकार होता है :

Active Voice	**Passive Voice**
(1) Help the disabled.	The disabled should be helped.
(2) Listen to me.	I should be listened to.
(4) Always speak the truth.	The truth should always be spoken.
(5) Love the kids.	The kids should be loved.

इस तरह के वाक्यों का Passive Voice में structure निम्न होता है :

Subject + should be + III form of verb.

(D) Sentences with Advice :- जिन वाक्यों में सलाह का भाव निहित होता है, उनकी Voice को Passive में बदलते समय 'You are advised to' का प्रयोग निम्न प्रकार किया जाता है :

Active Voice	**Passive Voice**
(1) Work hard.	You are advised to work hard.
(2) Get up early.	You are advised to get up early.

PASSIVE OF INFINITIVE

Active Voice में Infinitive वाले वाक्यों का सामान्यतया Structure निम्न प्रकार होता है :

Subject + is / am / are / was / were/ have / has / had + to + verb -I + object.

ऐसे वाक्यों का Passive structure निम्न प्रकार होगा :

Subject + is / am / are / was / were / have / has / had + to be + V-3 + by + agent.

Look at the following solved examples :

Active Voice	**Passive Voice**
(1) I am to finish this work.	This work is to be finished by me.
(2) They are to buy a TV.	A TV is to be bought by them.
(3) We were to buy a car.	A car was to be bought by us.
(4) You were to bring him here.	He was to be brought here by you.
(5) The students have to write notes.	Notes have to be written by the students.
(6) Harish had to complete this work.	This work had to be completed by Harish.

PASSIVE VOICE : MISCELLANEOUS STRUCTURES

(A) 'It is time to + V-1 + noun' structure वाले वाक्य :

इस तरह के वाक्यों का passive structure होगा – **It is time + for + noun + to be + V-3.**

Active Voice	**Passive Voice**
(1) It is time to close the office.	It is time for the office to be closed.
(2) It is time to supply food.	It is time for food to be supplied.

(B) 'There' से शुरू होने वाले वाक्य :

There +be form of verb + noun + infinitive. — Active Structure

इस तरह के वाक्यों का Passive structure निम्न होता है :

There + be form of verb + noun + to be + verb III form. — Passive Structure

Active Voice	**Passive Voice**
(1) There is a lot of work to complete.	There is a lot of work to be completed.
(2) There are six letters to write.	There are six letters to be written.

(C) Verbs showing, state of mind or feelings : कुछ Verbs ऐसी होती हैं जो कोई action व्यक्त नहीं करती है, बल्कि मानसिक स्थिति या भाव को व्यक्त करती हैं। इस प्रकार की Verbs की passive form में 'by' का प्रयोग नहीं किया जाता है, बल्कि उपयुक्त Preposition का प्रयोग किया जाता है। जैसे :

Active Voice	**Passive Voice**
(1) I know her.	She is known to me. (Preposition - 'to')
(2) He annoyed with me.	I was annoyed with him.(Preposition - 'with')
(3) This magazine has greatly interested me.	I have been greatly interested in this magazine. (Prep-'in')
(4) The news pleased her.	She was pleased with the news. (Prep-'with')
(5) Her behaviour annoyed him.	He was annoyed at her behaviour. (Prep.-'at')

इस तरह की कुछ verbs एवं उनके साथ आने वाले preposition निम्न हैं :

'Known to, amazed at, annoyed with (some person), annoyed at (something), startled at, vexed at, decorated with, filled with, surprised at, embodied in' etc.

(D) Verbs with Appropriate Prepositions:

कुछ verbs अपने बाद Prepositions के साथ ही object लेती हैं, ऐसी verbs के साथ passive form में भी preposition उसी तरह से लगा रहता है :

Active Voice	**Passive Voice**
(1) He *laughed* at me.	I was *laughed at* by him.
(2) The police is *enquiring* into the matter	The matter is being *enquired into* by the police.
(3) He *looks after* his parents.	His parents are *looked after* by him.

इस तरह की Verbs जो अपने साथ preposition के बाद object लेती है निम्न है :

Look at, look after, laugh at, smile at, deride at, mock at etc.

(E) कुछ Sentences की बनावट Active Voice में निम्न प्रकार की होती है :

Subject + ask + object + if / whether + clause.

इस तरह के वाक्यों में प्रथम भाग को ही Passive में बदला जाता है; शेष वाक्य में कोई परिवर्तन नहीं होता है:

Active Voice	**Passive Voice**
(1) I asked Rani, if she went to Jaipur.	Rani was asked if she went to Jaipur.
(2) He asked me, when I would complete my work.	I was asked when I would complete my work.

(F) Causative Verbs : जब किसी वाक्य में Causative verb का प्रयोग किया जाता है, तो उस वाक्य में Active voice में subject के बाद Causative verb आता है। इस तरह के वाक्यों को Passive voice में निम्न प्रकार परिवर्तित किया जाता है :

	Active Voice	**Passive Voice**
(1)	I made him polish my shoes.	He was made to polish my shoes.
(2)	He made me sing a song.	I was made to sing a song.
(3)	They made him king.	He was made king.
(6)	We elected him monitor.	He was elected monitor.

(G) कुछ वाक्य में 'They believed, People think, People say, We know, Everyone knows' जैसे शब्दों से वाक्य शुरू करके 'that he is .....' से वाक्य पूर्ण होता है। इस प्रकार के वाक्यों का Passive निम्न दो प्रकार से बन सकता है :

(1) It was/is believed that....

(2) He is known / said / believed to be....

Look at the following examples :

	Active Voice	**Passive Voice**
(1)	They believed that Mr. Shukla was very rich.	It was believed that Mr Shukla was very rich. Mr Shukla was believed to be very rich.
(2)	We know that some children go wise early.	It is known that some children go wise early. Some children are known to go wise early.
(3)	People consider that she is intelligent.	She is considered to be intelligent. It is considered that she is intelligent.
(4)	People say that he is a thief.	It is said that he is a thief. He is said to be a thief.
(5)	Everyone knows that he is a gangster.	It is known that he is a gangster. He is known to be a gangster.

(H) Double Passive:-

(1) They looted the shop and took away the money. *— Active*
The shop was looted and the money was taken away. *— Passive*

(2) She wrote the book and got published. *— Active*
The book was written and got published by her. *— Passive*

(3) The police arrested the thieves and sent them to jail. *— Active*
The thieves were arrested and sent to jail. *— Passive*

(I) Verbs with two objects :- जब वाक्य में दो objects होते हैं, तो हम जिस object को प्रमुखता देना चाहते हैं, उसे subject बनाया जाता है। सामान्यतया, व्यक्तियों (Indirect object) को प्रमुखता दी जाती है।

Look at the following examples :-

	Active	**Passive**
(1)	He gave me a purse.	I was given a purse by him. A purse was given to me by him.
(2)	Rahim teaches us English.	English is taught us by Rahim. We are taught English by Rahim.
(3)	The principal asked him a question.	A question was asked him by the principal. He was asked a question by the principal.
(4)	Rani gave him a letter.	A letter was given to him by Rani. He was given a letter by Rani.

MISCELLANEOUS SENTENCES

(1) He likes people to call him, 'Don'. — *Active*
He likes to be called 'Don'. — *Passive*

(2) No one can do any thing unless someone gives us accurate information. — *Active*
Nothing can be done unless we are given accurate information. — *Passive*

(3) One must do one's duty. — *Active*
Duty must be done. — *Passive*

(4) The officer wants his subordinates to obey him. — *Active*
The officer wants to be obeyed by his subordinates. — *Passive*

(5) He wants that he should be treated as king. — *Active*
He wants to be treated as king. — *Passive*

(6) Ram desires his wife to respect his parents. — *Active*
Ram desires his parents to be respected by his wife. — *Passive*

(7) I remember them taking me to library. — *Active*
I remember being taken to library. — *Passive*

(8) We saw them go out. — *Active*
They were seen go out. — *Passive*

(9) When he arrived home, police arrested him. — *Active*
When he arrived home he was arrested. — *Passive*

(10) I saw her sing a song. — *Active*
She was seen to sing a song. — *Passive*

(11) Brutus accused Caesar of ambition. — *Active*
Caesar was accused of ambition by Brutus. — *Passive*

(12) We clected him secretary of the society. — *Active*
He was elected secretary of the society. — *Passive*

ERRORS, MISTAKES AND BLUNDERS IN ACTIVE PASSIVE

Exercise-1 : ***Find the errors and justify your answer.***

1. The bank robbery case (A)/ was enquired (B)/two months ago but no (C)/report has been published yet (D).
2. The lonely lady puzzled (A)/ when she found some (B)/strange footprints (C)/near the door (D).
3. The poor boy was approached (A)/ to the principal (B)/ and requested him (C)/to forgive him for his mistake (D).
4. Two students were badly injured (A)/ and a dog killed in the (B)/ bus car accident (C)/ that took place yesterday (D).
5. It was advised by (A)/our family doctor (B)/ that the patient (C)/ must be taken care (D).
6. A new TV serial (A)/ is soon to be (B)/ telecasted by (C)/ the Star channel (D).
7. Having found guilty (A)/ of rape and murder, (B)/ the accused was sentenced (C)/to life imprisonment (D).
8. Ram expelled his (A)/ son from his house (B)/ because he was married (C)/ an other caste girl (D).
9. If you don't apologise (A)/ for having committed (B)/ the mistake you (C)/ won't be forgave (D).
10. An officer sent to my house (A)/ and all the documents (B)/ and articles were (C)/thoroughly checked (D).
11. When he seriously wounded (A)/ by a lorry (B)/he was immediately (C)/ helped by an unknown person (D).

12. Stones should not be (A)/ thrown others (B)/ by those who (C)/ live in glass houses (D).
13. I had never saw surch (A)/ a magnificient (B)/ building of a hotel (C).
14. The people was called him (A)/ an imposter and regarded him (B)/ as a 'Don' (C).
15. On 26th January all (A)/ the streets was (B)/ thronged with spectators (C).
16. Grammar is taught us (A)/ by a lady teacher (B)/ named Smt. Kumkum (C).
17. By whom (A)/ were you (B)/ taught to Grammar (C).
18. The dog was killed (A)/ by him (B)/ by an iron road (C).
19. Why was such (A)/ a nasty letter (B)/ was written (C)/ by your brother (D) ?
20. The wounded man (A)/ was being (B)/ help by some girls (C).

Explanations

1. (B) 'enquired' के बाद 'into' लिखना होगा। कुछ verbs अपने बाद preposition लेती हैं। ऐसी verbs को Passive में बदलते समय उसी Preposition को लिखना आवश्यक होता है। ऐसे अन्य उदाहरण देखे:
   She laughed at me.................... Active
   I was laughed at by her.............Passive
2. (A) 'The lonely lady *was* puzzled' होगा। Passive Voice में V-III के पहले be form of verb का प्रयोग होता है।
3. (A) यह Active Voice का वाक्य है। इसमें 'was' का प्रयोग गलत है।
4. (B) 'a dog *was* killed' होगा। Pasive में V-III से पूर्व auxiliary का प्रयोग (Tense के अनुसार) होता है।
5. (B) 'care' के बाद 'of' preposition का प्रयोग होगा।
6. (C) 'telecasted' की जगह 'telecast' ही होगा। 'Telecast' की III form 'telecast' ही है।
7. (A) 'Having been found' होगा। वाक्य का अर्थ है – अपराधी को बलात्कार एवं हत्या का दोषी पाये जाने के बाद ... (Having been found guilty...)
8. (C) 'he was married' की जगह 'he married' ही होगा। यह Active Voice का वाक्य है।
9. (D) 'forgave' की जगह 'forgiven' होगा।
10. (A) 'sent' से पहले 'was' का प्रयोग आवश्यक है।
11. (A) 'when he *was* seriously wounded' होगा।
12. (B) 'thrown *at* others' होगा।
13. (A) 'never *saw*' की जगह 'never seen' होगा।
14. (A) 'was' को delete करें। यह Active Voice का वाक्य है।
15. (B) 'the streets *were*' होगा।
16. (A) 'taught *to* us' होगा।
17. (C) 'taught Grammar' होगा। 'to' को delete करें।
18. (C) '*with* an iron rod' होगा।
19. (C) 'was written' की जगह केवल 'written' आयेगा। 'was' का प्रयोग शुरू में 'why' के साथ हो चुका है।
20. (C) '*helped* by some girls' होगा।

Exercise-2 : *Choose the best way to complete these passive voice sentences.*

1. Your jacket _____ over there.
   A can be hang up
   B can be heng up
   C can be hung up
   D can be hunged up
   E can hung up

2. She_____.

A have never been heard of
B has never been hearing of
C has never been heared of
D has never been heard of
E has never be heard of

3. She _____ by a bus.

A was been knocking down
B was being knocked down
C was knocked down
D was knock down
E was knocking down

4. Nothing _____ me.

A can be hald against
B can be held against
C can be hold against,
D can be holding against
E can held against

5. The protesters _____ by the police.

A are holding back
B are being holding back
C are being hold back
D are being held back
E are being hald back

6. The flood water _____ by barriers.

A was being kept back
B was being keep back
C was been kept back
D was being keept back
E was be kept back

7. Thirty more people _____ last week.

A were laid off
B were layed off
C were laying off
D were lie off
E were lied off

8. The keys _____.

A must have been left behind
B must been left behind
C must having been left behind
D must have be left behind
E must have been leaving behind

9. The criminal _____.

A were locked up
B locked up
C was locking up
D was locked up
E was lock up

10. The road _____.

A was blocking off
B was block off
C was blocking off
D was blocked off
E was been blocked off

11. Our allies _____ support.

A will be lend
B will be lended
C will be lent
D will been lent
E will being lent

12. _____ to you yet?

A Has the book been given back
B Have the book being given back
C Have the book been gave back
D Was the book been give back
E Have the books been given back

13. She _____ with a fine.
A was let off
B was letted off
C was letting off
D let off
E were let off

14. 3000 employees _____.
A were lied off
B were laying off
C were layed off
D were lain off
E were laid off

15. The old cinema _____.
A being pulled down
B is been pulled down
C is being pull down
D is being pulled down
E is being pulling down

16. The inconvenience _____ by this money.
A will made up for
B will been made up for
C will be made up for
D will being made up for
E will be make up for

17. The candle _____ by the draught.
A was being blown out
B was blown out
C was blewed out
D was blow out
E was blowed out

18. A story _____.
A will be making up
B will being made up
C will be made up
D will been made up
E will be maked up

19. My bank loan _____ in five years time.
A will paid off
B will be being paid off
C will be paying off
D will be paid off
E will be payed off

20. An idea _____ for discussion.
A put forward
B was put forward
C was putted forward
D was putting forward
E has put for forward

Answers

1. C, **2.** D, **3.** C, **4.** B, **5.** D, **6.** A, **7.** A, **8.** A, **9.** D, **10.** D,
11. C, **12.** A, **13.** A, **14.** E, **15.** D, **16.** C, **17.** B, **18.** C, **19.** D, **20.** B.

Exercise-3 : *Correct the mistakes and rewrite these passive voice sentences.*

1. A big chunk of his calf was being bitten off by the dog.
2. A plan to stop drug trafficking had been draw up.
3. He was running over by a bus as he was crossing the road.
4. His confidence will be build up by this.
5. I am being catched up by the stress of the last few weeks.
6. I have being done in by all that exercise.
7. More and more farmland is being eated up by cities.
8. Most of the land in the area has be bought up by property developers.

9. My money have been stolen.
10. One of the other prisoners was beat up.
11. Red meat have been cut out of my diet.
12. She are being brought up in a friendly atmosphere.
13. The engagement was being broken off just two days before the wedding.
14. The essays have be handed in on Monday.
15. The office had been being blown up by terrorists.
16. The rebels will being called on to stop fighting.
17. The road outside my house is being digged up.
18. The task is braked down into smaller, manageable mini-tasks.
19. This government could be bringing down by this scandal.
20. Unemployment must dealt with by the government.

Explanations

1. A big chunk of his calf was bitten off by the dog.
2. A plan to stop drug trafficking had been drawn up.
3. He was run over by a bus as he was crossing the road.
4. His confidence will be built up by this.
5. I am being caught up by the stress of the last few weeks.
6. I have been done in by all that exercise.
7. More and more farmland is being eaten up by cities.
8. Most of the land in the area has been bought up by property developers.
9. My money has been stolen.
10. One of the other prisoners was beaten up.
11. Red meat has been cut out of my diet.
12. She is being brought up in a friendly atmosphere.
13. The engagement was broken off just two days before the wedding.
14. The essays have to be handed in on Monday.
15. The office had been blown up by terrorists.
16. The rebels will be called on to stop fighting.
17. The road outside my house is being dug up.
18. The task is broken down into smaller, manageable mini-tasks.
19. This government could be brought down by this scandal.
20. Unemployment must be dealt with by the government.

BLUNDERS

Exercise : ***Correct the following sentences and justify the corrections.***

1. The car is being repairing by the machanic.
2. This letter was wrote by Ramesh .
3. This car has purchased by my landlord.
4. The kites were flew by the students.
5. The project will have completed by Sarita by tomorrow.
6. The ball is hitten by him.
7. Were food being cooked by the cook?
8. Is this book wrote by Suresh?

9. When will my pen return by you ?
10. Whom was the Ramayan written ?

Explanations

1. 'repairing' की जगह 'repaired' लिखें। Passive structure में verb की III form ही प्रयुक्त होती है।
2. 'wrote' की जगह 'written' लिखें।
3. सही वाक्य होगा–This car has *been* purchased by my landlord.
4. 'flew' की जगह 'flown' होगा। fly - flew - flown.
5. 'will have *been*' होगा। Future perfect के Passive structure का ध्यान रखें।
6. 'hitten' की जगह hit होगा। 'hit' की III form, hit ही है।
7. 'were' की जगह 'was' होगा।
8. 'wrote' की जगह 'written' होगा।
9. 'return' की जगह 'be returned' होगा।
10. सही वाक्य होगा– '*By* whom was the Ramayan written ?' होगा।

□□□

15

Preposition

Preposition के सम्बन्ध में छात्रों द्वारा बहुत-सी गलतियाँ की जाती हैं। बहुत-सी Verbs के साथ एक विशेष Preposition ही प्रयुक्त होता है। कुछ verbs के साथ कोई भी Preposition नहीं प्रयुक्त होता है। छात्रों को Preposition के अध्याय को बार-बार बहुत धैर्य से पढ़ना चाहिए।

Preposition, वाक्य में ऐसा शब्द है, जो noun /pronoun के पूर्व प्रयुक्त होता है एवं noun /pronoun का सम्बन्ध, वाक्य में प्रयुक्त अन्य शब्दों से व्यक्त करता है ।

Preposition is a word placed before a Noun or Pronoun, denotes the relation, the person or thing referred by it, has with something else.

A preposition is followed by a 'noun'. It is never followed by a verb.

A preposition cannot be followed by a verb. If we want to follow a preposition by a verb, we must use the '-ing' form which is really a gerund or verb in noun form.

Read the following examples:

(1) The food is on the table. (2) She lives in China.

(3) Mira is looking for you. (4) The letter is under your black book.

उपरोक्त वाक्यों में underlined words -**Prepositions** हैं , जो noun या pronoun का सम्बन्ध अन्य शब्दों से व्यक्त करते हैं।

जिस Noun / Pronoun से पूर्व, Preposition प्रयुक्त हुआ है, वह Noun/Pronoun, उस Preposition का Object कहलाता है।

POSITION OF PREPOSITION

(1) जब Preposition का Object-Interrogative Pronoun, जैसे : What,Who,Whom,Which,Where, etc. होता है तो Preposition को वाक्य के अन्त में लिखा जाता है । जैसे :

(a) What are you thinking of ? (b) What is he crying for?

यहाँ 'What' Interrogative Pronoun है, जो underlined words-Preposition 'for', 'of' का Object है ।

(2) जब Preposition का Object-Relative Pronoun, 'that' होता है, तो भी Preposition को वाक्य के अन्त में लिखा जाता है। जैसे :

(a) Here is the magazine that you asked for. (b) This is the dish that she is fond of.

(3) जब Object-Infinitive हो तो Preposition को Infinitive के बाद लिखा जाता है। जैसे :

(a) This is a good hotel to stay at. (b) I need a pencil to write with .

(4) कई वाक्यों में Relative Pronoun, Hidden किया हुआ (छुपा हुआ) रहता है। ऐसे वाक्यों में Preposition वाक्य के अन्त में आता है। जैसे :

(a) This is the house (where) I lived in.

(b) This is the girl (that) I told you of.

(5) कुछ वाक्यों में **Preposition** का प्रयोग शुरू में ही किया जाता है। सामान्यतया ऐसे वाक्य **Interrogative** होते हैं :

(a) By which train did you come ? (b) For whom was instructions given ?

SOME IMPORTANT PREPOSITIONS

(1) At / In / On

These are very commonly used prepositions.

Note the use of these prepositions in reference of 'Time' :

(i) 'At' is used for a PRECISE TIME,

(ii) 'In' is used for MONTHS, YEARS, CENTURIES and LONG PERIODS,

(iii) 'On' is used for DAYS and DATES

At **Precise Time**	**In** **Months, Years, Centuries and Long Periods**	**On** **Days, Dates**
at 3 o'clock	in May	on Sunday
at 10.30 am.	in summer	on Tuesdays
at noon	in the summer	on 6 March
at dinner time	in 1990	on 25th Jan., 2007
at bed time	in the 1990s	on Christmas Day
at sunrise	in the next century	on Independence Day
at sunset	in the Ice Age	on my birthday

(a) I have a meeting at 10 am. (b) That shop closes at midnight.

(c) Richa went home at lunch time. (d) Where will you be on Independence Day?

Note the use of the preposition of time 'At' :

Expression	**Example**
at night	The stars shine at night.
at the weekend	I don't usually work at the weekend.
at Christmas/Easter	I stay with my family at Christmas.
at the same time	We finished the test at the same time.
at present	He's not home at present. Try later.

Note the use of the prepositions of time 'In' and 'On' in these common expressions:

in	**on**
in the morning	on Tuesday morning
in the mornings	on Saturday mornings
in the afternoon (s)	on Sunday afternoons
in the evening (s)	on Monday evenings

लेकिन 'last, next, every' के साथ At, In, On का प्रयोग नहीं किया जाता है।

(i) I went to Maxico last May. (not in last May)

(ii) He's coming back next Sunday. (not on next Sunday)

(iii) I go home every Easter. (not at every Easter)

(iv) We'll call you this evening. (not in this evening)

Note the use of these prepositions in reference of 'Place' :

(i) 'At' is used for a POINT,

(ii) 'In' is used for an ENCLOSED SPACE,

(iii) 'On' is used for a SURFACE.

At	In	On
POINT	ENCLOSED SPACE	SURFACE
at the corner	in the garden	on the wall
at the bus stop	in Delhi	on the ceiling
at the door	in India	on the door
at the top of the page	in a box	on the cover
at the end of the road	in my pocket	on the floor
at the entrance	in my wallet	on the carpet
at the crossroads	in a building	on the menu
at the entrance	in a car	on a page

Look at the following examples :

(a) Ruma is waiting for you at the bus stop. (b) The shop is at the end of the lane.

(c) I live on the 4th floor at 21, Diamond Street in Kolkata. (d) When will you arrive at the school?

(e) Do you work in a company? (f) I have a meeting in Delhi .

(g) Do you live in India ?

(2) At/ In/ To/ Into

(A) 'At'- स्थिर अवस्था के लिये तथा 'In' गतिशील स्थिति में प्रयोग होता है :

(a) She is at home. (b) The train is in motion.

(B) 'At' छोटे स्थान हेतु तथा 'In' बड़े स्थान हेतु प्रयुक्त होता है :

(a) He lives at Alwar in Rajasthan. (b) A temple is situated at Madurai in Tamil Nadu.

(C) 'At'- Point of time हेतु, तथा 'in' Period of time हेतु प्रयोग किया जाता है :

(a) The train will arrive at 6 in the morning. (b) He will meet you in the morning.

(D) In/Into: 'In' का प्रयोग पूर्व में ही कोई वस्तु अन्दर होती है, उसके लिये किया जाता है, जबकी 'Into' का प्रयोग Movement (बाहर से भीतर की ओर गति) को बताता है :

(a) He jumped into the river. (b) There are three students in the class.

(E) To/Into : दोनों का प्रयोग गतिशीलता प्रदर्शित करता है। इनका प्रयोग वाक्य के अर्थ के अनुसार किया जाता है। 'To' का अर्थ–'को' तथा 'Into' का अर्थ–'अन्दर' होता है :

(a) He went to market. (b) He jumped into the well.

(3) On/ To/ Onto

On- समय हेतु :

(a) He will come on Monday. (b) Ram will go on 4th June.

To- स्थान हेतु :

(a) He will go to Delhi. (b) Ram will go to market tomorrow.

On/Onto

'On' का प्रयोग स्थिरता एवं गतिशीलता दोनो के सन्दर्भ में किया जा सकता है :

(a) Snow fell on the hills. (b) He is sitting on his suitcase.

'Onto' का प्रयोग मुख्य रूप से movement गतिशीलता के सन्दर्भ में तब होता है, जब level (तल) का change व्यक्त होता है :

(a) People climbed onto their roofs. (b) He lifted her onto the table.

(4) With/ By

'With' का प्रयोग Instrument हेतु, 'By' का प्रयोग Agent (कर्ता) हेतु किया जाता है।

(a) The snake was killed by him with a stick.
(b) The letter was written by Suresh with a pencil.

(5) Since/ For/ From

'Since' का प्रयोग Perfect Tense में होता है। 'For' का प्रयोग Perfect Tense में भी एवं अन्य Tenses में भी 'समय की अवधि' के लिये होता है। Since का प्रयोग Point of time व्यक्त करने हेतु किया जाता है, जैसे :
Since 6 O'Clock/Last night/Last Monday; Since Morning/Evening/Monday/January/2004 etc.
'For' का प्रयोग अवधि हेतु होता है, जैसे: for two hours/two days/two years/a long time/some time etc.
'From' का प्रयोग 'समय से कार्य होने' के सन्दर्भ में होता है। 'From' का प्रयोग Perfect Tense में नहीं होता, अन्य Tenses में होता है :

(a) He will go to college from next Monday. (b) It has been raining for two hours
(c) It has been raining since two O'Clock. (d) He worked for three hours.

'From' का प्रयोग स्थान के लिये भी होता है :

(a) He is from Mumbai. (b) Where do you come from ?

(6) For/ During

'For' का प्रयोग सामान्यतया 'अवधि' हेतु तथा 'During' का प्रयोग 'दौरान' के अर्थ में किया जाता है, जैसे :

(a) It rained all Sunday, but stopped during the night.
(b) He has been ill for three days

और, जैसे : During childhood, during middle ages, during holidays, during summer vacations ; for a month, for three days, for 15 years etc.

'for' का अर्थ– 'के लिये' भी होता है, अत: अर्थ के अनुसार 'for' का प्रयोग निम्न प्रकार भी किया जा सकता है :

(a) I went there for summer vacations.
(b) I rented my car for the summer only.

(7) Below / Under / Beneath

'Below' और 'Under' दोनों का अर्थ : 'नीचे' होता है। सामान्यतया 'Under' द्वारा वस्तु से Physical contact व्यक्त होता है; एवं 'Below' से Contact व्यक्त नहीं होता है। जैसे :

(a) He put the books under the pillow. (b) He placed the lamp below the Almirah.

'Under' का अर्थ 'Junior' भी होता है।

(a) He is working under me. or He is under me.

'Below' का प्रयोग 'dignity' के Reference में भी किया जाता है :

(a) It is below his dignity to beg for mercy.

Beneath : Something that is **beneath** another thing is under the other thing.
She could see the muscles of his shoulders beneath his T-shirt....

(8) In/ Within

'In' का अर्थ होता है– 'में'। यह दिये गये समय के अन्तिम बिन्दु को व्यक्त करने हेतु प्रयुक्त होता है। इसका तात्पर्य कार्य में लगने वाले समय को व्यक्त करना है।

'Within' का अर्थ होता है 'अन्दर-अन्दर'। यह दी गई 'समय सीमा' को व्यक्त करता है। 'Within' का प्रयोग तब किया जाता है, जब कार्य के उस समय-सीमा से पहले ही पूर्ण होने की सम्भावना होती है। जैसे :

(a) I will complete the work in a month. (b) I can repair the car within two hours.

(9) Ago/ Before

'Ago' का प्रयोग Past की घटनाओं हेतु तथा 'Before' का प्रयोग दो घटनाओं / कार्यों के सन्दर्भ में किया जाता है।

(a) He came three days ago.
(b) The train had left before he reached the station.

(10) Beside/Besides

'Beside' का अर्थ-'साथ में /बगल में' होता है जबकि 'Besides' का अर्थ -'अतिरिक्त '(in addition to) होता है।

(a) He was sitting beside Sarla. (b) He has a car besides a motor cycle.

(11) Between/ Among

'Between' का प्रयोग सामान्यतया, दो के मध्य, के लिए किया जाता है। Among का प्रयोग, दो से अधिक, के मध्य के सन्दर्भ में किया जाता है।

(a) He distributed his property between his two sons.
(b) He distributed his property among the poor.

'Between' का प्रयोग दो से अधिक के लिये तब किया जा सकता है, जब वे आपस में closely associated हों। जैसे:

(a) A treaty was signed between three parties.
(b) He inserted a needle between the closed petals of a flower.

(12) Among/ Amongst

दोनों का प्रयोग दो से अधिक के सन्दर्भ में होता है। यदि इनके बाद वाक्य में 'the' आता है तो किसी (Among/Amongst) का भी प्रयोग किया जा सकता है, लेकिन यदि इनके बाद स्वर (Vowel) से प्रारम्भ होने वाला शब्द है, [eg. 'us' in example (b) below] तो Amongst का प्रयोग किया जाता है। Amongst का प्रयोग कम प्रचलन में है :

(a) He distributed the toffees among/amongst the poor.
(b) He distributed the toffees amongst us.

(13) Of/ Off

'Of' सम्बन्ध स्थापित करने के भाव वाला Preposition है, जबकि 'Off' से दूर हटने का भाव व्यक्त होता है :

(a) He is a member of our family. (b) He is off duty now.

(14) Above/ Over

दोनों का अर्थ 'higher than' (ऊँचा) होता है। कई स्थितियों में दोनों में से किसी का भी प्रयोग किया जा सकता है जैसे :

(a) The helicopter is hovering above /over us.
(b) Flags were waved above/over our heads.

'Over' को कई अर्थों; जैसे - Covering (ढकना), on the other side of (दूसरी तरफ), across (आर-पार) में प्रयोग किया जाता है :

(a) I put a cloth over her. (b) There is a bridge over the railway line.

'Over' का प्रयोग meal/tea/lunch/drink आदि के सन्दर्भ में निम्न प्रकार किया जा सकता है :

(a) We had a chat over a cup of tea. (b) The matter was decided over the lunch.

लेकिन 'above' का प्रयोग उक्त अर्थों में नहीं किया जा सकता है।

'Above' का अर्थ 'earlier'or 'previously' (पूर्व) भी होता है।

(a) He lives at the above address. (Previously mentioned address)
(b) For details please see P-1 above.

(15) Make of / Make from

दोनों Prepositions किसी material (सामग्री) को इंगित करते हैं :

'Make of' का प्रयोग तब होता है जब वस्तु (उक्त सामग्री) की अवस्था में कोई परिवर्तन नहीं होता है :

(a) A note book is made of papers. (b) A house is made of bricks.

'Make from' का प्रयोग तब होता है, जब उक्त सामग्री की अवस्था बदल जाती है :

(a) Butter is made from milk. (b) Paper is made from grass.

उपरोक्त वाक्यों में सामग्री से आशय 'Papers', 'bricks', 'milk' और 'grass' से है।

(16) In/ With

(a) He writes with a pen. (b) He is writing in ink.

जब countable noun (e.g.– 'pen') होता है तो Instrument हेतु 'with' का प्रयोग होता है। जब uncountable noun (e.g.– 'ink') होता है तो 'in' का प्रयोग होता है।

'With' का प्रयोग कई अर्थों में होता है :

(1) साथ-साथ — He is playing with his sister .

(2) कारण — He is trembling with fear.

(3) सम्बन्ध — I have no relation with her.

(4) तरीका (Manner) — He fought with determination.

(5) सहमति — I agree with you.

(17) Opposite / In front of

'Opposite' का प्रयोग : 'विपरीत' एवं 'सामने' दोनों अर्थ में होता है। 'Infront of' का अर्थ- 'सामने' ही होता है:

If, Ram and Shyam are having a meal; Ram is sitting at one side of the table and Shyam at the other side. तो हम कहेंगे: 'Ram is sitting opposite Shyam'. हम यह नहीं कहेंगे कि 'Ram is sitting in front of Shyam'.

सड़क के दोनों तरफ के मकानों के लिए भी 'opposite' ही प्रयोग होगा :

His house is opposite to ours.

'In front' का प्रयोग निम्न प्रकार किया जाता है :

(a) He parked the car in front of the hotel. (b) He put the plates on the table in front of us.

Preposition + Gerund :- कुछ verbs एवं adjectives इस प्रकार के होते हैं, जिनके साथ Preposition के बाद हमेशा Gerund का प्रयोग होता है। इस तरह की Verbs निम्न हैं :

Abstain from
afraid of
proud of
good at
desist from
disqualified from
dissuade (one)from
prevent from
refrain from
hinder(one) from
prohibit(one)from
despair of
confident of
fond of
glad about
disappointed about/at
sorry about/for

desirous of
angry about/at
succeed in
clever at
repent of
think of
hopeful of
fortunate in
assist in
excel in
negligent in
perceive in
persist in
famous for
keen on
fed up with,
happy about/at

pride in
debar from
bad at
crazy about
successful in
bent on
insist on
meditate on
aim at
passion for
excuse for
tired of
worried about
excited about
interested in
sick of

For example :

(a) He prevented me from drinking cold water. (b) He insisted on trying again.
(c) He was debarred from taking examination. (d) He succeeded in achieving his goal.
(e) They are afraid of loosing the match.

ELLIPSIS IN PREPOSITION

कई बार वाक्यों में दो या अधिक शब्दों हेतु एक ही Preposition का प्रयोग कर दिया जाता है। ध्यान रखें, यदि एक ही Preposition दोनों शब्दों हेतु उपयुक्त है, तो यह एक शुद्ध / सही प्रयोग होगा अन्यथा दोनों शब्दों के साथ अलग-अलग Preposition लिखना होगा। (Ellipsis का अर्थ है : Omission अर्थात् 'एक को हटाना' ।)

(a) We should prevent damage and theft of public property. —*Incorrect.*

यहाँ 'damage' एवं 'theft' के लिये एक ही Preposition 'of' का प्रयोग किया गया है, जो उचित नहीं है, क्योंकि 'damage' के साथ 'to' एवं 'theft' के साथ 'of' का प्रयोग किया जाना चाहिए। अत: इस वाक्य को निम्न प्रकार से लिखा जाना चाहिए :

We should prevent damage to and theft of public property. —*Correct*

(b) He is neither ashamed nor sorry for his misdeeds. —*Incorrect.*
He is neither ashamed of nor sorry for his misdeeds. —*Correct*

(c) The design of this house is different and inferior to that of other house. —*Incorrect*
The design of this house in different from and inferior to that of other house. —*Correct.*

PREPOSITION OMITTED

निम्न स्थितियों में Preposition का प्रयोग नहीं किया जाता है :

(1) सामान्यतया Transitive Verbs के साथ Preposition का प्रयोग नहीं किया जाता है। इस तरह की verbs हैं - Reach, Resist, Resemble, Afford, Accompany, Attack, Assist, Pick, Pervade, Precede, Obey, Order, Combat, Benefit, Inform, Violate, etc.

(a) He ordered for a cup of tea. —*Incorrect*
He ordered a cup of tea. —*Correct*
(b) India attacked on Pakistan. —*Incorrect*
India attacked Pakistan. —*Correct*
(c) He informed to me yesterday. —*Incorrect*
He informed me yesterday. —*Correct*

(2) कुछ, समय व्यक्त करने वाले शब्दों, जैसे : morning, evening, day, night, month,week, year इत्यादि से पूर्व कोई Objective, जैसे : This, that, next, every, last etc. का प्रयोग हो तो , उक्त समय व्यक्त करने वाले शब्दों से पूर्व कोई Preposition नहीं लिखना चाहिए। जैसे:

(a) She is going to Jaipur next morning. (b) I met her last evening.

अन्यथा समय व्यक्त करने वाले उक्त शब्दों के पूर्व Preposition आता है। जैसे :-

(a) She went in the morning. (b) I met her in the evening.
(c) Ram is coming here on Sunday.

(3) Yesterday, today, tomorrow के पूर्व भी कोई Preposition नहीं आता है। जैसे:

(a) Please meet me tomorrow. (b) He is arriving today.
(c) He went yesterday.

(4) Home : 'Home' के साथ जब गति (Motion) व्यक्त करने वाली verbs, जैसे : 'go, get' इत्यादि का प्रयोग हो, तो 'Home' के साथ preposition का प्रयोग नहीं किया जाता है। जैसे :

(a) It tóok them three hours to get home. (b) I went home by bus.

लेकिन यदि 'home' के तुरंत पूर्व किसी phrase/word का प्रयोग हो तो preposition आता है; जैसे-

(a) She returned to her husband's home. (b) I went to his home.

'Home' के साथ 'at' का प्रयोग भी किया जाता है :

(a) You can do this work at home. (b) We can stay at home.

लेकिन 'in' के तुरंत बाद 'home' का प्रयोग नहीं किया जाता है। जैसे :

(a) You can do this job in your own home. *—Correct*
You can do this in home. *—Incorrect*

(b) We can live in our home. *—Correct*
We can live in home. *—Incorrect*

(5) स्थान एवं समय व्यक्त करने वाले शब्दों (जैसे–Last week, last month, abroad, minute, bit, inside, outside etc.) के साथ भी सामान्यतया Preposition नहीं लगता है। जैसे:

(a) He came here last month. (b) Sita is going abroad next week.
(c) Please wait a minute/bit. (d) Please come inside.
(e) Why are you standing outside ?

SOME IMPORTANT PREPOSITIONS

Prepositions के नीचे दिये गये वाक्य प्रयोग से ज्ञात होगा कि वाक्य के सन्दर्भ के अनुसार *एक ही शब्द के साथ भिन्न-भिन्न Prepositions का प्रयोग* किया जाता है। Prepositions का सही प्रयोग रटकर नहीं किया जा सकता है। छात्रों को इस हेतु Practice करनी चाहिये। वाक्य के अर्थ के अनुसार Prepositions का वाक्य में प्रयोग करना चाहिए।

A

(1) **Abide at (place)** : I will abide at the railway station till the train arrives.
Abide in (house) : She has been abiding in my house for the last three months.
Abide by (decision) : She will abide by my decision positively.
Abide with (person) : He will abide with his friend Suresh in all circumstances.

(2) **Angry at (thing)** : He is angry at your way of questioning.
Angry with (person) : Sita is angry with Ram.
Angry for (action) : He is angry for your laughing at her wife.

(3) **Arrive at (place)** : The train is going to arrive at the station within ten minutes.
Arrive in (country) : He is scheduled to arrive in India on next Monday.

(4) **Alight on (ground, thing)** : A large number of birds alight on the roof of my house.
Alight at, from (a place) : The groom alighted from the elephant at her gate.

(5) **Appeal to (person)** : I earnestly appealed to the principal to consider the matter again.
Appeal against (decision) : He appealed against the decision of the lower court.

(6) **Amuse at (thing)** : He is greatly amused at the indifferent attitude of his father.
Amuse with (action) : The boys amused themselves with throwing flowers at the girls.

(7) **Ask for (a thing)** : He asked me for some help.
Ask from (person) : He asked some help from me.

(8) **Affiliated to (University, Board)** : Our college is affiliated to the University of Punjab.
Affiliated with (a party) : Bajrang Dal is affiliated with BJP indirectly.

(9) **Annoyed at (thing)** : He became annoyed at my laughing.
Annoyed with (person) : He is annoyed with you.

(10) **Antipathy to (thing)** : He has a great antipathy to wine.
Antipathy against (person) You should not have any antipathy against your friend Jack.

(11) Answer to (person) : You have to answer to me for your conduct.
Answer for (action) : He was asked to answer for the misbehaviour.

(12) Arm against (danger) : We must arm ourselves against the danger of chemical weapons.
Arm with (weapon) : He armed himself with a revolver and a knife.

(13) Atone to (person) : I tried to atone to him by offering market price of the land.
Atone for (action) : He tried to atone for the mischief he had committed.

(14) Award for (action) : He was awarded a gold medal for winning 100 metres race.
Awarded to (person) : A silver medal will be awarded to the best sports girl.

(15) Antidote to (medicine) : Diamond is regarded as an antidote to the poison of the snake.
Antidote against (inflection) : Quinine is an antidote against Malaria.

(16) Argue against or about (a matter) : He went to argue against the topic of debate.
He argued well about the newly introduced bill.
Argue with (person) : Don't argue with me unnecessarily.

(17) Agree in (opinion) : Ganesh agrees with Ram in opinion expressed by him (Ram).
Agree to (proposal) : I cannot agree to his proposal of dividing the property.
Agree with (person) : I fully agree with you on this issue .
Agree on (subject) : After a lot of discussion all agreed on the terms of agreement.

(18) Accomplice with (person) : Her wife was an accomplice with the murderer.
Accomplice in (act) : His wife was an accomplice in the murder.

(19) Authority for (action) : You have no authority for instructing me as such.
Authority on (subject) : She is indeed an unquestionable authority on Physics.
Authority over (person) : He has no authority over me officially.

(20) Accused of (a crime) : He is an accused of murder.

(21) Accused by (a person) : He was accused by his wife .

B

(1) Blush for (fault) : She blushed for the misbehaviour of her husband.
Blush at (praise) : She blushed at the comments of her husband.

(2) Blind to (deeds, action) : He should not be blind to the misdeeds of his son Rakesh.
Blind in (one eye) His husband is blind in the right eye.

(3) Born of (parents) : He was born of an orthodox mother.
Born at, in (place) : He was born at general hospital at Alwar.

(4) Buy from (shop) : You can buy this item from any grocery shop.
Buy for (person) : I bought this ball pen for my son.

(5) Beg of, from (person) : I begged of him to give me some time to pay back.
I begged some rice from him.
Beg for (person) : I begged him for some rice.

C

(1) Close to (adjective) : His house is very close to the railway station.
Close with (shut) : She closed the door with a bang.
Close down (= to terminate the operation) : He closed down his shop within six months.
Close out (= to reduce the price) : He closed out the price of sugar to increase sales.

(2) Confer about (= consult of a matter) : Ram and Rahim confer together about nominating the secretary.
Confer with (= consult with a person) : I will confer with my father in this matter.

(3) **Contend for (thing) :** Mr. S. S. Shekhawat will contend for a seat in Vidhan Sabha.
Contend with (person) : You should not contend with a person like Lalu Singh.

(4) **Consist in (= remain) :** The beauty of this building consists in its style and grandeur.
Consist of (= composed of) : Our body consists of flesh, bone and blood.

(5) **Condemn to (punishment) :** He was condemned to death by the judge.
Condemn for (crime) : He was condemned for murder by the court.

(6) **Compare to (comparing two different kind of things) :** Don't compare water to milk.
Compare with (comparing two things of same class) : Kalidas was compared with Shakespeare by several renowned scholars.

(7) **Care for (= like) :** I do not care for drinks.
Care about (thing) : She takes full care about her sarees and makeup.

(8) **Consult on (matter) :** We were not consulted on the new issue of debentures.
Consult with (person) : You should consult with some expert before taking a final decision.

(9) **Controversy on (matter) :** A lot of controversy was raised on this issue.
Controversy with (person) : I do not have any controversy with any of the members on this matter.

(10) **Confide to (= to tell) :** You should not confide your secrets to any body.
Confide in (= to pose confidence) : I confided in him, but he deceived me.

(11) **Complain of (a thing) :** I complained of his misconduct to the boss.
Complain to (person) : I complained of his misbehaviour to his father.

(12) **Compete with(person) :** Can you compete with him ?
Compete for (job) : I will try my best to compete for this job.

(13) **Cause of (problem) :** He is the main cause of all this trouble.
Cause for (anxiety) : I do not have any cause for anxiety.

(14) **Clothed in (dressing) :** She was clothed in a silken dress.
Clothed with (Some quality) : She was clothed with shame.

(15) **Connect to (join) :** Connect the end of this rod to the other.
Connect with (= to relate) : I have no connection with her for the last three years.

D

(1) **Displeased at (thing) :** She is not displeased at such humourous jokes.
Displeased with (person) : Ram is greatly displeased with Sita.

(2) **Disqualified for (post) :** She was declared disqualified for the election .
Disqualified from (competing) : He was disqualified from taking part in the competition.

(3) **Dwell upon (to speak) :** The Chairman dwelt upon the importance of truth and honesty.
Dwell in (country) : The French dwell in France.
Dwell at (place) : These days Ram is dwelling at his friend's hotel.
Dwell among (people) : He is dwelling among the tribals.

(4) **Disgusted at (thing) :** She became disgusted at your silly joke.
Disgusted with (person or life) : I am very much disgusted with him .

(5) **Deal with (= to do with the matter) :** This book deals with the population problem in India .
Deal in (trade) : He deals in iron scrap.
Deal out (= distribute) : The principal should deal out equal treatment to all the teachers.

(6) **Differ on (point) :** I totally differ on this point.
Differ with (person) : I differ with you on this point.
Differ from (thing) : Your views entirely differ from that of mine.

(7) **Die of (a disease) :** He died of hunger.
Die from (some cause) : He died from hard labour.
(8) **Destined for (= created for) :** God had destined him for the post of President of India.
Destined to (subject to) : He is destined to such a pitiable condition.
(9) **Dine with (person) :** I am scheduled to dine with him tonight.
Dine on (thing) : I can't dine on same kind of menu daily.
(10) **Dispense with (= do with out) :** Jack can't easily dispense with her .
Dispense to (= distribute) : A judge must dispense equal justice to all.
(11) **Dispose of (= to sell) :** She wants to dispose of all the goods at the earliest .
Dispose to (state of things) : The news of his father's death disposed him to a deep sorrow.
(12) **Dispute with (person) :** Why are you disputing with your friends on such a trifle matter.
Dispute about (thing) : There was a great dispute about the nomination of chairman.

E

(1) **Embark on (a vessel) :** She embarked on the ship for Srilanka.
Embark in (new business) : He has embarked in the new business with full fervour.
(2) **Enter into (thing) :** They have entered into an agreement with Ramesh.
Enter upon (new course) : After marriage I entered upon a new way of life.
(3) **Exchange for (thing) :** She exchanged a book for a piece of art.
Exchange with (person) : I want to exchange my views with you.
(4) **Exult at (success) :** She was exulted at her brilliant success.
Exult over (an enemy) : Our army exulted over the enemy's force.
Exult in (misery) : One should not be exulted in the misery of others.
(5) **Eager for (fame) :** She is very much eager for making a name in society.
Eager in (to find) : He has involved himself eagerly in pursuit of finding the cause of miseries in life.
(6) **Equivalent for (word) :** Write a word equivalent for 'fear'.
Equivalent to (money, thing) : One million is equivalent to ten lacs.
(7) **Exact from (person) :** Heavy fines were exacted from the unruly students.
Exact in (adjective) : He is not exact in repayment.
(8) **Expert in (doing) :** He is expert in repairing automobiles.
Expert at (thing) : He is expert at English Grammar.
(9) **Enquire of (person) :** I enquired of him the secret of his happiness.
Enquire into (a matter) : The police enquired into the case of bank robbery.
(10) **Entrust with (a thing) :** I entrusted him with my camera.
Entrust to (person) : I entrusted my camera to him.

F

(1) **Fit out (equip) :** The ship was fitted out for Srilanka.
Fit up (furnishing) : He fitted up his house with all necessary furniture.
(2) **Fascinated with (person) :** I was fascinated with Rekha.
Fascinated by (thing) : I was fascinated by her manners and looks.
(3) **False to (person) :** One should not be false to one's friends.
False of (thing, heart) : He is not false of heart.
(4) **Fight for (= defend) :** Our army is ready to fight for the country.
Fight with (together) : We must not fight with our friends.
Fight against (thing) : We must fight against the evil of illiteracy.

(5) **Familiar to (thing) :** Your looks are quite familiar to that of Sachin.

Familiar with (person) : I am familiar with him.

G

(1) **Gaze at (= look attentively) :** Don't gaze at these girls, they are the cops .

Gaze on (= look strangely) : He stood gazing on the pathetic scene of accident.

(2) **Grieve for (person) :** She was extremely grieved for him.

Grieve at (event) : Everyone was grieved at the death of Rajeev Gandhi.

Grieve over (thing) : She grieved over my unfortunate loss.

(3) **Good for (nothing) :** He is a good for nothing fellow.

Good at (something) : She is good at swimming.

H

(1) **Held by (person) :** A condolence meeting was held by the staff yesterday.

Held in (esteem or contempt) : In the heart of every Indian,Gandhiji is held in great respect.

Held at (place) : A meeting was held at Hope Circus yesterday.

(2) **Hear of (something) :** I heard of this robbery from Sarla.

Hear from (person) : I heard of this robbery from Sarla.

Hear by (post) : I hear by this letter about your promotion.

(3) **Happen to (person) :** Please tell me what happened to you in Newyork.

Happen at (place) : This event happened at Red Square.

Happen on (come across) : While returning from market I happened on a gang of thieves.

(4) **Hidden from (view) :** The Neem tree has hidden your house from direct view.

Hidden by (person, thing) : My shoes were hidden by his sister.

I

(1) **Introduce to (person) :** Let me first introduce my friend to you.

Introduce into (make modifications) : The UPSC has introduced many changes into the syllabus of IAS exams.

(2) **Invest with (authority) :** The President invested him with the honour of Bharat Ratna.

Invest in (business) : I am ready to invest Rs. fifty lacs in this business.

(3) **Inquire for (a thing) :** I went there to inquire for my lost brief case.

Inquire into (matter) : The police will inquire into the cause of death.

Inquire about (concern) : She came here to inquire about the health of her son.

Inquire of (ask) : First inquire of the way, then move.

(4) **Involve in (thing) :** She seems to be involved in some serious trouble.

Involve with (person) : Don't involve yourself with such unruly persons.

(5) **Irritated at (thing) :** I was greatly irritated at his unruly behaviour.

Irritated against (person) : She was extremely irritated against her husband.

(6) **Impatient at (unexpected thing) :** He became impatient at the unexpected delay.

Impatient for (expected thing) : She is very much impatient for the arrival of her husband.

(7) **Indebted for (thing) :** I was indebted for your timely help.

Indebted to (person) : He is greatly indebted to Rani for her timely help.

J

(1) **Jest at (person) :** I don't like to jest at a lunatic person.

Jest with (thing) : We should not jest with the communal thing.

(2) **Judge of (= giving opinion) :** Without going in details, how can you judge of this matter.
Judge by (observing) : Judging by her qualifications, I think she is not fit for this job.

K

(1) **Know by (= recognize) :** A man is known by his actions.
Know for (quality) : He is known for his foolish decisions.

L

(1) **Live at (a small town) :** He lives at Alwar in Rajasthan.
Live in (in country, big place) : He is living at Alwar in Rajasthan.
Live on (food) : He lives entirely on breads.
Live for (devote) : We must live and die for the cause of truth.
Live with(a person) : I live here with my parents.
(2) **Liable for (crime) :** You are liable for the death of your wife.
Liable to (punishment) : He was held liable to imprisonment for three years.
(3) **Listen for (sound) :** I am listening for the voice of Asha Mangeshkar.
Listen to (= hear attentively) : We should listen to the advice of our elders.
(4) **Laugh at (= make fun) :** We must not laugh at our friends.
Laugh with (= indulge with) : Better to laugh with disabled than to laugh at disabled.

M

(1) **Married to (a woman) :** Ramesh was married to Sarla.
Married with (a man) : Sarla was married with Ramesh.
(2) **Moved with (sorrow) :** He was actually moved with a feeling of sorrow.
Moved to (tears) : On hearing the news of sudden death of his wife, all moved to tears.
Moved from (one's determination) : You can't move me from my decision with your logics
Moved at (a scene) : He was greatly moved at the sight of her mother's dead body.

O

(1) **Obliged to (person) :** I am very much obliged to you.
Obliged at (thing) : I am obliged at your timely help.
(2) **Occupied in (doing a job) :** He is fully occupied in writing a book.
Occupied by (thing) : That house is occupied by a marriage party.
(3) **Originate with (person) :** All the plannings were originated with him.
Originate in (place, cause) : A fierce fire was originated in Connaught Place yesterday.

P

(1) **Part from (person) :** I parted from my wife in Kumbh.
Part with (thing) : He is not ready to part with his furniture at any cost.
(2) **Prepare for (= be ready) :** I am preparing for the IAS examination this year.
Prepare against (danger) : We must prepare ourselves against the danger of water pollution.
(3) **Pray for (thing) :** My wife prayed for my success .
Pray to (make prayer) : I prayed to God to help me in facing the unwarranted problems.
(4) **Perish by (famine) :** Our district was perished by the drought last year.
Perish with (hunger) : During drought the cattle perished with starvation.
(5) **Plead with (person) :** He pleaded with the Principal for mercy.
Plead for (thing) : He pleaded with the King for mercy.

(6) **Play at (cards) :** They were playing at cards.
Play upon (musical instrument) : Harish played upon the violin in the party.

Q

(1) **Quick in (doing) :** He is quick in reasoning questions .
Quick of (understanding) : Ramesh is quick of understanding the questions.

(2) **Quarrel over (thing) :** You must not quarrel over the parental property.
Quarrel with (person) : We must not quarrel with our friends.

R

(1) **Responsible to (person) :** An MLA is responsible to the Legislative Assembly.
Responsible for (action) : She is responsible for the loss caused due to her neglience.

(2) **Reason with (person) :** I reasoned with him on each and every point in this matter.
Reason about (thing) : You can't reason about the importance of self respect .

(3) **Ready for (action) :** I am ready for the match.
Ready with (something) : I was totally ready with my arguments on that day .
Ready in (replying) : I always found her ready in her reply.

(4) **Revenge on (person) :** He revenged himself on his enemy.
Revenge for (action) : I will positively revenge for the insult inflicted on me by her.

(5) **Reduce to (= to decrease) :** His salary was reduced to Rs. four thousands only.
Reduce by (an amount) : His salary was reduced by three hundred rupees per month.

S

(1) **Share of (thing) :** I must be paid my share of profit.
Share with (person) : I do not share my lunch with anybody.

(2) **Skilful at (thing) :** He is skilful at numbers.
Skilful in (doing a thing) : He is skilful in mathematical calculations.

(3) **Succeed to (property) :** He succeeded to his uncle's empire.
Succeed in (doing) : This time she succeeded in IAS examination.

(4) **Start at (time) :** I started at 10 O'clock in the morning.
Start from (place) : I started at 10 O'clock in the morning from Delhi.
Started for (place) : I started at 7 O'clock in the morning for Delhi.

(5) **Struggle for (thing) :** We have to struggle hard for keeping peace in the country.
Struggle with (person) : We should not struggle with our neighbours.

(6) **Serve out (= distribute) :** Sweets were served out to the audience.
Serve up (= to give food) : A nice lunch was served up there in the function.

(7) **Speak for (person) :** You go there, I have already spoken for you to the secretary.
Speak about (thing) : He is speaking about 'Unemployment Problem'.

(8) **Starved to (death) :** She was starved to death by her husband.
Starved with (hunger) : He starved with hunger.

(9) **Suited for (action) :** She is not suited for the role of vamp.
Suited to (occasion) : Sad song does not suit to such a merry occasion.

(10) **Supply to (person) :** The Municipality is supplying water to all the colonies in the city.
Supply with (thing) : Government must supply poor with food and clothing.

T

(1) **Thankful for (thing) :** I am really thankful for your timely help.
Thankful to (person) : I am very much thankful to you for your kind favour.

(2) **Think over (= to consider) :** The society agreed to think over the case in the next meeting.
Think on (= meditate) : I have been thinking on this matter for the last many days.

(3) **Trust in (person) :** Trust in God and work hard.
Trust to (thing) : I trusted to his words, and he was right.

(4) **Tired of (disgusted) :** I am tired of your daily excuses.
Tired with (= exhausted) : You seems to be tired with the long run.

(5) **Talk with (person) :** I will talk with my father in this matter.
Talk about (thing) : I will talk about this matter with my parents.
Talk over (discuss) : All the members of the society talked over the issue for many hours.

U

(1) **Useful for (thing) :** The bag is very much useful for carrying load.
Useful to (person) : I found that these directives are useful to me for success in exam.

V

(1) **Vote for (person) :** Vote for me, please.
Vote on (a resolution) : After having cast votes on the resolution , all took lunch.

(2) **Vexed with (person) :** Why are you vexed with your wife ?
Vexed at (thing) : He is vexed at my jokes.

W

(1) **Wait at (place) :** I will wait at church near the hospital.
Wait for (person) : I will wait for you up to tomorrow.

(2) **Wake up (= to get up) :** She wakes up at 6 AM. daily.
Wake from (= to be awaken) : She waked from slumber and decided to take action.

(3) **Warn against (an action) :** I have already warned you, against your such negligence.
Warn of (danger) : I have already warned you of the risk involved.

Z

(1) **Zealous for (a thing) :** A dedicated worker is always zealous for achieving the target.
Zealous in (a cause) : We must be zealous in the cause of humanity.

APPROPRIATE PREPOSITIONS

कुछ शब्दों के साथ, सामान्यतया एक निश्चित Preposition का प्रयोग होता है। **यद्यपि यहाँ भी वाक्य के अर्थ को समझना आवश्यक है, तथापि, आगे दिये गये शब्द एवं उनके साथ प्रयुक्त निश्चित Prepositions को बार-बार Revise करने से इन Prepositions का सही प्रयोग समझ में आ जाता है। परीक्षाओं में Prepositions पर आने वाले Questions अधिकतर अग्र-लिखित में से पूछे जाते हैं :**

1. **Abundance of (wealth)**
2. **Assent to (a proposal)**
3. **Accustomed to (work)**
4. **Avail ourselves of (an opportunity)**
5. **Attain to (a position)**
6. **Addicted to (drinking , something)**
7. **Accede to (a request)**
8. **Abstain from (food, indulgence etc.)**
9. **Absolved from (a promise, a sin)**
10. **Acquiesce (an opinion, in proposal)**
11. **Adhere to (principles)**
12. **Afraid of (a ghost)**
13. **Abhorrent to (good nature)**
14. **Accession to (throne)**
15. **Assure of (a thing)**
16. **Absorbed in (study)**
17. **Acquit (someone) of a charge**
18. **Acquaintance with (a person)**

19. Beware of (cheating, dogs)
20. Comply with (one's wishes)
21. Condemn to (death)
22. Cured of (a disease)
23. Comply with (wishes)
24. Coducive to (health)
25. Despair of (success)
26. Desirous of (doing some thing)
27. Deprive of (something)
28. Devoid of (quality)
29. Duty of (the country)
30. Eligible for (a post)
31. Exception to (a rule)
32. Excuse for (a fault)
33. Envious of (aperson or a thing)
34. Exchange a thing (with a person)
35. Elder to (some member of the family)
36. Fatal to (one's cause)
37. Fearful of (death)
38. Furnish with (clothes, details)
39. Greedy of (money)
40. Heir to (ancestral property)
41. Healed of (a disease or wound)
42. Hopeful of (success)
43. Hostile to (a person)
44. Hunger after (fame)
45. Innocent of (a crime)
46. Intimate with (a person)
47. Invite to (dinner)
48. Insist on a (thing)
49. Intimate with(person)
50. Impertinent to (elders)
51. Insight into(a matter or thing)
52. Jealous of (a person)
53. Keep to (the left, the point)
54. Knock at (the door)
55. Match for (a person)
56. Key to (success)
57. Mourn for (the dead)
58. Mad with (anger)
59. Motive for (an action)
60. Need for (help)
61. Need of (a thing)
62. Notorious for (drinking, thing)
63. Occur to (mind)
64. Overwhelmed with (sorrow, grief)
65. Pay for (one's mistakes)
66. Passion for (study)
67. Peculiar to (a person or a thing)
68. Persist in (doing)
69. Pity for (poor, downtrodden)
70. Pleased with (a person)
71. Preface to (a book)
72. Proud of (a thing)
73. Pride on (a thing)
74. Prefer to (a thing)
75. Refrain from (doing some wrong)
76. Repent of (a mistake)
77. Respectful to (a person)
78. Rob (a person) of (a thing)
79. Sentence to (punishment)
80. Short of (money)
81. Side with (a person)
82. Shocked at (a loss)
83. Superior to (a thing)
84. Sure of (some fact)
85. Search for (a thing)
86. Sacred to (a cause)
87. Triumph over (difficulties)
88. Trouble to (person)
89. Vain of (beauty)
90. Want of (money)
91. Wanting in (wisdom)
92. Worthy of (a reward)
93. Yield to (an enemy)
94. Search for (a thing)
95. Sacred to (a cause)
96. Work at (subject, a project)
97. Surrender to (enemy, God)
98. Stick to (point)
99. Suspect of (something)
100. Translate into (language)
101. Touch upon (subject)
102. Slur on (character)

HIGH FREQUENCY PREPOSITIONS

Preposition 'FOR'

(A) The following nouns take the preposition 'for' after them:
apology, appetite, aptitude,affection, ambition, blame, candidate, contempt, craving,capacity, compassion, compensation, desire, esteem, fitness, fondness, guarantee, leisure, liking, match, motive, need opportunity, partiality, pretext, passion, pity, predilection, remorse, relish.

(B) The following verbs take the preposition 'for' after them:
Atone, canvass, care, clamour, feel, hope, mourn, pine, start, stipulate, sue, wish, yearn.

(C) The following adjectives and participles take the preposition 'for' after them:
anxious, celebrated, conspicuous, customary, designed, destined, eager, eligible, eminent, fit, good, grateful, notorious,prepared, proper, penitent, qualified, ready, sorry, sufficient, useful, zealous.

Preposition 'OF'

(A) The following nouns take the preposition 'of' after them:
assurance, abhorrence, charge, distrust, doubt, experience, failure, observance, proof, result, want.

(B) The following adjectives and participles take the preposition 'of' after them:-
accused, acquitted, afraid, apprehensive, apprised, assured, aware, bereft, bought, cautious, certain, characteristic, composed, confident, conscious, convicted, convinced, covetous, defrauded, deprived, desirous, destitute, devoid, diffident, distrustful, dull, easy, envious, fearful, fond, greedy, guilty, heedless, ignorant, informed, innocent, irrespective, lame, lavish, negligent, productive, proud, regardless, sanguine, sensible, sick, sow, subversive, sure, suspicious, tolerant, vain, void, weary, worthy.

(C) The following verbs take the preposition 'of' after them:
Acquit, beware, boast, complain, despair, die, disapprove, dispose, divest, dream, heal, judge, repent, taste.

Preposition 'TO'

(A) The following nouns take the preposition 'to' after them:
allegiance, approach, assent, alternative,access, accession, antidote, antipathy, exception, incentive, indifference, invitation , key, leniency, likeness, limit, menace, obedience, opposition, objection, obstruction, postscript, preface, reference, resemblance, repugnance, sequel, submission, supplement, succession, traitor, temptation.

(B) The following adjectives and participles take the preposition 'to' after them:

(a) acceptable, accessible, accustomed, abhorrent, addicted, adequate, adjacent affectionate, agreeable, akin, alien, alive, amenable, analogous, applicable, appropriate, beneficial, callous, common, comparable, condemned.

(b) conducive, conformable, congenial, consecrated, contrary, creditable, deaf, derogatory, detrimental, devoted, disastrous, due, entitled, equal, essential exposed, faithful, fatal, foreign, hostile, impertinent, incidental, inclined.

(c) indebted, indifferent, indispensable, indulgent, inimical, insensible, injured, irrelevant, favourable, hurtful, immaterial, impervious, indigenous, liable, limited, lost, loyal, material, natural, necessary.

(d) offensive, opposite, obedient, obliged, painful, partial, peculiar, pertinent, pledged, preferable, prejudicial, prior, profitable, prone, relevant, repugnant,reduced, related, responsible, restricted, sacred,subject, suitable, sensitive, serviceable, suited, supplementary,true, tantamount.

(C) The following verbs take the preposition 'to' after them:
accede, adhere, allot, aspire, assent, attain, allude, apologise,adapt, appoint, ascribe, attend, attribute, belong, consent, contribute, conduce, conform, lead, listen, object, occur, prefer, pretend, refer, revert, stoop, succumb, surrender, testify, yield.

Preposition 'FROM'

(A) The following nouns take the preposition 'from' after them:
abstinence, cessation, deliverance, descent, digression, escape, exemption, inference,

(B) The following verbs take the preposition 'from' after them:
abstain, alight, cease, debar, derive, derogate, desist, detract, deviate, differ, dissent, elicit, emerge escape exclude preserve, prevent, prohibit, protect, recoil, recover, refrain.

Preposition 'IN'

(A) The following adjectives and participles take the preposition 'in' after them :
accomplished , accurate, assiduous,absorbed, abstemious, backward, bigot, correct, defective,diligent, deficient, experienced, enveloped, fertile, foiled, honest, implicated, interested, involved, lax, proficient, remiss, versed.

(B) The following verbs take the preposition 'in' after them:
acquiesce, delight, employ, enlist, excel, fall, glory, increase, indulge, involve, persevere, persist.

Preposition 'WITH'

(A) The following adjectives and participles take the preposition 'with' after them :
acquainted, affected, beset, busy, compatible, complaint, consistent, contemporary, contented, contrasted, conversant, convulsed, delighted, deluged, disgusted, drenched, endowed, fatigued, fired, gifted, infatuated, infected, infested, inspired, intimated, invested, overcome, popular, replete, satisfied, touched.

(B) The following verbs take the preposition 'with' after them:
associate, bear, clash, coincide, comply, condole, cope, correspond, credit, deluge, disagree, dispense, expostulate, fill, grapple, intrigue, meddle, quarrel, remonstrate, side, sympathise, trifle, vie.

Preposition 'ON'

(A) The following verbs take the preposition 'on' after them:
comment, deliberate, decide, depend, determine, dwell, enlarge, embark, encroach,impose, insist, intrude, subsist, trample.

ERRORS, MISTAKES AND BLUNDERS IN USE OF PREPOSITIONS

Exercise : ***Rewrite the sentences after correction.***

1. She was neither ashamed nor sorry for her misbehaviour.
2. She neither objected nor approved of it.
3. Ram has no interest and passion for cricket.
4. We must prevent damage and theft of public property.
5. Please listen and reflect on this topic afterwards.
6. He asked from her a silly question.
7. The police investigated into the case.
8. Ram resembles to her father.
9. She resigned from her post.
10. Ram signed to the agreement.
11. The poet described about the nature
12. She must love to her children.
13. We have discussed on the merits of the issue.
14. In this article the author has described about poverty.

15. She criticised upon my action without logic.
16. A meeting was held on Hope Circus yesterday.
17. In the heart of every Indian,Gandhiji is held with great respect.
18. I was fascinated at her manners and looks.
19. I entrusted him by my camera.
20. The police will inquire in the cause of death.
21. You are liable to the death of your wife.
22. On hearing the news of sudden death of his wife, all moved in tears.
23. Why are you vexed at your wife ?
24. His salary was reduced with Rs. four thou sands only.
25. He succeeded for his uncle's empire.

Explanations

1. She was neither ashamed of nor sorry for her misbehaviour.
2. She neither objected to nor approved of it.
3. Ram has no interest in and passion for cricket.
4. We must prevent damage to and theft of public property.
5. Please listen to and reflect on this topic afterwards.
6. He asked her a silly question.
7. The police investigated the case.
8. Ram resembles his father.
9. She resigned her post.
10. Ram signed the agreement.
11. The poet described the nature.
12. She must love her children.
13. We have discussed the merits of the issue.
14. In this article the author has described poverty.
15. She criticised my action without logic.
16. A meeting was held at Hope Circus yesterday.
17. In the heart of every Indian,Gandhiji is held in great respect.
18. I was fascinated by her manners and looks.
19. I entrusted him with my camera.
20. The police will inquire into the cause of death.
21. You are liable for the death of your wife.
22. On hearing the news of sudden death of his wife, all moved to tears.
23. Why are you vexed with your wife ?
24. His salary was reduced to Rs. four thousands only.
25. He succeeded to his uncle's empire.

SPOTTING ERRORS (PREPOSITIONS)

Exercise : ***Find the errors and justify your answers.***

1. He was sleeping (A)/ in his room when a thief (B)/ entered into his house (C)/ and took away a lot of things (D).
2. In her concluding speech (A)/ she said almost nothing (B)/ worth listening to (C).
3. It was apparent for (A)/ everyone present (B)/ that if the patient did not receive (C)/ immediate medical aid (D)/ he would die (E).
4. He proposed me (A)/ that we should go to the Disco (B) and then have (C)/ dinner at a restra (D).
5. There appears (A)/ to be a little liaison (B)/ among the (C)/ two groups of the society (D) .
6. The team (A)/ complained to the manager (B)/ against the captain (C)/ and the poor facilities provided in the hotel (D).

7. Yesterday I met (A)/ a man (B)/ who was blind with the right eye (C).
8. The principal distributed (A)/ the sweets among our friends (B)/ who bade him farewell (C).
9. As per the invitation card (A)/ Rahim marries with Saira (B)/ on 13 th December, Monday (C).
10. The debacle of the congress party (A)/ admits no other explanation (B)/ than its (C)/ poor performance during the last five years (D).
11. The society does not (A)/ hold itself responsible (B)/ for the loss or damage to (C)/ any item (D).
12. In spite of being (A)/ very busy at project work (B)/ he saves time (C)/ to the relatives (D).
13. Some persons (A)/ get promotions (B)/ even if they are not (C)/ worthy for them (D).
14. While he was returning (A)/ from the office (B)/ a man attacked on (C)/ him with a dagger (D).
15. The decline of her moral (A)/ was caused by a lot of (B)/ factors that were once (C)/ fascinating to her (D).
16. He took me to a restra (A)/ and ordered for two cups (B)/ of cold coffee (C)/ which the waiter brought in an hour (D).
17. There are some animals (A)/ than can live both in water and land (C)/ without any difficulty (D) .
18. During his tour (A)/ to the south (B)/ he visited not only to Tamil Nadu (C)/ but also Karnataka (D).
19. The President Mr. Kalam (A)/ is much sought after (B)/ by school students and (C)/ is invited for many functions (D).
20. His mother is not well (A)/ but he (B)/ does not look for her (C) properly (D).
21. We may have to await for (A)/ a new political revival (B)/ to eradicate the (C)/ corruption from our economy (D).
22. When she was (A)/ in jail (B)/ she was debarred to send (C)/ a letter even to her son (D) .
23. Despite of the best efforts (A)/ put by the doctors (B)/ the condition of the patient (C)/ is deteriorating from bad to worse (D).
24. The militant yielded for (A)/ the temptation and fell (B)/ into the trap (C)/ of police (D).
25. Many people in India (A)/ are dying from hunger (B)/ but government seems (C)/ to be ignorant of such crude fact (D) .
26. In difficult times (A)/ she prefers keeping her counsel (B)/ rather than wandering (C)/ here and there for relief (D).
27. The persons who are (A)/ suffering from diabetes are (B)/ advised to substitute (C)/ saccharine by sugar (D).
28. He always says (A)/ that he prefers to go (B)/ home to stay in (C)/ a hotel at night (D)
29. Hardly had we settled down (A)/ for the rest (B)/ when we were startled by the (C)/ strange sound of trumpets (D).
30. He was able to (A)/ free himself with (B)/ the debts by (C)/ working day and night. (D).

Explanations

1. (C) 'into' को delete करें। 'go into', 'jump into' हो सकता है। ध्यान रखें : 'entered upon a career, enter into a conversation, enter into a project/business' आदि हो सकता है, पर 'enter into house' लिखना त्रुटिपूर्ण है।
2. (C) 'listening to' की जगह केवल 'listening' ही होगा। 'Listen' के बाद कोई object नहीं हो, तो 'to' का प्रयोग नहीं होता है । जैसे :

   Please listen to <u>me</u> (object)
   I was listening but heard nothing.
3. (A) 'apparent to' होगा।

4. (A) 'Proposed to'होगा। suggested to, 'proposed to' होता है।
5. (C) 'among' की जगह 'between' आयेगा; सामान्यत: 'between' का प्रयोग दो के लिए तथा 'among' का प्रयोग दो से अधिक के लिये किया जाता है।
6. (D) 'and about the poor ......' होगा
   (i) Complained to somebody.
   (ii) Complained against somebody.
   (iii) Complained about/of something प्रयुक्त होता है।
7. (C) 'blind in' होगा।
   'blind in left or right eye' या 'blind of an eye' या 'blind with both eyes' आदि प्रयुक्त होता है।
8. (B) 'among' की जगह 'amongst' होगा।

ध्यान रखें

यदि 'among' के बाद वाला शब्द किसी vowel sound से pronounced है तो 'amongst' आवेगा। यदि consonant sound से pronounced है तो 'among' ही आयेगा। 'among' एवं amongst दोनों का प्रयोग दो से अधिक के लिए किया जाता है। 'the'से पूर्व 'among' या 'amongst' में से किसी का प्रयोग हो सकता है। जैसे :

among the girls	Correct	amongst the girls	Correct
among our members	Incorrect	amongst our members	Correct
amongst them	Incorrect	among them	Correct

9. (B) 'with' का प्रयोग नहीं होगा। जब 'marry' का प्रयोग मुख्य verb के रूप में होता है तो इसके साथ कोई preposition नहीं प्रयुक्त होता हैं, जैसे :
   (a) Hari is married to Hina. (b) Hari marries Hina on next Monday.
10. (B) 'admits of' होगा। proposition 'of' का प्रयोग 'admits' के साथ होगा।
11. (C) 'Loss of' होगा। यदि दो words, 'or' या 'and' से संयुक्त हों एवं वे अलग-अलग prepositions लेते हों तो अलग-अलग propositions लगाने आवश्यक हैं।
12. (D) 'to'की जगह 'for' का प्रयोग होगा ; Save के साथ preposition निम्न प्रकार से प्रयुक्त होते हैं; Save for something, Save somebody from something :
   (a) He has saved some money for medicines.
   (b) She saved me from drowning.
13. (D) 'worthy of' होगा, क्योंकि 'worthy' के बाद 'of', preposition प्रयुक्त होता है।
14. (C) 'On'का प्रयोग अनुचित है। यदि 'attack' का प्रयोग verb के रूप में किया जावे तो इसके बाद object (him) आता है preposition (on) नहीं। लेकिन यदि 'make' के साथ 'attack' का प्रयोग होता है तो preposition 'on' आता है।
   China made an attack on India .
15. (A) 'decline in' होगा। Decline of empire/decline of a manआदि सही है । Decline in moral/ Decline in prices में 'decline' के साथ 'in' आता है ।
16. (B) 'order' के बाद 'for' का प्रयोग नहीं होगा क्योंकि 'order' एक transitive verb है, जिसके तुरंत बाद object आता है :
   (a) He ordered a glass of wine . (b) He ordered him to go to market.
17. (C) 'On land' आयेगा। यदि दो words 'and' या 'or' से संयुक्त हों एवं दोनों के साथ अलग-अलग preposition आता हो तो, अलग-अलग prepositions प्रयोग करने चाहिएँ।
18. (C) 'to' का प्रयोग गलत है। 'visited' का प्रयोग जब एक verb के रूप में किया जाता है तो , इसके बाद object आता है। लेकिन 'make' के साथ जब 'visit' का प्रयोग किया जाता है, तो 'to' का प्रयोग होता है :
   He made a visit to Agra last year.

19. (D) 'invited' के साथ 'to' का प्रयोग होगा; 'for' की जगह 'to' लिखें।
(a) I was invited to a party. (b) He was invited to lunch.
20. (C) 'Look after' होगा। 'look after' का अर्थ है देखभाल करना।
21. (A) 'await' के साथ 'for' नहीं प्रयुक्त होगा। 'wait for' होता है; 'await for' गलत है। जैसे :
(a) We are waiting for his arrival
(b) We are awaiting his arrival .
22. (C) 'debarred from sending' होगा। 'debar/ abstain/ refrain' के साथ यदि 'from' का प्रयोग हुआ हो तो, verb+ ing का प्रयोग होता है :
He abstained from drinking wine.
23. (A) 'Despite' के साथ 'of' नहीं आता है। 'Despite' का अर्थ होता है 'In spite of'.
24. (A) 'Yielded to' होगा। 'Yield to' का अर्थ होता है – समर्पण (yield to somebody, Yield to something) करना :
(a) She yielded to her lovers wish. (b) He yielded to his enemy.
25. (B) 'dying of hunger' होगा। 'die of hunger/die of a disease' प्रयुक्त होता है। 'die from over working/die from over drinking/die from food posioning' आदि प्रयुक्त होता है ।
26. (C) 'rather than' का अनुचित प्रयोग किया गया है। इसकी जगह 'to' का प्रयोग होगा। prefer, senior, junior, prior इत्यादि के साथ Preposition 'to' प्रयुक्त होता है।
27. (D) 'by' की जगह 'for' का प्रयोग करें । ध्यान दें – substitute something for something होता है।
28. (C) 'to stay in' की जगह 'rather than stay in' होगा; जब 'prefer' द्वारा दो 'verbs' की तुलना की जाती है तो 'prefer' के साथ 'rather than' का प्रयोग होता है। जैसे :
She prefers to write rather than to speak on telephone .
29. (C) 'Startled at' होगा। 'surprised/startled/amazed/astonished' के साथ preposition 'at' आता है।
30. (B) 'free himself from' होगा। 'free somebody from something या free from something' प्रयुक्त होता है।

BLUNDERS

Exercise : ***Rewrite the following sentences after correction :***

1. On which train did you come ?
2. What's the time in your watch?
3. I am to attend a meeting on 10 O' clock.
4. He was born in 26th January at Delhi in India.
5. The stars shine in night.
6. He distributed sweets between his four sons.
7. He killed the snake by a stick.
8. Ram will go in the market.
9. She is fond in going to parties.
10. He is writing with ink.

Explanations

1. 'On' की जगह 'by' का प्रयोग होगा।
2. '*by* your watch' होगी।
3. '*On* 10 O' clock' की जगह '*at* 10 O' clock' होगा।
4. सही वाक्य होगा– He was born *on* 26th January at Delhi in India.
5. '*In* night' की जगह '*at* night' होगा।
6. 'between' की जगह 'among' होगा ।
7. '*by* a stick' की जगह '*with* a stick' होगा।
8. '*in* the market' की जगह '*to* the market' होगा ।
9. 'fond *in*' की जगह '*fond* of' होगा।
10. 'with ink' की जगह 'in ink' होगा।

❑❑❑

16

Conjunctions

Conjunctions के सम्बन्ध में पूछे जाने वाले प्रश्न, अधिकांशतया Correlated Conjuctions के सम्बन्ध में पूछे जाते हैं, या विशेष Conjuction के साथ आने वाली Auxiliary verb की स्थिति के सम्बन्ध में पूछे जाते हैं। छात्र Conjunctions का अध्ययन करते समय उक्त बिन्दुओं पर ध्यान दें ।

Conjunction ऐसा शब्द है, जो शब्दों या वाक्यों को आपस में जोड़ता है । इसे *Sentence Linker* भी कहा जाता है।

Definition

A Conjunction is a word that joins words or sentences together.

1. He is honest and she is intelligent.
2. I shall either read or write a book.
3. Three and three make six.
4. Suresh and Ganesh are friends.

वाक्य (1) एवं वाक्य (2) में Conjunction 'and' एवं 'or' दो वाक्यों को जोड़ने का कार्य कर रहे हैं, जबकि वाक्य (3) एवं (4) में Conjunction 'and' दो शब्दों को जोड़ने का कार्य कर रहा है।

KINDS OF CONJUNCTION

(A) Coordinating Conjunctions

ये Conjunctions दो समान Rank के Sentences या Words को जोड़ते हैं। इस तरह के मुख्य Conjunctions हैं: For,And, Nor, But, Or, Yet, So . An easy way to remember these six conjunctions is to think of the word **'F A N B O Y S'**. Each of the letters in this somewhat unlikely word is the first letter of one of the coordinating conjunctions.

(B) Subordinating Conjunctions

इन Conjunctions द्वारा एक Subordinating Clause को अन्य Clause से जोड़ा जाता है। (Subordinating Clause वह Clause है जो अपने पूर्ण अर्थ के लिये अन्य Clause पर निर्भर होती है।)इस तरह के मुख्य Conjunctions हैं : after,although,as,as if,as long as,as though,because,before,even if,even though, if, if only, in order that, now that, once, rather than, since, so that, than, that, though, till, unless, until, when, whenever, where, whereas, wherever, while.

Examples:

After : We are going out to eat after we finish our work.

Since : Since we have lived in Mexico,we have gone to every exhibit at the Royal Hall.

While : While I was waiting in line for my turn , I ate my lunch.

Although : Although the line was long and the wait over at least three hours, the exhibit was indeed worth it

Even if : Even if you have already bought your ticket, you will still need to wait in queue.

Even though : Even though Jack fell asleep, the mobile salesman kept talking.

(C) Correlative Conjunctions

जो Conjunctions pairs में प्रयोग किए जाते हैं, उन्हें Correlative Conjunctions कहते हैं : जैसे : Either.......or, Neither................nor, Both..........and, Not only........but also.

Correlative conjunctions are always used in pairs. They join similar elements. When joining singular and plural subjects, the subject closest to the verb determines whether the verb is singular or plural.

CONJUNCTION/RELATIVE PRONOUN/ RELATIVE ADVERB/PREPOSITION

Conjunctions का कार्य मात्र वाक्यों या शब्दों को जोड़ना है, जबकि Relative Pronoun/Relative Adverb/Preposition न केवल Pronoun या Adverb या Preposition का भी कार्य करते हैं, अपितु वाक्यों को जोड़ते भी हैं :

(a) This is the pen <u>that</u> she gifted me.	Relative Pronoun
(b) This the place <u>where</u> I was born.	Relative Adverb
(c) He sat <u>beside</u> Shyam	Preposition
(d) He came <u>and</u> he worked.	Conjunction

वाक्य (a) में 'that' noun, 'pen' को भी Refer कर रहा है, एवं दो वाक्यों को जोड़ भी रहा है; इसी तरह वाक्य (b), एवं (c) में Underlined words, Adverb एवं Preposition का भी कार्य कर रहे हैं एवं दो वाक्यों को जोड़ भी रहे है; जबकि वाक्य (d) में Conjunction मात्र दो वाक्यों को जोड़ने का कार्य कर रहा है ।

Some Important Conjunctions

(1) Not only ....but also:

Not only ....but also एक Correlative Conjunction है। इसमें मुख्य बिन्दु यह है कि यदि 'Not only' का प्रयोग noun से पूर्व हुआ है तो 'but also' का प्रयोग भी noun से पूर्व ही होना चाहिए; यदि 'Not only' का प्रयोग verb से पूर्व है, तो 'but also' का प्रयोग भी verb से पूर्व होना आवश्यक है :

(a) Ram is watching not only T.V but also playing football. *—Incorrect*
Ram is not only watching T.V. but also playing football. *—Correct*

वाक्य (a) में 'not only' का प्रयोग noun (T.V.) के पूर्व हुआ है, जबकि 'but also' का प्रयोग verb (playing) के पूर्व हुआ है। यह गलत है।

(b) Not only Ram gave me five coins but also thanked me. *—Incorrect*
Ram not only gave me five coins but also thanked me. *—Correct*

यह नियम सभी Correlative Conjunctions, जैसे : Either.......or, Neither........nor, Both.....and, Though.......yet, Whether......or इत्यादि पर समान रूप से प्रभावी होता है। यह एक महत्त्वपूर्ण बिन्दु है।

(2) Neither.......nor

इसके लिए दोनों वाक्यों का negative होना आवश्यक है:

(a) He neither plays football nor hockey. *—Incorrect*
(b) He plays neither football nor hockey. *—Correct*

(3) Either ..... or :

(a) She will either pay the rent or will vacate the house. *—Incorrect*
(b) She will either pay the rent or vacate the house. *—Correct*

(4) No sooner did ....than.....

(1) 'No sooner did' का प्रयोग 'past tense' के वाक्यों में ही होता है।

(2) सबसे मुख्य बात है कि 'No sooner' के बाद 'did' का प्रयोग किया जाता है, **अतः पहले वाक्य में verb की first form ही प्रयोग करनी है, इसका ध्यान रखें :**

(a) No sooner she reached the station than the train arrived. —*Incorrect*
No sooner did she reach the station than the train arrived. —*Correct*

(b) No sooner did he came here than she went to market. —*Incorrect*
No sooner did he come here than she went to market. —*Correct*

(5) Hardly had......when

(1) 'Hardly' के साथ 'when' का प्रयोग होता है, 'than' या अन्य Conjunction का नहीं ।

(2) 'Hardly had' के बाद verb की III form आएगी लगेगी, यह एक महत्त्वपूर्ण बिन्दु है, इसका ध्यान रखें:

(a) Hardly had she reached the station than the train arrived. —*Incorrect*
Hardly had she reached the station when the train arrived. —*Correct*

(b) Hardly did he reached here when she went to market. —*Incorrect*
Hardly had he reached here when she went to market. —*Correct*

(6) Neither.......nor.........nor........nor एवं Either........or........or........or

कुछ विद्वानों का मत है कि Neither.......nor....nor....nor एवं Either....or....or....or का प्रयोग करना उचित नहीं है। इस सन्दर्भ में **Mr. Vallins** ने लिखा है कि

"The correct correlatives are 'either.....or' and 'neither.....nor'. Strictly speaking, we should not add another 'or' or 'nor' since 'either' and 'neither' imply two and two only.

लेकिन अन्य विद्वानों , जैसे: Mr T.S. Eliot, Jefferson, Fowler, H.Walker आदि के अनुसार 'Neither......nor,' 'Either.....or' के साथ और भी extra 'nor' एवं 'or' add किए जा सकते हैं।

Look at the following sentences:

(a) Either from the moralists point of view, or from the theologian's point of view or from the psychologist's point of view, or from that of the political philosopher, or judging by the ordinary standards of likeableness in human beings, Milton is unsatisfactory. T.S. Eliot.

(b) Neither the brilliancy of Haglitt, nor the harmony of De Quincey, nor the vigour of Macaulay, nor the eloquence of Ruskin, nor the purity of Goldsmith could for a moment be thought capable of expressing the meaning of lamb. H.Walker.

अतः 'Neither......nor.........nor.......nor...' एवं 'Either......or.......or.........or' का प्रयोग सही एवं मान्य है।

(7) No/Not/Never........or

यदि किसी वाक्य में no/not/never आये एवं उसके बाद कोई Alternative Conjunction प्रयुक्त करना हो, तो 'or' का प्रयोग होगा, 'nor' का नहीं।

look at the following sentences :

(a) I have no chair **or** stool.
(b) I have never read about her or heard of her.
(c) She does not speak **or** weep.
(d) He did not say or write anything.

(8) The use of 'That'

(A) 'That' का प्रयोग Direct Narration में नहीं किया जाता है। हमेशा Indirect narration में ही इसका प्रयोग होता है :

(a) He said to me, "That I will go there". —*Incorrect*
He told me that he would go there. — Correct

(B) Indirect narration में 'that' के बाद आने वाले वाक्य का tense, reporting verb यदि past में है तो past में ही होगा। वाक्य में आये pronoun भी आवश्यकतानुसार बदले जाते हैं। इस सम्बन्ध में Reported Speech के अध्याय में विस्तार में वर्णन किया गया है।

(C) Imperative/Optative/Interrogative/Exclamatory वाक्यों में 'that' का प्रयोग Conjunction के रूप में नहीं किया जाता है। इस सम्बन्ध में भी Reported speech के अध्याय में विस्तृत रूप से वर्णन किया गया है।

(a) He said that close the door. —*Incorrect*
He said to close the door. —*Correct*

(b) He said that may God grant you success. —*Incorrect*
He prayed for me that God might grant me success. —*Correct*

(c) He said that how beautiful the girl was. —*Incorrect*
He exclaimed with pleasure that the girl was very beautifl. —*Correct*

(d) He said that where were you going. —*Incorrect*
He asked me where I was going. —*Correct*

(D) कुछ verbs के साथ 'that' का प्रयोग करना आवश्यक है (that का छिपा देना गलत माना गया है), ऐसी verbs हैं: agree, assert, avert, assume, hold, calculate, conceive, learn, maintain, state, reckon, suggest, understand.

(a) I agree your proposal is very good. —*Incorrect*
I agree that your proposal is very good. —*Correct*

(b) He asserted he could do that. —*Incorrect*
He asserted that he could do that. —*Correct*

(c) He suggested we should go there. —*Incorrect*
He suggested that we should go there. —*Correct*

(E) कुछ verbs जैसे: believe, hope, suppose, think, presume, afraid of के बाद 'that' को छिपाना, अच्छी अंग्रेजी लिखने हेतु आजकल उचित माना जाने लगा है :

(a) I hope, he is right. (b) We presume you are innocent.
(c) I suppose you have a good dictionary. (d) I think he will come.

(F) 'That' v/s 'Whether'
'Whether' का प्रयोग Choice वाले वाक्यों में किया जाता है। 'Whether' के प्रयोग वाले वाक्यों में 'or not' का प्रयोग, Choice को व्यक्त करता है :

(a) I don't know whether she will go there or not.
(b) He does not know whether he will pass or not.

ध्यान रखें, इस तरह के वाक्यों में 'whether' की जगह 'that' का प्रयोग नहीं किया जा सकता है।

(9) However / But

'However' के साथ कभी भी 'But' का प्रयोग नहीं किया जाता है; या तो वाक्य में 'But' का प्रयोग होगा या 'However' का।

(a) But his behaviour, however, has not changed. —*Incorrect*
His behaviour, however, has not changed. —*Correct*

(b) But that, however, is not repairable. —*Incorrect*
But that is not repairable. —*Correct*

(10) Though, although and even though

'Though/although' के साथ कभी भी 'but' का प्रयोग नहीं किया जाता है; या तो 'yet' का प्रयोग किया जाता है या नहीं किया जाता है।

'Though', 'although' and 'even though' are used to show a contrast between two clauses:

(a) Our new neighbours are quite nice (this is good) though their two dogs bark all day long. (this isn't good.)

We can use 'though' or 'although' with no difference in meaning. But, some differences are:

(i) 'Though' is more common than 'although' in conversation or writing.

(ii) 'Though' (but not 'although') can come at the end of a sentence:

(b) My new bike is really fast. I don't like the colour, though.

(iii) **Though (but not although)** can also be used as an adverb:

(c) I'm not good at reasoning but I can help you with your Geography, though, if you want.

The meaning of **'though'** is similar to 'however', but 'though' is much more common than 'however' in conversation.

'Even though' can be used to make the contrast between two clauses stronger:

(d) My father got back from work really late, even though he had promised to take Mom to the cinema.

(e) Although he is poor, yet he is honest.

(f) Though he is poor, he is honest.

(11) Until/Unless

'Until' का प्रयोग समय के सन्दभं में होता है, जबकि 'Unless' का प्रयोग, Condition (शर्त) के सन्दर्भ में :

(a) I will stay here until you return.

(b) He will wait until the train arrives.

(c) He can't succeed unless he works hard.

(d) You cannot achieve your goal unless you try for that.

वाक्य (a) एवं (b) में 'Unless' का प्रयोग एवं वाक्य (c) एवं (d) में Until का प्रयोग करना गलत होगा।

(12) When and While :

'When' का अर्थ होता है, 'जब' 'While' का अर्थ होता है, 'जबकि' 'When' का प्रयोग उस स्थिति में किया जाता है, जब एक कार्य पूर्ण हो जाता है।

'While' का प्रयोग उस स्थिति में किया जाता है, जब दो कार्य साथ-साथ हो रहे होते हैं :

(a) When he came here, she was going to market.

(b) He was reading while I was playing.

(13) As if/As though

'As if' एवं 'As though' का अर्थ होता है, 'Suppose' 'मान लीजिए / मानो'। इनका प्रयोग करते समय इस बिन्दु का ध्यान रखें कि, इनके बाद Past Conditional का ही प्रयोग होगा, Present form का नहीं; Would/could/did/was/were/had gone/knew का प्रयोग हो सकता है, लेकिन will/can/do/does/is/have gone/know का नहीं हो सकता है :

(a) He behaves as if he were a king.

(b) She orders as though she were the boss.

(c) They asked us for arranging tea and breakfast as if they were our invitees.

(14) 'Because', 'As' and 'Since'

'Because', 'As' and 'Since' are used to answer the question: 'Why?'.

(i) They join two clauses in the same sentence:

(a) I lost my job because I was often late.

(b) Ram resigned because he wanted to spend more time with his family.

(ii) 'Because', 'As' and 'Since' show the relationship between the two clauses :

(a) Why did you resign from such a well-paid job, Ram ?

Because I wanted to spend more time with my family.

'Because' is more common than 'As' and 'Since' ***when the reason is the most important thing.***

The **'because-clause'** is usually placed after the main clause:

I went to Chennai for a holiday last October because I knew it would be warm and sunny every day I was there.

As and **Since** are used ***when the reason is already well-known and / or less important***. The **'As'** or **'Since-clause'** often comes at the beginning of the sentence and is separated from the main clause by a comma :

(a) **As my family had finished dinner when I got home, I went to this really good beer bar.** (I'm telling you about the beer bar. It's not so important 'why' I went there.)

(b) **Since it's your birthday, I'll make you breakfast in bed.** (I'm going to make you breakfast.(I know, and you know, it's your birthday.)

(c) Since I have no money, I can't go to the movie.

ERRORS, MISTAKES AND BLUNDERS IN USE OF CONJUNCTIONS

Exercise : ***Rewrite the following sentences after correction.***

1. I could neither contact Lila nor Sarla.
2. Neither he plays nor reads.
3. She both accused me and my friend Shyam.
4. Ram not only built a temple but also a mosque.
5. He has visited both to Newyork and Mexico.
6. English is not only difficult to speak but also to write.
7. She is as much noted for her beauty as for her wisdom.
8. I have both visited America and Russia.
9. He neither knows me nor my wife.
10. Ramesh neither went to Jaipur nor Delhi.
11. No sooner had he reached the station when the train arrived.
12. Though he is poor but he is trustworthly.
13. Hardly had she left the hospital, than it began to rain.
14. He had neither a car or a scooter.
15. There was much disturbance both in Jammu as well as in Pahalgaon.
16. One cannot be both present at New Delhi as well as at Jaipur.
17. He cannot either read nor write English.
18. She cannot run nor walk.
19. He has not any book nor any copy.
20. I have never seen her nor heard of her.
21. I do not know that when she will go.
22. I cannot say that where he is working now a days.
23. I understand she will attend the function.
24. I hope that you are well now.
25. I can assert it is right.
26. I cannot explain that why I like her so much.
27. I asked my assistant that bring a chair and my mobile.
28. I agree it is a good oportunity to invest the money.
29. As she started late, she will miss the train.
30. Since Raju is a poor fellow, he couldn't buy a new dress.
31. It was generally doubted that India would permit the use of her soil.
32. It is not doubtful whether she will attend the party.
33. Is there any doubt whether she will come ?
34. Keep your body fit like I do.
35. You are as dear to me as her.
36. Until he works hard, he can't pass.
37. Take an umbrella in case it may rain.
38. You wait here unless the train arrives.
39. You will succeed, if you will work hard.
40. If I had wings, I will fly to London.
41. It is a year since I have met her.
42. It is a month since she has left for U.S.A.
43. He speaks as if he was the master.
44. Ram orders as though he would be a millionaire.
45. Five years have passed since I had seen her.
46. A year passed since his wife died.
47. I was playing when he was watching T.V.
48. I will go when he will come.
49. I went there while he awoke.
50. I will meet you before I shall leave for home.
51. The reason is because he is not well.
52. If I won a lottery, I will buy a big house.
53. If he had worked hard, he would pass.

Explanations

1. I could contact neither Lila nor Sarla.
2. He neither plays nor reads.
3. She accused both me and my friend Shyam.
4. Ram built not only a temple but also a mosque.
5. He has visited both to Newyork and to Mexico. or He has visited to both Newyork and Mexico.
6. English is difficult not only to speak but also to write.
7. She is noted as much for her beauty as for her wisdom.
8. I have visited both America and Russia.
9. He knows neither me nor my wife.
10. Ramesh went neither to Jaipur nor to Delhi.
11. No sooner had he reached the station than the train arrived.
12. Though he is poor yet he is trustworthly.
13. Hardly had she left the hospital, when it began to rain.
14. He had neither a car nor a scooter.
15. There was much disturbance both in Jammu and in Pahalgaon.
16. One cannot be present both at New Delhi and at Jaipur.
17. He cannot either read or write English.
18. She cannot run or walk.
19. He has not any book or copy.
20. I have never seen her or heard of her.
21. I do not know when she will go.
22. I cannot say where he is working now a days.
23. I understand that she will attend the function.
24. I hope you are well now.
25. I can assert that it is right.
26. I cannot explain why I like her so much.
27. I asked my assistant to bring a chair and my mobile.
28. I agree that it is a good oportunity to invest the money.
29. As she started late, she missed the train.
30. Since Raju is a poor fellow he can't buy a new dress.
31. It was generally doubted whether India would permit the use of her soil.
32. It is not doubtful that she will attend the party.
33. Is there any doubt that she will come ?
34. Keep your body fit like me . or Keep your body fit as I do.
35. You are as dear to me as she.
36. Unless he works hard, he can't pass.
37. Take an umbrella in case it rains.
38. You wait here until the train arrives.
39. You will succeed, if you work hard.
40. If I had wings, I would fly to London.
41. It is a year since I met her.
42. It is a month since she left for U.S.A.
43. He speaks as if he were the master.
44. Ram orders as though he were a millionaire.
45. Five years have passed since I saw her.
46. A year has passed since his wife died.
47. I was playing while he was watching T.V.
48. I will go when he comes.
49. I went there when he awoke.
50. I will meet you before I leave for home.
51. The reason is that he is not well.
52. If I won a lottery, I would buy a big house.
53. If he had worked hard, he would have passed.

Exercise : *Find the errors and justify your answers.*

1. She was not (A)/ so well versed in English (B)/ that they (C)/ had expected (D) .
2. He not only comes (A)/ here for having lunch (B)/ but also for having a glimpse of (C)/ the beautiful sales girls (D).
3. I cannot permit you (A)/ to leave the class (B)/ unless the teacher comes (C)/ and instructs me in the matter (D) .
4. The patient would not (A)/ have died (B)/ when the doctor had (C)/ come in time (D).
5. Three years have passed (A)/ that I returned from (B)/ USA and settled here (C).

6. The captain asked (A)/ the players to go (B)/ to market and buy some fruits (C)/ as apples, oranges, bananas etc (D).
7. Both the rich (A)/ along with the poor (B)/ are responsible for a great many vices (C)/ with which our country is inflicted (D).
8. Since the festival of Diwali is approaching, (A)/ so my son has bought (B)/ many fireworks (C)/ as rockets, crackers etc (D).
9. The thief had (A)/ hardly put the cash (B)/ in his pocket (C)/ then the owner woke up (D) .
10. No sooner did we (A)/ find out a solution (B)/ to the problem (C)/ when another problem cropped up (D).
11. She has lots of money (A)/ and she dare not (B)/ purchase a new car (C).
12. She is not only (A)/ sympathetic to the rich patients (B)/ but also to the poor ones (C).
13. Because she is intelligent (A)/ therefore she secures highest marks (B)/ in her class(C).
14. It was almost five months ago (A)/ since she wrote a letter (B)/ to me (C)/ to remind me of my promise (D).
15. The inspector was doubtful (A)/ that the man who had been run over (B)/ by the truck had (C)/ lain there for more than a day (D).
16. He instructed me (A)/ that I should do (B)/ all the work as quickly (C)/ like him (D).
17. Seldom or (A)/ ever have I sent (B)/ a beggar away without (C)/ giving him something (D).
18. Seldom or ever (A)/ have I tried my (B)/ best to help my friends (C)/ who are in need (D).
19. The teacher advised (A)/ the students to (B)/ go through the notes as many times as possible (C)/ lest they would fail (D).
20. He asked me (A)/ that why I was not appearing (B) in the examination (C).
21. Most of the founding fathers (A)/ of our constitution are (B)/ so reverend as Ambedkar (C)/ if not more (D).
22. I don't know (A)/ if any of the members (B)/ of the society is conspiring (C)/ against the chairman or not (D).
23. This is the same dog (A)/ which bit her (B)/ while she was going (C)/ to the hospital (D).
24. This is not (A)/ such a big problem (B)/ which cannot be solved(C)/with some efforts (D).
25. As he is (A)/ a perfectionist (B)/ so he always insists (C)/ on regular practice (D) .

Explanations

1. (C) 'that' की जगह 'as' का प्रयोग होगा, क्योंकि यहाँ वाक्य का structure, 'so ....as' का है ।
2. (A) 'not only' का प्रयोग here not only for having lunch के साथ होगा ।

   'Not only...... but also' से दो subjects/objects/verbs/gerunds को जोड़ा जाता है। जैसे :

   (1) Not only Hari but also Krishna is playing . — *Subject*
   (2) I have invited not only Hari but also Krishna . — *Object*
   (3) He not only reads but also plays. — *Verbs*
   (4) She likes not only swimming but also singing . — *Gerunds*
3. (C) 'Unless' की जगह 'until' का प्रयोग होगा। समय के संदर्भ में 'until' का तथा condition के संदर्भ में 'unless' का प्रयोग किया जाता है ।
4. (C) 'when' की जगह 'If' का प्रयोग करें । conditional sentence की structure निम्न होती है :

   If he had come to me, I would have helped him .
5. (A) 'that' की जगह 'since' का प्रयोग होगा। In perfect tense 'since' is used to express point of time and 'for' is usd for period of time.
6. (D) 'as' की जगह 'like' का प्रयोग होगा। 'as' का प्रयोग nominative के साथ होता है, जबकि 'like' का प्रयोग objective के साथ होता है :

   (1) He supports a man like me. (2) He supports a man as I (support)

7. (B) 'along with the' की जगह 'and का प्रयोग होगा। 'Both' के साथ 'and' conjunction आता है ।

8. (D) 'as' की जगह 'like' का प्रयोग होगा। 'as' का प्रयोग nominative case के साथ होता है, 'like' का प्रयोग objective case के साथ।

9. (D) 'than' की जगह 'when' का प्रयोग होगा। 'hardly' के साथ conjunction when आता है।

10. (D) 'when' की जगह 'than' का प्रयोग होगा। 'No sooner' के साथ 'than'तथा 'Hardly', 'scracely' के साथ 'when' का प्रयोग होता है।

11. (B) 'and' की जगह 'but' का प्रयोग होगा। वाक्य में contrast है।

12. (A) 'not only' का प्रयोग, 'to the rich' के पहले होगा । वाक्य में 'but also' का प्रयोग 'to the poor' के पहले हुआ है अत: वाक्य में balance बनाने हेतु 'not only' का प्रयोग 'to the rich' के पहले करना होगा।

13. (B) 'therefore' का प्रयोग अनुचित है। 'because, as, since, for' आदि conjunction के साथ 'so/therefore' आदि का प्रयोग नहीं किया जाता है।

14. (B) 'since' की जगह 'that' का प्रयोग होगा; साधारणतया 'since' और 'for' का प्रयोग perfect tense में किया जाता है। वैसे भी 'ago' के बाद 'that' का प्रयोग होता है। The sentence is of past indefinite.

15. (B) 'that' की जगह 'whether' का प्रयोग होगा।

16. (D) 'like him' की जगह 'as he'होगा। यहाँ comparison दो nominatives, 'I' एवं 'he' में है, अत: 'as he' लिखना होगा।

17. (B) 'ever' की जगह 'never' का प्रयोग होगा। वाक्य का अर्थ-'कभी नहीं' या 'अधिकांशतया' नहीं है।

18. (A) 'or' की जगह 'if' का प्रयोग होगा। 'seldom' के साथ या तो 'seldom if ever' या 'seldom or never' आता है। वाक्य के संदर्भ के अनुसार इनका प्रयोग किया जाता है।

19. (D) 'would' की जगह 'should' का प्रयोग होगा। 'lest' के साथ हमेशा 'should' का प्रयोग होता है।

20. (B) 'that' को हटा दें। Indirect narration में 'wh' questions में कोई conjunction नहीं आता है।

21. (C) 'so' की जगह 'as' का प्रयोग होगा। 'so----as' का प्रयोग negative वाक्यों में होता है, जबकि 'as----as' का प्रयोग affirmative वाक्यों में :

(a) Rahim is not so intelligent as Shyam. (b) Rahim is as intelligent as Shyam .

22. (B) 'If' की जगह 'whether' का प्रयोग होगा। वाक्य की संरचना 'whether----or' पर आधारित है।

23. (B) 'which' की जगह 'that' का प्रयोग होगा। जब verb स्पष्ट होती है तो 'same' के साथ 'that' का प्रयोग किया जाता है।

This is the same chair that was missing.

जब verb स्पष्ट नहीं होती तो 'same-as' का प्रयोग सामान्यत: किया जाता है। जैसे :

This is the same chair as mine .

24. (C) 'which' की जगह 'as' का प्रयोग होगा। 'Such' is followed by 'as' or 'that'.

See the following examples:

(1) Such + noun + as ....
He is not such a person as I thought.

(2) Such .... that
His behaviour was such that I felt hurt.

(3) Such+ as + infinitive ....
Her ailment is not such as to cause worries.

25. (C) 'so' का प्रयोग नहीं होगा; As, because, for, इत्यादि के साथ so, therefore का प्रयोग नहीं होता है।

❑❑❑

17

Conditional Sentences

विभिन्न प्रकार के Conditional Sentences के Sentence structures में परस्पर अन्तर होता है। Conditional Sentence के errors सम्बन्धित प्रश्नों में Structures की गलती देकर प्रश्न दिये जाते हैं। छात्र ध्यान दें।

सामान्यतया conditional sentences में दो clauses होती है :

(1) If clause, **(2) Main clause**

'If' clause, condition को बताती है, एवं main clause कार्य के पूर्ण होने या न होने को व्यक्त करती है।

Conditional sentences को मुख्य रूप से तीन भागों में वर्गीकृत किया जा सकता है :

(1) जब If clause - Present tense में हो,

(2) जब If clause - Past tense में हो, और

(3) जब If clause - Past Perfect tense में हो।

(A) Conditional sentence- 'If' clause in present tense

(1) जब 'If' clause, present tense में होती है तो main clause में future tense निम्न निम्न प्रकार से प्रयोग में आ सकता है।

(a) If he runs fast, he will reach in time. (b) If the fog gets thicker, the plane may be late.

इस तरह के वाक्य, जिनमें 'If' clause present tense में है तथा main clause में future tense का प्रयोग होता है, ऐसे clause कार्य के पूरा होने की probability /ability को व्यक्त करते है। **ध्यान रखें जब main clause में future tense का प्रयोग किया है तो 'if' clause में will/shall etc. का प्रयोग नहीं होगा।**

(2) जब 'if' clause present में है एवं main clause भी present में है, तो ऐसे वाक्य स्वत: (automatic) ही कार्य के होने को व्यक्त करते है :

(a) If you heat ice it turns to water. (b) If you boil water it turns to vapours.

(3) If+ present continuous का प्रयोग वर्तमान में होने वाले कार्य या future arrangement को व्यक्त करता है। ये वाक्य वर्तमान काल को व्यक्त करते हैं :

(a) If you are waiting for a taxi, you should better go there.

(b) If you are looking for Raju, you may find him in the park.

(4) If + Present Perfect conditional sentence

(a) If you have finished dinner, I will ask the waiter for ice cream.

(b) If she has written the thesis ,I will send it to the professor.

(B) Conditional sentence - 'If' clause is in past tense

(1) यदि 'If clause' past tense में है तो main clause में 'would' का प्रयोग होता है। जैसे :

(a) If I had an umbrella I would lend it to you.[But I haven't an umbrella.]
यदि मेरे पास छतरी होती तो मैं तुम्हें दे देता। [लेकिन मेरे पास छतरी नहीं है।]

(b) If I had a briefcase, I would give it to her. [But I haven't a brief case.]
यदि मेरे पास ब्रीफकेस होता, तो मैं उसे दे देता। [लेकिन मेरे पास ब्रीफकेस नहीं है।]

ये वाक्य वर्तमान स्थिति को व्यक्त करते हैं। वस्तुत: 'If clause' में past tense का प्रयोग past action को व्यक्त करता ही नहीं है।

यहाँ ध्यान रखें, 'had' के बाद noun का प्रयोग हुआ है, एवं main clause में 'would' के बाद V-I का प्रयोग हुआ है।

If + subject + had + noun +...would + verb-I

(2) 'If clause' में verb की II form का प्रयोग, जैसे :

(a) If he tried to threaten me I would inform his father.
(But I don't expect that he will try to threaten me.)
यदि उसने मुझे धमकाने का प्रयास किया तो मैं उसके पिता को सूचित कर दूंगा।

(b) If a thief came into my room I would call you.
(But I don't expect a thief to come into my room.)
यदि चोर मेरे कमरे में आया तो मै तुम्हें बुलाऊंगा।

उपरोक्त वाक्य future action को सूचित करते हैं।

इस तरह के वाक्यों में भी 'if clause' में past tense का प्रयोग वास्तविक Past नहीं है, न ये किसी Past action को सूचित करता है। **इस तरह के वाक्यों में 'If clause' में verb की II form का तथा main clause में would +V-I का प्रयोग होता है :**

If +Subject +V - II + ... Would + V-I ....

Note *Main clause में 'would' की जगह might/could इत्यादि का भी प्रयोग किया जा सकता है। 'would' का प्रयोग certainty को व्यक्त करता है, जबकि 'might' का प्रयोग possibility तथा 'could' का प्रयोग ability को व्यक्त करता है। जैसे-*

(a) If he tried again he would pass. *(certain result)*
यदि उसने पुन: प्रयास किया तो पास हो जायेगा।

(b) If he tried again he could pass. *(ability)*
यदि उसने पुन: प्रयास किया तो पास हो सकता है।

(c) If he tried again he might pass. *(possibility)*
यदि उसने पुन: प्रयास किया तो उसके पास होने की सम्भावना है।

(3) यदि 'if clause' में भी Past Indefinite हो एवं main clause में भी Past Indefinite हो तो ऐसे वाक्य एक के बाद तुरंत दूसरा कार्य habitually / automatically होने को व्यक्त करते हैं। जैसे :

(a) If anyone abused him, he became angry
(यदि किसी ने उसे गाली दी, तो वह गुस्सा हो गया।)

(b) If there was a scarcity of milk, its prices went up.
(यदि कभी दूध की कमी हुई, तो उसकी कीमतें बढ़ीं।)

(c) If there was a short supply of any commodity, prices of that commodity increased.
(यदि कभी किसी चीज की कमी हुई, तो उसकी कीमतें बढ़ी।)

इस तरह के वाक्य habitual or automatic action को व्यक्त करते हैं। वाक्यों में past tense, past time के actions को ही व्यक्त करते हैं।

(C) Conditional sentences -'If' clause is in Past perfect tense

इस तरह के वाक्यों का structure निम्न प्रकार का होता है :

If+ Subject + had + V-III +.. .. would have +V-III....

(a) If he had come to me, I would have helped him. (But he didn't come to me.)
यदि वह मेरे पास आता, तो मैं उसकी सहायता करता।

(b) If she had invited me, I would have attended the function. (But she did not invite me.)
यदि वह मुझे आमंत्रित करती तो मैं कार्यक्रम में उपस्थित होता।

Note

(1) इस तरह के वाक्यों में main clause में 'would' की जगह 'could' या 'might' का भी प्रयोग किया जा सकता है। 'could' का प्रयोग ability को तथा 'might' का प्रयोग possibility को व्यक्त करता है। जैसे :

(a) If we had found her earlier we could have saved her life. (ability)
यदि हम उसे पहले ढूंढ लेते तो उसकी जान बचा सकते थे।

(b) If we had found her earlier we might have saved her life. (possibility)
यदि हम उसे पहले ढूँढ लेते तो सम्भवतया उसकी जान बचा सकते थे।

(2) 'Had' का प्रयोग Subject से पहले करने पर 'if' को omit किया जा सकता है। निम्न दोनों वाक्यों का अर्थ समान होता है :

(a) If he had come to me I would have helped him.

(b) Had he come to me I would have helped him.

(3) 'If clause' में past perfect continuous का भी प्रयोग निम्न प्रकार किया जा सकता है :

OTHER TYPES OF CONDITIONAL SENTENCES

(A) 'If clause' के साथ 'would' का प्रयोग करके निम्न प्रकार conditional sentence बनाये जा सकते है :

(a) If you would like to come I will arrange a party for you.
जब 'if' clause में would का प्रयोग होता है तो main clause में simple future का प्रयोग होता है।

(B) 'If + should' का प्रयोग करके निम्न conditional sentences बनते हैं :

(a) If you should have any difficulty in getting newspaper, ring at this number.

(b) If these packets should arrive in a damaged condition please inform the company at once.

इस तरह के वाक्यों को निम्न प्रकार भी लिखा जा सकता है :
Should these packets arrive in a damaged condition, please inform the company at once.
Should का प्रयोग यहाँ possibility को व्यक्त करता है, लेकिन ऐसी possibility, जिसका घटित होना मुश्किल (unlikely) है।

(C) 'If + were' के प्रयोग से भी conditional sentences बनते हैं :

(a) If I were you ,I would forgive him. (b) If I were you , I would punish him.

'If I were you' का यहाँ अर्थ –'यदि मैं तुम्हारी जगह होता' से है।

(D) Use of 'Until' & 'Unless' in conditional sentences

Until : 'Until' का अर्थ होता है : 'जब तक' यह समय के सन्दर्भ में प्रयुक्त होता है। 'Until' के साथ सामान्यतया वाक्य में Not का प्रयोग नहीं किया जाता है :

(a) Until he comes back, you will wait for him.
जब तक वह वापस न आ जाये, तुम उसका इन्तजार करोगे।

(b) I will stay here until you complete your work.
जब तक तुम अपना कार्य पूर्ण न कर लोगे, मैं यहीं रुकूंगा।

Unless: 'Unless' का अर्थ होता है - 'अगर नहीं'। यह एक नकारात्मक शब्द है। सामान्यतया 'Unless' के साथ भी 'not' का प्रयोग नहीं किया जाता है। 'Unless' का प्रयोग किसी अन्य शर्त के पूरी होने के सन्दर्भ में किया जाता है। जैसे :

(a) You cannot pass unless you attend the college.
अगर तुम कॉलेज में उपस्थित नहीं रहोगे, तो पास नहीं हो सकते।

(b) I cannot go to America unless I have a visa.
अगर मेरे पास वीसा नहीं होगा, तो मैं अमेरिका नहीं जा सकता।

See the difference:

(a) You will wait here *unless* the train arrives. —*Incorrect*
You will wait here *until* the train arrives. —*Correct*

(b) You cannot achieve your goal *until* you work hard. —*Incorrect*
You cannot achieve your goal *unless* you work hard. —*Correct*

'Unless' की जगह 'Until' एवं 'Until' की जगह 'Unless' का प्रयोग न करें। 'Until' का प्रयोग समय के सन्दर्भ में तथा 'Unless' का प्रयोग किसी शर्त (condition) के सन्दर्भ में किया जाता है।

(E) Use of 'In case' in conditional sentences

'In case' का प्रयोग conditional sentences में भविष्य में किसी घटना के होने की सम्भावना को व्यक्त करता है : 'In case' का अर्थ होता है 'यदि ऐसा हो'

(a) Inform me in case you need more money.
यदि तुम्हें और धन की आवश्यकता हो (यदि ऐसा हो), तो मुझे सूचित करो।

(b) Turn on the light in case you need my help.
यदि मेरी सहायता की आवश्कता हो (यदि ऐसा हो), तो लाइट जला देना।

(F) Use of 'So long' in conditional sentences

'So long' का अर्थ होता है - 'जब तक'। 'So long' का प्रयोग conditional sentences में निम्न प्रकार होता है :

(a) I shall support him so long he is here.
जब तक वह यहाँ है, मैं उसका समर्थन करूंगा।

(b) You can stay here so long the owner is out of station.
जब तक मालिक बाहर है, तुम यहाँ रुक सकते हो।

(G) Use of 'Provided' in conditional sentences

'Provided' का अर्थ होता है- 'शर्त है कि' 'provided' का प्रयोग conditional sentences में अग्रलिखित प्रकार होता है :

(a) I shall attend the meeting provided he also attends.
मैं मीटिंग में उपस्थित हूंगा, शर्त है कि वह भी मीटिंग में उपस्थित रहे।

(b) We shall support you provided you favour us .
हम तुम्हे समर्थन देंगे, शर्त है कि तुम हमारा पक्ष लो।

(H) Use of 'Suppose' in conditional sentences

'Suppose' का अर्थ होता है - 'मान लीजिए' या 'मान लो'। 'Suppose' का प्रयोग conditional sentences में निम्न प्रकार होता है :

(a) Suppose a monkey comes here, what will you do?
मान लो एक बन्दर यहाँ आ जाता है, तो तुम क्या करोगे ?

(b) Suppose she doesn't agree, what can you do?
मान लीजिए वह सहमत नहीं होती है, तो आप क्या कर सकते हैं ?

(I) Use of 'But for' in conditional sentence

'But for' का अर्थ है – 'यदि ऐसा न हुआ होता'। 'But for' का प्रयोग 'if it hadn't happened' के अर्थ में होता है।

(a) But for his help, Ramesh would have ruined.
यदि वह सहायता नहीं करता, तो रमेश बर्बाद हो गया होता।

(b) But for the flood, I would have arrived here yesterday.
यदि बाढ़ नहीं आई होती, तो मैं यहाँ कल ही आ गया होता।

(c) But for your company, I would have bored.
यदि तुम्हारा साथ न होता, तो मैं बोर हो गया होता।

Exercise : *Rewrite the following sentences after correction.*

1. If he came to me, I would have given him a pen.
2. Had he invited me, I would attend the function.
3. If he had telephoned me, I would have gave him the address.
4. If a monkey came here, what you will do?
5. If I had an umbrella, I would have given it to her.
6. If he will work hard, he will get promotion.
7. Unless he will ask me, I shall not help him.
8. If I had a briefcase, I will have lend it to her.
9. If you will heat ice, it may turn to water.
10. If you are looking for Sita, you would find her with Ram.
11. If I was you, I would dismiss him.
12. Unless he comes back, wait for him.
13. Until you work hard, you can't beat him.
14. Suppose she does not agree, what could you do?
15. If he tried again, he can pass.

Explanations

1. If he had come to me, I would have given him a pen.
2. Had he invited me, I would have attended the function.
3. If he had telephoned me, I would have given him the address.
4. If a monkey came here what would you do?
5. If I had an umbrella I would give it to her.
6. If he works hard, he will get promotion.
7. Unless he asks me I shall not help him.
8. If I had a briefcase, I would lend it to her.
9. If you heat ice, it turns to water.
10. If you are looking for Sita, you will find her with Ram.
11. If I were you, I would dismiss him.
12. Until he comes back, wait for him.
13. Unless you work hard, you can't beat him.
14. Suppose she does not agree, what can you do?
15. If he tried again he could pass.

❑❑❑

18

Question Tag

Question Tag को यद्यपि पूर्ण प्रश्न नहीं माना जाता है, तथापि Question Tag से सम्बधित विभिन्न नियमों का ध्यान न रखने पर बहुधा त्रुटियाँ हो जाती हैं। Question tag विषय से error सम्बन्धित प्रश्न इन्हीं नियमों पर आधरित होते हैं।

Question tag एक पूर्ण प्रश्न नहीं है, बल्कि यह एक कथन के पीछे जुड़ा पुछल्ला प्रश्न है। Question tag का प्रयोग आपसी वार्तालाप में किया जाता है। इसका उद्देश्य, श्रोता का ध्यान वक्ता के कथन की ओर आकर्षित करना या वक्ता द्वारा अपने कथन की पुष्टि चाहना होता है।

RULES FRAMING QUESTION TAG

(1) Question Tag बनाने के लिये Helping verbs, जिन्हें Anomalous finites भी कहते हैं (Total 24), का प्रयोग, subject के साथ किया जाता है। यदि Question tag, Negative है तो Anomalous verb का प्रयोग संक्षिप्त रूप (abbreviated form) में किया जाता है। जैसे : Isn't he ?, Aren't I ?, Won't they? etc.

(2) Question Tag का Structure निम्न होता है :

Helping Verb + Subject ? — **-Positive**

Helping Verb + n't + Subject? — **-Negative**

यदि वक्ता का कथन positive हो तो question tag, negative होता है। यदि कथन negative हो तो question tag , positive होता है।

वक्ता के कथन (statement) के बाद comma अंकित कर, Question Tag लिखा जाता है। **(ध्यान रखें: question tag, capital letter से शुरू नहीं किया जाता है।)**

(3) Question Tag के साथ noun नहीं प्रयुक्त होता है, pronoun का प्रयोग होता है :

(a) Ram is going to Jaipur, isn't he ? (b) Sita is not cooking, is she?

(4) यदि मुख्य कथन में कोई helping verb नहीं हो, तो question tag में do/does/did को काम में लेते है :

(a) He goes to office, doesn't he ? (b) They play football, don't they?

(5) यदि वक्ता के कथन का subject, एक personal pronoun है, तो Question tag में वही personal pronoun प्रयुक्त होता है। लेकिन यदि कथन में subject कोई noun (किसी का नाम) है, तो question tag में जो pronoun प्रयुक्त होगा, वह कथन में दिए Subject के gender (male or female), तथा Number (singular or plural) के अनुसार होगा। अर्थात यदि वक्ता के कथन में subject, male एवं singular है, तो Question Tag में pronoun 'he' का प्रयोग होगा। जैसे :

(a) They play, don't they? (b) He is watching TV, isn't he?

(c) Ram and Sita are swimming, aren't they? (d) We played a match, didn't we?

(6) यदि वक्ता के कथन में Subject-there, this, that, those, these हो, तो Question Tag में subject अग्रलिखित प्रकार से प्रयुक्त होता है।

कथन का Subject	Question Tag में Subject
There	There
One	One
This	It
That	It
These	They
Those	They

(a) There is a cow, isn't there? (b) One can hold it, can't one?

(7) यदि one, this, that, these, those का प्रयोग कथन में एक adjective की तरह हुआ है ; अर्थात यदि इनके साथ कोई noun आया है, तो Question Tag का subject, उक्त noun के gender एवं person के अनुसार आता है :

(a) One man can pull it, can't he? (b) This girl was present there, wasn't she?
(c) This book is very useful, isn't it? (d) That boy has no manners, has he?

(8) यदि वक्ता के कथन का subject- no one, none, anyone , someone, everyone, everybody, somebody या nobody है, तो Question Tag का subject, 'they' होगा। जैसे :

(a) None can say so, can they? (b) No one voted against the bill, did they?

(9) यदि वक्ता के कथन का subject-nothing, anything, something या everything हो, तो ध्यान रखें, Question tag का subject - 'it' होगा। जैसे :

(a) Everything is arranged, isn't it? (b) Something is missing, isn't it?

(10) यदि वक्ता के कथन का subject निम्न में से कोई होता है, तो question tag का subject -'we' होता है : All of us, Some of us, Any of us, None of us, Most of us, Everyone of us, Either of us, Neither of us etc.

लेकिन यदि 'us' की जगह 'you' या 'they' का प्रयोग किया हो तो question tag का subject - 'you' या 'they/them' होता है। जैसे :

(a) All of us are invited, aren't we? (b) Either of you can join, can't you?
(c) Neither of you can do it, can you? (d) None of us was present there, were we?

(11) जब कथन में 'I am' का प्रयोग होता है एवं Question Tag-negative में बनाना है, तो 'Amn't I' कभी भी न लिखें। इस हेतु 'Aren't I' लिखा जायेगा। लेकिन affirmative में Question Tag बनाना हो, तो 'Am I' लिखना सही है। जैसे :

(a) I am going to meet her, aren't I ? (b) I am not going there, am I ?

(12) 'Dare/Need' को semi modal auxiliary माना जाता है इनका प्रयोग main verb के रूप में भी किया जाता है। जब 'dare/need' का प्रयोग modal auxiliary की तरह किया गया हो, तो Question Tag में 'dare/need' का प्रयोग किया जाता है। जैसे :

(a) He dare not speak so, dare he? (b) She need not come here, need she?

(यहाँ 'dare not' एवं 'need not' का प्रयोग auxiliary की तरह हुआ है।)

लेकिन यदि 'dare/need' का प्रयोग मुख्य verb की तरह हुआ हो, तो Question Tag में किसी Auxiliary Verb का प्रयोग पूर्व में बताए गये नियमानुसार किया जाता है :

(a) He dares to speak like this, doesn't he? (b) He needs your help, doesn't he?

(यहाँ 'dare, need' का प्रयोग मुख्य Verb की तरह हुआ है।)

(13) यदि वक्ता के कथन में 'used to' का प्रयोग हुआ हो, तो Question Tag में 'usedn't' या 'didn't' का प्रयोग किया जा सकता है। यदि Question Tag affirmative में बनाना हो, तो 'used' या 'did' का प्रयोग किया जाता है। जैसे :

(a) She used to go to temple, usedn't she? or didn't she?
(b) He used to smoke, usedn't he ? or didn't he ?
(c) I never used to hit him, used I ? or did I?

SOME IMPORTANT POINTS

(1) कई बार वक्ता के कथन में 'not' का तो प्रयोग नहीं होता है, लेकिन ऐसे शब्दों का प्रयोग होता है जिनसे वाक्य का अर्थ negative हो जाता है, जैसे: Few, Little, Neither, None, No one, Nothing, Hardly, Rarely, Seldom, Scarcely, Never etc.

ऐसे कथन के साथ Question tag, Positive में बनता है। जैसे :

(a) None was present there, were they?
(b) I know little about U.S.A, do I ?
(c) Nobody believe it, do they?
(d) They said nothing about it, did they?

(2) यदि कथन एक Positive Imperative sentence (Imperative sentence में प्रार्थना या आदेश का भाव होता है।) हो, तो Question Tag, 'will' या 'won't' किसी से भी बन सकता है। लेकिन Negative imperative sentence का question tag हमेशा positive बनता है। जैसे :

(a) Open the gate, will you?
(b) Open the gate, won't you?
(c) Don't open the gate, will you?
(d) Go there, will you? or won't you?

इस तरह के Imperative sentence में, बात को अधिक प्रभावशाली बनाने के लिए, negative question tag का प्रयोग किया जाता है।

(3) यदि Imperative sentence से कोई नाराजगी जाहिर की जाती है, या नाराजगी व्यक्त करते हुए कोई कथन किया जाता है तो can't you?, question tag प्रयुक्त करना उचित रहता है। जैसे:

(a) Use your own vehicle, can't you ?
(b) Keep shut, can't you?

(4) 'Let's' (Let us) से शुरू हुए वक्ता के कथन के साथ question tag, 'shall we?' आता है; एवं 'Let him/ let you/let them' से शुरू वक्ता के कथन के साथ, question tag 'will you' प्रयुक्त होगा। जैसे :

(a) Let's play, shall we ?
(b) Let us sing, shall we?

ERRORS, MISTAKES AND BLUNDERS IN PUTTING TAG QUESTIONS

Exercise : ***Rewrite the following sentences after correction.***

1. He doesn't want to go to college today,is he ?
2. Let's pray to God, should we ?
3. You had met me before, didn't you ?
4. We couldn't enjoy the picnic, could they ?
5. He is a rude man,doesn't he ?
6. Everybody was watching the TV,wasn't he ?
7. Mrs.Saxena is a good lady, is she ?
8. Something must be done for us,needn't it ?
9. Someone might come,mightn't she?
10. He needs money,needn't he?
11. I needn't write, need he ?
12. Nisha need not go there, does she?
13. This book is very useful, doesn't it?
14. That boy has no manners, hasn't he?
15. None of us was present there, weren't we?
16. I am not going there, aren't I ?
17. They dare to meet the chairman, daren't they?
18. He used to smoke, doesn't he ?
19. Anyone can attend the function, don't they?
20. Those books are mine, aren't those?
21. She used to go to temple, don't she?
22. I know little about politics, did I ?
23. Go there, can you?
24. Please come here, can't you?
25. Use your own stationery, couldn't you?
26. Mind your own business, shall you?
27. Let them play, should you?
28. Consult a doctor, didn't you?
29. Few people can live in such circumstances, shall they?
30. I know little about U.S.A, does I ?

31. Everybody was watching the cricket match on TV, wasn't they?

32. He is a very wise man, doesn't he ?

33. Mrs. Meena is a good teacher, doesn't she?

34. We saw a rainbow in the sky yesterday, wasn't we?

35. Sita is a beautiful girl, is she ?

36. You should not smoke, will you?

37. Miss Neha does not play tennis,is she?

38. I am older than you, amn't I?

39. You always have your lunch at 1 o'clock, aren't you ?

40. I can do it for you, don't I ?

41. She doesn't want to go to college today,is she ?

42. Let's pray to Almighty,should we?

43. He had met you before, ddn't he ?

44. We couldn't enjoy the picnic,did we?

45. None can say so, can you?

Explanations

1. He doesn't want to go to college today, does he ?
2. Let's pray to God, shall we ?
3. You had met me before, hadn't you ?
4. We couldn't enjoy the picnic, could we ?
5. He is a rude man,isn't he ?
6. Everybody was watching the TV,weren't they?
7. Mrs.Saxena is a good lady, isn't she ?
8. Something must be done for us,mustn't it ?
9. Someone might come,mightn't they?
10. He needs money,doesn't he?
11. I needn't write, need I ?
12. Nisha need not go there, need she?
13. This book is very useful, isn't it?
14. That boy has no manners, has he?
15. None of us was present there, were we?
16. I am not going there, am I ?
17. They dare to meet the chairman, don't they?
18. He used to smoke, usedn't he ? or didn't he ?
19. Anyone can attend the function, can't they?
20. Those books are mine, aren't they?
21. She used to go to temple, usedn't she? or didn't she?
22. I know little about politics, do I ?
23. Go there, will you? or won't you?
24. Please come here, won't you?
25. Use your own stationery, can't you?
26. Mind your own business, can't you?
27. Let them play, will you?
28. Consult a doctor, won't you?
29. Few people can live in such circumstances, can they?
30. I know little about U.S.A, do I ?
31. Everybody was watching the cricket match on TV, weren't they?
32. He is a very wise man, isn't he ?
33. Mrs. Meena is a good teacher, isn't she?
34. We saw a rainbow in the sky yesterday, didn't we?
35. Sita is a beautiful girl, isn't she ?
36. You should not smoke, should you?
37. Miss Neha does not play tennis,does she?
38. I am older than you, aren't I?
39. You always have your lunch at 1 o'clock, don't you ?
40. I can do it for you, can't I ?
41. She doesn't want to go to college today, does she ?
42. Let's pray to Almighty,shall we?
43. He had met you before, hadn't he ?
44. We couldn't enjoy the picnic,could we?
45. None can say so, can they?

❑❑❑

19

Unenglish and Superfluous Expressions

इस chapter में ऐसे English expressions/ phrases का वर्णन किया जा रहा है, जिनका प्रयोग काफी प्रचलित है; इनमें *अंग्रेजी भाषा का हिन्दीकरण* किया गया प्रतीत होता है। ऐसे phrases expressions का प्रयोग किया जाना त्रुटिपूर्ण है, छात्रों को ऐसे phrases- expression का प्रयोग नहीं करना चाहिए :

(1) Females : 'Females' का प्रयोग women के लिए किया जाना गलत है। 'Females' से sex का ज्ञान होता हैं :

Male sex or Female sex :

(a) The females of my house do not agree to this proposal. —*Incorrect*

(b) The women of my house do not agree to this proposal. —*Correct*

(2) Family man : 'Family man' का प्रयोग बहुधा 'A man with a family' के संदर्भ में किया जाता है; यह गलत है, पूर्णतया Unenglish है।

(3) Family members/ Parliament members : इनकी जगह हमें Members of family or Members of Parliament का प्रयोग करना चाहिए।

(4) To give key to the watch :- घड़ी में चाबी भरने हेतु उक्त Phrase का प्रयोग करना अंग्रेजी का हिन्दीकरण है। इसकी जगह 'To wind the watch' का प्रयोग करना चाहिए।

(5) To eat food : यह पूर्णतया Unenglish है। I have eaten my food. इस तरह का प्रयोग पूर्णतया एक Unenglish प्रयोग है। English भाषा में अधिकांशतया खाने का नाम प्रयुक्त होता है :

(a) Have you had your lunch ? (b) Have you had your dinner ?

Break fast हेतु 'take' की जगह 'have' का प्रयोग करना चाहिए। I have *taken* my breakfast की जगह हमें लिखना चाहिए, I have *had* my break fast.

(6) Sick/Ill : 'Sick' का अर्थ शारीरिक बीमारियों के sense में नहीं करना चाहिए। 'Sick' का भावार्थ मानसिक थकान, परेशानियों के सन्दर्भ में होता है :

I am sick or He fell sick की जगह I am *ill* or He fell *ill* लिखना चाहिए।

'Sick' का प्रयोग निम्न अर्थ में सही है :

I am sick of this life --- means,I am tired of this life.

(7) Pulling on well : का अर्थ 'ठीक-ठाक खेंच रहे हैं' के अर्थ में करना गलत है। 'Pulling well' एक सही English Idiom है जिसका अर्थ है 'Working in Harmony'.

अत: यह लिखना कि 'We are pulling on well' गलत होगा। इसकी जगह 'We are pulling well together' कहना सही है।

(8) Etc :- 'Etc.' - etcetera की abbreviated form है। इसका अर्थ है : 'and others' इसका प्रयोग 'such as' या 'and' के साथ नहीं करना चाहिए :

There were many kinds of fruits in his shop, such as apples, mangoes, plums, pears etc. — *Incorrect*

या There were many kinds of fruits in his shop like apples, mangoes, plums and pears etc. — *Incorrect*

इन दोनों ही वाक्यों में 'etc.' का गलत प्रयोग किया गया है। इनकी जगह हमें लिखना चाहिए था :

There were many kinds of fruits in his shop, such as apples, mangoes, plums so on. — *Correct*

Or There were many kinds of fruits in his shop like apples, mangoes, plums, pears etc. — *Correct*

(9) Rather Very : 'Rather ' का अर्थ होता है – 'not very', 'a little' अत: 'Rather' के साथ 'very' का प्रयोग अनुचित है, गलत है :

She was rather very happy. — *Incorrect*
She was rather happy. — *Correct*
She was very happy. — *Correct*

(10) Comparative better : 'Comparative' शब्द के साथ 'better' (या किसी अन्य comparative degree adjective) का प्रयोग नहीं करना चाहिए । जैसे :

She is comparatively better. — *Incorrect*
She is comparatively good. — *Correct*
She is better. — *Correct*

(11) Keeping good health का प्रयोग सभ्य अंग्रेजी में मान्य नहीं है। जैसे :

I think now she is keeping good health. इसकी अपेक्षा यह कहना चाहिए :
I think now she is <u>well</u>.

(12) No mention/ No matter : 'Thanks' के प्रत्युतर में इन शब्दों का प्रयोग काफी प्रचलित है। इनकी अपेक्षा 'All right' or 'It's all right' कहना अधिक उपयुक्त है ।

(13) Generally/ Always : एक ही वाक्य में 'Generally' एवं 'Always' दोनों का प्रयोग करना गलत है । 'Generally' का अर्थ 'Always' को Contradict करता है :

Generally he is always late- इसकी जगह हमें मात्र यही कहना चाहिए कि, "Generally he is late".

(14) Tomorrow morning/ Next morning : यदि Present tense का वाक्य है तो हमें Tomorrow morning का प्रयोग करना चाहिए । एवं यदि past tense का कोई वाक्य है तो next morning का प्रयोग करना होता है :

(a) I will go to Jaipur tomorrow morning.
(b) I went to Jaipur the next morning .

(15) As best as he can : इस Phrase की जगह 'as well as he can' का प्रयोग करना चाहिए । 'as well' का प्रयोग एक comparison को व्यक्त करता है। ' best' के स्वयं एक superlative degree of adjective होने के कारण इसका comparative use गलत है ।

(16) Because/in order that/ so that : कारण (cause) को express करने हेतु 'because' का प्रयोग किया जाता है; जबकि Purpose (उद्देश्य) को express करने हेतु 'in order that' या 'so that' का प्रयोग किया जाता है। निम्न वाक्यों को देखें :

(a) We eat because we may live. — *Incorrect*
We eat so that we may live. — *Correct*
(b) I took medicine because I might get well. — *Incorrect*
I took medicine in order that I might get well. — *Correct*

(17) In respect of / With respect to :- ये दोनों Phrases अलग-अलग अर्थ में प्रयुक्त होते हैं। 'In respect of', से पूर्व adjective का प्रयोग होता है। इसका अर्थ है 'In point of some quality'.

He is senior to her in respect of service.

With respect to का प्रयोग किसी subject (noun) के संदर्भ में किया जाता है। जैसे :

We must have a discussion with respect to the proposal given by him.

(18) Both --- and, as well as, Not only ---- but also :-उक्त conjuctions का प्रयोग करते समय यह ध्यान में रखे कि जो fact ज्यादा महत्त्वपूर्ण है, उसे बाद में लिखें । जैसे :-

He was both expelled from the school and degraded from his class. —*Improper*

इसकी अपेक्षा हमें लिखना चाहिए :

He was both degraded from his class and expelled from the school . —*Proper*

इसी तरह Others as well as I declare this to be justified. —*Improper*

इसे हमें लिखना चाहिए :- I as well as others declare this to be justified. —*Proper*

इसी तरह :

Rahim was not only convicted of the crime, but also accused of it. —*Improper*

इसे निम्न प्रकार से लिखना चाहिए :

Rahim was not only accused of the crime but also convicted of it. —*Proper*

(19) Another/ other/ Any other : 'Another' का प्रयोग singular nouns के साथ, तथा 'other' का प्रयोग plurals के साथ किया जाता है। दोनों का प्रयोग affirmative sentences में किया जाता है। जबकि 'Anyother' का प्रयोग negative statements में करते हैं ।

(20) Fair sex :- Fair sex का प्रयोग 'women' हेतु किया जाता है। Strictly speaking, यह गलत है। In good English, Fair sex का प्रयोग 'women' हेतु करने को avoid करना चाहिए।

(21) Lately/ Latterly : 'Lately' एवं 'Latterly' दोनों का अर्थ recently से लिया जाता है लेकिन 'Latterly' का प्रयोग comparison हेतु Change of condition हेतु किया जाता है। 'Lately' means-'recent past'. 'Latterly' means- 'most recent':

(a) His wife has left him latterly. —*Incorrect*
His wife has left him lately. —*Correct*

(d) She has shown a different behaviour lately. —*Incorrect*
She has shown a different behaviour latterly. —*Correct*

यहाँ change of condition बताई गई है :

The old man was in a coma latterly; towards the end, at the end, finally.

Dad's health has not been good lately.

(22) Pass off :- समय (Time) के संदर्भ में 'pass off' का प्रयोग प्रचलित है, जैसे : The time passes off happily or The days pass off happily. इन दोनों वाक्यों में off का प्रयोग गलत है। 'pass off' का प्रयोग तब किया जाता है, जब किसी चीज के गुजरने के बाद, कोई अन्य चीज, घटना शेष नहीं रहती है। जैसे :

The event passes off peacefully and we resume our routine.

Time के संदर्भ में केवल 'pass' का ही प्रयोग करना चाहिए, यथा :

The time passes happily. The days pass happily .

(23) With a view to :- 'With a view' के बाद हमेशा gerund का प्रयोग होता है। Infinitive (to) का प्रयोग करना गलत है। जैसे :

I journeyed through the different countries of the world with a view to find out the source of true happiness . —*Incorrect*

अपितु, ऐसा लिखना चाहिए :

I journeyed through the different countries of the world with a view to finding out the source of true happiness . —*Correct*

(24) What to speak of : इसका प्रयोग सामान्यतया 'not to speak of / not to mention' के संदर्भ में किया जाता है। जैसे :

What to speak of lunch or dinner,there was no arrangement of breakfast even. —*Incorrect*

इसकी अपेक्षा यह कहना चाहिए :

There was no arrangement of breakfast even, not to mention lunch or dinner. —*Correct*

इसी तरह -He can hardly rise from the bed, what to speak of walking.

इसकी अपेक्षा यह कहना चाहिए :

He can hardly rise from the bed, not to speak of walking. —*Correct*

(25) What to do ? : यह एक Unenglish expression है। इसकी अपेक्षा यह कहना चाहिए 'What am I to do ?'

(26) To do the needful : इस phrase का उपयोग, अच्छी अंग्रेजी में मान्य नहीं है। इसकी अपेक्षा हमें निम्न phrases प्रयोग में लाने चाहिएँ :

Give the necessary instructions **or** Make the necessary arrangements.
or Give the necessary orders.

(27) Yes/ No : 'Yes' एवं 'No' में Answer देते समय निम्न गलतियाँ की जाती है :

Did you find your purse ? Yes, I did not find it yet. —*Incorrect*

इसकी जगह हमें लिखना चाहिए : No, I did not find it yet.

यदि प्रश्न का उत्तर Affirmative में हो तो Yes का प्रयोग करें, यदि उत्तर negative में हो, तो 'No' से शुरू करें ।

(28) Good or bad success :- 'Sucess' के साथ 'good' या 'bad' का प्रयोग करना गलत है। Sucess may be great or small, important or trivial, but never good or bad.

(29) Splitting of Words :- निम्न शब्दों को दो भागों में लिखना गलत है :

Incorrect	Correct	Incorrect	Correct
any body	anybody	can not	cannot
more over	moreover	some times	sometimes
else where	elsewhere	in as much	inasmuch
other wise	otherwise	in stead of	instead of
foot ball	football	head master	headmaster
work man	workman	post man	postman
arm chair	armchair	back-bite	backbite
tea spoon	teaspoon	half penny	halfpenny
not with standing	notwithstanding	mad man	madman

उपरोक्त शब्दों को लिखते समय इन्हें परस्पर मिलाकर लिखने का ध्यान रखें ।

(30) Combination of Words :- निम्न शब्दों को परस्पर मिलाकर लिखना गलत है :

Incorrect	Correct	Incorrect	Correct
everyone	every one	someone	some one
alright	all right	inspite of	in spite of
youngman	young man	underage	under age

SUPERFLUOUS EXPRESSIONS & UNNECESSARY WORDINESS

Unnecessary Wordiness : कई बार वाक्यों में अनावश्यक शब्दों का प्रयोग किया जाता है। इसे unnecessary wordiness कहा जाता है, जैसे :

(1) For a long period <u>of time</u> : यहाँ 'of time' लिखना अनावश्यक है, क्योंकि 'period' के अर्थ में 'of time' का अर्थ समाहित है।

(2) Return <u>back</u> : यहाँ 'back' लिखना अनावश्यक, है क्योंकि Return के अर्थ में back का अर्थ समाहित है।

(3) Cousin <u>brother</u>/Cousin <u>sister</u> में brother/sister लिखना अनावश्यक है, क्योंकि Cousin के अर्थ में brother/sister का अर्थ समाहित है।

(4) Retreat <u>back</u>/Recall <u>back</u>/Reimburse <u>back</u>/Recast <u>back</u> / Recede <u>back</u> : इनमें 'back' लिखना अनावश्यक है, क्योंकि Retreat /Recall /Reimburse / Recede/Recast में 'back' का अर्थ समाहित है।

(5) Restate/Repeat/Reborn/Rewrite/Reiterate/Rearrange/Rebuild के साथ **'<u>again</u>'** का प्रयोग गलत है, क्योंकि इन शब्दों केअर्थ में 'again' का अर्थ समाहित है।

(6) Supposing /Suppose के साथ '<u>if</u>' का प्रयोग गलत है।

(7) <u>Kindly</u> requested के साथ kindly का प्रयोग गलत है, क्योंकि Request हमेशा Kindly ही की जाती है ।

(8) Await के साथ **'<u>for</u>'** का प्रयोग गलत है, क्योंकि await का अर्थ- wait for होता है ।

(9) Comprise/despite के साथ 'of' का प्रयोग गलत है क्योंकि :
'Comprise' means-- 'Consist of' : 'Despite' means -- 'In spite of'

(10) Until/Unless/Forbid/Prohibit/Prevent/Dissuade/Deny/Refuse/Lest के साथ **'<u>not</u>'** का प्रयोग अनुचित हैं क्योंकि इनमें 'not' का meaning समाहित है।

(11) Flee के साथ away का प्रयोग गलत है, क्योंकि 'flee' का अर्थ ही 'run away' होता है।

(12) Coward के साथ <u>man</u> का प्रयोग गलत है क्योंकि 'coward' का अर्थ ही 'कायर आदमी' होता है इसमें 'man' का अर्थ समाहित होता है ।

(13) <u>Mutual</u> Agreement में mutual का प्रयोग अनावश्यक है, क्योंकि Agreement तभी होगा जब दोनों पार्टियाँ (mutually) स्वीकार करेंगी। इसी तरह, 'Mutual dislike of each other' में 'each other' का प्रयोग अनावश्यक है।

(14) <u>Two</u> twins में 'two' का प्रयोग गलत है।

(15) Bifurcated or divided into <u>four</u> quarters में 'four' का प्रयोग अनावश्यक है।

(16) Reason <u>because</u> का एक साथ प्रयोग अनुचित है या तो 'Reason' का प्रयोग करें या 'because' का ।

(17) Because के साथ **'<u>therefore, as</u>',** का प्रयोग गलत है।

(18) Equally, as good as, दोनों का साथ साथ प्रयोग गलत है। या तो वाक्य में 'equally' का प्रयोग करें या 'as good as' का।

(19) Consensus <u>opinion</u> में 'Opinion' लिखना अनावश्यक है। 'Consensus' में 'Opinion' का अर्थ समाहित है।

(20) Final conclusion में final लिखना अनावश्यक है क्योंकि 'conclusion' का अर्थ ही 'final' होता है।

(21) Spouse wife/husband में wife/husband का प्रयोग अनावश्यक हैए क्योंकि 'Spouse' के अर्थ में 'wife/husband' का अर्थ समाहित है।

(22) इसी प्रकार Consort husband/wife में 'husband/wife' का प्रयोग अनावश्यक है, क्योंकि 'Consort' का अर्थ होता है- 'husband or wife of a ruler.'

(23) Funeral <u>service</u> में 'service' का प्रयोग अनावश्यक है, क्योंकि 'Funeral' स्वयं एक Service है।

(24) Override/over take/over turn/over shoot आदि के साथ पुन: 'over' का प्रयोग करना गलत है।

(25) With bag and baggage में 'with' का प्रयोग करना अनावश्यक है, क्योंकि 'bag and baggage' का अर्थ 'with all belongings' होता है ।
He returned bag and baggage.

(26) **Mutual friend** एक Unenglish expression है, इसका प्रयोग करना गलत है। इसकी जगह 'Common friend' का प्रयोग किया जाता है।

(27) **Free ship या Lecturership** की जगह 'free studentship' या 'lectureship' का प्रयोग उचित है।

(28) **'An English teacher'** का अर्थ होता है 'A teacher who is an English' (Citizen of England), अत: 'An English teacher' की जगह 'A teacher of English' लिखना उचित है।

(29) **Passing marks** की जगह 'pass marks' लिखना उचित है।

(30) **Linking road / Linking language** की जगह link road/link language लिखना शुद्ध है।

FIND ERRORS, MISTAKES AND BLUNDERS IN FOLLOWING SENTENCES

Exercise-1 : *Rewrite the sentences after correction.*

1. He has been sick since Monday.
2. I eat my food at 8 P.M..
3. There were many kinds of bag in the shop, such as paper, leather, cloth, and canvas etc.
4. Ramesh said to me, "Sita was rather very happy on that day".
5. All his family members are planning to visit Jammu & Kashmir.
6. I give key to my wrist watch at 8 P.M. daily.
7. I eat my breakfast at 7 A.M. daily.
8. He said, "Today I am feeling comparatively better".
9. Sunita always wears blue saree on such functions generally.
10. She went to Delhi tomorrow morning.
11. We eat because we may live.
12. She didn't attend the meeting so that she was ill.
13. I took medicine, because I might get well soon.
14. Both he is a philosopher and a teacher.
15. Either he is a stupid or a rogue.
16. Others as well as Ram declares this an unethical act.
17. The females are not allowed to participate in the competition.
18. The days pass off happily.
19. With a view to study the urgent publications he joined the library.
20. Did you find your pen ? Yes, I didn't find it so far.
21. I can not play football today.
22. He achieved good success in B.A. examination.
23. He some times comes to visit his parents.
24. Everyone will be given a certificate .
25. Have you found your lost purse? No, I have found .
26. It is not the men but the fair sex, responsible for the present trend in fashion.
27. Not with standing the present degradation in the society, he believes in fair means even today.
28. Inspite of increase in turn over, the profit remains the same.
29. Ram discussed the matter with so many another fellows.
30. Ram and his other friend Shyam went to Jaipur yesterday.

Explanations

1. He has been ill since Monday.
2. I take my dinner at 8 P.M..
3. There were many kinds of bag in the shop, such as paper, leather, cloth, and canvas.
4. Ramesh said to me, "Sita was rather happy on that day".

5. All the members of his family are planning to visit Jammu & Kashmir.
6. I wind my wrist watch at 8 P.M. daily.
7. I have my breakfast at 7 A.M daily.
8. He said, " Today I am feeling better".
9. Sunita always wears blue saree on such functions.
10. She went to Delhi the next morning.
11. We eat so that we may live .
12. She didn't attend the meeting because she was ill.
13. I took medicine, in order that I might get well soon.
14. He is both a philosopher and a teacher.
15. Either he is a stupid or a rogue.
16. Ram as well as others declares this an unethical act.
17. The women are not allowed to participate in the competition.
18. The days pass happily.
19. With a view to studying the current publications he joined the library.
20. Did you find your pen ? No, I didn't find it so far.
21. I cannot play football today.
22. He achieved great success in B.A. examination.
23. He sometimes comes to visit his parents.
24. Every one will be given a certificate .
25. Have you found your lost purse? Yes, I have found it.
26. It is not the men but the women, responsible for the present trend in fashion.
27. Notwithstanding the present degradation in the society, he believes in fair means even today.
28. In spite of increase in turn over, the profit remains the same.
29. Ram discussed the matter with so many other fellows.
30. Ram and his another friend Shyam went to Jaipur yesterday.

Exercise-2 : ***Find the errors and justify your answers.***

1. All the members (A)/ of the club are (B)/ kindly requested (C)/to attend the meeting (D).
2. This is the wristwatch (A)/ which my uncle (B)/ brought it (C)/ for you (D).
3. She asked me (A)/ where I was going to (B)/ and what I had done (C)/ the previous day (D).
4. He will leave (A)/ for Mexico (B)/ on Monday (C)/ with bag and baggage (D).
5. This idea of the (A)/ Home Minister's (B)/ has put everyone (C)/ in serious thoughts(D) .
6. The teacher forbade (A)/ the students not to(B)/make a noise(C).
7. Rita, cousin sister of the (A)/ M.P said that she would (B)/ contest the next (C)/ election certainly (D).
8. "Harish is comparatively better (A)/ today and we hope that (B)/ he will recover soon", (C) / said Ramesh (D).
9. Yesterday in the night (A)/ he came by bus (B)/ and was disturbed (C).
10. In Jaipur she (A)/ came across with many (B)/of her friends (C)/ who had settled there after marriage (D).
11. Pakistan's support (A)/ to the terrorists in India (B)/ is universally condemned (C)/ by all (D).
12. Within two hours (A)/ we will approach (B)/ near Agra (C)/ by car (D) .
13. Suppose if (A)/ all problems are solved (B)/ what would you do then ? (C).
14. When he lent me (A)/ some money, he asked (B)/ to return it back (C)/ within a week (D).

15. Throughout the whole year (A)/ there was (B)/ not a single day (C)/ without any incidence of violence (D).
16. The recent incidents of corruption (A)/ amply illustrate about (B)/ the characters of (C)/ our political leaders (D).
17. The thing what (A)/ you like is (B)/ available in (C)/ that departmental store (D).
18. He denied that(A)/ he was not present(B)/ there at the time(C)/ the accident took place (D) .
19. The P.M. said (A)/ that it was his decision (B)/ and that nobody (C)/ could get it changed (D) .
20. The students (A)/ requested the teacher (B)/ to repeat the question (C)/ again (D).
21. The reason why (A)/ most of the people commit crime (B)/ is because they are unware (C)/ of the legal complications (D).
22. He doesn't hardly know (A)/ about the real factors (B)/ that have created (C)/ so many problems (D) .
23. My mother asked me (A)/ if I have sufficient enough money (B)/ to buy the books (C).
24. They were quite all right (A)/ when they went to the police station (B)/ to lodge an FIR (C).
25. He stayed in Jammu (A)/ for a very short period of time (B)/ and then went to (C)/ Kolkatta (D).
26. He reimbursed back (A)/ the money which I spent (B)/ on his medical treatment (C).
27. I have to attend (A)/ the funeral service (B)/of my dear departed friend (C)/ today (D).
28. Unless you do not (A)/ pass this examination (B)/ you cannot get the job (C).
29. I want to know (A)/ whether it is (B)/ the right and proper time (C)/ to start this business (D).
30. The second project (A)/ of this company was equally as (B)/ sucessful as (C)/ the first project (D).
31. He was (A)/ very friendly enough (B)/ to help me (C)/ when I was in trouble (D).
32. My friend asked (A)/ me if there was any place (B)/ in the (C)/ compartment for him (D).
33. I know (A)/ that more than hundred (B)/ students have applied (C)/ for freeship(D).
34. Each competitor (A)/ tried his best (B)/ to defeat one another (C)/ in the wrestling match (D).
35. He put his sign (A)/ at the foot of the (B)/ letter and posted it (C)/ immediately (D).
36. She ran as (A)/ faştly as she could (B)/ to catch the train (C) .
37. The officer advised me (A)/ to talk to the concerned clerk (B)/ in case I felt any (C)/ problem in the matter (D) .
38. Many pupils of this college (A)/ are working as teachers (B)/ in different (C)/ public schools (D).
39. He was (A)/ awarded cent percent (B)/ marks in (C)/ mathematics (D).
40. All his family members(A)/are social(B)/and cooperative(C) .
41. To what has (A)/ always puzzled me (B)/ is your insincerity (C)/ and carelessness(D).
42. According to me (A)/ every student should (B)/ go through the (C)/ notes given by the professors (D) .
43. One of my friends (A) / is in the teaching line (B)/ and presently settled (C)/ abroad .
44. Nowadays she (A)/ is living in foreign (B)/ but her husband (C)/ is in India (D).
45. Our English teacher said (A)/ that we should practice (B)/ regularly if we wanted to improve (C)/ our English (D).
46. I want to join (A)/ lecturership (B)/ because I think it is a (C)/ peaceful profession (D).
47. As my neighbourers (A)/ are very cooperative (B)/ so I do not have (C)/ any problem here (D).
48. The passing marks (A)/ are thirty there (B)/ but you have secured (C)/ only thirty two marks (D).
49. Both of them(A)/have not (B)/turned up in(C)/the court today (D).
50. We must wait (A)/ for quieter time before (B)/ the claims of civilization(C)/ can over ride over the claims of the party spirit(D).

Explanations

1. (C) 'Kindly' को delete करें। 'Kindly' का प्रयोग superfluous है; use either 'kindly' or 'requested'।
2. (C) 'It' का प्रयोग superfluous है।
3. (B) 'to' का प्रयोग superfluous है।
4. (D) 'with' का प्रयोग superfluous है; meaning of the phrase–'bag and baggage' includes 'with'।
5. (B) 'Home Minister' के साथ apostrophe ('s) का प्रयोग superfluous है।
6. (B) 'not' का प्रयोग 'forbade' के साथ superfluous है। 'forbade' का अर्थ ही negative होता है।
7. (A) 'sister' या 'brother' का 'cousin' के साथ प्रयोग superfluous है।
8. (A) 'Comparatively' और 'better' दोनों का एक साथ प्रयोग गलत है; या तो लिखना चाहिए - Harish is comparatively good या Harish is better लिखना चाहिए।
9. (A) 'Yesterday in the night' की जगह 'Last night' लिखना चाहिए; 'Yesterday night' लिखना भी गलत है।
10. (B) 'across' के साथ 'with' का प्रयोग superfluous है।
11. (D) 'by all' का प्रयोग 'universally' के साथ superfluous है।
12. (C) 'near' का प्रयोग 'approach' के साथ superfluous है।
13. (A) 'Suppose' के साथ 'if' का प्रयोग superfluous है।
14. (C) 'back' का प्रयोग 'return' के साथ superfluous है।
15. (A) 'whole' का प्रयोग superfluous है।
16. (B) 'Illustrate/discribe/discuss' के बाद object आता है; यहाँ 'about' का प्रयोग superfluous है।
17. (A) 'what' की जगह 'which' का प्रयोग होगा, या 'The thing' को हटाना होगा; 'what' के साथ किसी antecedent का होना आवश्यक है। जैसे :
    What you like most is this pen. The thing which you like most is this pen.
18. (B) 'not' का प्रयोग 'deny' के साथ गलत है। 'deny/refuse/prevent/forbid/until/unless' सभी negative हैं इनके साथ 'not' का प्रयोग नहीं होता है। शुद्ध वाक्य होगा – 'He denied that he was present there at the time the accident took place.'
19. (C) यहाँ 'that' का प्रयोग superfluous है।
20. (D) 'repeat' के साथ 'again' का प्रयोग superfluous है। Repeat/Recast/Rewrite के साथ 'again' का प्रयोग नहीं होता है।
21. (C) जिस वाक्य में 'Reason' का प्रयोग होता है उसी में 'beacuse' का प्रयोग superfluous है।
22. (A) 'hardly/scarcely' स्वयं 'negative' हैं इनके साथ 'not' या 'doesn't' का प्रयोग गलत है।
23. (B) 'Sufficient' एवं 'enough' का प्रयोग एक साथ नहीं होता है।
24. (A) 'quite' के साथ 'all' का प्रयोग गलत है ; या तो 'quite' को हटायें या 'all' को।
25. (B) 'of time' का प्रयोग superfluous है ; या तो 'for a short period' या 'for a short time' का प्रयोग करें।
26. (A) 'reimburse/return' के साथ 'back' का प्रयोग superfluous है।
27. (B) 'funeral' के साथ 'service' का प्रयोग superfluous है। 'funeral' स्वयं में 'service' है।
28. (A) 'Unless/until/forbid/refuse/deny/hardly/ scarcely' के साथ 'not' का प्रयोग नहीं करें, ये सभी negative हैं।
29. (C) 'right' या 'proper' में से या तो 'right' का प्रयोग होगा या 'proper' दोनों का प्रयोग एक साथ नहीं होता है। 'and' भी delete होगा।
30. (B) 'equally' का प्रयोग superfluous है। इन वाक्यों को देखें :
    Ram and Rahim are equally successful. Ram is as successful as Rahim.

31. (B) 'Very'का प्रयोग superfluous है।
32. (B) 'Place' की जगह 'room' शब्द का प्रयोग होगा; Car/compartment/train/bus' आदि में स्थान (space) होने के सन्दर्भ में 'room' का प्रयोग होता है।
33. (D) 'freeship' एक Unenglish expression है 'freestudentship' होगा।
34. (C) 'one another' की जगह 'the other' का प्रयोग होगा; 'each' के साथ 'other' का प्रयोग होता है ।
35. (A) 'sign' की जगह signature होगा; 'sign' एक verb है, जबकि 'signature' एक noun है ।
36. (B) 'fastly' की जगह 'fast' ही होगा। 'fast' एक adjective भी है एवं adverb भी। अत: इसे adverb की तरह प्रयोग करते समय इसमें 'ly' जोड़ने की आवश्यकता नहीं होती है :

He is a fast runner. --- adjective He ran fast. --- adverb
37. (B) 'Concerned clerk' का अर्थ होता है –'चिन्तित क्लर्क' । यहाँ 'concerned clerk' की जगह 'clerk concerned' होगा, जिसका अर्थ होता है –'संबंधित क्लर्क'।
38. (A) 'Pupils' की जगह students होगा pupils का अर्थ होता है-शिष्य; यहाँ वाक्य में 'शिष्य' शब्द का प्रयोग अनुचित है।
39. (B) 'Cent percent' एक Unenglish expression है! इसकी जगह 'hundred percent' होगा।
40. (A) 'All the members of his family' होगा। Standard english में 'family member' या 'family members' का प्रयोग गलत है।
41. (A) 'To' का प्रयोग superfluous है।
42. (A) 'According to me' की जगह 'In my opinion' होना चाहिए । First person (I, me) के साथ 'According' का प्रयोग Standard English में मान्य नहीं है; 'According to us', 'According to him'/ you आदि सही है।
43. (B) 'teaching line' की जगह 'teaching profession' लिखना चाहिए।
44. (B) 'in foregin' की जगह 'abroad' होगा या 'in foreign country' लिखना सही रहेगा।
45. (A) 'English Teacher' की जगह 'teacher of English' लिखना सही है; English Teacher का अर्थ–'अंग्रेज अध्यापक' होता है, न कि 'अंग्रेजी का अध्यापक'।
46. (B) 'lectureship' होगा 'lecturership' Unenglish expression है।
47. (A) 'Neighbourers' कोई english word नहीं है; सही word–'neighbours' है।
48. (A) 'Passing marks' की जगह 'pass marks' होगा।
49. (E) No Error. वाक्य सही है।
50. (D) 'over ride' के बाद 'over' का प्रयोग superfluous है।

❑❑❑

20

Spelling Rules

अंग्रेजी में सही Spelling writing के कुछ नियम हैं। Spelling (वर्तनी) में गलती अक्षम्य है; अत: Spelling में गलती को हर हालत में avoid करें।

SPELLING RULES

(1) कुछ words, एक syllable के होते हैं, जिनकी Spelling के अन्त में एक consonant आता है एवं उससे पहले एक vowel (a, e, i, o, u) आता है। यदि इस प्रकार के word में उक्त consonant के बाद किसी vowel letter के साथ कोई suffix (–'ing', 'ed') लगता है, तो इस consonant को Double कर देते हैं।

Look at the following words :

run	–	running	get	–	getting
rob	–	robbed	plan	–	planning

(2) एक से अधिक syllable वाले शब्द, जिनकी spellings, single vowel + single consonant से समाप्त होती हैं; इनमें अन्तिम consonant, double हो जाता है। जैसे -

begin	–	beginning	refer	–	referring
permit	–	permitted	transfer	–	transferring

Exceptions are :

suffer	–	suffered	offer	–	offered
benefit	–	benefited	differ	–	differed

(3) बहुत-से words जिनकी spellings के अन्त में 'l' आता है, वह 'l' उपरोक्त suffix जोड़ने पर double हो जाता है। जैसे -

quarrel	–	quarrelled	equal	–	equalled
distil	–	distilled	travel	–	travelled

Exceptions :

parallel	–	paralleled	Peril	–	Perilous

(4) (a) कुछ words की spellings के अन्त में 'e' आता है। ऐसे words के साथ उपरोक्त vowel से शुरू होने वाला suffix लगाने पर 'e' हट जाता है :

live	–	living	bite	–	biting
fame	–	famous	make	–	making
move	–	moving	blame	–	blaming

(b) लेकिन 'e' से अन्त होने वाले शब्दों के साथ consonant से शुरू होने वाला suffix लगाने पर 'e' भी अपनी जगह रहता है :

hope	–	hopeful	excite	–	excitement
engage	–	engagement	nice	–	nicely

Exceptions :

true	–	truly,	awe	–	awful
whole	–	wholly,	argue	–	argument

(5) जिन words की spellings–'ce' या 'ge' से समाप्त होती है उनके साथ a, o, u से शुरू होने वाला suffix लगाने पर 'e' यथास्थिति रहता है :

Replace	–	Replaceable	manage	–	manageable
Change	–	Changeable	marriage	–	marriageable

(6) जब कोई word, 'y' से समाप्त होता है, एवं 'y' से पहले कोई consonant आता है, तो suffix (except–ing) लगाने पर 'y', 'i' में बदल जाता है :

cry	–	cried	pity	–	pitiful
mercy	–	merciful	carry	–	carried

Exceptions :

Shy	–	Shyly	dry	–	dryly
Sly	–	Slyly			

लेकिन यदि 'y' के पहले कोई vowel आता है, तो 'y' यथास्थिति ही रहता है :

Pray	–	Prayed	buy	–	buyer
Play	–	Played	pay	–	payable

Exceptions :

say	–	said	pay	–	paid
lay	–	laid	day	–	daily

(7) यदि कोई word, 'll' से समाप्त होता है, तो उसके साथ 'full', suffix लगाने पर उक्त word एवं suffix दोनों में एक-एक 'l' ही रह जाता है :

Skill + full – Skilful , Will + full – wilful.

(8) जिन words की spellings 'ie' से अन्त हो और उनमें यदि 'ing' suffix जोड़ा जाये, तो 'ie' बदलकर 'y' हो जाता है :

die	–	dying	lie	–	lying
tie	–	tying	vie	–	vying

SPELLING RULES – BRITISH AND AMERICAN

1. कुछ words के अन्त में American English में 'or' रहता है, किन्तु British English में 'our' रहता है; जैसे-

American – **Labor, Color, Rumor,Humor,Neighbor etc;**
British – **Labour, Colour , Rumour, Humour, Neighbour.**

2. American English में कुछ शब्दों की spellings के अन्त में 'og' रहता है, किन्तु British English में 'ogue' आता है । जैसे-

American English – **catalog,dialog;**
British English – **catalogue, dialogue.**

3. American English में word के अन्तिम शब्द 'l' को double नहीं किया जाता है, किन्तु British English में 'l' double हो जाता है; जैसे-

American English – **Traveler, leveling**
British English – **Traveller, levelling**

4. बहुत से verbs की spellings के अन्त में American English में 'ize' रहता है, किन्तु British English में 'ise' या 'ize' दोनों प्रयुक्त होते हैं; जैसे-

American English – **realize, analyze;**
British English – **realise, realize,analyse.**

5. **American English में कुछ शब्दों की spellings के अन्त में 'ter' रहता है, किन्तु British English में 'tre' आता है; जैसे–**

American English – Theater, Meter, center;

British English – Theatre, Metre, centre.

कई अन्य शब्दों में भी American English एवं British English में spellings के अन्तर हैं; जैसे –

American	British
tire	tyre (on a vehicle)
program	programme
jail	gaol, jail
aluminum	aluminium
defense	defence
jewelry	jewellery

India में हम लोग British English का प्रयोग करते हैं, अत: हमें British English की spellings का ही ध्यान रखना चाहिये।

LIST OF COMMONLY MIS SPELT WORDS

Autumn
Accommodate
Accustom
Agility
Athlete
Accommodate
Acquaintance
Assailant
Aggregate
Acquiesce
Abbreviate
Ascetic
Annihilate
Appropriate
Aerodrum
Architecture
Acquiesce
Alcohol
Adherent
Abhorrence
Accessible
Acknowledgment
Acquittal
Apparatus
Amateur
Appetite
Acclamation
Affectionate

Conscience
Cigarette
Colloquial
Commemorate
Competition
Convenient
Conceive
Condemn
Curriculum
Deceive
Discernible
Deficiency
Dialogue
Descendant
Division
Dilemma
Deteriorate
Dysentery
Ecclesiastical
Etiquette
Erroneous
Exaggeration
Ecstasy
Equilibrium
Exchequer
Extravagance
Efficiency
Efficacious

Irresistible
Irrelevant
Irreparable
Indefatigable
Indigenous
Incorrigible
Juggler
Jealousy
Jubilee
Juvenile
Knave
Kitchen
Knee
Knight
Kneeled
Knives
Leniency
Leisure
Laurel
Luxurious
Lieutenant
Manageable
Magnificent
Martyr
Manoeuvre
Misdemeanor
Meagre
Moustache

Phenomenon
Physique
Psychology
Potato
Pharmaceutical
Pursue
Quarrel
Queue
Quinine
Rogue
Routine
Regrettable
Restaurant
Repetition
Referee
Rehearsal
Rupee
Sceptre
Scissors
Schedule
Strategy
Simultaneous
Symmetrical
Soliloquy
Sovereign
Stomach
Technique
Transience

Aesthetic
Alienate
Ambassador
Ambition
Assassin
Bankruptcy
Beneficent
Behaviour
Bequeath
Besiege
Bureaucracy
Budget
Buffoon
Circumstance
Commitment
Committee
Condescend
Connoisseur
Correspondence
Counterfeit
Catalogue
Convalesce

Embarrass
Fallacious
Fascinate
Facilitate
Felicitate
Freight
Favourable
Fourth
Genuine
Guarantee
Gorgeous
Grievance
Grotesque
Geometry
Grammar
Gazette
Harassment
Heinous
Heterogenous
Hygiene
Inflammable
Incarcerate

Mosquito
Missionary
Millionaire
Massacre
Museum
Mischievous
Musician
Noticeable
Nuisance
Neighbour
Necessary
Necessitate
Occurrence
Omitted
Oscillate
Ominous
Parallel
Pneumonia
Proletariat
Perceive
Proprietor
Perspicuous

Tenacious
Transgressor
Utterance
Vacation
Vaccination
Vicissitude
Vocabulary
Vicious
Villainous
Wednesday
Weigh
Woolen
Written
Writing
Xenomania
Xylography
Yawning
Yeoman
Zodiac
Zealous
Zootomy
Zythepsary

Exercise : ***Tick mark the word with correct spellings.***

1. (a) temperature (b) temprature (c) tempareter (d) temparetar
2. (a) definate (b) definite (c) difinite (d) difinte
3. (a) expirience (b) exparience (c) experience (d) exprience
4. (a) incident (b) insident (c) insidant (d) insidan
5. (a) extasy (b) ecstacy (c) acstasy (d) xstacy

Find out the wrongly spelt word :

6. (a) pompous (b) populous (c) prejudiced (d) pretentous
7. (a) exempleary (b) embarrass (c) envious (d) excellence
8. (a) dispose (b) dipose (c) demote (d) denote
9. (a) casual (b) candid (c) convercant (d) catastrophe
10. (a) procession (b) passion (c) posession (d) profession
11. (a) rein (b) neigh (c) neither (d) neice
12. (a) efficient (b) reticent (c) magnificient (d) deficient
13. (a) vocal (b) focal (c) mystical (d) vehical
14. (a) altogether (b) alrigt (c) almighty (d) allottee
15. (a) pretence (b) offence (c) dence (d) deference

Answers

1. (a) **2.** (b) **3.** (c) **4.** (a) **5.** (b) **6.** (d) **7.** (a) **8.** (b)
9. (c) **10.** (c) **11.** (d) **12.** (c) **13.** (d) **14.** (b) **15.** (c)

21

Use of Capital Letter and Punctuation

शुद्ध अंग्रेजी लेखन हेतु, Capital letters के प्रयोग का ज्ञान बहुत आवश्यक एवं महत्त्वपूर्ण है। Punctuation Marks के उचित प्रयोग की जानकारी न होने से, अर्थ का अनर्थ हो सकता है। Punctuation के अध्याय को ध्यानपूर्वक पढ़ें।

Alphabet :-अंग्रेजी भाषा 26 अक्षरों से बनी है, जिन्हें Alphabet कहते हैं :

A B C D E F G H I J K L M N O P Q R S T U V W X Y Z ;

ये Capital Letters कहलाते हैं; जबकि Small Letters को निम्न प्रकार लिखा जाता है :

a b c d e f g h i j k l m n o p q r s t u v w x y z.

Capital Letters एवं Small Letters की आकृति भिन्न होती है, लेकिन उच्चारण समान होता है।

English में A E I O U - 5 स्वर (Vowels) तथा 21 व्यंजन (Consonants) होते हैं। हिन्दी भाषा में 52 अक्षर (16 स्वर एवं 36 व्यंजन) होते हैं। हिन्दी भाषा में capital letter या small letter जैसा कोई अक्षर भेद नहीं होता है।

English में एक शब्द, कई प्रकार की ध्वनि हेतु प्रयुक्त होता है। जिन अक्षरों को स्वर (A E I O U) माना गया है उनका प्रयोग बहुत बार व्यंजन की तरह होता है अर्थात् उनसे बनने वाले शब्द का उच्चारण व्यंजन की तरह होता है। अत: अंग्रेजी भाषा में शब्दों के सही उच्चारण का बहुत महत्त्व है।अंग्रेजी भाषा में Alphabet का capital letter व small letter में अंतर किया गया है, अत: यह भी ध्यान रखना आवश्यक है कि कहाँ, किस word में capital letter का प्रयोग होता है। **सही अंग्रेजी लिखने हेतु capital letters के सही प्रयोग का ज्ञान होना आवश्यक है।**

USE OF CAPITAL LETTER - RULES

निम्न स्थितियों में Capital letter के प्रयोग करने का ध्यान रखें :

1. **First letter of a sentence: हर वाक्य हमेशा Capital letter से शुरू होता है।**
2. **Proper noun एवं proper adjective का पहला अक्षर Capital होता है। अर्थात्, किसी व्यक्ति, शहर, देश, राज्य, समुद्र, नदी, दिन, माह, ग्रन्थ, भवन, जाति, त्योहार तथा भाषा के नाम का पहला अक्षर Capital होता है।** जैसे- Ram, Delhi, India, Rajasthan, Indians, the Himalayas, The Ramayans, Sunday, December, The Rajputs, Diwali, English, Hindi, The Tajmahal.
3. **ईश्वर (God) या उसके लिये प्रयुक्त समस्त nouns एवं pronouns का पहला अक्षर; जैसे-**
   My God, Thou art merciful, The Lord, The Almighty, God is Omnipresent.
4. **पद का नाम, डिग्रियों के नाम का पहला अक्षर capital letter होता है :**
   Prime Minister, M.A., B.A.
5. **Pronoun 'I' एवं Injection 'O' जब किसी वाक्य में अकेले आयें, तो हमेशा capital letter में लिखे जाते हैं :**
   He is taller than I., O, my God !
6. **English Poem (कविता) में प्रत्येक लाईन का प्रथम अक्षर Capital letter होता है :**
   Thirty days has September,
   April , June and November...

7. **Inverted commas (" ") के अन्दर के वाक्य का पहला अक्षर Capital letter होता है :**
He said, "She will go to market".
8. **Initials एवं abbreviations के लिये प्रयुक्त अक्षर Capital letter होता है :**
Sh. M.K.Gandhi, S.D.O., G.M., R.M.P.
9. **उपाधियों के नाम, राजनैतिक दलों के नाम, समाचार पत्रों के नाम, मुख्य ऐतिहासिक घटनाओं के नाम, सार्वजनिक संस्थाओं के नाम, किताबों के नाम, Title या Heading के नाम का पहला अक्षर Capital letter होता है :**
Padma Bhushan, Congress, Janta Party, The Hindustan Times, The First World War, The Battle of Panipat, The Nirmal Shiksha Kendra, The General English Book, 'A Clever Monkey', 'A visit to Water Park'.
10. **अंग्रेजी में लिखे जाने वाले First, Middle एवं Last name का पहला अक्षर Capital होता है। जैसे-**
Shri Dipesh Jain, Suresh Chandra Gupta, Veer Pratap Singh, Man Mohan Singh.
11. **व्यक्ति के नाम के पहले लगने वाले Title का पहला अक्षर हमेशा capital letter में लिखा जाता है :**
Mr., Mrs, Miss, Sir, Madam, Dr., Lt., Prof.
12. **जब वाक्य में Father/ Uncle/ Mother/ Aunt etc. का प्रयोग Proper noun की तरह होता है, और जब इनके पूर्व my, his, her, your, the etc. का प्रयोग नहीं होता है, तब इनका पहला अक्षर Capital letter में लिखा जाता है। यदि इनके पहले my, his, her the, your etc. का प्रयोग होता है, तो इनका पहला अक्षर Small letter ही होगा। जैसे:**
(a) Father was happy but Mother was sad.
(b) I am waiting for Father.
(c) I dare not face Mother and Aunt.
(d) My father is a businessman.
वाक्य (a), (b), (c) में Father/ Mother/ Aunt Proper nouns की तरह प्रयुक्त हुए हैं।

PUNCTUATION

Punctuation :*The right use of putting in marks or stops in writing is called Punctuation.*

Punctuation marks

1. **Full stop (.)**
2. **Ellipsis (...)**
3. **Question mark (?)**
4. **Mark of Exclamation (!)**
5. **Comma (,)**
6. **Semi colon (;)**
7. **Colon (:)**
8. **Dash (–)**
9. **Hyphen (-)**
10. **Inverted Commas (" "), (' ')**

1. Use of Full stop or Period (.) :

1. Interrogative एवं Exclamatory sentences के अतिरिक्त सभी प्रकार के sentences के अन्त में full stop अंकित होता है; चाहे वह वाक्य सामान्य statement हो, command हो या sentence के मध्य में कोई प्रश्न (indirect question) हो। जैसे-
He is a good boy. (Statement)
Do not open the gate. (Command)
He asked me where I was. (Indirect question)
2. Initials एवं Abbreviations के बाद full stop का प्रयोग होता है :
R.K.Sharma, P.K.Jain, M.L.A., M.P., U.K.
(a) आजकल Mr, Mrs, Dr, Ltd. जैसे कई Abbreviations के बाद में full stop नहीं लगाया जाता है।
(b) यदि कोई वाक्य Abbreviations पर ही समाप्त होता हो तो वाक्य के अन्त में एक ही full stop आता है :
He is an M.L.A .

2. Ellipsis (... or ....) :

जब वाक्य में से कुछ शब्द या शब्दों का लोप (omit) किया गया हो, तो Ellipsis का प्रयोग किया जाता है :

1. यदि किसी वाक्य में से शुरू के या बीच के शब्दों का लोप (omission) किया गया हो तो Ellipsis में तीन full stops का प्रयोग किया जाता है। जैसे–
   ... a beautiful girl she ... with her sister.
2. यदि किसी वाक्य के अन्तिम शब्दों का लोप (omission) किया गया हो तो Ellipsis में चार full stops (....) का प्रयोग किया जाता है :
   Rahul went to Jaipur with ....

3. Question mark (?) – प्रश्नवाचक चिह्न :

1. Interrogative sentence के अन्त में तथा एक sentence में question पूछने वाले words (Question Tag), clause या phrase के बाद भी question mark प्रयुक्त किया जाता है :
   Who invited you to dinner? Open the window, will you?
   Whom shall we elect? Rahul? Meenakshi?
2. जब वाक्य में किसी प्रकार की अनिश्चितता या शंका या प्रश्न जैसा भाव हो, तो question mark प्रयुक्त किया जाता है :
   Gandhiji died in 1948?
   यह वाक्य 1948 के विषय में uncertainty का भाव प्रदर्शित करता है ।

4. Mark of Exclamation (!) – विस्मयबोधक चिह्न :

ऐसे sentences, clauses, phrases या single word जो अति आश्चर्य, अति दुखः, अति प्रसन्नता, आदेश, प्रशंसा या कामना का भाव प्रकट करते हैं, के बाद Mark of Exclamation (!) का प्रयोग किया जाता है :

Hurrah! We have won the match.
What a beautiful bird it is!

5. Comma (,) – अल्प विराम :

1. यदि किसी वाक्य में एक ही part of speech के तीन या अधिक (more than two)शब्द आते हैं, तो इन शब्दों को एक दूसरे से पृथक करने के लिए comma (,) का प्रयोग किया जाता है। अन्तिम शब्द से पहले यदि 'and' का प्रयोग हुआ है, तो वहाँ पर 'and' से पूर्व comma नहीं आता है।
   She purchased an eraser, a pen and some copies.
   उपरोक्त वाक्य में 'and' से पूर्व comma नहीं लगाया गया है, लेकिन कई ऐसे वाक्य भी होते हैं, जिनमें 'and' से पूर्व comma प्रयुक्त करना आवश्यक होता है। जैसे –
   Their equipment included airplanes, helicopters, artillery, amphibious vehicles, and tanks. यदि इस वाक्य में 'and' से पूर्व comma हटा दिया जावे तो यह समझा जा सकता है कि 'tanks' भी amphibious है।
   (amphibious means it can be used in land and water both.)
2. वाक्य के शुरू में आने वाले, adjective, adverb, participle या participle phrase के बाद भी comma का प्रयोग किया जाता है :
   Technically, the scheme is quite feasible.
3. Words of address, interjections, जो वाक्य को शुरू करने में प्रयुक्त होते हैं, जैसे : oh, yes, no, however, nevertheless, still, anyway, well, why, frankly, really, moreover, incidentally etc. के बाद Comma का प्रयोग किया जाता है :
   Ramesh, where have you gone?, Oh, she is here!
   Why, you can't say so?, Still, he must realise that he is my guest.

4. Direct speech में Reporting verb को Reported speech से अलग करने के लिये comma का प्रयोग किया जाता है :

He said to me, "I will come on Monday".

5. Compound sentence में छोटी-छोटी coordinating clauses को स्पष्ट रूप से पृथक-पृथक व्यक्त करने के लिये comma का प्रयोग किया जाता है :

He sold his house, sold his furniture, rented his computer, and left the city.

6. वाक्य में pair of words को पृथक करने के लिये (He is intelligent and trustworthy, devoted and dedicated, sincere and honest.) comma का प्रयोग किया जाता है तथा principal clause से noun clause, adjective clause तथा adverbial clause को अलग करने के लिये comma का प्रयोग किया जाता है :

Since he says so, she should obey him.

7. वाक्य के मध्य आने वाले words, phrases, या clauses के दोनों तरफ उन्हें स्पष्ट रूप से पृथक-पृथक दिखाने हेतु comma अंकित किया जाता है :

1. The treaty , as everybody knows, may be signed today.
2. Her way of cooking is as good as, or better than, yours.

8. जब किसी शब्द को महत्त्वपूर्ण बनाने के लिए उसे बार-बार प्रयुक्त किया जाता है, तो उनके बीच comma लगाया जाता है :

Come, come ; don't delay. Try, try, and try again.

9. वाक्य को सुन्दर बनाने हेतु कई बार कुछ शब्दों को omit कर दिया जाता है । इन शब्दों के स्थान पर comma लगाकर, इन शब्दों की पूर्ति की जाती है :

Rakhi is seventeen; Sarita, ten. (is-omitted)

10. किसी noun या Appositive या phrase in apposition को अलग एवं स्पष्ट दिखाने के लिये उसके पहले एवं बाद में दोनों तरफ comma लेते हैं :

Akbar, the great king, was a great religious scholar also.

11. Letter में Salutation या Subscription के बाद comma अवश्य लगाया जाता है :

My dear father, My dear friend, Yours faithfully, Yours sincerely.

12. जब दो Independent clauses आपस में and, but, or, yet, for, nor जैसे coordinating conjunctions से जुड़े हों तो इनके पहले comma लगाया जाता है :

She can't talk, nor can she walk. He is poor, yet he is honest.

13. Address लिखते समय House No, Street या अन्य सन्दर्भों को अलग-अलग स्पष्ट करने हेतु comma लगाया जाता है :

129, South West Block. 329, Kala Kua, Near Jain Temple, Alwar

Note *यदि Adjectives एक दूसरे से closely related हों तो comma का प्रयोग नहीं करते हैं। इसके लिए यह देखना चाहिये कि comma की जगह 'and' का प्रयोग करने पर यदि वाक्य अधिक स्पष्ट एवं सुन्दर लगता है तो 'and' लिखें अन्यथा comma प्रयोग करना चाहिये।*

(a) Three happy little children.
(b) A dozen colourful oranges.
(c) Ramesh lives in a small, beautiful and newly built cottage.
(d) Sarla bought a new, blaw and beautiful saree.

6. Semi colon (;)

Comma का प्रयोग वहाँ किया जाता है जहाँ Full Stop की अपेक्षा कम रूकने/ ठहरने की आवश्यकता होती है, जबकि Semi colon का प्रयोग वहाँ पर किया जाता है जहाँ Comma से कुछ अधिक लेकिन Full Stop से

कुछ कम रुकने/ठहरने की आवश्यकता होती है। **Semi colon वास्तव में comma एवं full stop के बीच की अन्तराल अवधि (ठहरने की) के लिए प्रयुक्त किया जाता है। Semi colon का प्रयोग निम्न स्थिति में किया जाता है :**

1. जब विभिन्न प्रकार के तथ्य एक series में, एक ही वाक्य में एक दूसरे के साथ आयें, तो इन्हें अलग एवं स्पष्ट रूप से व्यक्त/प्रदर्शित करने के लिये semi colon का प्रयोग किया जाता है :
   The nominated members are S.Krishnan, Chairman ; K.Krishnan, Vice Chairman; L.Krishnan, Secretary; and M.Krishnan,Joint Secretary .
2. जब दो Independent clauses के मध्य कोई conjunction न प्रयुक्त हुआ हो, तो उनके बीच में Semi colon का चिह्न प्रयोग किया जाता है :
   The hotel burnt down ; it was the biggest hotel in the city.
   The efforts must continue; war can be fruitless.
3. दो Independent clauses के मध्य therefore, hence, henceforth, however जैसे conjunctions प्रयुक्त हुये हों, तो इन conjunctions के पहले semi colon अंकित किया जाता है ।
   He was not well ; so, he could not attend the meeting.
   Registrations exceed all expectations; however, there is shortage of good teachers.
4. जब कोई Phrase, या कुछ शब्द, एक वाक्य में Introductory words या Explanatory words की तरह आते हैं, तो उस Phrase या उन words से पूर्व Semi colon का प्रयोग किया जाता है :
   She completes her work in time ; she never wastes her time in taking tea, in gossiping or in making useless calls.
   On the advice of a friend , he chose to invest in shares of some industries; *i.e.* Steel, I.T, and Petro products.

7. Colon-(:)

1. Colon का प्रयोग किसी उदाहरण या सूचि को शुरू करने हेतु किया जाता है, जैसे:
   The three committees are as follows: Finance, Administration and Sports.
2. वाक्य में, लम्बे quotation, statement या question से पूर्व colon का प्रयोग किया जाता है :
   This is the point : Can an officer insult a clerk for no material reason ?
   This I believe : Sincerity pays, if not today, after some time, but it pays.
3. जब किसी शब्द या Noun के बाद उसका definition या description दिया जाता है, तो उस शब्द या Noun के बाद colon का प्रयोग किया जाता है :
   Noun : Name of any person or a thing.
   Peacock : A large beautiful bird with blue neck and colourful feathers.
4. नाटकों (plays) की पटकथाओं में speaker के नाम के बाद colon का प्रयोग होता है :
   Ram : I shall forgive Ravana for his misdeeds.
   Laxman : I shall kill Ravana.
5. समय लिखते समय hours एवं minutes की digits के बीच colon का प्रयोग किया जाता है :
   10:30 A.M., 3:45 P.M.
6. Colon का प्रयोग वाक्य में 'For example' या 'Namely' के substitute की तरह भी किया जाता है :
   It is a city renowned for beautiful parks : Every lane is clean, parks are full of beautiful flowers, trees are planted at the road side and so many other such things.
7. Proportion या अनुपात लिखने के लिये colon का प्रयोग किया जाता है :
   15 : 3 :: 5 : 1   4 : 3 : 7

8. Dash (–)

Dash का प्रयोग निम्न स्थिति में किया जाता है–

1. यदि किसी वाक्य के मध्य में; विचारों में या grammatical construction में abrupt change हो, तो Dash का प्रयोग किया जाता है :

   He lost the game – but I am to go to hospital.

   He was passed in interview – but his father is ill.

2. वाक्य में किसी प्रकार की रुकावट को प्रदर्शित करने हेतु भी Dash का प्रयोग किया जाता है :

   "Rahul, don't go now – you are too late.

3. वाक्य में बोलते समय यदि वक्ता के स्वर में हिचकिचाहट (Hesitation) है, तो उस हिचकिचाहट को प्रदर्शित करने के लिये भी Dash का प्रयोग किया जाता है :

   "Well", he said, "You – you can't speak like this."

4. अपनी कही बात को स्पष्ट करने के लिये brackets की जगह भी dash का प्रयोग किया जाता है :

   The other man – Mukul.– didn't know me.

5. Long pause को प्रदर्शित करने के लिये , किसी चीज को महत्त्वपूर्ण बनाने के लिये भी dash प्रयुक्त करते हैं :

   That agreement was signed differently – it must be taken into account.

6. कभी-कभी colon की जगह भी dash का प्रयोग किया जाता है :

   I have demanded following things –

   1. One eraser, 2. One pen, and 3. One pencil.

7. Dash का प्रयोग बीच की संख्याओं; Page Numbers etc. को Omit करने के लिये भी किया जाता है :

   1985–91, Page No. 47–63.

9. Use of Hypen (-)

1. वाक्य का अन्तिम शब्द पहली पंक्ति में यदि पूरा नहीं आ पाता है एवं दूसरी पंक्ति में पूरा किया जाये, तो पहली पंक्ति में अपूर्ण शब्द के बाद Hyphen लगाया जाता है :

   Ram was not pre–
   sent yesterday in his shop.
   Sita is indeed an intelli–
   gent girl.

2. Twenty-one से Ninety-nine तक के Compound Numerals लिखते समय निम्न प्रकार से Hyphen लगाया जाता है :

   Thirty-nine feet, Thirty-seven miles.

3. बहुत से compound एवं complex words के भागों को अलग-अलग सा दिखाया जाता है; एवं उनके बीच Hyphen प्रयोग किया जाता है :

   Anti-government, Ex-President,
   Ex-wife, Pre-planned.

4. बोलने की हकलाहट, तुतलाहट को प्रदर्शित करने के लिये भी Hyphen प्रयोग किया जाता है।

   P-p-p-please madam, R-r-r-Rahul don't beat me.

10. Inverted Commas (" ")

Inverted commas को Quotation Marks भी कहा जाता है। ये Single ('....') भी प्रयोग में आते हैं, एवं Double ("....") भी।

Inverted Commas का प्रयोग निम्न स्थिति में किया जाता है :

1. Inverted Commas का प्रयोग Direct Narration में Reported Speech को बन्द करने के लिए निम्न प्रकार किया जाता है :
He said, "Where do you live?" • She said to me, "I am going to market."
2. किसी के कथन (Quotation) को भी Inverted Commas में बन्द किया जाता हैं। जैसे :
Shakespeare says, "Sweet are the uses of adversity."
Ram says, "Honesty is the best policy."
3. किसी पुस्तक, अखबार, कविता, लेख या कहानी के नाम को भी Inverted Commas में बन्द करके, उनको वाक्य में पृथक रूप से दिखाया जाता है। जैसे :
I haven't read 'Hamlet' so far? "An arrogant Hare" is a good story.
4. कई बार वाक्य में प्रयुक्त कुछ Phrases या Words को Inverted Commas द्वारा बन्द किया जाता है, जिसका उद्देश्य इन words या Phrases को अलग से दिखाना या उन पर विशेष ध्यान देना होता है। जैसे :
The Word 'Nature' is also used to mean the aptitude of a person.
Many persons were jailed under 'POTA' in Tamil Nadu.
5. यदि किसी quotation के अन्दर भी कोई quotation हो या Direct Narration के मध्य कोई quotation आये तो उसे भी Inverted Commas के मध्य रखा जाता है। इस सन्दर्भ में यह ध्यान रखें कि ये दोनों Inverted Commas अलग-अलग प्रकार के होंगे। अन्दर वाले Inverted Commas सामान्यतया Single होते हैं :
She said to me, "Have you read 'Godan' of Prem Chand."
Ram said to me. "Haven't you seen 'The Spider man' so far?"

ERRORS, MISTAKES AND BLUNDERS IN USING PUNCTUATION MARKS

Exercise : ***Rewrite the sentences after correction.***

1. If you dont understand it tell him.
2. he said to me what is his name.
3. try try and try again
4. ram and shyam went to punjab.
5. ram not shyam is responsible.
6. do what you were told.
7. oh you are here.
8. o lord help me.
9. gandhiji the father of the nation loved the poor.
10. the answer she said is this
11. hands up said the dy sp.
12. oh dear where have you been.
13. follow me ordered the jailer.
14. she is after all an orphan.
15. yes please he said
16. she said I cant do it
17. when you are ready tell me
18. Where have you been
19. you must you can you shall do it
20. it you try you will pass
21. I like reading he likes playing
22. ppp please try again he said
23. please move fast it is getting late
24. I want the following items pencil rubber and a pen
25. he said I can't agree with your policy divide and rule at this moment
26. raju do you follow me. sudha yes I do
27. the other girl gayatri sharma refused to accept the gift
28. no I dont remember it
29. ram is a hindu ashraf is a muslim
30. I saw the note welcome.

Explanations

1. If you don't understand it, tell him.
2. He said to me, "What is his name?"
3. Try, try and try again.
4. Ram and Shyam went to Punjab.
5. Ram, not Shyam is responsible.
6. Do, what you were told.
7. Oh! you are here.
8. O, Lord, help me.
9. Gandhiji, the Father of the Nation, loved the poor.
10. "The answer", she said, 'is this.'
11. "Hands up!" , said the Dy.S.P.
12. Oh dear! where have you been?
13. "Follow me!", ordered the jailer.
14. She is, after all, an orphan.
15. "Yes please", he said.
16. She said, "I can't do it."
17. When you are ready, tell me.
18. Where have you been?
19. You must, you can, you shall do it.
20. If you try, you will pass.
21. I like reading; he likes playing.
22. "P-p-p-please try again", he said.
23. Please move fast; it is getting late.
24. I want the following items : pencil, rubber and a pen.
25. He said, "I can't agree with your policy 'Divide and Rule'at this moment".
26. Raju : Do you follow me?
    Sudha : Yes, I do.
27. The other girl- Gayatri Sharma - refused to accept the gift.
28. No, I don't remember it.
29. Ram is a Hindu ; Ashraf is a Muslim.
30. I saw the note "Welcome".

❑❑❑

22

Practice Tests (Spotting the Errors)

How to Solve Questions of Spotting Errors

विभिन्न Competitive Examinations केअंग्रेजी विषय के प्रश्न-पत्र में 'Spotting the Errors' शीर्षक लगभग 10-15 प्रश्नों का समावेश होता है । अधिकांश प्रश्न Grammatical Rules पर आधारित होते हैं। यद्यपि यह कहना बहुत मुश्किल है कि मुख्यतया किस तरह की errors वाले प्रश्न परीक्षा में दिये जाते है, तथापि 'Spotting errors' से सम्बन्धित अधिकांश प्रश्न-Verbs, Nouns, Pronoun, Articles, Participles, Adjectives, Adverbs etc. के सही प्रयोग पर आधारित होते हैं। कई बार Unenglish expressions तथा Superfluous expressions से सम्बन्धित प्रश्न भी परीक्षा में आते हैं। **छात्रों को एक बात बहुत अच्छी तरह समझ लेनी चाहिए कि, अंग्रेजी में बिना व्याकरण की अच्छी जानकारी हुए, आपको अंग्रेजी प्रश्नपत्र को solve करने में, अच्छे अंक प्राप्त करने में, अवश्य ही परेशानी होगी ।**

Spotting errors के प्रश्नों के सही हल हेतु आप को सतत् Practice करने की आवश्यकता है । **नियम रटकर, अंग्रेजी के प्रश्नों को हल करना सम्भव नहीं है।**

PRACTICE TESTS (SPOTTING THE ERRORS) EXERCISES

Exercise-1

Directions (Qs. 1 to 10) : ***Read each sentence to find out whether there is an error. The error if any will be in one part of the sentence. The number of that part is the answer. If there is no error, write 'No Error'.***

1. Her and the (A)/other members of the group (B)/spoke to the person (C)/after their final victory (D).
2. In early India (A)/there has been very little to read (B)/ except for the books sent (C)/ from Britain (D).
3. Still remaining in the ancient castle (A)/are the Duke's collection of early Dutch paintings (B)/ which will be (C)/ donated to a museum (D).
4. Most students preferred (A)/courses in the classical arts to (B)/courses in science unless (C)/ they are science majors(D).
5. When she comes (A)/ to see us (B)/ she usually will bring(C)/ some thing with her (D).
6. Why did you (A)/ not told me (B)/ that the meeting (C)/ was postponed? (D).
7. I did not want (A)/ him to have spent (B)/ all the money at (C)/ the fair yesterday (D).
8. The assistant (A)/ is never found (B)/ wherever the manager (C)/ want him (D).
9. He picked up (A)/the books (B)/ and put it (C)/ on the table (D).
10. They decided (A)/ to talk it over (B)/ at dinner (C).

Exercise-2

1. I am not hungry (A)/ beside(B)/ I do not like eggs(C).
2. Economics are (A)/ nowadays included as a subject(B)/ in all colleges(C).
3. When he (A)/had got what (B)/ he wanted (C)/ he has gone home(D).
4. Of the two proposals (A)/ we think (B)/the second is (C)/ the most attractive (D).
5. If I wrote (A)/ to my father now (B)/ he will receive(C)/ the letter tomorrow (D).
6. This road is(A)/worst than(B)/any other road(C)/of the city (D).
7. The driver as well as (A)/ the conductor are (B)/ responsible for this accident(C).
8. Some peoples (A)/ feel that (B) no progress is possible (C)/ without discipline (D).
9. She told (A)/ her mother that (B)/ she is busy (C).
10. After listening to (A)/ little of songs (B)/ she switched off (C)/ the radio (D).

Exercise-3

1. We erect monuments (A)/ in the memory of great leaders (B)/ lest their achievements (C) / might be forgotten(D).
2. He will not escape (A)/ punishment unless (B)/ he does not speak (C)/ the truth (D).
3. Being a cold day (A)/ neither my friend (B)/ nor I was (C)/ in a mood to go to market (D).
4. Such students (A)/ who have not submitted (B)/ their T.C. will not be allowed (C)/ to appear in the examinations (D).
5. I went to the librarian and cashier (A)/ and they gave me (B) / all facilities required (C)/ to complete the project (D).
6. Milk is (A)/ the most perfect (B)/ food in the world (C).
7. What is there (A)/ which is a secret (B)/ between you and me(C) ?
8. By the death of Rajeev Gandhi (A)/ a great statesman and politician (B)/ were lost (C).
9. You had better (A)/ to stop (B)/ your work (C)/ for some time (D).
10. A severe cold (A)/ prevented the president (B)/ being present (C)/ at the function (D).

Exercise-4

1. I dislike (A)/ my child (B)/ watching T.V. (C)/ all the time (D).
2. These people (A)/ get their bath water (B)/ from the river (C)/ and their drink water from a well (D).
3. It was evident (A)/ to me that there (B)/ was any mistake (C)/ in that account (D).
4. He does not seem (A)/to be aware (B)/ as to (C)/ his merits (D).
5. He declared (A)/ at the top of his (B)/voice that (C)/ it was not possible(D).
6. Crossing the road(A)/ a car knocked (B)/ him down (C)/.
7. The captain (A)/ with all his team (B)/ were held responsible (C).
8. Bangladesh has come (A)/ into existence (B)/ thirty years ago (C).
9. No sooner did (A)/ she saw me (B)/ than she came up (C)/ and spoke to me (D).
10. No monument in the world (A)/ is so beautiful (B)/ as the Taj Mahal (C).

Exercise-5

1. Many a man(A)/ have been(B)/ working under me (C).
2. I told him(A)/ the story(B)/ in details(C)/ to make him understand it fully (D).
3. Different authorities(A)/ defines(B)/ intelligence in different ways (C).
4. The old man(A)/told his sons(B)/ that there was no such thing(C)/ like luck (D).
5. Everyone knows(A)/ that the tiger(B)/ is faster(C)/ of all animals (D).

6. Sakshi wrote an essay(A)/ so well that(B)/ her teacher was(C)/ very pleased with her (D).
7. The conference was(A)/ attended (B)/ by more than one hundred delegates (C).
8. This is(A)/ one of the most(B)/ interesting book(C)/ I have ever read (D).
9. Ram was happy(A)/ that Rita and her sister was going(B)/ by the same train(C)/ the next day (D).
10. The only criteria (A)/ to judge(B)/ a person(C)/ is to observe his behaviour (D).

Exercise-6

Directions : *(Qs. 1 To 10) Read each sentence to find out whether there is an error. The error, if any , will be in one part of the sentence. The number of that part is the answer. If there is No Error., the answer is E :*

1. No country can long endure (A)/ if its foundations (B) /were not laid deep (C) / in the material prosperity. (D)
2. Mahatma Gandhi did not solve (A) / all the future problems (B) / but he did solve (C) /problems of his own age. (D)
3. We now look forward for (A) /some great achievements (B)/ which to some extent (C)/ can restore the country's prestige once again. (D)
4. While Mahendra was away (A)/ on a long official tour (B)/ his office receive an important letter (C)/ which was marked 'Urgent' (D)
5. We will pack not only (A)/ the material properly (B)/ but will also deliver it (C)/ to your valued customers. (D)
6. We can not handle (A)/ this complicated case today (B)/ unless full details are not given (C) / to us by now. (D)
7. According to one survey (A)/ only those forests which were (B)/ not under village management (C)/ succumbed from fires recently. (D)
8. Our school is making (A)/ every possible effort (B)/ to provide best facilities (C)/ and personal attention for each child . (D)
9. We have done everything (A)/ that could be done (B)/ to avert the storm (C)/ which is now coming on. (D)
10. Jayesh loved his Guru immensely (A)/ and gave him fullest loyalty, (B)/ yet he had his own (C)/ independent way of thinking. (D)

Exercise-7

Directions : *(Qs. 1 To 10) Read each sentence to find out whether there is any error in it. The error, if any , will be in one part of the sentence. The number of that part is the answer. If there is No Error. , the answer is E :*

1. This laboratory of Physics is (A)/ not only equipped with (B)/ all state-of-the-art instruments (C)/ but also with outstanding physicists. (D)
2. No method of making other (A)/ people agree to (B)/ your view point is (C)/ as effective as this method. (D)
3. I was pretty sure that (A)/ he would support me (B)/ for changing the age-old (C)/and static structure of our organisation.(D)
4. I did not like his (A)/ comments on my paper (B)/ but I had no alternative (C)/ as I had agreed to keep quiet. (D)
5. The report is candid in admitting (A)/ that the investment by the government (B)/ in health and family planning sectors (C)/ have eroded considerably. (D)
6. He tried as he could (A)/ but Naveen did not (B)/ succeed in getting (C)/ his car to start up.(D)

7. Foolishly Madhu threw (A)/ some water on the electric heater (B)/ when it catches fire and (C)/ she got a shock. (D)
8. Rajesh was expecting (A)/ a telegram from his uncle (B)/ which would inform (C) / him whether he went or not. (D)
9. Neither of the plans (A)/ suits him and therefore (B)/ he decided not to (C)/ go out yesterday. (D)
10. In spite of the rumors (A) of an impending takeover(B)/ by the government, (C)/ Ramlal bought more shares of that company. (D)

Exercise-8

Directions : ***(Qs.1 to 10) Read each sentence to find out whether there is any grammatical or idiomatic error in it. The error, if any, will be in one part of the sentences. The number of that part is the answer. If there is No Error, the answer is E :***

1. Our housing society comprises (A)/ six block and thirty flats (B)/ in an area of (C)/ about thousand square meters (D)
2. They took to (A)/ reading 'Times' (B)/ for better knowledge(C)/ of the facts. (D)
3. As I was to reach early (A)/ I preferred train (B)/ instead of (C)/ bus. (D)
4. He did not go (A)/ to the city on foot (B)/ he went there (C)/ by the train. (D)
5. One of the most (A)/ widely spread (B)/ bad habit (C)/ is the use of tobacco. (D)
6. Myself and Ramanujam (A)/ will take care of (B)/ the function (C)/ on Saturday. (D)
7. All the doctors (A)/ were puzzled on the (B)/ strange symptoms (C)/ reported by the patient. (D)
8. India is in no way (A)/ inferior than the USA (B)/ in the fertility of soil (C)/ and richness of resourcess. (D)
9. The visitors (A)/ complained at (B)/ the poor accommodation (C)/ they were given. (D)
10 Amit's habit of (A)/ delaying his work (B)/ put his colleagues(C)/ to a lot of trouble. (D)

Exercise-9

Directions : ***(Qs. 1 to 10) One part of following sentences has an error; point out the portioin carrying error in the answer sheet. In case No Error is there, the answer is E :***

1. I have been to a few of his lectures (A)/ but understood little of (B)/what he has said.(C)
2. Not only the bandits robbed (A)/ the traveller of his purse (B)/ but also wounded him grieuously. (C)
3. The old woman has had the best medical facilities available (A)/ but she will not be cured (B)/ unless she does not have a strong desire to live. (C)
4. Frozen foods are so popular today(A)/ that many people wonder (B)/how they ever lived without them. (C)
5. We should never be (A)/ cent percent sure of our success (B)/ in any walk of our life.(C)
6. Smith including (A)/ all the members of his family (B)/ goes to the church every Sunday. (C)
7. The students of now-a-days (A)/ hesitate to talk (B)/ to their teachers. (C)
8. If you would have (A)/ practised regularly (B)/ you would have won the match. (C)
9. Kanchejungha is one of the(A)/ beautiful peak (B)/ of the (C)/Himalayan range. (D)
10. He is one of the (A)/ most intelligent (B)/ student (C)/ I have ever taught. (D)

Exercise-10

Directions : ***(Qs. 1 To 10) Read each sentence to find out whether there is any error in it. The error, if any , will be in one part of the sentence. The number of that part is the answer . If there is No Error the answer is E :***

1. Radha with (A)/ her brothers (B)/ and sisters (C)/ are present here. (D)
2. Men (A)/ proposes (B)/ but God (C)/ disposes. (D)

3. He gets (A)/ up (B)/ early at (C)/ the morning. (D)
4. The house (A)/ is built (B)/ in an (C)/ attractive manner. (D)
5. She worn (A)/ a necklace (B)/ studded (C)/ with diamonds. (D)
6. None (A)/ of these (B)/ students (C)/ was there. (D)
7. He (A)/ was not (B)/ blind (C)/ from birth . (D)
8. I said (A)/ that a interesting (B)/ face could (C)/ also be pretty. (D)
9. He love (A)/ his father (B)/ and his father (C)/ also loved him. (D)
10. Milking used (A)/ to be a task (B)/ or a duty cost (C)/on him. (D)

Exercise-11

1. The doctor (A)/ did not (B)/ ask Mohan (C)/ the time. (D)
2. How do (A)/ Vinoba appeal (B)/ to the (C)/ landlords ? (D)
3. Bats are (A)/ sometime seen (B)/ in our (C)/ houses. (D)
4. I am glad (A)/ Rex never saw (B)/ a trained(C)/ police dog jump.(D)
5. His (A)/ son met (B)/ him (C)/ on the door. (D)
6. The plane (A)/ was to (B)/ take of (C)/ at 6 A.M. (D)
7. This is (A)/ our attitudes (B)/ towards (C)/ Ahimsa and Truth .(D)
8. I caught him (A)/ from the hand (B)/ and began (C)/ to plead .(D)
9. We ought (A)/ not to (B)/ speak ill (C)/ for others. (D)
10. Radha works (A)/ harder than (B)/ I did (C)/ her age. (D)

Exercise-12

1. Krishna is (A)/ the taller (B)/ boy (C)/ in the class. (D)
2. Bhimma was (A)/ the man (B)/ who all (C)/ the Indians loved . (D)
3. I can (A)/ neither read (B)/ or speak (C)/ Hindi. (D)
4. I have been (A)/ suffering from (B)/ fever since (C)/ three days. (D)
5. The committee (A)/ is divided (B)/ over (C)/ this issue. (D)
6. The Planning Commission expects (A)/ the Gross Domestic Product to (B)/ grow by a satisfactory (C)/ rate during the year. (D)
7. The language used for writing text books (A)/ differs from other forms of writing (B)/ in its preference on (C)/ simplicity over style.(D)
8. One of the basics of good writing (A)/ is to have a (B)/ clear understanding of the target audience (C)/ and its requirements. (D)
9. This is an (A)/ excellent site for (B)/ a stadium which we (C)/ should like to acquire. (D)
10. If you absent (A)/ from college, your (B)/ name is likely to be (C)/ struck off the rolls. (D)

Exercise-13

Directions : ***(Qs. 1 to10) There is a mistake in each of the following sentences. Find out the part in which the mistake occurs. Write 'No Error' if you find none :***

1. The man(A)/ is (B)/ a (C)/social animal. (D)
2. Twenty five kilometers (A)/ from Bhubaneshwar to Cuttak (B)/ are (C)/ a long distance. (D)
3. The institute (A)/ imparts training (B)/ in (C)/ the French. (D)
4. Looking forward (A)/ to meet (B)/ you (C)/ soon .(D)
5. Pass on (A)/ the salt, (B)/ please, (C)/ do you ? (D)
6. He is (A)/ a mason (B)/ who (C)/ built my house . (D)
7. I cannot (A)/ make from (B)/ what you are saying (C)/ about him. (D)

8. What (A)/ you will think (B)/ if school boys (C)/ make fun of you ? (D)
9. The minister's speech (A)/ has been reported (B)/ in the newspaper. (C)
10. No sooner (A)/ we reached there (B)/ than it started raining. (C)

Exercise-14

Directions : ***(Qs 1 to 10) The following sentences contain errors in grammer, usage, diction (choice of words) and idiom. Some sentences may be correct. No sentence has more than one error. Select the numbered part that according to you contains the error. Its number is the answer :***

1. Being a very cold day (A)/ I would (B)/ not go out for (C)/ a morning walk . (D)
2. Such an act of cruelty (A)/ had never (B)/ be commited (C)/ before. (D)
3. If you will (A)/ insist upon (B)/ challenging me, (C)/ I will fight it out alone. (D)
4. Fifty years (A)/ have passed (B)/ since (C)/ Subhash Chandra Bose had died. (D)
5. A good house (A)/ and a good bank (B)/ account is what (C)/ he wants. (D)
6. Of all the (A)/ other teachers the (B)/ students respected the history (C)/ teacher the most. (D)
7. He is one of those persons (A)/ who listen (B)/ to all advice but keep (C)/ his own counsel. (D)
8. No one but (A)/ he knew (B)/ who was (C)/ setting the question paper. (D)
9. A box (A)/ of apples are (B)/ in (C)/ the car. (D)
10. The principal threatened to (A)/ inform to (B)/ his father about (C)/ his misdeeds. (D)

Exercise-15

Directions : ***(Qs. 1 to 10) Read each sentence to find out whether there is any error in it. The error, if any, will be in one part of the sentence. The number of that part is the answer. If there is No Error., the answer is E :***

1. Sharad was entrusted with (A)/ the task of co-ordination yesterday (B)/ but due to certain difficulties(C)/ he does not do it. (D)
2. One should make (A)/ his best efforts if (B)/ one wishes to achieve (C)/ success in this organisation. (D)
3. Having deprived from their (A)/ homes in the recent earthquake (B) they had no other option but (C)/ to take shelter in a school. (D)
4. The technician reminded (A)/ them to have a (B)/ throughly cleaning of the (C)/ machine after use. (D)
5. The villager told (A)/ us where was the (B)/ temple and even led (C)/ us to thes pot. (D)
6. The person who (A)/ they are referring (B)/ to is none other (C)/ than my close friend. (D)
7. Mahesh was kind enough (A)/ to inform us about the (B)/ conspiracy but declined to (C)/ name the person behind it. (D)
8. He told the policeman (A)/ that he would rather (B)/ starve to stealing to get (C)/ what he had been aspiring for. (D)
9. In spite of the workload yesterday (A)/ Nitin manages to play (B)/ it cool and continued (C)/ with his work as usual. (D)
10. The demand of the workers' (A)/ union that the dismissed (B)/employee to reinstated, has (C), been accepted by the management.(D)

Exercise-16

Directions : ***(Qs.1 to10) (i) In this section a number of sentence are given. The sentences are divied in three separate parts and each one is labelled (A), (B), and (C). Read each sentence to find out whether there is an error in any part. No sentence has more than one error. When you find an error in any one of the parts (A,B, or C) indicate your response. You many feel***

that there is No Error. in a sentence. In that case letter 'D' will signify a 'No Error' response. (ii) You are to indicate only one response for each sentence. (If you indicate more than one response, your answer will be considered wrong.) Error may be in grammar, word usage or idioms. There may be a word missing or there may be a word which should be removed. (iii) You are not required to correct the error. You are required only to indicate your response :

1. Thinking that he has finally found (A)/someone with similar interests, (B)/ the scholar tried to strike up a conversation. (C)/ No Error. (D)
2. Earlier this year, (A)/ 'Constantant' had entered the news via a video-tapted interview (B)/ telecasted by commercial television channel.(C)/ No Error. (D)
3. If you permit me to speak the truth, (A)/I shall say without hesitation (B)/ that you have done a mistake.(C)/ No Error. (D)
4. My friend is so rich that (A)/ he is having six houses in Mumbai (B)/ and four in Pune, (C)/ No Error. (D)
5. He asked me (A)/ if I am ill (B)/ and I answered that I was not . (C)/ No Error. (D)
6. He lost his new knife (A)/ shortly after (B)/ he bought it. (C)/ No Error. (D)
7. The ultimate problem of Physics (A)/ is to reduce matter by analysis (B)/ to its lowest condition or divisibility.(C)/ No Error. (D)
8. By the time (A)/ she finished typing (B)/ it was not hardly ten. (C)/ No Error. (D)
9. He like (A)/ his companions (B) were deceived. (C)/ No Error. (D)
10. He told me that you had left the school (A)/ a year ago (B)/ and seeking for a job.(C)/No Error.

Exercise-17

Directions : *(Qs. 1 to 10.) : (i) In this section, a number of sentences are given. The sentences are divided in three separate parts and each one is labelled as (A), (B), and (C). Read each sentence to find out whether there is an error in any part. No sentence has more than one error. When you find an error in any one of the parts (A, B, or C) indicate your response. You may feel that there is No Error. in a sentence. In that case. Write 'No Error'. (ii) You are to indicate only one response for each sentence (If you indicate more than one response, your answer will be considered wrong.). Errors may be in grammar, word usage or idioms. There may be a word missing or there may be a word which should be removed. (iii) You are not required to correct the error. You are required only to indicate your response :*

1. As I prefer coffee than tea (A)/ my friends always take the trouble (B)/ to get a cup of coffee, whenever I visit them. (C)/ No Error. (D)
2. There has been (A)/ little change in the patient's condition (B)/ since he was moved to the special ward. (C)/ No Error. (D)
3. The king was perturbed (A)/ to find evidences (B)/ against his own queen. (C)/ No Error. (D)
4. They begged her (A)/ not to go (B)/ but she was determined (C)/ and left the castle. (D)/ No Error. (E)
5. They cook meal, (A)/ lay the table, (B)/ clean the house and iron the clothes. (C)/ No Error. (D)
6. No sooner did (A)/ the doctor enter the house (B)/ then the patient died. (C)/ No Error. (D)
7. The drawing room was a mess (A)/ with all the furnitures (B)/ scattered in total disarray. (C)/ No Error.
8. The gap between what he preaches (A)/ and what he practises is too wide (B)/ to be accepted by anyone. (C)/ No Error. (D)
9. While flying over India (A)/ we had glimpses of the two sources of her culture (B)/ Ganges and Himalayas. (C)/ No Error. (D)
10. This picture (A)/ is the best (B)/ of the two. (C)/ No Error.(D)

Exercise-18

Directions : *(Qs. 1 to 10) : In this section, a number of sentences are given. These sentences are marked in three parts indicated by the letters (A), (B), and (C). Read each sentence to find out whether there is an error in any part of it. No sentence has more than one error. When you find an error in any one of the parts (A), (B), or (C), select that part as your answer. You may feel that there is No Error. in a sentence. In that case letter 'D' will signify a 'No Error' response. Errors may be in grammar, word usage or idioms. There may be a word missing or there may be a word which should be removed :*

1. Finishing the work (A)/ he was allowed rest (B)/ for half an hour. (C)/ No Error. (D)
2. The pirates, who had hidden the treasure on the island, (A)/ went back again (B)/ because they thought they can now remove it with safety.(C) / No Error. (D)
3. In those early days (A)/ the West paid lip-service (B)/ to United Nations. (C)/ No Error. (D)
4. Ten shillings (A)/ was charged (B)/ by him for the service. (C)/ No Error. (D)
5. To an amusing degree (A)/ he was addicted to read the jokes in punch aloud (B)/ even when he was alone. (C)/ No Error. (D)
6. Why not stop the first man you meet next and ask, (A)/ "could you tell me (B)/ what the time is?"(C)/ No Error. (D)
7. The invention of the internal combustion engine (A)/ is considered to be (B)/ a most unique development. (C)/ No Error. (D)
8. Put off (A)/ the fire (B)/ quickly. (C)/ No Error. (D)
9. A fight (A)/ took place (B)/ on the board of the ship. (C)/ No Error. (D).
10. Hardly the rains started (A)/ when a child in the corner (B)/ sent out a piercing wail. (C)/ No Error. (D)

Exercise-19

Directions : *(Qs. 1 to 10) : (i) In this Section, a number of sentences are given. The sentences are in three separate parts and each one is labelled (A), (B), (C). Read each sentence to find out whether there is an error in any of these part. No sentence has more than one error. When you find an error in any one of these parts choose that part as your response. You may feel that there is No Error. in a sentence, in that case choose (D) as your response. Errors may be in grammar, word usage, or idioms. There may be a word missing or a word which should be removed :*

1. Don't think you can say unpleasant things (A) / about someone behind his back (B) / and not found out. (C) / No Error. (D)
2. The Americans speak (A) / different from us (B)/ though our grammar is the same. (C)/ No Error. (D)
3. This is an instance (A)/ of the blind (B)/ leading the blinds (C)/ No Error. (D)
4. He took to drink (A) / to lessen (B) / his mental worries. (C) / No Error. (D)
5. My father could lead (A) / a full and happy life (B) / without spending lot of money. (C) / No Error. (D)
6. All India Radio broadcasted (A) / a very good programme (B) / this morning. (C) / No Error. (D)
7. There were so much cattle (A) / on the road that (D) / it was difficult to drive safely. (C) / No Error. (D)
8. What could have provoked him to behave (A) / in such a rude manner (B) / at dinner last night ? (C) / No Error. (D)

9. They were rich zamindars in the thirties (A) / but now they have fallen on the evil days (B) / and have lost much of their property. (C) / No Error. (D)
10. The foreign ambassador was (A) / both noted for his charming manners (B)/ as well as his wide knowledge of languages. (C) / No Error. (D)

Exercise-20

Directions : *(Qs. 1 to 10) : (i) In this Section a number of sentences are given. The sentences are marked in three separate parts and each one is labelled (A), (B), (C). Read each sentence to find out whether there is an error in any part. No sentence has more than one error. When you find an error in any one of the parts (A, B or C), indicate your response accordingly. You may feel that there is No Error. in a sentence. In that case letter (D) will signify a 'No Error' response. (ii) You are to indicate only one response for each sentence. (If you indicate more than one response, your answer will be considered wrongly. Errors may be in grammar, word usage or idioms. There may be a word missing or there may be a word which should be removed. (iii) You are not required to correct the error. You are required only to indicate your response :*

1. The news of the disturbance (A) / was braodcasted (B) / the same evening. (C) / No Error.(D)
2. Everyone visiting the house asked the young girl (A) / how could she kill the wolf (B) / single handed and without a weapon.(C) / No Error. (D)
3. While walking slowly in the park (a) / on a quiet summer afternoon (B) / a mad dog suddenly attacked him from behind. (C) / No Error. (D)
4. Since the attachment of air-conditioned sleeping cars to all important trains (A) / travelling became very pleasant (B) / especially during the summer season. (C) / No error.(D)
5. It is the newspapers (A) / that exposes us to the widest range (B) / of human experiences and behaviour. (C) / No Error.(D)
6. The method suggested in the lecture (A) / enables a student to learn more quickly (B) / and to have remembered for a longer period of time. (C) / No Error. (D)
7. Last month we celebrated (A) / the wedding of our sister for whom (B) / we have been looking for suitable alliance for three years. (C) / No Error. (D)
8. A leading textile manufacturer, one of the fastest growing in the industry, (A) / is looking for a marketing manager (B) / to look up the marketing network of the company. (C) / No Error. (D)
9. There was very heavy rain last night (A) / and the rivers have overflown their banks (B) / causing severe hardship to the people living by them. (C) No Error. (D)
10. The government warned the shopkeepers (A) / that if they persist in charging unfair prices (B) / their licences would be cancelled. (C) / No Error. (D)

Exercise-21

Directions : *(Qs. 1 to 10): Read each sentence to find out whether there is any error in it. The error, if any will be in one part of the sentence. The number of that part is the answer. If there is No Error, the answer is 'E' (Ignore the errors of punctuation, if any.) :*

1. Kamlesh asked the dealer (A) / what was the price (B) / of that bicycle and whether (C) / it is really made in Germany ? (D) / No Error. (E)
2. While luminaries of the dance world (A) / has no dearth of opportunities to display their art, (B)/ upcoming dancers suffer from (C) / an unfortunate lack of exposure. (D) / No Error. (E)
3. Scarcely had I (A) / finished washing the car (B) / than the master came (C) / and asked me to clean the floor of the house. (D) / No Error. (E)
4. The job is much worse than I expected (A) / if I would have realised (B) / how awful it was going to be, (C) / I would not have accepted it. (D) / No Error. (E)

5. I am trying to finish (A) / this letter for the last one hour, (B) / I wish you would (C) / go away or stop disturbing me. (D) / No Error. .(E)
6. I offered him part-time work (A) / but he turned it over (B) / saying that he would (C) / rather wait for a full-time job.(D)/No Error. (E)
7. He fixed a metal ladder (A) / for the wall below his window (B) / so as to be able to (C) escape if there was a fire. (D) / No Error. (E)
8. The foremost criteria of selection we adopted (A) / were the number of years of training (B) / a dancer had received (C) / under a particular Guru. (D) / No Error. (E)
9. He refused to disclose to his friends (A) / whether he will leave for England (B) /immediately after finishing his studies. (C) / No Error.(D)
10. Despite for her protests (A) / I decided to buy (B) / the saree which (C) / she did not like. (D) / No Error. (E)

Exercise-22

Directions : ***(Qs. 1 to 10) Read each sentence to find out whether there is any grammatical or idiomatic error in it . The error, if any, will be in one part of the sentence. The number of that part is the answer. If there is No Error, the answer is 'E'. (Ignore the errors of punctuation, if any.) :***

1. The principals of equal justice (A) / for all is one of (B) / the cornerstones of our, (C) / democratic way of life. (D) / No Error. (E)
2. The Trust has succeeded (A) / admirably in raising (B) / money for (C) / future programmes. (D) / No Error. (E)
3. Honesty, integrity and being intelligent (A) / are the qualities which (B) / we look for, when (C) / we interview applicants. (D) / No Error. (E)
4. In order to save petrol, (A) motorists must have to (B) / be very cautious (C) / while driving along the highways .(D) / No Error. (E)
5. If the by-stander had not been (A) / familiar with first -aid techniques,(B) / the driver which had met (C) / with the accident would have died. (D) / No Error. (E)
6. Not one of the children (A) / has ever sang (B) / on any occasion (C) / in public before. (D) / No Error. (E)
7. Neither the earthquake (A) / nor the subsequent fire (B) / was able to dampen (C)/ the spirit of the residents. (D) / No Error. (E)
8. The customer scarcely had (A) / enough money to pay (B) / to the cashier (C) / at the cash counter. (D) / No Error. (E)
9. The apparently obvious solutions (A) / to most of his problems (B)/ were overlook by (C) / many of his friends. (D) / No Error. (E)
10. By arresting the local criminals (A) / and encouraging good people (B) / we can end (C) / hostilities of that area. (D) / No Error. (E)

Exercise-23

Directions : ***(Qs. 1 to 10) In this section ten sentences are given. Each sentence has three parts, indicated by (A) ,(B) and (C). Read each sentence to find out whether there is an error. If you find an error in any one of the parts, (A, B, C), indicate your response. If a sentence has No Error, write No Error Errors may be in grammar, appropriate word usage or idioms :***

1. The flicker of light from the gas lamps (A) / indicated that the night (B) / was barely passed / (C).
2. India was committed to keep maintaining peace /(A) and solving all outstanding problems / (B) with her neighbours through dialogue. / (C)

3. Being the second Saturday of the month, /(A) he got up late and spent the whole day at home, / (B) doing his share of the household chores. / (C)
4. As economic restructuring in Central and Eastern Europe progresses, /(A) an estimated 15 million people may be out of work / (B) by the end of the year./ (C)
5. Such of those who have not paid the fees, /(A) the circular says,/ (B) will not be permitted to attend classes./ (C)
6. There is a good British Library in the city /(A) and anyone interested in books (B)/ can avail of the facility./ (C)
7. Those who are excessively careful (A)/ for their health (B)/ are not generally healthy./ (C)
8. Once we have agreed on (A)/ the fundamentals, there will hardly be (B)/ anything left to discuss about. / (C)
9. I did ask him (A)/ where you were (B)/ but he didn't tell me./ (C)
10. I will wait for you (A)/ at the office (B)/ till you will finish your wrok./ (C)

Exercise-24

1. We had swam (A)/ across the river (B)/ before (C)/ the sunset. (D) / No Error. (E)
2. Madhuri is (A)/ more prettier (B)/ than her (C)/ younger sister. (D)/ No Error. (E)
3. A cell (A)/ is the smallest (B)/ identifiable unit of life and cannot be (C)/ seen with a naked eye. (D)/ No Error.(E)
4. If a student needs advices about (A)/ carreers,(B)/ he or she should consult (C)/ the Carrer officer. (D)/ No Error.(E)
5. Had they have been in (A)/ my condition,(B)/ they would have felt (C)/ miserable and thought of committing suicide. (D)/ No Error. (E)
6. The Secretary of the worker's union (A)/ remarked that the present government is so selfish (B)/ that it cared very little (C)/ about solving anyone else's problem. (D)/ No Error. (E)
7. He don't know (A)/ the difference between (B)/ a ship and (C) a submarine.(D)/ No Error. (E)
8. Yesterday I met an old friend (A)/ when I are going (B)/ to the market.(C)/ No Error. (D)
9. Cattles (A)/ were grazing (B)/ in the meadows (C)/ near our farm .(D)/ No Error. (E)
10. You are really (A)/ senior than (B)/ me (C)/ in age. (D)/ No Error. (E)

Exercise-25

1. Make haste (A)/ lest (B)/ you should not miss (C)/ the train. (D)/ No Error. (E)
2. Many of us (A)/ do not know (B)/ to swim (C)/ at all. (D)/ No Error. (E)
3. His car is (A)/more bigger than (B)/that of any of us.(C)/ No Error. (D)
4. One of my uncles (A)/ is a doctor / in America.(C)/ No Error. (D)
5. This machine looks (A)/ good but is very (B)/ badly designed (C)/ and doesn't work good. (D)/ No Error.(E)
6. He is well-known for both (A)/ his kindness (B)/ as well as (C)/ his understanding. (D)/ No Error.(E)
7. Ramu closely (A)/ resembles to his father (B)/ not only in physical features (C)/ but also in habits. (D)/ No Error. (E)
8. After he had read the two first chapters (A)/ of the novel (B)/ he felt like reading (C)/ the book at one sitting. (D)/ No Error. (E)
9. India is (A)/ one of the leading (B)/ film producing country (C)/ in the world . (D)/ No Error. (E)
10. Hardly had (A)/ I left the house (B)/ then it began (C)/ to rain . (D)/ No Error. (E)

Exercise-26

1. He told me (A)/ that he wrote a letter (B)/ to his superior (C)/ for a certain reason. (D)/ No Error. (E)
2. The teacher told the boys (A)/ that one (B)/ ought to work hard (C)/ to earn one living. (D)/ No Error. (E)
3. The obstacles to which (A)/ Gandhiji had to surmount (B)/ were mostly (C) on the moral and spiritual grounds. (D)/ No Error. (E)
4. Unless you do not (A)/ take care of your health (B)/ you will continue (C)/ to suffer (D)/No Error. (E)
5 After Ravi (A)/ read the (B)/ magazines and newspapers, and watched the TV programme, he decided (C)/ to go out and meet some old friends. (D)/ No Error. (E)
6. Everyone agrees that (A)/ the Ganga is the holiest (B)/ of all other rivers (C)/ of India (D)/ No Error.(E)
7. The issues are (A)/ complex and (B)/ has been obscured (C)/ by other factors .(D)/ No Error. (E)
8. The bus was (A)/ hired by (B)/ the ladies (C)/ for its picnic .(D)/ No Error. (E)
9. If (A)/ it snowed tomorrow (B)/ we'll go (C)/ skating .(D)/ No Error. (E)
10. A quarrel arose between the five members (A)/ and for a time (B)/ it appeared as if the party (C)/ had been heading for a split.(D)/ No Error. (E)

Exercise-27

1. She had swam (A)/ across the river (B)/ before (C)/ we reached there. (D) / No Error. (E)
2. Sunita is (A)/ more prettier (B)/ than her (C)/ friend Anita. (D)/ No Error. (E)
3. Everyone of (A)/ the staff members present here (B)/ has given a day's pay (C)/ as their contribution (D)/ to the fund. (E)/ No Error. (F)
4. Found guilty (A)/ on murder (B)/ the accused was (C)/ sentenced to death. (D)/ No Error. (E)
5. The criminal was (A)/ sentenced to death (B)/ and was hung for his crime. (C)/ No Error. (D)
6. He said that (A)/ he will help me (B)/ in securing a decent job .(C)/ No Error. (D)
7. The recent symposium on censorship(A)/ indicated that to refrain with saying or writing (B)/ something, others might object,(C)/ to is a form of self-censorship. (D)/ No Error. (E)
8. The Indian way (A)/ of thinking is superior(B)/ to most of the (C)/ countries of the world. (D)/ No Error. (E)
9. I am certain that none (A)/ of these two books (B)/ is useful to the (C)/ students of the 8th standard. (D)/ No Error.(E)
10. The lawyer asked me (A)/ where had I (B)/ kept clothes (C)/ before taking a dip in the river (D)/ No Error. (E)

Exercise-28

1. Like most young (A)/ women living at homes, I can't really (B)/ talk about my ideas or what I really feel, to my parents. (C)/ No Error. (D)
2. The minister conferred /(A) with his colleagues (B)/ and agreed that the new projects on education (C)/ should be sanctioned immediately. (D)/ No Error. (E)
3. Sunil is (A)/ a best student (B)/ in our class (C)/ at present . (D)/ No Error. (E)
4. It is in 1929 (A)/ that we first (B)/ flew to (C)/ the United States .(D)/ No Error. (E)
5. Being a (A)/ fine day we went out (B)/ for picnic(C)/ at Okhla.(D)/ No Error. (E)
6. Many a man (A)/ have been (B)/ working (C)/ under me.(D)/ No Error. (E)
7. Please explain to me (A)/ how is a digital computer /(B)/ different from (C)/ an analogy computer. (D)/ No Error. (E)

8. I'll work for you (A)/ as long as (B)/ you'll pay (C)/ well. (D)/ No Error. (E)
9. Had you informed me earlier (A)/ I would have (B)/ certainly purchase (C)/ the car for you (D)/ No Error. (E)
10. It was seven o'clock (A)/ in the evening that (B)/ the train steamed (C)/ into the station.(D)/ No Error. (E)

Exercise-29

1. Even if he had been driving more slowly (A)/ it will have been quite impossible (B)/ to avoid the accident. (C)/ No Error. (D)
2. Would you please (A)/ stop from smoking (B)/ while the ceremony is in progress? (C)/ No Error. (D)
3. When I offered him to help (A)/ which he needed, (B)/ he persisted in refusing it (C)/ so I left him to his fate . (D)/ No Error. (E)
4. He reminded me (A)/ that he has (B)/ often told me not to (C)/ play with fire .(D)/ No Error. (E)
5. Our country need (A)/ a number of (B)/ self sacrificing and (C)/ devoted political leaders (D)/ No Error. (E)
6. Instead of (A)/ his busy and hard life (B)/ he still retains (C)/ freshness and robustness (D)/ No Error. (E)
7. The smuggler yielded (A)/ for the tempatation (B)/ and fell into (C)/ the police trap. (D)/ No Error. (E)
8. The girl said (A)/ that she preferred (B)/ the blue gown (C)/ than the black one. (D)/ No Error. (E)
9. Of the two principles (A)/ he put forward, the last one (B)/ was the more (C)/ difficult to understand. (D)/ No Error. (E)
10. All of us (A)/ surprised (B)/ to see an old man of (C)/ sixty taking part in the Marathon, held last month. (D)/ No Error. (E)

Exercise-30

1. The new railway line will greatly improve (A)/ transport and communication (B)/ in eastern part of the country (C)/ No Error. (D)
2. The receptionist asked me (A)/ who do I want (B)/ to meet in the office. (C)/ No Error. (D)
3. At last (A)/ he was married (B)/ with (C)/ a poor girl. (D)/ No Error. (E)
4. She said (A)/ that (B)/ she will help me (C)/ whenever I was in difficulty. (D)/ No Error. (E)
5. Neither Rakesh (A)/ nor (B)/ I are leaving (C)/ for Hyderabad.(D)/ No Error. (E)
6. Death (A)/ is (B)/ preferable (B)/ than life. (D)/ No Error. (E)
7. We were still talking (A)/ about what we should do (B)/ when we heard (C)/ the children shouting.(D)/ No Error. (E)
8. As soon as the peon rings (A)/ the first bell (B)/ then all the students assemble (C)/ on the play ground for prayer .(D)/ No Error. (E)
9. Have you (A)/ turned detective (B)/ that you keep your eye (C)/ on me like this? (D)/ No Error. (E)
10. She asked him (A)/ what it was that made him (B)/ so much stronger and braver (C)/ than any man .(D)/ No Error. (E)

Exercise-31

1. Being that he (A)/ is interested in getting himself examined (B)/ by a heart specialist (C)/ we must try our best to take him to a reputed doctor. (D)/ No Error. (E)
2. The vehicle which is stopped (A)/ by the policeman (B)/ contained a number (C)/ of smuggled watches (D)/ No Error. (E)

3. One should look for his (A)/ own faults first (B)/ and then those (C)/ of others (D)/No Error. (E)
4. Sitting under the shade (A)/ of a tree for a while (B)/ made us fresh (C)/ for the further journey (D)/ No Error. (E)
5. Although it is summer (A)/ yet the weather at the (B)/ hill station was (C)/ quite pleasant (D)/ No Error. (E)
6. To our surprise (A)/ we noticed that (B)/ every soldier and every sailor (C)/ was in his place (D)/ No Error. (E)
7. Neither he nor I (A)/ was able to (B)/ finish the task within (C)/ the time limit (D)/No Error. (E)
8. No sooner we entered (A)/ than he got up (B)/ and left the room. (C)/ No Error. (D)
9. The villagers fled away their houses (A)/ when they saw (B)/ the flood water rising.(C)/ No Error. (D)

Exercise-32

1. I know (A)/ he is having (B)/ a lot of books (C)/ on how to improve English. (D)/ No Error. (E)
2. The theory of relativity is (A)/ so complicated (B)/ as we cannot describe (C)/ it in a few sentences.(D)/ No Error. (E)
3. After the brief appearence before the waiting crowds, (A)/ he was taken (B)/ to the Governor chamber (C)/ for the swearing in ceremony.(D)/ No Error. (E)
4. Congress dissidents and (A)/ a wide range among the (B)/ opposition has mounted a (C)/ campaign to have the President renominated . (D)/ No Error. (E)
5. If I would have (A)/ worked regularly (B)/ I would have passed (C)/ the examination. (D)/ No Error. (E)
6. The gentleman (A)/ together with his (B)/ wife and daughter (C)/ were drowned . (D)/ No Error. (E)
7. No man (A)/ in our country (B)/ is as rich (C)/ as he is .(D)/ No Error. (E)
8. The teacher remarked (A)/ very angrily yesterday (B)/ that the boys have (C)/ all done it very badly. (D)/ No Error. (E)
9. A letter of recommendation (A)/ from the principal and (B)/ the head of English department have helped him to(C)/ get this lucrative job. (D)/ No Error. (E)
10. An Indian driver or carpenter has to work(A)/ about two hours to buy kilogram of rice (B)/ while his counterparts in Austria, the Netherlands and Switzerland (C)/need work only fifteen minutes for it. (D)/ No Error. (E)

Explanations (Ex.-1)

1. (A) 'her' की जगह 'she' लिखें । 'Her' एक Pronoun Object है जो कि subject की तरह प्रयुक्त नहीं हो सकता है ।
2. (B) 'has been' की जगह 'was' लिखा जाना चाहिये। जब वाक्य में Past tense (In early India) के बारे में चर्चा है, तो present perfect का use न होकर past tense का प्रयोग होगा ।
3. (B) 'are' की जगह 'is' होगा; subject, Duke's collection of early Dutch painting's है, जो collective noun है, singular है अत: verb 'are' की जगह 'is' आवेगी ।
4. (A) 'preferred' की जगह 'Prefer'आयेगा । (The sentence is in Present Tense.)
5. (C) 'will bring' की जगह 'brings' आयेगा । Subordinate clause का Tense, Principal clause के Tense के अनुसार ही होना चाहिये ।

6. (B) told की जगह 'tell' आयेगा Past interrogative में जब 'did' का प्रयोग होता है, तो verb की 1st form ही आती है ।
7. (B) 'to have spent' की जगह 'to spend' लिखना ही पर्याप्त है । 'have spent' का प्रयोग अनावश्यक किया गया है ।
8. (D) 'want' की जगह 'wants' आयेगा, 'Manager', singular number third person है; अत: wants आयेगा।
9. (C) 'put it' की जगह 'put them' होगा, यहाँ 'them' का प्रयोग 'Books' के लिये है जो plural है।
10. No Error.

Explanations (Ex.-2)

1. (B) 'beside' की जगह 'besides' लिखें ।
2. (A) 'economics' एक subject है, अत: इसके साथ 'is' का प्रयोग होगा ।
3. (D) 'has gone' की जगह 'went' लिखें। जब वाक्य में past tense है, तो present perfect का प्रयोग करना अनुचित है।
4. (D) 'the most' की जगह 'more' लिखें 'more', comparison हेतु काम आता है; यहाँ दो proposals का comparison किया जा रहा है most superlative degree है।
5. (A) 'wrote' की जगह 'write' लिखें।
6. (B) 'worst' की जगह 'worse' आयेगा। comparison हेतु comparative degree का ही प्रयोग होगा, superlative degree का नहीं।
7. (B) 'are' की जगह 'is' आयेगा; जब वाक्य में as well as; besides, in addition आये, तो पहले आए noun के अनुसार verb आयेगी। यहाँ पहला noun, 'driver' singular है अत: verb भी singular प्रयुक्त होगी।
8. (A) 'peoples' की जगह 'people' आयेगा। 'people' का यहाँ अर्थ individual व्यक्तियों से है।
9. (C) 'is' की जगह 'was' लिखें। Indirect narration में reported speech का tense, reporting verb के अनुसार होगा।
10. (B) 'little of' की जगह 'some of लिखें; 'little का use, uncountables हेतु किया जाता है।

Explanations (Ex.-3)

1. (D) 'might' की जगह 'should' लिखें। lest is always followed by 'should'.
2. (C) 'does not speak' की जगह 'speaks' लिखें। जब वाक्य में unless का प्रयोग हुआ है ,जो स्वयं negative है, तो double negative को avoid करें।
3. (A) 'being' से पहले 'it' लिखें। This is an example of unrelated participle.
4. (B) who की जगह 'as' or 'that' आयेगा such के साथ 'as' or 'that' का प्रयोग होता है।
5. (B) 'they' की जगह 'he' लिखें। यहाँ 'librarian' एवं 'cashier' दोनों शब्द, एक ही व्यक्ति को refer कर रहे हैं।
6. (B) 'most' को 'delete' करें, क्योंकि perfect स्वयं ही superlative है।
7. (B) which की जगह 'that' लिखें; interrogative वाक्यों में सामान्यतया 'that' pronoun का प्रयोग किया जाता है। What is followed by 'that' instead of 'which'.
8. (C) 'were' की जगह 'was' लिखें। 'statesman' एवं 'politician', ये दोनों शब्द, एक ही व्यक्ति को refer कर रहे हैं।
9. (B) 'to' को delete करें। यहाँ infinitive 'to' का प्रयोग गलत है।
10. (C) 'being' से पहले 'from' लिखें। 'prevented' is always followed by preposition 'from.'

Explanations (Ex.-4)

1. (B) 'my child' की जगह 'child's' होगा; noun के बाद में , जब gerund (यहाँ–watching) का प्रयोग होता है तो noun, possessive आता है।
2. (D) 'drink' की जगह 'drinking' आयेगा।
3. (C) 'any' की जगह 'some' लिखें। 'some' का प्रयोग affirmative में तथा 'any' का प्रयोग interrogative एवं negative में होता है।
4. (C) 'as to' 'की जगह of'लिखें, यहाँ aware के बाद preposition 'of' प्रयुक्त होगा।
5. No Error.
6. (A) 'crossing the road' की जगह 'When he was crossing the road' लिखें। This is an example of unrelated participle.
7. (C) 'were' की जगह 'was' आयेगा। यहाँ subject of the verb : 'captain' है, जो singular है।
8. (A) जब वाक्य में past time adverbs ago, yesterday etc हो, तो present perfect का प्रयोग नहीं किया जाता है। Change 'has come' to 'came'.
9. (D) 'saw' की जगह 'see'लिखें; did के साथ verb की first form आयेगी।
10. No Error.

Explanations (Ex.-5)

1. (B) 'have' की जगह 'has' आयेगा। 'many a' is followed by singular verb.
2. (C) 'details' की जगह detail आयेगा।
3. (B) 'defines' की जगह define लिखें। जब subject, 'authorities,' plural है, तो verb उसके अनुसार ही होगी।
4. (D) 'like' की जगह 'as' लिखें। 'such' के साथ सामान्यतया 'as'का प्रयोग होता है।
5. (D) 'of all animals' की जगह 'than any other animal' होना चाहिये।
6. (A) 'an essay' की जगह 'the essay' होना चाहिये। यहाँ 'essay' particular हो गया है।
7. No Error.
8. (C) 'Change book to books'. 'One of' is always followed by plural noun.
9. (B) Change 'was' to were, as the subject 'Rita and her sister' is plural .
10. (A) Change 'criteria' to 'criterion'; 'criteria' की singular form 'criterion' होता है।

Explanations (Ex.-6)

1. (C) Change '<u>were</u> not' to '<u>are</u> not laid deep'.
2. (B) Change to 'the problems of the future'.
3. (A) Change 'forward <u>for</u>' to 'forward <u>to</u>'.
4. (C) Change 'receive' to 'received'.
5. (A) Change part A to 'We will not only pack'.
6. (C) 'Avoid' using double negative. Part 'C'should be – 'unless full details are given'. Delete 'not'.
7. (D) Change 'from' to 'to'; Part 'D'should be – succumbed <u>to</u> fires recently'.
8. (D) Change 'for' to 'to'. Part 'D'should be – 'and personal attention <u>to</u> each child'.
9. (E) No Error.
10. (D) Delete 'independent.' Part 'D'should be – 'way of thinking'.

Explanations (Ex.-7)

1. (D) The word 'physicists' is meaningless. Part (D) of the sentence shoule be rewritten as – 'but also with beautiful furniture.'
2. (A) Change it to; 'No other method of making.'

3. (C) Change it to 'in changing the age-old'.
4. (E) No Error.
5. (D) Change 'have' to 'has'; the verb should agree with the subject investment.
6. (D) Change 'his car to start up' to 'his car start up'.
7. (C) Change 'when it catches fire' to 'when it caught fire'; क्योंकि वाक्य past tense में है और इसमें प्रयुक्त संज्ञाओं का वाक्य के tense साथ agreement होना आवश्यक है।
8. (D) Change 'he went or not' to 'he had gone or not'.
9. (B) Change 'suits him and therefore' to 'suited him therefore'. Superfluous use of 'and' plus incorrect use of tense.
10. (E) No Error.

Explanations (Ex.-8)

1. (B) वाक्य में प्रयुक्त 'six block and thirty flats' के स्थान पर 'six blocks and thirty flats' का प्रयोग होगा। 'six' is plural, so write 'blocks'.
2. (C) वाक्य में प्रयुक्त 'for better knowledge' के स्थान पर 'for the better knowledge' का प्रयोग होगा; 'knowledge' is particularised in the sentence.
3. (C) Change 'instead of' to 'to'.Preposition 'to' is used with 'prefer, senior, junior' etc.
4. (D) वाक्य में प्रयुक्त 'by the train' के स्थान पर 'by train' का प्रयोग होगा। In phrases like; by train, by wa..., by bus etc. we should not make any change.
5. (C) वाक्य में प्रयुक्त 'bad habit' के स्थान पर 'bad habits' का प्रयोग होगा; क्योंकि 'one of', के बाद noun या pronoun के plural form का प्रयोग होता है।
6. (A) वाक्य में प्रयुक्त 'Myself and Ramanujam' के स्थान पर 'Ramanujam and I' का प्रयोग होगा।
7. (B) Change 'puzzled on' to 'puzzled over'. Wrong use of preposition.
8. (B) Change 'inferior than' to 'inferior to'.Wrong use of preposition; since -inferior, superior,senior, junior, prefer etc. take preposition 'to'instead of 'than'.
9. (B) Change 'complained at ' to 'complained about'.Wrong use of preposition.
10. (E) No Error.

Explanations (Ex.-9)

1. (C) Change 'what he has said' to 'what he said'; Wrong use of tense.
2. (A) Change 'Not only the bandits robbed ' to 'The bandits not only robbed'; Improper placement of conjunction.
3. (C) Change 'unless she does not have a strong desire to live' to 'unless she has a strong desire to live'. Avoid double negative .
4. (E) No Error.
5. (B) Change 'cent percent' to 'hundred percent'. 'Cent percent' is a wrong expression.
6. (C) Delete 'the' before church.Wrong use of article 'the'.Public institutions, जैसे–church, temple, hospital, mosque, school, prison,college etc. के पहले 'The' उसी स्थिति में प्रयुक्त है जब व्यक्ति इन स्थानों पर किसी अन्य उद्देश्य से visit किया करते हैं।
7. (B) अगर वाक्य से dislike, hesitation तथा risk का बोध हो, तो हमें verb infinitive के बदले gerund का प्रयोग करना चाहिए; अत: यहाँ 'talking to their teachers' होना चाहिए।
8. (A) Change 'would have' to 'had'. See the structure of conditional sentences.
9. (B) Change 'peak' to 'peaks'. After 'one of', the noun is pluralised in such sentences.
10. (C) Change 'student' to 'students'. After 'one of,' noun is pluralised in such sentences.

Explanations (Ex.-10)

1. (D) Change 'are ' to 'is'. When two nouns are joined by the conjunction; 'with', 'as well as', 'together with,' 'besides' etc., the verb should agree with the first noun ('Radha' in this case); इसी कारण वाक्य में 'are present here' के स्थान पर 'is present here' का प्रयोग होना चाहिए।
2. (A) Change 'men' to 'man'.
3. (C) Change 'early at' to 'early in'; Wrong use of preposition.
4. (E) No Error.
5. (A) Change 'worn' to 'wore'. 'Wore' is the past of 'wear'.
6. (E) No Error. 'None' can be used as singular and as plural also.
7. (D) Change 'from' to 'by'; Wrong use of preposition.
8. (B) Change 'a' to 'an'; Wrong use of article.
9. (A) Change 'love' to 'loved' or 'used to love'; Wrong use of verb tense.
10. (C) Change 'a duty cost' to 'a duty cast',

Explanations (Ex.-11)

1. (D) Change 'the time' to 'about the time'; Wrong use of preposition.
2. (A) Change 'How do' to 'How did'; Wrong use of tense verb.
3. (B) Change 'sometime' to 'sometimes'; Wrong use of word.
4. (D) Change 'police dog jump' to 'police dog jumping'.
5. (D) Change 'on the door' to 'at the door'; Wrong use of preposition.
6. (C) Change 'of' to 'off'. Wrong use of phrase.
7. (B) Change 'attitudes' to 'attitude'.
8. (B) Change 'from the hand' to 'by the hand'; Wrong use of verb phrase.
9. (D) Change 'for' to 'of'; Wrong use of preposition.
10. (D) Change 'her age' to 'at her age'.

Explanations (Ex.-12)

1. (B) Change 'taller' to 'tallest'; Wrong use of degree of adjective.
2. (C) Change 'who' to 'whom'; Wrong use of pronoun.
3. (C) Change 'or' to 'nor'; Wrong use of conjuctions.
4. (C) Change 'since' to 'for'; 'For' used for period of time.
5. (B) Change 'is decided' to 'are decided'. Here 'committee' is not used as collective noun (a unit).
6. No Error.
7. (C) Change 'in its preference on' to 'in its preference to'; Wrong use of Preposition. 'Preference' के पश्चात् preposition के रूप में 'to' का प्रयोग किया जाता है।
8. No Error.
9. (D) Change 'should like to acqire' to 'would like to acqire'.
10. (A) Change 'if you absent' to 'if you absent yourself'; 'Absent' is to be used reflexively.

Explanations (Ex.-13)

1. (A) Delete 'the'; Wrong use of definite article 'the'.
2. (C) Change ' are' to 'is'; Wrong use of verb. Here 'twenty five kilometers' is used as a unit, so singular verb is used.

3. (D) Change 'the French' to 'French'. Do not use definite article 'the' before name of a language.
4. (B) Change 'to meet' to 'to meeting'. Wrong use of infinitive.
5. (D) Change 'do you' to 'won't you'. It is a request.
6. (B) Change 'a mason' to 'the mason'. Wrong use of article.
7. (B) Change 'make from' to 'make out'. Wrong use of preposition or phrasal verb .
8. (B) Change 'you will think' to 'will you think'. Proper use of Inversion is necesary in questions.
9. No Error. यह वाक्य शुद्ध है।
10. (B) Change 'we reached there' to 'did we reached there'; Wrong use of inversion.

Explanations (Ex.-14)

1. (A) It should be '<u>It</u> being a very cold day'. This is the problem of dangling participle.
2. (C) Change 'be' to 'been'.
3. (C) Change 'will insist' to 'insist'. Do not use 'will' after 'if' in such conditional sentences.
4. (D) Delete 'had'. It should be 'Subhash Chandra Bose died'.
5. (C) Change 'is' to 'are'; Wrong use of singular verb . When two nouns are joined with the conjunction 'and' use plural verb.
6. (D) Delete 'the' before 'most'; Wrong use of article 'the'.
7. (D) Change 'keep <u>his</u>' to 'keep <u>their</u>'. Pronoun 'their' refers to 'those persons' not 'he'.
8. No Error.
9. (B) Change 'are' to 'is'. Wrong use of plural verb with singular subject 'box'.
10. (B) delete 'to' after 'inform'.

Explanations (Ex.-15)

1. (D) Change ' he <u>does</u> not do it ' to 'he <u>did</u> not do it'; Wrong use <u>of</u> tense .
2. (B) Change ' his best' to 'one's best'; Wrong use of pronoun; 'one' का posessive –**one's** होता है, न कि 'his' .
3. (A) Change 'deprived <u>from</u>' to 'deprived <u>of</u> '; Wrong use of preposition.
4. (C) Change 'throughly' to 'through'; Unnecessary use of adverb.
5. (B) Indirect speech में Interogative word के बाद subject आता है और फिर verb .So it should be : The villager told us where <u>the temple was</u> and even led us to the spot.
6. (D) Change 'than' to 'but'.
7. (E) No Error.
8. (C) Change 'to' to 'than'. 'Rather' के बाद 'than' का प्रयोग किया जाता है, न कि 'to' का।
9. (B) Change 'manages to play' to 'managed to play'; Wrong use of tense verb. वाक्य Past Tense structure पर आधारित है।
10. (C) Change 'to reinstated' to 'be reinstated'.

Explanations (Ex.-16)

1. (A) It should be 'Thinking that he <u>had</u> finally found'. The sentence is in past tense so to use present perfect is incorrect.
2. (C) It should be '<u>telecast</u> by a commercial television channel'.The past of 'telecast' is 'telecast'.
3. (C) It should be 'that you have <u>made</u> a mistake' or 'you have <u>committed</u> a mistake'.
4. (B) It should be 'he <u>has</u> six houses in Mumbai'. Generally the verb 'have' is not used in continuous form.
5. (B) It should be 'if I <u>was</u> ill'.If the reporting verb is in past , the tense of the reported speech should also be in past.

6. (C) It should be 'he had bought it'.For the action completed first , use past perfect tense.
7. (B) It should be 'is to reduce matter by an analysis'.Use article a/an before countables.
8. (C) It should be 'it was hardly ten'.'Hardly' has negative meaning. Avoid using double negative .
9. (C) It should be 'was deceived'.If two nouns are joined with; 'like, in addition to, together with', etc. the verb will be as per the first noun.
10. (C) It should be 'and were seeking a job'. Use past verb before 'seeking'.

Explanations (Ex.-17)

1. (A) Part (A) should be: 'As I prefer coffee to tea.' 'Prefer' always take preposition 'to'
2. No Error.
3. (B) Part (B) should be: '.....to find evidence.....'
4. No Error.
5. No Error.
6. (C) Change 'then' to 'than'. 'Than' is used here in conjunctions.
7. (B) Noun 'furniture' can't be pluralised as 'furnitures'. Part (B) should be : '.....with all the furniture.'
8. No Error.
9. (C) Insert definite article 'the'. 'the Ganges and the Himalayas.'
10. (B) Change to 'is the better.....' For the comparison of two, use comparative degree.

Explanations (Ex.-18)

1. (A) Change the part 'A' to, 'After he finished the work'.
2. (C) Change 'can' to 'could]; ' because they thought that they could now remove it with safety'.The sentence is in past tense.
3. (C) Insert 'the' before 'United Nations.'
4. (B) Change 'was' to 'were '.
5. (B) Part 'B' should be, 'he was addicted to reading the jokes in punch aloud.' Gerund form is used in such sentence structures.
6. (A) Use either 'first' or 'next' in the sentence .Part 'A' should be, 'Why not stop the first man you meet and ask' OR 'why not stop the man you meet next and ask'.
7. (C) 'Unique' cannot be compared. Part 'C' should be, 'a unique development'.
8. (A) 'Put out' means - to extinguish; Part 'A' should be, 'put out.'
9. (C) Part 'C' should be, 'on the deck of the ship.'
10. (A) Always use auxiliary 'had' after 'hardly'. Part 'A' should be, 'Hardly had the rains started'.

Explanations (Ex.-19)

1. (C) Change 'and not found out' to 'and are not found out' . Use of preposition is necessary here.
2. (B) Change 'different' to 'differently'. Incorrect use of verb in place of adverb.
3. (C) Change 'leading the blinds' to 'leading the blind'. The 'blind' means 'the blind people'.
4. (A) Change 'took to drink' to 'took to drinking' .
5. (C) Change 'lot of money' to 'a lot of money'. 'A lot of' is a phrase.
6. (A) Change 'broadcasted' to 'broadcast.' Broadcast is the past of 'broadcast'.
7. (A) Change 'much' to 'many'. 'Much' is used for uncountables.
8. (A) Change 'What could have provoked him' to 'What provoked him'; Incorrect use of perfect tense.
9. (A) Change 'They were rich Zamindars in thirties'. to 'They had been rich Zamindars in thirties'.
10. (C) Change 'as well as' to 'and'; Incorrect use of conjunction as well as.

Explanations (Ex.-20)

1. (B) Change 'broadcasted' to 'broadcast' .
2. (B) Change 'how <u>could she</u> kill ' to 'how <u>she could</u> kill '; Incorrect use of inversion in indirect speech.
3. (A) Change 'While walking slowly in the park', to 'While <u>he was</u> walking slowly in the park'. This is a problem of unrelated participle.
4. (B) Change 'travelling <u>became</u> very pleasant.' to 'travelling <u>has become</u> very pleasant.'; Incorrect use of tense.
5. (B) Change 'exposes' to 'expose'; Incorrect use of singular verb.
6. (C) Change 'and to <u>have remembered</u> for' to 'and <u>to remember for</u>'. Incorrect use of perfect tense.
7. (C) Change 'we <u>have</u> been looking for' to 'we <u>had</u> been looking for'; Incorrect use of tense.
8. (C) Change 'look <u>up</u> the marketing' to 'look <u>after</u> the marketing'; Incorrect use of phrasal verb.
9. (B) Change 'have <u>overflown</u>' to ' have <u>overflowed</u>'. Incorrect use of Tense. Part (B) should be 'and the rivers have overflowed their banks'.
10. (B) Change 'persist' to 'persisted'. The sentence structure is in past.

Explanations (Ex.-21)

1. (D) Change 'it <u>is</u> really made' to 'it <u>was</u> really made'; Incorrect use of tense in indirect speech.
2. (B) Change '<u>has</u> no dearth of' to '<u>have</u> no dearth of'; Incorrect use of verb.
3. (C) Change 'than' to 'when'; Incorrect use of 'than' with 'scarcely'.
4. (B) Change 'if I <u>would have</u> realised' to 'if I <u>had</u> realised'. See the structure of conditional sentences.
5. (A) Change '<u>I am trying</u>' to 'I <u>have been</u> trying'; Incorrect use of tense.
6. (B) Change 'but he turned it <u>over</u>' to 'but he turned it <u>down</u>'; Incorrect use of phrasal verb.
7. (B) Change '<u>for</u> the wall below' to '<u>against</u> the wall below'; Incorrect use of preposition.
8. (A) Change 'criteria' to 'criterion'; 'Criteria' is plural of 'criterion'.
9. (B) Change 'will' to 'would'; The sentence structure is in past.
10. (A) Delete 'for'; Incorrect use of preposition

Explanations (Ex.-22)

1. (A) Change 'principal' to 'principle'; Incorrect use of word.
2. (D) Change 'future <u>programmes</u>' to '<u>its</u> future <u>programme</u>'.
3. (A) Change 'Honesty, integrity and being <u>intelligent</u>' to 'Honesty, integrity and <u>intelligence</u>' .
4. (B) Change 'must have to' to 'have to' or 'must'.
5. (C) Change 'which' to 'who'.'Who' is used for living persons.
6. (B) Change 'sang ' to 'sung'. Incorrect past participle of verb.
7. (C) Change '<u>was able to</u> dampen' to '<u>could</u> dampen'.
8. (B) Change '<u>enough</u> money' to '<u>any</u> money'.
9. (C) Change 'were <u>overlook</u>' to 'were <u>overlooked</u>' . In passive structure, third form of the verb is used .
10. (D) Change 'hostilities <u>of</u> that area' to 'hostilities <u>in</u> that area' .

Explanations (Ex.-23)

1. (C) Change 'was' to ' had'; Incorrect use of tense.
2. (A) Change ' to keep maintaining ' to ' to maintaining' .
3. (A) Change 'Being the second ' to 'It being the second'.It is a problem of unrelated participle.
4. No Error.
5. (A) Change 'Such of those who have not paid the fees' to ' They who have not paid the fees' .
6. (C) Insert 'himself' after 'avail'. 'Avail' is used reflexively.
7. (B) Change 'for' to 'of'; '.... of their health...'
8. (C) Omit 'about'; Part (B) should be : '....anything left to discuss.'
9. (B) Change pronoun 'you' to 'he'. Part (B) should be : '..... where he was.'
10. (C) Part (C) should be : '..... till you finish your work.' In such type of sentences, don't use 'will' after 'when , as soon as, till , after, as,' etc.

Explanations (Ex.-24)

1. (A) 'swam'की जगह 'swum' का प्रयोग होगा, क्योंकि 'swim' की Third form, 'swum' होती है।
2. (B) 'more' का प्रयोग नहीं होगा, क्योंकि Double comparatives का प्रयोग वाक्य में नहीं किया जाता है। Avoid using double compartives in a sentence.
3. (D) 'a'की जगह 'the'का प्रयोग होगा। 'with the naked eyes' is correct expression .
4. (A) 'advices'की जगह 'advice' का प्रयोग होगा; यहाँ 'advice' Uncontable Noun है। We cannot pluralise 'advice' as such (Advices).
5. (B) 'they' के बाद 'have' का प्रयोग नहीं होगा। This is a conditional sentence with following structure : 'Had they invited me, I would have attended the function.'
6. (B) 'is'की जगह 'was'होगा, क्योंकि Indirect Narration में है; और क्योंकि Reporting verb Past Tense में है, अत: Reported speech में भी Past Tense का प्रयोग होगा।
7. (B) 'don't' के बदले 'doesn't' का प्रयोग होगा। क्योंकि 'He' के साथ 'does not' का प्रयोग होता है, 'do not' का नहीं।
8. (B) 'are' की जगह 'was' का प्रयोग होगा। The sentence structure is in Past Tense.
9. (A) 'cattles'की जगह 'cattle' का प्रयोग होगा क्योंकि 'cattle' स्वयं plural noun है।
10. (B) 'than' की जगह 'to' का प्रयोग होगा। Superior, Senior, Junior, Inferior, Prior के साथ 'to' preposition प्रयुक्त होता है।

Explanations (Ex.-25)

1. (C) 'not'का प्रयोग नहीं होगा; **Avoid double negative.** 'Lest' का अर्थ ही negative होता है।
2. (C) 'to' के पहले 'how' का प्रयोग होगा। ध्यान दें इस तरह के वाक्यों में 'know' के बाद 'how/when/where/what' आदि में से अर्थ के अनुसार किसी एक का प्रयोग कर, infinitive का प्रयोग करते हैं, जैसे :
   (i) I do not know how to swim .
   (ii) I don't know how to play carrom.
   (iii) I do not know where to go.
3. (B) 'more'का प्रयोग नहीं होगा। क्योंकि Double Comparatives का प्रयोग वाक्य में नहीं किया जाता है; जैसे : He is stronger than you. (न कि more stronger)
4. No Error.

5. (D) 'good' की जगह 'well' का प्रयोग होगा; क्योंकि यह 'Work'(verb) की विशेषता बतलाता है, और यह काम एक Adverb ही कर सकता है, न कि Adjective. 'Well' एक Adverb है तथा 'good' एक adjective है। Adjective qualifies a noun.
6. (C) 'as well as'के स्थान पर 'and का प्रयोग होगा। The structure of the sentence is, 'Both ..... and'.
7. (B) 'resemble' के बाद 'to' का प्रयोग नहीं होगा। Always remember that, resemble is a Transitive Verb। अत: इसके बाद सीधे Object का प्रयोग किया जाता है। इसके बाद prepositions का प्रयोग गलत है।
8. (A) 'the two first'की जगह 'the first two' होगा, क्योंकि जब Ordinal Number (जैसे-first,second, third, last आदि) और Cardinal number (जैसे-one, two, three, four आदि) दोनों का प्रयोग एक साथ करना हो तो पहले Ordinal और तब Cardinal आता है।
9. (C) 'country' 'की जगह 'countries' का प्रयोग होगा; 'one of', 'most of' के बाद आने वाला NOUN Plural होता है।
10. (C)'than'की जगह 'when'का प्रयोग होगा। 'Hardly', 'Scarcely' के बाद conjunction 'when'का प्रयोग होगा। जैसे-(i) Hardly/ scarcely had she left the hotel when it began to rain.

Explanations (Ex.-26)

1. (B) 'he wrote' की जगह 'he had written'का प्रयोग होगा। जब Direct Narration में Reporting Verb, Past Tense में हो तथा Reported Speech में Simple past का प्रयोग हो तो Indirect Narration में Reported Speech को Past Perfect में बदला जाता है।
2. (D) 'one' पर 's (Apostrophe) का प्रयोग होगा। सही expression होगा-'one's living'.
3. (A) 'to'का प्रयोग Superfluous (अनावश्यक) है।
4. (A) 'do not'का प्रयोग गलत है। 'unless, until' के साथ 'Not' का प्रयोग नहीं होगा; 'unless' is itself negative.
5. (B) 'read' के पहले 'had' का प्रयोग होगा,क्योंकि जब Past की दो घटनाओं का वर्णन हो जिनमें एक पहले तथा दूसरी बाद में घटी हो, तो पहली घटना के लिए Past Perfect तथा दूसरी के लिऐ Past Indefinite Tense का प्रयोग करते हैं, जैसे :
   (i) After he had reached the station , the train arrived.
   (ii) The patient had died before the doctor reached here.
6. (C) 'other'का प्रयोग superfluous (अनावश्यक) है।
7. (C) 'has' की जगह 'have'का प्रयोग होगा; वाक्य का Subject "The issues' है जो कि Plural है।
8. (D) 'its'की जगह'a' का प्रयोग होना चाहिए; 'for a picnic' is correct phrase.
9. (B) 'snowed' की जगह 'snows' का प्रयोग होगा; क्योंकि 'Tomorrow' future को सूचित करता है, जबकि 'snowed', Verb 'snow' का Past है, जो Past Tense में प्रयुक्त होता है। The use of future and past tense like this is an incorrect combination.
10. (A) 'between' की जगह 'among'का प्रयोग होगा। 'between' is used for two and 'among' for more than two.

Explanations (Ex.-27)

1. (A) 'swam'की जगह 'swum' का प्रयोग होगा, क्योंकि 'swim' की Third form 'swum' होती है।
2. (B) 'more' का प्रयोग नहीं होगा, क्योकि Double comparatives का प्रयोग वाक्य में नहीं किया जाता है। Avoid using double compartives in a sentence.
3. (D) 'their' की जगह 'his'का प्रयोग होगा। With 'Everyone, Everybody, Anyone, Anybody'always use singular possessive pronoun(his or her).

4. (B) 'on' की जगह 'of' Preposition का प्रयोग होगा।
5. (C) 'hung' की जगह 'hanged' का प्रयोग होगा। Verb 'hang' has two forms and two meanings as per following:

	First form	Second form	Third form
(i)	Hang (लटकाना)	hung	hung
(ii)	Hang (फाँसी देना)	hanged	hanged

यही कारण है, कि 'hang' की V-I form और V-III form के रूप में confusion होता है।

(6) (B) 'will' की जगह 'would' का प्रयोग होगा; The reporting verb is in past.

(7) (B) 'refrain' के बाद 'with' का प्रयोग नहीं होगा, बल्कि 'from' का होगा, क्योंकि 'refrain, abstain, prohibit' आदि के बाद 'from' का प्रयोग होता है।

(8) (C) 'to' के बाद 'that of' का प्रयोग होगा, क्योंकि comparision 'the Indian way' तथा 'the way of most of the countries' के बीच है।

(9) (A) 'none' की जगह neither का प्रयोग होगा। दो व्यक्तियों या वस्तुओं के लिए 'neither' का प्रयोग होता है, जबकि दो से अधिक के लिए 'none' का प्रयोग होता है।

(10) (B) 'where had I की जगह 'where I had' का प्रयोग होगा। In Indirect narration the sentence changes from interrogative to affirmative.

Explanations (Ex.-28)

1. (B) 'homes' की जगह 'home' का प्रयोग होगा, क्योंकि 'at home' एक phrase है।
2. (E) वाक्य सही है।
3. (B) 'a' की जगह 'the' प्रयोग होगा। Superlative degree के Adjective से पहले 'the' का प्रयोग होता है।
4. (A) 'is' की जगह 'was' का प्रयोग होगा, क्योंकि 'in 1929' से Past time का बोध होता है। The whole sentence reflects action in the past.
5. (A) 'Being' के पहले 'It' का प्रयोग होगा। This is the prolem of unrelated participle.
6. (B) 'have' की जगह 'has' का प्रयोग होगा। 'Many a' के बाद singular noun and singular verb का प्रयोग होता है जैसे :
   (i) Many a <u>pen</u> is on the <u>stool</u>.
   (ii) Many a person comes here daily.
7. (B) 'is' का प्रयोग 'a digital computer' के बाद होगा; This is an assertive sentence, not an interrogative one.See the following examples:
   (i) I do not know where he lives (न कि, 'Where does he live' ?).
   (ii) I know what he says (न कि, 'What does he say' ?).
8. (C) 'you'll pay' के बदले 'you pay' होगा; जब principal clause में Future Indefinite Tense हो, तो Subordinate clause में Simple Present का प्रयोग होता है।
9. (C) 'Purchase' की जगह 'Purchased' का प्रयोग होगा; This is a conditional sentence with the following structure : Had + Sub + V–3 .... + would have + V–3 ....
10. (E) वाक्य शुद्ध है।

Explanations (Ex.-29)

1. (B) 'will'की जगह 'would'का प्रयोग होगा; When the sentence reflects an action in the past, it is incorrect to use 'will' .
2. (B) 'from' का प्रयोग Superfluous है।
3. (A) 'help'के पहले 'to'का प्रयोग नहीं होगा।
4. (B) 'has' की जगह 'had'का प्रयोग होगा; Reporting Verb में Past Tense का प्रयोग है, अत: Indirect narration में Reported Speech में Present Perfect का प्रयोग नहीं होगा, Past Perfect का प्रयोग होगा।
5. (A) 'need' की जगह 'needs'का प्रयोग होगा; वाक्य का Subject 'our' country' Singular Number में है।
6. (A) 'Instead of' की जगह 'In spite of'का प्रयोग होगा, क्योंकि 'Instead of' का अर्थ है-'के बदले में', किन्तु 'In spite of' का अर्थ है-'के बावजूद'।
7. (B) 'for' की जगह 'to' का प्रयोग होगा, क्योंकि 'yield' के बाद 'to' preposition का प्रयोग होता है।
8. (D) 'than'की जगह 'to' का प्रयोग होगा। Remember : use 'to' after; 'senior, junior, prefer, prior' instead of 'than'.
9. (B) 'last' की जगह 'latter' का प्रयोग होगा, क्योंकि दो व्यक्तियों या वस्तुओं के क्रम को बताने के लिए 'latter' का प्रयोग किया जाता है, किन्तु दो से अधिक व्यक्तियों या वस्तुओं के क्रम को बताने के लिए 'last' का प्रयोग होता है, जैसे :
   (i) Ramesh and Surersh are friends. The latter is an engineer.
   (ii) Ramesh, Suresh and Middha are friends. The last is a banker.
10. (B) 'surprised' के पहले were का प्रयोग होगा। This is a Passive structure.

Explanations (Ex.-30)

1. (C) 'eastern के पहले 'the' का प्रयोग होगा।
2. (B) 'who do I want ' के बदले 'whom I wanted ' का प्रयोग होगा; चूंकि वाक्य में Reporting Verb (asked), Past Tense में है, अत: Reported speech में भी Past Tense का ही प्रयोग होगा। In indirect narration the sentence changes to affirmative.
3. (C) 'with' की जगह 'to' का प्रयोग होगा।
4. (C) 'will' की जगह 'would' का प्रयोग होगा, क्योंकि वाक्य में Reporting verb' (she) 'said' Past Tense में है। The tense of the reported speech changes accordingly.
5. (C) 'are' की जगह 'am'का प्रयोग होगा। जब दो Subjects – Either....... or, Neither .... nor, Not only....... but also से जुड़ते हैं, तो Verb पास वाले Subject अनुसार प्रयुक्त होता है।
6. (D) 'than'की जगह 'to'का प्रयोग होगा, क्योंकि preferable, senior, junior, superior, inferior, prior, anterior, posterior etc. के बाद 'to' का प्रयोग किया जाता है, जैसे :
   (i) They are senior to me (न कि 'than me').
   (ii) I prefer tea to coffee.
7. (E) Sentence is correct.
8. (C) 'Then' का प्रयोग superfluous (अनावश्यक) है; As, Because, Since, As soon as के बाद- therefore, so, then, आदि का प्रयोग नहीं किया जाता है।
9. (E) वाक्य शुद्ध है।
10. (D) 'any' के बाद 'other' का प्रयोग होगा।

Explanations (Ex.-31)

1. (A) 'Being' की जगह 'that, because, since, as' आदि में से किसी एक का प्रयोग होगा; In this question Being is used in place of– that or because or since or as.
2. (A) 'is' की जगह 'was' का प्रयोग होगा। The sentence reflects an action in the past .
3. (A) 'his' की जगह 'one's' का प्रयोग होगा, क्योंकि 'one' का Possessive 'one's' होता है।
4. (A) 'under' की जगह 'in' preposition का प्रयोग होगा; Sit <u>in the shade</u> of a tree तथा Sit <u>under a tree</u> होता है।
5. (C) 'was' की जगह 'is' का प्रयोग होगा, क्योंकि वाक्य Present Tense (It is summer......) में है।
6. (E) वाक्य शुद्ध है।
7. (E) वाक्य शुद्ध है।
8. (A) 'No sooner' के बाद 'had' का प्रयोग होगा, क्योंकि 'No sooner' के बाद Auxiliary verb प्रयोग करना आवश्यक है। This is an example of inversion.
9. (A) 'fled'के बाद 'away' का प्रयोग Superfluous (अनावश्यक) है, क्योंकि 'fled'का अर्थ ही 'run away' होता है। This is an example of superfluous expression.

Explanations (Ex.-32)

1. (B) 'is having की जगह 'has का प्रयोग होगा। Possession बताने वाले verbs (जैसे- own, possess, have, belong आदि) का प्रयोग Continuous Tense में नही होता है, बल्कि Simple present में होता है।
2. (C) 'as' की जगह का 'that' का प्रयोग होगा, क्योंकि वाक्य का structure–'so........that' पर आधारित है। देखें :

   (i) He is so poor that he cannot buy a pen.

   (ii) She is so weak that she cannot climb up the stairs.
3. (C) 'Governor chamber' की जगह 'Governor's chamber' का प्रयोग होगा। This is the question of the use of apostrophe.
4. (C) 'has' की जगह 'have' का प्रयोग होगा, क्योंकि वाक्य का Subject – 'Congress dissidents and a wide range'है, जो Plural Number में है। If the suject is plural, the verb is plural.
5. (A) 'would have' की जगह 'had' का प्रयोग होगा। This is a conditional sentence with specific structure: If + Sub + had + V–III + Would have + V–III.
6. (D) 'were' की जगह 'was'का प्रयोग होगा। जब दो Subjects – 'with,as well as, along with, in addition to, besides, together with' आदि से जुड़ते हैं, तो Verb इन Conjuctions के पहले आने वाले Subject के Numberऔर Person पर निर्भर करता है। If this subect is singular, verb is singular; If subject is plural, verb is plural.
7. (A) 'No' के बाद 'other'का प्रयोग करना पड़ेगा। While making comparison, the item (being compared) is required to be excluded; eg.

   No other girl of this class is so/ as beautiful as Rani.
8. (C) 'have' की जगह 'had' का प्रयोग होगा; Reporting Verb Past Tense में है।
9. (C) 'have' की जगह 'has' का प्रयोग होगा, क्योंकि वाक्य का Subject – 'A letter' Singular Number में है।
10. (B) 'kilogram' के पहले 'a' का प्रयोग होगा, क्योंकि kilogram एक countable Noun है।

PRACTICE TEST (*MISCELLANEOUS*) EXERCISES

Rewrite the sentences after correction.

Exercise-1

1. His father gave him many advices.
2. The boys went to the college directly.
3. I am much pleased to see you both.
4. He has just returned back from London.
5. Because he does not work hard, therefore he will fail.
6. He does not know wrong from right.
7. The English is difficult to speak.
8. What to speak of food, even water was not available there.
9. Bible is a sacred book of Christians.
10. I am much thankful to you for this act of kindness.

Exercise-2

1. This book gives us many informations about Prithvi Raj.
2. The furnitures of office house are very costly.
3. He is one of the best poet the world has ever produced.
4. He asked from me that I had gone there or no.
5. Where you spent your last summer vacations?
6. The hen has lain two eggs.
7. He enjoys very bad health.
8. He never said anything of the kind.
9. I should be glad if you will come in the evening.
10. I am the one who am to blame.

Exercise-3

1. At his sight I trembled with fear.
2. We should pray God every day.
3. Open your book on page 78.
4. He was born in nineteen hundreds ten.
5. The subject to her essay is about politeness.
6. As I am ill, so I will not be able to attend office today.
7. I do not know who are you.
8. So quickly we walked that we reached the station in time.
9. I neither met Gopal or his sister.
10. English is not only difficult to read, but also to write.

Exercise-4

1. It is half past six in my watch.
2. He is true to his words.
3. The magistrate passed order for his an acquittal.
4. His family members have gone to Kashmir.
5. The examination begins from Monday.
6. He hesitated in complying with my request.
7. He was displeased at Mira going to the theatre last night.
8. He was angry at me not complying with his request.
9. Health is more preferable than riches.
10. His claim is prior than yours.

Exercise-5

1. He is the most happiest man living on this earth.
2. The elephant is larger than any animal.
3. Akbar was wiser than any king.
4. No girl in the class is so intelligent as Kanika.
5. This book is as good or even better than yours.
6. He is the worthiest and sympathetic man in the town.

7. He has been suffering from fever from Tuesday last.
8. He has been ill since ten days.
9. I have not seen him since a long time.
10. His brother died since a fortnight.

Exercise-6

1. We shall not be here before two months.
2. You must finish this work before two hours.
3. I except a letter from her in a week.
4. I received his letter long before.
5. The train will arrive just now.
6. Character, and not riches, win us respect.
7. Every flower and every leaf proclaim the glory of God.
8. The sum and substance of her speech are as follow.
9. Fifty rupees are not a large sum for that. painting.
10. Aesop's Fables are book everybody should read.

Exercise-7

1. The majority was present at the meeting.
2. The committee was divided in its opinions.
3. None but those having a teaching experience needs apply.
4. It were the girls that defied their teacher's orders.
5. Every one should be careful of one's health.
6. Neither the students nor the principal was there.
7. Walking along the Mall Road, his head dashed against a lamppost.
8. Being a fine day, they went to the river to enjoy a picnic.
9. Failing in the first attempt, no second attempt was made.
10. He has an urgent business at home.

Exercise-8

1. Ramesh has many businesses today.
2. There was not any temple there but I visited.
3. He as well as I am wrong.
4. We have come here to take your leave.
5. I cannot endure her separation.
6. Do you know who are you referring to?
7. You should follow their advice who are superior to you in intellect.
8. He dares not to speak against me.
9. I was greatly wondered at what met my eyes.
10. I admitted my brother to the D.A.V. College.

Exercise-9

1. He took admission in to the D.A.V. High School.
2. She did nothing but sang.
3. I am feeling feverish.
4. I intend to inform his misbehavior to his father.
5. Please excuse me for giving you this trouble.
6. He told these news to his mother.
7. Her arguments hold no water
8. Many kinds of fruits grow in Kashmir, such as apples, plums, pears, cherries, etc.
9. With regard my conduct, I beg to submit as follows.

Exercise-10

1. He packed his luggages.
2. He provided the blinds with food and clothes.
3. Scouts wear half pants.
4. There is no place in this compartment.
5. Give my B.C's to all.
6. He hit an over-boundary.
7. He saw a joker at the circus.
8. We had a good play of hockey.
9. I saw a theatre last night.
10. Won't you like to take part in drama?

Exercise-11

1. He is a tall gentleman.
2. These females have come here to take your advice.
3. He got a bad companionship.
4. Here is my cup; please fill.
5. I asked for my book, but he did not give me.
6. The boy who stand first he will get a prize.
7. I with some friend went for a walk.
8. The master tested the boy if he could speak English.
9. He is elder than me.
10. He will spend his remaining life here.

Exercise-12

1. This is a worth seeing building.
2. He got nearly cent percent marks.
3. He got an employment in a Nationalised Bank.
4. You should not make noise.
5. What a fun!
6. I do not care for you.
7. He does not care for his money.
8. He got angry before I said a word
9. If I would have worked hard, I would have passed.
10. I left playing.

Exercise-13

1. I take my food.
2. I want that I should get leave.
3. I like to play football.
4. He is troubling me.
5. He gave a speech.
6. He would not hear me.
7. I cannot pull on with my work.
8. He has ordered for a new suit.
9. He has disposed off his bicycle.
10. I put up with him.

Exercise-14

1. Keep this on the table.
2. I had a mind to play.
3. He cannot maintain his livelihood.
4. I struck a blow on his face.
5. He is reading at the High School.
6. He won his opponents.
7. They made a goal.
8. I hope she must come.
9. The committee is consisted of fifteen members.
10. Always fair out a written exercise.

Exercise-15

1. Open the light.
2. Shut the light.
3. His hand has been operated.
4. It is written in this letter that ....
5. He was very kind enough to comply with my request.
6. He did it anyhow.
7. To tell in brief ....
8. He told the story in details.
9. This book is much interesting.
10. He behaved cowardly.

Exercise-16

1. He lives miserly.
2. Never I had seen such a sight.
3. Though he is old, still he can run fast.
4. As he is old so he walks slowly.
5. If he works hard then he will pass.
6. Because he is clever therefore he gets good marks.
7. He did not attend the meeting because he was ill.
8. Until he does not apologizes, he must not be allowed to sit in the class.
9. No sooner I had reached the station, than the train started.
10. Not only he will go, but also he will stay there.

Exercise-17

1. Neither she comes nor she writes.
2. I am fond of all game as for an example tennis.
3. I want to know as to why I have not been allowed to sit in the examination.
4. He called her as a fool.
5. Supposing if he fails, What will he do?
6. He is ill since three months.
7. He wrote me a long letter.
8. I shall explain him this.
9. Send this letter on my address.
10. He suggested me this.

Exercise-18

1. He goes in the school.
2. He goes on his work.
3. He was favourite to his friends.
4. I did not ask any question to him.
5. From our class he did best.
6. The term begins from June 1st.
7. He will be cured from his fever.
8. There are many advantages from this.
9. He wasted much time in trifles.
10. There is a saying in Hindus.

Exercise-19

1. There is no harm to go there.
2. Write with ink.
3. He rides on a car.
4. This is a comfortable house to live.
5. This is the road to go.
6. I gave her a chair to sit.
7. He is called with different names.
8. He went away for doing some business.
9. We discussed about the matter.
10. When this was searched it was found.

Exercise-20

1. Due to illness, I can not go to school.
2. He walked all the way by foot.
3. The Bank will compensate the loss of the cheque.
4. I must go; there is no help.
5. There was a match between Delhi against Jaipur.
6. No mention.
7. He is running thirty.
8. In my opinion I think it is right.
9. In the way I met a woman.
10. It has its origin from a story in Ramayana.
11. We sat under the shade of a mango tree.
12. Tears streamed on her cheeks.
13. The match starts from four o'clock.
14. The holidays will commence from June the 20th.

Explanations (Ex.-1)

1. His father gave him many pieces of advice.
2. The boys went to the college direct.
3. I am very pleased to see both of you.
4. He has just returned from London.
5. He does not work hard, therefore he will fail.
   Or
   Because he does not work hard, he will fail.
6. He does not know right from wrong.
7. English is difficult to speak.
8. Not to speak of food, even water was not available there.
9. The Bible is a sacred book of the Christians.
10. I am very thankful to you for this act of kindness.

Explanations (Ex.-2)

1. This book gives us much information about Prithvi Raj.
2. The furniture of this office is very costly.
3. He is one of the best poets the world has ever produced.
4. He asked me whether I had gone there or not.
5. Where did you spend you last summer vacation?
6. The hen has laid two eggs.
7. He has very bad health.
8. He said nothing of the kind.
9. I should be glad if you would come in the evening.
10. I am the one who is to blame.

Explanations (Ex.-3)

1. At the sight of him I trembled with fear.
2. We should pray to God every day.
3. Open your book at page 78.
4. He was born in nineteen hundred and ten.
5. The subject of her essay is "Politeness".
6. As I am ill, I will not be able to attend office today.
7. I do not know who you are.
8. So quickly did we walk that we reached the station in time.
9. I met neither Gopal nor his sister.
10. English is difficult not only to read, but also to write.

Explanations (Ex.-4)

1. It is half past six by my watch.
2. He is true to his word.
3. The magistrate passed orders for his acquittal.
4. The members of his family have gone to Kashmir.
5. The examination begins on Monday.
6. He hesitated to comply with my request.
7. He was displeased at Mira's going to the theatre last night.
8. He was angry at my not complying with his request.
9. Heath is preferable to riches.
10. His claim is prior to yours.

Explanations (Ex.-5)

1. He is the happiest man living on this earth.
2. The elephant is larger than any other animal.
3. Akbar was wiser than any other king.
4. No other girl in the class is so intelligent as Kanika.
5. This book is as good as or even better than yours.
6. He is the worthiest and most sympathetic man in the town.
7. He has been suffering from fever since Tuesday last.
8. He has been ill for ten days.
9. I have not seen him for a long time.
10. His brother died a fortnight since.

Explanations (Ex.-6)

1. We shall not be here for two months.
2. You must finish this work within two hours.
3. I expect a letter for her in a week.
4. I received his letter long ago.
5. The train will arrive soon.
6. Character, and not riches, wins us respect.

7. Every flower and every leaf proclaims the glory of God.
8. The sum and substance of her speech is as follows.
9. Fifty rupees is not a large sum for that painting.
10. Aesop's Fables is a book every body should read.

Explanations (Ex.-7)

1. The majority were present at the meeting.
2. The committee were divided in their opinions.
3. None but those having teaching experience need apply.
4. It was the girls that defied their teacher's orders.
5. Every one should be careful of his heath.
6. Neither the principal nor the students were there.
7. As he was walking along the Mall Road, his head dashed against the lamp-post.
8. It being a fine day, they went to the river to enjoy a picnic.
9. Failing in the first attempt, he made no second attempt.
10. He has an urgent piece of business at home.

Explanations (Ex.-8)

1. Ramesh has much business today.
2. There was no temple there that I did not visit.
3. He is wrong as well as I.
4. We have come here to take leave of you.
5. I cannot endure separation from her.
6. Do you know whom you are referring to?
7. You should follow the advice of those who are superior to you in intellect.
8. He dares not speak against me.
9. I was greatly astonished at what met my eyes.

   Or I wondered greatly at what met my eyes.
10. I got my brother admitted to the D.A.V. College.

Explanations (Ex.-9)

1. He was admitted to the D.A.V. High School.
2. She did nothing but sing.
3. I feel feverish.
4. I intend to inform his father of his misbehavior.
5. Please excuse me for the trouble I am giving you.
6. He told his mother this news.
7. Her arguments will not hold water.
8. Many kinds of fruit, such as apples, pears, plums and cherries, grow in Kashmir.

   Or Many kinds of fruit-apples, pears, plums, cherries, etc. grow in Kashmir.
9. With regard to my conduct I beg to submit as follows.

Explanations (Ex.-10)

1. He packed his luggage.
2. He provided the blind with food and clothes.
3. Scouts wear shorts.
4. There is no room in this compartment.
5. Give my (kind) regards to all.
6. He hit a six.
7. We saw a clown at the circus.
8. We had a good game of hockey.
9. I saw a play last night.
10. Won't you like to act in the drama ?

Explanations (Ex.-11)

1. He is a tall man.
2. These women have come here to take your advice.
3. He got into bad company.
4. Here is my cup; please fill it.
5. I asked for my book, but he did not give it to me.
6. The boy who stands first will get a prize.
7. I went for a walk with some friends.
8. The master tested if the boy could speak English.
9. He is elder to me.
10. He will spend the rest of his life here.

Explanations (Ex.-12)

1. This is a building worth seeing.
2. He got nearly full marks.
3. He got employment in a Nationalised Bank.
4. You should not make a noise.
5. What fun !
6. I do not care what you do.
7. He does not take care of his money.
8. He got angry before I had said a word.
9. If I had worked hard, I would have passed.
10. I stopped playing.

Explanations (Ex.-13)

1. I have my food.
2. I want to get leave.
3. I want to play football.
4. He is giving me trouble.
5. He made a speech.
6. He would not listen to me.
7. I cannot manage my work.
8. He has ordered a new suite.
9. He has disposed of his bicycle.
10. I stayed with him.

Explanations (Ex.-14)

1. Put this on the table.
2. I intended to play.
3. He cannot earn a living.
4. I gave him a blow on the face.
Or I struck him in the face.
5. He is at the High School.
6. He beat his opponents.
7. They scored a goal.
8. I hope she will come.or She must come.
9. The committee consists of fifteen members.
10. Always make a fair copy of a written exercise.

Explanations (Ex.-15)

1. Turn on the light.
2. Turn off the light.
3. His hand has been operated upon.
4. This letter says that...
5. He was kind enough to comply with my request.
6. He managed to do it somehow.
7. In short....
8. He told the story in detail.
9. This book is very interesting.
10. He behaved in a cowardly manner.
Or He behaved like a coward.

Explanations (Ex.-16)

1. He lives in a miserly way.
2. Never had I seen such a sight.
3. Though he is old, yet he can run fast.
4. As he is old, he walks slowly.
5. If he works hard, he will pass.
6. Because he is clever, he gets high marks.
7. He did not attend the meetting because he was ill.
8. He must not be allowed to sit in the class until he apologizes.

9. No sooner had I reached the station than the train started.

10. He will not only go but also stay there.

Explanations (Ex.-17)

1. Neither does she come nor does she write.
2. I am fond of all games, for example, tennis.
3. I want to know why I have not been allowed to take the examination.
4. He called her a fool.
5. Supposing he fails, what will he do?

   Or If he fails, what will he do?
6. He has been ill for there months.
7. He wrote a !ong letter to me.
8. I shall explain this to him.
9. Send this letter at my address.
10. He suggested this to me.

Explanations (Ex.-18)

1. He goes to school.
2. He goes to his work.
3. He was a favourite with his friends.
4. I did not ask him any question.
5. He did best in our class.
6. The term begins on June 1.
7. He will be cured of his fever.
8. The advantages of this are many.
9. He wasted much time on trifles.
10. There is a saying among the Hindus.

Explanations (Ex.-19)

1. There is no harm in going there.
2. Write in ink.
3. He rides in a car.
4. This is a comfortable house to live in.
5. This is the road to go by.
6. I gave her a chair to sit on.
7. He is called by different names.
8. He went away on business.
9. We discussed the matter.
10. When this was searched for it was found.

Explanations (Ex.-20)

1. Because of illness, I cannot go to school.
2. He walked all the way on foot.
3. The Bank will compensate for the loss of the cheque.
4. I must go; there is no help for it.
5. There was a match between Delhi and Jaipur.
6. Please do not mention it.
7. He is in his thirtieth year. *Or* He is thirty.
8. In my opinion it is right.or I think it is right.
9. On the way I met a woman.
10. It has its origin in a story in the Ramayana.
11. We sat in the shade of a mango tree.
12. Tears streamed down her cheeks.
13. The match starts at four o'clock.
14. The holidays will commence on June 20.

PRACTICE TESTS (MISCELLANEOUS) EXERCISES

Exercise-1 : ***Find the errors in these quotations and correct them.***

1. Faith keeps many doubts in her pay. If I can not doubt, I should not believe.
2. No matter how bad things get you got to go on living, even if it will kill you.
3. As for death one gets used to it, even if it would be only other people's death you get used to.
4. No culture can live if it attempt to be exclusive.
5. They will say you are on the wrong road, if it would be your own.
6. A wise man admits his weaknesses. I would admit mine if I would have any.
7. If I am not willing to give 120 percent, somebody else would.
8. If I had been present at creation, I would give some useful hints.

9. If I did had my career over again? Maybe I'd say to myself, speed it up a little.
10. I would be a billionaire if I would want to be a selfish boss. That's not me.
11. If I repent of anything, it is very likely would be my good behaviour.
12. Miss a meal if you has to, but don't miss a book.
13. If I will spit, they will take my spit and frame it as great art.
14. If I had not started painting, I would raised chickens.
15. If it was not for dogs, some people would never went for a walk.
16. To buy books would be a good thing if we also can buy the time to read them.
17. Develop a passion for learning. If you did, you will never cease to grow.
18. Do something. If it work, do more of it. If it doesn't, do something else.
19. Do every act of your life as if it would be your last.
20. If I wasn't an actor, I will be a secret agent.

Exercise-2 : *Find the grammatical errors in conditionals in these quotations and correct.*

1. You must not blame me if I would talk to the clouds.
2. You can only be free if I will be free.
3. If you wants a thing done well, do it yourself.
4. If what happen does not make us richer, we must welcome it if it makes us wiser.
5. If it were not for hopes, the heart will break.
6. If it was a good script I will do it. And if it's a bad script, and they pay me enough, I'll do it.
7. If it looks like shit, smells like shit, mail it to your enemy... he would know what to do with it.
8. If it is not right, do not do it; if it was not true, do not say it.
9. If it fail, admit it frankly and try another. But above all, try something.
10. If I will play my best, I can win anywhere in the world against anybody.
11. If I will not be allowed to laugh in heaven, I don't want to go there.
12. If I were two-faced, will I be wearing this one?
13. If I die, I forgive you. If I shall live, we shall see.
14. If I could stop one heart from breaking, I shall not live in vain.
15. If I could not understand my friend's silence, I will never get to understand his words.
16. I wonder whether if I would have had an education I should have been more or less a fool than I am.
17. I don't jog, if I will die I want to be sick.
18. Every day is a gift - even if it will suck.
19. Believe and act as if it would be impossible to fail.
20. An idea was worth nothing if it has no champion.

Exercise-3 : *Find the grammatical errors in conditionals in these quotations and correct.*

1. We would accomplish many more things if we do not think of them as impossible.
2. No one would have doubted his ability to reign has he never been an emperor.
3. Never work before breakfast. If you had to work before breakfast, get your breakfast first.
4. My warning: If you don't drive your business you would be driven out of business.
5. Many people might have attained wisdom have they not assumed they already had it.
6. If youth would know; if age could.
7. If you think your boss is stupid, remember: you won't have a job if he was any smarter.
8. If you marry for money, you will surely have earned it.
9. If you will have to ask how much it costs, you can't afford it.

10. If you won't program yourself, life will program you!
11. If you do not care, your customer never would.
12. If you can counted your money, then you're not a rich man.
13. If you build a better mousetrap, you will have caught better mice.
14. If we spoke a different language, we would have perceived a somewhat different world.
15. If the blind lead the blind, both would fall into the ditch.
16. If I had no sense of humour, I would long ago commit suicide.
17. I won't belong to any organisation that would had me as a member.
18. I wish people that have trouble communicating just shut up!
19. I wish I would have the voice of Homer.
20. Advice is what we ask for when we already know the answer but wish we do not.

Exercise-4 : ***Find the errors in the following sentences. Briefly describe what is wrong and write the correct or improved version.***

1. A rentcharge is the right to receive an annual sum out of the income of land every year.
2. All of the solutions considered so far have only involved Legendre functions of even order.
3. Before spelling out exactly what this means, it is worth first asking whether translating machinery is necessarily irreversible.
4. Being in charge, the accusation was particularly annoying to me.
5. Finally, it enables the therapist to assess the effectiveness of his own clinical skills and, hopefully, to improve them in future.
6. He is a former student who I've not seen for years.
7. He is an unskilled labourer and works at odd jobs, but he don't do any of them very well.
8. However, there were other patients whose lives had ended by suicide.
9. I have now discussed the proposals for replacing all the computers with my colleagues.
10. It is felt that less people would be put off attending with other problems if the stigma of going to a clinic could be dispensed with.
11. It is just possible that you are one of those rare people who has never seriously tried to diet.
12. It may be open to challenge on certain grounds, i.e. if an emergency occurs.
13. It was the community in it's purest form.
14. It was thought necessary to determine legally that someone had attained the age when they were allowed to marry?
15. Jean Baptiste Lamarck (1744-1829) had supposed that the main cause of evolutionary change was because of the "inheritance of acquired character".
16. Kinship in these societies had to be completely different to what it was in capitalist society.
17. No matter what he says, he has and will always be in charge.
18. She could give a better response than that to I and to my friends.
19. The category of killings which has come to be known as involuntary manslaughter hasn't nothing to do with involuntariness.
20. The committee has not announced their decision yet.
21. The emphasis on revolution as ending every stage is, also, much more definately stated than in earlier works.
22. The esential feature of these results has been amply confirmed.
23. The experiment by Norcross (1958) which used a slightly different version of this procedure produced essentially the same outcome.

24. The first really useful realization of the Lie algebra of the Geroch group, was formulated by Kinnersley and Chitre (1977, 1978a, b).
25. The more aggressive technologies, those which need a great deal of energy and natural resources and cause extensive environmental pollution, represent a percentage of industrial production.
26. Jones and Smith argues that the problem began in December 1942.
27. At that time there were hardly any scholarly accounts of the period in question, the only really important biography was that of George V by Harold Nicolson.
28. The task - one that involved pedalling on a stationery bicycle - was equally demanding at all times.
29. They are, in fact, just the kind of things the natural philosopher might be interested in.
30. This has meant that elsewhere it has been very difficult to clearly assess the extent of the problem.
31. Though he has generally been considered anti-intellectual and disinterested in art theory, at this stage of his career he shared the concerns of his fellows of the Petit Boulevard for principles of colour.
32. When they were discussing the historical development which led to capitalism.

Exercise-5 : *Correct the errors / mistakes in the following sentences. The mistakes may be in; (a) grammar, (b) style, and (c) meaning.*

1. Although e-commerce is a modern phenomenon. It has become a valuable business tool.
2. I.T. is very common in business. It is very useful.
3. Computer science is the science of doing things with computers.
4. Zoology is the science of managing a zoo.
5. Although HKPU is in a convenient location, however the air pollution here is quite bad.
6. Engineering courses are more popular as IT courses.
7. The most busy students here are the third-year students.
8. There are a number of similarity between computing and business courses.
9. While Taiwan has a strong hardware industry, Hong Kong haven't.
10. E-mail is the most popular program on the Internet.
11. Plagiarism is defined as copying from text books.
12. Referencing correctly will make your assessment grades more higher.
13. Teachers should know that students can be categorised as either male or female.
14. E-business can be define as the process of doing business electronically.
15. Academic writing is defined as writing is formal, well-organised and well-referenced.
16. Hong Kong students' English language ability always correlates with their academic ability.
17. Hong Kong students they always have more better English as Mainland.

Explanations (Ex.-1)

1. Faith keeps many doubts in her pay. If I could not doubt, I should not believe.
2. No matter how bad things get you got to go on living, even if it kills you.
3. As for death one gets used to it, even if it is only other people's death you get used to.
4. No culture can live if it attempts to be exclusive.
5. They will say you are on the wrong road, if it is your own.
6. A wise man admits his weaknesses. I would admit mine if I had any.
7. If I am not willing to give 120 percent, somebody else will.
8. If I had been present at creation, I would have given some useful hints.
9. If I had my career over again? Maybe I'd say to myself, speed it up a little.
10. I would be a billionaire if I wanted to be a selfish boss.

11. If I repent of anything, it is very likely to be my good behaviour.
12. Miss a meal if you have to, but don't miss a book.
13. If I spit, they will take my spit and frame it as great art.
14. If I had not started painting, I would have raised chickens.
15. If it was not for dogs, some people would never go for a walk.
16. To buy books would be a good thing if we also could buy the time to read them.
17. Develop a passion for learning. If you do, you will never cease to grow.
18. Do something. If it works, do more of it. If it doesn't, do something else.
19. Do every act of your life as if it was your last.
20. If I wasn't an actor, I would be a secret agent.

Explanations (Ex.-2)

1. You must not blame me if I talk to the clouds.
2. You can only be free if I am free.
3. If you want a thing done well, do it yourself.
4. If what happens does not make us richer, we must welcome it if it makes us wiser.
5. If it were not for hopes, the heart would break.
6. If it is a good script I will do it. And if it's a bad script, and they pay me enough, I'll do it.
7. If it looks like shit, smells like shit, mail it to your enemy... he will know what to do with it.
8. If it is not right, do not do it; if it is not true, do not say it.
9. If it fails, admit it frankly and try another. But above all, try something.
10. If I play my best, I can win anywhere in the world against anybody.
11. If I am not allowed to laugh in heaven, I don't want to go there.
12. If I were two-faced, would I be wearing this one?
13. If I die, I forgive you. If I live, we shall see.
14. If I can stop one heart from breaking, I shall not live in vain.
15. If I can not understand my friend's silence, I will never get to understand his words.
16. I wonder whether if I had had an education I should have been more or less a fool than I am.
17. I don't jog, if I die I want to be sick.
18. Every day is a gift – even if it sucks.
19. Believe and act as if it were impossible to fail.
20. An idea is worth nothing if it has no champion.

Explanations (Ex.-3)

1. We would accomplish many more things if we did not think of them as impossible.
2. No one would have doubted his ability to reign had he never been an emperor.
3. Never work before breakfast. If you have to work before breakfast, get your breakfast first.
4. My warning: If you don't drive your business you will be driven out of business.
5. Many people might have attained wisdom had they not assumed they already had it.
6. If youth knew; if age could.
7. If you think your boss is stupid, remember: you wouldn't have a job if he was any smarter.
8. If you marry for money, you will surely earn it.
9. If you have to ask how much it costs, you can't afford it.
10. If you don't program yourself, life will program you!

11. If you do not care, your customer never will.
12. If you can count your money, then you're not a rich man.
13. If you build a better mousetrap, you will catch better mice.
14. If we spoke a different language, we would perceive a somewhat different world.
15. If the blind lead the blind, both will fall into the ditch.
16. If I had no sense of humour, I would long ago have committed suicide.
17. I won't belong to any organisation that would have me as a member.
18. I wish people that have trouble communicating would just shut up!
19. I wish I had the voice of Homer.
20. Advice is what we ask for when we already know the answer but wish we did not.

Explanations (Ex.-4)

1. A rentcharge is the right to receive an annual sum out of the income of land every year.
   - *Error:* Grammar – Duplication of meaning; 'annual' = 'every year'.
   - *Correction:* A rentcharge is the right to receive an annual sum out of the income of land.
2. All of the solutions considered so far have only involved Legendre functions of even order.
   - *Error:* Grammar - placing of 'only'
   - *Correction:* All of the solutions considered so far have involved only Legendre funtions of even order.
3. Before spelling out exactly what this means, it is worth first asking whether translating machinery is necessarily irreversible.
   - *Error:* Duplication – 'before' = 'first'.
   - *Correction:* Before spelling out exactly what this means, it is worth asking whether translating machinery is necessarily irreversible.
4. Being in charge, the accusation was particularly annoying to me.
   - *Error:* Dangling participle – the 'accusation' was not in charge.
   - *Correction:* Being in charge, I found the accusation particularly annoying.
5. Finally, it enables the therapist to assess the effectiveness of his own clinical skills and, hopefully, to improve them in future.
   - *Error:* 'hopefully' is an adverb, therefore should limit meaning of verb, but in this case it tells you nothing about the meaning of verb– 'improve'.
   - *Correction:* Finally, it enables the therapist to assess the effectiveness of his own clinical skills and, it is hoped, to improve them in future.
6. He is a former student who I've not seen for years.
   - *Error:* 'who'is the object, therefore it should be 'whom'.
   - *Correction:* He is a former student whom I've not seen for years.
7. He is an unskilled labourer and works at odd jobs, but he don't do any of them very well.
   - *Error:* Grammar - 'don't'.
   - *Correction:* He is an unskilled labourer and works at odd jobs, but he doesn't do any of them very well.
8. However, there were other patients whose lives had ended by suicide.
   - *Error:* Grammar– wrong use of prepositions; change 'by' to 'in'.
   - *Correction:* However, there were other patients whose lives had ended in suicide.

9. I have now discussed the proposals for replacing all the computers with my colleagues.
   - *Error:* Grammar – meaning confused by 'word order'.
   - *Correction:* I have now discussed with my colleagues the proposals for replacing all the computers.
10. It is felt that less people would be put off attending with other problems if the stigma of going to a clinic could be dispensed with.
   - *Error:* Grammar – 'less' is used for uncountable nouns; 'fewer' for countables.
   - *Correction:* It is felt that fewer people would be put off attending with other problems if the stigma of going to a clinic could be dispensed with.
11. It is just possible that you are one of those rare people who has never seriously tried to diet.
   - *Error:* The verb 'has' does not agree with 'people'; change 'has' to 'have'.
   - *Correction:* It is just possible that you are one of those rare people who have never seriously tried to diet.
12. It may be open to challenge on certain grounds, i.e. if an emergency occurs.
   - *Error:* Wrong use of 'i.e.'; change 'i.e.' to 'e.g.'
   - *Correction:* 'It may be open to challenge on certain grounds, e.g. if an emergency occurs'.
13. It was the community in it's purest form.
   - *Error:* Punctuation; 'it's'= 'it is'. change 'it's' to 'its'.
   - *Correction:* It was the community in its purest form
14. It was thought necessary to determine legally that someone had attained the age when they were allowed to marry?
   - *Error:* 'someone' is singular; 'they' is plural .
   - *Correction:* It was thought necessary to determine legally that someone had attained the age when he or she was allowed to marry?

   Or "It was thought necessary to determine legally that people had attained the age when they were allowed to marry".
15. Jean Baptiste Lamarck (1744–1829) had supposed that the main cause of evolutionary change was because of the 'inheritance of acquired character'.
   - *Error:* Grammar – duplication; 'cause' = 'because of'.
   - *Correction:* Jean Baptiste Lamarck (1744- 1829) had supposed that the main cause of evolutionary change was the 'inheritance of acquired characters'.
16. Kinship in these societies had to be completely different to what it was in capitalist society.
   - *Error:* Grammar – Wrong use of preposition 'to'; use–'from'.
   - *Correction:* Kinship in these societies had to be completely different from what it was in capitalist society.
17. No matter what he says, he has and will always be in charge.
   - *Error:* 'he has' should be 'he has been'; you can only join elemnts with the same grammatical role with 'and'.
   - *Correction:* No matter what he says, he always has been and will always be in charge.
18. She could give a better response than that to I and to my friends.
   - *Error:* 'me' not 'I'.
   - *Correction:* She could give a better response than that to me and to my friends.

19. The category of killings which has come to be known as involuntary manslaughter hasn't nothing to do with involuntariness.
   - *Error:* Double negative .
   - *Correction:* The category of killings which has come to be known as involuntary manslaughter has nothing to do with involuntariness.
20. The committee has not announced their decision yet.
   - *Error:* Grammar – singular followed by a plural; 'has' followed by 'their.'
   - *Correction:* The committee has not announced its decision yet. OR The committee have not announced their decision yet.

   Be careful : There is a problem with these collective nouns (see the chapter of 'noun'), which are grammatically singular but have a plural meaning.
21. The emphasis on revolution as ending every stage is, also, much more definately stated than in earlier works.
   - *Error:* Spelling mistake.
   - *Correction:* The emphasis on revolution as ending every stage is, also, much more, definitely stated than in earlier works.
22. The esential feature of these results has been amply confirmed.
   - *Error:* Spelling mistake.
   - *Correction:* The essential feature of these results has been amply confirmed.
23. The experiment by Norcross (1958) which used a slightly different version of this procedure produced essentially the same outcome.
   - *Error:* Punctuation; Use of commas.
   - *Correction:* The experiment by Norcross (1958), which used a slightly different version of this procedure, produced essentially the same outcome.
24. The first really useful realization of the Lie algebra of the Geroch group, was formulated by Kinnersley and Chitre (1977, 1978a, b).
   - *Error:* Punctuation – the comma interrupts the run of the sentence.
   - *Correction:* The first really useful realization of the Lie algebra of the Geroch group was formulated by Kinnersley and Chitre (1977, 1978a,b).
25. The more aggressive technologies, those which need a great deal of energy and natural resources and cause extensive environmental pollution, represent a percentage of industrial production.
   - *Error:* Meaningless use of "percentage".
   - *Correction:* The more aggressive technologies, those which need a great deal of energy and natural resources and cause extensive environmental pollution, represent a large percentage of industrial production.
26. Jones and Smith argues that the problem began in December 1942.
   - *Error*: "Jones and Smith" is plural; 'argue' should be plural.
   - *Correction:* Jones and Smith argue that the problem began in December 1942.
27. At that time there were hardly any scholarly accounts of the period in question, the only really important biography was that of George V by Harold Nicolson.
   - *Error:* Punctuation – run-on sentence; can't join two sentences with a comma.
   - *Correction:* At that time there were hardly any scholarly accounts of the period in question. The only really important biography was that of George V by Harold Nicolson. OR At that time there were hardly any scholarly accounts of the period in question, the only really important biography being that of George V by Harold Nicolson.

28. The task - one that involved pedalling on a stationery bicycle - was equally demanding at all times.
   - *Error:* Wrong use of the word – "stationery".
   - *Correction:* The task – one that involved pedalling on a stationary bicycle - was equally demanding at all times.
29. They are, in fact, just the kind of things the natural philosopher might be interested in.
   - *Error:* Preposition at end of sentence.
   - *correction:* They are, in fact, just the kind of things in which the natural philosopher might be interested.
30. This has meant that elsewhere it has been very difficult to clearly assess the extent of the problem.
   - *Error:* Grammar - Unnecessary splitting of infinitive – 'to asses'.
   - *Correction:* This has meant that elsewhere it has been very difficult to assess clearly the extent of the problem.

   Putting a word between the "to" and the verb is called splitting the infinitive. This is actually wrong because in English the infinitive is one word so cannot be split. Now a days putting one adverb between the infinitive is accepted reasonable in some cases by some grammarians.
31. Though he has generally been considered anti-intellectual and disinterested in art theory, at this stage of his career he shared the concerns of his fellows of the Petit Boulevard for principles of colour.
   - *Error:* Wrong use of "disinterested"; check your dictionary.
   - *Correction:* As per instruction given at the top, in the questions, full sentence should the written after correction 'Though............<u>uninterested</u>............colour.
32. When they were discussing the historical development which led to capitalism.
   - *Error:* Incomplete sentence
   - *Correction:* When they were discussing the historical development which led to capitalism, they stressed the structure between different stages and the universality of the historical process.

Explanations (Ex.-5)

1. The correct answer is: 'Although e-commerce is a modern phenomenon, 'it' has become a valuable business tool.' (One sentence only, because sentences starting with 'Although' always have two parts, separated by a comma.)
2. The correct answer is: 'I.T. is very common in business, <u>and</u> it is very useful.' (The original sentences are too short for academic writing, and there is no linking.)
3. The original sentence it: 'Computer science is the science of doing things with computers.' (Too obvious. This definition does not help a reader to understand what computer science is. Computer science is a complicated subject, and you need to write an extended definition to define it adequately; e.g.–'Computer science involves the design, assembly, programming and use of computers.')
4. The original sentence is: 'Zoology is the science of managing a zoo.' (Wrong meaning; zoology is the category of biology dealing with animals.)
5. The correct answer is: 'Although HKPU is in a convenient location, ~~however~~ the air pollution here is quite bad.' (Don't use 'however' and 'although' in the same sentence. In general, use only one conjunction for contrast, such as– 'however', 'but' and 'whereas', in one sentence.)
6. The correct answer is: 'Engineering courses are more popular ~~as~~ <u>than</u> IT courses.' (After the comparative adjective – 'more', use 'than'. Only use 'as' if something is 'the same as'.)

7. The correct answer is: 'The ~~most busy~~ busiest students here are the third-year students.' (Adjectives of two syllables that end in 'y', usually change their ending to 'ier' or 'iest', while chaning degree.
8. The correct answer is: 'There are a number of ~~similarity~~ similarities between computing and business courses.' (After 'a number of', use a plural noun.)
9. The correct answer is: 'While Taiwan has a strong hardware industry, Hong Kong ~~haven't.~~ hasn't.' or '..., Hong Kong doesn't.' (Always be careful of subject-verb agreement. Hong Kong is one thing (singular), so use 'hasn't' or doesn't, not 'haven't'. 'Hasn't' is a more obvious contrast to 'has', and 'doesn't' is also possible because 'doesn't' is the negative auxiliary verb for the third person singular in the present simple tense.)
10. The correct answer is: 'E-mail is the most popular type of program on the Internet. (It's a type of program. Eudora and Outlook are e-mail programs. Definitions must be accurate.)
11. The correct answer is: 'Plagiarism is defined as copying from text books without referencing and either quoting, summarising or paraphrasing.' (The original sentence is not detailed enough: Copying from text books is acceptable if the copied text is shown as a quote and has some referencing; e.g the author's family name, date of publication and page number.)
12. The correct answer is: 'Referencing correctly will make your assessment grades ~~more~~ higher.' ('High' is a one-syllable adjective, so change the ending rather than adding 'more'.)
13. The original sentence was grammatically correct. 'Teachers should know that students can be categorised as either male or female.'
14. The original sentence was grammatically correct, 'E-business can be defined as the process of doing business electronically.' (However, this definition is not very helpful to a reader who does not know what e-commerce is. A more extended definition would be more helpful; e.g.–'E-business can be defined as the process of enabling business transactions such as ordering over the Internet.')
15. The correct answer is: 'Academic writing is defined as writing which is formal…' (To give more information about a noun such as 'writing', you can use a relative clause. Relative clauses start with a relative pronoun such as 'which', then a verb; e.g 'is' is written, and then the rest of the clause.)
16. The correct answer is: 'HK students' English language ability ~~always~~ often correlates with their academic ability.' (Don't use 'always' to emphasise the frequency of an action in academic writing. Use a more accurate adverb of frequency, such as 'frequently' or 'often'. 'Correlates' means something is at the same level and increases or decreases at the same time. Therefore, if the students, are getting high marks in English, they are probably getting high marks in other academic subjects as well.)
17. The correct sentence is 'Hong Kong students sometimes have better English than Mainlanders.' This sentence contains many of the mistakes mentioned above, namely; One should not use two comparatives (here 'more' and 'better') in a sentence. Secondly, here comparision is between the Englishman and the Mainlanders' (not the Mainland) Third, for comparision here, we should use 'than' insteed of 'as'.

23

Words Often Create Confusion

HOMONYMS

English में ऐसे बहुत से शब्द हैं, जिनका उच्चारण लगभग एक जैसा होता है, लेकिन उनके अर्थ में अन्तर होता है; ऐसे शब्दों को **Homonyms or Homophones** कहा जाता है : जैसे- Access, Excess;Affect, Effect। इन शब्दों का उचित ज्ञान न होने पर, एक की जगह पर दूसरे शब्द को लिखने से सब कुछ गलत हो जाता है, अत: छात्रों को ऐसे शब्दों का बहुत ध्यानपूर्वक अध्ययन करना चाहिए। नीचे इस तरह के बहुत से शब्दों को बताया गया है :

1. **Affect** (to act upon, to pretend –प्रभाव डालना) : (a) She *affects* too much innocence.
   (b) The drought *affected* a large part of the district.
   Effect (result –प्रभाव) : Internet produces a bad *effect* on the young generation.
2. **Adapt** (accomodate–यथा काल व्यवहार) : One should *adapt* oneself to the new circumstances.
   Adept (expert –निपुण) : He is an *adept* in Folk dance.
   Adopt (take up –गृहण करना) : One should not *adopt* unfair means to secure good marks.
3. **Addition** (putting more –जोड़ना) : I am to buy two more copies in *addition* to this one.
   Edition (printing books –संसकरण) : The first *edition* of this book has sold like hot cakes.
4. **Accede** (agree –स्वीकार करना) : He will not *accede* to your request.
   Exceed (to be greater –सीमा से बाहर जाना, बढ़ाना) : Write an essay not *exceeding* three hundred words.
5. **Access** (approach, reach –पहुँच) : Now a days every person has an easy *access* to the temples irrespective to his caste.
   Excess (more than enough –अधिकता) : *Excess* of everything is bad.
6. **Accept** (to take –स्वीकार करना) : He can not *accept* this gift.
   Except (leaving out –सिवाय, बजाय) : *Except* Nisha everyone was present in the party.
7. **Alter** (change –बदलना) : You can not *alter* my opinion about her.
   Altar (place of offering –वेदी) : (a) S.C. Bose sacrificed everything at the *altar* of freedom.
   (b) In India incense is burnt at the altar in temples.
8. **Antic** (odd–strange –अपरिचित) : Yesterday, his behaviour was quite *antic*.
   Antique (ancient –प्राचीन) : I am fond of collecting *antique* items.
9. **Assay** (attempt –प्रयास, testing the purity of metals–धातुओं की शुद्धता की जाँच करना)
   (a) He *assayed* hard to secure top position.
   (b) He *assayed* the gold ornaments.
   Essay (a piece of composition–निबन्ध) : Write a brief *essay* on 'Indian Films'.
10. **All ready** (all are ready –सभी तैयार) : They were *all ready* to welcome the groom.
    Already (earlier –पूर्व में) : I have *already* informed him.

11. **Allusions** (indirect reference –अप्रत्यक्ष संकेत) : The poem is full of *allusions.*

Illusion (a deceptive show –माया, इन्द्रजाल) : Indian mythology regards the material world as an *illusion.*

12. **Apposite** (proper–योग्य) : His arguments were not *apposite* to the subject.

Opposite (contrary–विपरीत, In front of) : His house is *opposite* to the college.

13. **Assent** (agreement–स्वीकारोक्ति) : He gave his *assent* to the new proposal.

Ascent (going up–ऊपर चढ़ना) : He pushed the button and the elevator began its slow *ascent.*

14. **Arc** (part of circle–वृत्त खण्ड, चाप) : If a straight line is drawn in a circle it will divide it into two *arcs.*

Ark (covered floating vessel–ढका हुआ जहाज) : He crossed the Black Sea with his family in an *ark.*

15. **Aloud** (high volume–ऊँचा स्वर) : I can't hear you well, please speak *aloud.*

Allowed (permitted–इजाजत दी) : He was *allowed* to enter.

16. **Angle** (An angle of degree–कोण) : This is a ninety degree *angle.*

Angel (a divine messenger–फरिश्ता) : *Angels* reside in heaven while men reside on earth.

17. **Advice** (noun–सलाह) : I need your expert *advice* in this matter.

Advise (verb–सलाह देना) : Please *advise* me in this matter.

18. **Amiable** (lovable–प्यार योग्य) : She is not only a beautiful but also an *amiable* girl.

Amicable (friendly–मित्रवत) : Finally they came to an *amicable* settlement.

19. **Ail** (to be ill–बीमार होना) : What *ails* the Industry is to be sorted out.

Ale (a drink –शराब) : He has gone to the *ale*–house.

20. **All together** (in a body–साथ-साथ) : Let us move there *all* together.

Altogether (completely–पूर्णतया) : It seems *altogether* impossible to cross the river in night.

21. **Ad** (short for advertisement) : He has given an *ad* in the newspaper.

Add (short for addition) : *Add* two to three.

Aid (to assist–सहायता करना) : He has given *aid* of Rs 5000/–to the poor family.

Aide (an assistant) : He is a close *aide* to the Prime Minister.

22. **Aerie** (eagle's nest–घोंसला) : There is an *aerie* on this tree.

Airy (breezy–हवादार) : The room is quite *airy.*

23. **Aisle** (walkway–रास्ता) : (a) An *aisle* is a long narrow gap that people can walk along between rows of seats in a public building such as a church or between rows of shelves in a supermarket. (b) **The** *aisle* is also used in expressions such as **walking down the aisle** to refer to the activity of getting married : I am in no hurry to *walk down the aisle.*

Isle (island–द्वीप) : I have seen many *isles* but this is the best isle.

24. **All** (everything–सब) : He has donated *all* his property.

Awl (A small pointed tool for pricking or piercing holes, *esp.* such as– tool used by shoemakers– औजार, मोची का सूजा)

25. **Ate** (past tense of eat–खाया) : He *ate* two apples.

Eight (the number base of octal, seven, eight, nine–आठ) : I have *eight* pens.

26. **Auger** (a drill, a tool–बरमा, औजार) : I need an *auger* to make a hole.

Augur (foretell –भविष्य बतलाना, शकुन विचारना) : The recent communal riots do not *augur* well for the smooth running of government.

27. **Aural** (of hearing–सुनने सम्बन्धित) : He became famous as an inventor of astonishing visual and *aural* effects.
Oral (of the mouth–मौखिक) : He presented his ideas in a nice way *orally.*

28. **Auricle** (external part of the ear–कान का बाहरी हिस्सा)
Oracle (seer–श्रेष्ठ) : He regards himself as an *oracle* on architecture.

29. **Away** (distant–दूर) : Do not go far *away* from the house.
Aweigh (just clear of the bottom) M :

30. **Awed** (in a state of wonder–चकित, श्रद्धा युक्त भय होना) : *Awedly* she was unable to recall his name.
Odd (not usual)Ñ Find the *odd* word from the following passage.

31. **Aye** (Aye means yes–हाँ) : used in some dialects of British English :
'Do you remember your first day at school?' 'Oh *aye*. Yeah.'
Eye (ocular organ–आँख) : Her *eyes* are very beautiful.

32. **Bale** (package–गांठ) : I received thirty *bales* of cotton last month.
Bail (security–जमानत)Ñ The magistrate didn't grant him *bail* in the theft case.

33. **Berth** (sleeping place in train–ट्रेन में बर्थ) : I have booked two *berths* in Shatabdi Express.
Birth (coming to life–जन्म) : This is not the *birth* place of Buddha.

34. **Bare** (uncovered–नंगा, बिना ढका) : He came here *bare* footed.
Bear (to tolerate–सहन करना) : I cannot *bear* your insulting remarks.
Bear (an animal–रीछ) : There are three *bears* in that circus.
Beer (a kind of wine–बीयर) : I don't prefer to take *beer.*

35. **Blow** (to whistle–बजाना, फूँकना) : A cool wind is *blowing* ; Don't blow the whistle.
Below (under neath–नीचे) : Hitting *below* the belt is not allowed.

36. **Born** (to take birth–जन्म) : My wife was *born* in 1960.
Borne (supported–सहन किया) : He is suffering from water *borne* disease.

37. **Bad** (not good–बुरा) : He is a *bad* man.
Bed (sleeping place–बिस्तर) : I go to *bed* at 11P.M.

38. **By** (assistance–द्वारा) : A snake was killed *by* Raju with a stick.
Buy (purchase–खरीदना) : I want to *buy* a car.

39. **Beet** (a vegetable–चुकन्दर) : I prefer mango to *beet.*
Beat (to thrash–पीटना) : It is wrong to *beat* the students with a stick.

40. **Borrow** (to take loan–उधार लेना) : I have *borrowed* some money from Bank.
Burrow (a hole in earth–छेद, बिल) : A mouse lives in this *burrow.*

41. **Cell** (a small cottage–छोटी कोठरी) : There are more than twenty *cells* in that prison.
Sell (verb–to dispose off–बेचना) : He *sells* fruits and vegetables.
Sale (noun–act of selling–बिक्री) : I have purchased this dress from that shop on discount *sale.*

42. **Beach** (shore–किनारा) : Many people like to walk along the sea *beach.*
Beech (a kind of tree–पेड़) : There are many *Beech* trees near the railway station.

43. **Brake** (lever–ब्रेक) : I am going to get the *brake* wire changed .
Break (to make a part–तोड़ना) : Can you *break* this stick with your hands ?

44. **Bow** (bend–झुकना) : Let us *bow* to our mother–land India.
Bough (a branch of tree –टहनी) : Many birds are sitting on the *bough* of the tree.

45. **Bridal** (pertaining to marriage–शादी या दुल्हन से सम्बन्धित) : She is looking beautiful in her *bridal* dress.

Bridle (reins–लगाम) : It is not easy to *bridle* a vicious horse.

46. **Baron** (a landlord–जमींदार) : There was a time when all powers rested in the hands of rich *barons*.

Barren (not fertile–बंजर) : In *barren* land you can't cultivate any thing.

47. **Blue** (a colour–नीला) : I like *blue* colour; Sky is *blue*.

Blew (whistled–बजाई) : The refree *blew* the whistle again and again.

48. **Bait** (Food placed on a hook or in a trap to entice fish) : Let your *bait* fall gently upon the water.

Bate (to lessen–कम करना) : We listened with *bated* breath the stories of grand mother's travel.

49. **Bald** (hairless–गंजा) : She is *bald* headed.

Balled (गोला बनाना) : He picked up the sheets of paper and *balled* them tightly in his fists.

Bawled (cried aloud–जोर से पुकारना) : Some one in the audience *bawled* out 'once more'.

50. **Band** (a group–समूह) : A musical *band* is a group of musicians.

Banned (forbidden–प्रतिबन्धित) : Drinking is *banned* in Gujrat.

51. **Bard** (a poet–कवि) : People sometimes refer to William Shakespeare as the *Bard*.

Barred (enclosed by poles–घेरना) : The windows were closed and shuttered and the door was *barred*.

52. **Basal** (forming the base–आधार बनाना) : The *basal* layer of the skin was also torn.

Basil (a herb–तुलसी) : *Basil* is used in cooking also.

53. **Base** (the bottom support for anything–आधार) : The *base* of the bottle is very narrow.

Bass (the lowest musical pitch or range–धीमी आवाज, गायन में सबसे धीमा सुर) : A *bass* is also a man with deep singing voice.

54. **Bask** (to warm oneself pleasantly–गर्म करना, सेंकना) : Crocodiles *bask* on the small sandy beaches.

Basque (tight fitting bodice or tunic–कसे हुए कपड़े) : She was advised to wear *basque*.

55. **Baud** (bits per second)Ñ A unit of data transmission speed equal to one information unit per second·

Bawd (brothel manager–कुटनी) : She is the *bawd* of that brothel.

56. **Beau** (male friend–मर्द मित्र) : A woman's *beau* is her boy friend or lover.

Bow (a curve or bend–मुड़ा हुआ, नमस्कार, धनुष) : He *bowed* slightly for picking up his bag.

57. **Bell** (ding-ding–घंटी) : Don't try to *bell* the cat.

Belle (beautiful woman–सुन्दर स्त्री) : She was the *belle* in last night party .

58. **Besot** (to get drunk–नशे में होना) : He became so *besotted* with her that the even forgot his children.

Besought (past tense of beseech–विनती की) : She *besought* him to cut his drinking and reduce his smoking.

59. **Better** (superior–अच्छा) : It is always *better* to drive carefully.

Bettor (one who bets–जुआरी) : The person who bets is called a *bettor*.

60. **Bight** (a loop, a small bay–झूलन, छोटी खाड़ी) : The loop of a rope (रस्सा) is called *bight*.

Bite (a mouthful–गस्सा) : You can have a *bite* of chocolate.

Byte (eight bits–बाइट) : *Byte* is a unit of storage in computers.

61. **Bloc** (an alliance–मित्रगण) : A *bloc* is a group of countries which have similar aims and interest and that generally act together over some issue.

Block (A block in a town is an area of land with streets on all its sides–घरों की पंक्ति) : She walked four *blocks* down High Street.

62. **Boar** (wild pig–जंगली सूअर) : We can find wild *boars* in the valley.

Boer (a South African of Dutch descent) : He is a *boer.*

Boor (tasteless buffoon–स्वाद रहित) : If we refer someone as a *boor*, we think his behaviour and attitude rough and rude.

Bore (not interesting–अरुचिकर) : He *bored* me all through the meal with stories of the army life.

63. **Bode** (an omen–शकुन) : She says the way bill was passed *bodes* ill for the democracy.

Bowed (curved–मुड़ा हुआ) : He has *bowed* legs.

64. **Bole** (trunk–पेड का धड़ या तना) : He was standing behind the *bole* of a tree.

Bowl (dish–बर्तन) : Put all the soup in a large *bowl.*

65. **Boos** (disparaging sounds from audience–असंतोषजनक आवाज) : Demonstrators *booed* and jeered him.

Booze (whiskey–व्हिस्की) : I have five empty bottles of *booze*.

66. **Bough** (tree branch–पेड़ की टहनी) : I rested my fishing rod against a pine *bough.*

Bow (front of a ship; respectful bend–जहाज का उगता भाग) : I gave a theatrical *bow* and waved.

67. **Bra** (brassiere–पहनने की ब्रा) : She wears beautiful, coloured *bra.*

Braw (well-groomed–तैयार रहना) : He always keeps himself in *braw* shape.

68. **Braid** (a narrow piece of twisted thread or cloth used to decorate clothes) : He was wearing a coloured uniform with lots of gold *braid.*

Brayed (a donkey cried–गधे की आवाज) : The donkey *brayed* and tried to bolt.

69. **Braise** (cook with oil and water–पकाना) : I like *braised* cabbage.

Brays (loud, harsh cry of donkey–गधे की आवाज) : A donkey is *braying.*

70. **Bread** (a loaf–रोटी) : *Bread* is necessary for the living .

Bred (past tense of breed–नस्ल का भूतकाल) : He is an ill *bred* fellow.

71. **Brewed** (fermented–शराब बनाना, किण्वित करना) : I like nicely *brewed* beer.

Brood (family–परिवार, सोचना) : (a) A *brood* is a group of baby birds that were born at the same time to the same mother.

(b) If someone *broods* over something they think about it a lot, seriously .

72. **Bruise** (an injury–चोट) : How did you get that *bruise* on your cheek?

Brews (making beer–बीयर बनाना, किण्वित करता है) : I *brew* my own beer.

73. **Broach** (to raise a subject–शास्त्रार्थ करना) : At last I *broached* the subject of her early life.

Brooch (an ornament fastened to clothes, which has a pin at the back) : I have five *brooches.*

74. **Brows** (multiple foreheads–भौंहें) : Your *brows* are on your forehead.

Browse (grazing–चरना) : Three red deer were *browsing* near my lodge.

75. **Burger** (meat sandwich–बर्गर) : I do not like eating *burger.*

Burgher (merchant–व्यवसायी) : The *burghers* of a town are the people who live there, especially the richer or more respectable people.

76. **But** (excepting–लेकिन) : He is *but* a good man.

Butt (the thick end–मोटा सिरा) : A number of cigarette *butts* are lying there.

77. **Buyer** (one who purchases–खरीदार) : Only a prospective *buyer* can purchase this ouse.

Byre (a cow barn–गौशाला) : A *byre* is a cowshed.

78. **Check** (to verify, to stop–जाँचना) : He *checked* my passport. He checked me from leaving the function.

Cheque (bank document–चेक) : I issued a *cheque* favouring P.N.B.

79. **Calendar** (chart showing dates etc.–कलैण्डर) : I have only one *calendar* in my office.

Calender (to press paper,cloth etc.–प्रेस करना) : Please *calender* my dress.

80. **Cannon** (big gun–तोप) : A *cannon* of ancient time is placed near the Railway station.

Canon (rule–सिद्धान्त) : He believes in *canons* of justice.

81. **Canvas** (a kind of rough cloth–तिरपाल) : My shoes are made of *canvas.*

Canvass (to solicit votes–वोट मांगना) : Nowadays students are busy in *canvassing* for their friends.

82. **Casual** (accidental, occasional–आकस्मिक) : I was granted only one day *casual* leave.

Causal (showing cause– कारण बताने वाला) : There is a *causal* link between balanced diet and sound mind.

83. **Corpse** (dead body–लाश) : The *corpse* was covered with a white bedsheet.

Corps (a body of troops–सेना की टुकड़ी) : I want to join National Cadet *Corps.*

84. **Coma** (state of senselessness–बेहोशी) : The patient has been in *coma* since Monday.

Comma (mark of punctuation– कौमा) : One should be careful about proper use of *comma.*

85. **Cession** (to yield–छोड़ना) : India should not have made a *cession* of an inch of its land for the establishment of Pakistan.

Session (sitting of assembly or court–सत्र) : The winter *session* of parliament will be over tomorrow.

86. **Censer** (a pot in which incense is burnt–यज्ञ की वेदी) : Place some incense into the *censer.*

Censor (an official examination–सेंसर) : The *censor* board has awarded 'U' certificate to this film.

Censure (criticize adversely–निन्दा) : His conduct was *censured* by the parliament.

87. **Chord** (a string of musical instrument–तार) : He is playing with the *chords* of the violin.

Cord (a thin rope–रस्सी) : I need a fifteen fit *cord* for packing the luggage.

88. **Cease** (discontinue–छोड़ना) : He resigned and thus *ceased* to be the chairman of our society.

Seize (to catch–पकड़ना) : Heroin worth two lacs rupee was *seized* from his office.

Siege (surrounded–घेरना) : Akbar's army *sieged* the castle of Chittorgarh.

89. **Career** (profession–व्यवसाय) : For better *career* opportunities, join computer courses.

Carrier (one who carries–ले जाने वाला, वाहक) : Mosquitoes are *carrier* of virus.

90. **Coarse** (rough–खुरदरा) : Do not use a *coarse* cloth to clean the glasses.

Course (line of action–कार्य की दिशा) : A disciplined *course* of action is required to achieve success.

91. **Collision** (clashing–टक्कर) : In a *collision* between train and bus, three persons died on the spot.

Collusion (secret agreement for an evil plan–षड़यंत्र) : He planned to execute a robbery in *collusion* with the clerk.

92. **Cloth** (unstitched cloth–बिना सिले कपड़े) : I want to purchase *cloth* for a shirt and a trousers.

Clothe (stitched cloth–सिले हुये कपड़े) : I have given my *clothes* to washerman for drycleaning

93. **Capital** (centre of administration–राजधानी) : Delhi is the *capital* of India

Capitol (Roman temple of Jupiter, US Congress House–एक भवन का नाम) : A meeting of US congress will be held in *Capitol* tomorrow.

94. **Defy** (challenge –चुनौती, अनादर करना) : One should not *defy* the orders of one's superiors.
Deify (worship as God–ईश्वर की तरह पूजना) : Mr M.K.Gandhi is *defied* by all Indians.

95. **Complacent** (self satisfied–संतुष्ट) : He seems *complacent* with his job and earning.
Complaisant (polite–नम्र) : He is a man of very *complaisant* nature.

96. **Complement** (which completes–पूरक) : Husband and wife are *complementary* to each other.
Compliment (regards–अभिनंदन) : Please convey my best *compliments* to your parents.

97. **Cautious** (aware –जागरूक) : I am quite *cautious* of his activities.
Conscientious (careful, scrupulous–विवेकी, धार्मिक आस्था वाला) : My mother is very hard working, sincere and *conscientious* lady.

98. **Council** (assembly–सदन) : He was nominated to the *Council* of State .
Counsel (advice–सलाह) : He *counsels* in a right way.

99. **Credible** (believable–विश्वसनीय) : He is not a *credible* person.
Creditable (worthy of praise–प्रशंसनीय) : His achievements are indeed *creditable*.

100. **Cymbal** (a musical instrument–मंजीरा) : I like the melodious sound of the *cymbal*.
Symbol (sign–चिह्न) : What was the *symbol* for last Olympic Games?

101. **Current** (present–वर्तमान, ताजा) : What is the *current* news?
Currant (dried grapes–किशमिश) : I am fond of *currants*.

102. **Cite** (speak–कहना, दृष्टान्त देना) : He *cited* the example of bravery of Maharana Pratap.
Site (location–स्थान) : In my opinion this *site* for the departmental store is commercially viable.
Sight (view–दृश्य) : It was a pitiable *sight*.
Sight (vision–दृष्टि) : Get your eye *sight* checked at the earliest.

103. **Caste** (community–जाति) : He belongs to schedule *caste*.
Cast (to give–पासा फेंकना, साँचा, देना) : Please *cast* your votes in favour of me.

104. **Cattle** (animal–पशु) : *Cattle* were grazing in the field.
Kettle (vessel–पतीली) : Put the *kettle* on the gas-burner.

105. **Corporal** (pertaining to body–शारीरिक) : *Corporal* punishment is banned nowadays in all schools and colleges.
Corporeal (bodily, material–शरीर सम्बन्धित) : God has no *corporeal* existence.

106. **Cache** (hidden storage–कोई वस्तु या चीज छिपाने का स्थान) : A huge arms *cache* was discovered by police.
Cash (legal tender–नगद) : I do not accept *cash*, but cheque.

107. **Canter** (a moderate gallop–कदम चाल) : When a horse *canters*, it moves at a speed that is slower than a gallop but faster than a trot.
Cantor (singer–गायक) : A *cantor* is an official who sings liturgical music and leads prayer in a synagogue.

108. **Carat**–unit of weight for precious stones, equal to 200 milligrams.
Caret–proof-reader's insertion mark–छूटा हुआ शब्द दिखाने का चिह्न
Carrot–edible orange root–गाजर.
Karat–one 24th part of otherwise pure gold – 24 का भाग या पूर्ण सोना।

109. **Carol** (Christmas song–गाना) : *Carols* are Christian religious songs that are sung at Christmas.
Carrel (Study enclosure–अध्ययन कक्ष) : A small enclosure or study in a cloister.

110. Cause (generative force–कारण) : Smoking is the biggest *cause* of death.

Caws (sounds of crows–कौओं की आवाज) : When a crow *caws* it makes a loud sound.

111. Cent (one hundredth of a dollar–डॉलर का सौवाँ हिस्सा) : A dollar has hundred *cents.*

Scent (an aroma–सुगन्ध) : I like the aroma of freshly baked bread .

Sent (dispatched–भेजा) : I have sent you a packet of wool.

112. Scents (many things to smell–सुगन्ध) : Flowers are chosen for their *scent* as well as their look.

Sense (Physical abilities of sight, smell, hearing, touch and taste–चेतना) : She has a good *sense* of humour.

113. Cere –waxy fleshy covering at the base of the upper beak in some birds–पक्षियों मे चोंच का निचला हिस्सा

Sear (To sear something means to burn its surface with a sudden intense heat–झुलसाना) : Grass fires have *seared* the land near the farming village .

Seer (a prophet–सिद्ध पुरुष, भविष्य दर्शी) : *A seer* is a person who foretells about the future.

114. Chalk (calcareous earthy substance–चाक) : He writes on the board with a *chalk.*

Chock (wedge to keep wheels from rolling–रोक, रुंधना) : The small roads are *chock* a block with traffic.

115. Chard (spinach–like vegetable–सब्जी) : She is fond of *Chard.*

Charred (burnt–जला हुआ) : In the fire that broke out yesterday seven persons were *charred* to ash.

116. Chased (quickly followed–पीछा करना) : I *chased* the thief for 100 yards.

Chaste (virginal–पवित्र) : If you describe a person or their behaviour as *chaste*, you mean that they do not have sex with anyone, or they only have sex with their husband or wife.

117. Chews (masticating–चबाना) : *Chew* your food well and eat slowly.

Choose (to select–चुनना) : They will be able to *choose* their own leader through election.

118. Chile a South American country–एक देश 'चिली'

Chilli (dried pod of capsicum–मिर्च) : *Chillies* are used in cooking.

Chilly (uncomfortably cool–अत्यधिक ठंडा) : It was a *chilly* night.

119. Choir (church singers–गायक) : A *choir* is a group of people who sing together; for example–in a church or school.

Quire (The twentieth part of a ream of paper–कागज की रीम का बीसवाँ हिस्सा)

120. Collar (around your neck–कॉलर) : The *collar* of this shirt has worn out.

Choral (music sung by a choir–गीत) : His collection of *choral* music is very large and wonderful.

Coral (a hard substance formed from the bones of very small sea animals–मूंगा)

Corral (तबेला): a space surrounded by a fence where cattle or horses are kept.

121. Clack (a chattering sound–आवाज) : The windshield wipers *clacked* back and forth.

Claque (a group hired to applaud, sycophants–प्रशंसक) : Whenever our team scored a goal the *claque* made a superb clappings which further boosted the spirit of the team.

122. Claus (fat, jolly guy with presents–सांताक्लॉज) : Santa *Claus* comes to town on every Christmas.

Clause –Clause is a group of words, containing a verb, contractual unit–शब्द समूह

Claws (big fingernails–पंजा) : The cat tried to cling to the edge by its *claws.*

123. **Click** (ticking noise–क्लिक करना) : You can check your e mail with a *click* of your mouse.
Clique (exclusive group–अलग समूह) : *Clique* is a group of people that spend a lot of time together and seem unfriendly towards people who are not in the group.

124. **Climb** (ascend–चढ़ना) : He *climbed* the stairs.
Clime (climate–वतावरण) : She left Britain for the sunnier *climes* of Southern France.

125. **Coal** (black mineral–कोयला) : A number of families even today use he *coal* for cooking.
Cold (opposite to warm–ठंडा) : I like tea neither too hot nor too *cold*.

126. **Coax** (persuade–फुसलाना, बहलाना) : The government *coaxed* them to give up therir strike by promising them some temporary benefits.
Cokes (more than one soft drink–पेय, ईंधन, कोकीन) : Several kinds of *cokes* were available in the party.
Cocks (more than one male bird–मुग) : I have two beautiful *cocks*.
Cox (नाव में अधिकारी) : In a rowing boat , the *cox* is the person who gives instructions to the rowers.

127. **Coddling** (tenderly treating–स्नेह पूर्ण व्यवहार) : She *coddled* her youger daughter madly.
Codling (small, unripe apple–छोटे सेब) : A small unripe apple is also called codling

128. **Conch** (shellfish–शंख) : A *conch* is a shellfish with a large shell.
Conk (blow to the head–जोर की ध्वनि) : The dynamo *conked* out so we have no electricity.

129. **Coo** (a soft murmuring sound–धीमी आवाज) : 'Isn't she beautiful?' he *cooed*.
Coup (a successful stroke–सच्चा आघात) : He was sentenced to death for his involvement in the *coup*.
Copes (gets along with adversity–मुकाबला करना) : It was amazing how my mother *coped* with bringing up three children on less than Rs. one thousand a month.
Copse (a stand of trees–पेड़ों की पंक्ति) : A *copse* is a small group of trees growing very close to each other.
Cops (police officers–पुलिस अधिकारी) : I do not like the *cops* standing near my house.

130. **Creak** (A short high pitched sound–तेज ध्वनि) : The door *creaked* open by the storm.
Creek (small stream–जल की धारा) : If someone is up the *creek*, he is in a difficult situation.

131. **Desert** (a waste track of land–रेगिस्तान–noun; to forsake, त्यागना –verb) : Churu is a desert area in Rajasthan; He has deserted his wife.
Dessert (fruit served after dinner–भोजन के बाद फल आहार) : The *dessert* course after dinner was liked by all.

132. **Decry** (to cry down–निन्दा करना) : The Iraq policy of US government is *decried* by Indian Govt.
Descry (to see dimly–दूर से देखना) : Across the river you can *descry* a hut near the palm tree.

133. **Dye** (a verb–to colour–रंगना) : *Dye* my shirt in sky blue .
Die (expire–मरना) : He *died* from cholera.

134. **Dose** (quantity of medicine–दवा की खुराक) : I have already taken four *doses* of this medicine by now.
Doze (sleep–ऊँघना) : You were *dozing* in the class yesterday.

135. **Draught** (a quantity of liquid–तरल की मात्रा) : The patient was given a *draught* of medicine.
Drought (want of rain–सूखा) : Due to scanty rain, whole of the district is in the grip of *drought*.

136. **Dam** (surrounding area to stop flow of water–बांध) : A *dam* is being built up here to store the rainy water.

Damn (condemn–निंदा) : His behaviour is *damned* by all the members of the society.

137. **Dear** (loving–प्रिय) : He is my very *dear* friend.

Deer (an animal–हरिण) : I saw many *deer* in that forest.

138. **Deduce** (draw conclusion–नतीजा निकालना) : You can't *deduce* such a conclusion of the discussion.

Deduct (to take something–कम करना) : *Deduct* cash discount 3 % and make the payment by tomorrow.

139. **Deference** (respect–आदर) : I treat my elders with due *deference*.

Difference (dissimilarity–अन्तर) : There was a *difference* of opinion on this point.

140. **Decent** (good–बढ़िया) : Because of his *decent* behaviour, he was promoted to the post of General Manager.

Descent (coming down–नीचे उतरना) : That hill has a steep *descent* to the south.

Dissent (to differ–मतभेद) : He recorded his *dissent* on this proposal.

141. **Device** (noun–plan–योजना) : He used all *devices* to popularise the game.

Devise (verb–to plan–योजना बनाना) : You are to *devise* a plan to increase the turn over.

142. **Duel** (a fight between two–द्वन्द-युद्ध) : There was a *duel* between Dara Singh and Kingkong.

Dual (Double–दोहरा) : *Dual* system of governance is a bad governance.

143. **Disease** (illness–रोग) : Malaria is a curable *disease.*

Decease (death–मृत्यु) : The sudden decease of his father forced him to abandon his studies.

144. **Dart** (a pointed missile–बर्छी) : He died after being struck by a poisonous *dart.*

Dearth (a famine–अकाल) : In this time of crisis and *dearth,* our human resources must be conserved.

145. **Darn** (to mend–रफू करना) : She is *darning* the old socks to wear in winter.

Darne (a fish steak) : He had a *darne* with his lunch.

146. **Dine** (to eat–खाना) : He *dines* alone most nights.

Dyne (unit of energy–ऊर्जा मापने की इकाई) : Three *dyne* energy is needed to pull this pump.

147. **Dire** (desperate–भयानक) : He was in *dire* need of hospital treatment.

Dyer (one who dyes–रंगरेज) : Ram is working in the firm of drycleaners as *dyer.*

148. **Do** (an auxiliary in grammar–करना) : They do not know me; *Do* come tomorrow again.

Doe (a female deer–मादा हरिण) : There are several *does* in the forest.

Dough (uncooked bread–साना हुआ) : Roll out the *dough* into one large circle.

DOS (part of computer operating system) : He is learning *DOS* nowadays.

149. **Done** (completed–पूर्ण करना) : I have *done* my job.

Dun : Something that is *dun* is a dull grey –brown colour.

150. **Eruption** (bursting out–फटना) : There was an *eruption* of volcano near Gujarat border.

Irruption (invasion–आक्रमण) : The *irruption* of Mughals destroyed the glory of Rajput empire.

151. **Emerge** (to come out–बाहर आना) : He *emerged* successfully out of the miserable circumstances.

Immerge (to plunge into–डूबना) : He is *immerged* in mythological thoughts.

152. **Eminent** (distinguished–विशिष्ट) : Indira Gandhi was an *eminent* politician.

Imminent (impending–आसन्न, उपस्थित-प्राय) : Indian army is ready to face any *imminent* attack of Pakistan.

153. Eligible (fit to be chosen–योग्य) : He is *eligible* for the post.

Illegible (that which cannot be read–अपठनीय) : His writing is *illegible.*

154. Earn (to come to deserve–कमाना) : Companies must *earn* a reputation for honesty.

Urn (a jar–अस्थि-कलश, बर्तन) : An *urn* is a container in which a dead person's ashes are kept. An *urn* is a metal container used for making a large quantity of tea or coffee and keeping it hot.

155. Elude (to escape from–बचना) : He *eluded* the police for ten years.

Allude (refer–इशारा करना) : She also *alluded* to her rival's post marital troubles.

156. Epic (a narrative poem or story–काव्य) : Like 'Gone with the wind' it's an unashamed *epic* romance.

Epoch (a noteworthy period in history–ऐतिहासिक काल) : The birth of Christ was the beginning of a major *epoch* of world history.

157. Eunuchs (a castrated male person–हीजड़ा) : In India *eunuchs* are turning to politics.

Unix (operating system–ऑपरेटिंग सिस्टम) : *Unix* is a operating system in computers.

158. Ewe (female sheep–मादा भेड़) : A *ewe* is an adult female sheep.

Yew (a type of tree–पेड़) : is a evergreen tree which has sharp leaves.

You (the second person–तुम) : Where are *you* going?

159. Eyelet (small hole for laces–छोटे छिद्र) : My shoes have eight *eyelets.*

Islet (small island–छोटा द्वीप) : An *islet* is a small island.

160. Ere (before) : Take the water *ere* the clock strikes four.

Err (to make a mistake) : If you make a threat be sure to carry it out if he *errs* again.

Heir (one who will inherit–उत्तराधिकारी) : The younger prince was declared *heir* to the throne.

161. Facility (ease, opportunity–सुविधा) : *Facility* of STD is also available in this hotel.

Felicity (happiness–प्रसन्नता) : True *felicity* can't be enjoyed by a dishonest man.

162. Foul (unfair–अनुचित) : One can't achieve true success through *foul* means.

Fowl (a bird–पक्षी) : He is fond of *fowl's* meat.

163. Find (to get–पाना) : Go there, you will *find* a tree near the river.

Fined (to charge–जुर्माना) : The court *fined* him Rs. 20000 for the offence.

164. Floor (surface–फर्श) : Clean the *floor* with dettol and water.

Flour (wheat meal–आटा) : He has a *flour* mill.

165. Forth (onward–आगे आना) : He alone came *forth* to assist that poor lady .

Fourth (third–fourth–चौथा) : April is the *fourth* month of the year.

166. Farther (more distant–दूर) : Delhi is *farther* from Alwar in comparison to Jaipur.

Further (next–आगे) : Please settle the case without any *further* delay.

167. Faint (to swoon–बेहोश होना) : She *fainted* after taking wine yesterday .

Feint (pretension–दिखावा) : She made a *feint* of reading the book.

168. Fain (gladly–खुशी से) : She would *fain* on seeing me.

Feign (pretend–दिखावा) : When his boss scolded him, he *feigned* as a deaf.

169. Fair (pure, a show–पवित्र, मेला) : (a) : I believe in using fair means to achieve the target. (b) : Let us go to the fair.

Fare (passage money–यात्रा-किराया) : A strike was called by the bus operators, demanding hike in minimum *fare.*

170. Feat (an exploit–साहसिक कार्य) **:** A racing car is an extra ordinary *feat* of engineering.
Feet (plural of foot–पाँव) : Do not put your *feet* on the table.

171. Forego (go before–पहले जाना) : We have already discussed this point in *foregoing* lessons.
Forgo (to let go–त्याग देना) **:** I cannot *forgo* my rights.

172. Fairy (imaginary magic person–परी, अप्सरा) : Fairies are often represented as small people with wings.
Ferry (river–crossing boat–छोटी नाव) : They crossed the river by *ferry.*

173. Fey (whimsical–सनकी) : If you describe someone as *fey*, you mean that they behave in a shy, childish, or unpredictable way, and you are often suggesting that this is unnatural or insincere : Her *fey* charm and eccentric ways were legendary.
Fays (more than one fairy–एक से अधिक छोटे जीव)

174. Faze (to stun–आश्चर्य) : He was *fazed* to see such a big hall.
Phase (a part of the sequence–कला) : The crisis is entering a crucial *phase.*

175. Ferrate (a chemical salt containing iron and oxygen) :
Ferret (a domesticated polecat –छोटी बिल्ली) : A *ferret* is a small fierce animal which is used for hunting rabbits and rats.

176. Feted (celebrated–कार्य करने वाला) : If someone is *feted*, they are celebrated, welcomed or admired by the public.
Fetid (stinking–बदबूदार) **:** *Fetid* water or air has a very unplesant smell.

177. Few (not many–थोड़ा) : I gave a dinner party for a *few* close friends.
Phew (expression of relief) : *Phew*, what a relief I am feeling now!

178. File (a folder for holding papers–फाइल) : Please put this paper in a *file.*
Phial (a small glass bottle–छोटी बोतल, शीशी) : A *phial* is a small tube shaped glass bottle used to hold medicine.

179. Finish (to complete–समाप्त करना) : I will *finish* my work by tomorrow.
Finnish (from Finland–फिनलैंड के निवासी फिनलैंड की भाषा) : *Finnish* is the language spoken in Finland.

180. Flair (verve , talent–प्रवृति) : If you have a *flair* for a particular thing , you have a natural ability to do it well.
Flare (to spread–बढ़ाना) : Camp fire *flares* like beacons in the dark.

181. Flea (parasitic insect–मक्खी) : A *flea* feeds on the blood of humans or animals.
Flee (to run away–भाग जाना) : He tried to *flee* from the sight , but he was caught.

182. Flecks (many tiny specks–छोटा धब्बा जैसा) : His hair is dark grey with *flecks* of ginger.
Flex (to bend–मोड) : He slowly *flexed* his muscles and tried to stand.

183. Flew (past tense of fiy–उड़ा) : He *flew* many kites yesterday.
Flu (short for influenza–बुखार) : I got *flu* day before yesterday.
Flue (chimney pipe–चिमनी पाइप) : The *flue* of the chimney required to be changed.

184. Floe (sheet of floating ice–तैरती बर्फ की परत) : Ice *floe* is a large area of ice floating in the sea.
Flow (to glide along–बहना) : A stream *flowed* gently down into the valley.

185. For (in place of–के लिए) : It is enough *for* me.
Fore (in front–सामने) : There is no direct damage in the *fore* part of the ship.
Four (number after three–चार) : I have *four* pens.

186. Frees (releasing–छोड़ना) : He *frees* the bird from the cage.

Freeze (very cold–ठंडा) : (a) The trees are damaged by a freeze in December. (b) We want the government to freeze the prices.

Frieze (a wall decoration–दिवार सजाने की वस्तु) : A *frieze* is a decoration high up on the walls of a room or just under the roof of a building. It consists of a long panel of carving or a long strip of paper with a picture or pattern on it.

187. Friar (a monk –तपस्वी) : He is a *friar.*

Fryer (A utensil–बर्तन) : A *fryer* is a type of deep pan which is used to fry food in hot oil.

188. Gild (thin coating of metal–धातु का पत्तर चढ़ाना) : *Gilded* ornaments look more beautiful than the original.

Guild (group of persons from same profession–संघ, समाज, मण्डली) : Now-a-days all the workers have organised themselves into *guilds*.

189. Gage (security–जमानत) : I do not lend with out sufficient *gage*.

Gaze (to look attentively–एकटक देखना) : She stood *gazing* at herself in the mirror.

190. Gait (manner of walk–चाल) : That model girl has a graceful and sexy *gait*

Gate (large door–दरवाजा) : You should not enter through the main *gate*.

191. Goal (aim–उद्‌देश्य) : To achieve this *goal* you are to work hard.

Gaol (jail–जेल) : He has been to *gaol* earlier also.

192. Gaff (a barbed spear–भाला) : A *gaff* is a pole with a point or hook at one end, which is used for catching large fish.

Gaffe (a stupid mistake–मूर्खतापूर्ण गलती) : He made an embarrassing *gaffe* at the convention last weekend.

193. Galley (ship's kitchen–जहाज की रसोई) : The *galley* of this ship is well maintained and full of eatables.

Gally (to frighten or terrify–डराना) : He tried to *gally* the child with a mask of demon.

194. Gilt (gold–plated–धातु की परत चढ़ा हुआ) : This is a *gilt* ornament .

Guilt (culpable–अपराध, पातक पाप कर्म) : You aren't convinced of Mr. Charles *guilt.*

195. Gnawed (chewed–चबाना) : He *gnawed* his long fingernail.

Nod (head tilting–सर हिलाना) : 'Are you fine?' I asked . She *nodded* and smiled.

196. Gnu (African deer–अफ्रीकी हरिण) : I saw a *gnu* in the zoo.

Knew (past tense of know–जाना) : He *knew* me well.

New (not old–नया) : What is *new* in the market.

197. Gored (pierced by an animal's horns) : He was *gored* to death in front of his family.

Gourd (fleshy fruit with hard skin–फल) : I like *gourd* very much.

198. Gorilla (large ape–गोरिल्ला) : *Gorilla* has long arm, black fur and a black face.

Guerrilla (irregular soldier–अनियमित छापामार सिपाही) : The *guerrillas* threatened to kill their hostages.

199. Grade (–श्रेणी) : What *grade* are you going to get?

Grayed (turned gray–ग्रे रंग) : I like *grayed* colour walls.

200. **Graft** (to attach–जोड़ना) : The top layer of skin has to be *grafted* onto the burns.
Graphed (plotted–ग्राफ बनाना) : You can see a *graphed* diagram of the progress made by the country in population control.

201. **Grate** (a lattice–जाली) : A *grate* is a frame work of metal bars in a fireplace, which holds the coal or wood; A wood fire burned in the grate.
Great (extremely good–बड़ा, महान) : Gandhi was a *great* man.

202. **Grill** (to sear cook–पकाना) : A *grill* is a flat frame of metal bars on which food can be cooked over fire; Place the omellete under a gentle *grill*.
Grille (an iron framework–लोहे की जाली) : This helment has no protective *grille* to cover the face.

203. **Groan** (a long low sound uttered in pain–कराहना) : He opened his eyes and began to *groan* with pain.
Grown (has gotten larger–बड़ा बढ़ना) : Dad , I am a *grown* woman, I know what I am doing.

204. **Guise** (appearance–भेष, बहाना) : She presented the dance in the *guise* of a rabbit.
Guys (man–व्यक्ति) : Hi, *guys* .How are you doing?

205. **Hail** (frozen rain–ओले) : (a) : It is *hailing*. (b) : It hailed yesterday.
Hale (healthy–स्वस्थ) : May God keep you *hale* and healthy.

206. **Horde** (a gang–समूह) : A *horde* of mischievous students attacked the shopkeepers.
Hoard (to store–एकत्र करना) : *Hoarding* of sugar beyond the prescribed limit is an offence.

207. **Hair** (बाल) : She has black *hair.*
Heir (successor–उत्तराधिकारी) : He is an *heir* apparent to the throne.

208. **Hurt** (injury–चोट) : Your comments can *hurt* her feelings.
Hart (a male deer–हरिण) : I have a beautiful pair of *harts.*
Heart (an organ in the body–दिल) : He is suffering from *heart* disease.

209. **Humane** (Kind–दयालु, मानवीय) : UNO has advised the member countries to meet out *humane* treatment to the prisoners of war.
Human (pertaining to mankind–मनुष्य से सन्बन्धित) : You will find almost the same *human* nature everywhere.

210. **Heel** (part of shoe–जूते की एड़ी) : The *heels* of my shoe are pinching.
Heal (to cure–अच्छा होना) : This medicine will help you in quick *healing.*

211. **Hole** (a burrow–छेद) : A serpent live in this *hole*.
Whole (complete–सम्पूर्ण) : He ate *whole* of the breakfast.

212. **Hall** (a large room–बड़ा कमरा) : He has hired a *hall* for the concert.
Haul (उठाना) : (a) If you *haul* something which is heavy or difficult to move, you move it using a lot of effort; A crane had to be used to haul the car out of the stream...(b) If someone is hauled before a court or someone in authority, they are made to appear before them because they are accused of having done something wrong; He was hauled before the managing director and fired.

213. **Hammock** (rope bed–झूले वाली खाट) : A *hammock* is a piece of strong cloth or netting which is hung between two supports and used as a bed.
Hummock (low, rounded hill–छोटी पहाड़ी) : A *hummock* is a small raised area of ground, like a very small hill.

214. **Hangar** (garage for airplanes–हवाई ज़हाज रखने का स्थान) : Some repairing is going on in the *hangar* of the airport.

Hanger (from which things hang–लटकाने वाला) : I want to purchase a coat *hanger.*

215. **Ho** (an expression of admiration or surprise–हो-हो) : Ho ! you are here.

Hoe (a garden tool–औजार) : Today he is *hoeing* in the vineyard.

216. **He'll** (contraction of 'he will') : *He'll* come tomorrow.

Hill (smaller than a mountain–छोटी पहाडी) : There is a temple on that *hill.*

217. **Hear** (to listen) : I *hear* his voice.

Here (at this location–यहाँ) : Come *here.*

218. **Heard** (listened to–सुना) : I *heard* a strange sound yesterday in the night.

Herd (a group of animals–भीड़, झुण्ड) : They are individuals. They will not follow the *herd.*

219. **Hi** (greetings–हाय) : '*Hi* Luis', she said

High (way up–ऊँचा) : I looked down from the *high* window.

220. **Heroin** (narcotic–अफीम) : *Heroin* is a powder drug.

Heroine (female hero– नायिका) : My favourite *heroine* is Ash.

221. **Hew** (to chop–काटना) : He felled, peeled and *hewed* his own timber.

Hue (a colour–रंग) : The same *hue* will look different in different light.

222. **Higher** (farther up–अपेक्षाकृत ऊँचा) : He has gone to USA for *higher* studies.

Hire (to employ–किराये पर लेना) : Cars are available on *hire.*

223. **Him** (pronoun–उसको) : I know *him.*

Hymn (religious song–धार्मिक गीत) : I like singing *hymns.*

224. **Hoard** (store–एकत्र करना) : They have begun to *hoard* food and sugar .

Horde (a great many people–भीड़-भाड़) : This attracted *hordes* of tourists to Las Vegas.

225. **Hoarse** (rough voice–कर्कश ध्वनि) : His voice is *hoarse.*

Horse (equine–घोड़ा) : He has a black *horse.*

226. **Hold** (to grip–पकड़ना) : *Hold* the bucket please.

Holed (full of holes–छिद्रदार) : The wall seems to be *holed* by a drill.

227. **Holy** (with religious significance–पवित्र) : Ayodhya is a *holy* place for the Hindus.

Wholly (completely–पूर्णतया) : This approach for the urban area is *wholly* inadequate.

228. **Hostel** (inexpensive lodging for travelers–छात्रावास) : He is living in the college *hostel.*

Hostile (unfriendly–दुश्मनी) : Pakistan has not yet changed its *hostile* attitude towards India.

229. **Idle** (indolent–निकम्मा) : An *idle* man can't make any progress.

Ideal (visionary–आदर्श) : My teacher, Mr. Shrivastava is an *ideal* for me.

Idol (an image of a deity–मूर्ति) : A section of the Hindus believe in *idol* worship.

230. **Ingenious** (clever–चतुर) : He is an *ingenious* engineer.

Ingenuous (simple–सीधा) : His *ingenuous* attitude is liked by all.

231. **Incite** (to provoke–उत्तेजित करना) : His arrogant behaviour *incited* me a lot.

Insight (a clear vision–स्पष्ट देखना) : He is a man with considerable *insight.*

232. **Indite** (to compose–रचना) : Though he *indited* the letter carefully, yet it was not liked by the chairman.

Indict (to accuse –दोषारोपण करना) : He was *indicted* for theft and murder.

233. **In** (expressing inclusion–में) : He is *in* the room.

Inn (hotel–होटल, सराय) : This is a well maintained *inn.*

234. **Inc.** (short for incorporated) : *Inc.* is an abbreviation for 'Incorporated' when it is used after a company's name.

Ink (writing fluid–स्याही) : I have an *ink* pen.

235. **It's** (contraction of 'it is') : *It's* a large hotel.

Its (possessive pronoun) : I know *its* true position.

236. **Jealous** (envious–ईर्ष्या) : He is not liked by anybody beause of his *jealous* nature, .

Zealous (enthusiastic–उत्साही) : She is very *zealous* about her new book.

237. **Jewel** (precious stone–जवाहरात) : This watch contains many *jewels.*

Joule (unit of energy measure–ऊर्जा की इकाई) : In Physics *joule* is a unit of energy or work.

238. **Juggler** (one who juggles–जादूगर) : He is a good *juggler.*

Jugular (artery to head–सर की नस) (a) A *jugular or jugular* vein is one of the three important veins in your neck that carry blood from your head back to your heart. (b) If you say that someone **went for the jugular**, you mean that they strongly attacked another person's weakest points in order to harm him.

239. **Naughty** (mischievous–शैतान) : She is a *naughty* girl.

Knotty (difficult–कठिन) : This was indeed a *knotty* problem.

240. **Knap** (crest of a hill; break with a hammer–तोड़ना) : We unfurled the flag at the *knap* of the hill at 6.30 P.M., He knapped the glass box to uncountable pieces.

Nap (a short sleep–झपकी) : You should use your lunch hour to have a *nap* in your chair.

241. **Knead** (working bread dough–गूंदना) : He *kneaded* the mixture on a floured surface; She felt him *knead* the aching muscles.

Need (must have–आवश्यकता) : He *needs* your help.

242. **Knight** (chivalrous man–बहादुर) : He was *knighted* on the queens birthday.

Night (darkness–रात) : *Night* comes after day.

243. **Knit** (interlocking loops of yarn–बुनना) : She has already started *knitting* baby sweators.

Nit (louse egg–जूं के अंडे) : (a) *Nits* are the eggs of insects called lice which live in people's hair.(b) If you refer to someone as a *nit*, you think they are stupid or silly; I'd rather leave the business than work with such a nit.

244. **Knob** (handle–हैंडल का सिरा, घुंडी) : He turned the *knob* and pushed against the door.

Nob (rich person–धनी व्यक्ति) : The *nobs* who, live in that big house are very generous

245. **Knock** (to rap–ठोकना) : Someone had *knocked* him unconcious; I heard a *knock* at the front door.

Nock (a notch in an arrow–तीर के सिरा जैसा) : A 'V' shape cut or indentation in an edge or across a surface.

246. **Knot** (fastening in cord–गांठ) : He tied a *knot* at the end of the lace.

Naught (or nought is zero–शून्य) : Sales rose by nought point four percent last month.

Not (negation–नहीं) : He was *not* present in the party.

247. **Know** (to possess knowledge–जानना) : I *know* him.

No (negation–नहीं) : I have *no* pen.

248. **Knows** ('Only the shadow knows...'–जानना) : He *knows* me well.

Nose (नाक) : She has a big *nose*.

249. **Lightening** (make lighter–हल्का करना) : We had appealed to the court for *lightening* the punishment, but of no avail.
Lightning (electric discharge in clouds–बिजली चमकना) : There was occasional *lightning* in the sky last night.

250. **Loath** (unwilling–इच्छा विरुद्ध) : Nothing *loath* he did, as he was saying.
Loathe (to dislike greatly–घृणा करना) : I *loathe* her dressing pattern and arrogant way of talking.

251. **Latter** (antonym of 'former'–बाद वाला) : Between Ram and Shyam, the *latter* (Shyam) is a diligent student.
Later (comparative of late–देरी से आने वाला) : He came *later* than his friend.

252. **Lose** (to part with–खोना) : Where did you *lose* your briefcase.
Loose (to slack–ढीला करना) : He was wearing a *loose* cotton shirt.

253. **Lesson** (chapter–पाठ) : Learn your *lesson* well.
Lessen (to make less–कम करना) : Even this medicine has not *lessen* my pain.

254. **Last** (antonym to first–अन्तिम) : Bahadur Shah was the *last* emperor of India.
Latest (superlative of late–ताजा) : She always prefers *latest* design clothes.

255. **Lacks** (does not have–नहीं होना, अभाव) : He *lacks* the judgment and political acumen for the post of General Manager.
Lax (loose discipline–शिथिल, असावधान) : One of the point of contention is the *lax* security for the airport personnel.

256. **Lain** (past tense of lay or lie–लेटना) : He has *lain* there for sometime.
Lane (narrow road–गली) : Shyam lives at the end of the *lane*.

257. **Lam** (headlong flight–भागना) : If someone is on the *lam* or if they go on the *lam*, they are trying to escape or hide from someone such as the police or an enemy; He was on the lam for seven years.
Lamb (baby sheep–भेड़ का बच्चा) : A *lamb* is a young sheep.

258. **Lay** (to recline–समर्पण, फैलाना) : *Lay* a sheet of paper on the floor.
Lei (a flower necklace–फूलों का हार) : A garland made of flowers, feathers, shells, etc., often given as a symbol of affection.

259. **Lea** (a meadow–सूत की लम्बाई) : They live in a hut constructed in the *lea*.
Lee (A sheltered position–सुरक्षित स्थिति) : The *lee* of a place is the shelter that it gives from the wind or bad weather.
Lease (Rented–किराये पर) : She *leased* out her bungalow at a good rent.

260. **Leach** : (A dish consisting of sliced meat, eggs, fruits, and spices in jelly etc.–खाने का व्यंजन) :
Leech (sucking parasite–जोंक) : (a) A *leech* is a small animal which looks like a worm and lives in water. Leeches feed by attaching themselves to other animals and sucking their blood. (b) If you describe someone as a *leech*, you disapprove of them because they deliberately depend on other people, often making money out of them. They're just a bunch of-leeches cadging off others .

261. **Leak** (accidental escape of liquid–रिसना) : The roof is *leaking*.
Leek (variety of onion–प्याज) : I like *leek* vegetables.

262. **Lean** (angle of repose–झुकना) : They stopped to *lean* over the gate.
Lien (a claim on property–अधिकार) : Please mark my *lien* over the property.

263. **Liar** (tells falsehoods–झूँठा) : He is a *liar* and a cheat.

Lyre (stringed instrument–यंत्र) : A *lyre* is a stringed instrument that looks like a harp.

264. **Lichen** (a fungus–एक प्रकार का पौधा) : *Lichen* is a group of tiny plants like moss that grows on the surface of things such as rocks, trees and walls.

Liken (to compare–तुलना करना) : If you *liken* one thing or person to another thing or person, you say that they are similar. The pain is often likened to something being drilled through the side of the head.

265. **Lie** (an untruth–झूठ) : He is telling a *lie.*

Lieu (instead–बजाय) : He gave his T.V. to the landlord in *lieu* of rent.

266. **Loo** (British toilet–ब्रिटिश टॉयलेट) : I asked if I could go to the *loo.*

Lou (short for Louis) : Where has *lou* gone so early.

Low (not high–नीचा) : He put it down on the *low* table.

267. **Limb** (tree branch–अंग, पेड़ की शाखा) : The entire structure was hanging from the *limb* of an enormous leafy tree; She would be able to stretch out her cramped *limbs* for some time.

Limn (Illuminate–चमकना) : His face was *limned* in the dim glow from the burning match stick.

268. **Links** (pieces of chain– संयुक्त करता है, चेन के टुकड़े) : I have no *link* with that man.

Lynx (A lynx is a wild animal similar to a large cat.–बड़ी बिल्ली जैसा जंगली पशु ।)

269. **Literal** (taking words in their primary sense–मूलार्थक, वास्तविक) : He was saying no more than the *literal* truth.

Littoral (having to do with the shore–किनारा) : In geography the *littoral* means the coastal.

270. **Load** (cargo–सामान, भार) : I have just *loaded* my truck up.

Lowed (a cow mooed–रंभाना) : The cow *lowed* in agony.

271. **Loan** (allow to borrow–ऋण) : She has taken *loan* from a bank.

Lone (by itself–अकेला) : He was shot by a *lone* gunmen .

272. **Loch** (a lake–झील, समुद्र का सँकरा भाग) : A *loch* is a large area of water that is almost surrounded by land.

Lock (a security device–ताला) : I need a good *lock.*

273. **Loot** (ill–gotten gains–लूटना) : The trouble began when the students began the *looting* of shops.

Lute (stringed instrument–यंत्र) : A *lute* is a stringed instrument with a rounded body that is quite like a guitar and is played with the fingers.

274. **Lumbar** (lower part of back–पीठ का नीचे का हिस्सा) : *Lumbar* support is very im portant if you are driving a long way.

Lumber (dimensional wood–लकड़ी, भद्दी तरह से चलना) : Noun: It was made of soft *lumber.* Verb: He turned and lumbered back to his chair.

275. **Meat** (flesh–मांस) : I don't like eating *meat.*

Meet (to assemble–मिलना) : She came here only to *meet* me.

276. **Mead** (meadow–चरागाह) : I met a beautiful girl in the *meads* yesterday.

Meed (reward–प्रतिफल) : Kalidas has got a universal *meed* of praise.

277. **Metal** (iron, brass etc.–धातु) : Silver is a white *metal.*

Mettle (spirit, courage–साहस) : Our leaders have no *mettle* to fight against corruption.

278. **Metre** (poetic rhythm–छंद) : Can you tell me,in what *metre* Shelley's 'Skylark' is written?

Meter (a measuring instrument =100 cm., मीटर) : One *meter* is equal to hundred centimeters.

279. **Minor** (underage–नाबालिग, छोटा) : *Minors* are not allowed to open current account in Banks.
Miner (one who works in mine–खान पर काम करने वाला) : He is a *miner*, works in a coal mine.

280. **Moat** (a ditch surrounding a castle–किले के चारों ओर बनी खाई) : There is a bridge over the *moat* near main gate.
Mote (a particle of dust–धूल का कण) : You can not see small *mote* by naked eyes.

281. **Monetary** (pertaining to money–मुद्रा सम्बन्धित) : Have you any book on *monetary* theory?
Monitory (giving advice–सलाह देना) : He acted against the *monitory* advise of his friends and so failed.

282. **Male** (opp.to female–पुरुष) : A *male* candidate can't be posted against the post reserved for a woman .
Mail (post–डाक) : Have you received my *mail* ?

283. **Mite** (small thing–अल्प-मात्रा) : He contributed his *mite* for the service of mankind.
Might (strength–शक्ति) : Your *might* will be tested in battle against the foreign power.
Might (past of may–सकना) : He told me that he *might* come to attend the function.

284. **Marry** (to get married–विवाह करना) : I want to *marry* your sister.
Merry (joyous–आनन्द करना) : Don't lose heart and be *merry.*

285. **Main** (chief–मुख्य) : Ramesh is the *main* culprit in the bank robbery case.
Mane (long hair of an animal's neck–गर्दन के बाल) : His horse had a fine *mane*.

286. **Marshal** (a military officer–मार्शल) : He is a *marshal* of the court.
Martial (war like –युद्ध जैसा) : He has a *martial* spirit and courage to fight in odd circumstances.

287. **Maize** (corn–मक्का) : I like to eat maize cake.
Maze (labyrinth–घुमाव) : This castle has many hidden *mazes*.

288. **Mach** (speed of sound–ध्वनि की गति) : *Mach* is used as a unit of measurement in stating the speed of a moving object in relation to the speed of sound. For example, if an aircraft is travelling at Mach 1, it is travelling at exactly the speed of sound.
Mock (parody–व्यंग) : I thought you were *mocking* me.

289. **Made** (accomplished–बनाया) : The table is *made* of wood.
Maid (young woman–नौकरानी) : She is our *maid* servant.

290. **Mall** (A large shopping area.–खरीदारी की जगह)
Maul (savage–क्रूर, कूँचना) : He had been *mauled* by a tiger.
Moll (gangster's girlfriend–लड़की मित्र) : She is the *moll* of the don.

291. **Manner** (method–तरीका) : I am a professional and I have to conduct myself in a professional manner.She smiled in a friendly *manner*.
Manor (lord's house or a large private house–बड़ा व्यैक्तिक घराना, जागीर) : Thieves broke into the *manor* at night.

292. **Marc** (coarse brandy–ब्रांडी) : I don't like the taste of *marc*.
Mark (a sign–निशान) : He made some peculiar *marks* with a pen.

293. **Marquee** (a roof like projection over a theatre entrance–बड़ा टेंट) : (a) A *marquee* is a large tent which is used at a fair, garden party, or other outdoor event, usually for eating and drinking in.(b) A *marque* is a cover over the entrance of a building, for example a hotel or a theatre.
Marquis a nobleman ranking between a duke and a count

294. **Massed** (grouped together–समूह) : He could not escape the *massed* ranks of newsmen.

Mast (sail pole–पाल, जहाज का मस्तूल) : The *mast* of a boat are the tall upright poles that support its sails.

295. **Mews** (stables–घुड़साल) : The house is in a secluded *mews*.

Muse (creative inspiration–प्रेरणा) : (a) Noun : Once she was a nude model and *muse* to French artist Henri.(b) Verb: (Think) Many scholars muse on the role of President in Indian polity.

296. **Mince** (chop finely–टुकड़े करना) : I'll buy lean meat and *mince* it mysef.

Mints (aromatic candies–सुगन्धित खाद्य) : *Mint* is a herb with fresh tasting leaves.

297. **Mind** (thinking unit–मस्तिष्क) : *Mind* your business please.

Mined (looked for ore–खनिज कार्य) : The pit was shut down bcause it hadn't enough that could be *mined* economically.

298. **Missal** (hymn book–किताब) : A book containing the service of the *Mass* for the whole year; loosely a Roman Catholic book of prayers,

Missile (projectile–प्रक्षेपणास्त्र) : The football supporters began throwing *missiles,* one of which hit the captain of the rival team.

299. **Mist** (fog–कोहरा) : The *mist* made the flying impossible.

Missed (not hit–चूकना) : He scored four of the goals but *missed* a penalty.

300. **Moan** (to groan–कराहना) : She gave a low choking *moan* and began to tremble.

Mown (the lawn is freshly cut–घास काटी) : He has *mown* the lawn today itself.

301. **Mood** (emotional state–मानसिक स्थिति) : She is in a jolly *mood* today.

Mooed (what the loquacious cow did–गाय की ध्वनि, रंभाना) : When cattle especially cows *moo,* they make a long low sound that cattle typically make.

302. **Moor** (swampy coastland; to anchor–रुकना, लंगर डालना) : I decided to *moor* near some tourist boats.

More (additional–अपेक्षाकृत अधिक) : I need some *more* rice.

303. **Moose** (a large elk–बड़ा हरिण) : *Moose* are large type of deer have big flat horns.

Mousse (dessert of whipped cream and eggs) : *Mousse* is a sweet light food made from eggs and cream.

304. **Morning** (A.M.–प्रात:) : I get up early in the *morning.*

Mourning (remembering the dead–मृतक हेतु प्रार्थना, मातम) : On the death of Rajeev Gandhi, the whole of India was in the *mourning*.

305. **Muscle** (fibrous, contracting tissue–मांस-पेशी) : He is doing a lot of exercises to keep his *muscles* strong.

Mussel (mussels are a kind of shellfish that you can eat from their shells–एक प्रकार की मछली)

306. **Mussed** (made messy–गड़बड़ी) : His clothes are all *mussed* up.

Must (required–आवश्यक) : You *must* go there to get his support.

307. **Mustard** (spicy yellow sauce–सरसों) : This is fried in *mustard* oil.

Mustered (assembled for roll call–एकत्र होना, संग्रह किया) : He travelled through out India to *muster* support for his movement.

308. **Nice** (good–अच्छा) : She is a *nice* and beautiful girl.

Niece (daughter of brother–भतीजी) : I am to attend the marriage of my *niece* positively.

309. **Naval** (pertaining to ships and the sea–जहाज से सम्बधित) : He is captain in *naval* forces.

Navel (pertaining to the belly button–नाभी) : There is a black mole near her *navel.*

310. Nay (no–नहीं) : The Rajya Sabha can merely say yea or *nay* to such a bill.

Neigh (a horse's cry–हिनहिनाना) : The horse gave a loud *neigh.*

311. Our (plural of 'my'–हमारा) : This is *our* house.

Hour (a period of time–घंटा) : I have been waiting for you for half an *hour.*

312. Oar (used for rowing a boat–पतवार) : Life without aim is like a boat without an *oar.*

Ore (Mineral from which metal can be extracted–खनिज) : Iron is extracted from its *ore* by melting.

313. Ordinance (a rule–अध्यादेश) : The President has promulgated an *ordinance* for administering the minority community.

Ordnance (gun–युद्ध सामग्री) : There is an *ordnance* factory in Jamshedpur, Bihar.

314. Oohs : People say '*ooh*' when they are surprised, looking forward to something, or find something pleasant or unpleasant. (informal–ऊह) : '*Ooh* dear me, that's a bit of a racist comment isn't it.'; 'Red? *Ooh* how nice.'

Ooze : (स्राव, रिसकर, बाहर निकलना) : When a thick or sticky liquid *oozes* from something or when something *oozes* it, the liquid flows slowly and in small quantities : The lava will just *ooze* gently out of the crater; The wounds may heal cleanly or they may *ooze* a clear liquid.

315. Overdo (carried to excess–अधिक करना) : It is important never to *overdo* new exercises.

Overdue (past time for payment or some action–ठीक समय पर अदा न किया हुआ) : The meeting is long *overdue.*

316. Pray (entreat–प्रार्थना) : I *pray* to God every day.

Prey (hunt–शिकार) : Do not *prey* upon the innocent animals.

317. Principal (head of school or college–प्राचार्य) : Sh.R.C.Jha is the new *Principal* of our college.

Principle (rule–सिद्धान्त) : Do you understand anything about the *principles* of justice.

318. Prophecy (noun–foretold–भविष्यवाणी करना) : It is his *prophecy* that America will not attack Iraq.

Prophesy (verb–to foretell–भविष्यवाणी) : He *had prophesied* that Iraq would attack Kuwait.

319. Proffer (offer–प्रस्ताव) : Many lucrative proposals were *proffered* to him for acceptance.

Prefer (to choose–चुनना, अधिक आदर करना) : I *prefer* coffee to tea.

320. Practice (*noun*–अभ्यास) : *Practice* makes a man perfect.

Practise (*verb*–to practise) : Don't preach but *practise.*

321. Plain (easy, simple–साधारण) : One should try to write his thoughts in *plain* language.

Plane (to smoothen,level–चमकदार करना) : I use cream to *plane* my hair.

322. Peel (to remove the skin–छीलना) : You cannot eat a banana without *peeling* it.

Peal (sound of thunder or bells–घंटियों की ध्वनि) : I am hearing *peals* of trumpets.

323. Pare (to trim–टुकड़े करना) : *Pare* your nails and then polish them.

Pair (two–जोड़ी) : I have only three *pair* of shoes.

324. Peace (tranquillity–शान्ति) : *Peace* of mind is more precious than the materialistic richness.

Piece (fragment–टुकडा) : The dog found a *piece* of meat .

325. Price (value–कीमत) : What is the *price* of this shirt ?

Prize (reward–ईनाम) : She could not won any *prize* this time.

326. Persecute (to harass–परेशान करना) : Pakistani soldiers *persecuted* the Indians in a cruel manner.

Prosecute (to bring before a court–अभियोग चलाना) : He was *prosecuted* for murdering his wife.

327. Physic (medicine–दवा) : No *physic* can cure him of cancer.

Physique (bodily fitness–शारीरिक बनावट) : He possesses an attractive *physique*.

328. Prescribe (to direct–निर्देश देना) : The doctor has *prescribed* three doses of medicine after four hours daily.

Proscribe (to banish–देश निकाला देना) : The minister was *proscribed* by the king.

329. Patrol (going round–गश्त लगाना) : A chowkidar was *patrolling* at the main gate.

Petrol (oil–पेट्रोल) : *Petrol* is required to run vehicles.

330. Popular (familiar–लोकप्रिय) : Rajeev Gandhi was a very *popular* leader.

Populous (thickly inhabited–घनी आबादी वाला) : Delhi is a highly *populous* city.

Pail (bucket–बाल्टी) : I have two *pails* full of water.

Pale (yellowish apperance,wanted–पीला) : On seeing a lion, his face turned *pale*.

331. Paced (measured by footsteps–कदम) : This excellent thriller is fast *paced* and unbelievable.

Paste (thick glue–चिपकाना) : I need a tooth *paste*.

332. Pain (it hurts–दर्द) : I felt a sharp *pain* in my lower back.

Pane (a single panel of glass–काँच का पैनल) : The left *pane* of this window requires change.

333. Pair (a set of two–जोड़ा) : I need a new *pair* of socks.

Pare (cutting down–काटना) : Local authorities were instructed to *pare* their budget.

Pear (bottom–heavy fruit–नाशपाती) : I am fond of red *pears*.

334. Palate (मुँह मे ऊपर का भाग, तालु) : The top *part* of the inside of your mouth is called *palate*.

Pallet (छोटा, कठोर बिस्तर) : (a) A *pallet* is a narrow mattress filled with straw which is put on the floor for someone to sleep on. (b) A *pallet* is a hard, narrow bed. *He was given only a wooden pallet with a blanket.* (c) A *pallet* is a flat wooden or metal platform on which goods are stored so that they can be lifted and moved using a forklift truck. *The warehouse will hold more than 90,000 pallets storing 30 million Easter eggs.*

335. Pall (to become wearisome–अरुचिकर) : Already the allure of meals in hotels and restaurants began to *pall*.

Pawl (locks a ratchet–पहिये के दाँतों को रोकने का साधन) : A pivoted, usually curved, bar or lever whose free end engages with the teeth of a cog–wheel or ratchet so that it can only turn or move one way.

336. Pause (to hesitate–रुकना) : He talked for three hours non-stop without *pausing* for a minute.

Paws (foot of cat–पंजा) : The cat has white front *paws*.

337. Pea (round, green legume–मटर) : I like *peas* vegetable.

Pee (piss–पेशाब करना) : The driver was probably having a *pee*. He needed to pee.

338. Peak (mountain top–पहाड़ की चोटी) : He climbed up to the *peak* of the mountain.

Peek (secret look–चोरी से देखना) : On one occasion, she had *peeked* at him through a crack in the door.

Pique (नाराज होना) : (a) *Pique* is the feeling of annoyance you have, when you think someone has not treated you properly; Simi had gotten over her pique at Rue's refusal to accept the job. (b) If something *piques* your interest or curiosity, it makes you interested or curious;This phenomenon piqued Dr Mohit's interest... (c) If someone does something in a fit of *pique,* they do it suddenly because they are annoyed at being not treated properly; Lallu, in a fit of *pique,* left the Army and took up a career in the town.

339. Pearl (round, luminescent gem from an oyster–मोती) : She wore a string of *pearls* at her throat.

Purl (धातु का तार –Thread or cord of twisted gold or silver wire, used esp. for edging; edging etc. made from this.

340. Pedal (foot control–पैडल) : I am too tired to *pedal* again.

Peddle (to sell–बेचना) : He attempted to *peddle* his paintings around the city .

341. Peer (कुलीन पुरुष, सावधानी से देखना, पीर) : If you *peer* at something, you look at it very hard, usually because it is difficult to see clearly. I had been *peering* at a computer printout that made no sense at all... (b) In Britain, a *peer* is a member of the nobility who has or had the right to vote in the House of Lords; Lord Swan was made a life *peer* in 1981. (c) Your *peers* are the people who are the same age as you or who have the same status as you; His engaging personality made him popular with his *peers*.

Pier–(प्लेटफार्म) : A *pier* is a platform sticking out into water, usually the sea, which people walk along or use when getting onto or off boats.

342. Pi (3.1416–पाई) : *Pi* is a number, approximately 3.1416, which is equal to the distance round a circle divided by its width. It is usually represented by the Greek letter π.

Pie (good eating–स्वादिष्ट खाने की वस्तु, कचौड़ी) : A *pie* consists of meat , vegetables or fruit baked in pastry.

343. Pieced (assembled from pieces–पैबन्द लगाया, टुकड़े) : We will know the truth once the police have *pieced* all the facts together.

Piste (a ski run of compacted snow–बर्फ) : A track of firm snow for skiing on.

344. Pincer (claw–like gripping action–पंजे से पकड़ना) : The *pincers* of an animal, such as– a crab or a loberster are its front claws.

Pinscher (terrier–छोटा कुत्ता) : A short coated dog.

345. Pistil (डोडी) : seed–bearing organ of a flower.

Pistol (hand gun–पिस्तौल) : He was caught with a *pistol.*

346. Place (a location–स्थान) : This is a good *place* to live at.

Plaice (एक प्रकार की मछली) : *Plaice* are a type of flat sea fish.

347. Plait (braid–चोटी गूंथना, तह बनाना) : She parted her hair and then began to *plait* it into two thick braids.

Plate (a dish–थाली) : She pushed her *plate* away. She had eaten nothing.

348. Plum (purple fruit–बेर) : A *plum* is a small, sweet fruit with a smooth red or yellow skin and a stone in the middle.

Plumb (straight up and down–लम्ब, पाइप फिट करना (नल का)) : He knows how to *plumb* the pipe well.

349. Pole (a person from Poland–पोलैंड का निवासी) : He is a *pole*.

Pole (big stick–बड़ी लकड़ी, बल्ली) : I need a *pole* to climb up that house.

Poll (a voting–चुनाव कार्य) : More than 60 per cent of those *polled,* said that they approved of his record as Chairman.

350. Poor (no money–निर्धन) : A *poor* man can't afford a car.

Pore (careful study; microscopic hole– ध्यान में लीन होना, छोटा छिद्र) : We spent hours *poring* over the visa rules.

Pour (to flow freely–बहना) : He *poured* himself another drink.

351. **Precedence** (priority–प्राथमिकता) : Enjoy fully but don't let it take *precedence* over work.
Precedents (established course of action–परिपाटी, नजीर) : This case can set an important *precedent* for dealing with such cases in future.
Presidents (The chief–प्रधान) : The *president* is all in all of this society.

352. **Presence** (the state of being present–उपस्थिति) : The meeting took place in the *presence* of the Judge.
Presents (gifts–उपहार) : He gave a nice *present* to his friend on his wedding anniversary.

353. **Pride** (ego–गर्व) : We take *pride* in offering you the best services.
Pried (opened–खोलना) : I *pried* the top off a can of chilli.

354. **Profit** (money earned–लाभ) : The company has earned good *profit* in this quarter.
Prophet (seer–महान व्यक्ति) : He did it as per the instructions of the *prophet.*

355. **Pros** (benefits–फायदा) : Motherhood has both its *pros* and cons.
Prose (ordinary language–गद्य) : Shute's *prose* is stark and chillingly unsentimental.

356. **Quite** (altogether–पूरी तरह से) : I am *quite* well now.
Quiet (silent–शान्त) : Please keep *quiet.*

357. **Rein** (bridle–लगाम) : Keep the *rein* tight, otherwise you may be thrown out by the horse.
Reign (rule–शासन करना) : The *reign* of Akbar is known for communal harmony.

358. **Rite** (ceremony–रस्म) : Only a few *rites* were performed in his wedding.
Write (compose–लिखना) : I am to *write* a letter immediately.
Right (antonym of left–दायाँ) : This is my *right* leg.
Right (antonym to wrong–सही) : You have taken a *right* decision.
Wright (a worker–बनाने वाला) : He is a wonderful play *wright.*

359. **Raise** (to lift–ऊँचा उठाना) : I will *raise* this issue in parliament.
Raze (to destroy–नष्ट करना) : The storm *razed* many buildings to the ground.

360. **Route** (course–रास्ता) : By which *route* you came here?
Rout (flight–भगाना, छितराना) : The Pakistan armies were put to *rout.*

361. **Rap** (a sharp blow–थप्पड़) : He *rapped* her on the cheek.
Rape (to ravish–बलात्कार) : He *raped* a college girl.
Wrap (to enclose–बन्द करना) : The book was *wrapped* in a piece of white paper.

362. **Reclaim** (to win back–सुधारना) : He was *reclaimed* from his bad habits by his devoted wife.
Re-claim (to claim again–पुन: दावा करना) : He is thinking to *re–claim* the property on some other ground

363. **Recover** (regain–ठीक होना) : He has now *recovered* a lot from the weakness.
Re-cover (to cover again–पुन: ढकना) : *Re–cover* the sweets with some clean cloth.

364. **Road** (way–रास्ता) : The *road* has recently been repaired.
Rode (past of ride–सवारी की) : He *rode* on the horse yesterday.

365. **Ring** (an ornament for fingers–अंगूठी) : This *ring* is made of gold.
Wring (to twist,to squeeze–ऐंठना, निचोड़ना) : *Wring* the clothes well and put them on the ground.

366. **Rest** (respite–आराम) : I want some *rest* before starting the next assignment.
Wrest (snatch by force–छीनना) : Ram *wrested* a bag from Shyam.

367. **Roll** (to run over–नामावली, लोटपोट होना) : What is your roll number ? He *rolled* over the log to the right side of river.
Role (an actor's part–नाटक के पात्र का अभिनय) : I am playing the *role* of Ravana in this serial.

368. **Raise** (elevate–उठाना) : He *raised* is hand in support of the resolution.
Rays (thin beams of light–किरण) : The sun *rays* can penetrate water up to ten feet.
Raze (to tear down completely–नष्ट करना) : Many of villages have been *razed.*

369. **Read** (having knowledge from reading–पढ़ना) : I have *read* this novel.
Red (a primary colour–लाल रंग) : I like *red* colour shirt.

370. **Rede** (advice–सलाह) : It is always frutful to listen to the *rede* of your elders.
Reed (tall, thin water plant–नरकट, पेड़) : He has a beautiful *reed* plant.

371. **Real** (authentic–वास्तविक) : Yes it is a *real* story.
Reel (wavering move–चक्कर) : He lost is balance and *reeled* back.

372. **Recede** (to move backward–पीछे जाना) : As he *receded* she waved goodbye.
Reseed (to plant again–पुन: बीजारोपण) : He is trying to *reseed* the rose plant.

373. **Reek** (smells bad–गंदी बदबू) : Your breath *reeks* of stale cigar smoke.
Wreak (to inflict–बदला लेना) : She threatened to *wreak* vengeance on the men who toppled her some years ago.

374. **Retch** (heave–वमन करना, ओकाना) : If you *retch*, your stomach moves as if you are vomiting; The foul smell made me retch.
Wretch (wicked–नीच व्यक्ति) : Oh, what have you done, you *wretch*!

375. **Review** (a general survey or assessment–पुनर्विचार करना) : The P.M. *reviewed* the situation with his cabinet.
Revue (a series of theatrical sketches or songs) : A *revue* is a theatrical performance consisting of songs, dances, and jokes about recent events.

376. **Rheum** (watery discharge of mucous–नाक बहना) : *Rheum* is a mucous discharge caused by infection with a cold.
Room (partitioned space–कमरा) : I need a three *room* set.

377. **Rho**: (ग्रीक भाषा का 17वाँ शब्द) : seventeenth letter of Greek alphabet.
Roe (fish eggs–मछली के अंडे) : He is fond of cod's *roe*.
Row (aisle; pull an oar–पंक्ति, पतवार चलाना) : They were standing in *rows.*

378. **Rigger** (one who rigs–छल करने वाला) : A person who works with lifting–tackle; a person who erects and maintains scaffolding.
Rigour (discipline–अनुशासित) : He found the *rigours* of the tour too demanding.

379. **Rise** (to stand up–उठना) : The sun *rises* in the east.
Ryes (varieties of grain–राई) : I am fond of cheese on *rye.*

380. **Roam** (to wander–घूमना) : Barefoot cildren *roamed* the streets.
Rome (Italian capital–रोम) : *Rome* was not built in a day.

381. **Roil** (to make turbid) : (a–अशान्त) – If water *roils,* it is rough and disturbed. The water roiled to his left as he climbed carefully at the edge of the waterfall.
(b) Something that *roils,* a state or situation makes it disturbed and confused. Times of national turmoil generally roil a country's financial markets.
Royal (worthy of a king or queen–शाही) : He belongs to a *royal* family.

382. **Rood** (a cross–क्रॉस चिह्न) : A cross as an instrument of execution; The Cross on which Jesus suffered; the cross as the symbol of the Christian faith. He wears a golden *rood.*
Rude (coarse–असभ्य) : He is *rude* to her friends and obsessively jealous.

383. **Rot** (decay –सड़ना) : Sugary canned drinks can *rot* your teeth.
Wrought (made, worked–बनाया हुआ) : The recent results of presidential elections in USA *wrought* a change in US policy towards India.
Rote (by memory–रटना) : I am very sceptical about the value of *rote* learning.
Wrote (has written–लिखा) : He *wrote* a letter yesterday.

384. **Rough** (coarse–कठोर) : is hands are *rough*.
Ruff (pleated collar –कॉलर) : A *ruff* is a stiff strip of cloth or other material with many small folds (frills) in it, which some people wore round their neck in former times.

385. **Rude** (impolite–असभ्य) : I am unable to understand as to why she behaved so *rudely*.
Rued (regretted–पश्चाताप) : If you *rue* something that you have done, you are sorry that you did it, because it has had unpleasant results. (b) : If you *rue* the day that you did something, you are sorry that you did it, because it has had unpleasant results; You'll live to rue the day you said that to me, my girl.

386. **Rye** (grain–राई) : *Rye* is a kind of grain.
Wry (twisted–मुड़ा हुआ) : (a) If someone has a *wry* expression, it shows that they find a bad situation or a change in a situation slightly amusing; He allowed himself a wry smile...
(b) A *wry* remark or piece of writing refers to a bad situation or a change in a situation in an amusing way; There is a *wry* sense of humour in his work.

387. **Sooth** (truth–सच) : *Sooth* to speak, he is not a good boy.
Soothe (to calm–शांत करना) : You can't *soothe* his anger with lame excuses.

388. **Spacious** (enough space–विस्तीर्ण) : His office is quite *spacious* and well decorated.
Specious (attractive–आकर्षक) : With your *specious* look,you can't fool her.

389. **Stationary** (fixed –स्थिर) : Earth is not *stationary*, it moves round the sun.
Stationery (writing material, स्टेशनरी) : I am going to market to purchase several *stationery* items for the office.

390. **Straight** (opposed to curved –सीधा) : I believe in *straight* talks.
Strait (narrow –सँकरा) : The lane is too *strait* to pass through for an elephant.

391. **Sore** (painful –दर्दकारक) : I can't sing as my throat is *sore*.
Soar (to fly high –ऊँचा उड़ना) : Birds *soar* in sky.
Sour (not sweet –खट्टा) : The grapes were *sour*.

392. **Suit** (an action in court–दावा) : Bank has filed a civil *suit* against you for recovery of loan.
Suite (a set of room–कमरों का सेट) : I have reserved a *suite* for you in Alaska Hotel.

393. **Story** (a tale–कहानी) : My grand mother told me a *story* of an old man.
Storey (floor of a building–मंजिल) : I have taken a room at first *storey*.

394. **Serge** (a kind of cloth–एक प्रकार का कपड़ा) : This suit is made of *serge*.
Surge (move like waves तरंगों की तरह गति करना) : The waves of ocean *surge* violently in night.

395. **Shear** (to clip the wool–ऊन कतरना) : The sheep are being *shorn*.
Sheer (downright –एकमात्र) : He achieved success by the *sheer* force of his hard labour.

396. **Sun** (sun –सूर्य) : The *sun* is a star.
Son (पुत्र) : He is my *son*.

397. **Sole** (lower surface of shoe–जूते का तला, एकमात्र) : The *sole* of the right shoe requires repairing.
The sole aim of my life is to earn reputation in the society.
Soul (immaterial part–आत्मा) : You can't see *soul*. *Soul* is immortal.

398. **Stair** (step–सीढ़ी) : Let us go up the *stairs.*

Stare (gaze –घूरना) : It is wrong to *stare* at girls.

399. **Sing** (melodious sound–गाना) : She will *sing* a sweet song.

Swing (to oscillate–झूलना) : She has gone to enjoy *swing* ride.

400. **Sale** (to exchange for money–बिक्री) : This is not for *sale.*

Sail (to travel in water –तैरना) : Ships can *sail* in deep sea only.

401. **Sachet** (a small bag containing perfumed powder–छोटा पैकेट) : I found twenty *sachet* of coffee.

Sashay (to strut or flounce–चलना) : The models *sashay* down the catwalk.

402. **Sacks** (bags–थैले) : I found twenty *sacks* for potatoes.

Sax : short for *saxophone*

403. **Sane** (mentally normal–मानसिक रूप से स्वस्थ) : He is perfectly *sane.*

Seine (fishing net–मछली पकड़ने का जाल) : A large fishing net having floats at the top and weights at the bottom, so as to hang vertically in the water, the ends being drawn together to enclose the fish and the net usually hauled ashore.

404. **Saver** (one who saves–बचाने वाला) : Low interest rates are bad news for *savers.*

Savor (to relish a taste–स्वाद लेना) : People come here to *savor* the exquisite food provided by the owner.

405. **Sawed** (cut timber–लकड़ी काटना) : He *sawed* the timber very quickly.

Sod (–गुस्सा व्यक्त करना) : If someone uses an expression such as '*sod it*', '*sod you*' or '*sod that*', they are expressing anger or showing that they do not care about something.

406. **Scull** (rowing motion–नाव चलाना) : *Scull* are small oars which are held by one person and are used to move a boat through water.

Skull (head bone–खोपड़ी) : He was treated for a fractured *skull.*

407. **Seal** (to close–बन्द करना, मुहर) : He *sealed* the envelope and put on a stamp.

Seel (to close someone's eyes–आँखें बन्द करना, आँख मारना) : *Seel* the eyes of (a hawk etc.) by stitching up the eyelids.

408. **Seam** (row of stitches–सिलाई, सीवन) : (a) A *seam* is a line of stitches which joins two pieces of cloth together. (b) If something **is coming apart at the seams** or **is falling apart at the seams,** it is no longer working properly and may soon stop working completely; Britain's university system is in danger of *falling apart at the seams.* (c) : If a place is very full, you can say that it **is bursting at the seams;** The hotels of New Dehi were *bursting at the seams* during Asia Trade Fair.

Seem (appears–दिखना) : Everyone *seems* very busy here.

409. **Seamen** (sailors–नाविक) : He emigrated to work as *seaman.*

Semen (male discharge–वीर्य) : He is being treated for some *semen* problem.

410. **Sear** (scorched–मुरझाया या सूखा) : To *sear* something means to burn its surface with a sudden intense heat. Grass fires have seared the land near the farming villages of Haryana.

Seer (a person who sees) : A seer is a person who tells what will happen in the future.

411. **Serf** (slave–दास) : In former times, *serfs* were a class of people who had to work on a particular person's land and could not leave without that person's permission.

Surf (लहर, झाग) : *Surf* is the wave between rocks and the shore; surf is also 'the mass of white bubbles' that is formed by waves, as they fall upon the shore (a) : If you *surf,* you ride on big waves in the sea on a special board. I'm going to buy a surfboard and learn to surf... I'm going to be surfing bigger waves when I get to Australia! (b) If you *surf* the Internet, you spend time finding and looking at things on the Internet. (COMPUTING) No one knows how many people currently *surf* the Net.

412. Sewer (मल मार्ग) : A *sewer* is a large underground channel that carries waste matter and rain water away, usually to a place where it is treated and made harmless.

Sower (one who sows–बोने वाला)

Suer (one who *sues*–दावा करने वाला)

413. Shell The *shell* of a nut or egg is the hard covering which surrounds it; They cracked the nuts and removed their *shells*.

She'll (contraction of 'she will') : *She'll* cooperate you positively.

Shill (a decoy–प्रलोभन) : A decoy, an accomplice, *esp.* one posing as an enthusiastic or successful customer to encourage buyers, gamblers.

414. Sic (–इस प्रकार से) : You write *sic* in brackets after a word or expression when you want to indicate to the reader that although the said word looks odd or wrong, you intended to write it like that or the original writer wrote it like that; *The latest school jobs page advertises a 'wide range (sic) : of 6th form courses.*

Sick (ill–बीमार) : He is very *sick*. He needs medication.

Six (whole number–छ:) : I have *six* pencils.

415. Side (lateral–बगल) : There is a park on the left *side* of the road.

Sighed (breathed sorrowfully–आह भरी) : He *sighed* wearily.

416. Sign (displayed board bearing information–निशान) : Equations are generally written with a two bar equals (=) *sign*.

Sine (reciprocal of the cosecant) : Find the *sine* value of this angle.

417. Sink (to submerge–डूबना) : A fresh egg will *sink* and an old egg will float.

Synch (together in time–साथ-साथ, तालमेल के साथ) : If two things are out of *synch*, they do not match or do not happen together as they should. If two things are in *synch*, they match or happen together as they should. Normally, when demand and supply are out of *synch*, you either increase the supply, or you adjust the price mechanism...

418. Slay (kill–मारना) : He *slew* a man with a sword.

Sleigh (snow carriage–बर्फ पर चलने वाली गाड़ी) : A *sleigh* is a vehicle which can slide over snow. *Sleighs* are usually pulled by horses reindeers.

419. Slew (past tense of slay–हत्या की)

Slouch (to droop–झुकना)

Slough (a layer of dead tissue on a wound, a snakes cast skin–केंचुली) : When a plant *sloughs* its leaves, or an animal, such as– a snake *sloughs* its skin, the leaves or skin come off naturally. All reptiles have to slough their skin to grow...

Sloe (blackthorn berries–जंगली बेर) : A *sloe* is a small, sour fruit that has a dark purple skin. It is often used to flavour gin.

Slow (not fast–धीमा) : The traffic is heavy and *slow*.

420. Solace (comfort–आराम) : I founds *soalce* in writting when my friend died three months ago.

Soulless (lacking a soul–मृत) : If you describe a thing or person as *soulless*, you mean that they lack human qualities and the ability to feel or produce deep feelings; He is a *soulless person*.

421. **Some** (a few–कुछ) : Please give me *some* money.

Sum (result of addition–जोड़) : The *sum* of all the angles of a tringle is 180 degree.

422. **Soot** (black residue of burning–काजल) : *Soot* is black powder which rises in the smoke from a fire and collects on the inside of chimneys; *This wall is blackened by soot.*

Suit (clothes–पहनने का सूट) : I have a blue *suit.*

Suite (a set of rooms–कमरों का समूह) : We enjoyed our time during the week in a *suite* at London.

423. **Spade** (shovel–फावड़ा) : He used a *spade* for digging this pit.

Spayed (to sterilize a female animal–बधिया करना) : When a female animal is *spayed,* it has its ovaries removed so that it cannot become pregnant; All bitches should be spayed unless being used for breeding.

424. **Spoor** (trail of an animal–गंध से पशु की खोज करना) : The *spoor* of an animal is the marks or substances that it leaves behind as it moves along, which hunters canfollow.

Spore (single cell reproductive body–जीवाणु) : *Spores* are cells produced by bacteria and fungi which can develop into new bacteria or fungi.

425. **Staid** (reserved–गम्भीर) : If you say that someone or something is *staid,* you mean that they are serious, dull, and rather old–fashioned.

Stayed (remained–ठहरना) : In the old days the woman *stayed* at home and the man earned the livelihood.

426. **Stake** (a–दाव) : If something is *at stake*, it is being risked and might be lost or damaged if you are not successful; *The tension was naturally high for that game with so much at stake...* (b) If you *stake* something such as your money or your reputation **on** the result of something, you risk your money or reputation on it; *He has staked his political future on this election victory...* (c) If you have a *stake in* something such as a business, it matters to you, for example, because you own part of it or because its success or failure will affect you; *He was eager to return to a more entrepreneurial role in which he had a big financial stake.* (d) A *stake* is a pointed wooden post (खूँटा), which is pushed into the ground, for example in order to support a young tree. (e) : If you *stake* **a claim**, you say that something is yours or that you have a right to it. *Jasmine is determined to stake her claim as an actress...*

Steak (slice of meat–मांस का टुकड़ा) : He hates eating *steak.*

427. **Step** (a measure taken–कदम) : The next *step* is to put the theory into practice.

Steppe (a level, grassy, unforested plain–बिना जोता–बोया हुआ घास का मैदान) : *Steppes* are large areas of flat grassy land where there are no trees, especially the area that stretches from Eastern Europe across the south of the former Soviet Union to Siberia.

428. **Stile** (narrow passage–सँकरा रास्ता) : A *stile* is an entrance to a field or path consisting of a step on either side of a fence or wall to help people climb over it.

Style (mode–तरीका, शैली) : She had not lost her grace and *style.*

429. **Stoop** (a–झुकना) : If you *stoop*, you stand or walk with your shoulders bent forwards; *She was taller than he was and stooped slightly.* (b) If you *stoop*, you bend your body forwards and downwards; *He stooped to pick up the carrier bag of groceries...* (c) If you say that a person *stoops* to doing something, you are criticizing him because he does something wrong or immoral that they would not normally do; He had not, until recently, *stooped* to personal abuse... How could anyone *stoop* so low? (d) A *stoop* is a small platform at the door of a building, with steps leading up to it; They stood together on the *stoop* and rang the bell.

Stoup (a drinking cup–प्याला) : She served wine in beautiful *stoups.*

430. Succour (relief, assist–आराम) : Helicopters fly in appaling weather to succour ship wrecked mariners.

Sucker (one who sucks–चूसने वाला) : If you call someone a *sucker*, you mean that it is easy to cheat him.

431. Suede (split leather–एक प्रकार का चमड़ा) : He wore a *suede* jacket and jeans.

Swayed (a–प्रवृत करना) : When people or things sway, they lean or swing slowly from one side to the other; The people swayed back and forth with arms linked; The whole boat *swayed* and tipped. (b) If you are *swayed* by someone or something, you are influenced by them; Don't ever be swayed by fashion.(c) If someone or something *holds sway*, they have great power or influence over a particular place or activity; South of the Uk, a completely different approach seems to *hold sway*... (d) If you are under the sway of someone or something, they have great influence over you; How mothers keep daughters under their sway is the subject of the next five sections.

432. Sundae (आइसक्रीम) : A *sundae* is a tall glass of ice cream with whipped cream and nuts or fruit on top.

Sunday (first day of the week–रविवार) : Today is *Sunday.*

433. Team (a group of players–दल) : Our college *team* has won the trophy.

Teem (to be full of, abound –बहुतायत से उत्पन्न करना, बच्चा जनना) : Rajasthan is a state *teeming* with natural resources.

434. Toe (a part of foot–पैर का अंगूठा) : She hurt her left toe in an accident.

Tow (to draw by a rope–रस्सा बांध कर खींचना) : The boat was towed with a tree near the shore.

435. Tail (part of body –पूँछ) : Cow has a long *tail.*

Tale (story–कहानी) : My grand mother told me an interesting *tale.*

436. Their (belong to 'they'–उनका) : They have learnt *their* lesson.

There (at that place–वहाँ) : I am to go *there* now.

437. Throne (royal seat–सिंहासन) : All the brothers are fighting for the *throne.*

Thrown (III form of throw–फेंक दिया) : She has *thrown* her certificates into the river.

Thorn (impediment–काँटा) : You need a needle to get the *thorn* out.

438. Tenor (purpose –तात्पर्य) : The *tenor* of his speech was important from religious point of view.

Tenure (right of holding an estate –भूमि नियमन, पट्टा) : The Zamindari Abolition Act has finished the big problem of land *tenure* system in our country.

439. Tare (the seed of a vetch used in refence to its small size–एक प्रकार की घास) : When the harvest is gleaned the evil *tares* will be separated from the good wheat.

Tear (salty drops from eyes–आँसू) : Her eyes filled with *tears.*

Tier (a horizontal row–पंक्ति) : I have booked your seats in two *tier* compartment.

440. Taught (past tense of teach–पढ़ाया) : Who *taught* you english?

Taut (stretched tight–तना हुआ) : The clothes line is pulled *taut* and secured.

441. Tea (herbal infusion–चाय) : I am fond of *tea.*

Tee (golfball prop–गोल्फ से सन्बन्धित) : The *tee* was broken accidentally.

442. Tenner (English slang for a ten pound note–दस का) : I have only a *tenner* in my pocket.

Tenor (purpose–तात्पर्य) : The whole *tenor* of discussion has changed.

443. Tern (a shorebird–एक चिड़िया) : A *tern* is a small black and white seabird with long wings and a forked tail.

Terne (alloy of lead and tin–मिश्रित धातु) : This plate is made of *terne.*

Turn (rotate–घुमाव) : He *turned* left and went away.

444. The (denoting persons already mentioned–आर्टिकल) : *'The'* is the definite article.
Thee (objective case of thou–तुझे) : I missed *thee*, beloved mother!

445. Through (from end to end–बीच से) : Go straight *through* that door under the 'exit' word.
Throe (a spasm of pain–दर्द) : A violent physical spasm or pang, esp. in the pain and struggle of childbirth or death. Also, a spasm of feeling; mental agony; anguish.
Throw (to discharge through the air–फेंकना) : The crowd began *throwing* stones.

446. Thyme (herb–एक प्रकार का पौधा) : *Thyme* is a type of herb used in cooking.
Time (natures way of keeping everything from happening at once–समय) : What is the *time* by your watch.

447. Tic (twitch– मुख की पेशियों की एँठन) : If someone has a *tic*, a part of their face or body keeps making a small uncontrollable movement, either because they are tired or have a nervous illness.
Tick (small noise; parasitic bug–टिक-टिक) : He sat listening to the *tick* of the clock.

448. Tighten (to make tighter–जोर से बांधना) : I use my nail to *tighten* the screw on my torch.
Titan (a giant–बहुत बड़ा) : He is the richest business *titan* of our country.

449. Timber (wood for building–लकड़ी) : In Japan *timber* is used for construction of house.
Timbre (musical quality–ध्वनि) : The *timbre* of someone's voice or of a musical instrument is the particular quality of sound that it has. (FORMAL) : *His voice had a deep timbre.. The timbre of the violin is far richer than that of the mouth organ.*

450. Toad (frog–मेंढक) : A *toad* is a creature similar to frog.
Toed (to conform a policy–अनुसरण/स्वीकार करना) : He has never entirely *toed* the party line.
Towed (pulled ahead–ले जाना) : The policeman threatened to *tow* away my car.

451. Told (what was spoken–बोला) : He *told* me how to do it.
Tolled (a bell was rung–घंटी बजाई) : The pilgrims *tolled* the bell.

452. Track(narrow path or road–सँकरा रास्ता) : We set of once more, over a rough mountain *track*.
Tract (a plot of land–भूमि) : A vast *tract* of land is available for stadium.

453. Tray (a platter–ट्रे) : I need a *tray* for six cups of tea.
Trey (three–तिग्गी, तिड़ी) : The side of a die or a card marked with three pips or spots; a throw of die which turns up this side.

454. Troop (a company of soldiers–सिपाहियों का समूह) : Twenty thousands *troops* were deployed on the border.
Troup (a company of actors–ऐक्टर्स का समूह) : She belongs to an acrobatic performing *troup.*

455. Trussed (tied up–बांधना) : She *trussed* him quickly with a rope and gagged his mouth.
Trust (faith–विश्वास) : I *trust* you completely.

456. Umpire (a referee–अम्पायर) : You must not disobey the *umpire.*
Empire (dominion–राज्य) : The king was *unable* to manage his empire properly.

457. Vein (a blood vessel–शिरा) : *Veins* take the blood to heart from all parts of body.
Vane (weather cock–मुर्गा) : There is a *vane* at the top of the temple.

458. Vale (valley–घाटी) : The beautiful *vale* of Manali is worthseeing.
Veil (a cover–पर्दा) : Muslim ladies generally put a *veil* on her face.
Wail (to lament–विलाप करना) : Don't *wail* please, he is safe and sound.

459. Wave (unevenness–लहर) : The *waves* of ocean are rising higher and higher.
Wave (movement–हिलाना) : She *waved* her hand as the bus started.
Waive (relinquish–छोड़ना) : I request the officer to *waive* the punishment.

460. Waste (useless–व्यर्थ करना) : Don't *waste* your precious time.

Waist (part of body–कमर) : The boy had a chain round his *waist.*

461. Weather (atmosphere–मौसम) : It is cold *weather* today.

Whether (which of two–यदि) : I asked her *whether* she would come .

462. Vain (useless–व्यर्थ) : I made several requests to our Principal but all in *vain.*

Wane (to decrease–कम होना) : I see the moon *waning* these nights.

463. Vary (to change–बदलना) : Your actions vary from the promise you made.

Very (more–बहुत) : She is a *very* beautiful girl.

Wary (cautious-सतर्क) : Because of his *wary* nature, he was saved.

464. Vacations (holidays–छुट्टियाँ) : We are going to Delhi in summer *vacations.*

Vocation (occupation–पेशा) : What *vocation* you intend to join after graduation.

465. Verses (paragraphs–पद्य) : This *verse* describes three reasons of his failure.

Versus (against–विपरीत, बनाम) : India *versus* Pakistan is a greatly contesting cricket match.

466. Vial (narrow glass container–छोटा शीशे का पात्र, शीशी) : A *vial* is a very small bottle which is used to hold something such as perfume or medicine; Please give me a *vial* of rose perfume.

Vile (despicable, unpleasant–अरुचिकर) : She was in too *vile* a mood to work.

Viol (stringed instrument–यंत्र) : *Viols* are a family of musical instruments that are made of wood and have six strings. You play the *viol* with a bow while sitting down.

467. Vice (bad habit–गलत आदत) : She described that those responsible for offences are connected with *vices*, like drugs or gambling.

Vise (bench–mounted clamp–क्लैंप) : I need a good *vise* while I repair the furniture.

468. Weigh (to ascertain the weight–तौलना) : I am to purchase one *weighing* machine.

Way (passage–रास्ता) : This *way* leads to hospital.

469. Weight (weight–वजन) : He gained ten kg of *weight* within a month.

Wait (to attend–इन्तजार) : Don't *wait* for me, I will go myself.

470. Week (period of seven days–सप्ताह) : Monday is the first day of a *week.*

Weak (feeble–कमजोर) : Raju is too *weak* to walk.

471. Ware (article–सामान) : He has sold all his cook *wares.*

Wear (to put on–पहनना) : I like to *wear* silk sarees.

Wear (to diminish–घिसना) : My shirt has *worn* out .

472. Wine (drink –शराब) : Drinking *wine* is harmful for lever.

Vine (creeper–बेल) : The hut is covered with grape *vines.*

473. Wax (candle stuff–मोम) : Candles had spread pools of *wax* on the furniture.

Whacks (several blows–धमाका) : He gave the donkey a *whack* across the back with a stick. Someone *whacked* him on the head.

474. Wade (walk in shallow water–पानी में चलना) : Rescuers had to *wade* across a river to reach them.

Weighed (weight was measured–वजन किया) : He *weighed* approximately 270 kilos.

475. **Wain** (a wagon–छकड़ा, एक प्रकार की गाड़ी) : He has hired a *wain* for transporting his household goods.

Wane (decrease, fade–कम होना) : His interest in sports began to *wane*, a passion for golf developed.

476. **Want** (desire–इच्छा) : I *want* to become a surgeon.

Wont (inclined–आदत, अभ्यास) : (a) If someone is *wont to* do something, they often or regularly do it; Both have committed their indiscretions, as human beings are wont to do. (b) (accustomed) If someone does a particular thing as is their *wont*, they do that thing often or regularly; Ram woke early, as was his wont.

477. **War** (large scale armed conflict–युद्ध) : A *war* like situation is prevailed between India and Pakistan.

Wore (past tense of wear–पहना) : She *wore* a silken saree last night.

Ware (merchandise–सामान) : The box seems to contain glass *wares.*

478. **Warship** (naval implement of destruction–युद्धपोत) : *Warships* played a decisive role in the victory of our forces.

Worship (revere in a religious manner–पूजा) : I enjoyed *worshipping* God .

479. **Wary** (cautious–सावधानी) : People do not teach their wards to be *wary* of strangers.

Wherry (छोटी नाव) : A light rowing boat used chiefly on rivers and in harbours for carrying passengers.

480. **We** (us–हम) : *We* are going to market.

Wee (a–छोटा साइज, नन्हा) : *Wee* means small in size or extent.He just needs to calm down a wee bit. **(b)** : To *Wee* means to urinate; *Wee* is an informal word used especially by children; He said he wanted to wee; (c) *Wee* is also a noun.The baby has done a wee in his potty...

481. **We'd** (contraction of 'we would') : *We'd* meet you there positively.

Weed (wild plants–खर-पतवार) : If you don't care the garden it will be soon full of *weeds.*

482. **We're** (contraction of 'we are') : *We're* friends.

Weir (a low dam, or a fence in a river for catching fish–नदी का बन्धा, बांध) : A *weir* is a low barrier which is built across a river in order to control or direct the flow of water. (b) A *weir* is a wooden fence which is built across a stream in order to create a pool for catching fish.

Were (past tense plural of 'to be') : Where *were* you playing?

Whir or whir (prolonged swish or buzz–घरघराहट) : When something, such as-a machine or an insect's wing **whirrs**, it makes a series of low sounds so quickly that they seem like one continuous sound; The camera *whirred* and clicked.

483. **We've** (contraction of 'we have') : *We've* twenty pencils only.

Weave (to make cloth–कपड़े बुनना) : They were busy in *weaving* cotton fabrics.

484. **Wheeled** (having wheels–पहिया युक्त, पहियों पर ढोया) : We *wheeled* her out on the stretcher.

Wield (to apply or use–काम में लाना) : (a) If you *wield* a weapon, tool, or piece of equipment, you carry and use it; The assailant was wielding a kitchen knife. (b) : If someone *wields* power, they have it and are able to use it; He remains president, but wields little power at the company.

485. **Weld** (to join metal by melting its edges–वेल्डिंग करना) : Where did you learn to *weld*.

Welled (pouring forth–अधिक होना) : Her love for him *welled* stronger than ever.

486. **Wet** (watery–गीला) : She towelled her *wet* hair.

Whet (prime–भूख बढ़ाने या जगाने वाली वस्तु) : If someone or something *whets* your **appetite for** a particular thing, they increase your desire to have it or know about it, especially by giving you an idea of what it is like; A really good catalogue can also *whet* customers' appetites for merchandise.

487. **Which** (selection–किसका) : *Which* dress do you like most.

Witch (जादूगरनी) : In fairy stories, a *witch* is a woman, usually an old woman, who has evil magic powers; *Witches* often wear a pointed black hat, and have a pet black cat.

488. **While** (during–जबकि) : He was reading *while* she was cooking.

Wile (A crafty, cunning, or deceitful trick; a stratagem, a ruse.–चालाकी, धोके बाजी) : She used all her *wiles* to earn his favour.

489. **Whine** (annoying cry–दर्द भरी आवाज) : I can hear my dog *whining* in the courtyard.

Wine (fermented grape juice–दारू) : This is a nice *wine*.

490. **Whit** (insignificant amount–बहुत थोड़ी राशि) : He cared not a *whit* for the social, political or religious aspects of literature.

Wit (cleverness; sense of humor–चतुराई) : He was at his *wit's* end.

491. **Whither** (to which place, point, condition, etc.?–कौन-से स्थान को/से) : They knew not *whither* they went.

Wither (wilt–मुरझाना) : The flowers *withered* away within three hours..

492. **Whoa** (*Whoa* is a command that you give to a horse to slow down or stop.–वाह) : You can say *whoa* to someone who is talking to you, to indicate that you think they are talking too fast or assuming things that may not be true.

Woe (despair–दुख, निराशा) : She listened to my tale of *woes* very patiently.

493. **Yearn** (to long–इच्छा करना) : I am anxiously *yearning* to meet my wife.

Yarn (thread–धागा) : I have purchased three bundles of *yarn*.

494. **Yoke** (slavery–दास बनाना) : He is under the *yoke* of his master.

Yolk (yellow portion of an egg–अंडे की पीली जर्दी) : Some people eat only the *yolk* of an egg.

495. **Yore** (the past–भूतकाल) : *Yore* is used to refer to a period of time in the past; The images provoked strong surges of nostalgia for the days of *yore*.

You're (contraction of 'you are') : *You're* a great writer.

Your (belonging to you–तुम्हारा) : Which is *your* house.

496. **You'll** (contraction of 'you will') : *You'll* be asked to explain your conduct.

Yule (Christmas–क्रिसमस) : Every one makes enjoyment in his own way during *yule* time.

SPECIFIC USE OF WORDS (SIMILAR MEANING)

सही लिखने एवं शुद्ध बोलने हेतु न केवल शब्दों के अर्थ का ज्ञान आवश्यक है, अपितु उनके उचित प्रयोग का ज्ञान भी बहुत आवश्यक है। मात्र शाब्दिक अर्थ का ज्ञान, शब्द के उचित प्रयोग हेतु पर्याप्य नहीं है। इस अध्याय को पढ़ने से आपको यह स्पष्ट हो जायेगा :

1. **Abstain** (from a thing) : One should *abstain* from sex without condom.
   Refrain (from doing) : One should *refrain* from making unwarranted comments.
2. **Revenge** (to return injury for injury) : She *revenged* herself upon Ramesh, her former lover.
   Avenged (to punish the evil doers) : He has devoted the past three years to *avenging* his daughter's death.
3. **Allow** (giving permission for otherwise unreasonable thing) : The girls were *allowed* to talk in the class by the principal.
   Permit ('to give'a positive assent) : 'I was *permitted* to appear in the M.A. examination.'
4. **Anger** (a sudden feeling of unhappiness) : The people showed great *anger* at the news.
   Resentment (more lasting feeling of unhappiness) : My words could not lessen hers *resentment.'*
5. **Attain** (to get by labour) : 'We *attained* a high degree of success through quality management.
   Acquire (to have something permanently) : The students of this section have *acquired* a thorough knowledge of Naturopathy.'
6. **Ancient** (opposite to modern) : 'We can learn a lot by the events of *ancient* history of India.'
   Old (opposed to new and to young) : 'The *old* dressing pattern is liked by the people even today; '*Old* people prefer simplicity to show.'
7. **Astonishment** (extreme surprise with some perplexity or confusion) : 'I was *astonished* to see him driving a two wheeler.
   Surprise (arising on the occurrence of something unexpected) : 'Your failure in the examination has *surprised* everyone.'
   Wonder (surprise with admiration) : I *wondered* at his securing first position at all India level.
8. **Admit** (to acknowledge as true) : He didn't *admit* that he was present in the house.
   Confess (to acknowledge responsibility or guilt) : He *confessed* that he had stolen the bike.
9. **Reply** (to a letter) : He always *replies* in time.
   Answer (to a question) : *Answer* only five questions.
10. **Ability** (Intellectual quality) : He is promoted on the basis of his *ability* to perform in a better way.
    Capacity (capable to hold or achieve) : His *capacity* to work, regularly is praiseworthy.
11. **Bravery** (in the blood) : The *bravery* of Rajputs is well known.
    Courage (in mind) : He has the *courage* to speak the truth.
    Valour (a quality more than bravery or courage) : The black commandoes are known for their deeds of *valour.*
    Daring (rashness) : He is *daring* but not prudent.
    Boldness (a short lived quality) : He showed his *boldness* in catching the robber single handed.
12. **Battle** (a contest between two opposing armies) : 'The third *battle* of Panipat was the last nail in the coffin of the Mughal Empire.'
    War (a series of contests continued for a long time) : The world *war* I and II saw the pinnacle of inhumane face of the weapons made by the men.

13. **Begin** (used on all occasions) : 'The sooner you *begin* the better it is.
Commence (used only in official and formal language) : 'The examinations will *commence* on the 25th of May.'

14. **Beautiful** (used for girls) : She is a *beautiful* girl.
Handsome (used for man) : He is a *handsome* boy.

15. **Custom** (relates to community or society) : Wearing kumkum after marriage is a *custom* among the Hindus
Habit (relates to individual) : Smoking is a bad *habit.*

16. **Crime** (against law of the state) : Theft is a *crime.*
Vice (offence against morals) : Drinking is a *vice.*
Sin (against law of religion or society) : Abusing elders is a *sin.*

17. **Ceiling** (inner portion of roof) : I want to purchase one *ceiling* fan.
Roof (upper covering of house) : They are playing at the *roof* of their house.

18. **Cite** (is used for things or persons) : 'He *cited* the authority of the Supreme court Judgement.
Quote (is used for thisngs only) : 'He *quoted* passage after passage from Geeta.'

19. **Compulsion** (is physical, what is generally against our wishes) : 'He was *compelled* by the court to be present on the next date.
Obligation (is moral; what is imposed on us as a duty) :'We are *obliged* to maintain those who depend on us.'

20. **Confer** (conferring is an act of authority) : 'The government *confers* titles like Bharat Ratna, Padma Bhushan etc. on eminent persons.'
Bestow (an act of generosity / charity) : 'Many presents were *bestowed* on the refugees.'

21. **Character** (mental or moral nature) : 'A man of *character* overcomes all temptations.'
Conduct (one's actions) : 'None can blame you, if your *conduct* is good.'

22. **Contentment** (inner satisfaction when nothing more is required) : Actual happiness consists in *contentment.*
Satisfaction (fulfillment of one's desire) : She completed the preparations to my entire *satisfaction.*

23. **Contagious** (disease spread by contact) : Small pox is a *contagious* disease.
Infectious (disease spread through air or mosquitoes etc.) : Malaria is an *infectious* disease.

24. **Cool** (pleasant feeling) : A *cool* wind is blowing.
Cold (unpleasant feeling) : Weather is very *cold* today.

25. **Defend** (against an attack) : Indian army is capable to *defend* the nation against any attack.
Protect (relates to an approaching injury) : Woolen clothes *protect* us from cold.

26. **Deny** (relates to a past action) : He *denied* his involvement in the murder.

27. **Doubt** (a negative feeling) : I *doubt* his loyalty (I think that he is not loyal) :
Suspect (a positive feeling) : I *suspect* his involvement in the crime. (I am thinking that he was not involved)

28. **Discover** (relates to thing already in existence) : A new star was *discovered* by him.
Invent (a new thing is created) : Who *invented* telephone?

29. **Drown** (relates to living beings) : Many persons were *drowned* in this river last year.
Sink (relates to things) : A ship dashed against this rock and *sank,* last year.

30. **Wish** (used in reference to a remote thing) : I *wish,* I were a king.
Desire (used in reference to achievable things) : I *desire* to have a beautiful house and a name in the society.

31. **Want** (relates to a thing, which is absent) : I *want* to buy a car.
Need (relates to necessary things) : I *need* a pen to write with.

Require (to demand) : You are *required* to attend the meeting.

32. **Envy** (bad feeling) : He is *envious* of his friend's prosperity.
Jealousy (positive feeling of possessing something) : I am *jealous* of our ancestral heritage.

33. **Sufficient** (necessary for) : Two persons are *sufficient* for this job.
Enough (more than necessary) : I have *enough* money for the education of my children.

34. **Accident** (an unexpected happening) : Train *accidents* have become common now a days.
Incident (an ordinary occurrence) : Our newspapers are full of daily *incidents.*
Event (an important happening) : The third battle of Panipat was an important *event* in the history of India.

35. **Notorious** (in bad sense) : He is a *notorious* cheat.
Famous (in good sense) : Newyork is *famous* for multi- storeyed buildings.
Renowned (high reputation) : Shakespeare was a *renowned* dramatist.

36. **Excuse** (xourteously used for trifle matters) : Please *excuse* me for troubling you at this time.
Forgive (used for comparatively big offences) : Please *forgive* me for my speaking ill about your friend.
Pardon (generally used for asking repetition of something) : I beg your *pardon* (Please repeat, I was unable to understand earlier) :

37. **Freedom** (implies absence of restraint at the moment) : We enjoy several kinds of *freedom.*
Liberty (implies previous restraint) : The prisoner was set at *liberty.*

38. **Falsehood** (something said or done with wrong intentions) : 'He was guilty of *falsehood* when he spoke against the character of the Chairman.'
Lie (speak untrue words) : Never tell a *lie.*

39. **House** (refer to a dwelling unit) : I am going to purchase a new *house.*
Home (place to live with family association) : Men make houses, women make *homes.*

40. **Listen** (to hear attentively) : The teacher asked the students to *listen.*
Hear (to get through ears) : I am *hearing* your voice.

41. **Hope** (is used when what we anticipate is welcome) : I *hope* to get selected this time.
Expect (is used when what we anticipate is certain, whether welcome or not) : 'Every student is *expected* to carry out the instructions given in the notes.

42. **Hardly** (refers to degree) : You can *hardly* imagine how much I suffered because of her allegation.
Scarcely (refers to quantity) : Don't ask me, I have *scarcely* enough for my own use.'

43. **Idle** (having nothing to do, due to circumstances) : He has been sitting *idle* due to great slump in the market.
Lazy (habit of not doing things in active manner) : He is too *lazy* to reply letters.

44. **Sick** (mental feeling) : He is a *sick* man.
Ill (out of health) : She is *ill* nowadays.

45. **Libel** (written) : His statement in the press release amounts to *libel.*
Slander (spoken) : His public speech was taken note of and an action for *slander* is being initiated.

46. **Oral** (spoken words) : 'He was failed in *oral* examination.
Verbal (written words) : Teachers were abused *verbally* and assaulted physically.

47. **Presume** (pre decision of a thing) : I *presume* he is responsible for the loss in business.
Assume (assuming anything true) : I *assume* he will help you in case of need.

48. **Place** (to put) : *Place* the keys on the chair.
Keep (to put at some defined place) : *Keep* the books in the shelf.

49. **Possible** (can be done) : It is not *possible* to reach there by car .
Probable (likely to happen) : It is *probable* that she may agree with our proposal.

50. **Blunder** (a gross mistakes) : Disclosing business secrets to the rivals is a *blunder* on your part.
Mistake (small act) : It is a *mistakes* to go on leave without taking prior permission.
Error: (doing things against the recognised norms) : Your essay is full of grammatical *errors.*

51. **Praise** (for actions) : His actions are *praiseworthy.*
Admire (for qualities) : Everybody *admires* him for his benevolent nature.

52. **Prohibit** (has force of law) : The government has *prohibited* the cow slaughter.
Forbid (relating to personal life) : *Forbidden* fruits taste more sweet.

53. **Recollect** (remember after some efforts) : Can you *recollect* what exact words did he use ?
Remember (having in memory) : I *remember* his words well.

54. **Regret** (for a thing done or left undone) : I felt *regret* for not completing the job in time.
Sorrow (for big harm or evil) : Her husband's death caused her deep *sorrow.*

55. **Redress** (to correct something wrong) : 'The agrieved party looks to the court for *redress.'*
Relief (feeling happiness because something wrong did not happen) : I breathed a sigh of *relief.*

56. **Rob** (to take away by force) : He was *robbed* of his money and jewellery.
Steal (to take away secretly) : The thieves *stole* away all the goods from my house last Sunday.

57. **Talk** (speaking with others) : I want to *talk* to him on this matter.
Tell (to inform) : He *tells* me to wear neat dress.
Speak (to say in ordinary way) : He *speaks* loudly.
Say (to assert) : How did you *say* so ?

58. **Seem** (something assumed by our mind) : The moon *seems* moving very fast.
Appear (Impression of objects on us) : The statue *appears* to be of ancient time.

59. **See** (In an ordinary way) : I can *see* that house.
Look (see with some attention) : *Look* at that house.
Watch (to observe closely) : Keep a *watch* on that house.

60. **Scenery** (a view of landscape) : The *scenery* of Manali is indeed beautiful.
Scene (a place of any happening, a landscape) : He captured many beautiful *scenes* in his camera.

61. **Treaty** (a written or formal arrangement) : India and the USA have signed a *treaty.*
Truce (a temporary suspension of conflict) : On NewYear eve, a *truce* was announced by the fighting militant groups.

62. **Trifling** ('no importance' matter) : 'She never neglects even a *trifling* matter.'
Trivial ('a small matter, no seriousness) : 'Do not waste your time on *trivial* details.

63. **Trade** (small or large scale buying-selling; it can be within or out of the country) : India has a long history of *trade* with USA.
Commerce (on a large scale; generally with foreign countries) : They have made their fortune from industry and *commerce.*

64. **Empty** (having nothing in it) : The briefcase is *empty.*
Vacant (having some occupancy) : Only one berth is vacant in this compartment.

WORDS DERIVED FROM THE SAME ROOT

In English, we find several words, which are derived from the same root word. These words differ slightly in form but in many cases the meanings differ a lot. Such words are also called Paronyms.

अर्थात्, Paronyms ऐसे शब्दों को कहते हैं, जो एक ही parent word से बनते हैं। ये दिखने में काफी मिलते-जुलते से लगते हैं एवं कई बार इनका अर्थ काफी भिन्न होता है। नीचे ऐसे शब्दों को दिया गया है। छात्रों को ऐसे शब्दों का अध्ययन काफी ध्यानपूर्वक करना चाहिये।

1. **Alternate** (by turn) : He comes here on *alternate* days.
   Alternative (choice between two things) : There were *alternative* methods of travel available.
2. **Acceptance** (accepting a thing) : I am happy to learn that she has given her consent for the attending the court.
   Acceptation (interpretation) : There are several *acceptations* of the word 'Nature'.
3. **Access** (approach) : I was not allowed *access* to a lawyer.
   Accession (becoming sovereign) : Today is the 50th anniversary of the queen's *accession* to the throne.
4. **Act** (to do) : I shall *act* as per the wishes of my parents.
   Action (doing things) : His timely *action* saved him from the loss.
5. **Admission** (being admitted) : He has taken *admission* in evening college.
   Admittance (to let in) : He was denied *admittance* in the hall.
6. **Artist** (performer of fine art) : A poet is no less an *artist* than a sculpture.
   Artiste (performer in singing, dancing etc.) : The group consists of several *artistes.*
7. **Artistic** (having aesthetic values) : This painting is indeed very *artistic.*
   Artful (cunning, clever) : He wants to achieve success by *artful* means.
   Artificial (antonym of natural) : City life is becoming more *artificial* day by day.
   Artisan (well versed in hardicrafts) : The *artisans* of Nepal are very hardworking and efficient.
8. **Appropriation** (to take possession of) : He was charged for *appropriation* of Bank's fund.
   Appropriateness (suitability) : The work of Harivansh Rai Bachchan is renowned for its *appropriateness* in style.
9. **Affecting** (touching, pathetic) : The movie has many *affecting* scenes and situations
   Affectation (false pretense) : Political leaders speak with *affectation* and artfulness.
10. **Besides** (in addition) : *Besides* paying my debt, he also gave me money for the medicines.
    Beside (by the side) : In Republic day function none was sitting *beside* the President.
11. **Barbaric** (simple, used in good sense) : I like her *barbaric* simplicity.
    Barbarian (Primitive) : 'Johar'and 'Sati' are the *barbarian* customs.
    Barbarous (cruel-used in bad sense) : War is indeed a *barbarous* act.
12. **Barbarism** (uncivilised condition) : In some part of Bihar, absolute barbarism prevails even nowadays.
    Barbarity (cruelty) : Aurangzeb was notorious for his *barbarity.*
13. **Confident** (certain) : I am *confident* that she will come.
    Confidant (reliable) : He is a cheat, don't make him your *confidant.*
14. **Completion** (end) : After *completion* of this work you are to go to Kolkata.
    Completeness (perfection) : None can claim *completeness* of knowledge in any field.

15. **Ceremonious** (overdone formalities) : His greetings and salutations are too *ceremonious*.
Ceremonial (pertaining to ceremony) : Diwali is a *ceremonial* occasion for Hindus.
16. **Comprehensive** (involves all aspects) : This book gives us *comprehensive* knowledge of English.
Comprehensible (understandable) : His views on this subject are not only clear but *comprehensible* also.
17. **Considerable** (much) : I have spent a *considerable* time in solving this problem.
Considerate (thoughtful) : He being a *considerate* man, can't refuse to sign this proposal.
18. **Continuous** (uninterrupted) : He has been *continuously* working on computer for the last three hours.
Continual (occasional breaks) : There has been *continual* raining since yesterday
19. **Child-like** (in good sense-act like a child) : Her *child-like* face attracts everybody.
Childish (in bad sense -silly act) : His *childish* habits annoyed everybody.
20. **Complacent** (pleasing look) : Indian farmers are *complacent* in their look.
Complaisant (polite) : She is a *complaisant* and intelligent girl.
21. **Dependent** (to rely on) : I am not *dependent* on anybody for my livelihood.
Dependant (depend on others) : My younger brother is *dependant* on me.
22. **Disinterested** (without self-interest) : Mother Teresa rendered *disinterested* service to the downtrodden.
Uninterested (indifferent) : Amitabh is *uninterested* in politics.
23. **Divers** (several) : *Divers* are trying to reach the top.
Diverse (dissimilar-different) : *Diverse* opinions were given by the members on this proposal.
24. **Decided** (past of decide) : He *decided* to go to Europe the next week.
Decisive (that which decides some thing important) : The battle of Plassey was a *decisive* one.
25. **Destination** (the place to reach) : The last *destination* of this train is Puri.
Destiny (fate) : One can make his *destiny* with hard labour.
26. **Envious** (feeling envy) :You should not be *envious* of your friend's progress.
Enviable (a rousing envy) : His *enviable* posting made many jealous of him.
27. **Effectual** (creating desired effects) : He adopted the *effectual* means and so got the contract.
Efficacious (sufficient to have desired result) : Quinine is nowadays not *efficacious* in malaria.
28. **Egotist** (self conceited) : I can not discuss anything with an *egotist* like you.
Egoist (selfish,self interested) : He is an *egoist*, he believes that self interest is the base of all actions.
29. **Especially** (pertaining to exceptional degree) : Her mother was *especially* invited on the occasion.
Specially (for the purpose) : I came *specially* to attend the function.
30. **Exceptional** (unusual) : J.L.Nehru was a man of *exceptional* qualities.
Exceptionable (objectionable) : His speech was full of *exceptionable* remarks.
31. **Exposition** (description) : Tennin's *exposition* of Ramayan is incomparable.
Exposure (to open air, cold etc.) : Protect yourself from *exposure* otherwise you may catch cold.
32. **Economic** (relating to economy) : The *economic* condition of our country is not so good.
Economical (thrifty) : He is very *economical* in spending the money.
33. **Funeral** (ceremony after death) : More than ten thousand people attended the *funeral* of his father.

Funereal (gloomy) : He came to the office with a *funereal* countenance.

34. **Fatal** (deadly) : He received a *fatal* wound in his chest.
Fatalist (believes in fate) : I am not a *fatalist.*
Fateful (lucky, important) : Fifteen August is a *fateful* day in Indian history.

35. **Forceful** (commanding force) : He enjoys a *forceful* personality.
Forcible (under compulsion) : Police made a *forcible* entry in his house.

36. **Godly** (pious) : Mahatma *Gandhi* led a godly life.
God-like (like God) : Mahatma Gandhi was a *God-like* man.

37. **Graceful** (handsome-smart) : She has a *graceful* appearance.
Gracious (kind) : God is *gracious.*

38. **Honorary** (without any remuneration) : He was nominated '*Honorary*' Chairman of the society.
Honourable (deserve honour, respected) : I request the *honourable* Principal to come on the dais.

39. **Imaginary** (not real) : Equator is an *imaginary* line.
Imaginative (pertaining to imagination) : A good writer must have *imaginative* ideas.

40. **Industrious** (laborious) : Nothing is impossible for an *industrious* and sincere student.
Industrial (relating to industry) : Bhiwadi is an *industrial* town.

41. **Intelligent** (wise) : He is an *intelligent* guy.
Intelligible (understandable) : He delivered an *intelligible* speech on educational necessities of rural area.

42. **Judicial** (pertaining to legal system or Judge) : Government has ordered a *judicial* enquiry in the matter.
Judicious (prudent, wise) : Going for a war is not a *judicious* decision.

43. **Loudly** (high volume) : Please do not speak so *loudly* in library room.
Aloud (audible voice) : He spoke *aloud* so that all could hear him.

44. **Luxuriant** (refer more growth) : There is a *luxuriant* growth of vegetables in our kitchen garden.
Luxurious (luxury) : He is leading a *luxurious* life after the death of his father.

45. **Lovable** (worthy of love) : He is a *lovable* person.
Lovely (charming) : What a *lovely* girl she is !

46. **Limit** (boundary) : Keep yourself within the *limits*, otherwise you have to face the music.
Limitation (restrictions) : Being a girl, I have many *limitations.*

47. **Memorial** (statue, building to commemorate) : You can find many *memorials* at Rajpath, New Delhi.
Memorable (rememberable) : 26th January is a *memorable* day in Indian history.

48. **Momentary** (for a moment) : His anger is *momentary*, soon things will be okay.
Momentous (important) : The battle of Plassey was a *momentous* event in the history of India.

49. **Negligible** (unimportant) : There is a *negligible* difference between this shirt and the shirt we saw in that shop.
Negligent (careless) : She is generally *negligent* about her health.
Neglectful (careless about a thing) : She is so *neglectful* that she does not care even for her career.

50. **Officious** (over kind) : His *officious* attitude towards her creates doubts.
Official (relating to office) : As a responsible *official* of a company, you must behave properly.

52. **Practical** (antonym of theoritical) : He failed in *practical* examination; He is a practical business man.
Practicable (capable of being carried out) : This is not a *practicable* plan.

53. **Political** (relating to politics) : We should not trust the *political* statements of leaders.
Politic (sagacious, prudent) : It is not *politic* to argue with an intoxicated person.

54. **Pitiable** (relating to pity) : His condition is indeed *pitiable.*
Pitiful (feeling pity) : Seeing her pitiable condition every one became *pitiful.*

55. **Prophecy** (noun-forecast) : He made a *prophecy* that whole of the world would be destroyed in 2202.
Prophesy (verb-to forecast) : I can *prophesy* that within five years India will be a very powerful country.

56. **Respective** (particular thing or person) : After prayer, students should join their *respective* teams.
Respectful (full of respected) : One should be *respectful* to one's teachers, elders.

57. **Righteous** (just) : Her anger was *righteous* as no girl could tolerate such insult.
Rightful (just claim) : I am the *rightful* owner of this car.

58. **Regrettable** (causing regret) : It is quite *regrettable* that you are not taking care of your father.
Regretful (full of regret) : I am not at all *regretful* for my actions.

59. **Servility** (flattery) : I can't adopt an attitude of *servility* to get promotion.
Servitude (slavery) : Try to come out of this state of *servitude.*

60. **Sociable** (fond of getting social) : She has a *sociable* nature.
Social (relates to society) : She is not only *social* but also very cooperative.

61. **Sensuous** (used in good-sense for appreciation of beauty) : Keats was a *sensuous* poet.
Sensual (used in bad sense means voluptuous) : He was jailed for his *sensual* advancement towards his college friend.

62. **Sensitive** (touchy) : Cow slaughter is a *sensitive* issue for Hindus.
Sensational (exciting) : There are many *sensational* stories of murder in this magazine.

63. **Spirituous** (alcoholic) : Gujarat has banned the use of *spirituous* drinks in restaurants.
Spiritual (pertaining to soul) : She is a *spiritual* lady.

64. **Tolerant** (refers to a person, who respects different opinions) : Akbar was regarded as a *tolerant* king.
Tolerable (bearable) : Because of his *tolerable* nature, he didn't lodge F.I.R. against you.

65. **Temperament** (disposition) : Because of his violent *temperament*, he often gets into trouble.
Temperance (sobriety) : He should observe *temperance* in drinking and dancing.

66. **Temporal** (antonym to spiritual) : Nowadays people are ready to do anything for *temporal* gains.
Temporary (for a short time) : I offered her a *temporary* job.

67. **Transitory** (short lived) : The life is not eternal but *transitory.*
Transient (of short duration) : The world is *transient.*

68. **Union** (to be united) : *Union* is strength .
Unity (one ness) : There is no *unity* among different classes of the society.
Unison (harmony) : There was a good *unison* of Tabla and Violin in the conert.

69. **Virtual** (in effect) : Sanjay Gandhi was the *virtual* head of Congress Party.
Virtuous (of good moral values) : Sita was a *virtuous* lady.

70. **Wilful** (knowingly) : He was charged for *wilful* negligence.
Willing (ready) : I am *willing* to help her.

71. **Womanly** (used in good sense, affectionately) : My wife possess all *womanly* qualities.
Womanish (used in bad sense, means-cowardly and weak like woman) : Everyone likes to dominate a man of *womanish* temperament.

72. **Wait** (generally used intransitively) : Please *wait* for me .
Await (lie in wait) : A surprise *awaited* them at their home.

73. **Weary** (tired) : You look pale and *weary.*
Wearisome (tiring) :The journey was *wearisome.*

74. **Yield** (return) : What is the annual *yield* from the fields?
Yielding (submissive) : He is a man of *yielding* nature.

WORDS NOT USED IN GOOD SENSE

Certain words and phrases are seldom used in good sense. To use these words where a good sense is meant, will be quite ridiculous. It would be absurd to say ; **'He is a notorious scientist', or 'He concocted a good plan for the welfare of the poor'**. Students should learn these words well and try to understand the difference. Mere Hindi meanings of these words will not suffice to use these words properly.

Accident	—	They met with an accident.
Accomplice	—	Partner in some crime; He was an accomplice in the theft.
Addicted	—	To some bad habit, drinking, gambling etc.
Adversary	—	An opponent : one who can cause harm.
Airs	—	He should not give himself airs (conceited= airs).
Apprehensive	—	Of some danger, loss or injury.
Artisan	—	Who practises some art of inferior nature.
Blunder	—	A very serious mistake.
Catastrophe	—	A disastrous happening.
Coalition	—	Of men of divergent or opposite views : It refers a kind of partnership which is not homogeneous.
Commit	—	To do something wrong : as to commit a suicide.
Concoct	—	To make a plan for an evil purpose; He concocted a false story to deceive her.
Counterfeit	—	To imitate for a unlawful purpose;Counterfeit notes.
Concubine	—	A woman having sexual relations with many persons.
Cunning	—	Doing things cleverly but in a deceiving manner.
Credulity	—	A simpleton readiness to believe easily.
Dictator	—	A despot ruler , uses brutal force.
Despot	—	A tyrannical kind of ruler.
Demagogue	—	An unprincipled leader or a ring leader.
Effeminate	—	Womanly ('feminine' and 'womanly are used in good sense.)
Fabricate	—	To invent with a bad motive.He fabricated a false story.
Fancy	—	Imaginations which are not guided by reason.
Fine figure	—	Disgraceful or ridiculous figure; He cuts a fine figure (The phrase 'fine figure' is ironical.)

Fulsome — Full or excessive, so as to produce disgust, hatred.
Glaring — Conspicuous or something evil, as 'glaring error.'
Hasty — Quick to fault; rash, easily excited; patience-less.
Inveterate — Used for something bad, as 'an inveterate liar,' 'an inveterate enemy'.
Loiter — To linger at a time when greater haste is required.
Lonely — Depressed or sad due to being alone.
Minion — An unworthy favourite.
Notorious — Evil reputation.
Perpetrate — Used only for crimes or offences.
Plight — A sad or painful condition; She is in a sad plight.
Pocket — To put into one's pocket fraudulently, as "He pocketed the money fraudulently." Or to submit patiently to an insult, as "He pocketed the insult patiently.
Prone — To some vice or weakness, as "He is prone to fever".
Sheer — Used as ' sheer nonsense', 'sheer folly'. We never say 'sheer virtue' but perfect or pure virtue.'
Shrewd — Clever, but often in a sense, implying some dishonesty or cunningness.
To a degree — "He is insolent or dishonest to a degree (that is of high degree). This phrase is usually applied to some bad quality.
Totally — Always used for something bad; as 'totally incompetent,' 'totally blind'.
Trivial — Things of little importance. A trivial or common place subject.
Utter — An utter fool, an utter failure, always used for something bad.

WORDS USED IN A GOOD SENSE

Some words and phrases are used in a good sense only , so students should learn the proper use of these words. Mere knowledge of Hindi meanings of these words will not suffice to use them in proper manner. Students must learn the proper use of these words.

Age — She is of age (= grown up). She is under age(= a minor).
Breed — He is a man of (high) breed (= a well-breed man).
Bosom — He is my bosom (= fast friend)friend.
Family — He is a man of (high) family.
Feeling — He is a man of (tender and good) feeling.
Famous — He is a famous artist.
Form — The boatman pulled together in form (= in good form or style).
Order — Everything is in (proper) order.
Place — Everything was in place (= in its right place).
Position — He is a man of (good) position.
Principle — He is a man of (highly) principles.
Quality — He is a person of (good or high) quality.

Renowned — Shakespeare was a renowned dramatist.
Rank — Man of (high) rank.
Taste — His remark was not in taste (= in good taste).
Temper — He is out of temper (= ordinary or good temper).(But in 'temper' or in a temper' means in bad temper; as, " She said all that in a temper = in a rage")
Time — He arrived in time (= at the proper or right time).

SOME PECULIAR EXPRESSIONS

Some phrases can be used in certain or specific context. **It is necessary that you should be well conversant with such specific phrases. We are giving below some such important phrases for your knowledge .**

Bevy of ladies – We never say, "a bevy of gentlemen."

Bosom friend – We never speak of "bosom enemy."

Broad daylight – We do not speak of "broad moonlight," but "bright moonlight."

Burning question– We should not say, "burning problem."

Drawn battle – We never say, "a drawn fight" But we can say "a drawn match."

Fast friend– We do not speak of "a fast enemy"or "a fast foe."

Foregone conclusion– We never speak of "a foregone result"or "a foregone consquence."

Forlorn hope– We never say, 'forlorn success' or 'forlorn expectations'

Golden age – We do not speak of "the golden time or period."

Gratuitous insult – We do not speak of "gratuitous abuse."

Honest penny – We do not speak of " an honest six pence."

Implicit confidence,faith or reliance – We do not say, "implicit love or hatred."

Leading question – We should not say, "a leading inquiry."

Livelong day *or* **night** – We cannot say, "a livelong hour, or week, or year."

Maiden speech – We cannot say, "a maiden song"or "a maiden attempt."

Market rate *or* **market value** – We cannot say, "trade rate"or trade value."

Moot point – We cannot say, "a moot question." But we can say "an open question.

Open secret – We cannot say, "an open point."

Out of doors – We never say, "out of door "or "out of gates."

Retrench expenditure – We do not say, "retrench trade or business."

Sinews of war – We cannot say, "the muscles of war."

Snail's space – We cannot say, "snail's movement."

Spin in yarn *or* **yarns** – We never say, "spin a thread."

Standing army – We never say, "standing navy or regiment."

Standing joke – We never say, "a standing jest."

Standing nuisance – We never say, "a standing trouble."We may say, "a constant trouble."

Standing water – We can never say, "standing need."

Standing rule – We can never say, "standing practice or custom or habit."

Standing orders – Generally we do not say, "standing instructions."(In some offices we use Standing instruction')

Stubborn fact – We can never say, "an obstinate fact" or "a stubborn truth."
Sworn friends – We can never say, "a sworn enemy." We may say "an avowed enemy."
Stone's throw – We never say, 'pebble's throw' or 'brick's throw'.
Tall talk – We never speak of "lofty talk."
Vials of wrath – We cannot say, 'vials of anger or fury.'
Whirligig of time – We cannot say, "whirligig of period."
White lie – We do not say, "white falsehood" or 'black lie'.
Willing slave – We do not speak of "willing servant."
Watery grave– We do not say, " a watery tomb" or "watery burial".

ONE WORD SUBSTITUTIONS

1. Abdication — Voluntary renouncing throne.
2. Aborigines — Original inhabitants of a country.
3. Ablaut — A vowel change that accompanies a change in grammatical function. Same as "gradation." *Sing, sang, and sung.*
4. Accismus — Pretended refusal of something desired.
5. Acrolect — A variety of language that is closest to a standard main language, especially in an area where a creole is also spoken; *Standard Jamaican English*, where Jamaican Creole is also spoken.
6. Adianoeta — An expression that carries both an obvious meaning and a second, subtler meaning.
7. Adynaton — A declaration of impossibility, usually expressed as an exaggerated comparison with a more obvious impossibility; *"I will sooner have a beard grow in the palm of my hand than he shall get one of his cheek."* ***— William Shakespeare.***
8. Alexia — Inability to read, usually caused by brain lesions; word blindness.
9. Alliteration — Repetition of the same sound beginning several words placed clos[e] together, usually adjacent; Working and wandering as the worl[d] requires; How high is haughty head ?
10. Alphabetism — The expression of spoken sounds by an alphabet.
11. Ambigram — A word, phrase, or sentence written in such a way that it reads th[e] same way upside down as right; 'MOW,' this word (MOW) whe[n] turned upside down still says 'MOW.'
12. Anadiplosis — Rhetorical repetition of one or more words, particularly a word at th[e] end of a clause. *"Men in great place are thrice servants: servants o[f] the sovereign or state; servants of fame; and servants of business."* ***— Francis Bacon.***
13. Anagram — A rearrangement of a group of letters, especially a word that can be formed by rearranging the letters in another word; Heart = Earth; plum-lump.
14. Accessible — Which can be approached.
15. Acclimatize — To accustom one self in new climate.
16. Aggressor — One who attacks first.
17. Alimony — Allowance paid to wife on legal separation.

18. Altruist — One, who loves others.
19. Amateur — Who does thing for pleasure and not for money.
20. Ambassador — Person representing a state in a foreign country.
21. Ambidextrous — One, who can use either hand without any problem.
22. Ambiguous — That can be interpreted in any way.
23. Amnesia — Loss of memory
24. Amphibia — Animals that live both on land and in water, e.g, frog.
25. Anarchy — Absence of rule or law and order.
26. Annual — Which happens once a year.
27. Anomaly — Deviation from common rule.
28. Anonymous — Which does not bear the name of writer.
29. Antiseptic — Medicine used to save plants and animals from being rotten or decayed.
30. Anaphora — Repetition of a word or phrase at the beginning of successive phrases, clauses, or sentences; This royal throne of kings, this sceptred isle, this earth of majesty, this seat of Mars. This happy breed of men, this little world.
31. Antonym — Words, which are opposite in meaning.
32. Aphasia — Loss of speech.
33. Aquarium — Vessel in which fish & water plants are kept.
34. Aquatic — Animals that live in water.
35. Archaology — Study of Antiquities
36. Aristocracy — Government by the rich/aristocrats.
37. Ascetic — One, who tortures himself for the good of soul.
38. Atheist — One, who does not believe in existence of God.
39. Audible — Sound which can be heard.
40. Auditor — One, who audits the accounts.
41. Aurist — A specialist with regard to the ear.
42. Autobiography — Life history written by self.
43. Autocracy — Govt by one man.
44. Autograph — Getting signature of some important person in his handwriting.
45. Bachelor-hood — State of being unmarried.
46. Bankrupt — One, who can't pay the debts.
47. Bellicose — One, who is fond of fighting .
48. Belligerent — Persons nations etc. engaged in war.
49. Billingsgate — Coarsely abusive language (from the name of a London fish market.).
50. Bibliophile — One, who loves and collects books.
51. Biennial — Happening every second year.
52. Bigamy — Have two husbands or two wives at a time.
53. Biography — Life history of a person.
54. Biped — Animal having two feet.
55. Blasphemy — Speaking disrespectfully about sacred or religious objects.
56. Bookworm — One, who devotes full time in studying course books.
57. Botany — Study of plants.
58. Brigand — A bandit or robber, esp. one of a band living by pillage and ransom.
59. Brittle — Which can be easily broken.
60. Bullion — Gold or Silver before using for manufacturing ornaments.

61. Bureaucracy — Government run by officials.
62. Caducity — The infirmity of old age, senility.
63. Calligraphy — The art of beautiful handwriting; elegant penmanship.
64. Cannibal — One, who eats human flesh.
65. Centrifugal. — Anything tending to move away from centre.
66. Centripetal — Anything tending to move towards centre.
67. Century — One, hundred years.
68. Chrestomathy — A collection of choice literary passages, especially to help in learning language.
69. Coprolalia — Uncontrolled, excessive use of obscene or scatological language, sometimes accompanying certain mental disorders.
70. Cruciverbalist — A constructor of crossword puzzles; also, an enthusiast of word games, especially crossword puzzles.
71. Colleagues — Persons working in the same office.
72. Compatriot — Belonging to same country.
73. Congenital — Belongs to a person by birth.
74. Contemporaries — Persons living at the same time., *e.g.*, Ram and Valmiki were contemporaries.
75. Convalescence — Period of gradual recovery after illness.
76. Cosmopolitan — A citizen of the world, free from national boundaries.
77. Credulous — One, who easily believes others.
78. Cryptography — Study of secret writing and coded words
79. Curable — Which can be cured.
80. Cytology — Study of cell
81. Dead letter — An unclaimed letter.
82. Deaf — One who cannot hear.
83. Democracy — Government of the people, for the people, by the people.
84. Dermatology — Study of skin.
85. Digestible — That which can be digested.
86. Dilogy — An ambiguous speech.
87. Dittograph — A letter or word repeated unintentionally in writing or copying.
88. Dittology — Two distinct interpretations of the same text.
89. Dipsomania — A strong desire to take liquor
90. Divisible — That which can be divided.
91. Dotage — Extreme old age when one behaves like a child, a weakness of mind caused by old age.
92. Drawn — A game in which no party wins.
93. Dumb — One who can't speak.
94. Dysgraphia — Impairment of the ability to write, usually caused by brain dysfunction or disease.
95. Dyslexia — A learning disorder distinguished by impaired ability to recognize and comprehend written words.
96. Edible — A thing fit to eat.
97. Effeminate — Womanish in habits.
98. Eligible — One who is fit for the post.
99. Elision — The omission of a letter or syllable; *"Don't"* instead of "do not."
100. Emigrant — One who goes to live in a foreign country.

101. Employee — One, who is employed.
102. Employer — One, who employs.
103. Endemic — A disease prevailing in a locality.
104. Entomology — Study of insects
105. Endophoric — Characteristic of a reference to something outside the speech or text in which the reference occurs.
106. Epic — A long narrative poem.
107. Epanorthosis — Immediate rephrasing for emphasis, intensification, or justification. *"You, young lad, are most brave! Brave, did I say? No, heroic!"*
108. Epistrophe — Repetition of the same word or phrase at the end of successive phrases, clauses, or sentences.
109. Epicure — One, who is fond of sensuous enjoyment (delicateating and drinking).
110. Epilogue — A speech given after conclusion of drama.
111. Epitaph — Words inscribed on the tomb of the dead.
112. Etymology — Science; deals with formation of words.
113. Eucrasia — A good or normal state of health.
114. Etymon — An earlier form of a word in the same language or an ancestor language.
115. Examinee — One, who is taking examination.
116. Examiner — One, who examines the copies of examinees.
117. Exonym — A name by which one people or social group refers to another but which is not used by said group to refer to themselves.
118. Expatriate — To send (some one) out of native country; a person living in a counry which is not his own.
119. Expurgate — To remove all objectionable matter from a book or record.
120. Extempore — A speech without previous preparation.
121. Extradite — To send back the criminal to the country of his origin.
122. Fanatic (Bigot) — Unreasonably enthusiastic about religion.
123. Fastidious — Having very selective taste, hard to please.
124. Fatalist — One who believe in fate.
125. Feminist — One devoted to the welfare of women.
126. Foster child — Child brought by persons, who are not his parents
127. Franchise — Constitutional right to cast vote.
128. Fratricide — Murder of brother.
129. Garage — A shed for motor car.
130. Geology — Study of earth
131. Germicide — Which destroy germs.
132. Glossolalia — Fabricated, nonmeaningful speech, especially such speech, associated with a trance state or some schizophrenic syndromes.
133. Glottochronology — The determination of how long ago different languages evolved from a common source language.
134. Glutton — Fond of eating too much.
135. Gratis — Without any payment, free.
136. Gregarious — Animals, that live in flocks; of gregarious nature.
137. Harangue — A noisy and loud speech before a large gathering.
138. Haplology — The process by which a word is formed by removing one or two identical or similar adjacent syllables in an earlier word.

139. Hearse — Vehicle to carry dead bodies.
140. Herbivorous — Animals that live on Herbs.
141. Hendiadys — The use of a conjunction rather than the subordination of one word to another. e.g. use of 'nice and warm' for 'nicely warm'.
142. Heterography — A method of spelling in which the same letters represent different sounds in different words, as in ordinary English orthography.
143. Heterophemy — The unconscious saying, in speech or in writing, of something that one does not intend to say, especially when what is said is the reverse of what was intended.
144. Heterogeneous — Things of different nature.
145. Histology — Study of Tissue
146. Hobson–jobson — An Anglicized word or phrase corrupted from one or more words of an Asian language; Moochy, Mookhtyars, Moollah are such words.
147. Holonym — A concept that has another concept as a part; 'tree' is a holonym of 'dark', of 'trunk' or of 'limb.'
148. Homicide — Murder of a human being .
149. Homogeneous — Things of same nature.
150. Honeymoon — The first night of newly married couple.
151. Honorary — A post without any remuneration.
152. Hydra — A mythological serpant with many heads, an invertibrate marine creature.
153. Hydrophobia — A fear from water
154. Hygienist — One who cares fully of his health.
155. Hypothesis — A tentative assumption, made to derive a logical conclusion
156. Hypallage — Interchange of two elements in a phrase or clause from the order in which they would normally appear; *"A mind is a terrible thing to waste,"* instead of *"To waste a mind is a terrible thing."*
157. Hypercorrect — Characteristic of an incorrect linguistic construction in which the error is produced from a mistaken effort to be correct. *"Between you and I,"* which should be **"between you and me."**
158. Hyponym — A word that is more specific than a given word. e.g. : 'red' 'white' 'blue' etc. are the hyponyms of the word 'colour'.
159. Iconoclast — A person who attacks popular beliefs or established customs which he thinks mistaken or unwise.
160. Idiosyncrasy — Peculiar temper of an individual.
161. Idolatry — Worshiping of idols.
162. Ignorant — A person who has no knowledge of any happening.
163. Illegal — Unlawful.
164. Illegible — Which can not be read.
165. Illiterate — One, who can neither read nor write.
166. Illeism — The practice of referring to oneself in the third person.
167. Imitable — Which can be imitated.
168. Immigrant — A person from another country, who comes to our country to settle.
169. Immovable — Which can't be moved, fixed.
170. Imposter — One who assumes name or title of someone else for deceiving others.
171. Impregnable — A fort which can't be entered into.
172. Incorrigible — Cannot be corrected.

173. Ingressive — Characteristic of a speech sound produced with an inhalation of brea
174. Incredible — Which can't be believed.
175. Inevitable — That cannot be avoided.
176. Infallible — One who cannot make a mistake.
177. Infanticide — Murder of an infant.
178. Infection — A disease spread by through air, mosquitoes and other carriers.
179. Inimitable — Cannot be imitated.
180. Insomnia — Loss of sleep
181. Interpolate — Inserting new matter in a book.
182. Intervein — Anything pushed inside veins.
183. Invisible — That which cannot be seen.
184. Invulnerable — Cannot be wounded.
185. Irreparable — That can't be repaired.
186. Irrevocable — A decision that can't be revoked.
187. Isocolon — A sequence of parallel structures, having the same number of woı and sometimes the same number of syllables. *"What else can one do when he is alone in a jail cell, other than wı long letters, think long thoughts, and pray long prayers?"* ***– Martin Luther Ki***
188. Itinerant — One, who travel from place to place; itinerant musicians.
189. Kindergarten — A school for small children.
190. Kleptomania — An abnormal desire to steal.
191. Linguist — One who knows many languages.
192. Ligature — A character that combines two or more letters, such as in 'tl curved line connecting of such letters).
193. Lipogram — Writing, composed of words lacking a certain specific lette cacurved line connecting such letters.
194. Litotes — Understatement by negating the opposite; a type of meiosis. *"I not disappointed with the news."*
195. Loquacious — A continuous talker.
196. Lunar — Eclipse of moon, related to moon.
197. Maiden speech — Speech made for the first time.
198. Mammals — Animals which give milk.
199. Manuscript — Book written by hand.
200. Masochism — The condition or state of deriving (esp. sexual) gratification one's own pain or humiliation.
201. Materialistic — One for whom money is the most important thing.
202. Matins — Morning prayer in church.
203. Matricide — Murder of own mother.
204. Matrimony — State of being married.
205. Maxim — An established principle, a saying.
206. Meadow — A low level tract of uncultivated grassland.
207. Meditation — The action or practice of profound spiritual or religious reflectioı mental contemplation.
207. Melodrama — A sensational dramatic piece with crude appeals to the emotions ; usually a happy ending.
209. Mercenary — One, who fights for the sake of money.
210. Mesomorph — A person whose build is powerful, compact, and muscular.

211. Meteorology — Study of climate or weather.
212. Meticulous — Very particular even about small details.
213. Migratory — That moves from one place to another.
214. Misogamist — One, who hates the custom of marriage.
215. Misogynist — Hater of women.
216. Misologist — One who hates learning .
217. Mobocracy — Rule by mob.
218. Metonymy — Substitution of a word or phrase with another which it suggests. ***"The pen is mightier than the sword,"*** in which both "pen" and "sword" are substituted for "written prose" and "military."
219. Morphology — The study of structure and form of words in language, including inflection, derivation, and formation of compounds.
220. Monogamy — Marrying one at a time.
221. Morphology — Study of Animal and plant structure.
222. Narcotic — Medicine which induces sleep.
223. Neologism — New word coined by an author.
224. Neology — Study of formation of new words.
225. Notorious — A man with bad reputation.
226. Nosism — The practice of referring to oneself as "we"; a type of enallage.
227. Numismatics — Study of coins.
228. Obsolete — No longer in practice.
229. Oceanography — Study of ocean.
230. Odontology — Study of teeth.
231. Oligarchy — Government by a few.
232. Omnipotent — One, who is all powerful.
233. Omniscient — One, who knows everything.
234. Omnivorous — Who eats every thing.
235. Opaque — That which can't be seen through.
236. Ophthalmology — Study of eye.
237. Optics — Study of light.
238. Optimist — One who sees bright side of things.
239. Orthography — The study of correct spelling according to established usage.
240. Ornithology — Study of Birds.
241. Orography — Study of Mountain.
242. Orphan — A child whose parents are dead.
243. Orthodox — One, who believes in traditional values.
244. Orthography — Study of correct spelling of words.
245. Ostracize — To expel from society.
246. Pacifist — One, who believes in total abolition of war.
247. Paleontology — Study of Fossils.
248. Panacea — A remedy for all ills.
249. Pantisocracy — Government by all.
250. Pantomime — A dumb show, acting without words.
251. Palilogy — The repetition of a word or phrase in immediate succession, for emphasis, e.g. the answer is wrong, wrong, wrong.

252. Palindrome — A word, phrase, clause, or sentence that reads the same. regularly as it does when its letters are reversed; a type of palingram.
253. Palingram — A word, phrase, clause, or sentence that reads the same backwards after rearranging segments; *"Workmate did teamwork,"*
254. Pangram — A sentence that uses all the letters of the alphabet; a holalphabetic sentence.
255. Paragoge — The process by which a new word is formed by adding a letter or syllable to the end of another word. Same as "proparalepsis."; *"Climature,"* derived from *"climate."*
257. Paraprosdokian — Unexpected ending of a phrase or series.
258. Parasite — One who depends on others.
259. Parasol — A lady's umbrella.
260. Pathology — Study of Disease
261. Patricide — Murder of one's own father.
262. Patrimony — Properties inherited from one's father.
263. Patriot — One who loves own country.
264. Pedagogy — Study of Art of teaching
265. Pedantic — A style in which author displays his knowledge.
266. Perpilocutionist — One who expounds on a subject of which he has little knowledge.
267. Polyptoton — Repetition of a word in different forms, cases, or with different inflection, in the sentence.
268. Purr word — A word with positive connotations and therefore desirable to use in building and sustaining good public relations.
269. Pedestrian — One who travel on foot.
270. Pessimist — One who sees dark side of things.
271. Philanderer — One who enjoys by love making, a flirt.
272. Philanthropist — A lover of mankind.
273. Philately — Hobby of stamp collection
274. Philistine — Who does not care for art or literature, whose interests are material and commonplace.
275. Philogynist — Lover of womankind.
276. Philology — Study of words and their roots, of development of language.
277. Phonetics — Acoustics—study of sound.
278. Phrenology — Study of shape skull with regard to human character
279. Physiology — Study of normal function of living things.
280. Pioneer — One who leads others.
281. Plagiarism — Literary theft, using ideas and words of another person presenting them as own.
282. Platitudes — Commonplace remarks.
283. Plutocracy — Government by rich.
284. Polyandry — Marrying more than one husband at a time
285. Polygamy — Marrying more than one wife at a time.
286. Post mortem — An examination of body after death.
287. Primogeniture — Right of succession belonging to the first born.
288. Pseudonym — An imaginary name of author assumed to disguise himself.

289. Pugnacity — Tendency to quarrel.

290. Purist — One, who is particular about the purity of one's language, one who pays great attention to correct procedures (e.g. in the arts.)

291. Quadruped — Animal having four foot.

292. Rebel — One who take up arms against Government, one who resists control or authority.

293. Red tapism — Too much official formalities.

294. Regicide — Murder of a king.

295. Reticule — A lady's purse.

296. Retrospective — Which takes effect from some earlier date.

297. Sacrilege — Violating sanctity of some religious place.

298. Sadist — A person who derives (esp. sexual) pleasure from inflicting pain, suffering, humiliation.

299. Shrew — A woman with peevish nature.

300. Simultaneous — Happening at the same time.

301. Smuggle — Importing goods illegally without paying custom duties.

302. Solar — Eclipse of sun, retated to sun.

303. Soliloquy — Speaking one's thoughts aloud when alone.

304. Somnambulism — Walking in sleep.

305. Somniloquism — Talking in sleep.

306. Spokesman — One who speaks on behalf of other.

307. Stoic — One who is indifferent to pleasure and pain.

308. Suicide — Killing of self.

309. Snarl word — A word with negative connotations and therefore not desirable to use lest good public relations be undermined.

310. Superordinate — A word that is more generic than a given word.

311. Syllogism — Deductive reasoning in which a conclusion is derived from two premises. *"All human beings are mortal. I am a human being. Therefore, I am mortal."*

312. Synesis — Agreement of words to logic rather than grammatical form. *"The wages of sin is death."* — *Romans 6:23.*

313. Synchronize — Occurring two or more events at a time.

314. Teetotaller — One, who does not take alcoholic drinks.

315. Telltale — One, who enjoys talking about other's private affairs.

316. Thearchy — Government by the God.

317. Theist — One, who believes in the existence of God.

318. Theomania — A belief that one is God.

319. Transmigration — Passing of soul from one body to another after death.

320. Transparent — That which can be seen through.

321. Truant — A student, who left school or class without permission.

322. Truism — An often repeated truth.

323. Twins — Two babies born together.

324. Usurer — One, who lends money at higher (imaginary) rate of interest.

325. Utopia — A state of highest (imaginary) perfection.

326. Uxoricide — Murder of wife.
327. Valetudinarian — One who always thinks that he is ill.
328. Venial — An excusable fault.
329. Verbatim — Repetition– word by word.
330. Verbicide — The destruction of the sense or value of a word.
331. Verbose — Style full of words.
332. Vesper — Evening prayer in a church.
333. Veteran — A well and long experienced person in a particular occupation.
334. Wardrobe — An almirah where clothes are kept.
335. Widow — A woman whose husband has died.
336. Widower — A man whose wife has died.
337. Xenoepist — One with a foreign accent.
338. Zoology — Study of animals

FREQUENTLY USED SYNONYMS

Abstain	—	Refuse, Renounce, Avoid, Shun.
Abandon	—	Desert, Forsake, Leave, Relinquish.
Absurd	—	Ridiculous, Silly, Foolish, Preposterous.
Abhor	—	Hate, Detest, Loathe, Abominate.
Abase	—	Degrade, Disgrace, Humiliate, Demean, Dishonour, Stigmatize.
Aberration	—	Deviation, Wandering, Errant, Irregular, Weird, Abnormal.
Abbreviate	—	Curtail, Abridge, Compress, Shorten, Truncate.
Abut	—	Adjoin, Border, Verge on, Join.
Abet	—	Aid, Assist, Condone, Favour, Support, Promote.
Abstruse	—	Recondite, Hidden, Difficult, Profound.
Assiduous	—	Painstaking, Diligent, Industrious, Laborious, Meticulous.
Abundant	—	Ample, Copious, Plentiful, Bountiful.
Adequate	—	Enough, Sufficient, Proportionate.
Accommodate	—	Adapt, Adjust, Reconcile.
Acme	—	Summit, Apex, Zenith, Peak.
Acclaim	—	Applaud, Cheer, Celebrate, Extol.
Acquiesce(in)	—	Assent, Rest, Accede, Comply, Concur, Consent, Submit.
Admiration	—	Esteem, Praise, Respect, Approval, Approbation, Awe, Regard.
Adherent	—	Sticking to, Follower, Partisan, Devotee.
Affliction	—	Distress, Ordeal, Suffering, Sorrow.
Adversity	—	Misfortune, Calamity, Catastrophe, Hostility.
Ameliorate	—	Make better, Improve, Amend.
Ally	—	Colleague, Helper, Partner Accomplice.
Audacious	—	Bold, Brazen, Impudent, Daring
Astonish	—	Amaze, Surprise, Astound, Flabbergast
Assistance	—	Help, Aid, Succor, Collaboration, Sustenance
Aphorism	—	Maxim, Apothegm, Axiom, Proverb, Motto, Adage, A saying.
Apprehend	—	Seize, Know, Fear, Arrest, Understand.
Appraise	—	Evaluate, Estimate.
Antithesis	—	Contrasting, Reverse.

Alms	—	Dole, Gratuity, Charity.
Beg	—	Implore, Solicit, Supplicate, Beseech, Request, Plead.
Behaviour	—	Conduct, Demeanour, Deportment, Manner.
Base	—	Ignoble, Dishonourable, Mean, Low, Foundation, Lowest part of anything.
Bad	—	Evil, Wicked, Devilish, Naughty, Worthless.
Blame	—	Censure, Reprove, Condemn, Reproach.
Blessing	—	Benediction, The favour of God.
Banish	—	Exile, Ostracize, Deport.
Barbaric	—	Savage, Uncivilized, Primitive.
Bait	—	Snare, Trap, Decoy.
Brittle	—	Frail, Fragile (hard but easily broken, as-glass.).
Bizarre	—	Unusual, Grotesque, Fantastic.
Bewilder	—	Confound, Perplex, Befuddle, Befog, Baffle, Daze, Stun.
Belligerent	—	Warlike, Pugnacious, Hostile.
Bedlam	—	Pandemonium, Chaos, Mayhem, Clamour, Confusion.
Brave	—	Fearless, Intrepid, Dauntless, Valiant, Bold.
Burlesque	—	Mock, Imitate, Tease, Satirize, Ridicule, Jeer, Deride.
Browbeat	—	Intimidate, Bully, Frighten, Threaten.
Backlash	—	Repercussion, Reaction, Recoil.
Banal	—	Dull, Trite, Hackneyed, Prosaic, Commonplace, Uninteresting.
Bigoted	—	Biased, Prejudiced, Dogmatic, Opinionated.
Calm	—	Quiet, Tranquil, Peaceful, Sedate, Composed, Placid.
Cajole	—	Persuade, Flatter, Wheedle, Coax
Captious	—	Censorious, Hypercritical, Faultfinding.
Care	—	Solicitude, Anxiety, Misgiving, Foreboding.
Charlatan	—	Impostor, Mountebank, Quack, Chicane, Trickster.
Choleric	—	Irascible, Petulant.
Conceit	—	Pride, Vanity, Ego, Arrogance.
Colossal	—	Gigantic, Huge, Enormous, Mammoth, Vast.
Cynical	—	Misanthropic, Moody, Eccentric, Sardonic, Sarcastic.
Conversant (with)		Well versed, Acquainted.
Condign	—	Due, Merited, Well deserved, Suitable.
Condone	—	Pardon, Forgive, Excuse, Overlook.
Confess	—	Admit, Apologise, Own, Acknowledge.
Contingent (on)	—	Liable, Possible, Uncertain.
Constant	—	Eternal, Perpetual, Incessant, Continuous.
Cross	—	Crusty, Fretful, Ill-humoured, Bad tempered.
Cursory	—	Hasty, Superficial, Careless.
Concise	—	Short, Brief, Abridged, Compact.
Crafty	—	Cunning, Artful, Sly, Calculating.
Cruelty	—	Tyranny, Persecution, Brutality, Oppression, Ferocity.
Damage	—	Loss, Harm, Injury, Detriment.
Decay	—	Wither, Fade, Corrode, Decline.
Destitute	—	Needy, Forsaken, Orphan.
Didactic	—	Teaching, Instructive, Perfecting.

Denounce — Accuse, Condemn, Arraign, Decry, Censure.
Divine — Heavenly, Celestial, Graceful, Godlike.
Dangerous — Perilous, Risky, Hazardous, Precarious.
Dear — Expensive, Costly.
Definitive — Limiting, Final, Positive.
Desultory — Discontinuous, Irregular, Rambling.
Diffident — Modest, Bashful, Shy.
Discourse — Lecture, Sermon, Exhortation, Dissertation.
Dissipate — Scatter, Waste.
Economy — Management, Frugality, Thrifty, Judicious expenditure.
Effete — Exhausted, Old, Worn out, Tired.
Elicit — Draw out, Discover.
Elude — Baffle, Avoid, Cheat, Fool.
Emancipate — Free, Liberate, Release, Deliver, Uplift.
Emulate — Imitate, Copy, Rival.
Entice — Lure, Persuade, Allure, Entrap.
Extravagant — Prodigal, Wasteful, Squander.
Exquisite — Elegant, Fine, Matchless, Exclusive.
Exceptional — Anomalous, Unique, Extraordinary, Not included.
Extricate — Disentangle, Untangle.
Ephemeral — Transient, Short-lived.
Exterminate — Uproot, Eradicate, Eliminate, Destroy, Annihilate.
Exacerbate — Magnify, Heighten, Enlarge, Overstate, Amplify.
Exculpate — Absolve, Vindicate.
Exigency — Emergency, Distress.
Fascinate — Charm, Enchant, Mesmerize, Bewitch.
Fastidious — Dainty, Squeamish, Hard to please.
Fate — Lot, Destiny, End.
Fatuous — Silly, Purposeless.
Fight — Battle, Contention, Combat, Struggle, Conflict, Strife.
Fury — Anger, Rage, Wrath, Ire.
Fecund — Prolific, Fertile, Fruitful, Luxuriant, Productive.
Ferocious — Savage, Barbaric, Fierce, Wild, Uncivilized.
Fictitious — False, Imaginative, Illusionary, Fabricated, Fanciful.
Flagrant — Notorious, Outrageous, Disgraceful, Glaring, Wicked Scandalous.
Fortuitous — Chance, Accidental.
Forerunner — Precursor, Herald, Harbinger.
Forbid — Prohibit, Preclude, Inhibit, Debar.
Flippant — Pert, Frivolous, Impudent, Saucy.
Flamboyant — Bombastic, Ostentatious, Ornate.
Fatal — Deadly, Mortal, Lethal, Virulent.
Fallacy — Imperfection, Ambiguity, Quirk, Error.
Fallible — Imperfect, Erring, Wrong.
Furbish — Polish, Spruce, Renovate.
Fortitude — Strength, Firmness, Valour, Determination.

Guile	—	Fraud, Trickery, Cunning.
Gratification	—	Satisfaction, Enjoyment.
Garrulous	—	Talkative, Loquacious.
Humane	—	Kind, Generous, Benevolent, Compassionate.
Haughty	—	Arrogant, Proud, Egoist, Obstinate.
Humility	—	Politeness, Meekness, Modesty.
Hamper	—	Hinder, Block, Impede, Prevent.
Illiterate	—	Unlearned, Ignorant, Uneducated.
Impotent	—	Powerless, Disabled, Inadequate, Incapable.
Immaterial	—	Unimportant, Insignificant, Useless, Irrelevant.
Imminent	—	Threatening, Impending, Approaching.
Irresolute	—	Undecided, Wavering, Vacillating, Unsettled.
Indignant	—	Anger, Furious, Irate, Exasperated, Outraged.
Inanimate	—	Lifeless, Dead, Dormant, Stagnant, Extinct.
Ingenuous	—	Artless, Sincere, Naive, Innocent, Simple.
Insidious	—	Cunning, Clever, Inventive, Deceitful, Sly.
Intimate	—	Close, Confident, Inform, Cherished.
Inexorable	—	Relentless, Merciless, Apathetic, Harsh.
Impertinent	—	Irrelevant, Impudent, Insolent, Saucy, Disrespectful.
Jolly	—	Jovial, Merry, Cheerful, Affable.
Jubilant	—	Elated, Triumphant.
Joy	—	Delight, Pleasure, Ecstasy, Elation.
Knave	—	Fraud, Cheat, Scoundrel, Rogue.
Lament	—	Sorrow,. Mourn, Grieve.
Liberal	—	Generous, Kind, Tolerant, Permissive.
Lenient	—	Forbearing, Forgiving, Compassionate, Mild.
Lethargy	—	Laziness, Stupor, Sluggishness, Idleness.
Likeness	—	Similarity, Resemblance, Affinity.
Lively	—	Active, Enthusiastic, Agile, Brisk.
Loyal	—	Devoted, Faithful, Trustworthy, Honest.
Meagre	—	Small, Tiny, Inadequate, Scanty.
Mean	—	Low, Petty, Abject, Selfish.
Misery	—	Sorrow, Distress, Affliction, Grief.
Morbid	—	Unhealthy, Diseased, Ghastly, Horrid.
Mournful	—	Sad, Sorrow, Gloomy, Dejected.
Mighty	—	Powerful, Massive, Strong, Almighty.
Malice	—	Bitterness, Spite, Ill-will, Rancour, Malevolence.
Melancholy	—	Gloomy, Sad, Sorrow, Dejected.
Magnificent	—	Splendid, Grand, Good, Glorious.
Notorious	—	Infamous, Dishonourable, Flagrant, Blatant.
Notable	—	Memorable, Remarkable, Renowned, Eminent.
Obscene	—	Filthy, Indecent, Awful, Bawdy, Vulgar, Gross, Crude.
Obsolete	—	Antiquated, Old-fashioned, Extinct, Outworn.
Obtrude	—	Thrust, Pressure, Importunate, Interfere.
Obliterate	—	Destroy, Efface, Demolish, Erase.
Opportune	—	Timely, Convenient, Appropriate, Well-chosen.

Pensive	—	Thoughtful, Rational, Contemplative, Reflective.
Pathetic	—	Moving, Touching, Distressing, Lamentable.
Pious	—	Religious, Holy, Devout, God-fearing.
Perennial	—	Perpetual, Permanent, Long lasting, Constant.
Portray	—	Delineate, Depict, Draw, Sketch.
Possess	—	Have, Own, Acquire, Occupy, Seize.
Prate	—	Chatter, Babble, Tattle, Talkative, Garrulous.
Prodigal	—	Extravagant, Wasteful, Spendthrift, Squander.
Precocious	—	Premature, Forward, Advanced, Developed.
Philanthropist	—	Altruist, Charitable, Benevolent, Kind.
Patronize	—	Condescend, Stoop, Snub.
Penalize	—	Castigate, Chastise, Punish.
Picturesque	—	Charming, Pictorial, Scenic, Sylvan.
Prerogative	—	Privilege, Advantage, Exemption, Right.
Prohibit	—	Forbid, Interdict, Prevent, Ban.
Pillage	—	Plunder, Loot, Rob, Destroy, Steal.
Poignant	—	Touching, Moving, Heart-rending.
Quaint	—	Queer, Odd, Singular, Whimsical.
Quirk	—	Whim, Caprice, Fancy, Peculiarity.
Quip	—	Retort, Repartee, Remark, Jest.
Quarantined	—	Separated, Isolated, Restrained.
Qualm	—	Scruple, Doubt, Uncertainty, Suspicion.
Queer	—	Strange, Odd, Indifferent, Weird.
Questionable	—	Doubtful, Disputable, Accountable, Objectionable.
Quest	—	Search, Pursuit, Inquisitive, Crusade.
Quick	—	Alive, Swift, Keen, Fast.
Radiant	—	Brilliant, Bright, Intelligent, Beaming.
Refined	—	Elegant, Polished, Cultured, Sophisticated.
Rebellion	—	Mutiny, Revolt, Struggle, Fight.
Reiterate	—	Repeat, Rewrite, Emphasis.
Remorse	—	Repentance, Regret, Anguish, Grief.
Renown	—	Reputation, Fame, Famous, Distinguished.
Rejoice	—	Exult, Delight, Happy, Glad.
Relevant	—	Execute, Applicable, Pertinent, Implement.
Resistance	—	Opposition, Hindrance, Combat, Struggle.
Ruin	—	Destruction, Downfall, Wreckage, Devastation.
Rigid	—	Stiff, Unyielding, Stern.
Rash	—	Impetuous, Hasty, Foolhardy, Impulsive, Heedless, Brash.
Refute	—	Disprove, Answer, Deny.
Ricochet	—	Rebound, Reflect, Bounce, Carom.
Rut	—	Groove, Hollow, Furrow, Habit, Course, Routine, Practice.
Rural	—	Suburban, Rustic, Agrarian, Country.
Radical	—	Fundamental, Native, Original, Extreme, Progressive, Rebellious
		Rimy Frosty, Hazy, Blurred.
Remote	—	Far, Distant, Interior place, Aloof.